The Pottery of Mayapan

INCLUDING STUDIES OF CERAMIC MATERIAL FROM UXMAL, KABAH, AND CHICHEN ITZA

1

WITHDRAWN

*Published in Cooperation with the
Carnegie Institution of Washington*

PAPERS OF THE PEABODY MUSEUM OF ARCHAEOLOGY AND ETHNOLOGY

HARVARD UNIVERSITY, CAMBRIDGE, MASSACHUSETTS, U.S.A.

VOLUME 66

The Pottery of Mayapan

INCLUDING STUDIES OF CERAMIC MATERIAL FROM UXMAL, KABAH, AND CHICHEN ITZA

Robert Eliot Smith

PEABODY MUSEUM OF ARCHAEOLOGY AND ETHNOLOGY

HARVARD UNIVERSITY, CAMBRIDGE, MASSACHUSETTS

1971

LIBRARY OF CONGRESS CATALOG CARD NUMBER 73–158899

PRINTED AT HARVARD UNIVERSITY PRINTING OFFICE

CAMBRIDGE, MASSACHUSETTS, U.S.A.

Preface

The primary subject matter of this report is the pottery of Mayapan forming the fifth and final part of the study of Mayapan presented in the Carnegie Institution Publication 619 called *Mayapan, Yucatan, Mexico* (1962). Four subjects are handled in that publication: Part I. Literary sources for the history of Mayapan by Ralph L. Roys; Part 2. Civic and religious structures of Mayapan by Tatiana Proskouriakoff; Part 3. Residential and associated structures at Mayapan by A. Ledyard Smith; Part 4. the artifacts of Mayapan by Tatiana Proskouriakoff. In this fifth study, not only the pottery of Mayapan is considered but also much of the pottery of Yucatan, with special emphasis on the Puuc area and Chichen Itza.

The earlier literary sources for the pottery of Yucatan are: E. H. Thompson, 1897a,b, 1898, 1904; H. J. Spinden, 1913; R. C. Merwin, 1914; T. W. F. Gann, 1918; S. K. Lothrop, 1924; G. C. Vaillant, 1927, 1935; Morris, Charlot, and Morris, 1931; H. B. Roberts, 1931–1935; J. E. S. Thompson, 1941, 1945, 1957; G. W. Brainerd, 1940–42, 1951, 1953, 1958; H. Berlin, 1956; R. E. Smith, 1955b, 1958a; W. T. Sanders, 1960; E. W. Andrews, 1965; R. E. Smith and Gifford, 1965. Of this list two publications are of special value to the study of the pottery of Yucatan; *The chronological significance of Maya ceramics*, by George C. Vaillant (1927) and *The archaeological ceramics of Yucatan* by George W. Brainerd (1958). In addition to the well-developed chronological classification and the ex-

cellent pottery descriptions, both these works have been invaluable because of the wealth of illustration from all over Yucatan, including whole vessels and potsherds.

It is a pleasure to acknowledge the aid received from many sources in compiling this work. For his patience, forbearance, and many useful suggestions during its planning, writing, and completion, I am most grateful to H. E. D. Pollock. Many other colleagues both of the Carnegie Institution of Washington and of the Peabody Museum of Harvard University have given of their time and knowledge. Of these I am especially indebted to William R. Bullard, Jr., James C. Gifford, Tatiana Proskouriakoff, Jeremy A. Sabloff, A. Ledyard Smith, and Gordon R. Willey.

Alberto Ruz L., then Jefe de la Zona Maya del Instituto Nacional de Antropología e Historia de Mexico, was most cooperative and helpful in all our endeavors, as were all members of the Instituto, some of whom visited Mayapan during the period of excavation.

A number of artists are responsible for the illustrations. Most of the original pencil drawings were done by Alberto Garcia Maldonado; a few paintings by Hipolito Sanchez V., and the final inking and arrangement are by Avis Tulloch.

Robert E. Smith
Cambridge, Mass.
June, 1969

Throughout this report, the following abbreviations are used:
GWB   Brainerd, 1958
WTS   Sanders, 1960
RES   Smith, 1955a

For complete citation, see References, page 273.

Contents

1

Contents

2

ILLUSTRATIONS

TABLES

CHARTS

PART ONE

Procedures

Ceramic Planning and Study

This report is essentially concerned with the pottery of Mayapan, a site in the central western part of the State of Yucatan in Mexico. As stated in the preface, this report is part of a larger Mayapan study. Mayapan was selected for intensive research and excavation (1951–1955) for a number of reasons. Foremost of these was to study the later prehistoric career of the Maya in Yucatan, a career which had some documentation in historical records and in the native literature exemplified by the Books of Chilam Balam, the Ritual of the Bacabs, and the Maya codices. It was felt that field archaeology might help in the solving of problems and contradictions created by the literature. Another reason was to investigate the relation of the late historical disturbances to the military and cultural aggression from the Mexican highlands. In all these late historical manifestations Mayapan was the religious, political, and artistic center. Its period of ascendancy may be estimated at A.D. 1250 to 1450, the generally accepted date of abandonment. From approximately A.D. 1000 to 1200, Chichen Itza seemed to dominate at least a part of Yucatan, and prior to that, roughly A.D. 800 to 1000, the Puuc Area appears to have been the most culturally influential region in Yucatan.

Naturally, in planning the excavation of a site as large as Mayapan, a city surrounded by a wall, roughly oval, containing 4.2 sq. km., considerable thought was given to the part pottery was bound to play in the reconstruction of its history. In order to facilitate the recording of all material cultural finds, the area was divided into 500-m. squares, thus forming a huge grid and each square was given a letter. To assist further in the separation of different cultural manifestations, we chose five major lot designations, i.e., A, A-1, B-1, C-1, D-1. The simple letter "A" represents objects gathered from the surface in general surveys. "A" followed by a number refers to locations associated with house mounds; "B" lots represent findings from or near the Great Wall; "C" stands for material excavated in and near ceremonial

structures; and "D" lots include objects excavated in cenotes, sinkholes, and abandoned sascaberas. In addition to the lots from within the walls of Mayapan we will refer to "E" lots, which come from small sites in the vicinity of Mayapan; "G" lots from Chichen Itza and Balam Canche; and "P" lots from Uxmal and Kabah. The precise provenience of a vessel or potsherd is rarely mentioned here, but when it is, it can be traced through the lot number by consulting the list in the Appendix in Pollock et al. (1962), pp. 433–438, which either gives the lot location or makes reference to the *Current Report* in which the lot is described. In this report, in Appendix A is the list of cuts made at Uxmal, Kabah, and Chichen Itza and in Appendix B the list of the early, middle, and late lots excavated at Mayapan.

In pursuing the study of the pottery of Mayapan we wished not only to ascertain the changes made from one era to another and to recognize the trade specimens, but to determine by means of pottery something of the mode of life of those living in ceremonial centers and those in house mound groups. Further, it was important to understand the function of cenotes, some of which were used simply as a source of water and others for the practice of the "Cenote Cult." Therefore, with these objectives in mind, we saved all the pottery excavated within the confines of the Great Wall, which totaled approximately 400,000 potsherds, plus nearly 100,000 sherds collected outside the wall in a radius of about 12 km. A preliminary examination of the collection brought to light a number of important facts.

First, that the period of occupation at Mayapan could be separated into three distinct stages:

1. The preconstruction stage, indicated by the presence of material earlier than the Middle Postclassic Period. This pottery may occur in any lot, but is more likely to be present in early strata or on bedrock. In no case, however, with the single exception of pottery deeply placed below the fall of huge sections of the original dome of X-Coton Cenote, did material earlier than the Middle Post-

classic Period occur unaccompanied by the latter. Represented in these lower level lots were sherds from the Late Preclassic through the Early Postclassic forming a total of about 2 per cent of all sherds collected.

2. The construction stage, the period (A.D. 1250–1450) when the vast body of ceramic material was used whether manufactured at the site or elsewhere. This material could readily be separated into early and late by means of the stratigraphy. The early will be referred to as the Hocaba Ceramic Complex and the late, the Tases Ceramic Complex.

3. The postconstruction stage, immediately after the fall of Mayapan, during the Colonial Period, and in Modern times. There is no ceramic evidence of a major reoccupation of the site after the ruthless destruction of many of its principal buildings, statuary, and even pottery effigy censers. Nor is there any strong indication that people returned to worship as they did at Chichen Itza after it was abandoned, only a strong suggestion that certain former occupants returned to steal. Actually no pottery has been identified with certainty as belonging to the Protohistoric Period (1450–1511) i.e., between the fall of Mayapan and the coming of the Spaniards. In fact only a very small amount of pottery testifies to the presence of colonial people. As for the modern pottery it is only natural that a few artifacts should have been deposited in the last two hundred years considering the presence of the Rancho San Joaquin, actually within the Great Wall, during a great part of the nineteenth century. Since its abandonment, the site has been overrun by cattle, villagers have crisscrossed the ruins with trails to neighboring settlements, and treasure hunters and archaeologists have sunk pits in some of the more promising mounds. All in all it is amazing that more recent pottery was not found at the site.

Second, it was an important fact and something of a surprise to learn that Mayapan of the Great Wall did not appear until about fifty years after the final abandonment of Chichen Itza (A.D. 1200). The evidence for this conclusion is not altogether at Mayapan but in large part at Chichen Itza. At Mayapan we found a small amount (.29%) of Sotuta Ceramic Complex pottery mixed with the material from earlier ceramic complexes. The very fact that the Sotuta sherds were mixed with this early material suggests that they formed part of the pre-Mayapan construction stage. Furthermore, the finding at Mayapan of the Xcanchakan Black-on-cream Type in the Hocaba Ceramic Complex (Middle Postclassic Period) and at Chichen

Itza on the surface, often on top of fallen debris, and not in the occupational fill or refuse of that site, serves to prove that it was in use after the abandonment of Chichen Itza and at the time of the construction of Mayapan as a major center. Recent findings at Dzibilchaltun by E. Wyllys Andrews tend to justify Brainerd's Middle Mexican substage and to indicate that at Mayapan the appearance of the Xcanchakan Black-on-cream Type, the same as Brainerd's Coarse Slate, was introduced as a trade type into Mayapan from Dzibilchaltun or some nearby center of manufacture. Until further information comes from Dzibilchaltun, it would appear that the Middle Mexican substage must have existed from approximately A.D. 1200 to 1300. The Mayapan major construction presumably began about A.D. 1250 thus leaving fifty years for Brainerd's Middle Mexican stage to develop.

The final fact of importance is that no possible stratigraphy was found for the pottery earlier than the Hocaba Ceramic Complex of the Middle Postclassic Period. The 2.2 per cent admixture of early potsherds included a few Late Preclassic Period types, some Early and Late Classic, and a larger collection of Late Classic–Early Postclassic Transitional and Early Postclassic types. The pottery of the latter two periods, embracing the Cehpech Ceramic Complex and Sotuta Ceramic Complex, respectively, included such wares as Puuc Unslipped and Chichen Unslipped, Puuc Slate and Chichen Slate, and Puuc Red and Chichen Red. Without stratigraphy there resulted a confusing mass of sherds which of necessity had to be classified typologically in an effort to determine which types were associated with each of the different periods.

At this stage our knowledge of the ceramic content of the Classic and Early Postclassic periods in Yucatan was both limited and confused. I for one knew far more about the Formative Period pottery than that of any other period, due to the fact that in general the Late Formative pottery was nearly identical to Chicanel types as found at Uaxactun. Following Late Formative, the ceramic picture in Yucatan took a very different course than was the case in the Central Maya area. In the latter, the trend was to gloss ware as opposed to slate ware in the Northern Maya area. Actually, slate ware seems to have developed slowly along with other wares, most of which have regional significance, reaching its peak in the Late Classic–Early Postclassic Transitional Period or Cehpech Ceramic Complex. Most of the wares and associated types that go to make up the ceramic content of all these periods, and probably the slate of the Classic Period, were found at Mayapan together with other slate types which could be differentiated from each other, but not associated with their proper ceramic complexes. We presumed that these slate types along with red and unslipped types belonged to both the Cehpech and Sotuta Ceramic Complexes. In order to determine which wares and types belonged to which period and ceramic complex, we decided to procure fresh samples.

It seems appropriate to explain why, after the rather extensive pottery trenching done by the Carnegie Institution during the 1930's at Uxmal, Kabah, and Chichen Itza, further ceramic sampling was necessary. Several factors were responsible for the digging of more test pits and trenches at these sites. First, Brainerd's (1958) *The Archaeological Ceramics of Yucatan*, based on the work done by Carnegie Institution, had not yet appeared; secondly, a considerable portion of the potsherds collected at these sites had to be discarded because the paper identification tags had been destroyed by insects, and the provenience lost, before Brainerd could examine the material; and lastly, it was hoped that more conclusive ceramic sequences might be found at all three sites.

In March and April of 1954 E. M. Shook and the author dug a series of trenches at Chichen Itza. In February of 1956 Gustav Stromsvik opened a number of trenches at Uxmal and Kabah. As our five-year contract with the Mexican Government had expired in September 1955, Stromsvik's excavations were made under special permission from the Instituto Nacional de Antropología e Historia, and in cooperation with its work at those sites.

During the excavation of Mayapan from 1951 through 1955 other exploratory or reasonably careful investigations were made at neighboring sites within a radius of about 12 km. This included the sherd sampling of over 100 sites, resulting in a fair percentage of early material. More intensive digging was done at Santa Cruz, a small site about 1.5 km. southeast of Mayapan culminating in the finding of a well-stratified sequence from Formative to Late Postclassic (Smith, 1954b; 1955b). The village of Telchaquillo (Smith, 1954a,b), about 1.5 km. north of Mayapan, was chosen for further careful investigation. Here several trenches were dug in the plaza cenote and two major trenches were cut into the large mound situated south of the cenote in the Main Plaza, one on the south, the other on the west side. These trenches penetrated through several terrace walls and in the pottery lots, the Cehpech and Sotuta Ceramic Complex types were always more abundant than the Hocaba and Tases Ceramic Complex types. Actually, the farther into the mound we progressed, the greater became the predominance of the Cehpech and Sotuta over the Hocaba and Tases types. The fact remains, however, that the later types were always present. In other words, we have here the same situation which was encountered within the walls of Mayapan, an admixture of early with late pottery.

Method of Classification

Perhaps the most important factor in presenting a collection of pottery is the method of classification. There is no doubt of the desirability of providing a taxonomic framework suited to current needs for the analysis of ceramics in Mesoamerica and for our immediate needs in Yucatan. In view of the fact that such a framework, based on the type-variety concept (Wheat, Gifford, and Wasley, 1958; Phillips, 1958; Smith, Willey, and Gifford, 1960), has been developed by a group including archaeologists concerned with the southwestern and eastern United States, and the Mesoamerican area, it seems opportune to exemplify the concept with the material collected for this report which is representative of the ceramic history of Yucatan from Middle Preclassic to Colonial times. Brainerd (1958), using a stage-ware method of procedure, apportioned no distinctive or true phase names to the Yucatan Peninsula. He (1958, pp. 3–4) sidestepped the naming of phases and substituted a new set of sequent culture divisions to which he fits his ceramic complexes. He says,

Because of the large area covered and the considerable time depth reconstructed, I have decided to use generalized names for major sequent culture divisions in Yucatan, and have fitted the collections from various horizons and sites into this more general scheme. These divisions are meant only for Yucatan, and fit certain peculiarities in Yucatecan cultural history. They differ somewhat both in name and duration from others used elsewhere in the Maya area. The major divisions have been called stages in accord with Dr. Kidder's usage (Kidder, Jennings, and Shook, 1946, pp. 1–9). Their names have been chosen in an effort to designate general characteristics of each, and at the same time to avoid confusion with the increasing number of such terms now in use in Mesoamerican Archaeology.

He goes on to name these stages which, from earliest to latest times, are Yucatan Formative, Yucatan Regional, Yucatan Florescent, Yucatan Mexican, and Post-Conquest. These stages may be subdivided into early, middle, and late. Brainerd's stages do not take the place of the cultural periods, generally accepted, for the Maya area.

These are Formative, Classic, Postclassic, Protohistoric, and Colonial. However, his Formative stage does closely parallel the cultural period. His Early Formative is presumably earlier than either Kaminaljuyu–Las Charcas or Uaxactun–Mamom, Middle Formative may in time be found to equate with Las Charcas and Mamom but at present too little is known about it, and Late Formative is very closely associated with Uaxactun–Chicanel. The Yucatan Regional Stage is closely related to the Classic Period. Typologically, I have found virtually no Uaxactun–Matzanel types. Early Regional seems to equate with Uaxactun–Tzakol 1–3, Middle Regional with Tepeu 1 and Late Regional with Tepeu 2; however, I am reasonably certain that the cultural divisions for Yucatan do not necessarily have exactly the same temporal limits as do those for Uaxactun any more than that typologically the ceramic complexes of like divisions are identical. Yucatan Florescent appears to be closely allied with Uaxactun–Tepeu 3. The Mexican Stage, divided by Brainerd into Early, Middle and Late, belongs partly in the Postclassic Period and partly in the Protohistoric Period. His Early Mexican Substage and Zacualpa–Tohil, and Zaculeu–Qankyak apparently are contemporaneous and affiliated stylistically. The existence of Middle Mexican Substage, as suggested by Brainerd is doubtful, in my opinion, but recent findings at Dzibilchaltun seem to justify Brainerd's selection of it as a full stage. The Late Mexican Substage, part of the Protohistoric Period, is roughly contemporaneous with Zacualpa–Yaqui and Zaculeu––Xinabahul. Brainerd's Postconquest Stage and the Maya Colonial Period have much the same meaning. Chart 1 lists in chronological order Maya cultural periods, Yucatan cultural phases, Brainerd's stages, and correlations with phases of the central and southern Maya area.

The nomenclature used in Chart 1 for the cultural phases of Yucatan, omitted by Brainerd, was selected primarily from the provinces of Yucatan (Roys, 1957). Our interest, however, is in the ceramic complex which bears the same name as the phase. Complexes are all-inclusive analytical units in that each descriptively encompasses all the material of a certain kind that is known from a given phase. Thus a ceramic complex, a lithic complex, an architectural complex combine with other complexes to constitute the artifactual manifestations of an entire phase and when considered together as a whole they represent the total material content of a phase.

The pottery that is being considered as belonging to a ceramic complex is separated into wares, types, varieties, groups, and modes. It seems appropriate to define briefly these categories although later on they are more fully described.

A ware is defined as a ceramic assemblage in which all attributes of surface finish and of paste composition, with the possible exception of temper, remain constant.

A type represents an aggregate of visually distinct ceramic attributes already objectified within one or several varieties that, when taken as a whole, are indicative of a particular class of pottery produced during a specific time interval within a specific region.

The variety is viewed as the basic unit of analysis, which in due course, consequent upon an increased depth of total ceramic knowledge, either becomes the type (as the established variety) or one of a number of varieties within the type.

A group is a collection of closely related types that demonstrate a consistency in range of variation concerning form and color. The types of any given group are roughly contemporaneous (elements of the same ceramic complex) and are also always components of the same ware. Group is a term which is most useful for lumping like material, belonging to the same ware and sometimes not possible of separating into types, whenever the ware (fine orange, plumbate, slate, etc.) is associated with several phases. It might be noted that particular sherd fragments from decorated types within the same group may lack decoration and so be counted as plain. It is obvious, therefore, that total group counts can be quite important (see Chapter V under Slipping).

A mode is here defined as an attribute or cluster of attributes that displays significance in its own right. It seems best to study modes separately in order to view their individual behavior in crosscutting varieties and types through time and space.

Lists showing the major wares, types, and shapes as found in Uxmal, Kabah, Chichen Itza, and Mayapan are included with each ware analysis. A table (1a,b) listing the total sherd counts in all ceramic complexes at Mayapan (a), as well as at Uxmal,

Kabah, and Chichen Itza (b) is incorporated along with other tables (2–24) showing the association between pottery and various types of structure and ceramic depositories, and still other tables (25–40) used to indicate the link between the various ceramic techniques, ceramic types, and vessel forms in the different ceramic complexes. Tables 41–43, portraying the temper distribution by ware, form, and some decoration based on sherds from Uxmal, Kabah, and Chichen Itza, are included as an unchecked preliminary study by A. O. Shepard (see full explanation in Introduction to Chapter IV). A temper table for Mayapan was omitted because the paste composition was so strikingly uniform that a simple description seemed adequate. The original file cards listing the sherds collected by lot, ware, and form, too voluminous for this report, will be kept on file at the Peabody Museum, Harvard University, Cambridge, Massachusetts. A chronological chart of the phase correlations of Yucatan and the central and southern Maya areas is included along with two charts recording numerically by ceramic complexes all wares, groups, and types under early, middle, and late lots from Mayapan (Charts 1–3).

Comparatively few photographs have been used for the pre-Mayapan pottery because of the simplicity of the material and the accuracy of the drawings. Color is represented schematically when more than one color is involved. A key to the color scheme precedes the illustrations.

Sherd counts outside of tables are enclosed in square brackets, e.g., [28]. These counts and all tabulations, unless otherwise stated, refer to rim sherds and whole vessels. Whenever the variety does not accompany the type, the established variety is implied.

All color designations were taken from Munsell (1949) soil color charts. The readings were taken to match the color hue most predominant for the specimen.

Some measurements and vessel forms require definition, others are self-evident. *Bowl*: a vessel with unrestricted or slightly restricted orifice, whose height may be equal to, but not less than, one-third its diameter. *Dish*: a vessel with unrestricted orifice, whose height is between one-third and one-fifth its diameter. *Plate*: a vessel with unrestricted orifice, whose height is less than one-fifth its diameter. *Size of mouth*: small, medium, wide refer to ratio of neck diameter to body diameter. *Height of neck*: based on the exterior measurement taken vertically from lip to juncture of the neck and side: low, 1–3 cm.; medium high, 4–6 cm.; high, 7 cm. and over. *Thick-*

ness of side: based on the average side thickness of each vessel: eggshell, .1–.25 cm.; thin, .30–.5 cm.; medium thick, .6–.8 cm.; thick, .9–2 cm.; very thick, over 2 cm. *Lip diameter*: measured from outside edge of lip. *Height of vessel*: unless otherwise indicated, measurements do not include ringstand or pedestal base, feet, or appendages.

III

Excavation and Stratigraphy

In the introduction it has been pointed out that further excavation at key sites was needed to enlarge our knowledge of pre-Hocaba Phase pottery with particular emphasis on the contents of the two preceding ceramic complexes, Cehpech and Sotuta. The earlier pottery of the Formative and Early Classic periods encountered at Mayapan and vicinity is discussed by Smith (1955b, pp. 253–265) using as an example the pottery from Santa Cruz, a site a short distance southeast of Mayapan, where excellent early stratigraphy was found. To enlighten ourselves concerning the later pre-Hocaba phases, stratigraphic trenches were dug at Uxmal and Kabah in the Puuc region, the center of the Cehpech Ceramic Complex and at Chichen Itza, the only site where the Sotuta Ceramic Complex was known to abound. At all three sites the trenches or cuts were excavated using metrical (25 cm. levels) rather than natural stratigraphy except where the latter was obvious. A list of these cuts, the number of levels, and contents by ceramic complex is recorded in Appendix A. Maps (fig. 1,a and b) locating the cuts at Kabah and Uxmal by number are included in this report and a map of Chichen Itza (Ruppert, 1952, fig. 151) is used to designate the location of the nineteen cuts made there. Lists of each cut recording sherds by level, form, ware, and type are available at the Peabody Museum, Harvard University.

At Uxmal, trenching was done in ten carefully selected locations seven (Cuts 1–6, 8) of which proved productive. Nothing of real value would be gained by showing drawings of these cuts, especially since no real change from top to bottom could be noted in any of them.

Much the same results were obtained at Kabah as at Uxmal. Several more exploratory pits were sunk than the five cuts shown on Map 1a. A number of these were just off the causeway associated with the triumphal arch but little depth was attained and only a handful of pottery recovered.

At Chichen Itza nineteen trenches were dug but only five (Cuts 1, 10, 14, 16, 17) were used in the analysis. Of these five cuts, only Cut 1 showed a definite indication of the influence of the preceding Cehpech Ceramic Complex. In this cut the two lowest levels had 32.3 per cent Cehpech pottery. In no cut was it possible to note any difference in the age of Sotuta Ceramic Complex sherds by level; that is, no early or late Sotuta types were recognizable.

At Mayapan, although exploratory trenches were dug in cenotes, in a sascabera, and in a few instances in the main group, the bulk of the digging that produced pottery was associated with architectural excavation either ceremonial or mundane. A few temporal distinctions could be made in the pottery associated with buildings, at least enough to differentiate between early and late, Hocaba or Tases phases. This was also true for most trenches wherever dug. However, in view of the hundreds of cuts made, and the impracticability of creating a table for each, a method of presentation had to be devised that would cover the situation simply and adequately. By virtue of the few reasonably deep stratified cuts (cf. Tables 2–4, 24) available, an early-late sequence was determined naming the pottery types associated with each. A careful examination of the material in each cut or level made it possible to separate the lowest level lots having only the earliest or Hocaba Ceramic Complex types and those from the upper levels which contained an abundance of the latest or Tases Ceramic Complex types. In between these two clear-cut extremes was the residue, the middle lots, a mixture of both early and late, but with nothing wholly its own. These early, middle, and late lots are listed in Appendix B and they total 664; for location data see Proskouriakoff (1962b, Appendix).

Three (Tables 2–4, 24) of eight stratified cuts are individually tabulated according to ceramic complex, ware, and type by early, middle, and late levels and described as follows: in the House Mound or A Lots, A11, A7, A6 and their respective extensions A19, A18, A20 (Table 2) dug into Structure J49b (Ruppert and Smith, 1952, pp. 47–48, fig. 2,b); in the Ceremonial or C Lots, C61–64 (Table 3) excavated between Structures Q77 and Q162 (Shook, 1954b, pp. 98–99, fig. 2,a), and in the Cenote or D Lots, D55, D54, D53, D46, D45, D41 (Table 4) cut from a column made in Cenote Chen Mul (Smith, 1954a, pp. 223–225, fig. 3, section C–C[1] of sector H). Place and time percentages are also shown in Table 5, derived from Tables 2–4, and the same shown in Table 6, derived from Charts 2 and 3.

At Mayapan out of the huge accumulation of cultural remains resulting from five years' intensive excavation, two phases emerge as representative of the major occupation of the site, namely the period of construction. These are Hocaba of the Middle Postclassic and Tases of the Late Postclassic periods. It is true that indications are present of an earlier occupation covering the Tihosuco, Cochuah, Motul, Cehpech, and Sotuta phases in this order. The fact that all of the pre-Hocaba Phase sherds total only 2.2 per cent and the post-Tases (Chikinchel, Chauaca, and Modern phases) sherds a mere .03 per cent, clearly indicates the tremendous impact at Mayapan of the Middle and Late Postclassic people from A.D. 1250 through 1450.

Furthermore, using Tables 5 and 6 as a guide, it is possible to note the great strength and persistence of the Hocaba Ceramic Complex types even into the late lots, except in the ceremonial late lots where Tases types predominate. Clearly this is due to the increased use of the Chen Mul Modeled Type effigy censer in the Tases ceremonial practice (Chart 3 and Table 24).

Another item of interest ascertained from Chart 3 and Table 24 is the presence and persistence of Peto Cream Ware and its most prolific type, Xcanchakan Black-on-cream. Peto Cream Ware forms 1.4 per cent of the total sherds found at Mayapan, but within the early lots it totals 8.5 per cent, middle lots 2.1 per cent, dropping down to .4 per cent in the late lots. If we compare Peto Cream Ware with Mayapan Red Ware (Hocaba Ceramic Complex types), we find the latter forming 30 per cent of the total sherds found at Mayapan, 46.4 per cent of early lots, 40.9 of middle lots, and 24.9 of late lots. This constitutes a much more gradual diminution of a basic ware. Peto Cream appears more like a trade or luxury ware

at Mayapan primarily associated with the Hocaba Phase.

With the loss of Peto Cream Ware of the Hocaba Ceramic Complex, San Joaquin Buff Ware became a major type in the Tases Ceramic Complex. This ware is absent in the Hocaba Phase and first appears in the middle lots where it forms 1.1 per cent of all sherds in those lots and .9 per cent in the late lots. If only slipped wares of the Hocaba and Tases complexes are considered, however, the percentages reverse themselves (1.9 middle lots and 2.2 late lots) increasing the strength of San Joaquin Buff Ware in the late lots.

Considering the more prominent trade wares we find that Fine Orange of the Matillas Group registers .5 per cent in the early, .9 per cent in the middle, and 1 per cent in the late lots considering only the slipped wares. On the same basis Tulum Red Ware, which is lacking in the early lots, forms .1 per cent in the middle lots and .02 per cent in the late lots.

The middle lots, which are truly the residue of what is not definitely early because they do not rest on the bottom and do not include any clear-cut late types, nor form part of the upper level or surface stratum copiously supplied by the Tases Phase or later material, have no exact stratigraphic position. Some, which rest on limestone, may be part of a Tases Phase deposit; others, sandwiched between clear-cut early and late strata, may represent a true middle stratigraphic accumulation or may have been laid down in either early or late times. The problem has either been not to have enough truly middle stratigraphic lots or not to find stratigraphy in depth (three to eight levels), which would show gradual change and new development, thus indicating possible separation into three or more ceramic complexes. The fact that I have been unable to isolate a ceramic complex between the Hocaba and Tases complexes, however, does not preclude the existence of such an intermediate complex.

All of the ceramic material excavated has been listed on cards on file at the Peabody Museum, Harvard University by provenience, ware, and form so that future researchers may judge for themselves. In addition the middle lots are presented in Appendix C.

PART TWO

Ceramic Descriptions

IV

Wares, Groups, Types, and Varieties

A detailed analysis of types and varieties and their forms, under the ware with which they are associated and within the confines of the ceramic complex to which they belong, will be presented in Part Four, Chapter XII of this study. Here a more descriptive breakdown of ware, group, type, and variety is presented.

The most important factors in the study of pottery are its attributes. These attributes are observable inherent criteria which, when combined, are seen first as varieties, then as types, and finally as wares. An attribute by itself is no more than one distinguishing feature.

In practice some archaeologists first sort for varieties then types, and, ultimately, wares. I sort for wares, types, and varieties in that order. Each of these entities has its own special set of attributes.

DEFINITIONS

Ware. This is a ceramic assemblage in which all attributes of paste composition, with the possible exception of temper and surface finish, remain constant. A ware is not limited in time as are types and varieties. In conjunction with paste composition, texture is examined to note whether it is very coarse, coarse, medium, fine, or very fine. In the case of very coarse and coarse, the vessel would be quite porous and less so if very fine. A vessel of very fine texture is normally untempered.

Temper itself should be most carefully investigated and can lead to extremely important discoveries. It is not sufficient in certain cases such as calcite and ash tempers to record them merely as calcite and ash. They must be qualified if real value is to be attained, giving them their exact descriptive name such as clear calcite, cryptocrystalline calcite, saccharoidal calcite, or a variety of ashes (fine, with mineral inclusions, etc.). Naturally, this becomes absolutely necessary for calcite when dealing with material found in a limestone country like the Yucatan Peninsula or the Peten of Guatemala, and for volcanic ash when analyzing pottery from the Valley of Mexico or Mexican highland sites deeply covered with volcanic ash. If this more exact data is not sought, it is impossible to differentiate the material from diversified centers of manufacture within these primarily calcite or volcanic ash regions. Once this

has been done, it may result in very distinctive differences for many wares but, on the other hand, certain wares such as Puuc Slate may have a great variety of tempers including several kinds of calcite, volcanic ash, potsherd, clay lump, and combinations of a number of these (Tables 41–43). In Puuc Slate Ware there is a high correlation between paste and vessel shape which, when more is known about the pottery of the Yucatan Peninsula as a whole, may lead to the recognition of certain at present unknown centers of manufacture and the naming of new slate wares other than Puuc, Chichen, and Thin.

The temper findings associated with the Cehpech and Sotuta wares are the result of Anna O. Shepard's microscopic identifications of temper. Since a period of time has elapsed since Miss Shepard made these identifications and she has not checked her work, the author absolves her of any responsibility for their accuracy. These identifications of temper with a brief definition of each, provided by Miss Shepard several years ago, are incorporated in spite of the chance of error either in temper reading or description. The author assumes the entire responsibility for including these preliminary findings because he feels that errors would be minor and the benefits considerable. At Miss Shepard's request, however, her 40-page contribution on the paste composition of Uxmal, Kabah, and Chichen Itza pottery has been deleted.

This study involved microscopic examination, the purpose of which, aside from defining paste, was to ascertain what new evidence composition might throw on sources of the pottery and relations among prehistoric Yucatecan pottery-making people. Her reason for requesting the deletion was that the section on paste technology was out-of-date because, in the meantime, she had made intensive X-ray diffraction analyses of Yucatecan clays and tempering materials plus a series of semi-quantitative spectrographic analyses. Further discussion of temper and paste composition may be found in Appendix D. The Hocaba and Tases temper annotations are based on Brainerd's remarks and the author's personal observations. These latter are very general. It is clear from examination with a ten-power lens that ash, sherd, and fibrous tempering materials were not used in association with Mayapan Red Ware, Mayapan Unslipped Ware, and Peto Cream Ware, and that calcite temper in some form was employed. Brainerd (1958, pp. 54 and 57) states that all of these wares are believed to have calcite temper. Unfortunately Shepard was unable to find the time to analyze the Hocaba and Tases pottery paste for temper identification except for certain collections including lot C 35 which she considers too preliminary for use in this publication.

The attributes associated with surface finish are rough or smooth, unslipped or slipped, matte or lustrous. These are the essential things which may be observed relative to the surface finish. Additional techniques applied to the surface are primarily methods of decoration (Shepard, 1956, pp. 186–193) and these will be discussed under type. Examining the essential surface finish attributes more closely, we find that a rough finish is usually the result of very coarse or coarse-textured paste. This condition nullifies smoothing because drying shrinkage leaves coarse grains protruding. Smoothing of medium or fine-textured paste is readily discernible, even as to the method and tool used. An unslipped vessel may have a rough or smooth finish or may have a white calcareous coat. Slipped vessels may have a matte or lustrous finish. This luster may be produced by burnishing or polishing a slightly moistened surface with a smooth tool before firing. Arbitrarily, burnishing has been selected as producing a less lustrous finish than does polishing. Gloss represents the greatest luster. Furthermore, Shepard (1956, pp. 122–123) tells us that "certain clays become glossy on drying from suspension without any special treatment." She also speaks of two other methods of creating luster: "by applying a fusible material which will melt and flow in firing to form a smooth, compact coat, and by coating with a varnish-like substance after firing."

Group. This is a collection of closely related types that demonstrate a consistency in variation of form and color. The types of any group are (roughly) contemporaneous (elements of the same ceramic complex) and are always components of the same ware. The term "group" is most useful for lumping together like material, belonging to the same ware but too small or weathered to separate into types, or whenever the ware (Fine Orange, Plumbate, Slate, etc.) is associated with several phases.

Type. This represents an aggregate of visually distinct ceramic attributes already recognized within one or (generally) several varieties that, when taken as a whole, are indicative of a particular class of pottery produced during a specific time interval within a specific region. So far, in the consideration of ware, we have used up the following attributes: texture, color, and, occasionally, temper for paste composition leaving out hardness except in its extreme manifestations; smoothness, slipped or unslipped, matte, burnished, polished, or glossed, and sometimes color for surface finish. This leaves plain or decorated, decorative techniques, design styles, and form. Of these attributes, decorative techniques and form are used to segregate types; a minor change in a decorative technique or a design style varying from the norm may be sufficient to warrant the naming of a variety other than the established variety.

Variety. The ceramic variety is viewed as the basic unit of analysis, which in due course, as total ceramic knowledge increases, either becomes the type (as the established variety) or one of a number of varieties within the type. Recent experience, however, has shown that the type provides a more practical basis for ceramic analysis. Minor, but significant, variations within the type, either intrasite or intersite, may be analyzed on a varietal level.

In this report are mentioned many wares (together with their associated groups, types, and varieties), which are alphabetically listed and described below.

"Figure" or "fig." is omitted before illustrations appearing in this study. Asterisks refer to those groups, types, and forms found in the collections under consideration.

WARES LISTED AND DESCRIBED ALPHABETICALLY

ABALA RED WARE

Paste composition. Coarse texture; gray to buff color; generally calcite temper. *Surface finish.* Smoothed, but surface often lumpy or granulated because drying shrinkage leaves coarse grains protruding. Slipped and lightly rubbed, leaving a matte or burnished finish. Color is red (2.5 YR 6/6, 4/2, 4/4, 5/6, 3/6) ranging from light red, through weak red and reddish brown, to red and dark red.

Red Sacpokana Group. *Types and varieties.* Sacpokana Red Type, Sacpokana Variety (57, a–c; GWB, p. 96, figs. 33, a–f, 34); Choolac White-on-Red Type, Choolac Variety (*ibid.,* fig. 34, c, 1, 2). *Forms.* Jars with parenthesis rim; bowls, hemispherical and deep with recurving sides. *Quantity.* 27 rim, 47 body sherds. *Provenience.* Dzibilchaltun, Mani Cenote, Mayapan. *Ceramic complex.* Chauaca (A.D. 1550–1800).

BOLON BROWN WARE

Paste composition. Coarse texture; light brown to buff color; generally calcite temper. *Surface finish.* Smoothed, and usually retaining a smooth appearance. Slipped and lightly rubbed, leaving a matte or burnished finish. Color is brown (2.5 YR 4/2, 4/4; 7.5 YR 5/4).

Brown Oxcum Group. *Types and varieties.* Oxcum Brown Type, Oxcum Variety (57, d). *Forms.* Comals and bowls with restricted orifice. *Quantity.* 4 rim, no body sherds. *Provenience.* Mani Cenote and Mayapan. *Ceramic complex.* Chauaca (A.D. 1550–1800).

CAUICH COARSE-CREAM WARE

Paste composition. Coarse texture; buff, drab, cinnamon, and buff color range; predominantly sherd temper. *Surface finish.* Smoothed but often lumpy because drying shrinkage leaves coarse grains protruding. Slipped and burnished appearing opaque but not waxy. The slip tends to peel off. Color ranges from cream (5 YR 8/2) to gray

(5 YR 8/1) and rarely cinnamon (5 YR 7/6, 7.5 YR 7/4).

Cream Holactun Group. *Types and varieties.* Holactun Black-on-cream, Holactun Variety (10, a–j; GWB, p. 54, where it is called Holactun Slateware, figs. 41, e, 3; 53, a–d; 66, c), cinnamon-slip variety (10, a) not previously reported has 5 YR 7/6, 7.5 YR 7/4 color readings. *Forms.* Jars with vertical neck and both interior and exterior rim bolsters; jars with outcurving neck and direct or everted rim; large basins with globular body and ovoid rim bolster; basins with egg-shape body and ovoid to triangular rim bolster, and basins with flaring sides and T-rim bolster. *Quantity.* None at Mayapan. *Provenience.* Chichen Itza, Dzibilchaltun, Edzna, Holactun, Huaymil, Kabah, Labna, Sayil, Uxmal. *Ceramic complex.* Cehpech (A.D. 800–1000).

CHICHEN RED WARE

Paste composition. Medium texture; orange (2.5 YR 5/8), reddish brown (2.5 YR 5/6; 5 YR 4/4, 4/6; 10 YR 5/3), red (2.5 YR 4/6, 4/8), and pinkish cinnamon (2.5 YR 6/8) color; almost exclusively ash temper. *Surface finish.* Smoothed and well finished. Slipped, medium polished, and has a slight waxy feel. Some fire-clouding on many sherds. Dishes may have gray bases and floors resulting from firing in a reducing atmosphere. Rootlet-marking, sometimes a purplish color, is present. Colors range from red (10 YR 4/6, 4/8, 5/6; 2.5 YR 4/6, 4/8), reddish brown (2.5 YR 5/6, 6/6; 5 YR 5/6), and orange (2.5 YR 5/8).

Red Dzibiac Group. *Types and varieties.* Dzibiac Red Type, Dzibiac Variety (20, a–e; j, p, r–t; 21, c–h, j, m–p, t, u, y, dd, ee, hh, ii, kk; 27, f, g; GWB, pp. 55–56, where it is called Mexican Medium Redware; figs. 86, d–f, h, i; 88, a, b). Chan Kom Black-on-red Type, Chan Kom Variety (20, h; 21, q, r, z), sharp-incised variety (21, k, l), and cream-slip variety (black design painted on cream coat overlying red primary slip; 20, i); Xuku Incised Type, Xuku Variety (20, n, o; 21, j, m, v, x; GWB, pp. 55–56; figs. 85, b, 1–3, 13, c), groove-incised variety (20, g; 21, a, i), cream-slip variety (sharp-incised through cream slip or slipped band; 20, m, q; 21, b, w, cc, gg, jj; GWB, pp. 55–56; figs. 85, b, 5; 86, g, 4; 87, e–h, j, aa–cc), and black-slip variety (sharp-incised through black slip or slipped band; ibid., pp. 55–56; fig. 87, y, z); Holtun Gouged-incised Type, Holtun Variety (20, l, u; GWB, pp. 55–56; figs. 85, a, b, 4, 7–12, 14; 86, a–c, g, 5, 7–11; 87, u), cream-slip variety (gouged-incised through cream slip or slipped band; 20, f, k; 21, s, aa, bb, ff; GWB, pp. 55–56; figs. 86, g, 1–3, j, l, 3–7; 87, a–d, i, k–s, x), and black-slip variety (gouged-incised through black slip or slipped band; ibid., pp. 55–56; fig. 86, j, 2); Tiholop Gadrooned Type, Tiholop Variety (ibid., pp. 55–56; fig. 85, b, 6 pushed out method). Forms. Dishes with rounded sides; water jars, small mouth, high neck; storage jars, wide mouth, low neck; bowls with restricted orifice; bowls, grater; dishes, basal-break tripod; vases, cylindrical; dishes with flaring sides rounding to flat base, and pyriform vessels. Quantity. 28 rim, 119 body sherds. Provenience. Chichen Itza, Mayapan. Ceramic complex. Sotuta (A.D. 1000–2000).

CHICHEN SLATE WARE

Paste composition. Medium texture; a color range including reddish brown (2.5 YR 5/6; 5 YR 4/6, 5/8, 5/6, 4/4); orange (2.5 YR 5/8; 5 YR 6/8; 10 R 5/8); red (2.5 YR 4/6, 4/8, 6/8); pinkish cinnamon (2.5 YR 6/8, 6/6, 7/6); beige (2.5 Y 7/4; 10 YR 6/3, 7/4); buff (10 YR 6/4); gray (2.5 YR 8/0); and cream (10 YR 8/4). Ash temper is predominant, but other tempers such as clay lump, clear calcite, and sherd occur. Surface finish. Smoothed and well finished; slipped and polished, the slip being translucent with a waxy feel, and some examples have purple dendritic markings; color has a wide range including gray (10 YR 7/2, 8/1, 7/1, 8/2, 6/1, 6/2; 2.5 Y 7/2, 8/2, 8/0; 5 YR 7/2, 7/1; 5 Y 8/1, 7/2; 2.5 YR 8/0; 7.5 YR 8/0), buff (10 YR 7/3; 7.5 YR 6/2; 2.5 Y 5/2), pinkish yellow (10 YR 8/6, 8/3; 5 YR 9/2), brown (5 YR 4/6, 5/8; 7.5 YR 5/4; 2.5 YR 4/3), drab (10 YR 6/3; 2.5 Y 6/2), beige (10 YR 7/4), cinnamon (5 YR 7/4; 7.5 YR 7/6), and orange (5 YR 4/8, 6/6).

Slate Dzitas Group. Types and varieties. Dzitas Slate Type, Dzitas Variety (13, a, b, j–l, o; 14, e, g; 16, a; 27, b, h, i; GWB, p. 55, figs. 71, 73, 74); Balantun Black-on-slate Type, Balantun Variety (13, c–f, g–i, m, n; 14, a–d, f, h–j, m; 15, a–e, g, h; 16, b; 19, b–f; 27, a; 59, a; GWB, p. 55, figs. 71, a; 72, e, 1; 73, c, 2; 74, c, d, h); Balam Canche Red-on-slate Type, Balam Canche Variety (17; GWB, p. 56, fig. 75); Chacmay Incised Type, Chacmay Variety (sharp-incised, no illustration) and groove-incised variety (14, k, n; 15, i, j; 18, f; GWB, p. 55, figs. 71, d; 73, c, 18–21, 38–43, d, 12–26); Tekom Gouged-incised Type, Tekom Variety (14, g; GWB, p. 55, fig. 72, b, c, h); Mopila Gadrooned Type, Mopila Variety (no illustration); Nenela Modeled Type, Nenela Variety (no illustration); Timak Composite (incised and painted black) Type, Timak Variety (groove-incised, 14, l; 15, f; 59, j) and sharp-incised variety (13, m, n). Forms. Dishes with rounded sides; bowls with restricted orifice and bolster or direct rim; grater bowls; water jars with small mouth and high neck; tripod jars with wide mouth and low to medium neck; jars with wide mouth and low thick neck; tripod dishes with convex base; ladle censers; cylinder tripod bowls, and disk covers. Quantity. 170 rim, 467 body sherds. Provenience. Chichen Itza, Dzibilchaltun, Mani, Mayapan. Ceramic complex. Sotuta (A.D. 1000–1200). Remarks. This ware is called Mexican Medium Slateware by Brainerd (1958, p. 55, figs. 21, a, 7–9, e; 66, d, j, l, 3, 5, 18–21; 71, a, b, c, 1–15, 17–28, d; 72, a–h, k–o; 73, a, 1–6, 15–26, c, 1–13, 18–24, 38–53, d, 1–26, 31–35; 74, a, b, 1–17, 19–22, 24–28, c–i; 90, h, j–o). For minor differences between this and Puuc Slate Ware see the description of the latter.

CHICHEN UNSLIPPED WARE

Paste composition. Coarse texture; porous structure; wide color range including gray (10 YR 7/2, 7/1, 6/2, 6/1, 5/1, 4/1; 2.5 YR 7/2; 5 YR 8/1; 7.5 YR 6/0), beige (10 YR 7/4), cream (10 YR 8/4, 8/3; 7.5 YR 8/4), brown (2.5 YR 6/4, 5/6; 5 YR 4/4; 7.5 YR 5/4; 10 YR 5/4), which are most common, plus others such as cinnamon (7.5 YR 7/4, 7/6; 2.5 YR 6/8), red (10 R 5/4; 5 YR 5/6), fawn (5 YR 6/4), drab (10 YR 6/3), buff (7.5 YR 6/2; 10 YR 6/4), and orange (5 YR 6/6); usually gray limestone, rarely undifferentiated crystalline calcite or clay lump temper. Surface finish. Smoothed but without slip or polish. Often has medium-coarse, rarely fine striations. A white calcareous coat often used. Surface color is same or nearly the same as paste color, except for white coating.

Unslipped Sisal Group. Types and varieties. Sisal Unslipped Type, Sisal Variety (11, f, g, i–m; 12, a, g, i, j, l, m; 18, h; GWB, pp. 54–55, figs. 68, f, 1–14 which may belong to Sotuta, Hocaba, or Tases phases; 69, c; 70, a, c, j; 95, k, m; 97, k; 104, c, 2–5); Piste Striated Type, Piste Variety (11, a–e, n–v; GWB, pp. 54–55, fig. 68, *b*, some, *e*); Espita Appliqué Type, Espita Variety (12, *d, h*; GWB, pp. 54–55, figs. 69, *a, e, 2*; 70, some; 104, *c, 1*); Tibolon Blue-on-red Type, Tibolon Variety (12, *k*); Cumtun Composite Type, Cumtun Variety (a combination of painting and appliqué; 12, *b, c, e, f*; GWB, pp. 54–55, figs. 70, *f*; 97, *f*). *Forms.* Jars with medium-wide mouth, medium-high outcurving or nearly vertical neck; censers, hourglass; censers, tripod; censers, ladle; bowls, flaring sides; comals; bowls, rounded sides, and bowls with restricted orifice. *Quantity.* 16 rim, 161 body sherds. *Provenience.* Chichen Itza and Mayapan. *Ceramic complex.* Sotuta (A.D. 1000–1200).

DZIBILCHALTUN WARE

This ware is highly distinctive and therefore easily separated from other wares. Its most diagnostic attributes are paste hardness, lustrous but pimply surface, and medium-low flaring jar necks. Considering certain aspects it resembles Puuc Slate Ware. These resemblances include: the paste composition, although Dzibilchaltun Ware is harder; the waxy feel, although Puuc Slate Ware is waxier, and the general color scheme, although Dzibilchaltun Ware runs more to reddish-brown. Examining other aspects we find that it looks like Brainerd's (1958, pp. 50–51) Oxkintok Coarse Monochrome and Regional Coarse Redware. These likenesses take into account the medium to coarse-tempered paste; the often lumpy surface finish; the jar form, especially the medium-low flaring neck; and in some instances the slip color. In view of the fact that these observations are based on 326 jar sherds found at Mayapan, a relatively small quantity representing a single form, the ware name should be considered as temporary. There is a serious doubt, however, whether it is a slate ware. Perhaps it may be said to be an early manifestation of slate. *Paste composition.* Medium to coarse texture, hard, probably largely undifferentiated crystalline calcite temper with the possibility of a small percentage of gray limestone temper, and cinnamon, pink, pinkish cinnamon, and sometimes gray color. *Surface finish.* Lustrous adherent slip, usually with a lumpy surface resulting from imperfectly smoothed temper particles. The vessel is slipped on exterior to and often overlapping a lateral groove below which there is light striation. The neck interior is slipped. Usually these vessels are reddish brown in color. They may, however, range from red through brown to orange, with some gray areas resulting from firing in a reducing atmosphere.

Red Conkal Group. *Types and varieties.* Conkal Red Type, Conkal Variety (25, *cc–ee*; 60, *b*). *Forms.* A variety of vessel shapes are associated with this ware at Dzibilchaltun, but at Mayapan the jar is the only form encountered. This has a wide mouth, medium to low flaring neck, direct rim, globular or barrel-shape body, and concave base. *Quantity.* 68 rim, 258 body sherds. *Provenience.* Dzibilchaltun and Mayapan in Yucatan and Ichmul in Quintana Roo. *Ceramic complex.* Motul (A.D. 600–800), but could have its beginnings in Cochuah (A.D. 300–600). *Remarks.* There is a superficial resemblance between Dzibilchaltun Ware jars and certain Tulum Red Ware jars (WTS, fig. 5, *d*, 12–16). These Tulum Red Ware wide-mouth flaring-neck jars from Tulum and Ichpaatun are similar to the Dzibilchaltun Ware jars not only in form but likewise in color and hardness. They differ, however, in paste composition and surface finish. The Tulum Red Ware specimens have a finer paste texture and different tempering ingredients plus a better smoothed surface, but lack the high lustrous finish of the Dzibilchaltun Ware.

FINE BLACK WARE

Paste composition. Very fine texture; presumably untempered, and black color. *Surface finish.* Very well smoothed, slipped, and usually matte but sometimes lustrous. Color is a strong black, sometimes jet.

Black Yalcox Group. *Types and varieties.* Yalcox Black Type, Yalcox Variety (Berlin, 1956, fig. 4, *hh, ii, kk, uu*); Tekanto Incised (sharp-incised) Type, Tekanto Variety (*ibid.*, fig. 4, *ll, rr*), red-decorated variety (fig. 25, *x*); Xnoria Fluted Type, Xnoria Variety (Berlin, 1956, fig. 4, *mm*), and Xtab Composite Type, Xtab Variety (*ibid.*, fig. 4, *pp, qq*, incised plus punctate). *Forms.* At Mayapan jars and side-angle bowls; at Tecolpan bowls with restricted orifice, basal-break bowls, and tripod dishes. All thin walled. *Quantity.* 3 rim, 8 body sherds. *Provenience.* Many places, but here we are especially concerned with Mayapan and Tecolpan; other known sites for this ware are Dzibilchaltun and Palenque. *Ceramic complex.* Motul (A.D. 600–800).

FINE BUFF WARE

Paste composition. Very fine paste; no temper; buff (7.5 YR 7/4) or pinkish color. *Surface finish.* Well smoothed, slipped and polished on exterior only, usually a cream or buff color, sometimes a brown (10 YR 5/3).

Groups. None given. *Types and varieties.* Possibly Cerro Montoso Polychrome (Smith, 1958b, pp. 153–54) but too weathered to be certain. *Form.* Possibly a jar or tall vase with pedestal base (60, *g*). *Quantity.* 10 rim, 7 body sherds. *Provenience.* Cerro de las Mesas, Isla de Sacrificios, and Tres Zapotes in Veracruz; Champoton, Huaymil, and Jaina in Campeche; and Chichen Itza and Mayapan in Yucatan. *Ceramic complex.* Sotuta (A.D. 1000–1200).

FINE GRAY WARE

Like Fine Orange Ware, this ware undoubtedly occurs over a period of time and in at least three different ceramic complexes. However, comparatively little is known about it. Altar de Sacrificios and Seibal have Fine Gray Ware closely associated with the fine-orange Altar Group. On the Jonuta Horizon (Berlin, 1956, pp. 118–120, 127) the Fine Gray Ware appears to be a mixture of Late Classic forms and types and certain Proto-Postclassic or Cehpech forms and types. At Palenque (Rands and Rands, 1957, pp. 147–148) the Fine Gray Ware may be compared to some of the Jonuta Horizon types. Dzibilchaltun may have the largest collection of this ware, and possibly a phase breakdown can be made to indicate its entire span. According to our present knowledge, it appears to begin in Late Classic times and carry on into the Proto-Postclassic Period or the Cehpech Ceramic Complex in Yucatan, and at Altar de Sacrificios and Seibal into late Cehpech. However, very few sherds of this ware were encountered at Uxmal, Kabah, and Sayil (GWB, p. 51 and figs. 28, *e–g*; 35, *b*; 36, *b*, *d–g*, *i*; 53, *f*, *h*, *k*) in the Cehpech Ceramic Complex. Actually these few could belong to the earlier Motul Ceramic Complex. At Altar de Sacrificios and Seibal, however, the Fine Gray Ware seems to be linked with the fine-orange Altar Group and later. Perhaps the span is Late Classic into the late part of Cehpech. *Paste composition.* Very fine texture, no temper, color usually same as surface or a little lighter. *Surface finish.* Well smoothed, burnished or matte finish, occasionally may be slipped. Color is gray (5 Y 6.8/2.0; 7.5 YR 5.0/1.0). In some instances this ware may be confused with Fine Orange Ware which has been fired in a reducing atmosphere.

Gray Chablekal Group. *Types and varieties.* Chablekal Gray Type, Chablekal Variety (Berlin, 1956, figs. 4, *s*, *w*, *x*; 5, *n*, *pp*); Chicxulub Incised Type, Chicxulub Variety (both groove-incised and sharp-incised, the former most common, *ibid.*, figs. 4, *h*, *m*, *r*, *t–v*, *z*; 5, *o*, *ff–mm*, *qq–ss*, *ww*, *xx*); Cholul Fluted Type, Cholul Variety (*ibid.*, figs. 4, *j*; 5, *ee*); Telchac Composite Type, Telchac Variety (*ibid.*, fig. 4, *i*, *y*, groove-incised, sharp-incised, and punctated). See also Brainerd (1958, figs. 28, *e–g*; 35, *b*; 36, *b*, *d–g*, *i*; 53, *f*, *h*, *k*, and 109, *b*) for all types. *Forms.* Vessel shapes generally encountered are: jars with wide mouth and medium-high neck; bowls with flat base, nearly vertical, flaring, or outcurving sides; bowls with restricted orifice; double-bottom rattle bowls; tripod grater bowls; tripod basal-break dishes, some with basal flange; and miniature vessels. *Quantity.* No rim, 4 body sherds. *Provenience.* Acanceh, Ake, Calcetok, Chichen Itza, Dzebtun, Dzibilchaltun, Holactun, Kabah, Labna, Mayapan, Sayil, Sotuta, and Uxmal in Yucatan; Chilib, Edzna, Huaymil, Jaina, Tixchel and Xicalango in Campeche; Coba in Quintana Roo; Palenque, Tecolpan, and Yoxiha in Chiapas; Boqueron, El Coco, Estapilla, Huimango, Jonuta, Juarez, Las Minas, Tiradero, and Tortuguero in Tabasco, and Altar de Sacrificios, Seibal, and Uaxactun in Guatemala. *Ceramic complexes.* Motul (A.D. 600–800) and early and late Cehpech (A.D. 800–1000).

FINE ORANGE WARE

This is one of the most distinctive wares in the Maya aggregate. It covers a span of approximately 950 years and may be separated into six different groups alphabetically listed: Altar (Y Fine Orange), Balancan (Z Fine Orange), Cunduacan (U Fine Orange), Dzibilchaltun (Dzibilchaltun Fine Orange), Matillas (V Fine Orange), and Silho (X Fine Orange). When originally given to the different fine oranges, these letters were assumed to be temporary, until more was known and appropriate names could be found to replace them (Smith, 1958b, p. 151). The time has come, and the group names have been given.

The ware attributes common to all these groups are found under the two principal headings of paste composition and surface finish. In all cases the paste is of very fine texture, has no temper but may contain certain mineral inclusions, and is generally orange in color, often a shade lighter than the surface. This is a brittle ware with a clear, porcelainlike fracture, and when tapped gives a distinct ring. At all times the surface is well smoothed. Usually it is slipped, although occasionally slipping is doubtful. It may carry secondary white or black slip on interior, exterior, or both. It is burnished, rarely polished, and the slip color is usually orange (2.5 YR 5/8; 10 R 5/8; 5 YR 6/8, 5/8, 6/6), or reddish brown (2.5 YR 5/6; 5 YR 5/6; 7.5 YR 5/6; 10 R 4/3; 2.5 YR 3/6; 5 YR 4/4, 4/3; 10 YR 4/3), sometimes brown (2.5 YR 5/4; 5 YR 5/6; 7.5 YR 5/6, 5/8, 5/4), red (2.5 YR 4/6; 4/8; 7.5 R 3/6; 10 R 5/6, 4/6, 5/4, 4/4, 6/4), light brown (7.5 YR 6/6; 10 YR 4/2, 4/3, 5/2, 5/3), cinnamon (2.5 YR 6/8; 5 YR 6/6; 7.5 YR 7/6), or fawn (5 YR 6/4). When weathered this ware generally leaves chalky surfaces.

Fine-orange Altar Group. *Paste composition.* Very fine texture, no temper, even in color throughout the section, but color may run a shade lighter than surface at times. *Surface finish.* Well smoothed, usually slipped and lightly burnished, commonly orange in color. Color readings: orange (5 YR 5/8, 6/8; 10 R 5/8; 2.5 YR 5/8), reddish brown (5 YR 5/6; 2.5 YR 5/6; 7.5 YR 5/6). The black decoration is usually lightly applied and therefore a darker brown. *Types and varieties.* Altar Orange Type, Altar Variety (no illustration); Pabellon Modeled-carved Type, Pabellon Variety (9, *h–j, l*; 27, *l*; Smith and Gifford, 1966; RES, figs. 3, *h*; 10, *s*; 37, *c*, 9; 66, *b*, 4, 7; 86, *b–h, j–l, n, p*); Trapiche Groove-incised Type, Trapiche Variety (RES, fig. 86, *a*); Cedro Gadrooned Type, Cedro Variety (*ibid.*, fig. 3, *j*), and Tumba Black-on-orange Type, Tumba Variety (*ibid.*, fig. 3, *a*). *Forms.* Flaring-side bowls rounding to flat base; ringstand barrel-shape vases; flat-base barrel-shape vases; hemispherical bowls; and possibly ringstand cylindrical vases (27, *l*). *Quantity.* 5 rim, 36 body sherds. *Provenience.* Altar de Sacrificios, Kixpek, Nakum, Piedras Negras, San Agustin Acasaguastlan, Seamay Cave, Tikal, Uaxactun, and Zaculeu in Guatemala; Benque Viejo in British Honduras; San Salvador in El Salvador; Uxmal and Mayapan in Yucatan; Finca El Salvador Cave, Palenque, and Yaxchilan in Chiapas. *Ceramic complexes.* Tepeu 3 (A.D. 800–900), Cehpech (A.D. 800–1000), Boca (A.D. 800–900), and Jimba (A.D. 900–1000+). *Remarks.* At Altar de Sacrificios, in addition to the forms and types associated with the fine-orange Altar Group, there appear to be both fine-orange Balancan Group and fine-orange Silho Group specimens. In fact, only the Pabellon Modeled-carved Type and its two principal vessel shapes, a flaring-side bowl or dish rounding to flat base, and a barrel-shape vase with ringstand base as described by Adams (1963, figs. 51, *f, p*; 52; 53, *d–e*), form part of both the Boca and Jimba Ceramic complexes. All the other Fine Orange Ware

forms and types mentioned by Adams occur only in the Jimba Ceramic Complex, suggesting that they are of a later date. Presumably they would otherwise have been found in the earlier Boca Complex. Furthermore, certain of these later forms such as pyriform vases and grater bowls and certain types like the Provincia Plano-relief and Ixpayac Incised belong to either the Cehpech or Sotuta Ceramic complexes.

Fine-orange Balancan Group. *Paste composition.* Very fine texture, no temper, and color usually matches surface color, if anything a shade lighter. *Surface finish.* Well smoothed, usually slipped orange and lightly burnished. Other surface colors, white and black, are also used. Color readings are: orange (5 YR 6/6, 6/8; 10 R 5/8), reddish brown (5 YR 4/6; 2.5 YR 5/6; 7.5 YR 5/6), a cream white, and a strong black shading to a dark brown if thinly applied. The white often carries a higher polish than the orange or black slips. When weathered, the surfaces become chalky. *Types and varieties.* Balancan Orange Type, Balancan Variety (Berlin, 1956, figs. 3, *a, mm–vv*; 4, *j, g*); Caribe Incised Type, Caribe Variety (no illustration), red-paint variety (9, *a*), and groove-incised variety (9, *m*); Canizan Gadrooned Type, Canizan Variety (GWB, fig. 59, *e, 11*; 89, *e, 4*); Palizada Black-on-orange Type, Palizada Variety (9, *b, f*); Provincia Plano-relief Type, Provincia Variety (9, *d, e, g, k*); Tenosique Red-on-orange Type, Tenosique Variety (9, *c*). *Forms.* Usually some segment of a sphere or ovaloid both deep and shallow, and with either restricted or open orifice. Other less common shapes are the hemispherical bowl with ringstand base, the barrel-shape vessel, and the tripod dish with outcurving sides. *Quantity.* 19 rim, 67 body sherds. *Provenience.* Although many other sites in Mesoamerica may claim a few examples of the fine-orange Balancan Group, the center of concentration would appear to be somewhere in eastern Tabasco, possibly the Jonuta-Tecolpan region (including in addition Huimango and Juarez), or in southwestern Campeche near Los Guarixes. Other sites where this group occurs are: Atasta, Canbalam, Edzna, and Jaina in Campeche; Acanceh, Chichen Itza, Dzibilchaltun, Holactun, Kabah, Labna, Mayapan, Sayil, Uxmal, and Xcanatun in Yucatan; Palenque (?) in Chiapas; Altar de Sacrificios, Piedras Negras, Seibal, Uaxactun (?), and Utatlan in Guatemala. *Ceramic complex.* Cehpech (A.D. 800–1000) in the Puuc and at Mayapan and Jimba (A.D. 900–1000) at Altar de Sacrificios.

Fine-orange Cunduacan Group. *Paste composition* and *surface finish.* Same as that of the fine-orange Matillas Group. *Types and varieties.* Cunduacan Orange Type, Cunduacan Variety (Berlin, 1956, pp. 136–138, fig. 6, *g–s*); Buey Modeled Type, Buey Variety (*ibid.*, fig. 6, *t–w*). *Forms.* Tripod bowls with lateral ridge, sometimes notched, and solid slab feet, usually stepped; the same form without lateral ridge but with solid conical feet on the smaller vessels, and hollow cylindrical flat bottom or tapering to rounded bottom on the others; miniature vases with pedestal base; deep bowls; ladle censers; and human effigy censers of hourglass shape with a standing human figure attached to the exterior. *Quantity.* 3 rim, 13 body sherds. *Provenience.* Atasta in Campeche; Juarez and Tamulte in Tabasco; and Mayapan in Yucatan. *Ceramic complex.* Chikinchel (A.D. 1450–1550). *Remarks.* It is significant that none of the deep or shallow tripods, miniature vases, and deep bowls carries any decoration, whereas usually fine-orange Matillas Group shallow tripods are incised, and frequently other forms are decorated (Smith, 1958, p. 157). Furthermore, the foot forms in the two groups differ greatly. The hollow effigy foot much used in the Matillas Group is not found in the Cunduacan, whereas the thin solid slab foot so common in Cunduacan is lacking in Matillas. In addition two forms commonly used in Cunduacan ladle censers and miniature vases with pedestal bases, are missing in Matillas.

Fine-orange Dzibilchaltun Group. *Paste composition.* Very fine texture, probably untempered although untested microscopically, orange in color. *Surface finish.* Unslipped (?), or may bear areas of orange, clear white, black, or gray slip. All interiors have a red slip. The white slip is opaque with medium luster; the black slip is a thin stain. *Types and varieties.* Dzibilchaltun Orange Type, Dzibilchaltun Variety (no illustration); Xlacah Incised Type, Xlacah Variety (incised through white, GWB, p. 52, fig. 59, *g, 1–4, 8, 9, 12; h, 6*) red-slip variety (*ibid.*, fig. *g, 6*), and black-slip variety (*ibid.*, fig. *g, 5, 10, 11*). *Forms.* Bowls with outcurving sides and flat base; restricted orifice barrel-shape vessels; dishes with basal-Z-angle and flat base, and rarely hemispherical bowls. *Quantity.* None at Mayapan. *Provenience.* Acanceh and Dzibilchaltun in Yucatan, and Los Guarixes in Campeche. *Ceramic complex.* Motul (A.D. 600–800). *Remarks.* This brief outline of the fine-orange Dzibilchaltun Group has been taken largely from Brainerd (1958, p. 52, fig. 59, *g, 1–16; h,*

6) and had better be considered preliminary since Dr. E. Wyllys Andrews will soon be publishing a report on Dzibilchaltun wherein this fine-orange group will be far more thoroughly and accurately discussed. It has, however, been included more to indicate its presence in and especially its absence from many known sites.

Fine-orange Matillas Group. *Paste composition.* Very fine texture, no temper, orange (5 YR 6/6, 6/8, 7/8), cinnamon (7.5 YR 7/6, 7/4), pinkish cinnamon (2.5 YR 6/6, 6/8; 10 R 6/3, 6/6), beige (10 YR 7/3, 7/4), light brown (7.5 YR 6/4, 6/6), buff (10 YR 6/4), and pink (5 YR 7/6) in color. *Surface finish.* Well smoothed, slipped and lightly burnished, leaving a matte finish. The slip may be orange, red, or black, rarely cream, and when weathered the surfaces become chalky. Color readings are: orange (2.5 YR 5/8), red (10 R 5/6, 4/6, 5/4, 4/4, 6/4; 2.5 YR 4/6, 4/8; 7.5 R 3/6), reddish brown (2.5 YR 5/6, 3/6; 10 R 4/3; 10 YR 4/3), light brown (7.5 YR 6/6; 10 YR 4/2, 4/3, 5/2, 5/3), cinnamon (5 YR 6/6; 7.5 YR 7/6; 2.5 YR 6/8), and rarely fawn (5 YR 6/4). *Types and varieties.* Matillas Orange Type, Matillas Variety (55, *a*); Chilapa Gouged-incised Type, Chilapa Variety (55, *c, 2–4, 7, 8, 11, 12, 14, 18, 19; 75, q*); Grijalva Incised-polychrome Type; Grijalva Variety (55, *b, 1*); Nacajuca Black-on-orange Type, Nacajuca Variety (55, *d, 1–3, 5, 6*); Salto Composite Type, Salto Variety (55, *b, 3, 5, 6; c, 1, 5, 6, 9, 10, 13, 15–17*; these all have painted stripes or bands and some are accompanied by incised, others by gouged-incised, designs); Sayula Polychrome Type, Sayula Variety (55, *d, 4*); Villahermosa Incised Type, Villahermosa Variety (55, *b, 2, 4, 7–11*). All Matillas Group incising is sharp. *Forms.* Tripod dishes with basal ridge or flange which may be notched and with plain (solid conical, hollow cylindrical, hollow bulbous) or hollow effigy (moldmade human or animal heads) feet, the same shape of tripod dish without ridge or flange; a similar form with flange and ringstand; a tall-neck jar; a low-neck jar; bowls with restricted orifice; deep bowls with ringstand base; and hemispherical bowls. *Quantity.* 397 rim, 961 body sherds. *Provenience.* The real center of concentration is Tabasco at such sites as El Coco, Juarez, Las Minas, and Tamulte as well as Atasta in Campeche. Other sites where this fine-orange group is found include: Aguacatal, Champoton, Los Guarixes, and Tixchel in Campeche; Cancun, El Meco, Ichpaatun, Mulchi, San Miguel (Cozumel), and Tulum in Quintana Roo; and Dzibilchaltun and Mayapan in Yucatan. *Ceramic complexes.*

Hocaba and Tases at Mayapan (A.D. 1250–1450) and the Cintla Horizon in Tabasco.

Fine-orange Silho Group. *Paste composition.* Very fine texture, no temper, and a variety of colors. The most frequent colors are orange (5 YR 6/6, 6/8), pinkish cinnamon (2.5 YR 6/8, 6/6), and cinnamon (7.5 YR 7/4, 7/6); less important are brown (5 YR 4/4) and buff (10 YR 6/4). *Surface finish.* Well smoothed, usually slipped and lightly burnished. Surfaces, particularly when unslipped or weathered, often are powdery. Most sherds bear an opaque orange slip somewhat darker than the underlying paste. Besides the orange, bands or panels of cream, black, or red slip are used. The black appears like a dull stain. The cream is lustrous, clear in color, opaque, and quite thick. The red sometimes sparkles and is purplish — a specular hematite red. Color readings include: orange (2.5 YR 5/8), reddish brown (2.5 YR 5/6; 5 YR 4/3, 5/6); brown (7.5 YR 5/6, 5/8, 5/4; 5 YR 5/6; 2.5 YR 5/4); less frequently red (2.5 YR 4/8, 4/6), and pinkish cinnamon (2.5 YR 6/8). *Types and varieties.* Silho Orange Type, Silho Variety (22, *c, d, m, o–q*; 59, *d, e*; Smith, 1957b, figs. 6, *n*; 13, *a, c*; 15, *a*; 17, *a*); Calkini Gadrooned Type, Calkini Variety (*ibid.*, fig. 13, *b*); Champan Red-on-orange Type, Champan Variety (*ibid.*, fig. 4, *e, h*); Cumpich Incised Type, Cumpich Variety (groove-incised, 22, *a*; *ibid.*, figs. 4, *a, d*; 5, *d*); black-paint variety (22, *v*); Kilikan Composite Type, Kilikan Variety (22, *e, j, k*; *ibid.*, figs. 5, *c*; 9, *f–m*; 10, *a–c*; 11, *a–s*; 12, *c, d, f*; gouged-incised designs through orange slip plus black-painted designs), black-slip variety (*ibid.*, figs. 4, *k, l*; 6, *p, q*; 10, *d, l, m*; 12, *l*; gouged-incised designs through black slip plus black-painted designs), cream-slip variety (22, *r*; 59, *h*; *ibid.*, figs. 13, *f*; 14, *d, f*; 15, *i*; 16, *b–e, g*; gouged-incised through cream slip plus black-painted design), polychrome variety (*ibid.*, fig. 14, *l*; gouged-incised through cream, plus both black and polychrome bands); Nunkini Modeled Type, Nunkini Variety (27, *k*; *ibid.*, figs. 7, 13, *g, o, p*; modeled and unaccompanied by painted embellishment), black-paint variety (*ibid.*, figs. 7, *a–e, g*; 13, *h–n*; modeled plus painted black details), polychrome variety (*ibid.*, fig. 17, *h*, modeled plus red and black decoration); Pocboc Gouged-incised Type, Pocboc Variety (22, *i*; *ibid.*, figs. 6, *o*; 10, *n, o*; 12, *e, m*; 13, *e*; 16, *f*; gouged-incised through orange slip), black-slip variety (*ibid.*, fig. 6, *r*; gouged-incised through black slip), cream-slip variety (*ibid.*, fig. 17, *f*; gouged-incised through cream slip); Pomuch Polychrome Type, Pomuch

Variety (*ibid.*, fig. 5, *m* (?); 14, *g–k*; there is some question as to whether the drum shape belongs in this group); Yalton Black-on-orange Type, Yalton Variety (22, *b, f–h, l, n, t–v*; 59, *b, c, f*; *ibid.*, figs. 4, *b, c, f, i*; 5, *a, b, g–k*; 6, *a–m*; 8, *a–w*; 9, *a–e*; 10, *e–k*; 12, *a, b, h–k*; 13, *d*; 14, *a, b*; 15, *b, c*; 16, *a*; 17, *b, e*), cream-slip variety (22, *s*). *Forms.* The principal shapes include: jars, small mouth with high outcurving neck; jars, medium-size mouth with bulging neck; jars, wide mouth with low flaring neck; pyriform vases, either tripod or with pedestal base, and either globular body or with body angle; cylindrical vases with bell-shape pedestal base; bowls, hemispherical with either flat or ringstand base; bowls with restricted orifice and flat base or with three hollow bulbous feet; tripod grater bowl with flaring walls angling to convex base; and plates or dishes with three hollow bell-shape or bulbous feet. These and less important shapes are described by Smith (1957b, pp. 136–137; fig. 1). *Quantity.* 24 rim, 162 body sherds. *Provenience.* Canbalam, Champoton, Huaymil, and Jaina in Campeche; Chichen Itza, Dzibilchaltun, Mayapan, and Xulmil in Yucatan; Altar de Sacrificios and Uaxactun in Guatemala; Tecolpan and Tierra Blanca in Tabasco; San Miguel on the Isla de Cozumel in Quintana Roo, and the Isla de Sacrificios, Veracruz, Mexico. *Remarks.* On the basis of frequency of occurrence it would appear that the fine-orange Silho Group had its center of manufacture somewhere along the coast of Campeche (Smith, 1958b, pp. 153–157). The state of Veracruz and even the Isla de Sacrificios, which have large quantities of fine wares including Fine Orange Ware, lack any appreciable amount of the fine-orange Silho Group types. The forms, decorative techniques, and design styles of Veracruz Fine Orange Ware are quite different. Of the illustrated material from Isla de Sacrificios, that shown by Du Solier (1943, p. 76) has more fine-orange Silho Group sherds than any other. It would appear that a few fine-orange Silho Group vessels reached Veracruz through trade, and a few of the Veracruz Fine Orange Ware types found their way into Tabasco, Campeche, and Yucatan. After a considerable amount of investigation in Tabasco from the Veracruz border on the west to the Campeche border on the east, Berlin (1956) totaled a mere handful of fine-orange Silho Group sherds, whereas with a somewhat similar degree of investigation along the Campeche coast this ceramic group appears to be far better represented. As for the largest collections of this ware group, they may be found in quantitative order at Huaymil in Campeche and

Chichen Itza and Mayapan in Yucatan. *Ceramic complex.* Sotuta (A.D. 1000–1200).

FLORES WAXY WARE

Within this ware, the Black Chunhinta, red Joventud,* and cream Pital groups are known. *Paste composition.* Medium-coarse texture; buff to gray color; at Uaxactun, sherd temper plus small percentages of ash and calcite are used. *Surface finish.* Smoothed, slipped, and burnished, having a waxy feel. Slip is thin and soft. Crazing, rootlet-marking, and fire-clouding are present. Colors are red, black, variegated, orange, dirty cream or buff, reddish brown, and gray. Most common red is Vinaceous Tawny (2.5 YR 6/6, 10 R 6/6); Vinaceous Rufous (10 R 5/6) is less common. Other reds include: Kaiser Brown (2.5 YR 4/8, 4/6), Brick Red (7.5 R 3/6), Burnt Sienna (2.5 R 4/8, 4/6), Onion Skin Pink (10 R 7/6, 6/6) and Hay's Russet (7.5 R 4/6, 4/8). The orange is usually Ferruginous (10 R 5/7).

Red Joventud Group. *Types and varieties.* Joventud Red Type, Joventud Variety*; Guitara Incised Type, Guitara Variety (groove-incised) and sharp-incised variety; Resaca Impressed Type, Resaca Variety; Patos Appliqué Type, Patos Variety; and Desvario Chamfered Type, Desvario Variety. *Forms.* Flaring* or outcurving-side plates or dishes*, sometimes with thickened rim; cuspidor shape bowls; jars; restricted-orifice bowls; wide-everted rim plates; nearly cylindrical bowls, and rounded-side bowls. *Quantity.* Mayapan, 2 rim, no body sherds. *Provenience.* Mayapan and Uaxactun. *Ceramic complex.* Mamon (1500–800 B.C.). *Remarks.* The other groups, not encountered in these collections, are described and listed in earlier publications (RES; Smith and Gifford, 1966).

HOMUN UNSLIPPED WARE

Paste composition. Medium-fine texture, undetermined temper, and cinnamon (7.5 YR 8/5) to deep gray color. *Surface finish.* Smoothed, unslipped, and lusterless with pinkish buff (7.5 YR 8/4, 8/5) and olive (5 Y 5/2, 5/3) color.

Unslipped Yotolin Group. *Types and varieties.* Only the one type Yotolin Pattern — burnished, Yotolin Variety (GWB, p. 48, fig. 30, *c, 1–35*). *Forms.* Bottles with distinctive narrow neck and thickened rim. *Quantity.* None at Mayapan. *Provenience.* Mani Cenote and Balam Canche Cave.

Ceramic complex. Ecab (Early Formative according to Brainerd).

MAYAPAN BLACK WARE

Paste composition. Same as Mayapan Red Ware, color grayer or pinker. *Surface finish.* Slipped and burnished, much the same as Mayapan Red Ware except for color which varies from a strong black to a brownish black, and may have dark red areas.

Black Sulche Group. *Types and varieties.* Sulche Black Type, Sulche Variety (cf. for shape 38, *a,* 1, 3–9, 11 12; 40, *b,* 1, 2, 4; 41, *b,* 6, 8, 9; 44, *f, j*); Conil Plano-relief Type (no illustration, but a bowl form); Pacha Incised Type, Pacha Variety (groove-incised, cf. for shape 38, *a,* 2, 10), and Sacmuyna Modeled Type, Sacmuyna Variety (no illustration, a bird whistle). *Forms.* Water jars; tripod dishes with flaring sides; tripod dishes with rounded sides; bowls with restricted orifice; cylindrical vases; and figurines. *Quantity.* 64 rim, 1074 body sherds. *Provenience.* Mayapan. *Ceramic complex.* Hocaba and Tases (A.D. 1200–1450).

MAYAPAN COARSE WARE

Paste composition. Very coarse texture, heavily tempered with what appears to be calcite but was not examined by Shepard, red to reddish brown in color. Some appear to have been sunbaked, others fired. *Surface finish.* Imperfectly smoothed, unslipped, never striated, orange-red to reddish brown color. The forming of the vessel as well as the modeling of attached figures and application of ornaments are all extremely crudely done.

Unslipped Uayma Group. *Types and varieties.* Uayma Modeled Type, Uayma Variety (35, *a,* 18; 65, *i, o*; 66, *c,* 1–3). *Forms.* Effigy censers and figurines. *Quantity.* 18 rim (or head), 30 body sherds. *Provenience.* Mayapan. *Ceramic complex.* Tases (A.D. 1300–1450).

MAYAPAN RED WARE

This ware has its beginning in the Hocaba Ceramic Complex and continues on into the Tases Ceramic Complex with different types, varieties, and forms. The group associated with the Hocaba Ceramic Complex is the red Mama Group, and the group linked to the Tases Ceramic Complex is the red Panabchen Group. Ware attributes are consistently the same for both groups. *Paste composition.* Coarse texture, calcite temper, usually a cryptocrystalline, chalky white limestone, the material locally called sascab. Paste color is normally pink to pale red (5 YR 7/6, 8/2, 8/3), occasionally cream (10 YR 8/3, 8/4; 7.5 YR 8/4) or gray (10 YR 6/1; 2.5 Y 8/2; 10 YR 8/1, 8/2). *Surface finish.* Moderately well smoothed, slipped, and burnished, ranging from faintly lustrous to lustrous. Slip fits well with little popping or spalling. Other blemishes include rootlet-marking, fire-clouding, and sometimes crazing. Color variation on a single vessel is common, especially on the jar form, less so on other vessel shapes. These variations include red (10 R 4/8; 2.5 YR 4/8; 10 R, 4/6, 3/6, 5/6; 2.5 YR 4/6; 7.5 R 3/8), orange (2.5 YR 5/8; 5 YR 4/8; 10 R 5/8; 5 YR 6/8), reddish brown (2.5 YR 3/6, 5/6; 5 YR 5/6, 5/8), brown (2.5 YR 5/4; 5 YR 4/4), and gray, the result of fire-clouding.

Red Mama Group. *Types and varieties.* Mama Red Type, Mama Variety (38, *a*, 1, 4–9, 11, 17, 22, 23; *b*, 12, 13; *c*, 1–3; 39; 40, *b*, 1–10, 12, 13, 15–17; *c*, 3; 41, *a*, 7, 8; *b*, 7; 43, *i*, *q*; 44, *h*; 46, *a*, 3; 49, *h*; 74, *z*); Chapab Modeled Type, Chapab Variety (38, *a*, 22; 45, *g*); Dzonot Appliqué Type, Dzonot Variety (cf. 38, *b*, 9); and Papacal Incised Type, Papacal Variety (cf. 38, *a*, 2, 10; 39; 40, *b*, 11, 14, *c*, 5; 43, *d*, *j*, *p*; 47) which is commonly groove-incised with a few sharp-incised examples. *Forms.* Water jars with high necks; storage jars with high or low necks; tripod dishes or bowls with flaring or rounded sides; bowls with restricted orifice; tripod grater bowls; tripod deep bowls; cuspidor shape bowls; basins with bolster rim; cups with pedestal base; miniature jars; cylindrical vases; drums; and an effigy vessel. *Quantity.* 15,642 rim, 104,073 body sherds. *Provenience.* Acanceh, Chichen Itza, Dzibilchaltun, Mayapan, Tecoh, and Ucu in Yucatan; Champoton in Campeche; and Ichmul in Quintana Roo. *Ceramic complex.* Hocaba (A.D. 1200–1300). *Remarks.* The tripod dishes or bowls with either flaring or rounded sides are slipped on both interior and exterior.

Red Panabchen Group. *Types and varieties.* Mama Red Type, unslipped-exterior variety (40, *a*, 1–5; 41, *b*, 1–4, 10), black-and-red-on-unslipped variety (40, *a*, 6), black-on-unslipped variety (no illustration) and red-on-unslipped variety (no illustration); Panabchen Red Type, Panabchen Variety (37, *b*, *f*, *g*; 38, *d*, 2, 3; 41, *c*, 1–4, *d*; 43, *i*, *n–p*); Tzitz Red Type, Tzitz Variety (38, *d*, 4–7; 42, *b–d*); Dzitxil Openwork Type, Dzitxil Variety (37, *a*, *c*;

75, c); Pustunich Incised Type, Pustunich Variety (38, *d*, 1; 47, *n*; 49, *a*) of which more are groove-incised than sharp-incised; Yobain Plano-relief Type, Yobain Variety (47, *o*), and Tixua Gadrooned Type, Tixua Variety (no illustration, but jar body). *Forms.* Water jars with high neck; storage jars with low or high neck; jars with parenthesis rim; tripod dishes or bowls with flaring sides and sometimes a flange; tripod dishes or bowls with rounded sides; bowls with restricted orifice and sometimes a pedestal rather than a flat or concave base; tripod grater bowls; deep tripod bowls, sometimes with a basal flange; hemispherical bowls; basins; cylindrical vases; effigy vessels; miniature jars and tripod bowls; disk or scutate covers; tripod or pedestal-base cups; pedestal-base plate; and figurines. *Quantity.* 2,675 rim, 8,313 body sherds. *Provenience.* Acanceh, Chichen Itza, Dzibilchaltun, Mayapan, Tecoh, and Ucu in Yucatan; Champoton in Campeche; and Ichmul in Quintana Roo. *Ceramic complex.* Tases (A.D. 1300–1450). *Remarks.* The tripod dishes or bowls with either flaring or rounded sides, included in this group, are slipped on interior but not on exterior.

MAYAPAN UNSLIPPED WARE

This is a ware which has its beginning in the Hocaba Ceramic Complex and develops new types, varieties, and forms in the Tases Ceramic Complex. The group associated with the Hocaba Ceramic Complex is the unslipped Navula Group, and the group connected with the Tases Ceramic Complex is the unslipped Panaba Group. Ware attributes are consistently the same for both groups. *Paste composition.* Coarse texture and apparently heavily tempered with calcite, either cryptocrystalline, chalky white limestone, or a gray limestone. The paste colors are much the same as those of the surface. Frequently the predominant light gray (10 YR 6/1, 7/1, 8/1) will have a cinnamon core, and many are cinnamon (5 YR 6/6) clear through. *Surface finish.* Normally fairly evenly smoothed, sometimes imperfectly smoothed, never polished. The surface texture ranged from smooth through fine sandpaper finish to the coarseness of a wood rasp. Many vessels, especially jars, were lightly striated over part of exterior. Colors are light gray (10 YR 6/1, 7/1, 8/1) which is most abundant, then dark gray (10 YR 5/1), cinnamon (5 YR 6/6), beige (10 YR 7/3, 7/4), cream (10 YR 8/3, 9/2), and pink (2.5 Y 8/2).

Unslipped Navula Group. *Types and varieties.*
Navula Unslipped Type, Navula Variety (33, *f*; cf.
28, *b*, 2, *c*, 2, 4, 8–11; 29, *k*, *l*, *n*, *o*, *q*, *dd*; 33,
a–e; 61, *a*, 5, *c*, 1, 2); Yacman Striated Type, Yacman Variety (28, *a*, 14; 29, *f*; 61, *a*, 3; cf. 28, *a*, 1–
13, 15–25, *b*, 1, 3; 29, *j*, *m*, *p*; 31, *v*; 61, *a*, 1, 2, 4);
Cehac-Hunacti Composite Type, Cehac-Hunacti
Variety (30, *d*, *e*, *k*, *l*; 31, *a–c*, *e*, *h*, *i*, *l–p*; 62, *a–f*);
Hoal Modeled Type, Hoal Variety (32, *b–d*; 68, *a*,
1–3); Kanasin Red-on-unslipped Type, Kanasin Variety (cf. 28, *c*, 1, 3, 5–7; 60, *l*); Cehac Painted
Type, Cehac Variety (61, *e*, 3; cf. 31, *cc–ee*; 61,
e, 1, 2), and Hunacti Appliqué Type, Hunacti Variety (no illustration, none certainly without painting). *Forms.* Storage and cooking jars; effigy, tripod or pedestal-base jar and ladle censers; flaring-
side dishes with bolster rim or lug handles; basins;
restricted, deep, or grater bowls; small bowl, possibly a paintpot; tripod cup; figurines; and a
pestle. *Quantity.* 12,515 rim, 51,803 body sherds.
Provenience. Chichen Itza, Dzibilchaltun, and
Mayapan in Yucatan; Aguada Grande, Calderitas,
Chiquila, Cozumel, Ichpaatun, Tancah, and Tulum
in Quintana Roo; Atasta and Champoton in Campeche. *Ceramic complex.* Hocaba (A.D. 1200–
1300).

Unslipped Panaba Group. *Types and varieties.*
Chen Mul Modeled Type, Chen Mul Variety (30,
y; 31, *ff*, *hh*; 32, *e–pp*; 34; 35; 63; 64; 65, *a–h*,
j–o; 66, *a*, *d*; 67; 68, *b*; 69–73); Panaba Unslipped
Type, Panaba Variety (28, *b*, 2; 29, *a–e*, *g–i*, *r–u*, *w*;
30, *a*, *n*, *p*, *q*, *s*; 31, *g*, *q*, *gg*; 33, *g–i*; 61, *a*, 5, *b*;
d, 1, 2); Huhi Impressed Type, Huhi Variety (31,
k, *s*); Thul Appliqué Type, Thul Variety (30, *c*, *g–i*,
o, *r*, *t*; 31, *r*, *t*, *u*, *z–bb*; 62, *f*); Acansip Painted
Type, Acansip Variety (28, *a*, 13, 15; 29, *v*, *x–cc*;
30, *f*, *w*; 31, *f*, *x*; 61, *e*, 4); Acansip-Thul Composite
Type, Acansip-Thul Variety (30, *b*, *v*; 31, *d*; 61, *e*,
5); Chenkeken Incised Type, Chenkeken Variety
(mostly groove-incised except for sharp-incised
graters, 29, *hh*, *kk*, *ll*; 30, *m*; 31, *j*; 33, *j*); Chenkeken-Acansip Composite Type, Chenkeken-Acan-
sip Variety (groove-incised, 32 a), and Buleb Striated Type, Buleb Variety (29, *jj*). *Forms.* Storage
and cooking jars; effigy, tripod or pedestal-base
jar and ladle censers; restricted, deep tripod, grater, and thick bowls; flat-based dishes with flaring
sides; tripod dishes with flaring or rounded sides;
tripod, pedestal-base, and flat-base cups; basins;
pedestal-base vases; figurines; effigy vessels; ringstand plates; moulds; miniature bowls and jars;
disk-shape covers; masks; and stands. *Quantity.*
10,355 rim, 130,763 body sherds. *Provenience.*
Chichen Itza, Dzibilchaltun, and Mayapan in Yu-

catan; Aguada Grande, Calderitas, Chetumal Bay,
Chiquila, Coba, Cozumel, Ichpaatun, Isla Mujeres,
Tancah, and Tulum in Quintana Roo; Atasta and
Champoton in Campeche; Cintla in Tabasco.
Ceramic complex. Tases (A.D. 1300–1450).

METALLIC WARE

In my opinion this is not truly a ware. Actually a number of different wares may have this
metallic quality: Peten Gloss Ware may be vitrified in appearance (RES, p. 27) and Fine Orange
Ware occasionally looks like plumbate Ware because it has an iridescent appearance (Medellin
Zenil, 1955; Smith, 1958b, p. 159).

OCHIL UNSLIPPED WARE

Paste composition. Coarse texture, calcite temper, and light reddish brown (5 YR 6/4) in color.
Surface finish. Well smoothed, but unslipped, and
the same light reddish brown as paste.

Unslipped Yuncu Group. *Types and varieties.*
Yuncu Unslipped Type, Yuncu Variety (cf. R. H.
Thompson, 1958, fig. 35, *a*); Kinchil Composite
Type, Kinchil Variety (57, *e*) and Tetis Appliqué
Type, Tetis Variety (GWB, fig. 33, *g*). *Forms.* Stor-
age jars and restricted-orifice bowls. *Quantity.*
16 rim, 7 body sherds. *Provenience.* Mani and
Mayapan. *Ceramic complex.* Chauaca (A.D. 1550–
1800).

PASO CABALLO WAXY WARE

Paste composition. Medium-coarse texture;
buff color; and usually sherd temper. *Surface finish.* Smoothed, slipped, and burnished, having a
strong waxy feel. Slip is thin and soft. Crazing is
a distinguishing characteristic. Other surface blemishes are rootlet-marking and fire-clouding. Colors are red, occasionally black, orange, or a good
cream. The most common red is Vinaceous Rufous (10 R 5/6), closely followed by Burnt Sienna
(2.5 R 4/8, 4/6). Other reds include: Kaiser Brown
(2.5 YR 4/8, 4/6) and Hay's Russet (7.5 R 4/6, 4/8).
The orange is usually Ferruginous (10 R 5/7). The
buff Escobal, cream Flor, black Polvero, Usulutan
Sarteneja, and red Sierra* groups fall under this
ware.

Red Sierra Group. *Types and varieties.* Sierra Red
Type, Sierra Variety*; Laguna Verde Incised Type,
Laguna Verde Variety (groove-incised)*; Alta Mira
Fluted Type, Alta Mira Variety*; Union Appliqué

Type, Union Appliqué Variety; Lagartos Punctate Type, Lagartos Variety*; and Repasto Black-on-red Type, Repasto Variety. *Forms*. Wide-everted or thickened rim plates or dishes; recurving-side bowls*; flaring-side dishes* or bowls*; outcurving-side and thickened rim plates; rounded-side dishes; jars*; dome-shape covers; lateral-flange dishes or bowls; lateral-ridge bowls or dishes; low-neck bowls; restricted-orifice bowls; lateral-Z-angle dishes*; basal-angle plates or dishes; basal-ridge bowl; labial-flange dish, and recurving-side dish. *Quantity*. Mayapan, 30 rim, 12 body sherds. *Provenience*. Mayapan and Uaxactun. *Ceramic complex*. Chicanel (800 B.C.–A.D. 100). *Remarks*. The other groups, not recorded from these collections, are described and listed in earlier publications (Smith, 1955a; Smith and Gifford, 1966). The asterisk refers to those groups, types, and forms actually represented in these collections.

PETEN GLOSS WARE

Paste composition. Medium-coarse texture, medium-porous, normally buff color; tempers include ash, calcite, sherd, and dolomite (rare). Monochromes are usually ash tempered in Tzakol 1–3, Tepeu 1 and Tepeu 2 with a fair percentage of calcite, some of sherd, and rarely of dolomite. Calcite is predominant in Tepeu 3, and the few ash-tempered specimens are usually atypical in form. Dichromes and polychromes are predominantly ash tempered in Tzakol 1–3, Tepeu 1 and 2. A few Tepeu 2 polychromes are calcite tempered and atypical in design. *Surface finish*. Smoothed, slipped, and glossed. The high luster and character of the slip give the impression that a varnish was used, although apparently this was not the case. Crazing, characteristic of early waxy wares, disappears almost entirely in the Tzakol Ceramic Complex but comes back strongly in Tepeu, especially in Tepeu 3. Rootlet-marking, strong in Tzakol, falls off noticeably in Tepeu. Fire-clouding occurs throughout with a somewhat lower percentage in Tzakol. Orange gloss is most abundant in Tzakol monochromes, whereas red takes the lead in Tepeu 3. Black diminishes from an important surface color in Tzakol to lesser importance through Tepeu; the same is true of variegated and orange, and to a lesser degree of buff. Red and brown grow in importance as time advances. Cream has little importance at any time in gloss ware. Dichromes and polychromes are well represented in Tzakol 1–3 and Tepeu 1 and 2, rare in Tepeu 3.

PETEN GLOSS WARE COLOR PERCENTAGES BY CERAMIC COMPLEX**

Ceramic Complex	Weathered	Orange	Variegated	Red	Black	Brown	Gray	Buff	Cream
Tzakol 1–3	15.4	28.0	27.8	9.8	15.1	0.8	0.8	2.4	
Tepeu 1, 2	50.7	16.1	17.4	6.6	4.0	3.5	1.5	0.1	0.1
Tepeu 3	27.5	10.6	8.5	38.8	2.0	10.1	2.2	0.1	0.1

PETEN GLOSS WARE DICHROMES — PERCENTAGES**

Ceramic Complex	Red-on-orange	Black-on-orange	Black-on-gray	Red-on-gray	Red-on-buff	Black-on-cream	Red-on-cream	Black-on-red	Black-on-buff
Tzakol 1–3	44.9	6.1		28.2	24.5			6.1	
Tepeu 1, 2	6.3	39.6	5.4			17.1	10.8	18.0	2.7
Tepeu 3	39.5	28.9	31.5						

PETEN GLOSS WARE POLYCHROMES — PERCENTAGES**

Ceramic Complex	Orange slip	Buff background	Cream slip	Gray slip	Red slip	Weathered	Multi-color on buff	Multi-color on cream	Multi-color on orange	Red and orange on cream
Tzakol 1–3	30.4	37.2	7.0	0.5		24.9				
Tepeu 1, 2	49.4	4.4	19.5	9.0	0.2		1.4	6.5	5.1	4.5
Tepeu 3	87.5		6.3				6.2			

** Data references pertain only to ceramic material obtained from Uaxactun (Smith, 1955a).
For slip color readings see R. E. Smith (1955a).
Groups: In this one case the groups are associated with subwares including Bandera Gloss*, Petipet Gloss*, Marihuana Gloss*, and Cucas Gloss. (See Appendix E.)

PETO CREAM WARE

This ware was termed Coarse Slateware by Brainerd (1958, p. 57; figs. 19, 20, 24, 92). The name has been changed because none of the attributes associated with the ware bears any resemblance to Slate Ware as defined. The two common attributes of Peto Cream Ware and Chichen Slate Ware (Mexican Medium Slateware) are a black tricklelike decoration and a number of vessel forms. It is most likely that this ware had its beginning close to A.D. 1200 and was well developed when found at Mayapan, always associated with Mayapan Red Ware. At two sites, Dzibilchaltun and Tihoo in Yucatan, Peto Cream Ware has been found unassociated with Mayapan Red Ware. This suggests several things: that Peto Cream Ware may have an earlier beginning than Mayapan Red Ware; that it probably was not made in the same centers of manufacture as Mayapan Red Ware; and that it had its original source near Merida because of the close proximity of both Dzibilchaltun and Tihoo. *Paste composition.* Coarse texture, usually undifferentiated opaque or cryptocrystalline calcite, less frequently gray limestone, and colors range from beige (10 YR 7/3, 7/4) to cinnamon (7.5 YR 7/4) and reddish brown (7.5 YR 4/4), with beige and gray (10 YR 8/2) predominant. Pink (5 YR 7/6) and drab (10 YR 6/3) are also found. *Surface finish.* Smoothed, leaving a lumpy surface involving a fine textured slip covering a paste bearing protruding temper particles. The lightly burnished slip is opaque, usually cream in color but occasionally smudged to gray. A few sherds have a cinnamon (dull orange) slip. The color readings include: cream (10 YR 8/4, 8/3; 5 Y 9/2; 7.5 YR 8/4), beige (10 YR 7/4, 7/3; 2.5 Y 8/4), light gray (10 YR 8/2, 8/1; 2.5 YR 8/0), light brown (5 YR 5/3), and cinnamon (7.5 YR 7/4).

Cream Kukula Group. *Types and varieties.* Xcanchakan Black-on-cream Type, Xcanchakan Variety (52, *a–r, t–x*; 75, *l, m*) and sharp–incised variety (fig. 52, *s*); Kukula Cream Type, Kukula Variety (51, *a–c, f–h, j–l, o, p, s–v*; 75, *k*); thin variety (51, *d, e, i, m, q*); Pencuyut Incised Type, Pencuyut Variety (sharp-incised, 51, *r*); Cusama Plano-relief Type, **Cusama** Variety (51, *n*); and Mataya Modeled Type, Mataya Variety (52, *y*). *Forms.* Water and storage jars; tripod dishes with flaring or rounded sides; restricted-orifice, grater, and hemispherical bowls; tripod bowls with recurving sides; cylindrical vases; and basins. *Quantity.* 526 rim, 4,989 body

sherds. *Provenience.* Acanceh, Chichen Itza, Dzibilchaltun, Mani, Mayapan, Miraflores (Colonia), Oxkutzcab, Tihoo, and Ucu in Yucatan; Ichpaatun, San Miguel Cozumel, Tancah, Tulum, and Vista Alegre in Quintana Roo. *Ceramic complex.* Hocaba (A.D. 1200–1300).

PLUMBATE WARE

Like Fine Orange, this is a very distinctive ware and the only preconquest glazed ware so far recognized. It covers a span of approximately 500 years and may be separated into three different groups chronologically listed: San Juan, Robles, and Tohil.

The ware attributes of the only plumbate group, Tohil, encountered in these diggings are included under paste composition and surface finish. *Paste composition.* In all cases the paste is dense and fine textured, and sometimes appears to be untempered. According to A. O. Shepard, however (1948, pp. 91–92), "the paste contains numerous, clear, unaltered feldspar crystals which would not normally occur in clay." The color may be dark to medium gray; core dark to medium gray with very narrow margins, usually light gray, occasionally weak or moderate orange. Color readings: gray (2.5 YR 4/0), light gray (2.5 YR 6/0), and pinkish cinnamon (2.5 YR 6/8). *Surface finish.* Shepard says:

The hard, gray, lustrous surface of plumbate ware is its most distinctive feature and also the least understood. It is furthermore, of genuine interest as a ceramic achievement; the majority of the gray parts are harder than steel, and the hardest areas cannot be scratched by quartz. . . . The colors of plumbate are also unusual. Characteristic are olives and pale grays, rare in other wares; the grays are often contiguous to comparatively clear hues of orange and reddish brown, and metallic iridescence is not uncommon. The luster, in contrast to that produced by a mechanical polish, is vitreous and suggests a glaze.

Color readings: gray (5 Y 5/1, 6/1; 10 YR 5/2), reddish brown (2.5 YR 5/6; 5 YR 5/6), brown (7.5 YR 5/4, 5/6), olive (2.5 Y 4/2), and orange (2.5 YR 4/8). Crazing is common.

In contrast to the Tohil, the plumbate San Juan Group (Thompson, 1948, p. 47; fig. 55; Shepard, 1948, pp. 91, 124) has a somewhat different paste composition and quite different forms which include tall cylinders, collared squat jars, and bowls with basal molding. The plumbate Robles Group (Shook, 1947, pp. 182–183; Shepard, 1948, pp. 125–126) has been noted but not studied. At present it would appear that the San Juan Group belongs to the Late Classic Period and the Robles Group to the Late Classic-Early Postclassic Transition Period.

Plumbate Tohil Group. *Types and varieties.* Tohil Plumbate Type, Tohil Variety (23, *a, c, d*); Tumbador Incised Type, Tumbador Variety (groove-incised, 23, *b*; 60, *h–j*); Porvenir Gadrooned Type, Porvenir Variety (60, *k*); and Malacatan Modeled Type, Malacatan Variety (none found in these collections, but many illustrated; Shepard, 1948, and Smith, 1957a, figs. 4 and 5). *Forms.* Jars: standard, continuous curve, bulging neck, and girdled shoulder (some may have a pedestal base or three round-bottomed feet); vases: pyriform, tapered with either pedestal or tripod supports, lamp chimney, recurved, barrel-shaped, and cylindrical (most may be effigy); bowls: relatively shallow, composite silhouette with flat base or three round-bottomed feet. *Quantity.* Chichen Itza, 11 rim, 16 body sherds; Mayapan, no rim, 9 body sherds. *Provenience.* See Shepard (1948, pp. 105–114) and in addition to the Marquez Collection (Smith, 1957a, pp. 117–118; figs. 1–5) and Chichen Itza collection (GWB, fig. 91, *a–f*) there are a number of more recent findings. These include: La Victoria, Nebaj, Pompeya (Finca), and San Julian (Finca) in Guatemala; Mayapan (Yucatan), Estapilla and Naranjeno (Tabasco), Acala and Tecolpan (Chiapas), Chachalacas and Quiahuiztlan (Veracruz), and Colima in Mexico; Jacaltenango in Salvador. *Ceramic complexes.* Sotuta (A.D. 1000–1200) at Mayapan and others of the same time period: namely, Qankyak at Zaculeu, and Tohil at Zacualpa.

PUUC RED WARE

This is Brainerd's (1958, p. 53, figs. 18, *k*; 35, *f, h*; 51; 52; 58, *h, l, 2*; *i, 5, 7*; 87, *v, w*) Florescent Medium and Thin Redware. Puuc Red Ware closely resembles Chichen Red Ware, although it was felt that a sufficient difference existed to retain them as separate wares. These differences include temper — Puuc Red Ware figures about 60 per cent ash and most of the rest calcite to nearly 100 per cent ash for Chichen Red Ware; color, because Puuc Red Ware has a more uniform red than Chichen Red Ware; and blemishing in that Puuc Red Ware is surprisingly clear of disfiguring marks caused by fire-clouding, rootlet-marking, or crazing. *Paste composition.* Medium to fine texture, having a variety of tempers (Tables 41 and 42) with ash most common, followed by chalky calcite, calcite and potsherd combination, clear calcite, pot-

sherd, and rarely saccharoidal calcite. The color is red, reddish orange, or reddish brown, and closely approximates the slip color but may be slightly lighter. Usually Puuc Red Ware is thin-walled like Thin Slate Ware but a fair percentage has medium-thick to thick walls. These sherds are tripod dishes, beveled-rim ringstand bowls, and basins. The thin forms are those usually associated with Thin Slate Ware, namely: hemispherical bowls with direct rim and flat or ringstand base, or bead rim and three nubbin feet; cylindrical vases; and some jars. *Surface finish.* Very well smoothed. Slipped and polished with medium luster and less waxy in feeling than Puuc Slate Ware. The surface smoothness, luster, slight waxy feel, lack of blemishes, and oneness of slip-paste color, together with thinness and frequently vessel shape, tend to link Puuc Red and Thin Slate. The red slip color is uniform throughout, especially as it affects each individual vessel. The color readings are red (2.5 YR 4/8, 4/6; 10 R 4/4, 4/8), reddish orange (2.5 YR 5/8; 10 R 5/8), and reddish brown (2.5 YR 5/6). Blemishes are unusual except for the rare occurrence of dark blotches and very occasional purple dendritic markings.

Red Teabo Group. *Types and varieties.* Teabo Red Type, Teabo Variety (8, *a, d, e, g, j–l*); Becal Incised Type, Becal Variety (8, *n, p, q, v,* all sharp-incised), groove-incised variety (8, *c, u*); Opichen Gouged-incised Type, Opichen Variety (8, *o, t*); Tekax Black-on-red Type, Tekax Variety (8, *f, h, i*), orange variety (8, *b*); Sahcaba Modeled-carved Type, Sahcaba Variety (8, *m*); and Yaxumha Composite (incised and impressed) Type, Yaxumha Variety (8, *r, s*). *Forms.* Hemispherical bowls with direct rim and flat or ringstand base, or bead rim and three nubbin feet; restricted-orifice bowls with beveled rim and ringstand base; tripod dishes with flaring or outcurving sides; cylindrical vases; basins; and jars (rare). *Quantity.* Uxmal-Kabah, 582 rim, 1,208 body sherds; Mayapan, 40 rim, 109 body sherds. *Provenience.* Acanceh, Chacchob, Chichen Itza, Dzan, Dzibilchaltun, Hunacti, Kabah, Labna, Mayapan, Miraflores (Colonia), Mulchic, Oxkintok, Oxkutzcab, Sabacche, Sayil, Tecoh, and Uxmal in Yucatan; Canbalam, Cayal, Edzna, Jaina, and Tohkok in Campeche, and Cozumel, Ichmul, and Vista Alegre in Quintana Roo. *Ceramic complex.* Cehpech (A.D. 800–1000).

PUUC SLATE WARE

Brainerd (1958, pp. 52–53, figs. 10, *a–g*; 15, *a–e, j–l, o–r*; 21, *a–c, e, f*; 32, *a–e, g–h*; 35, *a, d, g, i–m*;

36, *a, c*; 40, *a–f*; 41–46; 47, *a–i*; 48, *a, c, n–x*; 49, *a–c, d, 1–8, 16, 28, e–j, l, 4–7, m*; 54–57; 58, *a–g, i, 1–4, 6, 8, 10, j*; 62, *e–g, k–n, p–r*; 66, *j, 2, 9, 10, 12*; 67; 68, *c*; 71, *c, 16, 29–37, e–i*; 72, *i, j*; 73, *a, 7–14, b, c, 14–17, 25–37, d, 27–30, e, f*; 74, *b, 18, 23*) calls this Florescent Medium Slateware. In ware attributes it differs little from Chichen Slate Ware. Differences include: paste temper with Chichen Slate having 98.6 per cent volcanic ash and Puuc Slate showing an equal use of ash and calcite; paste color with Chichen Slate almost exclusively red and Puuc Slate more often gray, brown, or beige, and less frequently red; light paste color appears to be correlated with calcite temper, and surface color of Chichen Slate Ware often has a pinkish hue because of red paste showing through, a rare phenomenon with Puuc Slate Ware. *Paste composition.* Medium texture sometimes grading to near fine, variety of tempering materials (Tables 41 and 42), and colors which follow closely those of the surface plus red or reddish brown. *Surface finish.* Smoothed and well finished; slipped and polished, the slip being somewhat translucent with a waxy feel; blemished including occasional crazing, often purple or white dendritic markings, some fire-clouding, and colored with a wide range of color readings. These are gray (10 YR 7/1, 10 YR 7/2, 10 YR 6/2; 5 YR 7/2), brown (7.5 YR 6/4, 5/4; 5 YR 3/4, 4/6, 5/6), beige (10 YR 7/3, 7/4), drab (10 YR 6/3; 2.5 YR 7/2), buff (7.5 YR 6/2, 7/2), fawn (5 YR 6/4), and cream (10 YR 8/3).

Slate Muna Group. *Types and varieties.* Muna Slate Type, Muna Variety (4, *a, b, h, j–m*; 5, *a–j, l–n, p, q, v–aa, cc–ff, hh*; 6, *a–d, f, g, l, p, bb–ee, ii, jj*; 26, *b, 2–6, 10–15, 18*), notched variety (6, *m*); Sacalum Black-on-slate Type, Sacalum Variety (4, *g*; 5, *u*; 6, *z*; 26, *b, 1, 7–9, 17, 23*; 60, *d*), Tekit Incised Type, Tekit Variety (4, *c*; 5, *r, s, gg*; 6, *e, j, k, o, q, r, ff*, all sharp-incised), Akil Impressed Type, Akil Variety (5, *k, o, t*; 6, *h, t, w*; 26, *b, 4, 5, 16, 21, 22*), Chumayel Red-on-slate Type, Chumayel Variety (4, *e, f*; 5, *bb*; 6, *y, aa*; 26, *b, 19*; 60, *c*), modeled variety (4, *d*), and incised variety (4, *i*), Yaxnic Modeled Type, Yaxnic Variety (6, *gg, hh, kk–mm*; 26, *c, 2, 4*), Nohcacab Composite (incised and impressed) Type, Nohcacab Variety (6, *i, n, s, u, v*), and Xaya Gouged-incised Type, Xaya Variety (6, *x, nn*; 26, *c, 20*). *Forms.* Basins; jars; tripod flaring-sided dishes; beveled-rim ringstand bowls; bowls with rounded sides; effigy censers; flutes; a cylindrical vase; and a flat-based dish. *Quantity.* Uxmal-Kabah, 3,464 rim, 17,123 body

sherds; Mayapan, 633 rim, 2,645 body sherds. *Provenience.* Ake, Chacchob, Chichen Itza, Dzibiac, Dzibilchaltun, Hunacti, Kabah, Labna, Mayapan, Miraflores (Colonia and Quinta), Mulchic, Oxkutzcab, Sayil, Soblonke, Tecoh, Tihoo, Ucu, Uxmal, Xcanatun, Xulmil, and Yaxuna in Yucatan; Aguada Grande, Coba, Cozumel, Ichmul, Tancah; Vista Alegre, Xcaret, and Xelha in Quintana Roo; Canbalam, Cayal, Dzibilnocac, Edzna, Huaymil, Jaina, Queja, Santa Rosa Xtampak, Tohkok, and Xpuhil in Campeche. *Ceramic complex.* Cehpech (A.D. 800–1000).

PUUC UNSLIPPED WARE

Brainerd (1958, p. 52, figs. 14, *c, e, 1–9*; 35, *c*; 37, *a, 1–17, 20–27, b, 1–10, 13–18, 37–39, 43, 44, 51, c, 8–19, 21–29*; 38; 39; 65, *d*; 68, *b, 15, 17–20, d*; 69, *b*) calls this Florescent Unslipped Ware. *Paste composition.* Coarse and porous texture. Temper (Tables 41 and 42) usually clear calcite for jars with a few gray limestone and a few potsherd examples, whereas for censers potsherd temper prevails with a few examples of clear calcite or, more rarely, saccharoidal calcite. Color normally is the same as surface but in some cases varies. Color readings: Pink to pinkish cinnamon (5 YR 7/6; 2.5 YR 6/6, 7/4), brown (2.5 YR 5/6; 5 YR 5/4, 5/6; 7.5 YR 5/4), fawn (5 YR 6/4), and cinnamon (7.5 YR 7/4). *Surface finish.* Smoothed but without polish or slip. Usually coarse striated. A large percentage of the censers and some jars have a white calcareous coating. Color for jars is commonly beige, cream, or gray, whereas for censers the light browns and cinnamon seem to be dominant. Color readings: beige (10 YR 7/3, 7/4), light brown (2.5 YR 5/4, 6/4; 5 YR 5/4; 7.5 YR 6/4; 10 YR 5/3), fawn (5 YR 6/4), cream (10 YR 8/3, 8/4), cinnamon (7.5 YR 7/4), gray (10 YR 6/2), and buff (10 YR 6/4).

Unslipped Chum Group. *Types and varieties.* Chum Unslipped Type, Chum Variety (3, *n–q, w*), Yokat Striated Type, Yokat Variety (2, *h–p, r–y, aa*; 3, *u, v*; 26, *a*), neck-interior variety (2, *a–g*), Oxkutzcab Appliqué Type, Oxkutzcab Variety (3, *a, f, i–l*), Halacho Impressed Type, Halacho Variety (2, *q, z*; 3, *d, e, h, m, r–t*; 28, *c, 2*; 60, *m*), Yiba Modeled Type, Yiba Variety (3, *x–bb*), and Tepakan Composite (appliqué and impressed) Type, Tepakan Variety (3, *b, c, g*). *Forms.* Jars; censers, hourglass, basin, or ladle; bowls, flaring, rounded or restricted; figurines, and flutes. *Quantity.* Uxmal-Kabah, 771 rim, 15,822 body sherds; Mayapan, 294 rim, 2,263 body sherds. *Provenience.*

Same as Puuc Slate Ware. *Ceramic complex.* Ceh-pech (A.D. 800–1000).

SAN JOAQUIN BUFF WARE

This ware is associated only with the Tases Ceramic Complex. It is mentioned by Brainerd (1958, figs. 23, *c*; 94, *a*, two of which have added black in design) but called red-on-orange. *Paste composition.* The same as Mayapan Red Ware. *Surface finish.* Often imperfectly smoothed before slipping, slipped and burnished, faintly lustrous to lustrous. Buff is the most constant slip color, but the range includes many others. Color readings: buff (7.5 YR 7/4; 10 YR 7/6; 2.5 Y 7/4, 8/4, 9/4), cinnamon (7.5 YR 7/6; 10 YR 8/4; 5 YR 6/6), brown (7.5 YR 5/6, 6/6; 5 YR 4/6, 5/6, 5/8; 2.5 YR 5/6), beige (10 YR 7/4, 7/3), cream (10 YR 8/4), pink (7.5 YR 8/6), orange (10 R 5/8; 2.5 YR 5/8), and drab (10 YR 6/3). Red as found in the decoration has a range (10 R 4/8, 4/6, 3/6, 3/4; 2.5 YR 4/8, 4/6; 5 YR 4/8, 5/8; 7.5 R 3/6), and the black is a generally strong black.

Buff Polbox Group. *Types and varieties.* Polbox Buff Type, Polbox Variety (50, *a–c*; 75, *i*, *j*), Tecoh Red-on-buff Type, Tecoh Variety (53, *a*, *b*, 1–15), outline-incised variety (53, *b*, 16), Pele Polychrome Type, Pele Variety (54; 75, *n*), and Kimbila Incised Type, Kimbila Variety (sharp-incised, 50, *d*). *Forms.* Storage, water, and parenthesis-rim jars; tripod dishes with flaring sides; hemispherical, restricted, and deep bowls; potstands; basins; cylindrical and tripod vases; and covers. *Quantity.* 952 rim, 2,443 body sherds. *Provenience.* Acanceh, Chichen Itza, Mani, and Mayapan. *Ceramic complex.* Tases (A.D. 1300–1450).

TELCHAQUILLO BRICK WARE

This ware, found only on the surface at Mayapan, could conceivably belong to the Tases, the Chikinchel, or the Chauaca ceramic complexes but perhaps the Tases Ceramic Complex is more logical. If it formed part of the Chauaca it would represent 74.8 per cent of that complex or 96 per cent of the Chikinchel which is highly improbable for such a specialized ware. *Paste composition.* Very coarse texture, friable paste containing vitrified gray to blackish particles. Some appear splintery and some seem to contain inclusions of sherd temper together with vitrified fragments. This indicates that they are vitrified sherd. Number of vitrified particles varies from sherd to sherd; vitrifaction complete in some, partial in others. There-

fore it may be said that temper is vitrified potsherd. Color of paste is normally red (2.5 YR 4/6), rarely orange (2.5 YR 5/8). *Surface finish.* Slipped and lightly burnished on exterior or convex surface which was first smoothed vertically, leaving light striations. The interior or concave surface is smoothed and often crazed. All interiors show fire-blackening up to about 2 cm. of small end. Color when readable is red (10 R 4/4).

Red Moyos Group. *Types and varieties.* Moyos Red Type, Moyos Variety (36, *a*, *b*; 75, *d*), Cozil Incised Type, Cozil Variety (groove-incised, 36, *c*). *Forms.* Only one form which looks like the section of a gutterlike drain but more likely served as a candle-flame shield. *Quantity.* 74 rim, 229 body sherds. *Provenience.* Mayapan. *Ceramic complex.* Tases (A.D. 1300–1450).

THIN BLACK WARE

This ware is much the same as Peten Gloss Ware except for thinness which approximates eggshell. *Paste composition.* There is little data, but it appears to follow closely the paste of Peten Gloss Ware. *Surface finish.* The finish like Gloss Ware is glossy and thinly slipped. Blemishes are rare. In general the black color is strong. The two groups in this ware are Black Discordia (Tzakol 2, 3) and Black Uman (Motul).

Black Discordia Group. *Types and varieties.* Catzim Incised (sharp-incised) Type, Catzim Variety* and Discordia Black Type, Discordia Variety. *Forms.* Pitchers with gutter spout and ringstand or pedestal base; wide-mouth jars with gutter spout and ringstand base; hemispherical bowls; and a tripod cylindrical bowl.* *Quantity.* Mayapan, 1 rim, no body sherds. *Provenience.* Mayapan, Yucatan and Uaxactun, Peten, Guatemala. *Ceramic complex.* Tzakol 2, 3 (A.D. 360–600).

Black Uman Group. *Types and varieties.* Bokaba Incised (sharp-incised) Type, Bokaba Variety* and Uman Black Type, Uman Variety.* *Forms.* Side-angle bowls* and jars.* *Quantity.* Mayapan, 8 rim, 8 body sherds. *Provenience.* Mayapan. *Ceramic complex.* Motul (A.D. 600–800).

THIN SLATE WARE

Brainerd gave this ware the same name and he illustrated (1958, p. 53; figs. 4, *p*; 10, *h*; 15, *i*, *s*; 18, *j*; 21, *d*; 32, *d*, *e*; 35, *e*; 48, *b*, *d–m* (possibly); 50; 51, *a–c*; 61, *b*, *e*, *f*, *j*, *l*) most of the types. *Paste composition.* Fine texture, mostly saccharoidal calcite temper, and usually the same color as slip, although a few have red paste. *Surface finish.* Unusually well smoothed, slipped, and polished with medium luster, less waxy than Puuc Slate Ware, and generally free from blemishes except for vertical crazing which is common to all deep vessels. Other blemishes rarely encountered are fire-clouding and dendritic purple markings. The slip color is generally gray to cream, usually lighter than Puuc Slate Ware. Color readings: gray (10 YR 6/2, 7/1, 8/2; 2.5 Y 7/2), beige (10 YR 7/3), cream (2.5 Y 8/2), and light brown (10 YR 6/3) usually associated with Chichen Itza.

Thin-slate Ticul Group. *Types and varieties.* Ticul Thin-slate Type, Ticul Variety (7, *a, d, e, h–j, n, o, q–s, u, v, z–bb*; 26, *d*; 58, *c, d*), Xul Incised Type, Xul Variety, normally sharp-incised (7, *k, l, w–y*), Tabi Gouged-incised Type, Tabi Variety (7, *b, c, m, p, t*; 58, *e, f*), and Tikihal Circle-shading Type, Tikihal Variety (7, *f, g*). *Forms.* Hemispherical and deep bowls; cylindrical vases; tripod dishes with flaring sides; basins; jars, and a disk cover. *Quantity.* Uxmal-Kabah, 934 rim, 2,412 body sherds; Mayapan, 56 rim, 92 body sherds. *Provenience.* Acanceh, Ake, Chanpuuc, Chichen Itza, Dzebtun, Dzibilchaltun, Kabah, Labna, Mani, Mayapan, Miraflores (Colonia and Quinta), Oxkintok, Sayil, Uxmal, and Yaxuna in Yucatan; Aguada Grande, Calderitas, San Miguel Cozumel, and Tancah in Quintana Roo, and Hochob in Campeche. *Ceramic complex.* Cehpech (A.D. 800–1000).

TULUM RED WARE

This ware is undoubtedly a product of the east coast of the Yucatan Peninsula. It may well have derived from Mayapan Red Ware, but the development source of neither of these wares is quite certain. As for the name Tulum Red Ware, Shepard is the first to have used it in print (1958, p. 452). Sanders (1960, pp. 237–243) describes it in detail. *Paste composition.* Fine texture, calcite plus quartz grains temper (Shepard, 1958, p. 452), and uniformly pale orange in color. The ware is hard and breaks with a sharp, clean fracture. *Surface finish.* Well smoothed, slipped, and burnished, giving a medium to light luster. The color is a uniform red (10 R 4/6, 4/8, 3/6), varying little on a single vessel or from vessel to vessel. A small but consistent percentage, however, ranges from light to dark brown (7.5 YR 5/6, 5/8, 5/4). There are few blemishes except for some fire-clouding. *Remarks.* The uniformity of slip color, the

care with which the smoothing is done, the fineness and hardness of the paste, the addition of stray fine grains of quartz to calcite temper, the carelessness of the postfire incising, the use of a double incised line, and the style of design differentiate Tulum Red Ware from Mayapan Red Ware. The closest similarities are to be found in the slip color and vessel form. Sanders (1960, p. 239) mentions bolstered-rim jars which are "larger, higher-necked vessels, with much thicker walls and coarser paste than the direct rim type." Perhaps these are Mayapan Red Ware jars.

Red Payil Group. *Types and varieties.* Payil Red Type, Payil Variety (48, *b, j–n, p*), Palmul Incised Type, Palmul Variety, all sharp-incised (48, *a, c–h, o, q*), and Kanlum Plano-relief Type, Kanlum Variety (48, *i*). *Forms.* Jars, wide mouth, with high or low neck; tripod dishes with flaring sides; hemispherical or restricted-orifice bowls; and a basin. *Quantity.* 33 rims, 36 body sherds. *Provenience.* Quintana Roo with special emphasis on Tulum and Ichpaatun. Elsewhere only at Mayapan have Tulum Red Ware sherds been identified. *Ceramic complex.* Tases (A.D. 1300–1450).

TUTUL XIU RED WARE

This ware is called Red Slip over Striated Ware by Brainerd (1958, p. 48; fig. 31, *e, 19, 20, 26, 27*). *Paste composition.* Medium-coarse texture, untested temper except at Holactun where it is sherd (*ibid.*, p. 49), cinnamon to buff and gray color. *Surface finish.* Smoothed and finely striated, then slipped. Burnished, leaving a medium luster. Color is a strong red (10 R 4/6, 4/8; 7.5 R 3/8).

Red Tipikal Group. *Types and varieties.* At present writing there is only one type and one variety, a Tipikal Red-on-striated Type, Tipikal Variety (no illustration other than those by Brainerd). *Forms.* Jars only. *Quantity.* No rim, 4 body sherds at Chichen Itza; no rim, 4 body sherds at Mayapan. *Provenience.* Holactun, Mani, and Mayapan. *Ceramic complex.* Tihosuco (800 B.C.–A.D. 100).

USIL RED WARE

This ware is like the Flaky Redware described by Brainerd (1958, pp. 49, 50; figs. 4, *a–e*; 6, *a, 8–15, 22–29, b, c*; 17, *f, 36–44*; 18, *a, 1–7*; 65, *c, 31–36*). *Paste composition.* Coarse texture, untested temper, brown and buff to gray in color. *Surface finish.* Smoothed, then slipped and lightly polished, leaving a lustrous finish. Color is a strong red (10 R 5/6, 5/8, 4/6, 4/8) grading at times to dark grays and brown (5 YR 6/4). The flaking or peeling that occurs on many sherds results from a difference in the coefficient of expansion of slip and body. But since this same phenomenon occurs on many other wares, it is not a particularly good criterion to use in naming a ware.

Red Xanaba Group. *Types and varieties.* Xanaba Red Type, Xanaba Variety (25, a), Caucel Black-on-red Type, Caucel Variety (no illustration, but have vertical tricklelike parallel lines). *Forms.* Jars only at Mayapan and Chichen Itza for our findings; Brainerd illustrates basins and bowls as well. *Quantity.* Chichen Itza, no rim, 3 body sherds; Mayapan, 6 rim, 21 body sherds. *Provenience.* Acanceh, Chichen Itza, Mayapan, and Yaxuna in Yucatan, and Coba and Tancah in Quintana Roo. *Ceramic complex.* Cochuah (A.D. 300–600).

XCANATUN UNSLIPPED WARE

Brainerd (1958, p. 48; figs. 12, a; 65, a) calls this Formative Unslipped Ware. It seems to have been difficult to identify with certainty, because he has illustrated only a few jars. *Paste composition.* Coarse texture, usually calcite less frequently sherd temper, and gray and cinnamon in color. *Surface finish.* Smoothing is rough to moderately even; some have medium-coarse striation over part of exterior. Color ranges from light through dark gray to beige and cinnamon (no actual readings taken).

Unslipped Saban Group. *Types and varieties.* Saban Unslipped Type, Saban Variety (GWB, 1958, fig. 12, a) and Chancenote Striated Type, Chancenote Variety (*ibid.*, fig. 65, a). *Forms.* Only jars noted. *Quantity.* 7 rim, 27 body sherds. *Provenience.* Chichen Itza, Mayapan, and Oxkintok in Yucatan. *Ceramic complex.* Tihosuco (800 B.C.–A.D. 100).

YUCATAN CHALKY WARE

This ware was originally called Lustrous Streaky Brown (Smith, 1954b, fig. 6, j; 1955b, pp. 262–263, fig. 3, qq) and placed in Late Classic to Proto-Postclassic. *Paste composition.* Medium texture, friable and chalky, temper untested, gray in color. *Surface finish.* Thinly slipped over a somewhat irregular surface, glossy, and usually reddish brown color. The streaky effect is caused by the

application of the slip in unequal strength and thickness and by the tool used.

Brown Chuburna Group. *Types and varieties.* Chuburna Brown Type, Chuburna Variety (25, bb; 60, a). *Forms.* Storage jars and hemispherical bowls. *Quantity.* Chichen Itza, no rim, 6 body sherds; Mayapan, 10 rim, 9 body sherds. *Provenience.* Chichen Itza, Dzibilchaltun, and Mayapan. *Ceramic complex.* Cochuah (A.D. 300–600).

YUCATAN GLOSS WARE

This ware is covered by Brainerd (1958, pp. 50–51; Flaky Dichrome, figs. 1, g–i, k; 6, a, e–g, j; 17, g, 1–9; 63, a; 64; Regional Coarse Redware, figs. 2, a–e; 8, a–c, e–g, 1; 18, a, c, e; 20, c; Regional Medium Redware, figs. 2, f, g; 4, f, i; 8, d, h–k; 18, d, g, h; 19, h, 5, 6; 66, k; Regional Polychrome, figs. 3, b, c; 9, e, f; 19, g, 3; 30, a; 60, b; 63, a–d; 90, c; Oxkintok Coarse Monochrome, figs. 11; 12, g; 13, a–g, i, j; 41, e, 1, 4) by means of the various wares just listed. These various wares are here considered as types: Flaky Dichrome becomes Valladolid Incised-dichrome Type; Regional Coarse Redware and Regional Medium Redware combine in the Batres Red Type; Regional Polychrome is broken up into two types: an early, Timucuy Orange-polychrome Type and a late, Tituc Orange-polychrome Type; Oxkintok Coarse Monochrome is changed to the Maxcanu Buff Type. In addition an orange type, Popola Gadrooned was found and a black-on-orange, Motul Ceramic Complex type, Teya Black-on-orange was mentioned by Brainerd (*ibid.*, fig. 2, h, caption) but not found in our digging.

Yucatan Gloss Ware closely approximates Peten Gloss Ware. It is possible that in both cases they have been made to encompass too much. In both instances they include types of medium and coarse paste texture, both calcite and ash temper, various degrees of smoothing, and medium to high luster. It even may be that the most clear-cut break is between polychromes and monochromes. *Paste composition.* Medium to coarse texture, mostly calcite but some ash temper, buff (2.5 YR 8/2), and gray (2.5 YR 8/0) color. *Surface finish.* Smoothed but in many instances some lumpiness persists, slipped, has medium to high luster, and enjoys a variety of slip colors including red, buff, and orange. Color readings: red (10 R 4.2/10, 4.5/9, 5.2/10; 2.5 YR 5/5; 5 YR 6.6/4.5), buff (1 Y 4.2/4.5, 7.2/6; 5 YR 5.8/7), and orange (10 R 5/8; 2.5 YR 5/8, 6/8; 5 YR 6/8, 5/8). Red Batres, buff Maxcanu, and orange Timucuy groups fall under this ware.

Red Batres Group. *Types and varieties.* Batres Red Type, Batres Variety (25, *b*). *Forms.* Lateral flange bowls at Mayapan; Brainerd (1958, p. 51) records jars, basins, bowls with basal ridge, and hemispherical bowls. *Quantity.* Mayapan, 3 rim, 1 body sherd. *Provenience.* Acanceh, Chichen Itza, Mayapan, and Yaxuna in Yucatan, and Coba in Quintana Roo. *Ceramic complex.* Cochuah (A.D. 300–600).

Buff Maxcanu Group. *Types and varieties.* Maxcanu Buff Type, Maxcanu Variety (GWB, fig. 11, *a*). *Forms.* Jars at Mayapan; Brainerd (*ibid.*, pp. 50–51) records jars, basins, basal-break bowls, and large, very shallow, rounded bowls. *Quantity.* Mayapan, 13 rim, 88 body sherds. *Provenience.* Holactun, Maxcanu, and Mayapan in Yucatan. *Ceramic complex.* Cochuah (A.D. 300–600).

Orange Timucuy Group. *Types and varieties.* Timucuy Orange-polychrome Type, Timucuy Variety (10, *m*; 25, *e–o, v*) and Valladolid Incised-dichrome Type, Valladolid Variety (sharp-incised, 25, *c, d*; GWB, figs. 6 and 64) in Chakan or early Cochuah; Tituc Orange-polychrome Type, Tituc Variety (GWB, figs. 9, *e, f*; 19, *g, 3*; 30, *a*; 60, *b*; 63, *a, 12*) and Popola Gadrooned Type, Popola Variety (no illustration) belonging to the Cochuah Ceramic Complex. *Forms.* Jars, many with high necks; basal-flange and basal-Z-angle bowls. *Quantity.* Kabah, 1 rim, 6 body sherds; Chichen Itza, no rim, 3 body sherds; Mayapan, 85 rim, 230 body sherds. *Provenience.* Acanceh, Balam Canche Cave, Chichen Itza, Kabah, Labna, Mani, Mayapan, Oxkintok, Sayil, and Yaxuna in Yucatan. *Ceramic complex.* Cochuah (A.D. 300–600).

YUCATAN OPAQUE WARE

Brainerd (1958, pp. 48–49; figs. 4, *o*; 5, *a–f*; 16; 17; 31; 60, *a*; 65, *c*; 107, *a*), describes two wares which fit into this category: Formative Monochrome and Formative Flaky Red. The major difference between these two wares is the generally waxy feel of the former and the flakiness of the latter. The problem here is whether a waxy finish can also be flaky or whether a flaky finish can be waxy. In other respects the two wares have much in common. The actual examples involved in this report are opaque to waxy rather than flaky.

Yucatan Opaque Ware closely approximates Paso Caballo Waxy Ware but is more opaque and less waxy. *Paste composition.* Medium-coarse to coarse texture, untested temper, cinnamon to buff and gray color. *Surface finish.* Smoothed, opaque burnished slip, medium lustrous, rarely flaky, and commonest colors are red and orange-red, often with gray or yellow splotches. Some are dull gray to black. Fire-clouding and crazing are not uncommon. Red Nolo and black Ucu groups fall under this ware.

Red Nolo Group. *Types and varieties.* Nolo Red Type, Nolo Variety (24, *c*; GWB, figs. 65, *c, 12*; 107, *a, 5*), Kiba Incised Type, Kiba Variety, sharp-incised (*ibid.*, fig. 31, *e*) and groove-incised variety (24, *j*), and Kini Composite Type, Kini Variety (both incised and punctate decoration, not found in our digging, GWB, figs. 31, *c, 44*; 60, *a, 23*). *Forms.* Basal-break dishes, jars, and wide-everted rim bowls. *Quantity.* Chichen Itza, 1 rim, no body sherds; Mayapan, 6 rim, 18 body sherds. *Provenience.* Acanceh, Chichen Itza, Dzibilchaltun, Holactun, Kabah, Mani, Mayapan, Sayil, and Yaxuna in Yucatan. *Ceramic complex.* Tihosuco (800 B.C.–A.D. 100).

Black Ucu Group. *Types and varieties.* Ucu Black Type, Ucu Variety (24, *i*) and Yaxkukul Composite (groove-incised and punctated) Type, Yaxkukul Variety (10, *n*; GWB, fig. 17, *a, 8*; *d, 1*). *Forms.* Jars, basal-break bowls, and lateral-flange bowl. *Quantity.* Kabah, no rim, 1 body sherd; Mayapan, 1 rim, no body sherds. *Provenience.* Holactun, Kabah, and Mayapan in Yucatan. *Ceramic complex.* Tihosuco (800 B.C.–A.D. 100).

V

Methods of Decoration

There are two basic methods of decorating pottery: (1) altering the surface by penetration, by modeling or molding, or by inlay; and (2) adding to the surface with paint or plastic elements.

PROCESSES INVOLVING ALTERATION OF THE SURFACE

TECHNIQUES OF PENETRATION

Carving (Tables 25–27). At present we recognize four main types of carved decoration: plano-relief, flat-carving, modeled-carving, and gouged-incising. By the first and second methods the background is scraped off or cut away, the design thus standing out in relief. If in the process of removing the background, the remaining design is shaped and modeled, the technique is called modeled-carving. When small areas are gouged out in the development of the design, with no attempt at modeling and no effect of plano-relief or flat-carving, we use the term gouged-incising, as incising always accompanies the gouging.

Plano-relief (Table 25). This term is applied to a technique of decoration that first appears at Uaxactun in Tzakol 3 (RES, pp. 42–43). It has been variously called carving, champlevé, scraped surface, and engraving. It was done by cutting or scraping away the slip in such a way as to leave the design in the plane of the original surface, unmodified save for the sharp incising of details. Although the areas so isolated are normally polished, their edges are sharp; this indicates that the work was done after the vessel had been dried. Actually it was usually undertaken after firing. The background may be treated in several ways: a, left unaltered; b, crosshatched; c, filled with reed-impressed circles; d, filled with punctations; e, filled with paint which may be cinnabar or other red or blue.

An examination of the material from Uxmal, Kabah, and Mayapan, the only three sites under consideration with plano-relief decoration, shows that only background types a and e were encountered.

In this context the earliest use of this technique was found at Mayapan on two basal-flange tripod (?) bowls with unaltered background (25, *p*) of the Delirio Plano-relief Type, Peten Gloss Ware, Tzakol Ceramic Complex. However, it was most used in the Cehpech Ceramic Complex in the Provincia Plano-relief Type, fine-orange Balancan Group, all with unaltered background (Table 25). This technique did not appear in either the Sotuta or Hocaba collections, but was represented in small quantity in the Hocaba-Tases or middle lots where four wares carried plano-relief decoration. These were Peto Cream Ware, Cusama Plano-relief Type; Mayapan Red Ware, Yobain Plano-relief Type with blue-filled background; Mayapan Black Ware, Conil Plano-relief Type, and Tulum Red Ware, Kanlum Plano-relief Type. The representation in the Tases or late lots was even smaller and embraced but two wares: Mayapan Red and Tulum Red.

Flat-carving. This form of decoration was obtained by cutting away parts of the vessel surface to a considerable depth during the leather-hard stage so as to leave the design in relief. Details were usually added in sharp incising. Rarely used in the Maya area. Three examples, however, can be offered: two bowls of the Horcones Ceramic Complex at Chiapa de Corzo (Lowe, 1962, pls. 13, *m*, *n*; 15, *u*, *v*) and a cylinder tripod of the Esperanza Phase at Kaminaljuyu (KJS, fig. 177, *a*). Not found in the material under consideration.

Modeled-carving (Table 26). This kind of carving is similar to flat-carving. It differs in that after cutting away parts of the vessel surface to a considerable depth during the leather-hard stage so as to leave the design in relief, the raised areas were then modeled by hand or tool to produce a gently rounded relief. Various terms have been used in describing this technique: carved, modeled, engraved, champlevé, sculptured. Unlike plano-relief, the excised areas are rarely filled with paint. Stamped and moldmade examples of this type are included in this survey because the original from which the mold was cast had to be modeled-carved. A listing of the distribution up to 1955 is given by Smith (1955a, pp. 43–45).

Modeled-carving on pottery appears to have been initiated in late Tzakol-Esperanza-Teotihuacan III times and carried through to the Early Postclassic Period. In Yucatan it has so far been found only in association with the Cehpech Ceramic Complex.

Gouged-incising (Table 27). This is applied to a type of decoration produced by scooping or gouging out small areas to accentuate a sharp-incised design.

A review of this technique is given by Smith (1955a, p. 45 and Table a, 2, on file in Peabody Museum, Harvard University). Since 1955, however, considerable new material has been added because of the excavations in the lowland Maya area at such sites as Barton Ramie in British Honduras, Tikal and Altar de Sacrificios in Guatemala, Palenque and Chiapa de Corzo in Chiapas, Mexico, and Dzibilchaltun in Yucatan, Mexico. Considering that the final reports on the ceramic findings at these sites have not been published, only those specimens will be referred to that have been mentioned or illustrated in preliminary papers.

At Barton Ramie in the Spanish Lookout Ceramic Complex two types are listed (Willey, Bullard, Glass, and Gifford, 1965, fig. 220): Big Falls Gouged-incised (red Belize Group) and Calabaso Gouged-incised (brown Tialipa Group). In the New Town Ceramic Complex two more types are mentioned (*ibid.*, fig. 247): Mauger Gouged-incised (red Augustine Group) and Bluefield Gouged-incised (red Paxcaman Group, wherein a close relationship to Tulum Red Ware is probable) types. At Tikal in the Early Classic Period a polished black ware restricted-orifice bowl with pedestal base (Shook and Kidder II, 1961, p. 6), a black ware cylindrical bowl with fitted cover (W. R. Coe, 1965, p. 30), and a Tiquisate Ware cylinder tripod (*ibid.*, p. 27) are excellent examples of this technique. Although a number of examples embellished with this method of decoration were found at Altar de Sacrificios, the final report has

not as yet been published. At Palenque, on the other hand, no examples of this technique were noted in the published literature. At Chiapa de Corzo in the Horcones Ceramic Complex a polished black ware tripod dish with nearly vertical sides is illustrated (Lowe and Agrinier, 1960, fig. 43, *a*; pl. 21, *i*), and in the Frailesca Region, also belonging to the Horcones Ceramic Complex, a dish or low bowl with vertical sides and flat base is shown by Navarrete (1960, fig. 32, *g*). So far no type names have been given to these Chiapas gouged-incised specimens. At Dzibilchaltun, although gouged-incised examples were probably present, none has been mentioned or illustrated in the existing literature.

At Mayapan, associated with the Cehpech, Sotuta, Hocaba, Hocaba-Tases, and Tases ceramic complexes 136 gouged-incised sherds were found. Both preslip and postslip gouging-incising were practised and they seem to be equally distributed. The percentage of sherds with this technique to total sherds found was .034. It is interesting to note that this method of decoration is rarely used in the pre-Cehpech ceramic complexes in Yucatan; in fact no examples were unearthed in our digging.

Cehpech. In this ceramic complex the gouged-incised technique was little used. Of the total number of sherds of this complex found at Uxmal and Kabah, only 130 or .28 per cent were gouged-incised. Of these, 80, or 61.5 per cent, were preslip executed and 50, or 38.5 per cent, postslip. At Mayapan only 2 Cehpech sherds conformed to this method of decoration.

Sotuta. In this ceramic complex the gouged-incised technique was also sparingly used. Of the total number of sherds of this complex found at Chichen Itza, only 95, or .5 per cent, were gouged-incised. Of these 84, or 88.4 per cent, were preslip executed and 11 or 11.6 per cent postslip. At Mayapan just 22 Sotuta Ceramic Complex sherds with this method of decoration were identified.

Hocaba. In this ceramic complex at Mayapan the gouged-incised technique was very sparingly used. Only 4 sherds, all of the fine-orange Matillas Group, were so embellished. This forms .02 per cent of the total Hocaba sherd count.

Hocaba-Tases. In this Mayapan middle lot collection only 16 gouged-incised examples, or .02 per cent of the Hocaba-Tases total sherd count, were discovered. They all belong to the fine-orange Matillas Group.

Tases. Although in this ceramic complex 89 gouged-incised specimens were encountered, they formed only .05 per cent of the total Tases sherd count. These, also, all belong to the fine-orange Matillas Group.

Chamfering. This technique consists of slicing back the vessel wall to create a series of clapboardlike horizontal steps. It has been found in the Mamom Ceramic Complex at Uaxactun (RES, pp. 45–46) and in the late Classic or Tepeu 2 Ceramic Complex at Nakum (Tozzer, 1913, fig. 86). Elsewhere it occurs early at Kaminaljuyu (Shook, 1951, possible fig. 1, g). A possible example of the Uaxactun Desvario Chamfered Type (RES, fig. 14, b, 8) was noted in a sherd lot from Dzibilnocac, Campeche, and an excellent specimen of this technique was observed on a polished black cylinder tripod from Mirador, Chiapas (Peterson, 1963, fig. 13). Thus this method of decoration was used in the Middle Preclassic, the Early Classic, and the Late Classic periods and distributed over various parts of the Maya area. It did not occur, however, in the material under consideration.

Fluting. This method of decoration is accomplished by making shallow, wide, semicircular, close-set, usually contiguous, channels in the wet clay. Fluting is widely distributed in time and space (RES, p. 46) but it is rarely associated with the Yucatan material under study. Brainerd (1958, fig. 50, f) illustrates a Thin Slate Ware vessel. Actually only two examples were found at Mayapan, both vertically fluted jar body sherds belonging to the Alta Mira Fluted Type, Paso Caballo Waxy Ware of the Chicanel Ceramic Complex (no illustration).

In Mesoamerica this technique seems to occur with greatest frequency in the Preclassic and Classic periods. During the Postclassic Period fluting appears to have been largely superseded by gadrooning.

Gadrooning (Table 28). This is a form of decoration which combines grooving and modeling. Deep vertical grooves, sometimes with curved upper ends, appear to have been made in the globular vessel (jar body, bulging neck of jar, pyriform vase, or barrel-shape vase) wall, and the intervening areas were then thrown into higher relief by slicing or trimming to give a melonlike effect. The same effect may be attained by pressing out the vessel wall. Shepard defines this technique for plumbate vessels (1948, p. 17). Another method of creating the melon form other than by gadrooning is by vertical grooving of globular vessel bodies.

On reviewing the findings at Uaxactun and elsewhere (RES, p. 45; Table a, 3), we learn that this is essentially an Early Postclassic technique with occasional examples equally distributed in the Preclassic, Early Classic, and Late Classic periods.

At Chichen Itza in the Sotuta Ceramic Complex gadrooning was associated with four wares: Fine Orange Ware, Silho Group, Calkini Gadrooned Type; Chichen Red Ware, Tiholop Gadrooned Type; Chichen Slate Ware, Mopila Gadrooned Type; and Plumbate Ware, Tohil Group, Porvenir Gadrooned Type. It formed but a very small percentage (.06) of the total Chichen Itza Sotuta sherds recovered. At Mayapan the Plumbate Ware, Porvenir Gadrooned Type, was represented and it totaled .25 per cent of the Sotuta sherds found. In addition a single Mayapan Red Ware sherd of Tixua Gadrooned Type was found in the Hocaba-Tases middle lots.

Impressing (Table 29). This was produced by pressure of various sorts upon the wet clay. Impressing falls easily into three basic categories involving ways of doing: (1) manual, including thumb, finger and nail, (2) by means of natural tools such as reed, concentric reed, split-reed, shell, corncob, textile, mat, etc., and (3) by using manufactured tools like a stamp. Stamping, a rather special form of impressing, is the making of "marks or figures by means of the impression of a die, pattern or the like" (Funk and Wagnalls Dictionary (1931). In addition, most of these procedures may be adapted directly to the vessel wall or placed on an appliqué fillet or flange or even on a modeled molding.

Impressing was used moderately by the pre-Columbian potters of Yucatan, beginning in the Cehpech Ceramic Complex and ending in the Chauaca Ceramic Complex. Prior to Cehpech no impressing was noted in association with the collections under study for this report, although this technique was commonly used in the Preclassic and Classic phases at Uaxactun to the south.

At Mayapan, associated with the Cehpech, Sotuta, Hocaba, Hocaba-Tases, Tases, and Chauaca ceramic complexes, 3,852 impressed sherds were found. This formed 1 per cent of the total sherds involved. Of the many varieties of impressing encountered, thumb-impressed on a fillet comprised 93.6 per cent, direct nail-impressed 3.9 per cent, direct thumb-impressed 2.5 per cent, and reed, split-reed, stamped, and nail-impressed on a fillet formed negligible percentages. Notable among the varieties of impressing not present were the following: textile, which had been observed only in its capacity as an aid to adherence between two layers of plaster applied to huge jars (60, *n–q*) and not as a means of decorating; rocker-stamping, a natural tool category; and mat, which was noted on the base of a cylindrical vessel from Moxviquil, Chiapas (Smith, 1958, fig. 4, *f*), not part of this collection.

Cehpech. In this ceramic complex impressing is very modestly represented. Of the total number of sherds of this complex found at Uxmal and Kabah, only 242 or .52 per cent were impressed. The variety percentages were as follows: direct nail-impressed, 25.2; thumb-impressed on a fillet, 23.5; reed-impressed on a fillet, 17.4; direct thumb-impressed, 14.5; direct reed-impressed, 9.1; stamp-impressed usually on a basal molding, 5.4; concentric reed-impressed on basal bolding, 3.7; and direct split-reed, 1.2. At Mayapan only 11 Cehpech sherds had any sort of impressing, with direct nail-impressed constituting 45.4 per cent, direct reed-impressed 18.2 per cent, concentric reed-impressed on a basal molding 18.2 per cent, and thumb-impressed on a fillet and stamped basal molding each 9.1 per cent.

Sotuta. Even in the Chichen Itza collection impressing was extremely rare and wholly confined to Chichen Unslipped Ware. Of the total number of sherds, only 29 examples or .15 per cent were impressed. At Mayapan only 17 sherds or 1.4 per cent, all of Chichen Unslipped Ware, were embellished with impressed decoration.

Hocaba. Impressing had much the same experience in this ceramic complex as it had in the Sotuta Ceramic Complex. In other words, it was rarely used and almost wholly confined to Mayapan Unslipped Ware, the single exception being a Mayapan Red Ware jar sherd. Of the total number of sherds involved, only 52 examples or .21 per cent were impressed, all from Mayapan. Furthermore, 96.2 per cent were of the thumb-impressed-fillet variety and only 3.8 per cent had nail-impressed bands.

Hocaba-Tases. In this collection of middle lots at Mayapan impressing reached its peak, involving 1,455 sherds or 1.7 per cent of Hocaba-Tases total sherd count. Of these sherds 98.6 per cent had thumb-impressed fillets and 1.4 per cent had nail-impressed bands. The vast majority belonged to Mayapan Unslipped Ware.

Tases. In this ceramic complex impressing occurred on 2,303 specimens or .82 per cent of all Tases sherds. All were manually impressed with the following variety percentages: thumb-impressed-fillet, 90.8; nail-impressed, 5.2; thumb-

impressed, 4.0; and nail-impressed-fillet, .04.

Chauaca. At Mayapan a total of 102 sherds were associated with this ceramic complex. Of these 15 impressed specimens, 14.7 per cent, were identified. All 15 were restricted-orifice bowl sherds belonging to Ochil Unslipped Ware, Kinchil Composite Type, and the impressing was thumb on a fillet (57, *e*).

Incising (Table 30). Incising is cutting lines into the surface by means of a pointed implement. It may be done while the paste is plastic, leather-hard, after the vessel has been dried, or after firing; it may precede or follow slipping and/or polishing. The nature of the lines (depth, width, section, or slant) depends on the sort of tool employed, the amount of pressure exerted, and the paste texture (Shepard, 1956, pp. 195–203; figs. 14, 15). *Sharp-incising* was done with a sharp-pointed implement at any time after the vessel had been shaped. The lines are normally narrow, deep in relation to width, and tend to be V-shape in section. *Groove-incising* was ordinarily done with a round-pointed implement, which pressed down rather than cut into the clay, sometimes, apparently, by means of an implement with gougelike point which removed clay. The lines are shallow in relation to width; they are rounded in section when produced by the round point, more nearly half-rectangular in section when produced by the gouge. Groove-incising is practicable only when the clay is soft. It is normally done before slipping. *Slant-grooving* is produced by means of either a gouge inclined to one side or a knife inclined to the surface. In both cases the result is a slanted V-shape trough done while the paste is plastic and usually supplemented by incised lines (KJS, p. 184, fig. 74). *Light-incising*, so far associated only with the Correlo Incised-dichrome Type, consists of marking a slipped vessel with a medium-sharp incision which does not quite penetrate to the paste (RES, figs. 16, *e*, 9; 84, *k*). *Fine-incising* may be accomplished with a fine pointed tool or thin sharp knife. There are no doubt many examples of this technique; one is found at Uaxactun in the Mamom Ceramic Complex (*ibid.*, pp. 31–32, fig. 14, *d*, 1, 9). *Scratching* or doodling, probably a better term hardly qualifies as decoration. It appears on finished vessels or, seemingly more often, on sherds, and consists of random lines or crude drawings made with a sharp point. The technique derives its name from the fact that these sherds appear to have been used as a scratch pad for adults or as a medium for amusing children interested in drawing (*ibid.*, fig. 65). For discussion of when the incising was done, *see* Smith, (*ibid.*, p. 37) and Shepard (1956, pp. 195–203).

Actually incising plays a fairly strong part in the ceramic decorative aggregate. Considered by ceramic complex, an interesting breakdown is noted. Although the early complexes including Tihosuco, Cochuah, and Motul were poorly represented in the collections from Kabah, Uxmal, Chichen Itza, and Mayapan, incising was present.

At Mayapan, associated with the Cehpech, Sotuta, Hocaba, Hocaba-Tases, and Tases ceramic complexes, 11,646 incised sherds were found. Of these 9,700 or 83.3 per cent were groove-incised and 1,946 or 16.7 per cent sharp-incised. The percentage of incised to total sherds involved was 2.9. Several varieties of incising failed to show up in any of the Yucatan ceramic complexes discussed: fine-incising, light-incising, and slant-grooving. Scratching or doodling, always linked with postfire sharp-incising, was encountered sporadically. Since this form of incising is not truly decoration, it was not given type names but simply included under postfire sharp-incising. Another reason for this lumping was the difficulty of deciding whether serious decoration, sometimes imperfectly done, was intended or whether doodling was the objective.

Tihosuco. During this complex both sharp-incising and groove-incising were used.

Cochuah. At this time preslip sharp-incising was most common, especially as it concerned the Valladolid Incised-dichrome Type. Even the majority of trade types such as Pita Incised were generally preslip sharp-incised (25, q–s), rarely groove-incised (25, t).

Motul. The few examples found were either postfire incised or postslip, prepolish sharp-incised. The former belonged to the Bokoba Incised Type, the latter to the Tekanto Incised Type. Two Peten Gloss Ware trade types of the Tepeu 2 Ceramic Complex were present at Mayapan, one with a preslip sharp-incised design (Geronimo Incised Type), the other with a groove-incised decoration (Carmelita Incised Type).

Cehpech. In this complex sharp-incising was well represented. Associated with Puuc Slate Ware, the Tekit Incised Type was usually preslip incised, rarely postslip or postslip, prepolish. With Thin Slate Ware, the Xul Incised Type was more often postslip incised, whereas the Puuc Red Ware associated Becal Incised Type, although normally preslip sharp-incised, did have a number of preslip groove-incised specimens. On the other hand, the Caribe Incised Type of the fine-orange

Balancan Group appeared to be all preslip groove-incised. Of the 46,767 Cehpech Ceramic Complex sherds found at Uxmal and Kabah, only 419 or .9 per cent were incised. Of these 388 were sharp-incised and 31 groove-incised. At Mayapan a total of 6,259 Cehpech sherds were encountered, of which 65 or 1 per cent, including 48 sharp-incised and 17 groove-incised, had incised decoration.

Sotuta. In this ceramic complex sharp-incising was more plentiful than groove-incising. The Chacmay Incised Type of Chichen Slate Ware was commonly sharp-incised, less frequently groove-incised. For Chichen Red Ware, the Xuku Incised Type was more often sharp-incised than groove-incised, whereas for the Silho Fine-orange Group and the Tohil Plumbate Group all the incising was of the grooved variety. Considering the 18,768 Sotuta Ceramic Complex sherds excavated at Chichen Itza only 536 sherds or 2.8 per cent were incised. Of these 458 were sharp-incised and 78 groove-incised. At Mayapan 1,191 Sotuta sherds were encountered, of which 18 or 1.5 per cent had incised decoration. Of these 13 were groove-incised and 5 sharp-incised.

Hocaba. In this ceramic complex at Mayapan groove-incising predominated over sharp-incising. Only three wares were embellished by incising: Mayapan Red Ware, Papacal Incised Type, had 80.8 per cent of the groove-incised variety and 19.2 per cent of the sharp-incised variety; Fine Orange Ware of the fine-orange Matillas Group, Villahermosa Incised Type, with a very small total was entirely sharp-incised, and Mayapan Unslipped Ware, Chenkeken Incised had 2 sharp-incised sherds. In addition Peto Cream Ware, Xcanchakan Black-on-cream Type, incised variety had 1 grater bowl example. Of the 24,568 Hocaba Ceramic Complex sherds found in the earliest and usually the lowest levels at Mayapan, 871 or 3.5 per cent were incised, and of these 80 per cent were groove-incised and 20 per cent sharp-incised.

Hocaba-Tases. In this instance the middle lots between early or Hocaba and late or Tases are considered. As in the Hocaba Ceramic Complex, groove-incising (83.1 per cent) prevailed over sharp-incising. Six wares were involved, but only three were associated with any appreciable percentage of incising. These included Fine Orange Ware of the Matillas Group (28.2), Tulum Red Ware (27.9), and Mayapan Red Ware (10.1), the first two high percentages reflecting trade wares. Mayapan Red Ware was separated into the early or Papacal Incised Type with 4,073 sherds and the late or Pustunich Incised Type with 7 sherds, a total of 4,080; of which 3,535 were groove-incised and 545 were sharp-incised. Fine Orange Ware of the Matillas Group totaled 96 Villahermosa Incised Type sherds and 20 Salto Composite Type sherds, all sharp-incised. Mayapan Unslipped Ware had 43 Chenkeken Incised Type sherds: 31 sharp-incised, 12 groove-incised. Tulum Red Ware totaled 12 Palmul Incised Type sherds, all sharp-incised. Peto Cream Ware had 4 Pencuyut Incised and 3 Xcanchakan Black-on-cream, incised variety sherds, all sharp-incised. Finally San Joaquin Buff Ware had 2 Kimbila Incised Type sherds; one was groove-incised, the other sharp-incised. Of the 86,420 middle lot sherds recovered, 4,261 or 4.8 per cent were incised, and of these 83.3 per cent were groove-incised and 16.7 per cent sharp-incised.

Tases. Groove-incising continued to prevail over sharp-incising at Mayapan by 5,420 to 1,001 sherds. The number of wares decorated with incising increased from two in Hocaba, five in the middle lots, to eight in the late or Tases lots. Likewise the number of wares with an appreciable percentage of incised decoration increased from three to four. These four comprise Telchaquillo Brick Ware (11.2), Mayapan Red Ware (8), and two trade wares, Tulum Red (46.2) and Fine Orange of the Matillas Group (18.7). Mayapan Red Ware incising was divided between the early Papacal Incised Type which had 5,335 groove-incised and 782 sharp-incised sherds and the late Pustunich Incised Type with 11 sharp-incised and 3 groove-incised sherds. Fine Orange of the Matillas Group separated into three types, all sharp-incised: 117 Villahermosa Incised; 31 Grijalva Incised-polychrome; and 12 Salto Composite of the sharp-incised rather than gouged-incised variety. Mayapan Unslipped Ware had two types with incising, the Chenkeken-Incised with 24 groove-incised and 23 sharp-incised, and the Chenkeken-Acansip Composite Type with 25 sherds, all groove-incised. Telchaquillo Brick Ware had 33 Cozil Incised Type sherds, all groove-incised. Tulum Red Ware through its Palmul Incised Type numbered 12 sherds, all sharp-incised. San Joaquin Buff Ware by means of its Kimbila Incised Type totaled 9 sharp-incised sherds. Mayapan Black Ware with its Pacha Incised Type had 2 examples, both sharp-incised. Peto Cream Ware had 2 Xcanchakan Black-on-cream Type, sharp-incised variety grater bowls. Of the 279,156 Tases Ceramic Complex sherds found, 6,421 or 2.3 per cent were incised and of these 84.4 per cent were groove-incised and 15.6 per cent, sharp-incised. Scratching or doodling was responsible for 5 of the latter sherds.

Notching (Table 31). Notching is the embellishment of a vessel by a cut, generally V-shape, or nick into any edge (angle, fillet, flange, lip). This practice is represented at Uxmal and Kabah in the Cehpech Ceramic Complex by 29 sherds (19 Puuc Slate Ware and 10 Puuc Red Ware) or .06 per cent of the total number involved. All notches were associated with different parts of tripod dishes: flange, 41.4 per cent; Z-angle, 31 per cent; side-base angle, 27.6 per cent. At Chichen Itza only 2 sherds carried notching. These were tripod basal-break dishes of Puuc Slate Ware. At Mayapan in the Hocaba Ceramic Complex a single example, a tripod basal-flange dish of Mayapan Red Ware, was found. In the Hocaba-Tases or middle lots, 38 sherds with this technique were located, forming .04 per cent of the total count there. In the Tases Ceramic Complex 34 examples or .01 per cent emerged. Of these 72 sherds, 49 examples or 68.1 per cent were tripod basal-flange dishes associated with the fine-orange Matillas Group. Other wares represented included: Mayapan Red with 20 examples or 27.8 per cent found in both complexes, Mayapan Unslipped with 2 sherds of the middle lots, and San Joaquin Buff with 1 example from the Tases or late lots.

Perforating (Table 32). This device consists of embellishing vessels by cutting through their walls. The result is openwork decoration. Not included are "crack-lacing" mending holes which occur throughout, although infrequently; or vents, associated with censers, feet, and musical instruments; suspension holes; or even figurine face openings such as eyes, mouth, and nostrils. Here I consider only perforations made primarily for decorative purposes. In these collections feet rarely had decorative perforations in addition to the necessary vent or vents.

The largest assemblage of decorative perforation or openwork was found at Chichen Itza in the Sotuta Ceramic Complex linked with the Tinum Red-on-cinnamon Type ladle censer (Mixtec-type censer, Wauchope, 1948, pp. 148–149, fig. 66). These totaled 53 examples or .28 per cent, and the two complementary decorative techniques were incising and openwork. At Mayapan 15 fragments belonging to this type censer were found: 5 in the Hocaba and 10 in the Hocaba-Tases ceramic complexes. The most noteworthy perforated examples encountered at Mayapan, however, were the bowl clusters of Mayapan Red Ware, Dzitxil Openwork Type. Of these, 10 occurred in the middle lots, all complemented by incising, and 20 were found in the Tases Ceramic

Complex, where perforation alone was used. The only other form at Mayapan associated with this technique was the tripod or pedestal-base jar censer. Mostly these sherds were found in the middle lots (14 to 1 in the late lots), and they involved a guilloche band both incised and perforated. To sum up, there were 60 examples of perforating: 25 per cent of the Sotuta Ceramic Complex and 75 per cent of the Tases Ceramic Complex.

Punctating (Table 33). Punctation is embellishing a vessel by punching depressions into the wet clay usually with the point of a sharp, rarely a blunt, instrument. If these punches are elongated into dashes, the result is dash punctation, or if they appear as cuneiform dents made with an awl, the product is awl punctation. Another variety is roulette punctation, rarely encountered in Mesoamerica; the rouletting of two Uaxactun specimens (RES, figs. 7, *d*; 70, *b*, 11) possibly was done with a shell. Punctation is used as an outline, as a filler of design or background, as banding, as a design element or accessory, but rarely for the making of a complete design.

Only two examples, both sharp-pointed, one used for design outlining, the other as a design accessory, were found in the collections under review. The former, from Kabah, belonged to a flaring-side dish of Yaxkukul Composite Type, Yucatan Opaque Ware of the Tihosuco Ceramic Complex. The latter from Mayapan, a deep bowl of **Salto Composite Type**, white-slip variety, fine-orange Matillas Group, was associated with the Hocaba-Tases middle lots. All others, although from the Yucatan area under observation, came from collections used by Brainerd (1958).

As these examples clearly show (Table 33), the vast majority of specimens embellished by punctation were of the sharp-pointed variety; only a few enjoyed dash punctation. Considering their design function, the following percentages were noted: outlining, 42.4; design filler, 39.4; background filler, 9.1; design accessory, 9.1. Other varieties of punctation, such as blunt, awl, or roulette, were not noted in this area.

Texturing. There are three main types of texturing: raking or striating (the latter term is used throughout this report); roughening; and textile or other forms of impressing for purposes of roughening the surface. Any of these texturing devices may be used for a dual purpose, both decorative and practical, or individually as a form of decoration, or as a means of roughening the vessel surface for practical reasons. Here we are interested in the decorative rather than the utilitarian purpose.

Striating (Table 34). With this technique a vessel is textured by stroking the surface with a frayed twig, a bunch of reeds, or a shell edge so as to produce a series of parallel scores. Striating, found occasionally on the neck and generally on the shoulder and body of unslipped jars and exterior of several unslipped bowl forms, occurs throughout all the ceramic complexes. It may be coarse, that is uneven, rough and ragged, medium-coarse, or fine, which means even, neat, and sharp. Besides its texture, striating has a depth coefficient here expressed by light, medium-deep, and deep.

Striating was used extensively by the pre-Columbian potters of Yucatan beginning in the Tihosuco Ceramic Complex and continuing to the present day. In the early complexes, Tihosuco through Sotuta at Mayapan, striating was responsible for texturing 36.3 per cent of the total number of sherds. 29.4 per cent of this total, however, belonged in the Cehpech Ceramic Complex. In the Hocaba Ceramic Complex the percentage of striated specimens was 14.9; in Hocaba-Tases, 20.6, and in Tases, 8.3. The kind of striation varies with the ceramic complexes: deep-coarse (2, *w–y*, *aa*) prevailed exclusively in Tihosuco and Cochuah, and largely in Cehpech; light-coarse (2, *s*, *u*; 28) dominated in Motul, Hocaba, Hocaba-Tases, and Tases and had a relatively small representation in Tihosuco and Cehpech; medium-deep-coarse (2, *t*, *v*; 11, *q*, *s*, *u*) and spaced medium-deep-coarse (11, *r*, *t*, *v*) prevailed in Sotuta and was rarely noted in other complexes; light-fine (11, *n–p*) was found in very small quantity only in Sotuta.

Roughening (Table 35). This technique renders the surface rough, gives it a rasplike appearance something like coarse sandpaper. The tool or tools used to produce this effect are not easy to determine. So far this rasplike roughening has been noted only in association with the Hocaba, Hocaba-Tases, and Tases ceramic complexes. In some instances there may be slight differences in roughness but not sufficient to warrant different groupings. This type of texturing formed a small percentage (.5) of the total sherd count in these ceramic complexes: Hocaba, .4; Hocaba-Tases, .8; Tases, .4. In Table 35 the totals are marked approximate because exact counts of this feature were not kept in all instances.

Impressing. This technique is commonly used for decorating (Table 29). It is rarely employed for texturing even in a practical sense. It has been used to roughen a surface so that a plaster coating would better adhere, however (60, *n–q*).

TECHNIQUES OF MODELING AND MOLDING

Since whatever is made in a mold first had to be modeled, the two techniques will be considered for the most part as one — modeling. Most modeling, however, had to do with figurines, effigies, and miscellaneous objects, and since these, with the exception of large figurines, effigy censers, and effigy vessels, were usually applied to either vessels or figures, they will be considered as a technique under appliqué.

Modeling (Table 36). The combined modeling or molding techniques are primarily concerned with effigy censers, effigy vessels, and figurines, most of which are embellished with appliqué adjuncts (Tables 37 and 38). Many are part modeled and part moldmade; often the head is moldmade, less frequently the body. The head may be made in a mold and then have features (a long nose, a beard, whiskers, and tusks) or other devices added.

Effigy censers. For a complete description of how these are made, see Chapter XV under Hocaba Ceramic Complex, Mayapan Unslipped Ware, Hoal Modeled Type effigy censers; and Chapter XVI under Tases Ceramic Complex, Mayapan Unslipped Ware, Chen Mul Modeled Type effigy censers.

Cehpech. In this ceramic complex effigy censers with associated modeled figures are rare. Evidence is present, however, at Uxmal and Kabah through an arm and head (6, *ll*, *mm*, respectively). Quite large effigy censers were encountered at Xcaret, Quintana Roo. These also seemed to be of Puuc Slate Ware (Proskouriakoff, 1957, pp. 333–334).

Sotuta. In this complex, modeled effigy censers were not encountered, only those with appliqué features.

Hocaba. In this complex for the first time modeling of effigy censers occurred in appreciable quantity. These censers are of the Hoal Modeled Type (32, *b–d*; cf. 68, *a*), and may be distinguished from the later effigy censer of the Chen Mul Modeled Type by the figure not being overburdened with appliqué ornamentation, and the cylindrical vessel having a low pedestal.

Hocaba-Tases. Hoal Modeled Type effigy censers continue (68, *a*, 2, 3) but in smaller quantity, and the Chen Mul Modeled Type in three size

categories (large, medium, and small, 32, *y*; 66, *d*, 1–3, 7, 10; 68, *b*, 3, 7, 10; 70, *a*, 4) takes over in an impressive manner. The figures associated with these censers, except for the faces, are modeled. The faces are usually moldmade. Certain facial additions and many adornos are appliquéd. At this time another effigy censer type is noted, the Uayma Modeled Type. These are crudely made of Mayapan Coarse Ware, usually orange-red to reddish brown in color; although most of the figure is crudely modeled, appliqué adornments are used.

Tases. Hoal Modeled Type effigy censers (32, *c*, *d*; 68, *a*, 1) have nearly disappeared and Uayma Modeled Type effigy censers are found in small quantity; on the other hand, the Chen Mul Modeled Type (32, *e–x*, *z*; 66, *d*, 4–6, 8, 9, 11–13; 67; 68, *b*, 1, 2, 4–6, 8, 9, 11, 12; 69; 70; 71, *a*, 1) has multiplied in all sizes.

Effigy vessels. As shown in Table 36, effigy vessels are of four principal forms: jars, rectangular altars (may or may not be vessels), cups, and miscellaneous. They occur in all the ceramic complexes under consideration except Cehpech and Hocaba, and are made in many of the wares.

Sotuta. The effigy vessel, although present, forms but a small percentage. It is found at Chichen Itza in vase form of Fine Orange Ware, Nunkini Modeled Type (GWB, fig. 79, *l*), and in bowl form (a frog?) of Chichen Slate Ware, Balam Canche Red-on-slate Type, modeled variety (*ibid.*, fig. 75, *l*). It occurs in the Marquez collection, formerly located in Merida, in pyriform vase form (a monkey) of Fine Orange Ware, Nunkini Modeled Type (Smith, 1957b, fig. 7, *q*) and in jar form (a frog) also of Nunkini Modeled Type (*ibid.*, fig. 13, *o*, *p*). Even at Mayapan a few jar sherds of Fine Orange Ware, Nunkini Modeled Type (27, *k*) occur.

Hocaba. No effigy vessels noted.

Hocaba-Tases. In this complex, actually the middle lots between complexes, 73 vessels and fragments have been noted. Made in Mayapan Unslipped Ware, the Chen Mul Modeled Type (47 examples), including miscellaneous vessel forms representing a monkey (32, *mm*), a jaguar (32, *nn*), humans or gods (32, *oo*, *pp*), a merchant god (64, *a*), the old god, Itzamna (64, *c*), and turtles with human head in mouth (64, *d*, *j*, *k*, *n*, *o*), are nearly always modeled. Exceptions are most of the human or god heads, which are moldmade, and cup forms with god or human representations on one side including moldmade Chacs, the long-nosed god (63, *b*, *f*), and a modeled face with Pinocchio nose (63, *j*). Others (26 examples) are made in Mayapan Red Ware, Chapab Modeled Type. These include cups, most of which have moldmade Chac gods (45, d; 75, g) placed on one side of vessel often modified by appliqué; jars with modeled face (45, e) and a humpback (45, b; 75, f) with moldmade head and modeled body.

Tases. There are more effigy vessels (461 examples) in this late complex than in earlier complexes. In Unslipped Mayapan Ware, Chen Mul Modeled Type (378) there is a new form portraying rectangular altars (no illustration). Regular forms are jars representing toads or frogs (64, l), birds, monkeys (63, c), a death's head face (63, d), and a rabbit (64, m), all modeled except for a few moldmade heads; miscellaneous vessel forms depicting turtles (64, p), diving gods supported by a dog (64, e, h) or a bird (64, f), a warrior (64, b), and a grotesque head (32, ll), which are mostly modeled except for some moldmade human or godlike heads; and cups, usually with moldmade faces modified by appliqué devices, representing Chac gods (30, y; 31, hh; 63, a, e, h, i) and human heads (31, ff; 63, g). Other effigy vessels (83) are made in Mayapan Red Ware, Chapab Modeled Type, including vases with modeled, moldmade, and appliqué diving god on one side (45, a; 75, e), and modeled fragments of other vessels (45, f, h); jars with a bird modeled to the shoulder (42, a); and cups with modeled faces on one side probably representing the Chac deity (30, x, z–bb).

Figurines. As indicated in Table 36, figurines, including whistles and flutes in human or animal form, may be modeled or moldmade (sometimes the entire figure is moldmade, sometimes only the face), hollow or solid, may have articulated limbs, and may be found in ceramic complexes from Cehpech through Tases with the possible exception of Sotuta. They occur in a variety of wares both unslipped and slipped.

Cehpech. At Uxmal modeled figurine limbs, some articulated, and one moldmade head, plus a few modeled flute sherds, are noted. Altogether the Uxmal finds totaled 19 Puuc Unslipped Ware, Yiba Modeled Type examples, whereas Kabah had only 3. At Mayapan two flutes (26, c, 1, 2; 66, b, 1) of Puuc Slate Ware, Yaxnic Modeled Type and one figurine whistle (26, c, 3) of Puuc Red Ware, Sitpach Modeled Type were found. It is possible that the four flute tube fragments (3, x, y) found at Uxmal were of Puuc Slate Ware with slip weathered off. A Puuc Slate Ware tubular fragment (6, ll) from Uxmal may have belonged to a flute.

Sotuta. Only a figurine mold was encountered.

Hocaba. Only three figurine fragments were found at Mayapan in this ceramic complex. They belonged to the Mayapan Unslipped Ware, Hoal Modeled Type: one modeled and two moldmade (weathered, no illustration).

Hocaba-Tases. At Mayapan in the middle lots or Hocaba-Tases intermediate complex a total of 164 figurines occurred. The majority were moldmade and usually hollow and human (35, a, 4–6, 8, 10, 11, 13, 14, 16, 17) or grotesque (35, a, 9); some were solid and human (35, b, 1, 2, 4, 6, 7, 9), including an articulated limb specimen (35 b, 5) and a jaguar head (35, b, 8). Others were hollow and modeled, including some bodies and a pisote whistle (35, c, 1), or solid and modeled, especially articulated limbs. All these belong to the Chen Mul Modeled Type. Unslipped but coarse figurines also turned up. These hollow and modeled specimens (35, b, 18; 65, i) pertain to the Uayma Modeled Type. In addition, 8 examples both modeled and moldmade, solid and hollow, were slipped red and associated with the Chapab Modeled Type (37, e, a head and 65, p, a complete figure with articulated limbs).

Tases. Intermingled with the material in this ceramic complex were 194 figurines. Of these 183 were of Mayapan Unslipped Ware, Chen Mul Modeled Type with 101 moldmade (hollow, 35, a, 1–3, 12, 15; 65, e, or solid, 35, b, 3) and 82 modeled (hollow, 35, c, 3; 65, j, k, or solid, 65, l, m; and articulated, cf. 35, b, 5); 6 were associated with Mayapan Coarse Ware, Uayma Modeled Type, both hollow and solid, but all modeled; 4 belonged to Mayapan Red Ware, Chapab Modeled Type with 3 hollow moldmade (37, d; 45, i) and 1 solid modeled (no illustration); 1, a hollow modeled bird (no illustration), may be included in Mayapan Black Ware, Sacmuyna Modeled Type.

Molds. This form is always modeled and rare in the collections under consideration. A single fragmentary example of Fine Orange Ware, Silho Group, Nunkini Modeled Type occurred at Mayapan. Three specimens (66, a, 3, 4) of Mayapan Unslipped Ware, Chen Mul Modeled Type, were found in the Hocaba-Tases or middle lots and 14 (66, a, 1, 2, 5) in the Tases Ceramic Complex, all at Mayapan.

Masks. These are also rare and so far have proved to be moldmade. The ten examples found came from Mayapan and belong to Mayapan Unslipped Ware, Chen Mul Modeled Type. Six (34, a–c, f) were recovered from the middle lots (Hocaba-Tases) and 4 (34, d, e) from the Tases Ceramic Complex; 34, f, a monkey, is the only animal represented in this group.

PROCESSES INVOLVING ADDITIONS TO THE SURFACE

TECHNIQUES OF PLASTICITY

Appliqué (Tables 37 and 38). Since all appliquéd pieces save the rare moldmade examples were modeled, the combined modeled-and-appliqué will be considered here as appliqué. This concerns all applied objects including adornos and appendages such as feet, flanges, handles, spouts, and supports. In all cases the modeled or moldmade embellishments were applied to the surface of the vessel or figure.

Adornos (Table 37). This category signifies applied ornamentation or adornment and includes a number of items. They conform to three main groups: (1) simple vessel attachments, (2) human or animal figure adornment or accoutrement, and (3) small heads or figures, either human or animal, used as ornaments. The total number of sherds representing these pottery vessels and ceramic objects amounted to 60,924, resulting in the following percentages: censers, 98.4; effigy vessels, .5; figurines, .4; jars, .3; vases, .1; cups, .1; bowls, .09, and dishes .09.

In the first group the principal items are buttons or disks, fillets, spikes, flanges, and bosses or lugs. Buttons or disks appear first in the Sotuta Ceramic Complex and are abundantly used through the Tases Ceramic Complex. They are associated principally with a variety of censer forms but also with figurines, cups, effigy vessels, vases, and bowls. Fillets, usually impressed, occur throughout and are most often associated with censers, but do appear on other vessels such as jars, dishes, vases, and bowls. Spikes likewise are found in all ceramic complexes herein considered and are usually linked with censers, but occasionally cups and bowls bear them. Flanges, both vertical and horizontal used as decoration rather than as part of the vessel form, are noted first in the Cehpech Ceramic Complex and continue through the Tases. They are found mostly on censers, rarely on a jar or vase. Bosses or lugs (other than handles) are rare and usually associated with jars of the Tases Ceramic Complex.

The second group, primarily linked with the Hocaba-Tases and Tases ceramic complexes, includes effigy censers, figurines, and effigy vessels with adornment and accoutrement of the associated human and animal figures.

The adornment includes representations of bone, clay, jade, shell, and stone jewelry, actual examples of which have been found at Mayapan and described by Tatiana Proskouriakoff (1962b). Those of bone (*ibid.*, figs. 38, 39, and 41 which include perforated teeth), clay (*ibid.*, fig. 50, *h*, *i*), jade (*ibid.*, figs. 25, *a*, *b*, *d*; 26, *b–i*, *m–p*), metal (*ibid.*, fig. 48, copper finger rings, *a–n*; copper bells, *t–dd*), iron pyrites (*ibid.*, fig. 26, *k*), shell (*ibid.*, figs. 42–45) and stone (*ibid.*, fig. 26, *a*, *j*).

In most cases actual examples may be identified on the pottery figures in the form of anklets (64, *l*; 75, *e*), armbands (64, *a*; 67, *a*; 70, *a*, 4, 6, 7, 13, 18, 20; 71, *d*, 2), bracelets (32, *j*, *n*; 64, *a*, *c*, *f*, *l*; 65, *f*; 67, *a–d*; 70, *a*, 1, 2, 7, 8, 10–12, 14–24; 71, *a*, 1; 75, *e*, *f*), collars (64, *b*, *e*, *f*; 66, *d*, 1; 67, *c*, *e*; 68, *b*, 1; 70, *a*, 1–3, 5; 71, *a*, 1, 2), earplugs (30, *y*, *z–bb*; 31, *hh*; 32, *e*, *g*, *h*, *j*, *k*, *m*, *n*; 35, *a*, *b*; 63, *a*, *b*, *d–f*, *h*, *i*; 64, *a–f*, *j*, *k*, *n*, *o*; 65, *a–h*, *p*; 66, *d*, 1–3, 7–9, 11; 67; 68, *b*, 1, 3, 4, 8–10, 12; 69, *h*, *t*; 71, *d*; 75, *e–g*), leg bands (75, *e*), necklaces (32, *j*; 64, *l*; 65, *f*; 66, *d*, 2; 75, *e*), nose ornaments (32, *i*; 65, *f*), pectoral ornaments (67, *a*, *e*), and pendants (64, *a*; 65, *f*; 75, *e*). In addition there are various other devices; namely, beaded bands (32, *f*, *j*, *m*; 68, *b*, 6; 69, *i*; 73, *d*, 1–3), beards (32, *e*; 66, *d*, 7; 68, *b*, 9), bells (67, *a*; 70, *a*, 1, 2, 8, 13, 21, 24), bowknots (67, *c*; 68, *b*, 4, 8; 71, *e*, 1; 73, *c*, 4; 75, *e*), braids or twists (31, *ff*; 32, *g*, *n*; 63, *g*; 64, *d*; 67, *b*, *d*, *e*; 68, *b*, 1; 70, *a*, 18; 72, *g–k*; 73, *b*, *c*, 1–3), cylinders (32, *k*; 67, *c*; 71, *e*, 6), a hand (73, *d*, 4), feathers (32, *e*, *g*, *k*, *m*, *n*; 64, *e*, *g*; 67; 71, *a*, 5; *e*, 8–10; 72, *o–q*; 73, *a*, 1, 2, 5–7), flat zoomorphic adornos (72, *jj–pp*), a paddlelike de- (72, *f*), rattles (72, *w*, *x*), ropes (70, *a*, 27), scrolls of "ram horn" type (73, *a*, 3, 4), scrolls of simple type (32, *k*, *m*, *n*; 67, *a–d*, *f*), scrolls of spiral type (71, *e*, 4), S-shape (71, *e*, 5), serpent eyes (67, *d*; 73, *d*, 5–8), tassels (32, *g*; 67, *b*, *e*; 71, *e*, 7; 75, *e*), T-shape (71, *e*, 2, 3), tusks (30, *x*, *y*, *aa*, *bb*; 31, *hh*; 32, *e*, *j*, *k*, *m*, *n*; 63, *a*, *b*, *e*, *f*, *h–j*; 65, *i*; 67, *c*, *d*, *f*; 68, *b*, 2, 8, 9; 75, *g*), and whiskers (32, *e*, *h*, *m*; 66, *d*, 7; 67, *f*; 68, *b*, 6, 9). There is also accoutrement, including appliqué items of clothing and ornaments other than jewelry as well as objects carried. These comprise Atlatls (70, *a*, 24), bags or pouches (32, *k*, *n*; 67, *c*, *d*; 72, *dd*), balls of masa or copal (32, *g*, *n*; 64, *d*, *e*; 67, *a*, *b*, *n*; 70, *a*, 11, 20, 25; 72, *aa–cc*, *hh*), bibs (32, *g*, *k*, *n*; 64, *c*; 67, *b–d*), capes (64, *d*), cones (32, *k*; 64, *f*; 67, *c*), fans (32, *z*; 64, *c*, *g*; 65, *g*; 73, *c*, 8), flaps for headdresses (32, *g, k, n*; 66, *d,* 1; 67, *a–d*; 68, *b*, 1, 2; 75, *e, f*), flaps for loincloths (32, *g, k, n*; 64, *a, d*; 66, *d,* 1; 67, *a–e*; 75, *e*), flaps for sandals (32, *g, k, n*; 67, *a–e*; 68, *b,* 1; 70, *b,* 1–6, 9), flowers and buds (72, *a–e, l, m, s–v, ee–gg, ii*; 73, *c,* 5–7), fruits and vegetables (70, *a,* 26), headdresses of bonnet, crown, or cap style (32, *g, j, k*; 35, *a,* 1–6, *b,* 5; 64, *b*; 65, *a, b, h*; 66, *d,* 7; 67, *b, c*; 68, *b,* 2, 4, 7, 8, 10, 11; 69, *b, h, m, q*; 71, *a,* 2, 3; 75, *e*), headdresses of animal or bird helmet style (32, *e, f, l–n*; 66, *d,* 1; 67, *a, d, f*; 68, *b,* 5, 6, 9; 69, *a, c, i–k*; 71, *a,* 5), headdresses of turban style (32 *h*; 35, *a,* 7–12; *b,* 1–4; 63, *a*; 64, *a, c, d*; 65, *c, d, f, g, p*; 66, *c,* 1, *d,* 2–4, 8–10; 69, 1), headdresses of rectangular style (71, *a,* 1, 4), shields (64, *b*; 65, *h*; 67, *e*; 70, *a,* 19), spears (64, *b*; 65, *h*), torchlike devices (32, *n*; 72, *n, r, y, z*), and a vessel (32, *n*).

The third group embraces small heads of figures either human or animal, used as ornaments and attached to the figures associated with effigy censers or effigy vessels. The various forms include an alligator (32, *l*), unidentified animals (32, *bb–dd, mm, nn*; 70, *b,* 16, 17; 72, *oo, pp*), bats (69, *c*; 71, *c,* 5), birds (32, *e, f, m, ee–ii*; 66 *d,* 1; 67, *f*; 68, *b,* 6; 69, *a, i*; 71, *c,* 1–4; 72, *ll*), death heads (68, *b,* 7; 69, *m*; 71, *a,* 2, 3, 6–11) a deer (72, *nn*), a dog (72, *mm*), fish (72, *jj, kk*), human heads (32, *aa, ll, oo, pp*; 70, *a,* 4), jaguars (67, *a*; 69, *j, k*; 71, *c,* 7), and serpents (32, *n*; 71, *a,* 4; *b*). This group, like the second, is almost entirely associated with the Hocaba-Tases and Tases ceramic complexes.

Appendages (Table 38). This grouping covers decorated accessories: feet and other supports, such as pedestal and ringstand bases, handles, spouts, and flanges, all of which are applied, usually welded onto vessel base or wall.

The *feet* are of three basic forms: cylindrical, slab, and effigy, either animal or human. Embellishment of these foot forms is accomplished by three principal techniques: stamping (mold-pressed), modeling, and forming in a mold. Incising and painting are sometimes used as supporting techniques. Cylindrical feet with rounded bottoms far outnumber those with flat bottoms. All those considered have a mold-pressed decoration on the front. These stampings represent "fat-cheeked" heads on cylindrical round-bottom feet, full-length or nearly full-length figures with collars and a distinctive hairdo usually associated with cylindrical flat-bottom feet, and full-length obese figures possibly representing the "fat god" which occur on both rounded and flat-based cylindrical feet. These forms are illustrated in 6, *p, gg, hh, kk*; 7, *o, aa,* and also in Brainerd's publi-

cation (1958, figs. 58 and 62). They are used on Puuc Slate Ware, Thin Slate Ware, and occasionally Puuc Red Ware tripod basal-break or basal-Z-angle dishes. This type of foot has been noted only in the Cehpech Ceramic Complex. The terraced solid slab foot, on the other hand, although well represented in Cehpech (*ibid.,* at Mayapan, fig. 15, *q, l*; at Mani, fig. 32, *h,* 24; at Uxmal, fig. 45, *i,* 10; at Sayil, fig. 46, *f,* 37; and at Chichen Itza, figs. 66, *j,* 2; 67), is rare in other complexes, both earlier where only the hollow notched slab (KJS, 1946, figs. 175, *c*; 177, *b*; 197, *a–c* and RES, figs. 52, *a,* 13; 78, *m*) has been noted in the Early Classic Period, and later where a single solid terraced slab occurs in San Joaquin Buff Ware at Mayapan (no illustration); a number of sherds have been noted in the Cunduacan Fine-Orange Group (Berlin's U Fine-Orange, 1956, fig. 6, *i, j*) from Juarez, Tabasco, and Atasta, Campeche, respectively. Moldmade animal and human effigy feet are found at Mayapan, increasing in importance from Hocaba through Tases, associated with Mayapan Red Ware, San Joaquin Buff Ware, and the Fine-Orange Matillas Group. The animal effigy feet form 80.9 per cent and the human 19.1 per cent of those encountered at Mayapan. Elsewhere, however, the effigy foot perhaps occurs first in the Early Mexican Stage as found by Brainerd (1958, fig. 88, *d,* 6, Chichen Red Ware or fig. 91, *c, e,* Plumbate Ware) and Wauchope (1948, fig. 57, various Tohil wares, but may occur in Late Pokom as well). This gives the effigy foot a Late Classic or Tepeu 2 (RES, fig. 58, *c,* 3) through Late Postclassic or Tases (Table 38) range.

The other supports which carry decoration are the *ringstand base* and the *pedestal base.* Rarely is the former found in other than the Cehpech Ceramic Complex; one example from Tepeu 3 at Uaxactun (*ibid.,* fig. 1, *h, i*) which may be contemporaneous, and a single specimen (21, *jj*) of Chichen Red Ware, Xuku Incised Type, cream slip variety from the Sotuta Ceramic Complex. The pedestal form, however, appears to be not only more abundant but more widely spread both in space and time. Besides those listed in Table 38, a number have been noted from Uaxactun (RES) all belonging to the Tzakol 2 Ceramic Complex and all of Peten Gloss Ware: rounded-side bowls with pedestal base; Lucha Incised Type (*ibid.,* fig. 23, *b,* 2, 5); Positas Modeled Type, openwork variety (*ibid.,* fig. 23, *b,* 1); and Pita Incised Type, openwork variety (*ibid.,* fig. 71, *b,* 4).

Decorated *handles* are extremely rare, occurring in these collections only in the Cehpech and Sotuta ceramic complexes usually associated with ladle censers (for a Cehpech specimen see GWB, fig. 39, *h*, 7; for Sotuta-Tohil specimens see 12, *h*; Wauchope, 1948, figs. 66; 67, *h*; 68 and Brainerd, 1958, fig. 97, *h–j*). A very rare example of horizontal strap handles decorated with appliqué spikes found on a typical Cehpech "hourglass" form censer from Acanceh is illustrated by Brainerd (*ibid.*, fig. 19, *c*). An equally rare ladle example found in the Tzakol Ceramic Complex at Uaxactun is illustrated by Smith (1955a, fig. 84, *a*).

Decorated *spouts* are lacking in these collections. On the other hand, decorated *flanges*, which form an integral part of the vessel shape, are present throughout from Cehpech through Tases, although in Sotuta the flange, plain or decorated, is extremely rare except in association with censers. Brainerd (1958, fig. 86, *a, b*) does illustrate a few terraced examples on an unusual vessel form belonging to Chichen Red Ware (Brainerd's Medium Redware), Xuku Incised Type. Otherwise in Cehpech, Hocaba, Hocaba-Tases, and Tases there is a reasonable representation of the decorated flange, both terraced and notched (Table 38). In Early Classic times at Uaxactun flanges were painted (RES, fig. 76, *a*), incised (*ibid.*, fig. 20), and rarely gadrooned (*ibid.*, fig. 20, *n, q*), whereas in Late Classic they were notched or terraced (*ibid.*, figs. 37, *a*; 64, *a*, 3; 84, *h*).

TECHNIQUES INVOLVING COLOR

Painting (Tables 39 and 40). Painting furnishes a distinct contribution to the ceramic art of the five ceramic complexes under consideration: Cehpech, Sotuta, Hocaba, Hocaba-Tases, and Tases. It has two well-established main divisions, positive and negative. The former, predominant in the collections under review, subdivides into prefire and postfire painting. Prefire painting is well represented. Negative painted examples are rare and always of the reserve-space technique. The negative resist technique was not observed. Postfire painting used abundantly especially in the Tases Ceramic Complex, may include design painting on a primary white calcareous coating, the simple addition of blue or red paint, and the application of stucco which is then painted. The first two categories are almost exclusively associated with ceremonial pottery (Tables 36 and 37). The stuccoed-and-painted class is usually coupled with slipped pottery. Only a few examples of the stuccoed-and-painted technique were found (Table 40).

Positive prefire painting (Table 39). Although positive prefire painting was used at Mayapan in all five ceramic complexes under review, it formed a greater percentage of the decorated types in Cehpech, Sotuta, and Hocaba than in Hocaba-Tases or Tases. In fact, considering the relatively small number of sherds identified with the earlier Cochuah-Tzakol and Motul-Tepeu 1, 2 ceramic complexes, the percentages of this technique are both higher and better than average, 52.3 and 6.4, respectively.

At Mayapan, associated with the Cehpech, Sotuta, Hocaba, Hocaba-Tases, and Tases ceramic complexes, 8,666 positive prefire painted sherds were found. The percentage of these to total number of sherds involved was 2.2.

Cochuah. At Mayapan the positive prefire painted examples of this ceramic complex formed 52.3 per cent of all sherds of that complex. This percentage may be divided into 85.7 local and 14.3 Peten-like.

Motul. The total sherds found at Mayapan representative of this ceramic complex was small and the percentage of positive prefire painted specimens was 6.4, considerably less than that of Cochuah. In this instance the entire lot appeared to have its roots in the Peten of Guatemala.

Cehpech. In this complex positive prefire painting was moderately well represented wherever found except at Kabah and Chichen Itza where it registered average or below. Percentages at the sites reviewed were: Uxmal, 11; Kabah, 2.1; Chichen Itza, 1.3; and Mayapan, 10.3. The groups and associated types of this complex in order of abundance comprised: cream Holactun Group, 58 per cent (Holactun Black-on-cream Type); slate Muna Group, 36.9 per cent (Sacalum Black-on-slate Type, Chumayel Red-on-slate Type, and Nohcacab Composite Type); fine-orange Balancan Group, 3.9 per cent (Tenosique Red-on-orange Type, Palizada Black-on-orange Type, Provincia Plano-relief Type, and Caribe Incised Type, red-paint variety), and red Teabo Group, 1.2 per cent (Tekax Black-on-red Type, Tekax Variety and orange variety, and Opichen Gouged-incised Type, black-slip variety). The vessel shapes decorated in this manner included: jars, 52.1 per cent; basins, 41.9 per cent; bowls, 5.2 per cent and dishes, .7 per cent.

Sotuta. Positive prefire painted examples were well represented at Chichen Itza, 18.5 per cent of all sherds, and somewhat less so at Mayapan where they formed 7.1 per cent of all the Sotuta Ceramic Complex sherds. The groups and associated types of this complex included in order of abundance: slate Dzitas Group, 92.3 per cent (Balantan Black-on-slate Type, Balam Canche Red-on-slate Type, Chacmay Incised Type, black-paint variety, and Timak Composite Type); fine-orange Silho Group, 5.3 per cent (Yalton Black-on-orange Type, Yalton Variety and cream-slip variety, Pomuch Polychrome Type, and Cumpich Incised Type, black-paint variety); red Dzibiac Group, 2.1 per cent (Chan Kom Black-on-red Type, Chan Kom Variety and cream-slip variety and Xuku Incised Type, black-paint variety), and miscellaneous groups, .3 per cent (Cerro Montoso Polychrome Type and Cenotillo Gray-polychrome Type). The vessel shapes embellished with this technique comprised: jars, 51.8 per cent; basins or large restricted-orifice bowls, 34.3 per cent; dishes, 8.9 per cent; vases, pyriform or cylindrical, 3.2 per cent; bowls, 1.5 per cent, and ladle censers, .3 per cent.

Hocaba. Positive prefire painted examples formed 9.2 per cent of all sherds assigned to this ceramic complex. The groups and associated types involved were: cream Kukula Group, 99.5 per cent (Xcanchakan Black-on-cream Type and Mataya Modeled Type) and fine-orange Matillas Group, .5 per cent (Nacajuca Black-on-orange Type and Salto Composite Type). The vessel shapes that accompanied these painted types comprised: jars, 91.2 per cent; tripod dishes, 5.8 per cent, and restricted-orifice bowls, 3 per cent.

Hocaba-Tases. In this ceramic complex positive prefire painting is less important than in the preceding complexes at Mayapan. It formed 2.7 per cent of all sherds attributed to the Hocaba-Tases Ceramic Complex. The groups and associated types involved included in order of abundance: cream Kukula Group, 73.7 per cent (Xcanchakan Black-on-cream Type, Xcanchakan Variety and incised variety); buff Polbox Group, 24.5 per cent (Tecoh Red-on-buff Type and Pele Polychrome Type); fine-orange Matillas Group, 1.7 per cent (Salto Composite Type, Nacajuca Black-on-orange Type, Sayula Polychrome Type, and Grijalva Incised-polychrome Type), and red Mama Group, .1 per cent (Mama Red Type, black-on-unslipped variety and red-on-unslipped variety). The vessel shapes associated with these painted types included: jars, 80.5 per cent; tripod dishes, 13.3 per cent; hemispherical or deep bowls, 3.9 per cent; restricted-orifice bowls, 2.2 per cent, and tripod grater bowls, .1 per cent.

Tases. In this ceramic complex positive prefire painting reached its lowest percentage, 1.2. The groups and associated types involved included in order of abundance: buff Polbox Group, 63.8 per cent (Tecoh Red-on-buff Type and Pele Polychrome Type); cream Kukula Group, 33.9 per cent

(Xcanchakan Black-on-cream Type); fine-orange Matillas Group, 2.2 per cent (Salto Composite Type, Grijalva Incised polychrome Type, and Nacajuca Black-on-orange Type), and red Mama Group, .1 per cent (Mama Red Type, black-on-unslipped variety). The vessel shapes associated with these painted types included: jars, 71.7 per cent; tripod dishes or bowls, 23.7 per cent; hemispherical or deep bowls, 2.1 per cent; restricted-orifice bowls, 1.8 per cent; basins, .5 per cent; potstands, .1 per cent; vases, .1 per cent, and grater bowls, less than .1 per cent.

Positive postfire painting (Table 40). Postfire painting techniques, although present in the Cehpech and Sotuta ceramic complexes, enjoyed far greater popularity in the Hocaba through Tases. As mentioned before, they comprised three techniques: the simple addition of blue or red paint to the unslipped surface; the painting of designs on a primary white calcareous coating; and the application of a stucco coating to be embellished with painted decoration. This last was usually done on a slipped surface.

The *addition of paint*, usually directly to the unslipped surface, rarely to a primary calcareous coating, is the application of a single color to cover the entire vessel or to cover special areas of the vessel. The color most used was blue or blue green. Red may be employed in the same manner. The special areas covered were the rim, the exterior, or a cluster of spikes and the space in which they were set. The *painting of designs* on a white calcareous coating was in a variety of colors and shades such as red, orange, blue, green, yellow, brown, and black, and the designs were numerous and varied. The *stuccoed-and-painted* technique, the number two process in the Kidder, Jennings, and Shook description (1946, pp. 218–219), was simply the painting of designs upon a stucco background using many different colors.

Positive postfire painting played a very strong role in Yucatan ceramic decorative art, especially in the later Postclassic ceramic complexes. At Mayapan in the Hocaba, Hocaba-Tases, and Tases ceramic complexes it formed 37.3 per cent of the total number of sherds involved. Perhaps the best way to examine this artistic development is by ceramic complex.

Cehpech. During this ceramic complex, positive postfire painting was extremely rare. At Mayapan only a single sherd was found with this technique, and at Uxmal the occurrence was a mere .2 per cent of the sherds in that collection. At Uxmal the groups, associated types, special techniques, and vessel shapes of this complex in order of abundance included: unslipped Chum Group (Chum Unslipped Type and Yiba Modeled Type), addition of paint technique, 89.7 per cent, associated with ladle censers (44.2 per cent), flaring-sided bowls (21.2 per cent), restricted-orifice and deep bowls (17.3 per cent), and flutes (17.3 per cent); unslipped Chum Group (Yiba Modeled Type), painting of designs on a white calcareous coating technique, 1.7 per cent, represented by one flute fragment; and thin-slate Ticul Group (Ticul Thin-slate Type), stuccoed-and-painted technique, 8.6 per cent, associated with round-sided bowls (40 per cent), a restricted-orifice bowl (20 per cent), a deep bowl (20 per cent), and a tripod, recurving-sided dish (20 per cent).

Sotuta. At Mayapan no sherds with this decorative technique representing this ceramic complex were encountered. At Chichen Itza a fair number of examples were found, totaling 1.9 per cent of this collection. The groups, associated types, special techniques, and vessel shapes of this complex in order of abundance at Chichen Itza comprised: unslipped Sisal Group (Cumtun Composite Type), painting of designs on a white calcareous coating technique, 69.5 per cent, entirely represented by hourglass censers; unslipped Sisal Group (Tibolon Blue-on-red Type and Cumtun Composite Type), addition of paint technique, 27.1 per cent, associated with flaring-sided censers (71.6 per cent) and tripod flaring-sided censers (28.4 per cent); slipped Tinum Group (Tinum Red-on-cinnamon Type), addition of paint technique, 3.4 per cent, entirely represented by ladle-handle censers.

Hocaba. In this ceramic complex at Mayapan only one positive postfire painting technique was recognized, the painting of designs on a white calcareous coating. The sherds with this decorative technique totaled 3.3 per cent of all Hocaba sherds. The groups, associated types, and vessel shapes in order of abundance included: unslipped Navula Group (Hoal Modeled Type, Cehac-Hunacti Composite Type and Cehac Painted Type) associated with effigy censers (69.1 per cent), tripod jar censers (16.9 per cent), pedestal vase or jar censers (13.4 per cent), figurines (.3 per cent), and a tripod cup (.1 per cent).

Hocaba-Tases. In this collecting level at Mayapan positive postfire painting became increasingly popular, totaling 17.4 per cent of all sherds. The groups, associated types, special techniques, and vessel shapes in order of abundance included: unslipped Panaba Group (Chen Mul Modeled Type, Acansip Painted Type, Acansip-Thul Composite Type, and Chenkeken-Acansip Composite Type),

unslipped Navula Group (Cehac-Hunacti Composite Type and Hoal Modeled Type), and unslipped Uayma Group (Uayma Modeled Type) with painting of designs on a white calcareous coating technique, 99.8 per cent, associated with large, medium, and small effigy censers (75.6 per cent), tripod or pedestal-base censer jars (11.6 per cent), tripod censer jars (5.8 per cent), pedestal-base censer jars (5 per cent), figurines (1.2 per cent), effigy vessels (.3 per cent), pedestal-base cups (.2 per cent), pedestal-base vases (.1 per cent), tripod deep bowls (.06 per cent), and miscellaneous (.06 per cent); and unslipped Panaba Group (Cehac Painted Type and Chen Mul Modeled Type), addition of paint technique, .2 per cent, represented by tripod cups (95 per cent) and flat-base cup (5 per cent).

Tases. At Mayapan, in this ceramic complex, positive postfire painting reached its greatest popularity. The sherds encountered having this decorative technique totaled 47.1 per cent of all sherds from this complex. The groups, associated types, special techniques, and vessel shapes in order of abundance, comprised: unslipped Panaba Group (Chen Mul Modeled Type, Acansip Painted Type, Chenkeken-Acansip Composite Type, and Acansip-Thul Composite Type), unslipped Navula Group (Cehac-Hunacti Composite Type and Hoal Modeled Type), and unslipped Uayma Group (Uayma Modeled Type), with painting of designs on a white calcareous coating technique, 99.9 per cent, associated with large, medium, and small effigy censers (97.6 per cent), tripod censer jars (1.1 per cent), pedestal-base censer jars (.4 per cent), effigy vessels (.3 per cent), tripod or pedestal-base censer jars (.3 per cent), figurines (.1 per cent), pedestal-base vases (.04 per cent), tripod deep bowls (.02 per cent), pedestal-base cups (.02 per cent), tripod cups (.01 per cent), tripod flaring-side bowls (.01 per cent), and miscellaneous (.01 per cent); and unslipped Panaba Group (Cehac Painted Type, Chenkeken-Acansip Composite Type, and Chen Mul Modeled Type), with addition of paint technique, .03 per cent, represented by tripod cups (80 per cent) and tripod flaring-side bowls (20 per cent).

Negative painting (Table 39). This technique was rarely found in Yucatan and then only in the reserve-space style. This process, which is accomplished before firing, may be done either freehand or by using protective forms made of any solid material. For a more complete description consult Smith (1955a, p. 61). Other than at Mayapan a single example was noted at Uxmal on a hemispherical bowl of Puuc Red Ware, Tekax

Black-on-red Type (8, *i*) and at Chichen Itza eight sherds belonging to a pedestal-base vase of the Tunkas Red-on-gray Type (23, *g*). In the middle levels of Hocaba-Tases at Mayapan one jar sherd was found of San Joaquin Buff Ware, Tecoh Red-on-buff Type (53, *a*, 11). A few more examples occurred in the Tases Ceramic Complex at Mayapan. These totaled eight and were all in San Joaquin Buff Ware, Tecoh Red-on-buff Type associated with a jar (53, *a*, 10), a tripod flaring-side dish (53, *b*, 5), and 6 potstand fragments (53, *b*, 14).

Slipping. Possibly this heading is unnecessary because of the simplicity and frequency of the technique. A slip is a refined clay added to the surface to form a relatively thin, closely adhering, body concealing covering. Slips vary in color, quality, and thickness. Once applied they may be treated in many different ways, such as: left unburnished or matte, burnished or polished, and frequently decorated in the various ways covered in this report. Descriptions of the slipped wares and groups are to be found in the section on wares and are also listed in Charts 2 and 3.

It is of interest to note that at Mayapan slipped wares formed 32.2 per cent, unidentified wares 10.6 per cent, and unslipped wares 52.2 per cent of all sherds counted. However, this distribution of unslipped and slipped wares did not hold true when considering the material by ceramic complex. Slipped wares formed the following percentages: Cehpech, 59.1; Sotuta, 85.1; Hocaba, 64.9; Hocaba-Tases, 50.6; Tases, 24.7; Chauaca, 79.5, thus showing that slipped wares held a more prominent role in Sotuta and Chauaca than they did in the other sites especially Tases. The poor showing of slipped wares in the Tases Ceramic Complex was due largely to the tremendous increase in the manufacture of effigy censers and other ceremonial vessels.

It should be noted that the quantity of undecorated slipped sherds from Mayapan and elsewhere in the collections under consideration is swelled by sherd fragments from decorated types within the same group which lack decoration. This gives a disproportionately large total to the plain slipped sherds by comparison with other type or variety units. It is obvious, therefore, that total group counts can be quite important (Willey, Bullard, Glass, and Gifford, 1965, pp. 320–321). At Mayapan the plain slipped type percentage of all slipped sherds totaled 85.3 (89.3 in Cehpech, 83.7 in Sotuta, 79.7 in Hocaba, 81.8 in Hocaba-Tases, and 88.1 in Tases). At Uxmal and Kabah the plain slipped type percentage for all Cehpech slipped sherds was 84.4, and at Chichen Itza for all Sotuta slipped sherds was only 63. The principal reason for the lower percentage of the Sotuta undecorated slipped sherds is that Sotuta decoration covered a larger portion of the vessel.

VI

Types Of Design

The designs associated with the Uxmal, Kabah, Chichen Itza, and Mayapan collections may be treated under four titles: abstract, naturalistic, conventionalized (i.e., simplified, part of the whole, etc.), and hieroglyphic. Elements, excluding glyphs, are the simplest units; they may be used separately or as part of more complex decorations. Compositions are simple or complex combinations of elements forming a unit. Patterns are repetitions of elements or compositions.

In the present chapter comparative date other than the material being studied is rarely introduced. Such an effort will be more valid in the very near future, when a number of most important Maya ceramic studies will be available. Examples of all types of design are illustrated.

The following enumeration of designs, in alphabetical order, listed under the four types, includes: the name of the device; description and remarks if necessary; ceramic complex, type and variety names, vessel form, illustration reference; and the relative quantity. The last includes five categories: present, meaning a single example; rare, 2–4; moderate 5–9; well represented, 10–15; and abundant, 16 plus. "Figure" or "fig." is omitted before illustrations from this volume.

ABSTRACT DESIGN

a b c d

Bowknot. A central disk and wedge-shaped wings giving the effect of a bowknot or bow tie. Occurrence: *Tepeu 1*, Saxche Orange-polychrome Type pedestal-base jar (cf. GWB, fig. 3, *b*); *Sotuta*, Dzibiac Red Type, scratched variety jar (20, *j*); Holtun Gouged-incised Type jar (20, *l*); *Tases*, Chen Mul Modeled Type effigy censer earplug painted design (32, *j*), headdress adornment (32, *k*), and appliqué adornment (73, *c*, 4). Quantity: moderate.

a b c d

Braid, guilloche, or twist. This is an ornamental braid or twist formed by two or more intertwining strands or intersecting lines. Usually it is a horizontal band, sometimes vertical. Most are curvilinear but some are rectilinear. Occurrence: *Tzakol*, Delirio Plano-relief Type cylindrical tripod (25, *p*); *Cehpech*, Xaya Gouged-incised Type cylindrical vase (6, *nn*) and jar (58, *g*); Nohcacab Composite Type tripod dish (26, *b*, 20); Tabi Gouged-incised Type cylindrical vase (7, *m*; 58, *f*) bowl (7, *p*; 10, *k*), and basin (7, *t*); Yaxumha Composite Type tripod dish (8, *s*); *Sotuta*, Tekom Gouged-incised Type tripod jar (14, *q*); Holtun Gouged-incised Type tripod pyriform vase or jar (20, *u*) and tripod dish (21, *aa*; 59, *n*); Cumtun Composite Type hourglass censer (12, *e*); Yalton Black-on-orange Type pedestal-base pyriform (Smith, 1957b, fig. 8, *n*); Kilikan Composite Type tripod pyriform (*ibid.*, figs. 11, *m*, *n*; 15, *f*, *h*) and tripod hemispherical bowl (*ibid.*, fig. 16, *d*); *Hocaba-Tases*, Chenkeken Incised Type, openwork variety jar censer (31, *j*); Papacal Incised Type jar or deep bowl (47, *m*); Pustunich Incised Type restricted-orifice bowl (47, *n*); Yobain Plano-relief Type rounded-side bowl (47, *o*); Dzitxil Openwork Type candlestick cluster (37, *a*); Uayma Modeled Type figurines (35, *a*, 18); Chen Mul Modeled Type effigy vessel (64, *d*); Tecoh Red-on-buff Type wide-mouth jar (53, *a*, 11). *Tases*, Chen Mul Modeled Type cup (31, *ff*; 63, *a*, *g*), effigy censer (32, *g*, *n*; 67, *b*, *d*, *e*; 68, *b*, 1; 72, *g–i*, *y*; 73, *b*; *c*, 1–3); Thul Appliqué Type tripod deep bowl (31, *u*); Cehac-Hunacti Appliqué Type pedestal-base cylindrical vase (30, *d*; 62, *d*); Pustunich Incised Type restricted-orifice bowl (cf. 47, *n*); Chilapa Gouged-incised Type deep bowl with ringstand base (55, *c*, 7), tripod dish (55, *c*, 2; 75, *q*); Salto Composite Type restricted-orifice bowl (55, *c*, 10); Tecoh Red-on-buff Type potstand (53, *b*, 14). Quantity: abundant.

a

b

Checkerboard pattern. May be painted or incised. Occurrence: *Cochuah*, Valladolid Incised-dichrome Type jar (GWB, fig. 6, *g*, 3); *Sotuta*, Dzibiac Red Type, scratched variety tripod (?) dish (21, *ii*). Quantity: rare.

a

b

c

Chevron. V-shaped elements, often used in bands placed horizontally or vertically. Chevrons may belong to a design group based on oblique lines which at times develop into the zigzag (see chevron-and-circle). Occurrence: *Cehpech*, Tekit Incised Type drum (14, *o*) and basal-flange dish (6, *r*, ladder-sided chevron); Red-on-cream Type, incised variety cylindrical vase, not identified as to ware (23, *h*); *Hocaba-Tases*, Papacal Incised Type jar (47, *g*); Palmul Incised Type wide-mouth low-neck jar (48, *f*); Tecoh Red-on-buff Type tripod dish (53, *b*, 2) and ringstand restricted-orifice bowl (53, *b*, 10); *Tases*, Cozil Incised Type reflector (36, *c*); Papacal Incised Type jar (38, *b*, 8); Mama Red Type, incised variety flange (40, *c*, 8); Chilapa Gouged-incised Type tripod dish (75, *q*); Chen Mul Modeled Type effigy censer (32, *h*, painted decoration); Pele Polychrome Type tripod dish (54, *c*). Quantity: well represented.

Chevron-and-circle. V-shape elements usually concentric plus centrally located circles used in bands and placed vertically. This is essentially a zigzag motif. Occurrence: *Hocaba*, Villahermosa Incised Type tripod dish with or without flange (cf. 55, *b*, 4); *Hocaba-Tases*, Villahermosa Incised Type tripod dish with or without flange (cf. 55, *b*, 4); *Tases*, Villahermosa Incised Type tripod basal-flange dish (55, *b*, 4); Salto Composite Type tripod dish (55, *b*, 3); Grijalva Incised-polychrome Type tripod basal-flange dish (55, *b*, 1). Quantity: moderate.

a

b

Circle. Simple or concentric, it may be incised, impressed, carved, or painted. Occurrence: *Tzakol*, Pita Incised Type hemispherical bowl (25, *q*; 60, *f*); *Cochuah*, Timucuy Orange-polychrome Type jar (10, *m*; 25, *o*); Tituc Orange-polychrome Type basal-flange bowl (cf. GWB, fig. 30, *a*, 29, 30, 32). *Cehpech*, Halacho Impressed Type hourglass censer (3, *e*) and basin censer (3, *s*); Akil Impressed Type tripod basal-flange dish (6, *t*; 26, *b*, 21, 22) and jar (cf. GWB, fig. 21, *a*, 21); Nohcacab Composite Type tripod basal-flange dish (6, *v*) and tripod dish (26, *b*, 20); Yaxumha Composite Type tripod dish (8, *s*); Tenosique Red-on-orange Type round-sided bowl (9, *c*); Pabellon Modeled-carved Type hemispherical bowl (9, *j*); *Sotuta*, Cumtun Composite Type censer with pedestal base (12, *e*); Xuku Incised Type, scratched variety jar (20, *j*); Xuku Incised Type, cream-slip variety tripod dish (21, *gg*); Chan Kom Black-on-red Type jar (20, *h*); Yalton Black-on-orange Type restricted bowl (22, *l*) and pyriform tripod vase (cf. Smith, 1957b, fig. 6, *j*); Kilikan Composite Type pyriform tripod vase (*ibid.*, fig. 11, *l*); Cerro Montoso Polychrome Type pyriform pedestal-base vase (23, *e*; *ibid.*, fig. 14, *g*, *j*). *Hocaba*, Xcanchakan Black-on-cream Type restricted-orifice bowl (cf. 52, *l*). *Hocaba-Tases*, Cehac-Hunacti Composite Type pedestal-base jar censer (31, *a*, *c*; 62, *c*); Palmul Incised Type jar (48, *g*); Chilapa Gouged-incised Type hemispherical bowl (55, *c*, 14); Xcanchakan Black-on-cream Type restricted-orifice bowl (52, *l*). *Tases*, Cehac-Hunacti Composite Type pedestal-base jar censer (31, a); Thul Appliqué Type tripod deep bowl (31, u, aa); Chen Mul Modeled Type effigy censer (32, m, n; 70, a, 6); Papacal Incised Type jar (47, h, i); Villahermosa Incised Type deep ringstand bowl (55, b, 9, 10); Chilapa Gouged-incised Type restricted-orifice ringstand bowl (55, c, 12, 19) and deep ringstand bowl (55, c, 18); Salto Composite Type restricted-orifice bowl (55, c, 10) and restricted-orifice ringstand bowl (55, c, 16); Tecoh Red-on-buff Type bulging-neck jar (53, a, 22), wide-mouth jar (53, a, 13), tripod jar (53, a, 17) and tripod dish (53, b, 1, 6); Pele Polychrome Type tripod dish (54, a). Quantity: abundant.

a   b   c

Circle-and-bar. These may be incised (b), gouged-incised (a), or painted (c). Occurrence: Sotuta, Holtun Gouged-incised Type, cream-slip variety jar (20, k); from the Marquez collection (Smith, 1957b) there is a Yalton Black-on-orange Type pedestal-base pyriform vase (ibid., fig. 8, p), a Cerro Montoso Polychrome Type pedestal-base pyriform vase (ibid., fig. 14, j), and a Pocboc Gouged-incised Type low-neck tripod jar (ibid., fig. 16, f); Hocaba-Tases, Papacal Incised Type pedestal base and flange (43, p); Chen Mul Modeled Type figurine (65, f) and design on armband of effigy censer fragment (70, a, 4; Thompson, 1957, fig. 2, a); Tases, Pele Polychrome Type tripod dish (54, a). Quantity: moderate.

a   b

Circle-and-dot. Simple or concentric, it may be incised, gouged-incised, carved, modeled, or painted. Occurrence: Cochuah, Timucuy Orange-polychrome Type jar (10, m); Tituc Orange-polychrome Type basal-flange bowl (cf. GWB, figs. 30, a, 18, 29, 32); Cehpech, Tekit Incised Type tripod dish (6, k) and deep bowl (6, ff); Becal Incised Type cylindrical vase (8, v); Pabellon Modeled-carved Type hemispherical bowl (9, j); Sotuta, Holtun Gouged-incised Type, cream-slip variety tripod dish (21, ff); Cerro Montoso Polychrome Type lamp-chimney vase (23, e); Hocaba-Tases, Chilapa Gouged-incised Type hemispherical bowl (55, c, 14); Tases, Chen Mul Modeled Type effigy censer (32, k, n; 68, b, 6, painted decoration) and effigy

vessel (64, p, painted decoration); Pele Polychrome Type tripod dish (54, a). Quantity: well represented.

Circle-and-squiggle. Like a corkscrew. Occurrence: Tases, Tecoh Red-on-buff Type jar (53, a, 13). Quantity: present.

Circle chain. A chain differs from a band in the linking together of the device in question. Occurrence: Tases, Tecoh Red-on-buff Type tripod dishes (53, b, 1, 6). Quantity: rare.

a   b

Crescent, arc, or semicircle. These may be simple or concentric on occasion. Occurrence: Tzakol, Delirio Plano-relief Type basal-flange bowl (25, p); Cochuah, Tituc Orange-polychrome Type basal-flange bowl (cf. GWB, fig. 9, a, 11; f, 10). Motul, Tekanto Incised Type, red-decoration variety bowl angling to base (25, x). Cehpech. Tekit Incised Type bowl (6, ff); Nohcacab Composite Type tripod dish (6, s); Opichen Gouged-incised Type, black-painted variety tripod dish (8, t); Sotuta, Xuku Incised Type, sharp-incised variety deep bowl (21, v); Xuku Incised Type, cream-slip variety tripod dish (21, gg); Holtun Gouged-incised Type, cream-slip variety tripod dish (21, ff); Chan Kom Black-on-red Type jar (20, h); Kilikan Composite Type, cream-slip variety tripod dish (cf. 59, h); Yalton Black-on-orange Type jar (22, b); Hocaba, Xcanchakan Black-on-cream Type jar (52, f); Tases, Pustunich Incised Type jar (49, a); Tecoh Red-on-buff Type tripod jar (53, a, 22) and tripod dish (53, b, 6); Chilapa Gouged-incised Type deep bowl (55, c, 18); Salto Composite Type basal-flange dish (55, c, 1) and restricted-orifice deep bowl (55, c, 13); Chen Mul Modeled Type effigy censer (32, n, painted). Quantity: abundant.

a   b   c

Crescent-and-dot. Used individually and as a band. Occurrence: *Cehpech*, Nohcacab Composite Type tripod dish (6, *u*); Sahcaba Modeled-carved Type hemispherical bowl (8, *m*); *Sotuta*, Balantun Black-on-slate Type tripod dish (19, *f*); Yalton Black-on-orange Type restricted-orifice bowl (22, *l*); *Hocaba-Tases*, Chen Mul Modeled Type turtle effigy vessel (64, *n*); *Tases*, Salto Composite Type deep bowl (55, *c*, 6). Quantity: moderate.

Crescent-and-semidisk. Occurrence: *Sotuta*, Kilikan Composite Type, cream-slip variety tripod dish (22, *r*); Yalton Black-on-orange Type tripod dish (22, *u*). Quantity: rare.

a   b   c   d

Cross. Both the Greek Cross (a, b) and the St. Andrew's Cross (*c*, *d*) are used. *Tzakol*, Pita Incised Type, sharp-incised variety hemispherical bowls (25, *q–s*); *Sotuta*, Holtun Gouged-incised Type, cream-slip variety pyriform vase (20, *f*); Xuku Incised Type, cream-slip variety tripod dish (21, *cc*); Dzibiac Red Type, scratched variety dish (21, *kk*); Balantun Black-on-slate Type, scratched variety rounded-side dish (13, *f*); Cerro Montoso Polychrome Type lamp-chimney vase (cf. Smith, 1957b, figs. 2, *x*; 14, *k*); *Hocaba-Tases*, Chen Mul Modeled Type pedestal-base cup (63, *b*, painted decoration); *Tases*, Nacajuca Black-on-orange Type tripod dish (55, *d*, 2). Quantity: moderate.

Crosshatch. This is a device resembling the "make a space" sign in correcting proofs. Occurrence: *Sotuta*, Xuku Incised Type, cream-slip variety rounded-side dish (59, *p*); Holtun Gouged-incised Type, cream-slip variety pyriform vase (20, *f*).

Quantity: present. Remarks: only one (20, *f*) was found in collections which were under consideration. The others, including 59, *p*, are from Chichen Itza and illustrated by Brainerd (1958, fig. 87, *aa*, *cc*).

a   b

Crosshatching. This device may be attained by horizontal and vertical lines or diagonal lines. Occurrence: *Motul*, Bokoba Incised Type side-angle bowls (25, *y–aa*). *Cehpech*, Tekit Incised Type basin (4, *c*) and tripod dish (6, *e*); Xul Incised Type tripod dish (7, *y*); Becal Incised Type tripod basal-flange dish (8, *p*); *Sotuta*, Timak Composite Type tripod grater bowls (13, *m*, *n*); Xuku Incised Type tripod grater bowl (21, *j*); Xuku Incised Type, black-paint variety tripod grater bowl (21, *k*); Dzibiac Red Type, scratched variety dish (21, *ii*); *Hocaba*, Chenkeken Incised Type flat-base dish (29, *kk*); Xcanchakan Black-on-cream Type, incised variety tripod grater bowl (52, *s*); *Hocaba-Tases*, Chen Mul Modeled Type effigy vessel (64, *c*, painted) and figurine (65, *f*, painted); Chilapa Gouged-incised Type restricted-orifice deep bowl (55, *c*, 11); Salto Composite Type deep bowl (55, *b*, 5) and restricted-orifice deep bowl (55, *c*, 15); *Tases*, Chen Mul Modeled Type figurine (35, *a*, 3, painted); Papacal Incised Type drums (39, *e*, *n*); Villahermosa Incised Type deep bowls (55, *b*, 8, 10); Salto Composite Type restricted-orifice deep bowl (55, *c*, 10); Tecoh Red-on-buff tripod jar (53, *a*, 22). Quantity: abundant.

a   b   c   d

Cursive M. The M-like device may be shorter or longer than an actual M or N. The most common decorative techniques employed are incising and painting. The latter is a late manifestation. Occurrence: *Cehpech*, Provincia Plano-relief Type flaring-side bowls rounding to flat base (9, *d*, *e*, *g*; cf. GWB, figs. 59, *b*; *c*, 10, 13, 16, 17; *d*, 3, 8, 9, 13, 15, 21, 22; 89, *e*, 7); *Hocaba-Tases*, Papacal Incised Type tripod basal-flange deep bowl (43, *i*), which undoubtedly represents something entirely different from the earlier examples.

Quantity: moderate. Remarks: the Cehpech examples seem to be cursive replicas of scroll appendages (GWB, fig. 59, a).

a   *b*

Dab. This device is commonly found on the rim of a vessel forming a band of rim dabs (a). It is spaced at intervals and probably made with a finger. Less frequently it appears on other parts of the vessel, especially the floor (b), but on these occasions the resemblance is more to a blotch than a finger dab. Occurrence: *Cehpech*, Sacalum Black-on-slate Type tripod dish (6, z), and ringstand beveled-rim bowl (26, b, 23); Chumayel Red-on-slate Type flaring-side bowl (6, y) and tripod flaring-side dish (26, b, 19); Holactun Black-on-cream Type basin with ovoid rim bolster (10, c) and jars (10, g, h); *Sotuta*, Balantun Black-on-slate Type rounded-side dishes (13, c–f) and a jar (27, a); *Hocaba*, Xcanchakan Black-on-cream Type jar (52, c), tripod grater bowl (52, s), and tripod rounded-side bowls (52, p, q); *Hocaba-Tases*, Xcanchakan Black-on-cream Type jars (52, a, b, d), rounded-side bowl (52, r), and tripod recurving-side bowls (52, t, u). Quantity: abundant. Remarks: this device is well illustrated by Brainerd (1958) for Cehpech with Sacalum Black-on-slate Type ringstand-base rounded-side bowl (fig. 32, e, 10), tripod basal-break dishes (figs. 32, h, 5, 6; 35, j, k; 47, a, b, f–i; 62, g, l; 67, a), and ringstand-base beveled-rim bowl (fig. 49, b); for Sotuta with Timak Composite Type tripod dish (fig. 72, a) and Balantun Black-on-slate Type rounded-side dishes (fig. 74, c, d).

a   *b*

Dash line and pendent dashes. May be painted, incised, or punctated. Occurrence: *Tzakol*, Pita Incised Type rounded-side bowl (25, r, s; 60, f); *Motul*, Tekanto Incised Type, red-decoration variety side-angle bowl (25, x); *Tepeu 2*, Geronimo Incised Type side-angle bowl (25, u; 60, e); *Cehpech*, Tekit Incised Type tripod dish (6, k); Tabi Gouged-incised Type tripod dish (cf. GWB, fig. 50, i, 1); Opichen Gouged-incised Type hemispherical ringstand bowl (8, o); Provincia Plano-relief Type tripod plate (9, k); Pabellon Modeled-carved Type

hemispherical bowl (9, j); *Sotuta*, Tinum Red-on-cinnamon Type, openwork variety ladle-handled censer (11, w); Chankom Black-on-red Type, cream-slip variety jar (20, i); Xuku Incised Type bowl (21, v); Xuku Incised Type, cream-slip variety tripod dish (21, gg); Holtun Gouged-incised Type, cream-slip variety dish (21, s); Kilikan Composite Type, cream-slip variety tripod dish (22, r); Tumbador Incised Type jar (60, j); *Hocaba*, Papacal Incised Type basal-flange deep bowl (cf. 43, i); *Hocaba-Tases*, Papacal Incised Type jars (47, a, d) and tripod basal-flange deep bowls (43, i, n, o); Pustunich Incised Type bowl (47, r); Palmul Incised Type jars (48, c); Salto Composite Type ringstand-base deep bowl (55, b, 5); Tecoh Red-on-buff Type pedestal-base rounded-side bowl (53, b, 10); *Tases*, Cozil Incised Type reflector (36, c); Villahermosa Incised Type deep bowl (55, b, 8); Chilapa Gouged-incised Type tripod dishes (55, c, 3, 4), deep bowl (55, c, 18), and ringstand restricted-orifice bowl (55, c, 19); Salto Composite Type ringstand deep bowl (55, c, 5) and restricted-orifice deep bowls (55, c, 10, 13). Quantity: abundant.

a   *b*

Diamond. Occurrence: *Cehpech*, Becal Incised Type, groove-incised variety tripod hemispherical bowl (8, c); *Tases*, Chen Mul Modeled Type effigy censer adorno (73, c, 3). Quantity: rare.

a   *b*   *c*

Diamond-and-triangle pattern. This is formed by fairly well-spaced crosshatching with the resulting diamonds and triangles usually embellished by centrally placed circle or dot. Occurrence: *Cehpech*, Xul Incised Type hemispherical bowl (7, k); *Hocaba-Tases*, Villahermosa Incised Type deep bowl (55, b, 7); Tases, Papacal Incised Type jar (47, c). Quantity: rare.

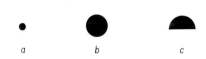

a   *b*   *c*

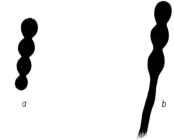

a   *b*

Dot, disk, part-disk. Variations of the same element, the disk being an enlarged dot and the part-disk a portion of a disk. Dots may be used as filler, outline, in clusters, or as part of a design, rarely forming a design or element unassisted. A dot may be painted or punctated. Disks and part-disks usually are painted or modeled; sometimes they are pendent. Occurrence: *Tihosuco*, Yaxkukul Composite Type dish (10, *n*; GWB, fig. 60, *a*, 23); *Cochuah*, Valladolid Incised-dichrome Type jars (cf. *ibid.*, figs. 6, *a*, *16, 18, 20*; 64, *g*) and bowls (cf. *ibid.*, figs. 6, *d*, 2; 63, *a*, 1); Timucuy Orange-polychrome Type basal-Z-angle bowl (cf. *ibid.*, fig. 63, *a*, 5) and jar (10, *m*); Tituc Orange-polychrome Type basal-flange bowl (cf. *ibid.*, fig. 30, *a*, 30); *Tzakol*, Dos Arroyos Orange-polychrome Type basal-flange bowls (cf. RES, fig. 26, *b*, 6, 8); *Tepeu 1*, Bejucal Brown-on-buff Type rounded-side bowl (10, *p*); *Cehpech*, Tekit Incised Type rounded-side bowl (6, *ff*); Nohcacab Composite Type tripod dishes (cf. GWB, fig. 57, *a*; *c*, 1–9, punctation); Tabi Gouged-incised Type cylindrical vase (cf. GWB, fig. 48, *f*, punctation); Tikihal Disk-shading Type hemispherical bowl (7, *f*, *g*); Chumayel Red-on-slate Type flat-base bowl (6, *y*); Sacalum Black-on-slate Type tripod dishes (26, *b*, 17; cf. GWB, fig. 47, *b*, *i*); Tekax Black-on-red Type hemispherical bowl (8, *h*) and reserve-space variety hemispherical bowl (8, *i*); Sahcaba Modeled-carved Type hemispherical bowl (8, *m*); Pabellon Modeled-carved Type hemispherical bowls (9, *h*, *i*); *Sotuta*, Balantun Black-on-slate Type jars (14, *f*) and tripod dish (19, *f*); Balam Canche Red-on-slate Type jar (17, *a*), restricted-orifice bowl (17, *f*), and ladle censers (17, *g*, *h*); Chan Kom Black-on-red Type jar (20, *h*); Yalton Black-on-orange Type tripod dish (22, *u*); *Hocaba-Tases*, Villahermosa Incised Type restricted-orifice deep bowl (55, *b*, 7); Xcanchakan Black-on-cream Type jars (52, *a*, *b*; 75, *l*, *m*); Pele Polychrome Type tripod dish (54, *b*) and tripod bowl (54, *e*); *Tases*, Chen Mul Modeled Type effigy censer headdress (71, *a*, 5, painted) and face (69, *n*, painted); Salto Composite Type ringstand deep bowl (55, *c*, 6); Tecoh Red-on-buff Type jars (53, *a*, 10, 13) and tripod dish (53, *b*, 6); Pele Polychrome Type tripod dish (54, *c*). Quantity: abundant.

Dot chain. Dots or disks linked together, at times trailing off into a plain tricklelike line. Occurrence: *Cehpech*, Sacalum Black-on-slate Type jar (cf. GWB, figs. 40, *g*; 42, *c*); Holactun Black-on-cream Type basin (10, *b*); *Sotuta*, Balantun Black-on-slate Type jars (14, *f*; cf. GWB, fig. 71, *a*); *Hocaba*, Xcanchakan Black-on-cream Type tripod rounded-side dish (52, *q*) and jar (cf. GWB, fig. 92, *a*); Xcanchakan Black-on-cream Type, incised variety grater bowl (52, *s*). Quantity: moderate.

a   *b*   *c*   *d*   *e*

Dot-encircled devices. These designs are usually painted; a few are modeled and appliqué. In some instances the dots may be disks. Occurrence: *Cochuah*, Tituc Orange-polychrome Type basal-flange bowl (cf. GWB, fig. 30, *a*, 32); *Cehpech*, Sacalum Black-on-slate Type incurved-rim ringstand bowl (26, *b*, 23); a miniature vessel of undetermined type (GWB, fig. 48, *n*), Caribe Incised Type barrel-shape vase (Smith, 1958b, fig. 1, *f*); *Hocaba-Tases*, Chen Mul Modeled Type figurine (64, *c*, painted); *Tases*, Chen Mul Modeled Type effigy censer adorno (72, *a*), headdress (68, *b*, 2), fan (32, *z*), and various parts of personage (32, *j*, *k*, *n*, painted); Pele Polychrome Type tripod dish (54, *a*; 75, *n*). Quantity: moderate. Remarks: the device *b* is found at Topoxte on Topoxte Red jars (information from W. R. Bullard, Jr.).

Fence pattern. Occurrence: *Cehpech*, Holactun Black-on-cream Type basin (10, *c*). Quantity: present.

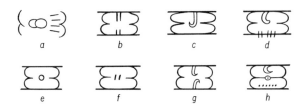

Figure-eight arrangements. Occurrence: *Tases,* Chilapa Gouged-incised Type ringstand restricted-orifice bowl (55, c, 19). Quantity: present. Remarks: actually this device is predominantly linked with the fine-orange Silho Group of the Sotuta Ceramic Complex. Various ceramic types are represented but usually this design is painted black and associated with tripod pyriform vases (Smith, 1957b, figs. 6, h, i; 11, k; GWB, fig. 76, q), pedestal-base cylindrical vases (Smith, 1957b, fig. 12, h, j; GWB, fig. 78, g, h, p), and a tripod dish (*ibid.,* fig. 81, h).

Loop. Occurrence: *Hocaba-Tases,* Chen Mul Modeled Type effigy censer adorno (73, b, 2); *Tases,* Chen Mul Modeled Type effigy censer adorno (72, j, l); Tecoh Red-on-buff Type tripod bulging-neck jar (53, a, 22). Quantity: rare. Remarks: although the Chen Mul Modeled Type examples represent either a looped flower stem or the end knot of a twist, they nevertheless constitute loops.

Mat pattern. A single example found. Occurrence: *Tases,* Papacal Incised Type jar (47, t). Quantity: present.

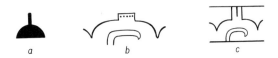

"Handbells." The example found in these collections is not of the simple "handbell" form (a) encountered in the Early Classic Period but a more elaborate variant or different device (b, c) associated with the Sotuta Ceramic Complex. Occurrence: *Sotuta,* Yalton Black-on-orange Type tripod dish (22, u) or Kilikan Composite Type lamp-chimney vase (Smith, 1957b, fig. 14, l). Quantity: present. Remarks: the "handbell" is most prevalent as a decorative device in the Tzakol Ceramic Complex at Uaxactun, usually as a rim or basal band (RES, figs. 25, b, 4; 26, b, 7, 8; 27, a, 4; b, 2, 4; 30, b, 2; c, 1, 4; 35, a, 4, 6; 38, a, 3).

Nose ornament device. Occurrence: *Cehpech,* Sahcaba Modeled-carved Type hemispherical bowl (8, m); *Hocaba-Tases,* Xcanchakan Black-on-cream Type tripod dish (52, o); Chen Mul Modeled Type seated figurine (65, f, ring at nose). Quantity: rare.

Ovoid or concentric ovoid. Elliptical (a), concentric (b), or solid flat oval shape (c). Occurrence: *Cehpech,* Provincia Plano-relief Type bowl with flaring sides rounding to flat base (9, g; 58, i; GWB, figs. 36, j; 59, b; 59, d, 8); *Sotuta,* Balam Canche Red-on-slate Type dish with flaring sides rounding to flat base (17, h); Yalton Black-on-or-

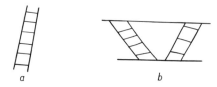

Ladder. This device may represent jaguar tail (a) or the sides of a triangle (b). Occurrence: *Cehpech,* Tekit Incised Type tripod basal-flange dish (6, r); *Sotuta,* Yalton Black-on-orange Type jar (22, b). Quantity: rare.

ange Type pedestal-base pyriform vase (Smith, 1957b, fig. 9, *a*); *Hocaba-Tases*, Chilapa Gouged-incised Type restricted-orifice deep bowl (55, *c*, 11); *Tases*, Chen Mul Modeled Type head (69, *q*; Thompson, 1957, fig. 1, *a*; painted decoration). Quantity: rare.

Ovoid-and-bar. Occurrence: *Hocaba-Tases*, Chilaap Gouged-incised Type hemispherical bowl (55, *c*, 14); *Tases*, Salto Composite Type deep bowl (55, *c*, 6) and restricted-orifice deep bowl (55, *c*, 16); Chilapa Gouged-incised Type restricted-orifice deep bowl (55, *c*, 12). Quantity: rare.

Ovoid-and-scroll. Occurrence: *Sotuta*, Pocboc Gouged-incised Type pyriform vase (22, *i*). Quantity: present.

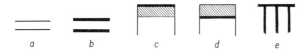

a   b   c   d   e

Parallel stripes and/or lines. These include incised, either sharp (*a*) or grooved (*b*) and painted, both prefire and postfire, decoration. If painted, the lines and stripes may be in the same color, usually red or black (*c, e*) or in different color combinations (*d*). Occurrence: *Tihosuco*, Yaxkukul Composite Type, groove-incised variety outcurving-side dish (10, *n*); *Tzakol*, Pita Incised Type, sharp-incised variety hemispherical bowls (25, *q–s*; 60, *f*); Delirio Plano-relief Type tripod basal-flange bowl (25, *p*, sharp-incised); *Cochuah*, Timucuy Orange-polychrome Type jars (25, *g–j, l*) and basal-Z-angle bowls (25, *v*); *Motul*, Bokoba Incised Type, sharp-incised variety side-angle bowls (25, *y–aa*); Tekanto Incised Type, red-decorated variety side-angle bowl (25, *x*, sharp-incised); *Tepeu*, Geronimo Incised Type, sharp-incised variety flaring-side bowl (25, *u*); Carmelita Incised Type, groove-incised variety cylindrical vase (cf. Berlin, 1956, fig. 4, *ll*); Saxche Orange-polychrome Type rounded-side bowl (10, *l*); *Cehpech*, Tekit Incised Type, sharp-incised variety jars (5, *s*; 14, *p*), tripod basal-Z-angle dish (6, *o*),

tripod basal-flange dish (6, *r*), tripod flaring-side dishes (6, *j, k*; 19, *g*), rounded-side bowl (6, *ff*), and basin (4, *c*); Xul Incised Type, sharp-incised variety tripod dish (7, *y*) and rounded-side bowl (7, *k*); Becal Incised Type, sharp-incised variety tripod basal-flange dish (8, *q*), tripod lateral-flange plate (8, *n*), flaring-side dish (26, *e*, 4), tripod cylindrical vase (8, *v*), and tripod basal-Z-angle dish (26, *e*, 2); Nohcacab Composite Type, sharp-incised variety jar (5, *r*) and tripod dish (26, *b*, 20); Becal Incised Type, groove-incised variety barrel-shape vase (8, *u*); Caribe Incised Type, groove-incised variety cylindrical vase (9, *m*), rounded-side bowl (9, *a*); Provincia Plano-relief Type, sharp-incised variety bowls with flaring sides rounding to flat base (9, *d, e, g*; 58, *i–k*) and tripod plate (9, *k*); Sahcaba Modeled-carved Type, groove-incised variety hemispherical bowl (8, *m*); Pabellon Modeled-carved Type, groove-incised variety hemispherical bowls (9, *h–j*), barrel-shape vase (9, *l*), and cylindrical vase with rattle bottom (27, *l*); Xaya Gouged-incised Type, sharp-incised variety tripod bolster-rim dish (6, *x*) and cylindrical vase (6, *nn*); Tabi Gouged-incised Type, sharp-incised variety cylindrical vase (7, *m*) and hemispherical bowls (7, *b, c, p*; 58, *e*); Opichen Gouged-incised Type, black-painted variety ringstand hemispherical bowl (8, *o*, sharp-incised) and tripod dish (8, *t*, sharp-incised); Yaxumha Composite Type, sharp-incised variety tripod dish (8, *s*); Tekax Black-on-red Type, orange variety hemispherical bowl (8, *b*); Palizada Black-on-orange Type pear-shape bowl (9, *f*); *Sotuta*, Chacmay Incised Type, groove-incised variety restricted-orifice bolster-rim bowls (15, *i j*) and wide-mouth low-neck jars (14, *k, n*); Timak Composite Type, groove-incised variety wide-mouth low-neck jar (14, *l*) and restricted-orifice bolster-rim bowl (15, *f*); Xuku Incised Type, groove-incised variety jars (20, *g*), restricted-orifice bowl (21, *a*), and cylindrical vases (21, *i*); Xuku Incised Type, sharp-incised variety jars (20, *o*) and flaring-side dish (21, *v*); Xuku Incised Type, cream-slip variety jars (20, *m, q*, sharp-incised), tripod flaring-side dishes (21, *cc, bb*), rounded-side dishes (21, *w*; 59, *p*), terraced-ringstand bowl (21, *jj*), and restricted-orifice bowl (21, *b*); Cumpich Incised Type, groove-incised variety jar (21, *a*); Tumbador Incised Type, groove-incised variety retricted-orifice bowl (23, *b*) and jars (60, *h–j*); Tekom Gouged-incised Type, sharp-incised variety tripod wide-mouth jar (14, *q*); Holtun Gouged-incised Type sharp-incised variety jar (20, *l*) and a pyriform vase (20, *u*); Holtun Gouged-incised Type, cream-slip variety pyriform vase (20, *f*, sharp-incised), jar (20, *k*, sharp-incised), and tripod dishes

(21, *aa*, *bb*, *ff*; 59, *l–n*, sharp-incised); Pocboc Gouged-incised Type, sharp-incised variety pyriform vase (22, *i*) and a tripod dish (cf. 59, *g*); Kilikan Composite Type, cream-slip variety tripod dishes (22,*r*, sharp-incised); Kilikan Composite Type, groove-incised variety tripod jar (22, *e*) and pyriform vases (22, *j*, *k*); Chan Kom Black-on-red Type, cream-slip variety jar (20, *i*); Balam Canche Red-on-slate Type jars (17, *b*, *c*); Yalton Black-on-orange Type jars (22, *b*; 59, *b*), tripod dishes (22, *t*, *u*; cf. 59, *f*), pyriform vases (22, *g*, *h*), restricted-orifice bowl (22, *l*), and a cylindrical vase (27, *j*); Cumpich Incised Type, black-paint variety tripod grater bowl (22, *v*); Kilikan Composite Type tripod dish (22, *r*); Cerro Montoso Polychrome Type lamp-chimney vase (23, *e*); Cenotillo Gray-polychrome Type cylindrical vase (23, *f*); *Hocaba*, Papacal Incised Type, groove-incised variety jars (cf. 38, *a*, 2, 10), tripod dishes (cf. 40, *b*, 11, 14), and drums (cf. 39, *a–c*); Villahermosa Incised Type tripod dishes with or without flange (cf. 55, *b*, 2, 4); Nacajuca Black-on-orange Type restricted-orifice bowl (55, *d*, *1*) and tripod dish (cf. 55, *d*, 2); Xcanchakan Black-on-cream Type jars (52, *g*, *i*, *j*); *Hocaba-Tases*, Papacal Incised Type, groove-incised variety water jars (38, *a*, 2, 10; 74, *a*, *b*), tripod dishes (cf. 40, *b*, 11, 14), drums (39, *a–c*), storage jar (47, *m*), and flaring-side bowls (43, *d*; 47, *r*); Papacal Incised Type, sharp-incised variety jars (47, *a*, *d*, *f*, *g*), restricted-orifice bowl (47, *n*) and a drum (39, *h*); Villahermosa Incised Type, sharp-incised variety tripod basal-flange dishes (cf. 55, *b*, 2, 4) and a restricted-orifice deep bowl (55, *b*, 7); Salto Composite Type, sharp-incised variety ringstand deep bowls (55, *b*, 5, 6); Palmul Incised Type, sharp-incised variety jars (48, *c–h*) and tripod flaring-side dish (cf. 48, *o*); Cusama Plano-relief Type, sharp-incised variety hemispherical bowl (51, *n*); Yobain Plano-relief Type, sharp-incised variety hemispherical bowl (47, *o*); Chilapa Gouged-incised Type, groove-incised variety restricted-orifice bowl (55, *c*, 11) and hemispherical bowl (55, *c*, 14); Salto Composite Type, sharp-incised variety restricted-orifice bowl (55, *c*, 15); Xcanchakan Black-on-cream jars (52, *a*, *b*, *h*, *k*; 75, *l*, *m*); Tecoh Red-on-buff Type parenthesis-rim jar (53, *a*, 20), tripod dish (53, *b*, 2), and pedestal-base restricted-orifice bowl (53, *b*, 10); Pele Polychrome Type tripod dish (54, *b*) and tripod everted-rim bowl (54, *e*); Sayula Polychrome Type restricted-orifice bowl (55, *d*, *4*); Uayma Modeled Type figurine (65, *i*); Chen Mul Modeled Type bird figurine (65, *g*), effigy ves-

sel (64, *c*), and small effigy censer (66, *d*, 1); Acansip Painted Type pedestal-base cup (30, *w*); Acansip-Thul Composite Type pedestal-base cup (30, *v*); *Tases*, Papacal Incised Type, groove-incised variety water jars (cf. 38, *a*, 2, 10; 74, *a*, *b*), tripod flaring-side dishes (40, *b*, 11, 14) and drums (39, *e*, *i*, *j*, *l–o*); Papacal Incised Type, sharp-incised variety low to medium-neck jars (47, *h*, *i*, *k*, *l*), high-neck storage jar (cf. 47, *a*), small-mouth low-neck jar (47, *b*), drums (39, *d*, *f*, *k*), and a tripod basal flange dish (40, *c*, 8); Pustunich Incised Type, sharp-incised variety restricted-orifice bowl (cf. 47, *n*), miniature jar (49, *a*), and jar (47, *p*, scratched); Villahermosa Incised Type, sharp-incised variety tripod basal-flange dishes (55, *b*, 2, 4) and ringstand deep bowls (55, *b*, 8–10); Grijalva Incised-polychrome Type, sharp-incised variety tripod basal-flange dish (55, *b*, 1); Salto Composite Type, sharp-incised variety tripod dish (55, *b*, 3) and ringstand restricted-orifice bowl (55, *b*, 6); Palmul Incised Type, sharp-incised variety high-neck jars (48, *a*; cf. 48, *e*), low-neck jars (cf. 48, *c*, *f*), and a tripod outcurving side dish (48, *o*); Cozil Incised Type, groove-incised variety reflector (36, *c*); Kanlum Plano-relief Type, sharp-incised variety low-neck jar (48, *i*); Chilapa Gouged-incised Type, groove-incised variety ringstand restricted-orifice bowls (55, *c*, 12, 19), ringstand deep bowls (55, *c*, 7, 18), and tripod dishes (55, *c*, 2–4); Salto Composite Type, groove-incised variety restricted-orifice bowls (55, *c*, 10, 13); Salto Composite Type, sharp-incised variety ringstand restricted-orifice bowls (55, *c*, 9, 16) and tripod basal-flange dish (55, *c*, 1); Mama Red Type, black-and-red-on-unslipped variety tripod dish (40, *a*, 6); Tecoh Red-on-buff Type tripod jar (53, *a*, 17), tripod bulging-neck jars (53, *a*, 19, 22), parenthesis-rim jars (53, *a*, 18, 21), water jars (53, *a*, 15, 16), tripod dishes (53, *b*, 1, 3, 6), bolster-rim basin (53, *b*, 4), potstand (53, *b*, 14), and cylindrical vases (53, *b*, 13, 15); Pele Polychrome Type tripod dishes (54, *a*, *c*, *d*); Grijalva Incised-polychrome Type tripod basal-flange dish (55, *b*, 1); Salto Composite Type tripod dish (55, *b*, 3) and restricted-orifice bowl (55, *c*, 9); Nacajuca Black-on-orange Type restricted-orifice bowl (55, *d*, 6); Chen Mul Modeled Type effigy censers (32, *e*, *g*, *j*, *k*, *m*, *n*; 67, *f*; 71, *a*, 5), figurines (35, *a*, 1–3), and an effigy vessel (64, *f*); Acansip Painted Type tripod flaring-side dishes (29, *v*, *x*, *y*) and a tetrapod square dish (29, *cc*); Cehac-Hunacti Composite Type jar censers (31, *e*; 62, *e*). Quantity: abundant.

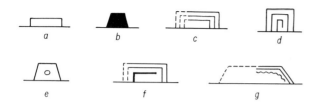

Platform and platform combinations. This includes the simple (*a, b*), concentric (*c, d*) forms with circle (*e*), with wavy line (*g*), or with right angle (*f*). Occurrence: *Tepeu 2*, Geronimo Incised Type, sharp-incised variety side-angle bowl (25, *u*; 60, *e*); *Cehpech*, Tekit Incised Type, sharp-incised variety jar (5, *gg*) and tripod basal-Z-angle dish (6 *q*); Opichen Gouged-incised Type ringstand rounded-side bowl (8, *o*); *Sotuta*, Xuku Incised Type, sharp-incised variety vase (cf. GWB, fig. 86, *g, 4*); Xuku Incised Type, cream-slip variety rounded-side bowl (21, *w*, sharp-incised); Cumtun Composite Type censer (12, *c*, painted); Chan Kom Black-on-red Type, cream-slip variety jar (20, *i*); *Hocaba-Tases*, Chilapa Gouged-incised Type restricted-orifice bowl (55, *c*, 11, sharp-incised); Salto Composite Type restricted-orifice bowl (55, *c*, 15, sharp-incised); *Tases*, Mama Red Type, incised-flange variety tripod basal-flange dish (40, *c*, 10); Pustunich Incised Type, sharp-incised variety jar (47, *p*); Salto Composite Type tripod basal-flange dish (55, *c*, 1, painted black); Dzitxil Openwork Type bowl cluster (37, *c*). Quantity: well represented.

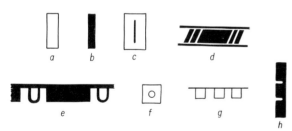

Rectangle and rectangle combinations. This device may be plain (*a*) or solid black (*b*) or other color; it may be associated with a dash (*c*), bars (*d*), U (*e*), a circle (*f*), or it may be pendent either plain (*g*) or red (*h*). Occurrence: *Tzakol*, Pita Incised Type, sharp-incised variety hemispherical bowl (25, *r*); *Cochuah*, Timucuy Orange-polychrome Type basal-Z-angle bowl (25, *v*); *Cehpech*, Tekit Incised Type sharp-incised variety tripod dish (6, *k*) and rounded-side bowl (6, *ff*); Provincia Plano-relief Type tripod plate (9, *k*, sharp-incised); *Sotuta*, Holtun Gouged-incised Type, cream-slip

variety tripod dish (21, *bb*); Kilikan Composite Type tripod pyriform vase (cf. Smith, 1957b, fig. 11, *s*, reserve-space black-painted); Pomuch Polychrome Type lamp-chimney vase (*ibid.*, fig. 14, *i*); *Hocaba*, Hoal Modeled Type effigy censer leg ornament (68, *a*, 3, painted); *Hocaba-Tases*, Palmul Incised Type, sharp-incised variety jars (48, *e, g, h*); Xcanchakan Black-on-cream Type jar (52, *k*); *Tases*, Kimbila Incised Type sharp-incised variety high-neck jar (50, *d*); Kanlum Plano-relief Type wide-mouth low-neck jar (48, *i*); Tecoh Red-on-buff Type tripod bulging-neck jar (53, *a*, 22) and parenthesis-rim jar (53, *a*, 18); Grijalva Incise-polychrome Type tripod basal-flange dish (55, *b*, 1, painted decoration); Chen Mul Modeled Type effigy censer heads (69, *c, h*; Thompson, 1957, fig. 2, *i, e*, respectively). Quantity: well represented.

Reverse angle. Similar to reverse curve (S-shape). Occurrence: *Cochuah*, Timucuy Orange-polychrome Type rounded-Z-angle bowl (GWB, fig. 63, *a*, 6); *Cehpech*, Tabi Gouged-incised Type hemispherical bowl (7, *c*); *Sotuta*, Yalton Black-on-orange Type lamp-chimney vase (cf. Smith, 1957b, fig. 8, *n*) and pedestal-base cylindrical vase (*ibid.*, fig. 12, *k*); *Hocaba*, Xcanchakan Black-on-cream Type jars (52, *g, i, j*); *Hocaba-Tases*, Chenkeken-Acansip Composite Type jar (32, *a*, groove-incised); Yobain Plano-relief Type hemispherical bowl (47, *o*); Xcanchakan Black-on-cream Type jars (52, *a, b*; 75, *l, m*); *Tases*, Cozil Incised Type, groove-incised variety reflector (36, *c*). Quantity: moderate. Remarks: some of these may be intended S-shape or reverse curve bands (52, *a, b, g, i, j*).

Right angle. This is also an L-shape device. Occurrence: *Cehpech*, Tekit Incised Type, sharp-incised variety rounded-side bowl (6, *ff*); Tabi Gouged-incised Type, sharp-incised variety deep bowl (7, *b*) and rounded-side bowl (7, *c*); *Sotuta*, Xuku Incised Type, cream-slip variety tripod dish (59, *o*); *Tases*, Cozil Incised Type, groove-incised variety candle-flame shield (36, *c*); Chilapa Gouged-incised Type, sharp-incised variety tripod dish (55, c, 3); Chen Mul Modeled Type effigy censer (32, k, painted decoration). Quantity: moderate.

S-shape or reverse-curve. Occurrence: *Tzakol*, Pita Incised Type, sharp-incised variety rounded-side bowl (60, f); *Tepeu 2*, Geronimo Incised Type, sharp-incised variety flaring-side bowl (25, u; 60, e); *Sotuta*, Balantun Black-on-slate Type water jars (14, a, h; 27, a); Yalton Black-on-orange Type jar (22, b); Timak Composite Type low-neck jar (59, i); *Hobaca-Tases*, Chenkeken Incised Type, groove-incised variety flanged censer (30, m); Salto Composite Type restricted-orifice deep bowl (55, c, 15); *Tases*, Papacal Incised Type, sharp-incised variety jar (47, e); Tecoh Red-on-buff Type wide-mouth high-neck jar (53, a, 10, negative painted reserve-space technique reverse S-shape); Chilapa Gouged-incised Type wide-mouth low-neck jar (55, c, 8) and barrel-shape bowl (55, c, 12); Salto Composite Type restricted-orifice deep bowl (55, c, 10); Chen Mul Modeled Type effigy censer adorno (71, e, 5). Quantity: well represented.

"Sausage." An elongated element rounded at both ends which may be slightly curved. Occurrence: *Cehpech*, Sacalum Black-on-slate Type tripod dish (6, z, possible sausages); Chumayel Red-on-slate Type tripod dish (6, aa, possible sausages); *Hocaba*, Xcanchakan Black-on-cream Type wide-mouth low-neck jar (52, e). Quantity: rare.

Scallop. One of a series of semicircular curves along an edge, as for ornament. Occurrence: *Tepeu 1*, Bejucal Brown-on-buff Type rounded-side bowl (10, p). *Cehpech*, Palizada Black-on-orange Type flaring-side bowl rounding to flat base (9, b); Tenosique Red-on-orange Type rounded-side bowl (9, c); Provincia Plano-relief Type, cream-slip vari-ety flaring-side bowl rounding to flat base (9, d, painted-black decoration); *Sotuta*, Cumtun Composite Type pedestal-base censers (12, b, e, flange); Kilikan Composite Type pedestal-base hemispherical bowl (cf. Smith, 1957b, fig. 4, j, painted-black decoration); Tinum Red-on-cinnamon Type, open-work variety ladle-handled censer (11, w); *Hocaba-Tases*, Chen Mul Modeled Type figurine (65, h, shield); *Tases*, Chen Mul Modeled Type effigy vessel (64, p) and effigy censer (67, e, shield); Tecoh Red-on-buff Type potstand (53, b, 14). Quantity: well represented. Remarks: U, crescent, or semicircle bands may closely resemble the scalloped variety. Examples of these nonscalloped bands are found in most ceramic complexes. Here a few are mentioned: *Cehpech*, Opichen Gouged-incised Type, black-painted variety tripod dish (8, t); *Sotuta*, Kilikan Composite Type, cream-slip variety tripod dish (22, r); *Hocaba*, Xcanchakan Black-on-cream jar (52, i); *Tases*, Chen Mul Modeled Type effigy censer (32, e, painted).

  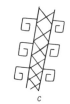

Scroll, angular. This design form has roots in Mesoamerica much earlier than the time period which this study covers. Occurrence: *Cochuah*, Valladolid Incised-dichrome Type jars (cf. GWB, fig. 64, h, n); *Cehpech*, Xul Incised Type, sharp-incised variety rounded-side bowl (7, k); *Sotuta*, Xuku Incised Type, sharp-incised variety rounded-side bowl (21, x); Xuku Incised Type, cream-slip variety rounded-side dish (59, p, sharp-incised); Balam Canche Red-on-slate Type jar (17, c); *Tases*, Kimbila Incised Type, sharp-incised variety jar (50, d); Tecoh Red-on-buff Type tripod jar (53, a, 22). Quantity: moderate.

Scroll, hook. An abbreviated scroll something like the hook of a crochet needle. Occurrence: *Motul*, Geronimo Incised Type, sharp-incised variety side-angle bowl (25, u; 60, e); *Cehpech*, Provincia Plano-relief Type flaring-side bowl rounding to flat base (9, e; 58, j); *Sotuta*, Timak Composite Type grater bowl (13, m, painted decoration); Yalton Black-on-orange Type tripod dishes (22, u; 59, f); Yalton Black-on-orange Type, cream-slip variety tripod dish (22, s); Cerro Montoso Polychrome Type lamp-chimney vase (23, e); *Hocaba*, Xcanchakan Black-on-cream Type flaring-side dish (52, w); *Hocaba-Tases*, Palmul Incised Type, sharp-incised variety jar (48, g); *Tases*, Chen Mul Modeled Type effigy censer (32, m, bordering headdress); Cozil Incised Type, groove-incised variety reflector (36, c); Palmul Incised Type, sharp-incised variety wide-mouth jar (48, a); Villahermosa Incised Type, sharp-incised variety tripod basal-flange dish (55, b, 2) and a ringstand deep bowl (55, b, 8). Quantity: well represented.

Scroll, meander. Occurrence: *Sotuta*, Holtun Gouged-incised Type cylindrical vase (59, q); Holtun Gouged-incised Type, cream-slip variety tripod dishes (59, l, m); Kilikan Composite Type tripod jar (22, e) and pyriform vase (22, k); Kilikan Composite Type, cream-slip variety tripod dishes (22, r; 59, h). Quantity: moderate.

Scroll, "ram horn." Generally used in combination with the other elements to form a band or as part of a complicated design, rarely found alone. Occurrence: *Cehpech*, Pabellon Modeled-carved Type hemispherical bowl (9, i); *Sotuta*, Holtun Gouged-incised Type, cream-slip variety pyriform vase (20, f) and tripod dish (21, bb); Xuku (?) Incised Type, sharp-incised variety vase (57, g); *Hocaba*, Xcanchakan Black-on-cream Type hemispherical bowl (52, p); *Hocaba-Tases*, Papacal Incised Type, sharp-incised variety jar (47, f); *Tases*, Papacal Incised Type, sharp-incised variety jar (47, h); Chen Mul Modeled Type effigy censer (32, n, painted decoration); Tecoh Red-on-buff Type tripod dish (53, b, 3). Quantity: moderate.

Scroll, simple curvilinear. In addition to the simple curvilinear scrolls (a, b), various combinations are included: the scroll band (c), scrolls in alternate rotation and transverse reflection (d), and scrolls-and-Tau motif (e). Occurrence: *Cehpech*, Provincia Plano-relief Type pedestal-base hemispherical bowl (58, a) and flaring-side bowl rounding to flat base (9, g; 58, i); Tekax Black-on-red Type hemispherical bowl (8, h); *Sotuta*, Tinum Red-on-cinnamon Type, openwork variety ladle-handled censer (11, w); Xuku Incised Type, sharp-incised variety vase (57, g); Holtun Gouged-incised Type, cream-slip variety pyriform vase (20, f); Yalton Black-on-orange Type jar (22, b); *Hocaba*, Hoal Modeled Type effigy censer fragment (32, d); Papacal Incised Type, groove-incised variety tripod basal-flange dish (40, c, 5); Xcanchakan Black-on-cream Type jars (52, g, j); Tecoh Red-on-buff Type wide-mouth high-neck jar (53, a, 10, both positive scrolls and a negative S-shape); *Hocaba-Tases*, Papacal Incised Type, sharp-incised variety jar (47, a); Pustunich Incised Type, groove-incised variety flaring-side bowl (47, r; 74, v); Palmul Incised Type, sharp-incised variety wide-mouth jar (48, e); Chilapa Gouged-incised Type hemispherical bowl (55, c, 14); Xcanchakan Black-on-cream Type jar (52, h); Tecoh Red-on-buff Type pedestal-base restricted-orifice bowl (53, b, 10); Chen Mul Modeled Type small effigy censer (66, d, 1); *Tases*, Papacal Incised Type, sharp-incised jars (47, h, i, k); Salto Composite Type tripod basal-flange dish (55, c, 1); Villahermosa Incised Type, sharp-incised variety ringstand-base deep bowls (55, b, 9, 10); Chilapa Gouged-incised Type wide-mouth low-neck jar (55, c, 8); Tecoh Red-on-buff Type tripod jar (53, a, 17); Chen Mul Modeled Type effigy censers (32, g, j, k, m, n; 67, a; 71, a, 5). Quantity: abundant.

Scroll, spiral. Occurrence: *Cehpech*, Pabellon Modeled-carved Type hemispherical bowl (9, i); Chumayel Red-on-slate Type tripod dish (26, b, 19); *Sotuta*, Balam Canche Red-on-slate Type small-mouth jar (17, a); *Tases*, Chen Mul Modeled Type effigy censer adorno (71, e, 4). Quantity: rare.

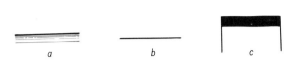

Single stripe or line. These are straight lines which usually encircle the vessel. They may be groove-incised (a), sharp-incised (b), or painted (c). Occurrence: *Tihosuco*, Kiba Incised Type, groove-incised variety flaring-side bowl (24, j); *Tzakol*, Pita Incised Type, groove-incised variety basal-flange bowl (25, t); *Cehpech*, Xul Incised Type, sharp-incised variety deep bowl (7, l); Becal Incised Type, groove-incised variety cylindrical vase (26, e, 5); Caribe Incised Type, red-painted variety rounded-side bowl (9, a); *Sotuta*, Xuku Incised Type, sharp-incised variety rounded-side dish (21, x); Xuku Incised Type, groove-incised variety restricted-orifice bowl (27, g); Chan Kom Black-on-red Type jar (20, h); Yalton Black-on-orange Type, cream-slip variety tripod dish (22, s); *Hocaba-Tases*, Chenkeken Incised Type, openwork variety jar censer (31, j, groove-incised); *Tases*, Salto Composite Type hemispherical bowl (55, c, 17); Tecoh Red-on-buff Type hemispherical bowls (53, b, 7, 8). Quantity: well represented.

Spatter. This form of decoration is accomplished by scattering paint over a surface in drops. Occurrence: *Cehpech*, Sacalum Black-on-slate Type ringstand-base incurved-rim bowl (26, b, 23, accidental spattering); *Sotuta*, Balantun Black-on-slate Type small-mouth high-neck jars (14, b, f) and basins (15, a–c). Quantity: moderate.

Squiggle. Occurrence: *Sotuta*, Yalton Black-on-orange Type jar (59, c; cf. Smith, 1957b, fig. 4, b; GWB, fig. 76, a). Quantity: present.

Step-fret. Sometimes called a grecque, this is a combination of the step or, more commonly, the half-terrace, and the scroll, angular (a, c) or curvilinear (b). Occurrence: *Cochuah*, Valladolid Incised-dichrome Type jars (GWB, figs. 6, a, 2; 64, d, i–k, m); *Motul*, Bokaba Incised Type sharp-incised variety side-angle bowls (25, y–aa); *Cehpech*, Tabi Gouged-incised Type deep bowl (7, b) and rounded-side bowl (7, c, 58, e); Opichen Gouged-incised Type tripod dish (8, t); Xaya Gouged-incised Type low-neck jar (58, g); *Sotuta*, Timak Composite Type grater bowl (13, m); Xuku Incised Type, cream-slip variety tripod dish (21, cc, sharp-incised); *Hocaba-Tases*: Papacal Incised Type, sharp-incised variety jar (47, g); Tecoh Red-on-buff Type parenthesis-rim jar (Proskouriakoff and Temple, 1955, fig. 12, c); Salto Composite Type restricted-orifice deep bowl (55, b, 6). Quantity: abundant.

Steps. Occurrence: *Cehpech*, Xaya Gouged-incised Type basin with strap handle (6, x); *Sotuta*, Tinum Red-on-cinnamon Type, openwork variety ladle-handled censer (11, y); *Tases*, Tecoh Red-on-buff Type jar (53, a, 12) and pedestal-base vase (53, b, 12). Quantity: rare.

Tassel. Occurrence: *Cehpech*, Tenosique Red-on-orange Type, scratched variety rounded-side bowl (9, c); *Tases*, Chen Mul Modeled Type effigy censer adornos (32, g, in two different places). Quantity: rare.

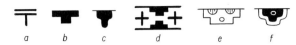

a   *b*   *c*   *d*   *e*   *f*

Tau and tau combinations. The tau or T-shape may be either thin (*a*) or thick (*b*, *c*). When reversed the thick type becomes a single terrace (*d*). Combinations include tau-and-cross (*d*), possible face (*e*), and tau-and-circle (*f*). Occurrence: *Cochuah*, Tituc Orange-polychrome Type, interior-striated variety jars (cf. GWB, figs. *63, b, 2; 64, b, e*); *Sotuta*, Yalton Black-on-orange Type tripod pyriform vase (cf. Smith, 1957b, fig. *6, g*); *Hocaba*, Xcanchakan Black-on-cream Type tripod dish (52, *x*); *Hocaba-Tases*, Xcanchakan Black-on-cream Type jar (52, *h*, scrolls-and-tau) and restricted-orifice bowl (52, *l*); *Tases*, Cozil Incised Type, groove-incised variety reflector (36, *c*); Chilapa Gouged-incised Type tripod dish (55, *c*, 3, tau-and-circle); Tecoh Red-on-buff Type bulging-neck jar (53, *a*, 19, tau-and-cross); Chen Mul Modeled Type effigy censer loincloth flap (67, *e*, painted) and adornos (71, *e*, 2, 3). Quantity: moderate.

a   *b*

Terrace. Occurrence: *Tases*, Chen Mul Modeled Type effigy censer earplug (32, *j*, painted) and loincloth flap (67, *e*, painted). Quantity: rare. Remarks: these include all terraced flanges (Table 38).

Terrace, split. Consists of two half-terraces or a single terrace split down the center. Occurrence: *Sotuta*, Yalton Black-on-orange Type tripod pyriform vase (cf. Smith, 1957b, fig. *6, g*); Xuku Incised Type, cream-slip variety tripod dish (cf. GWB, fig. 87, *h*); *Tases*, Tecoh Red-on-buff Type bulging-neck jar (53, *a*, 19). Quantity: rare.

  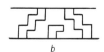

a   *b*

Terrace-and-right-angle. Occurrence: *Sotuta*, Xuku Incised Type, cream-slip variety tripod dish (59,

o; cf. GWB, figs. *86, j, 5; 95, a, 1*). Quantity: present.

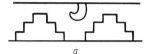

a   *b*

Terrace-and-scroll. Frequently the hook scroll is used. Occurrence: *Sotuta*, Cerro Montoso Polychrome Type lamp-chimney vase (23, *e*; cf. Smith, 1957b, fig. 14, *j*; GWB, fig. 89, *a*); Yalton Black-on orange Type pedestal-base pyriform vase (cf. Smith, 1957b, fig. 8, *m*), tripod pyriform vase (*ibid.*, fig. 15, *c*), pedestal-base cylindrical vase (GWB, fig. 78, *t*), and tripod dish (*ibid.*, fig. 80, *g*); *Hocaba-Tases*, Papacal Incised Type, sharp-incised variety basal-flange deep bowl (43, *n*); Palmul Incised Type, sharp-incised variety flanged bowl (48, *q*). Quantity: rare.

Terrace-and-U. Occurrence: *Sotuta*, Yalton Black-on-orange Type tripod pyriform vase (22, *g*), tripod dish (22, *t*), and rounded-side bowl (cf. GWB, fig. 87, *z*). Quantity: rare.

a   *b*   *c*   *d*   *e*

Triangle. May be painted, incised, or openwork, and reproduced as solid (*a*), open (*b*), hatched horizontally (*c*), crosshatched (*d*), and containing dots (*e*). Occurrence: *Cochuah*, Timucuy Orange-polychrome Type high-neck jar (10, *m*); *Motul*, Bokaba Incised Type, sharp-incised variety side-angle bowl (25, *z*); *Cehpech*, Tekit Incised Type, sharp-incised variety tripod dish (19, *g*) and basal-flange dish (6, *r*, plain and ladder); Nohcacab Composite Type tripod dish (26, *b*, 20, sharp-incised); Tabi Gouged-incised Type rounded-side bowl (7, *c*; 58, *e*); Xul Incised Type, sharp-incised variety basal-flange bowl (7, *x*) and basal-Z-angle bowl (7, *w*); Becal Incised Type, sharp-incised variety tripod dish (8, *n*); Opichen Gouged-incised Type hemispherical bowl (8, *o*); Chumayel Red-on-slate Type, incised-variety basin with square rim bolster (4, *i*); *Sotuta*, Tinum Red-on-cinnamon Type, openwork variety ladle-handled censer (11, *y*); Balam Canche Red-on-slate Type restricted-orifice bowl (17, *d*); Yalton Black-on-orange Type, cream-slip variety tripod dish (22, *s*); *Hocaba-Tases*, Chilapa Gouged-incised Type ringstand restricted-orifice bowl (55, *c*, 11); Salto Composite Type ringstand restricted-orifice bowl (55, *c*, 15); Chen Mul Modeled Type figurine (35, *a*, 10, painted black); Acansip Painted Type pedestal-base cup (30, *w*); Xcanchakan Black-on-cream Type water jar (52, *a*; 75, *m*); Tecoh Red-on-buff Type ringstand restricted-orifice bowl (53, *b*, 10); *Tases*, Chilapa Gouged-incised Type tripod dish (75, *q*); Salto Composite Type ringstand deep bowl (55, *c*, 5) and restricted-orifice bowl (55, *c*, 13); Tecoh Red-on-buff Type rounded-side bowl (53, *b*, 8); Pele Polychrome Type tripod dish (54, *c*). Quantity: abundant.

stricted-orifice basins (15, *a–e*, *g*, *h*; 16, *b*), tripod recurving-side dishes (19, *b–e*), tripod outcurving-side dish (19, *f*), rounded-side dishes (13, *c*, *d*, *g*), and tripod grater bowl (13, *n*); Timak Composite Type wide-mouth low-neck jar (14, *l*) and restricted-orifice basin (15, *f*); Balam Canche Red-on-slate Type wide-mouth low-neck jar (17, *b*); Chan Kom Black-on-red Type rounded-side dish (21, *r*) and tripod dish (21, *z*); Xuku Incised Type, black-paint variety tripod grater bowls (21, *k*, *l*); *Hocaba*, Xcanchakan Black-on-cream Type jars (52, *c*, *i*, *j*), tripod grater bowl (52, *s*), and tripod rounded-side dish (52, *q*); *Hocaba-Tases*, Xcanchakan Black-on-cream Type jars (52, *a*, *b*, *d–h*), restricted-orifice bowls (52, *m*, *n*), tripod rounded-side dish (52, *o*, *r*), and tripod recurving-side dishes (52, *t–v*); *Tases*, Tecoh Red-on-buff Type parenthesis-rim jar (53, *a*, 21). Quantity: abundant.

Triangle-and-circle. Occurrence: *Hocaba-Tases*, Salto Composite Type ringstand restricted-orifice bowl (55, *c*, 15). Quantity: present.

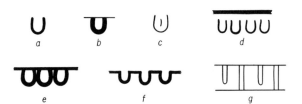

U-shape. May be simple (*a*), concentric (*b*), with dash (*c*), with bars (*g*), used in a band (*d*) or as a chain band (*e*, *f*). Occurrence: *Cochuah*, Timucuy Orange-polychrome Type basal-Z-angle bowl (25, *v*); *Cehpech*, Tekit Incised Type, sharp-incised variety tripod dish (6, *k*); *Sotuta*, Dzibiac Red Type, scratched variety rounded-side dish (21, *kk*); Xuku Incised Type, cream-slip variety jar (20, *m*, sharp-incised); Holtun Gouged-incised Type, cream-slip variety pyriform vase (20, *f*); Pocboc Gouged-incised Type pyriform vase (22, *i*); Kilikan Composite Type small-mouth jar (22, *e*); Yalton Black-on-orange jar (22, *b*) and pyriform vases (22, *g*, *h*); Tumbador Incised Type, groove-incised variety (60, *j*); *Hocaba*, Xcanchakan Black-on-cream Type jar (52, *i*); *Hocaba-Tases*, Pele Polychrome Type tripod everted-rim bowl (54, *e*); *Tases*, Pustunich Incised Type, sharp-incised variety miniature jar (49, *a*); Villahermosa Incised Type, sharp-incised variety ringstand deep bowl (55, *b*, 10); Chilapa Gouged-incised Type tripod dish (55, *c*, 2); Tecoh Red-on-buff Type wide-mouth jar (53, *a*, 13); Chen Mul Modeled Type effigy censers with painted decoration on headdress (32, *e*; 69, *b*) or front flap (32, *g*, *n*). Quantity: abundant.

Trickle. Usually black to brown but may be red; commonly rather thick (*a*), but may be relatively thin (*b*). Strictly speaking, this is not a true trickle but is painted on with a freedom which occasionally allows the paint to run down. Perhaps the term "controlled trickle" would be more apt. In this study trickle is first noted in the Cehpech Ceramic Complex. Actually, it is found earlier in Yucatan. Brainerd illustrates examples associated with his Regional Stage which he calls Trickle on Flaky Redware (1958, fig. 7). Occurrence: *Cehpech*, Sacalum Black-on-slate Type basins (4, *g*; 16, *c–e*, *g*; 26, *b*, 7–9), small-mouth jars (5, *u*; 26, *b*, 1), and ringstand incurved-rim bowl (26, *b*, 23); Chumayel Red-on-slate Type basins (4, *e*, *f*; 16, *f*) and small-mouth jar (5, *bb*); Holactun Black-on-cream Type basins (10, *a*, *b*) and jars (10, *d*, *g*, *h*); *Sotuta*, Balantun Black-on-slate Type small-mouth high-neck jars (14, *a–d*, *f*, *h–j*; 27, *a*; 59, *a*), re-

a   b

Wavy line. Occurrence: *Cochuah*, Timucuy Orange-polychrome Type jar (25, *l*), basal-Z-angle bowls (cf. GWB, fig. 30, *a, 24, 25*), and rounded-Z-angle bowl (*ibid.*, fig. 63, *a, 9*); Tituc Orange-polychrome Type basal-flange bowls (*ibid.*, figs. 19, *g, 3; 30, a, 7, 33; 60, b, 10; 63, a, 12*); Tituc Orange-polychrome Type, interior-striated variety jar (*ibid.*, fig. 63, *b, 3*); *Tepeu 2*, Geronimo Incised Type, sharp-incised variety side-angle bowl (25, *u*); *Hocaba-Tases*, Palmul Incised Type, sharp-incised variety jar (48, *h*); *Tases*, Pele Polychrome Type tripod dish (54, *a*). Quantity: rare. Remarks: the wavy line appears to be quite well represented in the Cochuah Ceramic Complex from the Puuc

site collections illustrated by Brainerd but not in the collections associated with this report.

Y-shape, cursive. Occurrence: *Cehpech*, Sahcaba Modeled-carved Type hemispherical bowl (8, *m*). Quantity: present.

Zigzag line. Occurrence: *Sotuta*: Balam Canche Red-on-slate Type restricted-orifice bowl (17, *d*). Quantity: present.

NATURALISTIC DESIGN

a   b

Animal. For the most part these resemble the dog but they may represent some other doglike animal. They may be moldmade (a) or modeled (b). Occurrence: *Hocaba-Tases*, Hoal Modeled Type effigy censer adornos (68, *a, 2*); *Tases*, Mama Red Type tripod dishes with moldmade animal feet (40, *b, 17; c, 18–20; 74, q, r*); Tecoh Red-on-buff Type tripod dishes with moldmade animal feet (53, *b, 1, 6*); Pele Polychrome Type tripod dishes with moldmade animal feet (54, *a, c, d*); Fine-orange Matillas Group moldmade animal feet for tripod dishes (56, *a*); Chen Mul Modeled Type effigy censer animal head adornos (32, *bb, cc*, moldmade; 32, *dd; 72, mm–pp*, modeled). Quantity: abundant (especially in form of effigy feet).

Bat. Occurrence. *Tases*, Chen Mul Modeled Type effigy censer adornos or possibly figurine fragments (71, *c, 5, 6* modeled). Quantity: rare.

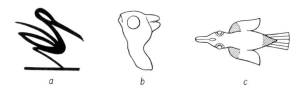

a   b   c

Bird. Often painted (a) and sometimes modeled (b, c). Occurrence: *Sotuta*, Cumpich Incised Type, black-paint variety tripod grater bowl (22, *v*); Kilikan Composite Type pyriform vase (22, *k*, painted black); Kilikan Composite Type cream-slip variety tripod outcurving-side dish (22, *r*, painted black); Yalton Black-on-orange Type pedestal-base pyriform vase (cf. Smith, 1957b, fig. 9, *b*); *Tases*, Thul Appliqué Type wide-mouth, low-neck jar (28, *a, 21, 23*, modeled); Chen Mul Modeled Type effigy censer bird adornos (32, *ee–ii; 42, a; 71, c, 1–4*; all modeled). Quantity: well represented.

Crossed bones. Occurrence: *Hocaba-Tases*, Chen Mul Modeled Type effigy censer loincloth flap (Thompson, 1957, fig. 2, *b*, painted decoration.) Quantity: present.

Death's head. The actual effigy censer figures, effigy vessels, and figurines representing the death's head are omitted here since they have been discussed and recorded elsewhere. The only examples are the modeled and appliqué adornos. Occurrence: *Hocaba-Tases*, Chen Mul Modeled effigy censer headdress adornos (68, *b*, 7; 71, *a*, 2, 6); *Tases*, Chen Mul Modeled effigy censer headdress adornos (69, *m*; 71, *a*, 3, 7–11). Quantity: well represented.

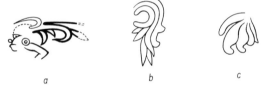

Feathers. They may be painted (*a*), incised (*b*), or modeled (*c*). Occurrence: *Cehpech*, Becal Incised Type, black-band variety tripod cylindrical (?) vase (8, *v*, sharp-incised); Caribe Incised Type, groove-incised variety cylindrical vase (9, *m*); Pabellon Modeled-carved Type hemispherical bowl (9, *j*); *Sotuta*, Yalton Black-on-orange Type restricted-orifice bowl (22, *n*); Pabellon Modeled-carved Type double-bottom cylindrical vase (27, *l*); *Tases*, Chapab Modeled Type wide-mouth jar (42, *a*); Salto Composite Type, Salto Variety, ring-stand-base deep bowl (55, *c*, 5); Chen Mul Modeled Type effigy censer headdresses (32, *e*, *g*, *k*, *m*, *n*; 67; 71, *a*, 5; 73, *a*, 1, 2, 5–7; 75, *e*). Quantity: abundant.

Fish. Usually painted (*a*), they are sometimes modeled (*b*). Occurrence: *Hocaba-Tases*, Pele Polychrome Type tripod dish (54, *b*); *Tases*, Pele Polychrome Type tripod dish (54, *a*; 75, *n*); Chen Mul Modeled Type effigy censer adornos (72, *jj*, *kk*). Quantity: rare.

Flower. Occurrence: *Hocaba-Tases*, Chen Mul Modeled Type effigy censer loincloth flap (Thompson, 1957, fig. 2, *b*, painted decoration). Quantity: present.

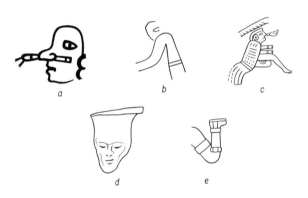

Human. The actual effigy censer figures, effigy vessels, and figurines representing humans are omitted here since they have been discussed and recorded elsewhere. The remainder may be painted (*a*), incised (*b*), carved (*c*), moldmade (*d*), or modeled (*e*). Occurrence: *Cehpech*, Muna Slate Type tripod basal-Z-angle dish with mold-pressed fat-cheek face feet (6, *p*); Yaxnic Modeled Type mold-pressed feet for tripod dishes (6, *gg*, *hh*, *kk*); Ticul Thin-slate Type tripod outcurving-side dish with mold-pressed fat-cheek face on feet (7, *o*) and mold-pressed human figure on feet (7, *aa*); Sahcaba Modeled-carved Type hemispherical bowl (8, *m*); Provincia Plano-relief Type flaring-side bowls rounding to flat base (9, *e*, *g*; 58, *i*, *j*); Pabellon Modeled-carved Type hemispherical bowl (9, *j*); Tabi Gouged-incised Type cylindrical vase (58, *f*); *Sotuta*, Yalton Black-on-orange Type restricted-orifice bowl (22, *n*); Kilikan Gouged-incised Type pedestal-base cylindrical vase (cf. Smith, 1957b, fig. 17, *c*); Cerro Montoso Polychrome Type lamp-chimney vase (cf. GWB, fig. 89, *a*); *Hocaba*, Hoal Modeled Type effigy censer fragment depicting leg of possible diving god (32, *b*); *Hocaba-Tases*, Xcanchakan Blackon-cream Type rounded-side dish (52, *o*); Chen Mul Modeled Type effigy censer arm adorno (70, *a*, 4, moldmade and painted); Mama Red Type tripod dish with moldmade feet (40, *b*, 15; *c*, 16); Fine-orange Matillas Group moldmade feet (56, *c*, 1, 3, 10, 12); *Tases*, Mama Red Type moldmade feet (40, *b*, 16; *c*, 13–15); Papacal Incised Type, scratched variety jar (47, *s*); Chapab Modeled Type effigy vessel, double-boiler form (45, *a*; 75, *e*; diving god); fine-orange Matillas Group moldmade feet (56, *c*, 2, 4–9, 11). Quantity: abundant.

Serpent or snake. This decoration may be painted (*a*) or modeled (*b*). Occurrence: *Sotuta*, Yalton Black-on-orange Type jars (59, *c*; cf. Smith, 1957b, fig. 4, *b*; cf. GWB, fig. 76, *a*) and pedestal-base pyriform vase (cf. Smith, 1957b, fig. 9, *a*, *e*); Cerro Montoso Polychrome lamp-chimney vase (cf. *ibid.*, fig. 14, *k*; cf. GWB, fig. 89, *a*); *Hocaba-Tases*, Chen Mul Modeled Type effigy censer headdress adorno (71, *b*, 4; *Tases*, Chen Mul Modeled Type effigy censer headdress adornos and other adornos (71, *a*, 4; *b*, 1–3, 5–9). Quantity: well represented.

CONVENTIONALIZED DESIGN

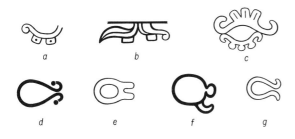

Eye-associated devices. Usually painted around or under both eyes of either the personage or the animal represented in his headdress; rarely modeled and appliqué. Occurrence: *Sotuta*, Cumtun Composite Type censer (12, *e*, modeled and appliqué); *Hocaba-Tases*, Palmul Incised Type jar (48, *h*); Chen Mul Modeled Type effigy censer fragment (73, *d*, 6); *Tases*, Chen Mul Modeled Type effigy censers (32, *j*, *k*, *l*, *m*; 68, *b*, 9; Thompson, 1957, fig. 1, *b*, *c*, all painted directly around or under eye of personage; 32, *n*; 71, *a*, 4; 73, *d*, 5, modeled and appliqué to headdress); Pele Polychrome Type tripod dish (54, *d*). Quantity: well represented.

Flower, budlike or floral representation. Occurrence: *Hocaba-Tases*, Yobain Plano-relief Type rounded-side bowl (47, *o*). Quantity: present. Remarks: this design, although encountered only once in the collections used in this analysis, was closely associated with the Sotuta Ceramic Complex in other collections from Chichen Itza and Huaymil. The best examples include: Holtun Gouged-incised Type, cream-slip variety tripod grater bowl (59, *n*; GWB, fig. 86, *j*, 7); Yalton Black-on-orange Type tripod dishes (Smith, 1957b, figs. 5, *j*; 17, *e*) and pedestal-base pyriform vases (*ibid.*, figs. 8, *w*; 12, *a*, *b*); Pocboc Gouged-incised Type tripod restricted-orifice bowl (*ibid.*, fig. 16, *g*), jar (GWB, fig. 77, *f*), and pyriform vase (*ibid.*, fig. 77, *i*); Kilikan Composite Type, creamslip variety restricted-orifice bowl (*ibid.*, fig. 80, aa); Kilikan Composite Type restricted-orifice bowl (*ibid.*, fig. 80, *z*), tripod bowl (59, *g*; GWB, fig. 80, *a*), rounded-side bowl (Smith, 1957b, fig. 4, *l*), pedestal-base pyriform vases (*ibid.*, figs. 9, *m*; 10, *a*, *d*; 12, *f*, *g*), and tripod pyriform vases (*ibid.*, figs. 10, *l*; 11, *r*, *s*; GWB, fig. 77, *m*).

a   *b*   *c*

Flowers, quatrefoil. An ornament with four lobes or leaflike appendages. It may be negative painted (*a*), painted (*b*), or gouged-incised (*c*). Occurrence: *Cehpech*, Tekit Incised Type, sharp-incised variety basin (4, *c*); *Sotuta*, Kilikan Composite Type pyriform vase (22, *j*); *Hocaba-Tases*, Cusama Plano-relief Type deep bowl (51, *n*); *Tases*, Tecoh Red-on-buff Type bulging-neck jar (53, *a*,

19) and tripod dish (53, *b*, 5, negative painted); Chen Mul Modeled Type effigy censer earplug painted decoration (32, *j*). Quantity: rare. Remarks: actually this design is moderately well represented in the Sotuta Ceramic Complex as shown by findings in other collections from Chichen Itza and Huaymil. Examples include: Holtun Gouged-incised Type jars (GWB, fig. 85, *b*, *7*, *12*), tripod barrel-shape vase (*ibid.*, fig. 86, *c*), tripod dish (*ibid.*, fig. 87, *a*, *r*), and a hemispherical bowl (*ibid.*, fig. 87, *u*); Yalton Black-on-orange Type pedestal-base pyriform vase (Smith, 1957b, fig. 8 *v*); Cerro Montoso Polychrome Type lamp-chimney vase (*ibid.*, fig. 14, *j*); Kilikan Composite Type pedestal-base pyriform vase (*ibid.*, fig. 10, *b*) and tripod pyriform vases (*ibid.*, figs. 10, *l*; 11, *g*); Pocboc Gouged-incised Type tripod restricted-orifice bowl (*ibid.*, fig. 16, *f*), pyriform vase (GWB, fig. 77, *c*), and tripod bowl (*ibid.*, fig. 80, *b*); Pocboc Gouged-incised Type, cream-slip variety tripod dish (*ibid.*, fig. 81, *j*).

GLYPHIC DESIGN

Affix, "comb." This derives its name from its likeness to a woman's hair comb. Morley (1915, pp. 65, 66) refers to one of the four constant elements used in forming the "introducing glyph" as comblike lateral appendages. The month signs Zec and Mac often have the "comb" as an affix (Thompson, 1950, figs. 16, 18). Thompson refers to many other instances of the use of the "comb" as an affix (*ibid.*, p. 322; 1962, p. 44, Glyph 25). Occurrence: *Cehpech*, Sahcaba Modeled-carved Type hemispherical bowl (8, *m*); *Tases*, Tecoh Red-on-buff Type tripod wide-mouth jar (53, *a*, 17). Quantity: rare.

Glyph band (?). The fragmentary examples under consideration may or may not be decorative or functional glyph bands. Occurrence: *Cehpech*, Tekit Incised Type, sharp-incised variety basin (4, *c*) and rounded-side bowl (6, *ff*); *Hocaba-Tases*, Papacal Incised Type sharp-incised variety jar (47,

d); *Tases*, Salto Composite Type, black-slip variety restricted-orifice deep bowl (55, *c*, 10). Quantity: rare.

Glyph band, possibly functional. Occurrence: *Cehpech*, Pabellon Modeled-carved Type hemispherical bowls (9, *h–j*); *Tases*, Tecoh Red-on-buff Type tripod dish (53, *b*, 5, negative painted). Quantity: rare.

Miscellaneous symbols, ahau. Occurrence: *Sotuta*, Cerro Montoso Polychrome Type lamp-chimney vase (23, *e*); *Hocaba-Tases*, Tecoh Red-on-buff Type wide-mouth jar (53, *a*, 11); *Tases*, Papacal Incised Type, sharp-incised variety jar (47, *h*, possible ahau set in tau form). Quantity: rare.

Miscellaneous symbols, glyph of god D (Itzamna?). Occurrence: *Tases*, Mama Red Type, unslipped-exterior variety tripod dish (40, *a*, 6, black motif on exterior). Quantity: present.

Miscellaneous symbols, possible kin sign. Occurrence: *Cehpech*, Provincia Plano-relief Type, cream-slip variety bowl with flaring sides rounding to flat base (9, *e*). Quantity: present.

"Sky band" symbols, diagonal cross (St. Andrew's). See under "Cross," p. 51 above. Sky bands are discussed and illustrated by Smith (1955a, p. 73).

"Sky band" symbols, Lamat-Venus glyph. Thompson illustrates several examples (1962, pp. 108–110, Glyph 510). Occurrence: *Sotuta*, Dzibiac Red Type, scratched variety rounded-side dish (21, *p*). Quantity: present.

"Sky band" symbols, kin sign. The Maya day sign or sun symbol, therefore the fundamental unit for the measurement of time. It has many variants (see RES, p. 74). It is suggested that this may be a kin variant. Occurrence: *Hocaba*, Xcanchakan Black-on-cream Type tripod flaring-side dish angling to convex base (52, x). Quantity: present. Remarks: Thompson (1962, Glyph 721) illustrated a somewhat similar glyph about which he stated "The examples on the Chipoc pottery vessel may be something different as they have a dot in each of the four quarters. Yet, they are not Glyph 510." The Chipoc reference is illustrated by Smith (1952, fig. 3).

VII

Modes

In this report a mode is considered to be a selected attribute or cluster of attributes that displays significance in its own right. Modes differ from types which refer to the entire artifact by referring to its parts. Here we presume to select the attributes which have significance.

This significance, considered as cultural relevance, may be sought in the areas of time, space, and function. The attributes involved are selected from basic ceramic categories: namely, paste composition; surface finish; form, including some complete vessels as well as modes of rim, base, and various kinds of appendages; decorative techniques; and specific designs. Rarely is a single attribute by itself sufficient as a time or space marker. For example the basal flange is a useful diagnostic, but without the aid of other traits it would not establish either the time or the area of manufacture, because the basal flange is associated with the Early Classic, Late Classic, Proto-Postclassic, Middle Postclassic, and Late Postclassic periods. In Early Classic it is usually linked with ring-base Peten Gloss Ware bowls, in Late Classic with tripod polychrome Peten Gloss Ware dishes, in Proto-Postclassic with Puuc Slate Ware tripod dishes, and in Middle and Late Postclassic with tripod dishes of either Mayapan Red Ware or the fine-orange Matillas Group.

We shall first consider the modes associated with paste composition, followed by a listing of the other categories. Under each category the mode or mode cluster is described, placed in time and space, and wherever possible identified as to function.

PASTE COMPOSITION MODES

Paste composition embraces texture, hardness, temper, and color. Texture bears a direct relation to the kind of temper used and the manner in which it is prepared. Hardness in this report is made use of only when it is extreme. Temper is a most valuable attribute and is used effectively for those wares and types analyzed by Shepard. Color is described throughout and occasionally has modal significance when associated with other attributes.

Calcite plus quartz grains temper. This temper, combined with fine texture, uniformly pale orange color, and fairly high degree of hardness, describes the paste composition of Tulum Red Ware. *Ceramic complex*: Tases, A.D. 1300–1450. *Provenience*: Ichpaatun and Tulum in Quintana Roo and Mayapan in Yucatan. *Illustrations*: 48, WTS, figs. 4, 5, and 6, a. Remarks: ibid., pp. 237–242, gives a good description of this ware, which also includes that of the paste.

Fiber temper. This is an unusual temper for the Peninsula of Yucatan and is associated with unslipped basins of the Cetelac Fiber-temper Type. These belong to Brainerd's (1958, p. 50) Early Regional Stage. *Ceramic complex*: Cochuah, A.D. 300–600. *Provenience*: Coba in Quintana Roo and Yaxuna in Yucatan. *Illustrations: ibid.*, fig. 1, e. *Remarks*: not found in the collections under discussion but an excellent time and area marker for Maya pottery.

Saccharoidal calcite temper. When this temper is linked with fine-textured light gray to cream-colored paste and thin-walled vessels, Thin Slate Ware is indicated. There are other attributes of surface finish and form (see Thin Slate Ware, p. 30) which complete the description of this most distinctive ware. However, considering the rare use of saccharoidal calcite temper with other definitely coarser and thicker wares, this mode cluster is usually sufficient for identification. Ce-

ramic complex: Cehpech, A.D. 800–1000. *Provenience*: see Thin Slate Ware, p. 30. *Illustrations*: 7; 26, *d*; 58, *c–f*; GWB, figs. 4, *p*; 10, *h*; 15, *i, s*; 18, *j*; 21, *d*; 32, *d, e*; 35, *e*; 48, *b, d–m*; 50, 51, *a–c*; 61, *b, e, f, j, l*.

Sherd temper. When this temper is combined with a coarse textured paste and a lumpy opaque cream slip, Cauich Coarse-cream Ware is strongly suggested. If black trickle is added to certain jar or basin forms, the identification becomes certain and we recognize the Holactun Black-on-cream Type. *Ceramic complex*: Cehpech, A.D. 800–1000. *Provenience*: Chichen Itza, Dzibilchaltun, Kabah, Labna, Sayil, and Uxmal in Yucatan and Edzna, Holactun and Huaymil in Campeche. *Illustrations*: 10, *a–j*; GWB, figs. 41, *e, 3*; 53, *a–d*; 66, *c*. *Remarks*: Brainerd calls this ware Holactun Slateware.

Untempered well-kneaded fine-textured paste. This by itself merely indicates a fine ware: Fine Black, Fine Buff, Fine Gray, and Fine Orange. Each of these wares may be separated into groups based on differences of form, decorative technique, and design style. Only one of the four fine wares mentioned, however, has been sufficiently studied to be followed accurately through time and space. This is Fine Orange Ware, first noted in the Late Classic Period as the fine-orange Dzibilchaltun Group, continuing through successive ceramic complexes with fine-orange Balancan, Altar, Silho, and Matillas groups, ending in the Protohistoric Period with the fine-orange Cunduacan Group. The identifying modes for these wares and groups will appear under form, decorative technique, and specific design categories.

SURFACE FINISH MODES

Surface finish involves smoothing, slipping, and the attaining of a matte or a lustrous appearance. The last is produced by burnishing or polishing, by glazing, and by using certain clays which become glossy on drying from suspension without any special treatment. Surface finish also embodies color, roughening, and blemishes.

Glazing. This technique is used only in connection with Plumbate Ware in Mesoamerica. Although there are three plumbate groups (San Juan, Robles, and Tohil), only the plumbate Tohil group appears to have been traded into Yucatan. The sheen associated with glazing is easily differentiated from other lusters because of its vitreous quality and often metallic iridescence. The vessel forms and decorative techniques help in determining the age. *Ceramic complex*: Sotuta, A.D. 1000–1200. *Quantity*: Chichen Itza, 27 sherds; Mayapan, 9 sherds. *Provenience*: Chichen Itza and Mayapan in Yucatan and Huaymil in Campeche. Many other sites are listed by Shepard (1948, pp. 105–114) plus the Marquez collection (Smith, 1957a, pp. 117–118) and a number of more recent findings (see Plumbate Ware, p. 27). *Illustrations*: 23, *a–d*; 60, *h–k*; GWB, fig. 91, *a–f*; Shepard, 1948; Smith, 1957a, figs. 1–5.

Glossiness. This kind of luster is attributed to a large collection of pottery (RES, pp. 26, 27), mostly from the Peten of Guatemala but to a lesser degree from the Yucatan Peninsula. The former is Peten Gloss Ware, the latter Yucatan Gloss Ware. When the name gloss was given it was assumed that all pottery so termed attained its luster because the clay became glossy on drying from suspension. Since that time it has become apparent that this is only true of part of the group; another part achieved its luster by means of polishing. This glossiness, which has a higher degree of luster than most other lustrous wares, when associated with certain other distinctive attributes becomes a useful mode. Yucatan Gloss Ware appears to be mostly of the Early Classic Period, whereas Peten Gloss Ware is equally distributed between the Early and Late Classic. These gloss wares separate into groups, however, whose identifying modes will appear under form, decorative technique, and specific design category. *Ceramic complexes*: Cochuah, Tzakol, Motul, and Tepeu 1, 2, A.D. 300–800. *Quantity*: total of all sherds at the site for Yucatan Gloss Ware includes 420 at Mayapan, 7 at Kabah, 3 at Chichen Itza, and none at Uxmal; and for Peten Gloss Ware, 278 at Mayapan, 7 at Kabah, 3 at Chichen Itza, and 4 at Uxmal. *Provenience*: Acanceh, Balam Canche, Chichen Itza, Dzibilchaltun, Kabah, Labna, Mani,

Mayapan, Oxkintok, Sayil and Yaxuna in Yucatan; Dzibilnocac, Edzna, Huaymil, and Xtampac in Campeche; Aguada Grande, Calderitas, Cedral (El), Coba, Ichpaatun, Kantunil Kin, San Miguel, and Tancah in Quintana Roo. *Illustrations*: 10, *l, m, p*; 25, *c–w, y–bb, ff, gg*; GWB, figs. 1, *g, i*; 2, *h*; 3; 4, *m*; 6; 9; 19, *g, 3*; 30, *a, b*; 60, *b*; 63; 64; WTS, fig. 10, *g*; Smith, 1957a, figs. 6; 7.

Roughening of surface. This gives the appearance of a sandpaper or wood rasp finish (Chapter V, p. 39). It is a mode used on ladle censer exteriors and a variety of unslipped utilitarian vessels (Table 35) belonging to Mayapan Unslipped Ware. *Ceramic complexes*: Hocaba and Tases, A.D. 1200–1450. *Quantity*: see Table 35. *Provenience*: Mayapan. *Illustration*: none. *Remarks*: the ladle censers found in the Cehpech and Sotuta ceramic complexes are more carefully smoothed on interior than on exterior but do not have the coarse sandpaper or wood rasp finish noted on those from the Hocaba and Tases ceramic complexes.

Striating. See Chapter V under texturing and Table 34.

Unslipped exterior. This feature is associated primarily with tripod flaring-side or rounded-side dishes and basins of Mayapan Red Ware. These dishes all have solid conical feet. *Ceramic complex*: Tases, A.D. 1300–1450. *Quantity*: Hocaba-Tases had a total of 1,748 sherds or 4 per cent, and Tases a total of 5,969 sherds or 7.2 per cent. These percentages are of the slipped wares in each complex. *Provenience*: Mayapan. *Illustrations*: 41, *a*; 41, *b*, 1–4, 10.

Vertical crazing. This is a mode identified exclusively with Thin Slate Ware. Although a blemish, it is a strong time and area marker. *Ceramic complex*: Cehpech, A.D. 800–1000. *Quantity*: no accurate count, but a very high percentage of all Thin Slate Ware. *Provenience*: Acanceh, Ake, Chanpuuc, Chichen Itza, Dzan, Dzebtun, Dzibilchaltun, Kabah, Labna, Mani, Mayapan, Oxkintok, Sayil, Uxmal, and Yaxuna in Yucatan; Aguada Grande, Calderitas, San Miguel de Cozumel, and Tancah in Quintana Roo; and Hochob in Campeche. *Illustrations*: 7; 58, *c–f*; GWB, figs. 4, *p*; 10, *h*; 15, *i, s*; 18, *j*; 21, *d*; 32, *d, e*; 35, *e*; 50; 51, *a–c*; 61, *b, e, f, j, l*.

Waxiness. This finish like glossiness must be linked with other attributes to form a mode cluster to be significant. Otherwise by itself it covers a wide area and a long time span; it is associated with a number of different wares and a variety of forms. The wares are Flores Waxy Paso Caballo Waxy, Puuc Red, Puuc Slate, Thin Slate, Chichen Red, and Chichen Slate; the area is most of the Maya area, and the time span stretches from the Middle Preclassic Period through the Early Postclassic Period with a hiatus during most of the Classic Period. The identifying modes for these wares will appear under form, decorative technique, and specific design category. *Ceramic complexes*: Mamom, Chicanel, Cehpech, and Sotuta, 1500 B.C.–A.D. 100 and A.D. 800–1200. *Quantity*: percentage of all sherds at Uxmal, 59.8 at Chichen Itza, 57.1; at Kabah, 43, and at Mayapan, 1.1. *Provenience*: Maya area (check the above listed wares). *Illustrations*: 4–8, 13–17, 19–21, 24, *a, b, d–h*; 26, *b*; *c, 2–4*; *d, e*; 27, *a–c, f–i*; 58, *c–h*; 59, *a, i, j–q*.

FORM MODES

Vessel shape and the various parts that combine to make a vessel include some of the most diagnostic attributes. A listing of the vessels and vessel parts considered as significant and therefore as modes follows in alphabetical order, beginning with complete vessels or objects and followed by vessel appendanges and vessel parts.

COMPLETE VESSELS

Basin, flaring side, flat bolster rim, two vertical strap or lug handles. This form may have ovoid bolster rim. *Wares*: Mayapan Red and Mayapan Unslipped. *Ceramic complexes*: Hocaba and Tases, A.D. 1200–1450. *Quantity*: Mayapan Unslipped Ware has 51 sherds in Hocaba, 66 in Hocaba-Tases, and 224 in Tases; Mayapan Red Ware has 5 sherds in Hocaba, 156 in Hocaba-Tases, and 849 in Tases. *Provenience*: Mayapan. *Illustrations*: 29, *f, g*; 46, *b*. *Remarks*: when this form carries a rounded, square, or triangular bolster it can belong only to the Tases Ceramic Complex.

Basin, flaring or rounded side, T-shape bolster rim. Two other distinguishing characteristics of this form are a narrow offset base and usually lack of handles. *Ware*: Cauich Coarse-cream. *Ceramic complex*: Cehpech, A.D. 800–1000. *Quantity*: Holactun Black-on-cream Type has 238 sherds from Uxmal and 11 from Kabah. *Provenience*: Kabah, Mayapan, and Uxmal in Yucatan. *Illustrations*: 10, *a*; GWB, fig. 53 *c, d*. *Remarks*: Brainerd's Holactun Slateware.

Basin, restricted orifice, flat bolster rim, two horizontal strap handles. The body may be globular, slightly pear-shape, or rounded side; bolster is rarely rounded or triangular. *Wares*: Mayapan Red and Peto Cream. *Ceramic complexes*: Hocaba, Hocaba-Tases, and Tases, A.D. 1200–1450. *Quantity*: Peto Cream Ware has 63 sherds in Hocaba, 16 in Hocaba-Tases, and 17 in Tases; Mayapan Red Ware has 92 in Hocaba, 213 in Hocaba-Tases, and 643 in Tases. *Provenience*: Acanceh, Chichen Itza, Dzibilchaltun, Mani, and Mayapan in Yucatan; Ichpaatun and Tulum in Quintana Roo. *Illustrations*: 41, *a*; 51, *j–l*; 52, *m, n*; 74, *e*; GWB, figs. 19, *i, 7, 9*; 20, *a, 20, 21*; *b, 14–21*; 24, *e, 1–11*; 27, *j, 7–24*; 94, *g, 6*; WTS, figs. 5, *f, 5–7, 15, 16*; 7, *b, 8*.

Basin, restricted orifice, ovoid bolster rim, two vertical strap handles. The body may be globular or pear-shape; bolster is occasionally rounded. *Ware*: Chichen Slate. *Ceramic complex*: Sotuta, A.D. 1000–1200. *Quantity*: Chichen Slate Ware has 2,034 sherds from Chichen Itza and 214 from Mayapan. *Provenience*: Chichen Itza, Dzibilchaltun, and Mayapan. *Illustrations*: 15; 16, *a, b*; 27, *h, i*; GWB, fig. 73, *d*.

Basin, rounded side, ovoid bolster rim, two horizontal strap handles. This form is large and has a flat base. *Ware*: Cauich Coarse-cream. *Ceramic complex*: Cehpech, A.D. 800–1000. *Quantity*: Cauich Coarse-cream Ware has 373 sherds from Uxmal. *Provenience*: Holactun (?) and Uxmal. *Illustration*: 10, *c*. *Remarks*: Brainerd's Holactun Slateware.

Basin, rounded side, rounded bolster rim, two vertical strap handles. Rarely ovoid, square, or triangular bolster rim. *Wares*: Puuc Red, Puuc Slate, and Thin Slate. *Ceramic complex*: Cehpech, A.D. 800–1000. *Quantity*: Puuc Slate Ware has 7,568 sherds from Uxmal, 2,604 from Kabah, 317 from Chichen Itza and 331 from Mayapan; Thin Slate Ware has 257 sherds from Uxmal, and Puuc Red Ware has 15 sherds from Uxmal and 2 from Mayapan. *Provenience*: Acanceh, Chichen Itza, Dzibilchaltun, Kabah, Labna, Mani, Mayapan, Oxkintok, Sabacche, Sayil, Uxmal, and Yaxuna in Yucatan;

San Miguel Cozumel, Tancah, and Xelha in Quintana Roo. *Illustrations*: 4, *a–k*; 7, *k, v*; GWB, figs. 10, *c*; 15, *e, o*; 21, *b*; 32, *g*; 41, *d, 11–20, f*; 43; 44; 52, *c, e, f*; 73, *d, 27–30*; WTS, fig. 11, *a, 24, 26–27, 42–46*.

Bowl, cluster. This is a cluster of four small deep rounded-side bowls surrounding and attached to a similarly shaped centrally placed fifth bowl. This cluster is attached to and supported by a single large pedestal. The pedestal may be flaring or nearly vertical and usually has a bolster rim at base, which may be confused with Mayapan Red Ware jar rims when only sherds are involved. These may have been candlestick clusters or a condiment vessel. *Ware*: Mayapan Red. *Ceramic complexes*: Hocaba-Tases and Tases, A.D. 1300–1450. *Quantity*: Mayapan Red Ware has 14 sherds in Hocaba-Tases and 87 sherds in Tases. *Provenience*: Mayapan. *Illustration*: 37, *a–c*.

Bowl, deep, recurving side, ringstand base. *Wares*: Mayapan Red and Fine Orange of the Matillas Group. *Ceramic complexes*: Hocaba-Tases and Tases, 1300–1450. *Quantity*: Mayapan Red Ware has 3 sherds in Hocaba-Tases and 7 in Tases; the Matillas Group has 7 sherds in Hocaba-Tases and 56 in Tases. *Provenience*: Mayapan. *Illustrations*: 43, *l*; 55, *c, 5*.

Bowl, deep, recurving side, ringstand base and apron flange. *Ware*: Mayapan Red. *Ceramic complexes*: Hocaba-Tases and Tases, A.D. 1300–1450. *Quantity*: Mayapan Red Ware has 5 sherds in Hocaba-Tases and 1 in Tases. *Provenience*: Mayapan. *Illustration*: cf. 43, *m*, a jar close to a deep bowl in form.

Bowl, deep, recurving-side tripod. Some have nearly vertical sides. The feet are usually solid conical for Mayapan Unslipped Ware specimens and solid conical, hollow cylindrical with rounded botton, or hollow oven-shape for Mayapan Red Ware vessels. *Wares*: Mayapan Red and Mayapan Unslipped. *Ceramic complexes*: Hocaba-Tases and Tases, A.D. 1300–1450. *Quantity*: Mayapan Red Ware has 110 sherds in Hocaba-Tases and 86 in Tases; Mayapan Unslipped Ware has 23 sherds in Hocaba-Tases and 245 in Tases. *Provenience*: Mayapan. *Illustrations*: 31, *w, x, y, bb*; 43, *b, c–g, j*.

Bowl, deep, recurving-side tripod with apron flange. The feet are hollow cylindrical with rounded bottom. *Ware*: Mayapan Red. *Ceramic complexes*: Hocaba, Hocaba-Tases, and Tases, A.D.

1200–1450. *Quantity*: Mayapan Red Ware has 21 sherds in Hocaba, 26 in Hocaba-Tases, and 11 in Tases. *Provenience*: Mayapan. *Illustrations*: 43, *h, i*.

Bowl, grater, tripod. This form was not found earlier than the Sotuta Ceramic Complex in the collections used in this report. Brainerd did not discover any earlier examples in his material as described and illustrated in his Yucatan ceramic report (1958, figs. 74 and 80, captions). There are suggestions of the earlier appearance of this form mentioned by Brainerd, but these are all hard to accept as truly grater bowls. On the other hand, Michael D. Coe (1961, figs. 26, *f–k*; 52, *p–s*; 53, *j*) illustrates a considerable number of Middle Formative grater bowls from La Victoria, Guatemala. More recently in excavations made at Altar de Sacrificios, Richard E. W. Adams (1963) identifies a number of grater bowls in Fine Gray Ware of a group associated with the Jimba Ceramic Complex (presumably chronologically linked with late Tepeu 3). In my opinion this linkage suggests that these examples may be precursors to those of the Early Postclassic Period, since in addition to being grater bowls some have hollow bulbous feet, also an Early Postclassic Period or Sotuta Ceramic diagnostic. Another instance of this late Tepeu 3–early Jimba association occurs at Seibal in Burial 1, where a Fine Gray Ware bulbous-footed grater bowl was found with three fine-orange Altar Group vessels, a Tepeu 3 style polychrome tripod dish (also with hollow bulbous feet), and an unslipped jar (verbal information from J. A. Sabloff). These Fine Gray Ware graters are formed differently from any that follow. Some have inwardly inclined sides angling to a convex base (cf. RES, fig. 50, *b*, 7–9, for vessel form only); others have outcurving sides and nearly flat bases (cf. *ibid.*, fig. 75, *b*, 4, for vessel form only), and the feet may be hollow bulbous or solid conical. Some of the so-called bulbous feet are near oven-shape, but a few examples of the true bulbous do occur. To sum up, the grater bowl appears to have been introduced into the Yucatan Peninsula in Sotuta times, elsewhere as early as Middle Preclassic.

Bowl, grater, tripod, flaring sides angling to a convex base. These have hollow bulbous feet. *Ware*: Fine Orange of the fine-orange Silho Group. *Ceramic complex*: Sotuta, A.D. 1000–1200. *Quantity*: 1 possible Yalton Black-on-orange Type sherd. *Provenience*: Chichen Itza and Marquez Collection. *Illustrations*: 22, v (probably a grater); GWB,

fig. 80, *l–p*; Smith, 1957b, fig. 5, *h, i*.

Bowl, grater, tripod, rounded side, convex base. These have hollow oven feet and wide open orifice. *Wares*: Mayapan Red, Mayapan Unslipped, and Peto Cream. *Ceramic complexes*: Hocaba, Hocaba-Tases, and Tases, A.D. 1200–1450. *Quantity*: Mayapan Red Ware has 161 sherds in Hocaba, 509 sherds in Hocaba-Tases, and 572 sherds in Tases; Mayapan Unslipped Ware has 2 sherds in Hocaba, 31 sherds in Hocaba-Tases, and 22 sherds in Tases; Peto Cream Ware has 1 sherd in Hocaba, 7 sherds in Hocaba-Tases, and 1 in Tases. *Provenience*: Acanceh, Chichen Itza, Dzibilchaltun, and Mayapan. *Illustrations*: 33, *j*; 46, *a*; 51, *r*; 52, *s*; GWB, figs. 20, *a, 10, b, 40*; 26, *a*; 92, *g, 5, 7*; 96, *i*.

Bowl, grater, tripod, rounded side, flat base. These have hollow oven-shape or hollow bulbous feet and a nearly restricted orifice. *Wares*: Chichen Red and Chichen Slate. *Ceramic complex*: Sotuta, A.D. 1000–1200. *Quantity*: 384 Chichen Slate Ware sherds and 31 Chichen Red Ware sherds. *Provenience*: Chichen Itza. *Illustrations*: 13, *m, n*; 21, *j–m* (*m* suggests the scroll or Turkish slipper foot); GWB, fig. 74, *h–j*.

Bowl, hemispherical, bead rim, flat base. *Ware*: Thin Slate. *Ceramic complex*: Cehpech, A.D. 800–1000. *Quantity*: 634 sherds at Uxmal; 25 sherds at Kabah, and 1 sherd at Mayapan. *Provenience*: Acanceh, Chichen Itza, Kabah, Labna, Oxkintok, Sayil, and Uxmal in Yucatan. *Illustrations*: 7, *f*; GWB, figs. 4, *p, 15, 34*; 18, *j, 6*; 50, *a, 5–15*; *b, 5–7*; *k, 32–49*; 51, *b, 5–8*; *c, 11*; all may have flat bases.

Bowl, hemispherical, bead rim, tripod. The foot type is a solid nubbin and the base is flat. Obviously, without the base this form is easily confused with the simple flat-base variety. *Wares*: Puuc Red and Thin Slate. *Ceramic complex*: Cehpech, A.D. 800–1000. *Quantity*: Thin Slate Ware has 101 sherds at Uxmal, 7 at Kabah, and 8 at Mayapan; Puuc Red Ware has 199 sherds at Uxmal, 20 at Kabah, and 13 at Mayapan. *Provenience*: Acanceh, Chichen Itza, Kabah, Labna, Oxkintok, Sayil, and Uxmal in Yucatan. *Illustrations*: 7, *h*; 8, *c, d*; GWB, figs. 4, *p, 15, 34*; 18, *j, 6*; *k, 5*; 50, *a, 5–15*; *b, 5–7*; *k, 32–49*; 51, *b, 5–8*; *c, 11*; *e, 10–15*; *g*; *h, 1*; *j*; *k, 4, 5*; *l, 1–20*.

Bowl, recurving side, tripod with hollow bulbous feet. This form may have dish dimensions. It is well represented, has a convex base, and sometimes outcurving sides. *Wares*: Chichen Red and Chichen Slate. *Ceramic complex*: Sotuta, A.D. 1000–1200. *Quantity*: Chichen Slate Ware has 85 sherds from Chichen Itza and 8 from Mayapan; Chichen Red Ware has 12 sherds from Chichen Itza. *Provenience*: Chichen Itza and Mayapan. *Illustrations*: 19, a–e; 21, z; GWB, figs. 74, b; 87, g, j, t, 16.

Bowl, recurring side, tripod with hollow oven-shape feet. This form may have dish dimensions. It is rare and has a convex or flat base. *Ware*: Peto Cream. *Ceramic complex*: Hocaba, A.D. 1200–1300. *Quantity*: 5 Xcanchakan Black-on-cream Type sherds. *Provenience*: Acanceh, Mani, and Mayapan. *Illustrations*: 51, u; 52, t–v; GWB, figs. 19, i, 5; 20, b, 32; 24, a, 1, 4, 6, 8, 11–13.

Bowl, ringstand base, exterior rim bevel. The rim may be slightly incurved, body is rounded, the ringstand undecorated or terraced, and the lip pointed, sometimes flat. *Wares*: Puuc Red and Puuc Slate. *Ceramic complex*: Cehpech, A.D. 800–1000. *Quantity*: Puuc Slate Ware has 198 sherds from Mayapan, 172 from Uxmal, 103 from Kabah, and 3 from Chichen Itza; Puuc Red Ware has 14 sherds from Uxmal and 8 sherds from Mayapan. *Provenience*: Acanceh, Chanpuuc, Chichen Itza, Dzebtun, Dzibilchaltun, Holactun, Kabah, Labna, Mani, Mayapan, Oxkintok, Sayil, and Uxmal. *Illustrations*: 4, l, m; 26, b, 23; 60, d; GWB, figs. 15, c, l, 4–8, r; 21, f; 32, c; 35, g; 49, a–c, d, 16, e–h; 51, h, 3, i, n.

Bowl, ringstand base, restricted orifice. The body may be globular or have a side angle, and the base may have a pedestal. *Wares*: Fine Orange of the Matillas Group, Mayapan Black Ware, Mayapan Red, and San Joaquin Buff. *Ceramic complexes*: Hocaba (rare) and Tases, A.D. 1200–1450. *Quantity*: Mayapan Red Ware has 5 sherds in Hocaba, 120 sherds in Hocaba-Tases, and 89 sherds in Tases; Fine Orange Ware, Matillas Group has 2 sherds in Hocaba, 54 sherds in Hocaba-Tases, and 68 sherds in Tases; San Joaquin Buff Ware has 16 sherds in Hocaba-Tases and 6 sherds in Tases; Mayapan Black Ware has 7 sherds in Hocaba-Tases. *Provenience*: Mayapan. *Illustrations*: 44, l, m; 53, b, 10; 55, b, 6; c, 15; 74, aa, bb; GWB, fig. 28, c, 18 (possibly).

Censer basin, bolster rim. This form may have a pedestal base, placing it in the censer class, or it may have a flat base establishing it as a basin.

No entire rounded-side bolster-rim vessels have been found. The bolsters may be ovoid, rounded, triangular, or square. *Ware*: Puuc Unslipped. *Ceramic complex*: Cehpech, A.D. 800–1000. *Quantity*: 44 sherds at Uxmal and 3 at Kabah. *Provenience*: Kabah, Sayil, and Uxmal in Yucatan. *Illustrations*: 3, r–t; GWB, figs. 37, c, 11, 12; 39, e, 23, 25–27, 29, f, 10. The bolsters are often embellished by thumb-impressing or reed-impressing.

Censer bowl, pedestal base, and two vertical strap handles. These bowls have flaring sides and usually a flat bolster rim as well as a bolster-rim pedestal. The temper is normally a gray limestone. *Ware*: Chichen Unslipped. *Ceramic complex*: Sotuta, A.D. 1000–1200. *Quantity*: 45 sherds at Chichen Itza. *Provenience*: Chichen Itza and Mayapan. *Illustrations*: 12, g; GWB, figs. 22, g; 23, d; 69, c; 70, a, c. *Remarks*: this form differs from the Cehpech hourglass censer in having handles and normally a larger pedestal, often with flat bolster rim. In addition it has gray limestone temper compared to potsherd or, rarely, clear calcite for the Cehpech variety of hourglass censer.

Censer bowl, tripod with two vertical strap handles. This bowl has flaring sides, either a bolster or direct rim, flat base, and three large, hollow, bulbous feet. The temper is usually a gray limestone. *Ware*: Chichen Unslipped. *Ceramic complex*: Sotuta, A.D. 1000–1200. *Quantity*: 407 sherds at Chichen Itza and 1 sherd at Mayapan. *Provenience*: Chichen Itza and Mayapan. *Illustration*: 12, f.

Censer, effigy, modeled with little appliqué adornment. The vessel form is that of a low pedestal-base cylindrical vase. The figure, partly modeled on and partly applied to the vessel wall, is usually in an upright position facing out. *Ware*: Mayapan Unslipped Ware, the Hoal Modeled Type. *Ceramic complex*: Hocaba, A.D. 1200–1300. *Quantity*: percentages of the Hoal examples within the unslipped of each complex follow: Hocaba, 11.5 or 562 sherds; Hocaba-Tases, .3 or 117 sherds; Tases, .002 or 3 sherds. *Provenience*: Mayapan and unknown. *Illustrations*: 32, b–d; 68, a; GWB, figs. 99, a, b; 100, a; 101, a. *Remarks*: both Mayapan and Xcaret have examples of this form in Puuc Slate Ware, the Yaxnic Modeled Type (6, mm). These belong to the Cehpech Ceramic Complex. Although the Hoal Modeled Type is a Hocaba product, fragments were encountered in higher levels.

Censer, effigy, modeled with plentiful appliqué adornment. The vessel form is cylindrical with a high pedestal base. The figure, partly modeled and partly moldmade, is usually created independently in full round and attached to the vessel. It is placed on one side of the censer in a standing position. Clearly these censers belong to an assembly line, mass production technique. *Ware*: Mayapan Unslipped Ware, the Chen Mul Modeled Type. *Ceramic complex*: Tases, A.D. 1300–1450. *Quantity*: these censers in all sizes first occur at the Hocaba-Tases levels where they total 9,936 sherds or 28.7 per cent of Mayapan Unslipped Ware of the Hocaba-Tases lots. In the Tases Ceramic Complex, however, 128,118 sherds form 77.2 per cent of the Mayapan Unslipped Ware in that complex, showing the tremendous increase in the use of these censers. *Provenience*: Aguada Grande, Calderitas, Cancun, Chetumal Bay, Chiquila, Cozumel, Ichpaatun, Isla Mujeres, Las Grecas, Palma Playa, and Tulum in Quintana Roo; Chichen Itza, Mani, and Mayapan in Yucatan. *Illustrations*: 32, e–kk; 67; 68, b; 69–73; GWB, figs. 27, a, b; 93, i–o; 98; 99, b–d; 100, b; 101, b, c; Gann, 1918, fig. 67, pl. 20; Lothrop, 1924, figs. 29, c; 30, b, c, g, k–m, o, p; pls. 9, g–l; 10, a–d, g, h, l, m; WTS, figs. 8, a, 1–9, 11, b, 3–8, 10–29, 32, 33, e; 16; 18, a–c. *Remarks*: large, medium, and small effigy censers are found. The large size is predominant.

Censer, hourglass. Essentially this is a flaring-side bowl with pedestal base and no handles. It may have thickened, T-shape, everted bolster or direct rim, often has appliqué spikes and/or fillets, and a white calcareous coat on exterior. The color is usually brown and the temper potsherd. *Ware*: Puuc Unslipped. *Ceramic complex*: Cehpech, A.D. 800–1000. *Quantity*: 246 sherds at Uxmal, 11 sherds at Kabah, and 4 sherds at Mayapan. *Provenience*: Chichen Itza, Holactun, Kabah, Mayapan, Oxkintok, Sayil, and Uxmal in Yucatan. *Illustrations*: 3, a–k; GWB, figs. 39, a–c, d, 4–9, 12, e, 16, 19, f, 9, 10, j, 7, k, 9, 11; 69, b; 104, b. *Remarks*: an early example of this form is illustrated from Uaxactun (RES, fig. 17, b, 8). A Late Classic Period or Regional-Florescent-stage transition specimen according to Brainerd (1958, fig. 19, c) has horizontal handles in addition to normal Cehpech Ceramic Complex features. Then there are Early Mexican substage specimens (*ibid.*, figs. 69, c and 70, a) from Chichen Itza which have two vertical strap handles. From a still later context Berlin (1956, fig. 6, u) illustrates a censer consisting of a modeled figure attached to an hourglass

vessel. This effigy censer is of Fine Orange Ware of the Cunduacan Group which belongs to the Chikinchel Ceramic Complex.

Censer jar with pedestal base. This form has a high flaring or outcurving neck, usually a direct rim, globular body, and high flaring or outcurving pedestal base. It may be embellished with appliqué spikes, buttons, and impressed fillets. A very few have a horizontal lateral flange. *Ware*: Mayapan Unslipped. *Ceramic complexes*: Hocaba, Hocaba-Tases, and Tases, A.D. 1200–1450. *Quantity*: 46 sherds in Hocaba, 1,690 sherds in Hocaba-Tases, and 714 sherds in Tases. *Provenience*: Chichen Itza and Mayapan in Yucatan; Calderitas and Tulum in Quintana Roo. *Illustrations*: 31, a–c; GWB, fig. 97, a; WTS, fig. 8, b, 31, d, 1.

Censer jar, tripod. This form has a medium-high flaring neck, normally a direct rim, globular body, convex base, and hollow oven-shape feet, rarely solid oven or hollow cylindrical with rounded bottom. The exterior usually has a white calcareous coat and may be painted and decorated with appliqué fillets and buttons. *Ware*: Mayapan Unslipped. *Ceramic complex*: Hocaba, continuing into Tases, A.D. 1200–1450. *Quantity*: 63 sherds in Hocaba, 1,300 sherds in Hocaba-Tases, and 1,765 sherds in Tases. *Provenience*: Mayapan. *Illustrations*: 31, e; 62, e.

Censer jar, tripod, ladle handle. This form, called the "Mixtec type" by Wauchope (1948, pp. 148–150), is a tripod flaring-neck jar with one elongated foot serving as a handle. The bodies are perforated to represent rather complicated geometric designs. *Ware*: not named, but the type is Tinum Red-on-cinnamon. *Ceramic complex*: Sotuta, A.D. 1000–1200. *Quantity*: 53 sherds at Chichen Itza and 15 sherds at Mayapan. *Provenience*: Chipal, Patal, Zacapa, Zacualpa, and Zaculeu in Guatemala; Copan in Honduras; Chichen Itza, Isla de Sacrificios, Mayapan, Mitla, and Oaxaca in Mexico. *Illustrations*: 11, h, w, y; 27, d, e; GWB, fig. 97, h–j; Butler, 1940, fig. 24, k; Dieseldorff, 1933, figs. 66, 68, 70; Galindo y Villa, 1905, pl. 18; Joyce, 1914, pl. 18, 6; Longyear, 1952, fig. 102, k; C. Seler, 1900, p. 325; E. Seler, 1904, fig. 84; Spinden, 1928, pl. 28; Wauchope, 1948, figs. 66; 67, h; Woodbury and Trik, 1953, figs. 79; 80; 246, m, o.

Censer, ladle. This form appears to change little from its beginnings in the Cehpech Ceramic Complex through the Tases Ceramic Complex. The principal changes from early to late are two: vessel wall thickness and size of bowl-handle aperture. The earlier ladle censers have thinner walls and smaller bowl-handle apertures. Brainerd suggests that the ladle censer had a very insignificant usage in Cehpech. He emphasizes its presence during the Sotuta or Early Mexican substage but remarks (1958, fig. 68, caption), "They are also probably absent in the Late Mexican substage in Yucatan." This leaves Sotuta and Hocaba (his Middle Mexican substage) as the time of ladle censer ascendancy in Yucatan. Actually this closely approximates our findings, except that ladle censers are quite well represented in Tases. *Wares*: Chichen Slate (Balam Canche Red-on-slate Type), Chichen Unslipped, Fine Orange of Cunduacan Group, Mayapan Red, Mayapan Unslipped, and Puuc Unslipped. *Ceramic complexes*: Cehpech, Sotuta, Hocaba, Hocaba-Tases, and Tases, A.D. 800–1450. *Quantity*: percentages of all sherds found in a particular ceramic complex such as at Uxmal in Cehpech, .15 (50 Puuc Unslipped Ware sherds); at Chichen Itza in Sotuta, 1 (173 Chichen Unslipped Ware sherds and 11 Chichen Slate Ware sherds of Balam Canche Red-on-slate Type); at Mayapan in Hocaba, .45 (110 Mayapan Unslipped Ware sherds), in Hocaba-Tases, 1.65 (1,400 Mayapan Unslipped Ware sherds and 28 Mayapan Red Ware sherds), and in Tases, .75 (2,096 Mayapan Unslipped Ware sherds). *Provenience*: Chichen Itza, Labna, Mayapan, Sayil, and Uxmal in Yucatan; Chiquila, Ichpaatun, Km. 14, Tancah, Tulum, and Yuukluuk in Quintana Roo, Juarez in Tabasco, and Tula in Hidalgo. *Illustrations*: 3, *n, o*; 12, *h, j*; 17, *g*; 33, *a–e*; 37, *h*; 63, *g–i*; 75, *b*; Acosta, 1945, fig. 20, *q*; Berlin, 1956, fig. 6, *o*; GWB, figs. 23, *b, 1–3, f*; 39, *d, 1, f, 1, g, 1, h, 7*; 68, *f*; 75, *e*; 104, *c, 4, 5*; WTS, figs. 8, *c*; 17, *o–s*. *Remarks*: the matter of thickness being a late trait does not appear to agree with the illustrations from the Quintana Roo survey (WTS, fig. 8, *c*). The three thinnest are from Ichpaatun, Tulum, and Yuukluuk (*ibid.*, fig. 8, *c, 3, 4, 8*), all single period late sites. Although the thicker specimens are from sites with earlier complexes, they may be associated with an accumulation of late material. Not only is the ladle censer well represented in the Tases Ceramic Complex, it was even found present in the Chikinchel by Berlin (1956, fig. 6, *o*) with his U Fine Orange (Cunduacan Group) specimen from Juarez. Another late characteristic not always present is a rough, rasplike, exterior surface finish found in the Hocaba through Tases ceramic complexes.

Comal. See under **Plate, comal-like.**

Cover. The cover is an extremely rare item in these collections. In fact it is rare in Yucatan. Among those encountered, however, are three main forms: disk, scutate, and pyramidal. The disk-shape cover may be separated into those carefully fashioned often with beveled rim, sometimes augmented by a handle, or rarely supporting a flange, and those made from reused potsherds. The well-made disk type may rest on a ledge (GWB, fig. 3, *b*), whereas those with a flange (*ibid.*, fig. 40, *c, 10, 11*) rest on the vessel top, the flange fitting inside to prevent the cover from sliding off. The scutate cover is formed like a shield and usually has a handle (37, *f*). The pyramidal cover likewise has a handle (GWB, figs. 70, *f*, and 75, *d*). *Wares*: Puuc Slate, Puuc Unslipped, Thin Slate, Chichen Slate, Mayapan Black, Mayapan Red, Mayapan Unslipped, and San Joaquin Buff. *Ceramic complexes*: Cehpech, Sotuta, Hocaba-Tases, and Tases. *Quantity*: Uxmal, 2 reused sherd disks and 1 disk with grooved rim; Chichen Itza, 2 disks with beveled rim; Mayapan from Hocaba-Tases Ceramic Complex, 8 well-made disks of which one has a handle, 2 reused sherd disks, and 23 scutate covers, most with handles; Mayapan from Tases Ceramic Complex, 13 well-made disks of which 10 have handles and most have beveled edge, 10 reused sherd disks, and 2 scutate covers, one of which has a handle. *Provenience*: Chichen Itza, Kabah, Maxcanu, Mayapan, Sabacche, Sayil, and Uxmal. *Illustrations*: 2, *r*; 5, *hh*; 7, *bb*; 13, *o*; 29, *ii, jj*; 37, *f, g*; 44, *d*; 49, *g*; 74, *w, x*; 75, *a*; GWB, figs. 23, *b, 6*; 40, *c, 10, 11, d, 26, 27, 64*; 41, *a, 1, b, 19, 60, c*; 42, *g, 1–6, 8*; 53, *b, 17, 19, 20, 29*; 70, *f*; 75, *d*; 92, *c, l*; 97, *1, 8, 9*.

Cup. This vessel form is small; it may have cylindrical, pear-shape, or barrel-shape walls, tripod, pedestal, or flat base. It may be undecorated (398 sherds) or decorated in various ways including modeled (57 sherds), painted (50 sherds), and appliqué (33 sherds); unslipped (497 sherds) or slipped (41 sherds). From a very weak beginning this form grew more and more popular, as witnessed through the associated ceramic complexes: Hocaba, 6 examples (1.1 per cent of all cups encountered); Hocaba-Tases or middle lots, 100 examples (18.4 per cent), and Tases, 432 examples (80.5 per cent).

Cup, flat base. This form is rare and forms only 1.5 per cent of all cups found at Mayapan. *Ware*: Mayapan Unslipped. *Ceramic complexes*: Hocaba-Tases and Tases, A.D. 1300–1450. *Provenience*: Mayapan. *Illustrations*: 31, *hh*; 63, *j*. *Remarks*:

7 are effigy cups.

Cup, pedestal base. This form is well represented forming 20 per cent of all cups found at Mayapan. *Wares*: Fine Orange of the fine-orange Cunduacan Group, Mayapan Red, and Mayapan Unslipped. *Ceramic complexes*: Hocaba, Hocaba-Tases, Tases, and Chikinchel, A.D. 1200–1500. *Provenience*: Atasta and Mayapan. *Illustrations*: 30, v–bb; 45, d; 61, e, 4, 5; 63, a, b; Berlin, 1956, fig. 11, e. *Remarks*: 29 are effigy.

Cup, tripod. This is the most abundant cup form, totaling 78.5 per cent of all cups found at Mayapan. *Wares*: Mayapan Red and Mayapan Unslipped. *Ceramic complexes*: Hocaba (a single specimen), Hocaba-Tases, and Tases, A.D. 1200–1450. *Provenience*: Chichen Itza and Mayapan in Yucatan; Nohmul and Santa Rita in British Honduras; and Tancah in Quintana Roo. *Illustrations*: 31, cc–ff; 61, e, 1–3; 63, e–h; GWB, figs. 93, s; 100, g; Gann, 1918, pl. 11; T. and M. Gann, 1939, pl. 6, 2; WTS, figs. 8, b, 30; 15, h. *Remarks*: 21 from Mayapan are effigy.

Dish, flaring side, flat base, flat bolster rim. This form is not well represented but is distinctive. Found only in Mayapan Unslipped Ware, it decreases in percentage as it progresses chronologically. *Ware*: Mayapan Unslipped. *Ceramic complexes*: Hocaba, 55 sherds (1.1 per cent); Hocaba-Tases, 147 sherds (.42 per cent), and Tases, 123 sherds (.09 per cent). *Provenience*: Mayapan. *Illustrations*: 29, dd; 61, c, 2; GWB, fig. 22, e, 1.

Dish, flaring side, tripod. This form with flat or slightly convex base, usually supported by solid conical feet, is well represented in various ceramic complexes. It also includes dishes, sometimes bowls, with outcurving sides, and other foot forms such as solid slab, hollow oven, and hollow cylindrical in Cehpech or hollow oven, hollow cylindrical, and hollow effigy in the later complexes. *Wares*: Mayapan Black, Mayapan Red, Mayapan Unslipped, Puuc Red, Puuc Slate, Thin Slate. *Ceramic complexes*: Cehpech, Hocaba, Hocaba-Tases, and Tases. *Quantity*: this form has the following percentages as compared with all sherds in their respective ceramic complexes: 12.3 (4,928 Puuc Slate Ware, 489 Puuc Red Ware, and 330 Thin Slate Ware) in Cehpech at Uxmal and Kabah; 4.1 (995 Mayapan Red Ware) in Hocaba at Mayapan; 9.4 (8,035 Mayapan Red Ware, 60 Mayapan Unslipped Ware, and 19 Mayapan Black Ware) in Hocaba-Tases at Mayapan, and 6.6 (18,276 Maya-

pan Red Ware, 205 Mayapan Unslipped Ware, and 42 Mayapan Black Ware) in Tases at Mayapan. *Provenience*: Acanceh, Chichen Itza, Coba, Dzan, Dzebtun, Dzibalchen, Dzibilchaltun, Holactun, Kabah, Labna, Mani, Mayapan, Oxkintok, Sayil, Tabi, Uxmal, and Yaxuna in Yucatan; El Diez, San Miguel, and Tancah in Quintana Roo for Cehpech forms; Chichen Itza and Mayapan for Hocaba through Tases forms. *Illustrations*: 6, a–k, m; 7, o, r, s, u, y; 8, j–l, s, t; 26, b, 11–19; 29, r–aa; 40, a, b; 74, m–o; GWB, figs. 10, g; 15, a; 18, k, 13–18; 21, c; 32, h; 35, i–m; 45, a–e, 1–15, f, g; 46, a–e, 3–8, f, 1–20; 47, a–i; 48, a; 52, j, 5, m, 1–8; 58, d; 62, e–f, k, m, p–r; 67, a, d–g, 1.

Dish, flaring side, tripod with basal-Z-angle. This form usually has a flat base which on occasion may be slightly convex. Some have outcurving sides and all have hollow feet, in most cases cylindrical with either flat or rounded bottom. *Wares*: Puuc Red, Puuc Slate, and Thin Slate. *Ceramic complex*: Cehpech. *Quantity*: 208 sherds in all with 152 of Puuc Slate Ware, 54 of Puuc Red Ware, and 2 of Thin Slate Ware combining to form .4 per cent of all sherds from Uxmal and Kabah in the Cehpech Ceramic Complex. *Provenience*: Acanceh, Chichen Itza, Holactun, Kabah, Labna, Mayapan, Sayil, Temax, and Uxmal in Yucatan; and Ichpaatun in Quintana Roo. *Illustrations*: 6, o–q; 7, w; 26, e, 2; GWB, figs. 18, k, 11; 45, e, 22, 25–30, h, 5; 46, c, 26, 29–31, d, 8, 12–14, e, 1, 2, 10, 11, f, 22; 52, i, j, 3, 4, k, l, 1, 2, 6–8, 10, 13, 16; 58, c; 62, n; 67, g, 15, 22; WTS, fig. 4, c, 16. *Remarks*: this form has an early history in the Maya area dating back to the Protoclassic Period in the Peten and British Honduras. It continued in the Early Classic Period, but dwindled in popularity in the Late Classic Period and in Tepeu 3.

Dish, outcurving side, tripod with basal flange. Some are bowls and these have a convex rather than slightly convex or rarely flat base. This form is usually supported by hollow feet either oven or cylindrical. The base convexity is apt to be more pronounced in the later complexes, especially in connection with Tulum Red Ware specimens. *Wares*: Mayapan Red, Puuc Red, Puuc Slate, and Tulum Red. *Ceramic complexes*: Cehpech, Hocaba, Hocaba-Tases, Tases. *Quantity*: this form has the following percentages as compared with all sherds in their respective ceramic complexes: .2 (69 Puuc Slate Ware, 40 Puuc Red Ware, and 4 Thin Slate Ware) in Cehpech at Uxmal and Kabah; .04 (9 Mayapan Red Ware) in Hocaba at Mayapan; .02 (21 Mayapan Red Ware) in Hocaba-Tases at

Mayapan, and .008 (23 Mayapan Red Ware) in Tases at Mayapan. *Provenience*: Chichen Itza, Kabah, Labna, Mayapan, Sayil and Uxmal in Yucatan and Ichpaatun and Tulum in Quintana Roo. *Illustrations*: 6, *l*, *r–t*, *v*, *w*; 7, *x*; 8, *p–r*; 26, *b*, 21, 22; 40, *c*, *1–10*; GWB, figs. 45, *e*, *17–19*; *i*, *3*; 46, *c*, *32*, *34*, *d*, *15*, *f*, *21*, *23*, *24*; 52, *m*, *14*; 58, *a*, *b*; 67, *g*, *2*, *6*, *8*, *9*; 95, *l*; WTS, fig. 4, *c*, *1–15*, *17–27*. *Remarks*: the basal-flange tripod dish appears in the Maya area late in the Early Classic Period but continues on through the Late Classic with more strength than the tripod basal-Z-angle dish. It dwindles in popularity during the Tepeu 3 and Cehpech ceramic complexes, however, and does not reappear until the Middle and Late Postclassic periods and then only sparingly.

Dish, outcurving side, tripod with hollow bell-shape feet. Occasionally this form may have flaring sides. *Ware*: Fine Orange of the Silho Group. *Ceramic complex*: Sotuta. *Quantity*: 16 sherds at Chichen Itza and 7 sherds at Mayapan. *Provenience*: Chichen Itza and Mayapan. *Illustrations*: 22, *r–u*; GWB, fig. 81, *a*, *j*.

Dish, outcurving side, tripod with convex base. The feet may be bulbous or oven-shape. The sides are sometimes recurving, always rounding to base. *Wares*: Chichen Slate and Peto Cream. *Ceramic Complexes*: Sotuta and Hocaba. *Quantity*: this form has the following percentages to all sherds in their respective ceramic complexes including 1 (184 Chichen Slate Ware) in Sotuta at Chichen Itza and .3 (79 Peto Cream Ware) in Hocaba at Mayapan. *Provenience*: Acanceh, Chichen Itza, and Mayapan in Yucatan. *Illustrations*: 19, *a–e*; 51, *u*; 52, *v–x*; GWB, figs. 20, *b*, *32*; 24, *a*, *1*, *11–13*.

Dish, rounded side, flat base. Infrequently this form has plate dimensions, frequently the base is concave, and sometimes the sides may be flaring but rounding to base. The dish is slipped and polished all over including the base. It is more abundant in Chichen Red Ware, 45.1 per cent, than in Chichen Slate Ware, 14.8 per cent. *Wares*: Chichen Red and Chichen Slate. *Ceramic complex*: Sotuta, A.D. 1000–1200. *Provenience*: Chichen Itza and Mayapan in Yucatan, and Tula in Hidalgo. *Illustrations*: 13, *a–f*; 21, *n–r*; GWB, figs. 74, *a*, *c*, *d*; 88, *a*; Acosta, fig. 20, *a*, *i*, *k*.

Dish, rounded side, tripod. Usually this form is supported by hollow oven-shape feet, but other feet such as solid conical, solid oven, or solid cylindrical are used on occasion. *Wares*: Mayapan

Black, Mayapan Red, Mayapan Unslipped, and Peto Cream. *Ceramic complexes*: Hocaba, Hocaba-Tases, and Tases. *Quantity*: this form comprises the following percentages of all sherds in their respective ceramic complexes at Mayapan: 2.1 (431 Mayapan Red Ware, 85 Peto Cream Ware, and 1 Mayapan Unslipped Ware) in Hocaba; 1 (813 Mayapan Red Ware, 63 Peto Cream Ware, 16 Mayapan Black Ware, and 4 Mayapan Unslipped Ware) in Hocaba-Tases, and .5 (1,437 Mayapan Red Ware, 46 Mayapan Unslipped Ware, and 6 Mayapan Black Ware) in Tases. *Provenience*: Chichen Itza and Mayapan. *Illustrations*: 29, *x*; 33, *i*; 41, *b*; 51, *q*; 52, *o–r*; GWB, figs. 26, *c*, *22*, *34*; 92, *m*; 94, *h*, *30*, *31*; 95, *i*; 96, *e*, *n*.

Drum. This musical instrument has many forms, has been identified from the Classic Period to conquest times in Mesoamerica, and occurs over a widespread area. Tepeu 1 examples from Uaxactun are discussed and illustrated by Smith, 1955a, p. 100, fig. 41, *b*. Somewhat later (Tepeu 2 and San José IV–V) specimens are portrayed by Satterthwaite (1938, pp. 416–428, fig. 1, *a*), Smith and Kidder (1951, p. 72, fig. 83, *d*), and Thompson (1939, p. 153, fig. 91, *i*; pl. 22, *b*, 2). The Thompson drums are said to have vertical handles. In my opinion instead of a vertical handle they are joined by a second drum which is attached near the lip of the base and the center of the upper section. A possible example (from Tabasco) of this double drum is illustrated by Rickards (1910, p. 78, bottom photograph, top of the stand). However, the main preoccupation here is with the Yucatan ceramic complexes principally associated with Mayapan, and these are Cehpech, Sotuta, Hocaba, Hocaba-Tases (middle lots) and Tases.

Cehpech. The drum form encountered in this ceramic complex may be similar to that of one of the two drum forms linked with the Classic Period (RES, fig. 41, *b*, 1). No complete drums were found. The closest examples are two illustrated by Brainerd (1958, fig. 62, *i*, *j*). *Ware*: Puuc Slate. *Types*: Muna Slate, Tekit Incised, and Akil Impressed. *Quantity*: at Uxmal-Kabah 213 possible drum sherds occurred, forming 1.03 per cent of the associated Puuc Slate Ware. *Provenience*: Chichen Itza, Kabah, Labna, Mayapan, Sayil, and Uxmal. *Illustrations*: 5, *k*, *l*, *n*, *r–t*; 14, *o*, *p*; 27, *c*; GWB, figs. 37, *c*, *1–7*, *20*; 39, *e*, *7–14*, *f*, *7*, *g*, *2*, *3*; 40, *d*, *25*, *e*, *2*, *20*; 41, *b*, *16–18*, *53*; 42, *f*, *10–12*, *g*, *7*; 62, *i*, *j*; 72, *k*, *4–20*.

Sotuta. A number of examples were found very closely resembling those encountered in the Cehpech Ceramic Complex. The only differences included thinner walls, a brownish slip color, and ash temper for those associated with the Sotuta Ceramic Complex as opposed to mostly thick walls, beige, buff or drab slip color, and sherd temper for those linked with the Cehpech Ceramic Complex. *Ware*: probably Puuc Slate. *Quantity*: 3 Puuc Slate Ware sherds from Chichen Itza; 28 sherds from Mayapan. *Provenience*: Chichen Itza and Mayapan. *Illustrations*: 14, *o, p*; 27, *c*; GWB, fig. 72, *k, 4–20*. *Remarks*: the differences between the Cehpech and Sotuta specimens may be due to manufacture in a different center (Chichen Itza) rather than at a different time. The same slip color difference is found in Thin Slate Ware examples from the Puuc sites as compared to those from Chichen Itza. The latter are brownish compared to a pearl gray or gray for those from the Puuc. Brainerd (1958, fig. 72, caption) states "... *k, 4–20*: Belong with the Puuc and Chenes fragments which are probably rims of drums, cf. figs. 37, *c*; 39, *e, 10–14*; 62, *i; j*. The thinness and somewhat different form and slip color of these specimens suggest that this style of drum may have lasted into Early Mexican times." Another form of drum which may belong to the Sotuta Ceramic Complex is illustrated by Smith (1957b, fig. 17, *g, i*) from the Marquez Collection in Merida. The two specimens are of Fine Orange Ware, possibly of the fine-orange Silho Group.

Hocaba, Hocaba-Tases, and Tases. The drums associated with these ceramic complexes may be of two forms: one as suggested in the reconstruction (39, *a*) and possibly another more like the Cehpech high-neck, pear-shape body form. *Ware*: Mayapan Red. *Type*: Papacal Incised. *Quantity*: at Mayapan a total of 193 possible drum sherds were found: 7 or .05 per cent in Hocaba; 64 or .16 per cent in Hocaba-Tases, and 122 or .15 per cent in Tases. *Provenience*: Mayapan. *Illustrations*: 39, *a–o*; 74, *f, g*; GWB, fig. 25, *a*.

Effigy vessel. This category includes many forms: namely, cups, cylindrical vases, jars, pyriform vases, and curiously shaped vessels. Only the latter are considered here; the others are discussed under their particular form names. At Mayapan a total of 700 effigy vessels were found. The curiously shaped forms are all of Mayapan Unslipped Ware, Chen Mul Modeled Type. *Ceramic complexes*: Hocaba-Tases and Tases, A.D. 1300–1450. *Quantity*: a total of 496 sherds or vessels embracing a variety of effigies: 313 animals (toads, turtles, jaguars, and rabbits), 74 altars or platforms, 60 birds, 24 diving gods, 17 warriors, and 8 humans. *Provenience*: Ak 1 and Bacalar in Quintana Roo; Chichen Itza

and Mayapan in Yucatan; Juarez in Tabasco; and Progreso and Santa Rita in British Honduras: *Illustrations*: 32, *ll–pp*; 64; Berlin, 1956, figs. 6, *ii*; 12, *a, c*; GWB, figs. 93, *e*; 96, *b*; Gann, 1900, pl. 35; Gann, 1918, figs. 18, 51; pls. 21, 22, and WTS, fig. 8, *a*, 10.

Figurine. This form may be extremely valuable as a mode (consult Table 36 and figurines in Chapter V), because the method of manufacture and the style undergo not only a temporal change, but frequently an areal one as well. Therefore, figurines are excellent time and region markers and they reveal a variety of functions, since they may be toys, idols, or musical instruments. These last are included, if of the effigy type, because of the difficulty of distinguishing ordinary figurines from whistle or rattle figurines when dealing with fragments. Figurines are associated with a number of early ceramic complexes both Preclassic and Classic, but here we are interested in those beginning with the Cehpech and ending with the Tases.

Cehpech. In this ceramic complex, although not abundant, figurines are found in various wares and forms. *Wares*: Puuc Red, Puuc Slate, and Puuc Unslipped, also possibly Fine Orange of the fine-orange Balancan Group. *Quantity*: Yiba Modeled Type, including 9 with articulated limbs, 9 bodies, 2 whistle mouthpieces, and 1 moldmade head, totaled 18 from Uxmal and 3 from Kabah. Sitpatch Modeled Type, 1 monkey whistle from Mayapan. Fine-orange Balancan Group a possible modeled seated figurine fragment from Mayapan. *Provenience*: Holactun, Kabah, Mayapan, Sayil, Uxmal, and Yaxuna in Yucatan. *Illustrations*: 3, *z, aa*; 26, *c, 3*; 56, *b, 1*; GWB, figs. 54, *f, g, k, l, t, u, cc–mm*; 55, *h, p, q, t–y, aa, bb, dd*.

Sotuta. No figurines identified in this ceramic complex.

Hocaba. In this ceramic complex a few figurine sherds were found. *Ware*: Mayapan Unslipped Ware, Hoal Modeled Type. *Quantity*: 3 including 1 head and 2 body sherds, totaling .01 per cent of all Hocaba sherds. *Provenience*: Mayapan. *Illustration*: none.

Hocaba-Tases. In this middle lot collection the figurine develops and becomes somewhat more important, totaling 164 or .19 per cent of all sherds in the lot. *Wares*: Mayapan coarse, Mayapan Red, and Mayapan Unslipped. *Quantity*: Chen Mul Modeled Type, including 115 hollow moldmade of which 1 has articulated limbs, 26 hollow modeled of which 7 have articulated limbs, and 11 solid moldmade, totaled 152. Chapab Modeled

Type, including 4 solid modeled articulated limbs, 2 hollow modeled bird whistles, and 2 moldmade of which one is hollow and the other has articulated limbs, totaled 8. Uayma Modeled Type, consisted of 4 hollow modeled specimens. *Provenience*: Mayapan. *Illustrations*: 35, *a*, 4–6, 8–11, 13, 14, 16–18; *b*, 1, 2, 4–9; *c*, 1, 2; 37, *e*; 65, *a–d*, *f–i*, *p*.

Tases. In this late Mayapan ceramic complex the figurine has decreased in abundance from its peak in the middle lots. At this time it totaled 194 or .07 per cent of all sherds found in Tases. *Wares*: Mayapan Black, Mayapan Coarse, Mayapan Red, and Mayapan Unslipped. *Quantity*: Chen Mul Modeled Type, including 98 hollow moldmade, 73 hollow modeled and 12 solid of which 8 are modeled, 3 moldmade, and 1 with articulated limbs, totaled 183. Uayma Modeled Type, both hollow and solid, had 6 modeled examples. Chapab Modeled Type, including 3 hollow moldmade and 1 solid modeled specimen, totaled 4. Sacmuyna Modeled Type had 1 modeled bird head. *Provenience*: Chichen Itza and Mayapan. *Illustrations*: 35, *a*, 1–3, 7, 12, 15, *b*, 3, *c*, 3; 37, *d*; 45, *i* (possibly); 65, *e*, *j–m*, *o*; 66, *c*; GWB, figs. 29, *b*; 90, *p–r*; 93, *d*, *r*, *u*, *v*, *z–cc*; 95, *d*.

Flute. This may be described as a tubular wind instrument of small diameter with holes along the tube. Actually in this context the term flute includes the flageolet, oboe, piccolo, and pan-pipes, as well as the flute. A number of examples are of the multiple-mouth type with three mouth openings or slits besides a number of stops along the tubes. Most, if not all the examples noted, are effigy flutes. *Wares*: Puuc Slate and Puuc Unslipped. *Ceramic complex*: Cehpech, A.D. 800–1000. *Quantity*: Kabah, 2 Yiba Modeled Type sherds; Mayapan, 1 Yiba Modeled Type and 1 Yaxnic Modeled Type; Uxmal, 10 Yiba Modeled Type fragments and 1 Yaxnic Modeled Type example. *Provenience*: Dzibilchaltun, Holactun, Kabah, Labna, Mayapan, Sayil, and Uxmal in Yucatan. *Illustrations*: 3, *x*, *y*, *bb*; 6, *ll*; 26, *c*, 1, 2, 4; 66, *b*, 1, 2; GWB, figs. 54, *a–e*, *h*, *i*, *m–s*; 55, *b–g*, *i*, *k–o*, *r*, *s*, *z*; 56, *h–n*, *p*. *Remarks*: in determining whether or not the example in 6, *ll* belongs to a flute, compare it to the specimen illustrated by Brainerd (1958, fig. 56, *m*, *n*). Marti (1955, pp. 79–141) illustrates many interesting flute types. For further information on the flute consult Table 36 and Chapter XIII, the Cehpech Ceramic Complex.

Jar. This vessel has a globular or pear-shape body with a neck rising somewhat abruptly from the upper part of the body or shoulder. All these jars, save the cooking jar, have a sharply formed base (flat, concave, rarely convex). Cooking jars may have rounded bottoms, often missing because they have disintegrated through constant burning. Water jars and some storage jars have handles. Slipped jars are nearly always unslipped on the interior, thus making possible the identification of most curvate sherds. Seldom do restricted-orifice bowls with globular body lack interior slip.

This vessel form is perhaps the most important in our present study, both quantitatively and usefully. The jar is responsible for 41 per cent of all sherds found at Mayapan from the Cehpech through the Chauaca ceramic complexes. From a utilitarian viewpoint there are three principal usages for the jar: water carrying, 40.7 per cent; storage, 30 per cent, and cooking, 28.9 per cent. A fourth category combines the special jar forms and totals .4 per cent. It must be noted, however, that certain of these forms assuredly served more than one purpose, just as forms other than jars were used for both cooking and storage.

In selecting jars with modal qualifications, those easily identifiable have been chosen. These will be studied in alphabetical order.

Jar, bulging neck, tripod. This form has a high neck (with a bulge located just above neck-body junction or midway between this junction point and the lip), direct rim, globular body, flat base, and three cylindrical feet with rounded bottoms. *Wares*: Fine Orange of the Matillas Group, Mayapan Red, and San Joaquin Buff. *Ceramic complexes*: Hocaba-Tases and Tases, A.D. 1300–1450. *Quantity*: 64 Tzitz Red Type, 43 Tecoh Red-on-buff Type, and 11 Matillas Orange Type totaling 12 Hocaba-Tases and 106 Tases sherds. *Provenience*: Mayapan. *Illustrations*: 38, *d*, 4–7; 42, *c*; 53, *a*, 19, 22; 55, *a*, 3; GWB, fig. 23, *a*, *14*, *15*. *Remarks*: a Peto Cream Ware (thin specimen), Kukula Cream Type appears to have a bulging neck (51, *e*). No specific function is attributed to these jars.

Jar, "Chultun." Brainerd (1958, figs. 42, *c*, *d*; 105, *g*, *h*, captions) calls these "chultun jars." They embrace two typical Cehpech Ceramic Complex forms: the Puuc Slate Ware high thick vertical neck jar with barrel-shape body and two vertical handles connecting the neck to the shoulder (*ibid.*, figs. 40, *a*; 42, *c*, *d*; 105, *g*); and the Cauich Coarse-cream Ware jar which is much the same except for its rim which may be thickened or T-shape (*ibid.*, figs. 40, *g*; 53, *a*, *12–20*; 105, *h*).

Wares: Cauich Coarse-cream and Puuc Slate. *Ceramic complex*: Cehpech, A.D. 800–1000. *Quantity*: no count of these two exact forms was made but several hundred are involved in the Mayapan collection. At Uxmal and Kabah combined, the totals came to 2,692 or 13.1 per cent of Puuc Slate Ware sherds and 802 or 35.4 per cent of Cauich Coarse-cream Ware sherds. *Provenience*: Acanceh, Chanpuuc, Chichen Itza, Holactun, Kabah, Labna, Mani, Mayapan, Oxkintok, Sabacche, Sayil, Uxmal, Xul, and Yaxuna, all from Yucatan. *Illustrations*: 5, *a–h, x–bb*; 10, *d, h, j*; 26, *b, 3*; GWB, figs. 10, *a, 20–23*; 15, *j, 1–3, p, 10*; 21, *a, 12–18*; 32, *b, 16–21*; 40, *a–d, e, 15–29, f, g*; 41, *a, 8–16, 32–34, b, 20–29, 43–52, 64*; 42, *b, 17–19, c, d, e, 20–25, f, 4–8*; 53, *a, 12–20*; 66, *c*; 72, *i*; 105, *g, h*. *Remarks*: the term "chultun jar" used for these vessels by Brainerd (1958, fig. 105, *g, h*) is apropos because they are shaped like a chultun and because they were probably used to ladle water out of chultuns.

Jar, corrugated neck. This jar is of two forms: those with medium-high nearly vertical necks (14, *l*); and those with low nearly vertical (14, *k*) or bolster-grooved (14, *n*) necks. All have horizontal neck-grooving, presumably two horizontal strap handles, and flat or slightly concave base. *Wares*: Chichen Slate and Peto Cream. *Ceramic complexes*: Sotuta and Hocaba, A.D. 1000–1300. *Quantity*: only 3 sherds found in the Chichen Itza cuts and none at Mayapan. Brainerd (1958, see below) illustrates considerably more than this. *Provenience*: Chichen Itza, Dzibilchaltun, and Mayapan in Yucatan. *Illustrations*: 14, *k, l, n*; 59, *i*; GWB, figs. 20, *a, 2, 3, 6*; 71, *d*; 92, *f, 11–13*; 106, *a, 1*. *Remarks*: the function of these vessels is not known.

Jar, flaring neck, tripod. These jars have a low flaring neck, direct rim, wide mouth, globular body, convex base, and three hollow, oven-shape or rounded-bottom cylindrical feet. *Wares*: Mayapan Red and San Joaquin Buff. *Ceramic complex*: Tases, A.D. 1300–1450. *Quantity*: a very few including 1 Panabchen Red Type and possibly 3 Tecoh Red-on-buff Type. *Provenience*: Mayapan. *Illustrations*: 43, *b*; 53, *a, 17*. *Remarks*: the function of this rare and specialized form is not clear.

Jar, high neck, bolster rim. Jars of this category have high to medium-high outcurving or flaring neck, wide mouth, ovoid, rounded, flat, triangular or square bolster rim, pear-shape or globular body, two horizontal strap handles, and a slightly concave base. *Wares*: Mayapan Red and San Joaquin

Buff. *Ceramic complexes*: Hocaba, Hocaba-Tases, and Tases, A.D. 1200–1450, for Mayapan Red Ware, but only Hocaba-Tases and Tases, A.D. 1300–1450, for San Joaquin Buff Ware. *Quantity*: percentage of red Mama Group jars of this category to all slipped sherds in Hocaba, 4.7; in Hocaba-Tases, 13.3, and in Tases, 20; the same for buff Polbox Group jars of this category in Hocaba-Tases, .4 and in Tases, 1.3. *Provenience*: Mayapan. *Illustrations*: 38, *a, 13–18, b, 1–5*; 53, *a, 1–10, 13*; 74, *j, l*; GWB, fig. 25, *b, d, 2–7*. *Remarks*: these most likely were storage vessels.

Jar, high neck, globular body, flat base. These high, nearly vertical neck vessels have direct, rarely a flat bolster rim, globular body, two horizontal strap handles, and a flat base. *Wares*: Mayapan Unslipped and San Joaquin Buff. *Ceramic complexes*: Hocaba-Tases and Tases, A.D. 1300–1450. *Quantity*: percentage of buff Polbox Group jars of this category to all slipped sherds in Hocaba-Tases, .24 and in Tases, .45. Only one Panaba Unslipped Type vessel occurred in the Hocaba-Tases middle lots. *Provenience*: Mayapan. *Illustrations*: 50; 61, *b*; 75, *i, j*. *Remarks*: these high-neck, medium-wide to wide-mouth vessels may be water jars.

Jar, high neck, globular body, tripod. This rather special jar form has an unusually high neck, almost equal to the globular body height. The three feet are hollow cylindrical with rounded bottoms. *Ware*: Mayapan Red, Tzitz Red Type. *Ceramic complexes*: Hocaba-Tases and Tases, A.D. 1300–1450. *Quantity*: percentage of red Panabchen Group jars of this category to all slipped sherds in Hocaba-Tases, .06 and in Tases, .65. *Provenience*: Mayapan. *Illustrations*: 42, *b*; 75, *h*. *Remarks*: this is a special type of vessel whose function is not clear.

Jar, high neck, pear-shape body, flat base. This is the principal water jar of the late period. Besides the high or medium-high nearly vertical, flaring or outcurving neck, it has a direct rim or rounded, flat, or square bolster rim, pear-shape body, two horizontal strap handles, and flat or slightly concave base. *Wares*: Mayapan Black and Mayapan Red. *Ceramic complexes*: Hocaba, Hocaba-Tases, and Tases, A.D. 1200–1450. *Quantity*: percentage of red Mama Group jars of this category to all slipped sherds in Hocaba, 50.2; in Hocaba-Tases, 43.8, and in Tases, 36.3; the same for black Sulche Group jars of this category in Hocaba, .2; in Hocaba-Tases, .6, and in Tases, .9. It is chronologically interesting to note that the red Mama Group percentages diminish, whereas those of the black Sulche Group increase. *Provenience*: Chichen Itza and Mayapan in Yucatan, and Ichpaatun and Tulum in Quintana Roo. *Illustrations*: 38, *a*, 1–12; 74, *a–d*; GWB, figs. 25, *c* and others; 94, *c*, *f*, 7–13; 96, *c*; WTS, fig. 5, *a*. *Remarks*: a special feature of these jars is the variety of colors (orange, brown, and reddish brown) that blend into the basic red of any one vessel.

Jar, huge storage. These huge size jars have high to medium-high flaring or outcurving necks, wide mouth, rounded or square bolster rim, pear-shape body, two vertical strap handles, and a convex base. Frequently the entire exterior of vessel is covered with a thick coat of plaster, hiding handles and bolster. A fair percentage (9.5) of these vessels from all complexes have red on bolster and neck interior. These are the Kanasin Red-on-unslipped Type. It is interesting to note that this type is most abundant in the Hocaba-Tases or middle lots. *Ware*: Mayapan Unslipped. *Ceramic complexes*: Hocaba, Hocaba-Tases, and Tases, A.D. 1200–1450. *Quantity*: percentage of unslipped Navula Group huge jars as compared to all unslipped sherds in Hocaba, 2; in Hocaba-Tases, 3.1, and in Tases, 2.9. The Kanasin Red-on-unslipped Type jars form a small percentage of huge jars in each complex: Hocaba, 2; Hocaba-Tases, 25.3; Tases, 6.2. *Provenience*: Mayapan. *Illustrations*: 28, *c*; 60, *l*; GWB, fig. 22, *g*, *1–10* (possibly).

Jar, low neck, wide mouth, lightly striated. This is the principal Middle and Late Mexican Period cooking vessel. It also has a flaring or vertical neck, thin globular body, flat or slightly convex base. A few have zoomorphic lug handles. *Ware*: Mayapan Unslipped. *Ceramic complexes*: Hocaba, Hocaba-Tases, and Tases, A.D. 1200–1450. *Quantity*: percentage of unslipped Navula Group jars of this category to all unslipped sherds in Hocaba, 68.6; in Hocaba-Tases, 50.5, and in Tases, 13.7. *Provenience*: Chichen Itza, Mani, and Mayapan in Yucatan, and Ichpaatun, Tulum, and Vista Alegre in Quintana Roo. *Illustrations*: 28, *a*; 61, *a*, 1–4; GWB, figs. 14, *f*, *2–9*; 22, *a*, *c*; 93, *a–c* (*c*, *15*, *17* are unknown at Mayapan); WTS, fig. 6, *e* with few exceptions. *Remarks*: there is a tendency for the Hocaba or early type to lack a shoulder angle below which later jars are striated. In the early type the striation reaches to the neck or very close to it.

Jar, low neck, wide mouth, horizontal strap handles. This jar form usually has a flaring or out-

curving, rarely vertical neck, direct or thickened and sometimes slightly triangular or flat bolster rim, globular or squat body which may have two horizontal handles, and a flat or concave base. *Ware*: Mayapan Red. *Ceramic complexes*: Hocaba, Hocaba-Tases, and Tases, A.D. 1200–1450. *Quantity*: percentage of red Mama Group jars of this category to all slipped sherds in Hocaba, 17.8; in Hocaba-Tases, 10.3 and in Tases, 7.3. *Provenience*: Mayapan. *Illustrations*: 38, *b*, 7, 11–13, 21, *c*; GWB, fig. 25, *h*, *j*, *k*, *1–4*, *9*, *11*, *r*. *Remarks*: like Mayapan Red Ware water jars, these have a variety of colors (orange, brown, and reddish brown) that blend into the basic red of any one vessel. This is a storage jar form.

Jar, medium-high neck, wide mouth, horizontal strap handles. In Chapters XV and XVI, under Mayapan Red Ware this form is combined with high-neck storage jars which usually have bolster rims, whereas this storage jar form normally has a direct rim. *Wares*: Mayapan Red and Mayapan Unslipped. *Ceramic complexes*: Hocaba, Hocaba-Tases, and Tases, A.D. 1200–1450. *Quantity*: in the red Mama Group, a somewhat lesser share of the high-neck, bolster-rim, storage jar count mentioned above. The percentage of the unslipped Navula Group jars of this category to all unslipped sherds in Hocaba, 5.4; in Hocaba-Tases, 1.5, and in Tases, 0.5. *Provenience*: Chichen Itza and Mayapan. *Illustrations*: 28, *b*; 38, *b*, 1–6, 8, 10, 14–20, 22; GWB, figs. 25 (by selection); 94, *f*, *12*. *Remarks*: this form in the red Mama Group, like the water jar, has a variety of colors (orange, brown, and reddish brown) that blend into the basic red of any one vessel. The unslipped Navula Group vessels are extremely uniform, having a medium-high slightly flaring neck, direct rim, globular or pear-shape thin body, two horizontal strap handles, and a flat base. They may be smoothed or striated.

Jar, outcurving high neck with interior striations. These storage (?) vessels have medium-wide to wide mouth, high outcurving or flaring medium-thick neck, overhanging, everted, or direct rim; a few have rim flange or rim molding, thin to medium-thick globular body, no bases associated. *Ware*: Puuc Unslipped. *Ceramic complex*: Cehpech, A.D. 800–1000. *Quantity*: percentage of Yokat Striated Type, neck-interior variety jars to all unslipped sherds in the collections from Uxmal, 6.2; from Chichen Itza, 1.7; from Kabah, .14; from Mayapan, .04. *Provenience*: Chichen Itza, Dzibilchaltun, Holactun, Kabah, Mayapan, and Uxmal. *Illustrations*: 2, a–g; GWB, figs. 14, a, 3–16; 37, a, 8–12, b, 30–36; 68, b, 1, 9, 10, 23.

Jar, outcurving high neck, narrow mouth, globular body. This vessel may occasionally have a pear-shape body. All have medium-high to high outcurving or vertical neck, direct, slightly everted or bolster rim, medium-thick body, two horizontal strap handles, and slightly concave or flat base. *Wares*: Fine Orange, of the Silho Group, Peto Cream, Chichen Red, and Chichen Slate. *Ceramic complexes*: Sotuta, Hocaba, Hocaba-Tases, and Tases. *Quantity*: percentage of slate Dzitas Group jars to all slipped sherds in the collection from Chichen Itza, 38.7; the same for the red Dzibiac Group, 8, and the fine-orange Silho Group, .9; percentage of cream Kukula Group jars to all slipped sherds from Mayapan in Hocaba, 12.9; in Hocaba-Tases, 3.8; in Tases, 1. *Provenience*: Acanceh, Chichen Itza, Mani, and Mayapan. *Illustrations*: 14, a–j; 17, a, c; 20, a–d; 22, c; 27, a, b; 52, a–c, f; 59, a, c; GWB, figs. 19, i, 13, 14, 20, 21; 20, b, 4–7; 21, a, 7–9; 24, c; 28, c, 1; 71, a, c, 1–5, 19–26; 76, a, b, 6–13; 85, a, c; 92, a, f, 1–5, 17; 106, a, 3, 8, 9, b. *Remarks*: in this form category there should be no problem in distinguishing between the different wares and types involved, since each is highly distinctive. Furthermore, there is little doubt but that they all functioned as water jars. Many, with the exception of the Fine Orange Ware specimens, were found at cenote water holes. Brainerd (1958, fig. 71, caption) suggests that this jar form "was introduced by copying from X Fine Orange jar necks, cf. fig. 76, a, b, and this chronologically links the appearance of the two types." The Peto Cream Ware examples are copies of the Chichen Slate Ware jar of this shape carrying on into the Hocaba Ceramic Complex and later.

Jar, outcurving low neck, sharp neck-body angle. This jar may have been used for cooking. It has a wide mouth, low to medium-high outcurving or flaring medium-thick to thick neck, rounded, triangular, or square bolster, pinched and thickened rim, globular body, and flat or slightly convex base. *Ware*: Puuc Unslipped. *Ceramic complex*: Cehpech, A.D. 800–1000. *Quantity*: percentage of unslipped Chum Group jars to all the sherds in the collection from Uxmal, 25.5; from Kabah, 52.7; and in the Cehpech collection from Mayapan, 40.7. *Provenience*: Acanceh, Chichen Itza, Holactun, Labna, Kabah, Mani, Mayapan, Oxkintok, Sabacche, Sayil, and Uxmal in Yucatan. *Illustrations*: 2, h–p; 26, a, 1–12; GWB, figs. 14, c, e;

37, a, b, d; 38; 65, d; 68, a, b, 15, 17–20, d, e. *Remarks*: the T-shape rim did not occur in Uxmal and Kabah collections but were found at Mayapan. These may be an early Cehpech style (26, a, 9–12; GWB, fig. 14, c includes several and 14, e shows a single example).

Jar, outcurving low neck, continuous curve. This like the Cehpech sharp neck-body junction jar was probably used for cooking. The continuous-curve jar has a medium-wide mouth, low to medium-high outcurving or nearly vertical neck, ovoid, rounded or medial rim bolsters, rarely direct or everted rims, mostly globular body and probably a flat base. *Ware*: Chichen Unslipped. *Ceramic complex*: Sotuta, A.D. 1000–1200. *Quantity*: percentage of unslipped Sisal Group jars to all the sherds in the collection from Chichen Itza, 18.9; percentage of unslipped Sisal Group jars to all the Sotuta Ceramic Complex sherds in the Mayapan collection, 13.3. *Provenience*: Chichen Itza and Mayapan. *Illustrations*: 11, b, d, f, k; GWB, figs. 22, c, 8, 16; 68, b, 1–11, 28–30. *Remarks*: the two outstanding attributes that differentiate this jar form from that immediately preceding are: the continuous-curve neck-body junction of the Sotuta jar compared to the sharp angle neck-body junction of the Cehpech jar and the Piste Striated Type with medium-deep-coarse and spaced medium-deep-coarse striation compared to the deep-coarse striation associated with the Yokat Striated Type. Those with medial rim bolster (11, e) have a special temper, a white carbonate with a fine lamellar structure (Table 43).

Jar, parenthesis rim. This kind of rim in an exaggerated form resembles the profile of a bicycle tire. The vessel has a high vertical, flaring, or bulbous neck, globular body, and probably slightly concave base. *Wares*: Abala Red, Mayapan Red, San Joaquin Buff, and Tulum Red. *Ceramic complexes*: Hocaba-Tases, Tases, and Chauaca, A.D. 1300 to present time. *Quantity*: red Panabchen Group parenthesis-rim jar percentage of all sherds in Hocaba-Tases middle lots, .4; Tases, .9. Buff Polbox Group parenthesis-rim jar percentage of all sherds in Hocaba-Tases, .2; Tases, .04. Red Payil Group parenthesis-rim jar percentage of all sherds in Hocaba-Tases, 0.4; Tases, none. Red Sacpokana Group parenthesis-rim jar percentage of all sherds in the Chauaca Ceramic Complex, 64.8. *Provenience*: Mani and Mayapan in Yucatan; Ichpaatun and Tulum in Quintana Roo. *Illustrations*: 38, d, 1–3; 48, k; 53, a, 18, 20, 21; 57, a–c; GWB, figs. 25, d, 1; 33, a, b, 19–24; 34, f, 4, 5,

26, 27; 106, *d*; WTS, 1960, fig. 5, *c*, 1–14. *Remarks*: this rim form appears to be linked only with jars. It has not been recognized earlier than the Middle Postclassic Period in Yucatan and probably in the Maya area. Its greatest center of manufacture and use was in Quintana Roo where the ware in use was Tulum Red. In most instances this was a large jar but unfortunately it customarily broke at the neck-body junction, thus leaving the exact body form in doubt. Brainerd (1958, fig. 106, *d*) gives us a reconstruction based no doubt on the modern jar form. The most likely function of this jar was to carry water, since large numbers have been recovered at or near water holes. In Cehpech there is an everted parenthesis-rim type (5, *v*, *w*) that is not closely allied to the later parenthesis-rim form.

Jar, taper neck. This rather large vessel, sometimes having three strap handles, was probably used for transporting water. The form comprised a medium-thick to thick neck which rises from a reduced neck-body angle, tapering in as it approaches the rim which is usually everted; the body tends to be more pear-shape than globular and some have two vertical strap handles. *Ware*: Puuc Slate. *Ceramic complex*: Cehpech, A.D. 800–1000. *Quantity*: Uxmal, 41 sherds or .12 per cent of all sherds in the Uxmal collection; Kabah, 3 sherds or .02 per cent of all sherds in the Kabah collection; Mayapan, at least 2 sherds present. *Provenience*: Kabah, Mani, Mayapan, Sayil, Uxmal, and Yaxuna in Yucatan. *Illustrations*: 5, *u–w*; GWB, figs. 10, *b*, 6, 9–11; 32, *a*; 36, *c*; 40, *d*, 63; 41, *a*, 35, 40, 47, *b*, 2, 3, 33, 49; 42, *e*, 8, 9, 11–16; 49, *j*, 21; 105, *f*, 2–4. *Remarks*: the taper-neck jar may owe its beginnings to Coarse Regional Redware at Yaxuna (GWB, fig. 8, *b*), Maxcanu Buff Type at Mayapan (25, *ff*, *gg*), and Oxkintok Coarse Monochrome of the Regional stage (GWB, fig. 11, *a*), all considered to belong to the Cochuah Ceramic Complex of the Early Classic Period. It is possible that some one of these types carried over into the Motul Ceramic Complex, thus establishing continuity to Cehpech.

Mask. This form has been discussed in Chapter V under techniques of modeling and molding (Table 36). The mask is a rare item in the collections under discussion. They are all moldmade and mostly represent humans, but Xipe Totec, death, a monkey, and a grotesque are also present. *Ware*: Mayapan Unslipped; Chen Mul Modeled type. *Ceramic complexes*: Hocaba-Tases, and Tases, A.D. 1300–1450. *Quantity*: 6 in Hocaba-Tases and 4 in Tases. *Provenience*: Chichen Itza and Mayapan. *Illustrations*: 34; GWB, figs. 29, *f*, 2, 3; 95, *g*. *Remarks*: the small masks, which like their larger counterparts have suspension holes, were used possibly as pendants or on small clay figures.

Miniature vessels. These comprise jars (71.5%) and bowls (26.9%). The former are mostly of the wide-mouth, low to medium-high neck, and globular body variety. The latter include deep bowls, with flat base or tripod; restricted-orifice bowls; rounded-side tripod bowls, and hemispherical bowls. Two specimens remain unidentified except for being very small. *Wares*: Mayapan Red Ware and Mayapan Unslipped. *Ceramic complexes*: Hocaba, Hocaba-Tases, and Tases. *Quantity*: Hocaba, 1 example; Hocaba-Tases, 82 specimens, and Tases, 47 specimens. *Provenience*: Chichen Itza and Mayapan. *Illustrations*: 28, *a*, 12; 33, *g*, *h*; 49; 61, *d*; GWB, fig. 93, *t*. *Remarks*: cups, which might be called miniature in many instances, are discussed earlier in this chapter. A fair number of miniature vessels occur in the Cehpech Ceramic Complex although none was encountered in these collections. Brainerd illustrates a number of examples of Puuc Slate Ware from such sites as Chichen Itza (*ibid.*, figs. 72, *i*, 1–3; 75, *a*); Sabacche (*ibid.*, fig. 40, *b*); and various collections (*ibid.*, fig. 48, *n–x*, ware not given for *n*, *x*). He also shows an unslipped Florescent jar from Chanpuuc (*ibid.*, fig. 15, *g*) and a highly polished, black-slipped miniature bottle and redware vessel with black paint from Labna (*ibid.*, fig. 103, *f* and *i*).

Mold. This form has been discussed in Chapter V and listed in Table 36. It is extremely rare. *Wares*: Fine Orange of the Silho Group and Mayapan Unslipped Ware. *Ceramic complexes*: Sotuta, Hocaba-Tases, and Tases. *Quantity*: Sotuta, a single example; Hocaba-Tases, 3 fragments, and Tases, 14 fragments. *Provenience*: Chichen Itza and Mayapan. *Illustrations*: 66, *a*; GWB, figs. 29, *d*; 98, *j*. *Remarks*: Brainerd (1958, fig. 56, *t*, *v*) illustrates two examples from Labna presumably of the Florescent stage. The mold suggests an early form of mass production. However, from the small quantity of reproduced moldmade objects (effigy censer heads excepted) many such items must have been traded.

Plate. This is a vessel with unrestricted orifice, whose height is less than one-fifth its diameter. In the dish category there are always a few that are really plates by actual measurement. Then there is the comal which is really a plate with a special function — that of a griddle used for frying tortillas. Actually few plates of any kind were encountered in these collections. An alphabetical listing follows.

Plate, comal-like. The few very low, flat-base plates found in the several different ceramic complexes may have been used for toasting tortillas, cacao beans, seeds, nuts, and so on. However, if this toasting function was of real concern to these Maya people it would seem logical for them to have manufactured more than are suggested by the very few sherds encountered. As a rule in the areas where the comal is found the accumulation is considerable. Brainerd (1958, fig. 97, *k*, caption) writes "The comal fragments shown under *k* (see also fig. 66, *g*) document only a very sparse appearance of this form in Yucatán. The Mayapan collections lack comales entirely, as do all other collections from Yucatán." *Wares*: Bolon Brown and Chichen Unslipped. *Ceramic complexes*: Sotuta and Chauaca. *Quantity*: Chichen Unslipped Ware, Sisal Unslipped Type, 6 sherds found on surface may belong to Chauaca Ceramic Complex; Bolon Brown Ware, Oxcum Brown Type, 3 sherds. *Provenience*: Chichen Itza and Mayapan. *Illustrations*: 18, *h*; 57, *f*; GWB, figs. 66, *g*; 97, *k*). *Remarks*: the comal or plate appears to have been used more on the east coast (WTS, figs. 6, *b*; 9, *c*, 46–50; 11, *d*) at Ichpaatun, Tancah, and Calderitas, both early and late, than in Yucatan.

Plate, rounded side, pedestal base. This unusual form may have had a ceremonial function. *Ware*: Mayapan Red. *Ceramic complex*: Tases, A.D. 1300–1450. *Quantity*: Panabchen Red Type, 12 sherds. *Provenience*: Mayapan. *Illustration*: 41, *d*.

Plate, rounded side, ringstand base. This form has direct rim and is shallow. *Ware*: Mayapan Unslipped. *Ceramic complexes*: Hocaba-Tases and Tases, A.D. 1300–1450. *Quantity*: Hocaba-Tases, 25 sherds; Tases, 45 sherds. *Provenience*: Mayapan. *Illustration*: 29, *gg*. *Remarks*: early examples of this form may be found at Oxkintok in Thin Monochrome Ware of Oxkintok Regional stage (GWB, fig. 12, *d*, *e*).

Potstand. This form is extremely rare. It has flaring rims both top and bottom, a bulging central area, and is open at both ends. One specimen has three sets of two circular suspension holes located at the rim. *Ware*: San Joaquin Buff. *Ceramic complex*: Tases, A.D. 1300–1450. *Quantity*: Tecoh Red-on-buff Type, 6 examples. *Provenience*: Mayapan. *Illustration*: 53, *b*, 14.

Shield for candle flame. This is perhaps the most unusual item from the Mayapan collections. On seeing a nearly complete example, the first impression is that it represents some sort of a roofing tile. On closer examination, however, it appears more tubular than a tile; possibly it is a drain or conduit section. One end is very thick and may have offsets, but against the conduit theory is the scorching and fire-blackening over all the central part interior leaving unburnt about 3.5 cm. at top and 5 cm. at bottom. The most likely theory, considering everything, is that this item is a candle-flame shield. *Ware*: Telchaquillo Brick Ware. *Ceramic complexes*: Hocaba-Tases middle lots and Tases, A.D. 1300–1450. *Quantity*: Hocaba-Tases, 7 sherds and Tases, 296 sherds. *Provenience*: Mayapan. *Illustration*: 36, *a*–*c*.

Stand. This shape might also be a platform, composed of a disk upheld by a pedestal base. Brainerd (1958, fig. 71, *e*–*i*, caption) writes "The pedestals *e*–*i* (also see fig. 72, *n*, 2–5) are so called because the term is noncommittal as to function. These are not lids; they would be difficult to use as such. Only noticeable wear is on the tops, the incised designs on which would limit their usefulness as tortilla forming tables (the making of tortillas is uncertain for pre-Conquest Yucatán). The absence of this form in the Puuc collections led us to believe it of Early Mexican age, but discovery of fragments in the Chenes area in sites free of other Mexican-stage ceramics makes a Florescent dating possible." *Ware*: Chichen Slate, Peto Cream, and Mayapan Unslipped, Panaba Unslipped Type. *Ceramic complexes*: Sotuta, Hocaba, Hocaba-Tases and Tases, A.D. 1300–1450. *Quantity*: Hocaba-Tases, 3 sherds and Tases, 3 sherds. *Provenience*: Chichen Itza and Mayapan. *Illustrations*: Mayapan, none; GWB, figs. 24, *d*; 71, *e*–*i*; 72, *n*, all from Chichen Itza.

Vase. This form belongs to the ceremonial rather than utilitarian category. Because of its height it lends itself to decoration in many techniques and in many design motifs. Its many forms include: barrel-shape; cylindrical with flat base, pedestal base, or tripod; lamp-chimney; and pyriform, either tripod or with pedestal base. These vase forms will be considered separately and in alphabetical order.

Vase, barrel-shape, flat base. Only one certain flat-base example is present, but this form is known as belonging in both the Cehpech and Tases cera-complexes. *Wares*: Mayapan Red and Puuc Red. *Ceramic complexes*: Cehpech and Tases. *Quantity*: Puuc Red Ware, 4 sherds from Uxmal; Mayapan Red Ware, 1 complete vessel with cover (44, *d*). *Provenience*: Mayapan and Uxmal. *Illustrations*: 8, *u*; 44, *d*. *Remarks*: it is interesting to compare two barrel-shape vase types from Uaxactun. These are fine-orange Altar Group, Tumba Black-on-orange Type (RES, fig. 3, *a*) and Peten Gloss Ware, Tinaja Red Type (*ibid.*, fig. 50, *a*, 22). Another excellent Fine Orange example, possibly of the Altar Group, is from Yucatan (GWB, fig. 59, *a*).

Vase, barrel-shape, ringstand base. Unlike the flat-base, barrel-shape vase, this is not represented by a single complete vessel. However, because of minor details of form and decoration it seems correct to place these examples with the ringstand type. *Ware*: Fine Orange of the Altar Group. *Ceramic complex*: Cehpech, A.D. 800–1000. *Quantity*: Uxmal, 2 sherds. *Provenience*: Uxmal. *Illustration*: 9, *l*. *Remarks*: this form linked with several types is found at Uaxactun associated with Peten Gloss Ware, Cucas Subware including the Monica Plano-relief Type, and the Portia Gouged-incised Type of the red Tinaja Group and the Torro Gouged-incised Type of the black Achote Group (RES, fig. 44, *e, g,* and *f*, respectively). It was also encountered near Labna (GWB, fig. 47, *k*) in Thin Slate Ware (?).

Vase, cylindrical, flat base. This form is present in varying quantities throughout the collections under consideration. The ceramic complexes involved are Cehpech, Sotuta, Hocaba, and Tases.

Cehpech. A comparison of form attributes for the cylindrical, flat-base vase throughout the various ceramic complexes reveals very little variance. Therefore, in order to differentiate among them a careful study of the wares, decorative techniques, and specific designs must be made. *Wares*: Fine Orange of the Balancan Group, Puuc Red, Puuc Slate, and Thin Slate. *Quantity*: Ticul Thin-slate Type sherds, 218 Uxmal, 4 Kabah, 4 Mayapan; Tabi Gouged-incised Type sherds, 21 Uxmal; Teabo Red Type sherds, 16 Uxmal, 2 Mayapan, 1 Kabah; Becal Incised Type sherds, 3 Uxmal, 1 Mayapan; Caribe Incised Type sherds, 6 Uxmal. This totals 276 sherds for Cehpech. *Provenience*: Kabah, Mayapan, Oxkintok, Sayil, and Uxmal in Yucatan; Jonuta in Tabasco. *Illustrations*: 6, *nn*; 7, *m, n*; 9, *m*; 26, *e, 3, 5*; 58, *f*; Berlin, 1956, fig. 3, *z, aa*; GWB, figs. 4, *p, 51–55*; 50, *d*; 51, *b, 9, 10,*

15, *c, 14–16, l, 46*; 88, *i, 10*; 103, *m*; 109, *d, 5, 6*. *Remarks*: an example of this form with modeled-carved decoration (Sahcaba Modeled-carved Type) is illustrated from Uaxactun (RES, fig. 44, *m*). The specimen from Jonuta (Berlin, 1956, fig. 3, *z, aa*) belongs to the Provincia Plano-relief Type. The vase from a private collection in Merida (53, *f*) belongs to the Tabi Gouged-incised Type. The plano-relief and modeled-carved techniques are strongly linked with Cehpech, whereas the gouged-incised technique is more closely allied to the Sotuta Ceramic Complex. The specific designs that associate these vessels with the Cehpech are the cursive M, reclining or seated human figures, and the braid or twist. This last is equally used in the Sotuta Ceramic Complex.

Sotuta. This form is rare and quite strange to this complex. There is some doubt how to classify the examples given. *Wares*: Chichen Red and unknown ware of Cenotillo Gray-polychrome Type. *Quantity*: 2 Xuku Incised Type sherds, and 4 Cenotillo Gray-polychrome Type sherds. *Provenience*: Chichen Itza. *Illustrations*: 21, *i* and 23, *f*. *Remarks*: both types might more properly be affiliated with the Cehpech Ceramic Complex.

Hocaba. The flat-based cylindrical vase does not occur very often, and no complete specimens were encountered. *Ware*: Mayapan Red. *Quantity*: 18 Mama Red sherds. *Provenience*: Mayapan. *Illustration*: GWB, fig. 23, *a, 16*. *Remarks*: Brainerd (*ibid.*, fig. 92, *j*) illustrates a vase from Chichen Itza of Peto Cream Ware, Xcanchakan Black-on-cream Type.

Tases. A single black example. *Ware*: Mayapan Black. *Quantity*: 1 Sulche Black Type sherd. *Provenience*: Mayapan. *Illustration*: none.

Vase, cylindrical, pedestal base. This form was more popular for approximately the same period as the preceding vase type.

Cehpech. In general the pedestals of this complex are lower than those of the Sotuta. *Ware*: Fine Orange of the Altar Group, Puuc Red, and Thin Slate. *Quantity*: Ticul Thin-slate Type sherds, 219 Uxmal; 5 Kabah, 3 Mayapan; Tabi Gouged-incised Type sherds, 21 Uxmal; Xul Incised Type sherd, 1 Mayapan; Pabellon Modeled-carved Type sherds, 39 Mayapan; Teabo Red Type sherds, 17 Uxmal, I Kabah; Becal Incised Type sherds, 2 Uxmal. *Provenience*: Kabah, Mayapan and Uxmal. *Illustrations*: 7, *i*; 27, *l*; GWB, fig. 50, *c, f*. *Remarks*: 79.5 per cent of these vases are undecorated, 12.7 per cent are modeled-carved, 6.8 per cent are gouged-incised, and 1 per cent incised.

Sotuta. These vases all have flaring pedestals,

but the Chichen Red Ware have convex bases as compared to flat bases for the Fine Orange Ware, Silho Group. *Wares*: Chichen Red and Fine Orange, Silho Group. *Quantity*: Dzibiac Red Type sherds, 18 Chichen Itza. Yalton Black-on-orange Type, grooved variety sherds, 4 Mayapan; Kilikan Composite Type sherds, 4 Mayapan; 1 Pomuch Polychrome Type sherd from Mayapan. *Provenience*: Chichen Itza and Mayapan in Yucatan; Isla de Sacrificios, Veracruz and Tlaxcala, Tlaxcala in Mexico; Uaxac Canal, Huehuetenango in Guatemala. *Illustrations*: 27, *j*; GWB, figs. 72, *c*; 78; 79, *r, s*; 86, *f*, and 89, *o*.

Hocaba, Hocaba-Tases, and Tases. These cylindrical vases have a direct rim, nearly vertical or outcurving sides, convex base, and a flaring pedestal support. *Wares*: Mayapan Red, Mayapan Unslipped, Peto Cream, and San Joaquin Buff. *Quantity*: Mayapan Red Ware sherds, 2 Hocaba, 49 Hocaba-Tases, and 232 Tases; Mayapan Unslipped Ware sherds, 55 Hocaba, 13 Hocaba-Tases, and 214 Tases; Peto Cream Ware, one Hocaba example; San Joaquin Buff Ware sherds, 2 Tases. *Provenience*: Chichen Itza and Mayapan in Yucatan and El Meco in Quintana Roo. *Illustrations*: 30, *a–t*; 44, *a, b*; 51, *v*; 53, *b*, 13, 15; 62, *d*; GWB, figs. 90, *s, t*; 92, *b*; 95, *h*; 97, *d*. *Remarks*: an example of this form of Chiquila Censer Ware from El Meco is illustrated by Sanders (1960, fig. 15, *f*). It has an openwork design of diamonds and triangles.

Vase, cylindrical, tripod. These vases may have solid cone or solid nubbin feet; the bases, although usually convex, may be flat. The ceramic complexes that have this form are Cehpech, Hocaba-Tases, and Tases.

Cehpech. A very rare form in this complex. *Ware*: Puuc Red. *Quantity*: 3 Becal Incised Type sherds. *Provenience*: Uxmal. *Illustration*: 8, *v*. *Remarks*: tripod vases either cylindrical or nearly so are illustrated by Brainerd (1958). A churn shape with hollow oven feet of Puuc Red Ware from Chunkatzin (*ibid.*, fig. 51, *f*) closely resembles in form the churn-shape vases of Chichen Red Ware from Chichen Itza (*ibid.*, fig. 86, *a–d*). A Thin Blackware specimen with recurving sides and hollow oven feet from Uxmal (*ibid.*, fig. 53, *e*) may belong to the Cehpech Ceramic Complex. A Puuc Slate Ware specimen with vertical walls and solid conical feet from Merida (*ibid.*, fig. 103, *b*) may be a Thin Slate Ware copy.

Hocaba-Tases and Tases. Generally this form has solid conical feet and a convex base. *Wares*: Mayapan Red and San Joaquin Buff. *Quantity*: Maya-

pan Red Ware sherds, 11 Hocaba-Tases, 52 Tases; San Joaquin Buff Ware sherds, 1 Hocaba-Tases, 2 Tases. *Provenience*: Mayapan. *Illustrations*: 44, *c*; 53, *b*, 16.

Vase, lamp chimney, pedestal base. This vase form is a very rare item in these collections. *Ware*: Fine Buff. *Ceramic complex*: Sotuta. *Quantity*: 7 Cerro Montoso Polychrome Type sherds. *Provenience*: Chichen Itza. *Illustration*: 23, *e*. *Remarks*: this form in either Fine Orange Ware or Fine Buff Ware is illustrated by Brainerd (1958, figs. 79, *o*; 89, *a*) from Chichen Itza; by Du Solier (1943, pp. 76, *a, e*; 77, *b*; 78, *n, o*) and Nuttall (1910, pl. 11) from the Isla de Sacrificios, Veracruz; by Smith (1957b, fig. 14) from either Huaymil or the Isla de Jaina in Campeche.

Vase, pyriform, tripod. This is a well-known vessel form at Chichen Itza during Toltec times. The specific shape found in these collections has a tapering neck, pear-shape body, convex or flat base, and three hollow bulbous feet. *Wares*: Fine Orange of the Silho Group and Chichen Red. *Ceramic complex*: Sotuta. *Quantity*: fine-orange Silho Group sherds, 67 from Chichen Itza, and 153 from Mayapan; red Dzibiac Group sherds, 14 from Chichen Itza. *Provenience*: Chichen Itza and Mayapan in Yucatan; Huaymil and Isla de Jaina in Campeche. *Illustrations*: 20, *f, r–u*; 22, *g*; GWB, 77, *m, jj*; 86, *e*; Smith, 1957b, figs. 1, *b*; 6; 13, *c–m*. *Remarks*: other pyriform shapes are described and illustrated by Smith, 1957b and 1958b.

VESSEL APPENDAGES

(Table 38). This category embraces handles, lugs, spouts, and supports including feet, pedestals, ring bases, and ringstand bases. In Table 38 only decorated appendages are listed.

Handles. Five principal handle types are recognized in the Maya area: basket, ladle, loop, lug, and strap. The basket type is very rare, the loop almost as scarce, the ladle and lug handles quite well represented, and the strap handle abundant.

The *basket handle* is normally flat, arches across the vessel mouth from one side to the other, and is attached to the rim or just below. Three examples have been noted: one from Mayapan middle lots (Hocaba-Tases) of a Navula Unslipped Type slightly restricted bowl (29, *q*); 2 from Chichen Itza, a Pocboc Gouged-incised Type restricted bowl (GWB, fig. 80, *z*) and a polychrome spouted jar of uncertain ware and type (*ibid.*, fig. 89, *h, 1*).

Ladle handles as the term implies, are for ladle censers, either the bowl or the tripod jar type. In either case they are tubular. The bowl or dish type handle usually opens into the bowl, while the tripod jar censer ladle handle does not. A few instances where the bowl type fails to have a bowl-handle opening are depicted in the following illustrations: 33, *e*; GWB, figs. 39, *f, 1*; and 68, *f, 12* representing the Hocaba-Tases, Cehpech, and Sotuta ceramic complexes, respectively. The great majority, however, have a bowl-handle aperture and thus could be used to blow clouds of incense smoke by applying the lips to the handle end. For further information on ladle handles consult Table 38 and ladle censers earlier in this chapter.

Loop handles are circular in section and may be placed on the vessel either vertically or horizontally. Some lug handles if it were not for their smallness might have been called loop handles. But even considering this possibility, they are extremely rare in these collections. *Ware*: Mayapan Red. *Ceramic complex*: Tases. *Quantity*: 1 Chapab-Modeled Type effigy vessel. *Provenience*: Santa Cruz, just outside the wall of Mayapan. *Illustration*: 45, *c*. Remarks: two examples, both of the Cehpech Ceramic Complex, are illustrated by Brainerd (1958, figs. 4, *p* and 15, *j, 2*). The first is of Thin Slate Ware from Chichen Itza, the second of Puuc Slate Ware from Chanpuuc.

Lug handles refer to a variety of perforated and unperforated lugs that serve or may serve as handles. These are bird heads, hook, slab-shape, spike, and twisted lump in form. They constitute a distinctive but small part of the Middle and Late Postclassic Period ceramic assemblage and occur only rarely in the Late Classic-Early Postclassic Transitional Period. The connection in the latter period is with the Puuc Slate Ware "Chultun jar" form. *Wares*: Mayapan Black, Mayapan Red, Mayapan Unslipped, and Puuc Slate. *Ceramic complexes*: Cehpech, Hocaba, Hocaba-Tases, and Tases. *Quantity*: At Kabah in Cehpech, 1 Puuc Slate Ware jar; at Mayapan in Hocaba, 19 lugs or .08 per cent of all sherds in Hocaba; in Hocaba-Tases, 78 lugs or .09 per cent, and in Tases, 238 lugs or .09 per cent. *Provenience*: Chanpuuc, Chichen Itza, Kabah, Mayapan, Sabacche, and Santa Cruz in Yucatan; Ichpaatun and Tulum in Quintana Roo. *Illustrations*: 5, *z*; 28, *a*, 16–24; 29, *a–e, g–j, m–o*; 31, *r, t, u, aa*; 43, *t*; 44, *n–p, r–v*; 46, *b, 1–3*; 49, *d–h*; 61, *a, 2*; GWB, figs. 15, *g*; 22, *a, 36–38*; 23, *a, 12*; 40, *b* (?); 66, *b, 12*,

39; 72, *i, 1–3*; 103, *i*; WTS, fig. 6, *c*, 4, 6, 17, 19, 20, 23, *d*. *Remarks*: the lug handles and lugs listed above are found on a variety of types and forms within the types, such as: basins of Yacman Striated Type, Panaba Unslipped Type, and Mama Red Type; restricted-orifice bowls of Navula Unslipped Type, Yacman Striated Type, Mama Red Type, and Sulche Black Type; low-neck, wide-mouth cooking jars of Yacman Striated Type; deep bowls of Thul Appliqué Type and Mama Red Type; miniature jars of Mama Red Type, Navula Unslipped Type, and Chum Unslipped Type; water jars of Muna Slate Type; a miniature vessel of Tekax Black-on-red Type, and miniature jars of Muna Slate Type.

Strap handles are formed like broad belt straps which hold the belt in place. They may be placed on the vessel either vertically or horizontally, rarely diagonally. Position on the vessel varies according to the vessel shape and function. In the Yucatan Peninsula area strap handles, usually two to a vessel and rarely three, enjoyed a long, widespread, and copious supremacy. Just when the potters of the Peninsula started using this type handle is not certain. The earliest illustrated specimen is a Tancah Red jar from Tancah of Late Formative Stage with three vertical handles (WTS, fig. 9, *b*, 1 and page 251). Far from being discarded as a usable form, it still occupies a prominent place among present-day handles in that area (Thompson, 1958, figs. 3–6, 39–41). *Wares*: Abala Red, Cauich Coarse-cream, Chichen Red, Chichen Slate, Chichen Unslipped, Mayapan Red, Mayapan Unslipped, Peto Cream, Puuc Red, Puuc Slate, Thin Slate, and San Joaquin Buff. *Ceramic complexes*: Cehpech, Sotuta, Hocaba, Hocaba-Tases, Tases, and Chauaca. *Quantity*: an exact enumeration of handles with associated vessel forms in the different types would be duplication, since these have been given under various vessel form modes as well as in Part Four.

However, here follows a listing of the association of vertical and horizontal strap handles with vessel form within the various ceramic complexes: Vertical: in Cehpech with Puuc Slate Ware basins, jars, and a bowl, Thin Slate Ware basins, and Cauich Coarse-cream Ware jars; in Sotuta with Chichen Unslipped Ware tripod or pedestal-base censers, Chichen Slate Ware basins, and Chichen Red Ware restricted bowls or basins; in Hocaba, Hocaba-Tases, and Tases with Mayapan Unslipped Ware huge storage jars and basins and Mayapan Red Ware basins. Horizontal: in Cehpech with Cauich Coarse-cream Ware basins; in Sotuta with Chichen Slate Ware jars and Chichen Red Ware jars; in Hocaba, Hocaba-Tases, and Tases with Mayapan Unslipped Ware wide-mouth, medium-high-neck jars and restricted bowls, Mayapan Red Ware water jars, both low-neck and medium-high-neck storage jars, restricted-orifice, direct or bolster-rim bowls, deep bowls or jars, and Peto Cream Ware water jars; in only Hocaba-Tases and Tases with San Joaquin Buff Ware jars both large and small; in Chauaca with Abala Red Ware parenthesis-rim jars. *Provenience*: Acanceh, Chanpuuc, Chichen Itza, Dzebtun, Dzibilchaltun, Kabah, Labna, Mani, Mayapan, Oxkintok, Sabacche, Sayil, Uxmal, Xul, and Yaxuna in Yucatan; Ichpaatun, Tankah, Tulum, and Vista Alegre in Quintana Roo. *illustrations*: 4, *a–i*; 5; 6, *x*; 7, *v*; 10, *c*, *h*; 12, *f*, *g*; 14; 15; 16, *b*, *d*; 20, *e*; 21, *f*; 28, *a*, 14, *b*, *c*, 1; 29, *f*, *p*; 38, *a*, *b*, 14, 15, *c*, 1, 3; 41, *a*, 1, 2; 43, *a*; 44, *q*; 46, *b*, 9, 10; 50; 52, *a*, *b*, *g*; 53, *a*, 1–4; 57, *a–c*; 58, *c*; 59, *a*; 60, *c*, *l*; 61, *a*, 5, *b*; 74, *e*, *j–l*; 75, *i*, *j*, *l*, *m*; GWB, figs. 10, *b*, 7, 12, 24; *c*, 11, 18; 15, *f*, 1, *k*, 3; 20, *a*, 7; 21, *a*, 19, 20; 24, *e*, 12; 25, *v*; 27, *j*, 27; 32, *a*, *b*, 38, *g*, 11; 33, *d*; 35, *a*, *c*; 36, *a*, *b*; 40, *a*, *d*, *e*, *g*; 42, *b*, 22, 42, *c*, *d*, *e*, 24; 43, *b*, *c*, 20, *d*, 36–38; 44, *b*, *e*, 4; 53, *a*, 12–20, *c*, 10; 68, *b*, 3, 11, 26, 31; 69, *c*, *d*, 1, *e*, 4; 70, *a*, *c*, 16; 71, *a*; 72, *l*, 4, 6, 8; 73, *b*, *f*; 92, *a*; 93, *c*, 17; 94, *c*, *f*, 4, 22; 104, *c*, 2, 3; 105, *f–h*; 106 *a*, 1, 9, *b*, *c*, 1, 2, *d*; WTS, figs. 6, *a*, 40, *d*, 9; 9, *a*, 7, 8, 19; 11, *a*, 46. *Remarks*: the use of three handles occurs early in Cehpech. Later two handles are the custom. Vertical handles are used exclusively in Cehpech except for Cauich Coarse-cream basins; again in Sotuta they prevail on all forms except jars, and in Hocaba through Tases they are only found on Mayapan Unslipped Ware huge jars and all basins, both unslipped and slipped. This shows a gradual taking over by the horizontal strap handle until the Chauaca Ceramic Complex and modern times, when a few vertical handles are employed.

Spouts. These are indeed rare items in the Yucatan Peninsula region, especially at Mayapan. In the Maya area four basically different spout types are recognized: coffee pot, effigy, gutter, and tubular. The only type encountered in the collections under consideration is the tubular spout. *Wares*: Mayapan Red and Peto Cream. *Ceramic complexes*: Hocaba and Tases, A.D. 1200–1450. *Quantity*: 10 Mama Red Type water jars and 2 Xcanchakan Black-on-cream Type water jars, all of the Hocaba Ceramic Complex; 1 Mama Red Type low-neck small jar, 1 Tzitz Red Type high-neck jar, and 1 Xcanchakan Black-on-cream Type water jar, all of the Tases Ceramic Complex. *Provenience*: Mayapan. *Illustrations*: 38, *a*, 23;

49, *l. Remarks*: Brainerd illustrates a couple of tubular spouts associated with Fine Orange Ware of the Silho Group or possible Fine Buff Ware (1958, fig. 89, *h*, 1, 2) from Chichen Itza, and another with Late Formative Monochrome (fig. 60, *a*, 30) from Kabah. He also depicts tubular spouts with an ovoid cross section of Late Formative Monochrome (fig. 17, *c*, 1–3) from Holactun and a single gutter spout of a Puuc Slate Ware tripod bowl (fig. 67, *c*) from Chichen Itza. Smith illustrates an example of the gutter spout on a Pocboc Gouged-incised Type tripod dish of the fine-orange Silho Group from the Marquez collection (1957b, figs. 1, *e*, 4; 17, *f*).

Supports. These embrace all foot forms and annular forms. Support totals and percentages are based on an actual count of the examples surely identifiable, whether attached to a vessel or disconnected.

Foot forms. These are many and varied, totaling 5,405 examples (3 bell-shape, 220 bulbous, 1 cloven, 2,393 conical, 377 cylindrical, 377 effigy, 125 nubbin, 1,855 oven-shape, 53 slab, and 1 "Turkish slipper"). They may be linked to a single ceramic complex or distributed throughout.

Bell-shape feet (22, *r*) are rare in these collections. The 3 bell-shape feet found at Chichen Itza are associated only with Fine Orange Ware, Silho Group tripod dishes, and total 1.5 per cent of all Sotuta Ceramic Complex foot specimens.

Bulbous feet, all hollow, occur in ceramic complexes from Sotuta through Tases. In Sotuta they form 64.2 per cent of all feet. They are associated with Chichen Slate Ware tripod dishes (19, *a*, *b*, *f*), tripod grater bowls, and tripod wide-mouth jars (14, *q*); with Chichen Unslipped Ware tripod censer bowls (12, *f*); with Chichen Red Ware tripod grater bowls (21, *j*) and tripod basal-break dishes (GWB, fig. 86, *i*, *j*, 2); and with Fine Orange Ware, Silho Group tripod pyriform vases (22, *g*) and a tripod jar (22, *e*). In Hocaba, the percentage is 8.3, and the Mayapan Red Ware tripod dish (GWB, fig. 26, *c*, 44) is the only related form. In Hocaba-Tases the percentage is .3, and the Mayapan Red Ware tripod flaring-side dish (*ibid.*, fig. 26, *c*, 44) is the only associated form. In Tases the percentage is 2.3, and the associations include Mayapan Red Ware tripod dishes (consult 40, *b*, 7) and tripod wide-mouth jars, Mayapan Unslipped Ware tripod basal-break dishes and tripod censer jars (no illustration of last three examples), and San Joaquin Buff Ware, Pele Polychrome Type tripod dish (no illustration). Considering all foot forms from all ceramic complexes and sites under study, the bulbous foot totals 4.1 per cent. *Remarks*: in these collections the hollow bulbous foot had a strong beginning in the Sotuta Ceramic Complex where it may have been introduced through a trade ware, Fine Orange of the Silho Group. Later in Hocaba through Tases it diminishes in popularity and in Chikinchel and Chauaca is not found. Adams, however (see earlier in this chapter under tripod grater bowls), does associate this foot form with the Jimba Ceramic Complex at Altar de Sacrificios.

Cloven feet, a solid example (not illustrated) occurs in the Tases Ceramic Complex associated with a Mayapan Unslipped Ware tripod deep bowl.

Conical feet, both solid and hollow but principally solid, are well represented in Cehpech, Hocaba, Hocaba-Tases, and Tases ceramic complexes. Only one hollow specimen was found in the Sotuta Ceramic Complex. In Cehpech the solid conical feet form 31.7 per cent and the hollow conical .2 per cent of all feet found in that complex. They are associated mainly with Puuc Slate Ware tripod dishes with flaring or outcurving sides (6, *a–d*) and rarely with Thin Slate Ware dishes of the same form (7, *r*). The percentage of this foot form is approximately the same at both Uxmal, Kabah, and even Mayapan considering only Cehpech feet. These percentages are 34.1, 32.5, and 29.6, respectively. In Hocaba only solid conical feet occurred, and they form a mere 6.9 per cent of all feet found in that complex. These are linked with Mayapan Red Ware tripod dishes with flaring or outcurving sides (cf. 40, *b*, 1–5) and a Mayapan Unslipped Ware tripod cup (61, *e*, 3). In Hocaba-Tases both solid and hollow conical feet are present and they form 41.2 per cent and .4 per cent, respectively, of all feet encountered in that complex. The solid examples are associated with Mayapan Red Ware tripod dishes with flaring or outcurving sides (40, *a*, 2, 5; cf. 40, *b*, 1–5), rounded-side bowls (41, *b*, 2–4), deep bowls (43, *d*, *f*, *j*), grater bowls (no illustration), and cylindrical vases (44, *c*), and with Mayapan Unslipped Ware tripod cups (31, *dd*), flaring-side dishes (cf. 29, *r*, *s*), deep bowls (31, *q*, *y*), miniature vessels (no illustration), and a grater bowl (no illustration). The few hollow specimens are linked with Mayapan Red Ware tripod flaring-side dishes (cf. 53, *b*, 1 for dish form). In Tases both solid and hollow conical feet occur and they form 53.8 per cent and .7 per cent, respectively, of all feet found in that complex. The solid examples are linked with Mayapan Red Ware tripod dishes having flaring or outcurving sides (40, *a*, 1, 3, 4, *b*, 1–

5), deep bowls (43, *e*), grater bowls (46, *a* for bowl form), rounded-side bowls (41, *b*, 1, 10), cylindrical vases (cf. 44, *c*), and high-neck jars (cf. 42, *b* for jar form); with Mayapan Unslipped Ware tripod cups (31, *cc*, *ee*, *ff*), deep bowls (31, *u*, *v*, *x*, *z–bb*), flaring-side dishes (29, *r*, *s*, *aa*), and a grater bowl (cf. 33, *j* for bowl form); with San Joaquin Buff Ware tripod flaring-side dishes (no illustration) and Mayapan Black Ware tripod flaring-side dishes (no illustration). The hollow specimens are associated with Mayapan Red Ware tripod flaring-side dishes (40, *b*, 6, 14), rounded-side dishes (41, *b*, 8), and a grater bowl (cf. 46, *a* for bowl form); with Mayapan Unslipped Ware tripod rounded-side bowls (cf. 33, *i* for bowl form), and with San Joaquin Buff Ware tripod flaring-side dishes (cf. 54, *b*, for dish form). In the overall picture, considering all foot forms from all ceramic complexes and sites being studied, the conical (mostly solid) rates the highest percentage, 44.3.

Cylindrical feet are both hollow and solid. The hollow may have a flat, closed, or (rarely) open base, or a rounded base. The solid has a rounded base. The cylindrical foot form occurs at Uxmal, Kabah, Chichen Itza, and Mayapan in the Cehpech, Sotuta, Hocaba, Hocaba-Tases, and Tases ceramic complexes. In Cehpech this foot type, hollow, closed flat base, and hollow, rounded base, forms 7.7 per cent of all feet. These feet are linked with Puuc Slate Ware tripod dishes (6, *o*, *ee* and *gg*, *hh* for form), with Thin Slate Ware tripod dishes (7, *z* and *o*, *aa* for form), and with Puuc Red Ware tripod dishes (GWB, figs. 18, *k*; 52, *i*, *k*, *m*, 21). In the Sotuta Ceramic Complex this foot form may not have been used. A few examples were encountered at Chichen Itza in predominantly Sotuta levels, but these may belong to Cehpech Puuc Red tripod dishes (21, *dd*, *ee*). In Hocaba only 3 feet, 2 hollow with rounded bottom and 1 hollow with closed flat base, were found forming 1.4 per cent of all feet. These are associated with Mayapan Unslipped Ware tripod censer jars (cf. 31, *e*) and with a Mayapan Red Ware tripod dish (cf. 40, *b*, 12). In Hocaba-Tases this foot form, including hollow and solid types, formed 7.4 per cent of all feet; the hollow totaling 6.9 per cent (flat closed base, 5.3 per cent, open base .1 per cent, and rounded base 1.5 per cent) and the solid, .5 per cent. The hollow flat-base feet are associated with Mayapan Red Ware tripod dishes with flaring or outcurving sides (40, *b*, 13), with San Joaquin Buff Ware tripod dishes (no illustration), and with Tulum Red Ware tripod outcurving-side dishes (48, *l*). The hollow rounded-base feet are linked with Mayapan Red

Ware tripod high-neck jars (cf. 42, a–c), deep bowls (43, i), and grater bowls (cf. 46, a, 3 which approaches the cylindrical); with San Joaquin Buff Ware tripod dishes (54, b); and with Fine Orange Ware, Matillas Group tripod dishes (cf. 55, a, 5 and b, 3 for dish forms). The solid cylindrical rounded-base feet (probably belonging to conical group) are associated with Mayapan Red Ware tripod rounded-side dishes (41, b, 3 a close approximation). In Tases much the same situation pertains as in Hocaba-Tases, with hollow and solid specimens forming 7.5 per cent of all feet; the hollow totaling 7.1 per cent (flat, closed base, 6.6 per cent and rounded base, .5 per cent) and the solid, .4 per cent. The hollow flat-base feet are associated with Mayapan Red Ware tripod dishes with flaring or outcurving sides (40, b, 12, c, 2) and with San Joaquin Buff Ware tripod dishes (no illustration). The hollow rounded-base feet are connected with Mayapan Red Ware tripod high-neck jars (42, a–c); with San Joaquin Buff Ware tripod dishes (cf. 54, b); and with a Mayapan Unslipped Ware tripod bowl (cf. 33, i for bowl form). The solid cylindrical feet are linked with Mayapan Red Ware tripod flaring-side dishes (cf. 40, a, b for dish form) and a tripod rounded-side dish (cf. 41, b for dish form), and with a Mayapan Unslipped Ware tripod bowl (cf. 33, i for bowl form). In the overall picture, counting all foot forms from all ceramic complexes and sites being studied, the cylindrical types total 7 per cent.

Effigy feet (Table 38), usually hollow, occur in all ceramic complexes under consideration, except Sotuta. They are of two kinds, impressed cylindrical (flat or rounded base) and moldmade animal or human heads. In Cehpech only the impressed type is found and it forms 6.5 per cent of all feet. These are associated with Puuc Slate Ware tripod dishes (6, p, gg, hh, kk); with Thin Slate Ware tripod dishes (7, o, aa); and with Puuc Red Ware tripod dishes (GWB, fig. 58, h, 1, 2). In Hocaba only 4 specimens of the moldmade effigy foot are recorded and these, 2 animal and 2 human, form 1.8 per cent of all feet. The associations are with Mayapan Red Ware tripod dishes (cf. 40, b, 15–17, c, 13–20) and with Fine Orange Ware, Matillas Group tripod dishes with or without basal flange (cf. 55, b, 1; 56, a, c). In Hocaba-Tases moldmade effigy feet form 7.7 per cent of all feet; 4.7 per cent animal and 3 per cent human. These are linked with Mayapan Red Ware tripod dishes (40, b, 15, c, 16; cf. 40, b, 16, 17, c, 13, 14, 16–20); with Fine Orange Ware, Matillas Group tripod dishes with or without basal flange (56, c, 1, 3, 10, 12; cf. 55, b, 1; 56, a, c, 2, 5–9, 11), and

with San Joaquin Buff Ware tripod dishes (cf. 53, b, 1, 6; 54, a, c, d). In Tases these feet total the same 7.7 per cent of all feet as in Hocaba-Tases, but the animal type comprises a larger part, 6.5 per cent, compared to 1.2 per cent for the human type. They are connected with Mayapan Red Ware tripod dishes (40, b, 16, 17, c, 13–15, 17–20); with San Joaquin Buff Ware tripod dishes (53, b, 1, 6; 54, a, c, d); and with Fine Orange Ware, Matillas Group tripod dishes with or without flange (55, b, 1; 56, a, b, 2, 4–9, 11). In the overall picture, considering all foot forms from all ceramic complexes and sites involved, the hollow effigy foot totals 7 per cent.

Nubbin feet, usually solid, rarely hollow, occur predominantly in Cehpech and have been identified at all the Puuc sites as well as at Chichen Itza and Mayapan. In the Cehpech Ceramic Complex solid nubbin feet total 13.1 per cent of all feet. They are linked with Thin Slate Ware tripod rounded-side bowls with direct or bead lip (7, h) and tripod flaring-side dishes (no illustration) and with Puuc Red Ware rounded-side bowls with bead lip (8, c, d; GWB, fig. 51, g, j) and flaring-side dishes (ibid., fig. 52, m, 35 ?). In the overall picture, of all foot forms from all ceramic complexes and sites under consideration, the solid nubbin foot totals 2.3 per cent. *Remarks*: prior to Cehpech the nubbin foot had a modest vogue in the Late Preclassic Period with both tripods and tetrapods at Uaxactun (RES, figs. 7, k; 16, f, 1; 52, b, 14; 70, a, 67–70) in Guatemala. One of these shows traces of the Usulatan technique (ibid., fig. 70, a, 70. Some of the Uaxactun examples might be called small truncated cone-shape feet.

Oven-shape feet mainly hollow, sometimes solid, are well represented throughout the ceramic complexes under consideration. This form, when it is sometimes slightly elongated, is difficult to differentiate from the hollow rounded-base cylindrical foot; it may narrow slightly near the foot-body junction, thereby resembling the hollow bulbous foot. The hollow oven-shape feet form 35.2 per cent and the solid oven-shape, .2 per cent of all feet in the Cehpech Complex. The hollow oven feet are associated with Puuc Slate Ware tripod dishes (6, f); with Puuc Red Ware tripod dishes (8, j, k) and a possible hemispherical bowl (8, b); and with Thin Slate Ware tripod dishes (GWB, fig. 4, p. 64). The solid oven feet are linked with a Puuc Slate Ware tripod dish (no illustration) and a Fine Orange Ware, Balancan Group, tripod deep bowl (no illustration). In Sotuta the hollow oven-foot form totals 33.9 per cent and the solid type, 2.6 per cent. The hollow type is linked predominantly with Chichen Slate Ware tripod grater bowls (13, *m*, *n*; GWB, fig. 74, *i*) and, rarely, flaring-side dishes (*ibid.*, fig. 74, *b*, 27) and with Chichen Red Ware tripod rounded-side bowls (*ibid.*, fig. 87, *v*). The solid type is associated with Chichen Slate Ware tripod dishes (no illustration) and a Chichen Red Ware tripod rounded-side bowl (cf. *ibid.*, fig. 87, *v* for bowl form). In Hocaba this foot form totals 81.6 per cent (hollow oven-shape, 80.7 per cent and solid oven, .9 per cent). The hollow examples are associated with Mayapan Red Ware tripod dishes with flaring or outcurving-sides (cf. 40, *b*, 8–11), rounded-side dishes (cf. 41, *b*, 6), grater bowls (46, *a*, 3), and deep bowls (cf. 43, *g*); with Mayapan Unslipped Ware tripod censer jars (cf. 31, *h*, *i*); and with a Fine Orange Ware, Matillas Group tripod dish (GWB, fig. 28, *a*, 24). The solid examples are linked with Mayapan Unslipped Ware tripod censer jars (cf. 31, *e* for jar form). In Hocaba-Tases oven-shape feet form 42.7 per cent of all feet in that complex (hollow type, 39 per cent and solid type, 3.7 per cent). The hollow feet are linked with Mayapan Red Ware tripod dishes (40, *b*, 9; 74, *m*), rounded-side dishes (cf. 41, *b*, 6), grater bowls (46, *a*, 1, 2, 4), deep bowls (cf. 43, *g*), and high-neck jars (cf. 42, *b* for jar form); with Mayapan Unslipped Ware tripod, flaring-side dishes (cf. 29, *s* for dish form); and with Peto Cream Ware rounded-side dishes (52, *o*). The solid feet are connected with Mayapan Red Ware tripod flaring-side dishes (40, *b*, 2 for dish form) and grater bowls (46, *a*, 2 for bowl form) and with a Mayapan Unslipped Ware tripod censer jar (cf. 31, *e* for jar form). In Tases the oven-shape foot forms 28.1 (24.9 hollow and 3.1 solid) per cent of all feet in that complex. The hollow feet are associated with Mayapan Red Ware tripod dishes with flaring or outcurving sides (40, *b*, 8, 10, 11), grater bowls (cf. 46, *a*), high-neck jars (42, *a*–*c*, for jar form), rounded-side bowls (41, *b*, 6), deep bowls (43, *g*), and low-neck jars (43, *b*); with Mayapan Unslipped Ware tripod censer jars (31, *e* for jar form and 31, *h*, *i* for foot form); with San Joaquin Buff Ware tripod jars (53, *a*, 17, 22); and with Fine Orange Ware, Matillas Group tripod dishes (GWB, fig. 28, *a*, 24). The solid specimens are linked with Mayapan Red Ware tripod flaring-side dishes (40, *b*, 2 for dish form), grater bowls (46, *a* for bowl form), a high-neck jar (42, *b* for jar form), and a deep bowl (31, *v*). In the overall picture, counting all foot forms from all ceramic complexes and sites under consideration, the oven-shape types total 34.3 per cent, making them second percentagewise to the conical foot form.

Slab feet (Table 38) in these collections are always solid and they may be plain or sometimes terraced. Mainly they occur in the Cehpech Ceramic Complex, although a few examples turned up in the middle lots of Mayapan. Berlin (1956, fig. 6, *i*, *j*, *l*) illustrates specimens that belong to the Chikinchel Ceramic Complex from Juarez in Tabasco and Atasta in Campeche, all of Fine Orange Ware, Cunduacan Group (formerly U Fine Orange). In Cehpech solid slab feet form 5.3 per cent (5 per cent plain, .3 per cent terraced) of all feet in that complex. The greatest number occurred at Mayapan, next at Kabah, and then Uxmal and Chichen Itza in that order. They are associated with Puuc Slate Ware tripod dishes with flaring or outcurving sides (6, *bb*, *cc*; 26, *b*, 13, 19). In Hocaba-Tases they are linked with Mayapan Red Ware tripod flaring-side dishes (29, *z*, *cc* for vessel form; GWB, fig. 94, *h*, 32). In the overall picture, considering all foot forms from all ceramic complexes and sites being studied, the slab feet total .9 per cent. *Remarks*: a curious concentration of slab feet is noted in the eastern part of central Yucatan at Yaxuna (GWB, fig. 10, *d*–*g*), Chichen Itza (*ibid.*, fig. 67), and Dzebtun (*ibid.*, fig. 35, *i*–*m*) all linked with Puuc Slate Ware tripod dishes.

"Turkish slipper" feet are very rare. In the Sotuta Ceramic Complex at Chichen Itza they are represented by a single example associated with a Chichen Red Ware tripod grater bowl (21, *m*) and in the Tases Ceramic Complex at Mayapan by one specimen connected with a Mayapan Red Ware tripod dish (40, *c*, 12). Sanders (1960, fig. 6, *a*, 48, 55) illustrates two "Turkish slipper" feet belonging to Tulum Red Ware found at Ichpaatun, Quintana Roo.

Annular forms. These are more numerous than foot forms. In all ceramic complexes they include 6,709 pedestal, no ring, and 439 ringstand bases.

Pedestal bases are a tall (in proportion to the vessel size) form of support. Pedestals may be flaring, outcurving, or nearly vertical, and they may have a basal rim bolster. On rare occasions they may be enclosed to form a double bottom; since this enclosure is usually filled with pottery pellets or stone pebbles, the result is a rattle bottom. The pedestal support is found in all the ceramic complexes with which this report is concerned, from Cehpech through Chikinchel. Its beginnings, however, appear to date back as far as the Ocos Phase at La Victoria (Coe, 1961, fig. 23, *a*), and by the Early Classic Period at Uaxactun (RES, fig. 23, *b*) this form is well established. In Cehpech pedestals form 19.6 per cent of all annular supports in that ceramic complex. They are linked particularly with Puuc Unslipped Ware hourglass censers (3, a), with Thin Slate Ware pedestal-base cylindrical vases (7, i), and rarely with Puuc Slate Ware and with one Fine Orange Ware, Balancan Group rounded-side bowl (58, a). In Sotuta they form 99.7 per cent of all annular supports in that complex. Pedestals are associated mainly with Chichen Unslipped Ware hourglass censers (12, a) and a pedestal-base cylindrical vessel (cf. 30, u for form); with Fine Orange Ware, Silho Group pedestal-base cylindrical vases (GWB, fig. 78, a, b, f–h) and pyriform vases (Smith, 1957b, figs. 8, 9); with Fine Buff Ware lamp-chimney vases (23, e); with Chichen Red Ware cylindrical vases (GWB, fig. 86, f); with a Chichen Slate Ware vessel (ibid., fig. 72, c), and with a Tunkas Red-on-gray Type vessel (23, g). In Hocaba the pedestal support is the only annular support recorded for that ceramic complex. Pedestals are connected with Mayapan Unslipped Ware, Hoal Modeled Type effigy censers (68, a) totaling 74.6 per cent and Cehac-Hunacti Composite Type pedestal-base censer vases or jars, 23.3 per cent. The remainder include Mayapan Red Ware cylindrical vases (cf. 44, a, b) and a Peto Cream Ware cylindrical vase (51, v) and bowl (no illustration). In Hocaba-Tases the pedestal forms 97.7 per cent of all annular supports in that ceramic complex. They are associated principally with Mayapan Unslipped Ware, Chen Mul Modeled Type effigy censers (cf. 32, g, k, n; 67, a–e) and Cehac-Hunacti Composite Type pedestal-base censer jars or vases (31, a–c; 62, a–c; cf. 30, a, d–g; 62, d), which together total 90.2 per cent of the pedestal supported vessels. The remainder include Mayapan Unslipped Ware, Hoal Modeled Type effigy censers (68, a, 2, 3), Mayapan Unslipped Ware cups (30, v, w; 61, e, 4, 5), Mayapan Coarse Ware effigy censers (no illustration), Mayapan Red Ware pedestal-base, restricted-orifice bowls (44, l, m; 74, aa, bb), cylindrical vases (cf. 44, a, b), bowl clusters (37, a), cups (45, d; 63, b), jars (43, m, o), and Mayapan Black Ware pedestal-base, restricted-orifice bowls (cf. 44, l, m, for vessel shape). In Tases the pedestal forms 99.6 per cent of all annular supports in that ceramic complex. They are linked mainly with Mayapan Unslipped Ware, Chen Mul Modeled Type effigy censers (32, g, k, n; 67, a–e), and Cehac-Hunacti Composite Type pedestal-base censer jars or vases (30, a, d–g; 62, d; cf. 31, a–c; 62, a–c), which together total 95.6 per cent of the pedestal supported vessels. The remainder comprise Mayapan Red Ware bowl clusters (37, b, c; 75, c), cylindrical vases (44, a, b), restricted-orifice bowls (cf. 44, l, m; 74, aa), plates (41, d), cups (30, x, z–

bb, deep bowls or jars (43, a; cf. 43, l, m, o; 74, bb), and a miniature bowl (no illustration); Fine Orange Ware, Matillas Group vessels (55, b, 11), and San Joaquin Buff Ware vessels (53, b, 12, 13, 15). Remarks: the closed-base or double bottom pedestals, not found at Mayapan, did occur at Moxviquil, Chiapas (58, a), and at Jonuta, Tabasco (Berlin, 1956, fig. 3, bb), in Fine Orange Ware, Balancan Group; at Uxmal, Yucatan, in Thin Slate Ware (GWB, fig. 50, c), and from the Marquez Collection in Fine Orange Ware, Silho Group (Smith, 1957b, fig. 12, e).

Ring bases are indeed a rarity in the ceramic complexes under consideration. This very low annular base, much in evidence in the Early Classic Period and rare in the Late Classic Period, did not occur in these collections from Cehpech through Chikinchel.

Ringstand bases, low forms of pedestal supports, may be flaring, outcurving, or vertical. In some cases this type is terraced (Table 38) and like the pedestal may be closed, forming a double or rattle bottom (27, l; Smith, 1958b, fig. 4, f). In Cehpech, ringstands form 80.4 per cent of all annular supports in that ceramic complex. They are associated mainly with Puuc Slate Ware beveled rim ringstand bowls (4, l, m; 26, b, 23; 60, d) which total 64.9 per cent of ringstand vessels in this ceramic complex. The remainder include Fine Orange Ware, Altar Group vases (27, l), Puuc Red Ware beveled rim ringstand bowls (same as Puuc Slate) and hemispherical bowls (8, o), Thin Slate Ware hemispherical bowls (7, e), and Puuc Unslipped Ware vessels (unattached ringstands). In Sotuta a single ringstand was found connected with a Chichen Red Ware bowl (21, jj). It is a terraced example. In Hocaba no ringstands were encountered. In Hocaba-Tases the ringstand base forms 2.3 per cent of all annular supports, most of which are linked with Mayapan Unslipped Ware plates (cf. 29, gg), others with Fine Orange Ware, Matillas Group deep bowls (55, b, 5) and restricted-orifice bowls (55, b, 6), with San Joaquin Buff Ware restricted-orifice bowls (53, b, 10), and with Mayapan Red Ware deep bowls (cf. 43, l for bowl form). In Tases, ringstands form only .4 per cent of all annular supports. Half of these are associated with Mayapan Unslipped Ware plates (29, gg). The remainder are linked with Mayapan Red Ware deep bowls (cf. 43, l for bowl form), an effigy vessel (45, a), and a plate (cf. 29, gg for plate form); with Mayapan Unslipped Ware miniature vessels (33, g, h) and a censer jar (31, d); and with a Fine Orange Ware, Matillas Group deep bowl (55, c, 5).

VESSEL PARTS

In this category the most significant vessel parts not already dealt with are basal-Z-angles, flanges, necks, and rims. Bases and bodies are omitted here since their significance if any has been considered under vessel form.

Z-angle This vessel part has two principal types: the lateral-Z-angle and the basal-Z-angle.

Lateral-Z-angle. This type occurs in the Late Preclassic Period (RES, fig. 16, *f*, 4) on relatively deep bowls.

Basal-Z-angle. This form appears for the first time at Uaxactun in Tzakol 1, but at Holmul it is found in the earliest Holmul I grave (Merwin and Vaillant, 1932, pl. 18, *c*), thus connecting with the Protoclassic Period. It is missing in the Late Classic assemblage at Uaxactun and elsewhere in the Maya area so far as I have been able to ascertain. It is revived in Tepeu 3 at Uaxactun (RES, figs. 42, *a*, 10; 51, *d*, 1), which is another link with forms of the Cehpech assemblage in Yucatan. In Cehpech the basal-Z-angle forms .52 per cent of all sherds found at Uxmal, .26 per cent at Kabah, and a total of 11 sherds at Mayapan. This vessel form is associated with tripod dishes of Puuc Slate Ware (6, *o–q*), Puuc Red Ware (26, *e*, 2; GWB, fig. 52, *i*, *k*), and Thin Slate Ware (7, *w*). In the ceramic complexes following Cehpech no basal-Z-angles were noted in the collections under consideration. Sanders, however, illustrates two Tulum Red Ware tripod bowls from Ichpaatun (1960, fig. 4, *c*, 16 and 26) which may belong to this form, although *c*, 16 seems more like a base-side angle and *c*, 26 more like a basal flange.

Flange. This vessel part has two main categories, the horizontal and the vertical. The horizontal flanges are basal, lateral, and rim, any of which may be incised, notched, plain, scalloped, or terraced. The vertical type is usually painted and associated with censers. Decorated flanges are listed in Table 38. At Mayapan the basal flange totaled 91 per cent and the lateral flange, 9 per cent; at Uxmal the basal flange formed 55.3 per cent, the lateral flange 39.4 per cent, and the rim flange 5.3 per cent; at Kabah the basal flange totaled 94.9 per cent and the lateral flange 5.1 per cent; and at Chichen Itza the lateral flange formed 92.4 per cent and the vertical flange 7.6 per cent.

Basal flange. This type is located at the juncture of base and side pointing diagonally down-ward. When it points almost vertically downward, it is called an apron flange. In Cehpech the basal flange is encountered at Kabah, Uxmal, and Mayapan, forming small percentages at each (.3, .2, and a mere 2 sherds, respectively). It is linked with tripod dishes of Puuc Slate Ware (6, *l, r–t, v, w*; 26, *b*, 21, 22), Puuc Red Ware (8, *p–r*), and Thin Slate Ware (7, *x*). A few of these flanges are terraced or notched (Table 38), and several are the apron type. In Sotuta the basal flange was not encountered. In Hocaba 13 basal-flange specimens occurred at Mayapan. These are associated with Mayapan Red Ware tripod deep bowls (43, *h*) and tripod dishes (40, *c*, 3, 5) where the flanges, sometimes of the apron type, are either terraced or notched, and with Fine Orange Ware, Matillas Group tripod dishes (cf. 55, *a*, 4, 5). The percentages by wares are 84.6 Mayapan Red and 15.4 Fine Orange. In Hocaba-Tases the percentages of basal flanges from Mayapan total .2 of all sherds in that complex. These are connected with Fine Orange Ware, Matillas Group tripod dishes (cf. 55, *a*, 4, 5, *b*, 1, 4, *c*, 1, *d*, 5) whose flanges rarely show decoration, and with Mayapan Red Ware tripod deep bowls (43, *i*), tripod dishes (40, *c*, 7, 9), and pedestal-base deep bowls (43, *m–o*) whose flanges, sometimes of the apron type, are either terraced or notched. The percentages by wares are 72.6 Fine Orange and 27.4 Mayapan Red. In Tases basal flanges from Mayapan total .1 per cent of all sherds in that complex. These are associated with Fine Orange Ware, Matillas Group tripod dishes (55, *a*, 4, 5, *b*, 1, 2, 4, *c*, 1), whose flanges rarely show decoration, and with Mayapan Red Ware tripod dishes (40, *c*, 1, 2, 4, 6, 8, 10) and tripod deep bowls (cf. 43, *h*, *i*) whose flanges, sometimes of the apron type, are either terraced, notched, or plain. The percentages by wares are 89.2 Fine Orange and 10.8 Mayapan Red. This flange is also present during Hocaba through Tases times at Tulum and Ichpaatun (WTS, fig. 4, *c*) in Quintana Roo.

Lateral flange. This type is sometimes called a medial flange and placed somewhere above the base and below the lip but not close enough to the lip to be considered a rim flange. Like many of the basal flanges it points diagonally downward. In the various ceramic complexes the lateral flange is found at Chichen Itza, Uxmal, Kabah, and Mayapan, forming small percentages at each (.3, .2, .01, and .01, respectively). In Cehpech it is associated with Puuc Unslipped Ware hourglass censers (3, *d–f, i*). Some of these flanges are scalloped, some terraced, and others notched. Two forms (*e* and *i*) have both upper and lower lateral flanges. In addition there is the single notched example of a Puuc Red Ware tripod (8, n). In Sotuta this flange type is linked with Chichen Unslipped Ware hourglass censers (12, b, e), most of which are scalloped. In Hocaba a few lateral flanges are connected with Mayapan Unslipped Ware pedestal-base vase or jar censers (30, n–q). Two of these out of a total of four are terraced. In Hocaba-Tases this flange type is associated with Mayapan Unslipped Ware tripod jar or pedestal-base vase censers (30, m). In Tases it is linked with Mayapan Unslipped Ware pedestal-base vase or jar censers (30, l, r–t) and may be plain or terraced.

Rim flange. This type is closely allied to the labial flange and is found only in Cehpech of those complexes being studied. The labial flange is quite well represented in Preclassic times by Brainerd's (1958, figs. 5, d, 5; 31, c, 43, 44) Formative stage monochrome vessels from Yaxuma and Mani as well as many from elsewhere. In our collection from Uxmal the rim flange is linked with a few Puuc Unslipped Ware jars (2, g) and a Cauich Coarse Cream Ware basin (10, e). Brainerd (1958, fig. 58, c, d) illustrates excellent examples of Puuc Slate Ware from Temax and Kabah. This type was not observed in any later complexes.

Vertical flange. This type is rare in these collections and associated only with the Sotuta Ceramic Complex by means of Chichen Unslipped Ware hourglass censers (12, e) from Chichen Itza. In other parts of the Maya area this feature is more in evidence: at Uaxactun in Tzakol (Ricketson and Ricketson, 1937, pl. 85, e–g) on cylindrical potstands; at Tzimin Kax and Hatzcap Ceel, British Honduras, in Holmul V (Thompson, 1931, fig. 14, b and pl. 27, respectively) on cylindrical censers; at Palenque, Chiapas, also in the Late Classic Period (Ruz, 1958, figs. 10–12, pls. 29–33) on cylindrical objects lacking bottoms and decorated with modeling, appliqué, and painting; from the Peten either Late Classic or later (Smith, 1944, fig. 2, a–e) on bottomless cylinders smaller but similar to those from Palenque.

Neck. This vessel part forms the upper section of a jar and is not connected with any other vessel shape except for a few effigy vessels which virtually have a jar form. Necks may be high, medium, or low. The distinguishing features are the way the neck is fashioned and the degree and curvature of its inclination, i.e., bulging and vertical or corrugated and vertical. Necks may be bulging, corrugated, flaring, outcurving, tapered, or

vertical. These features are described under jars in this chapter.

Rim. This forms the upper part of a vessel and encompasses the lip. There are many kinds of rim including bead, bolster, bulging, direct, everted, incurving, inset, overhanging, parenthesis, pinched, rim molding, scalloped, T-shape, and thickened. "Direct" is omitted in the analysis because it is too universally used to be significant as a mode. The nondirect rims form 20 per cent of all those in the collections, including those from Chichen Itza, Kabah, Mayapan, and Uxmal.

Bead rim. This type, sometimes called a bead lip, is really a miniature bolster. Earlier in this chapter it is discussed under the hemispherical bowl with bead rim, either flat base or tripod, belonging to Puuc Red Ware and Thin Slate Ware. In Cehpech besides hemispherical bowls, cylindrical vases occasionally have bead rims. These are associated with Thin Slate Ware (GWB, fig. 50, e, 18, 21, 23) and Puuc Red Ware (*ibid.*, fig. 51, l, 46). In addition there is one Puuc Slate Ware jar specimen (5, cc). In the collections under consideration this rim form does not appear to have been used in any ceramic complex other than Cehpech except for Sotuta with a single Fine Orange Ware, Silho Group restricted-orifice bowl (22, n) from Chichen Itza. At Uxmal this feature is present on 5.3 per cent of all rim sherds; at Kabah on 2.3 per cent, and at Mayapan on .3 per cent. The earliest bead rim so far observed occurs at Uaxactun in Mars Orange Ware (RES, fig. 14, d, 6) and belongs to the Mamom Ceramic Complex. Later it is found in Tzakol 2 and 3 (*ibid.*, figs. 12, q and 32, a, 8; and 23, a, 14, respectively). Then skipping Tepeu 1 and 2, it appears in Tepeu 3 at Uaxactun associated with a restricted-orifice bowl and a barrel-shape vase (*ibid.*, fig. 50, a, 10–14; 75, b, 8) which Brainerd (1958, fig. 51, l, 26–34) nearly duplicates in Puuc Red Ware from Uxmal. This is an instance of the close relationship between the Cehpech and Tepeu 3 ceramic complexes. Another Tepeu 3 example of the bead rim involves an Asote Orange Type tripod bowl (RES, fig. 12, o) from Uaxactun.

Bolster rim. This is a padded rim which bellies outward like a cushion. Bolster rims may be flat, medial, ovoid, rounded, square, or triangular in form. The bolster is located at the tip of the rim except for the medial rim bolster found in Sotuta on Chichen Unslipped Ware jars (11, e), placed just below the rim edge. Percentages for total number of bolsters to all rim sherds in each complex amount to: 30.3 in Cehpech at Uxmal, 39.4 at Kabah, and 36 at Mayapan; 22.9 in Sotuta at Chichen Itza and 55.9 at Mayapan; 27.2 in Hocaba at Mayapan; 11.6 in Hocaba-Tases at Mayapan; and 9.2 in Tases at Mayapan. These percentages are a reasonable reflection of the use of the bolster in Cehpech, Sotuta, and Hocaba. They are less so in Hocaba-Tases or Tases because of the vast number of effigy censer fragments which tend to distort the picture in these two complexes. By deducting the effigy censers, the percentages would read 12.4 for Hocaba-Tases and 12.6 for Tases. Of all the nondirect rim forms, the bolster rim is by far the best represented throughout, totaling 72.3 per cent.

Flat bolsters have a little more bulge than rim moldings. Although found in all complexes, they are rare in both Cehpech and Sotuta. In Cehpech none is noted in the material from Uxmal and Kabah, and they total 2.4 per cent of the Cehpech bolsters from Mayapan. These Cehpech bolsters are associated with Puuc Unslipped Ware storage jars (no illustration). In Sotuta a single Fine Orange Ware, Silho Group restricted-orifice bowl (22, *m*) occurs at Chichen Itza, and three Chichen Red Ware specimens are present at Mayapan, including 2 high-neck jars and 1 restricted-orifice bowl (no illustrations). In Hocaba the flat bolster totals 56.4 per cent of all bolsters in that ceramic complex. It is associated with Mayapan Red Ware jars (38, *a*, 8, 9; 74, *c*), restricted-orifice bowls (41, *a*, 7, 8), basins (cf. 46, *b*, 9, 10), and drums (cf. 39, *c*, *m*); with Mayapan Unslipped Ware dishes (29, *kk*), basins (29, *f*), jars (cf. 28, *c*, 9), and flat-base dishes (cf. 29, *dd*, *ee*); and with Peto Cream Ware restricted-orifice bowls (cf. 52, *m*, *n*), jars (52, *e*), and tripod rounded-side dishes (no illustration). In Hocaba-Tases this bolster type forms 62.6 per cent of all its bolsters. It is linked with water jars (38, *a*, 10, 12; 74, *a*), restricted-orifice bowls (41, *a*, 6), storage jars (no illustration), basins (cf. 46, *b*, 9, 10), and a drum (39, *c*; 74, *g*); with Mayapan Unslipped Ware flat-base dishes (cf. 29, *dd*, *ee*, *kk*), huge jars (cf. 28, *c*, 9), restricted-orifice bowls (no illustration), effigy censers (no illustration), tripod jar censers (no illustration), cooking jars (no illustration), and a censer vase (30, *m*); with Peto Cream Ware water jars (52, *a*; 75, *m*) and restricted-orifice bowls (51, *k*), and with a San Joaquin Buff Ware storage jar (cf. 53, *a*, 10). In Tases the flat bolster totaled 30.9 per cent of all bolsters. It is linked with Mayapan Red Ware water jars (cf. 38, *a*, 8, 9, 12), storage jars (38, *a*, 13), basins (46,

b, 9, 10), restricted-orifice bowls (41, *a*, 4, 9), bowl clusters (37 *c*), and drums (39, *m*).

Medial bolsters, broad and shallow in form, are located on the rim just below the lip. As bolsters they are nearest to the ovoid type and must not be confused with the Cehpech rim flange which, although similarly placed just below the lip, protrudes farther outward and is narrow. The medial rim bolster is found only in the Sotuta Ceramic Complex and is associated with Chichen Unslipped Ware storage jars (11, *e*). This form totals 4.1 per cent of the Sotuta bolsters from Chichen Itza.

Ovoid bolsters are most abundant in the Sotuta Ceramic Complex, whether from Chichen Itza or Mayapan. In Cehpech at Uxmal they total 9 per cent of all bolsters in that complex, 8.2 per cent at Mayapan, and .5 per cent at Kabah. This bolster form is linked with Cauich Coarsecream Ware basins (10, *b*, *c*); with Thin Slate Ware basins (7, *t*); with Puuc Unslipped Ware basinlike censers (3, *r*); and with Puuc Slate Ware basins (4, *g*; 16, *e*). In Sotuta at Chichen Itza these bolsters form 68.6 per cent and at Mayapan 87 per cent of all bolsters. They are associated with Chichen Unslipped Ware storage jars (11, *c*) and tripod censers (12, *f*) and with Chichen Slate Ware restricted-orifice basins (15, *a*, *b*, *d*–*j*). In Hocaba at Mayapan the percentage of ovoid bolsters to all others is 6.9. This bolster form is linked with Mayapan Unslipped Ware tripod jar censers (no illustration) and a pedestal-base (?) vase (30, *k*); with Mayapan Red Ware restricted-orifice bowls (41, *a*, 2, 3), water jars (38, *a*, 17), and a tripod rounded-side bowl (no illustration); and with Peto Cream Ware storage jars (no illustration). In Hocaba-Tases at Mayapan the percentage of ovoid bolsters to all others is 2.6. They are connected with Mayapan Unslipped Ware cooking jars (no illustration) and effigy censers (no illustration); with Mayapan Red Ware restricted-orifice bowls (cf. 41, *a*, 2, 3) and a tripod rounded-side dish (no illustration); with San Joaquin Buff Ware storage jars (cf. 53, *a*, 11); and with Peto Cream Ware water jars (cf. GWB, fig. 24, *c*, 15). In Tases at Mayapan the percentage of ovoid bolsters to all others is 4.3. They are associated with Mayapan Unslipped Ware huge or large jars (28, *c*, 7), cooking jars (no illustration), and effigy censers (68, *b*, 2) and with Mayapan Red Ware tripod rounded-side bowls (no illustration).

Rounded bolsters are reasonably well represented throughout, being most used in Cehpech and least in Hocaba. In Cehpech the rounded bolster totals 78.6 per cent at Uxmal, 84.2 per cent at Kabah, and 37.4 per cent at Mayapan of all bolsters found in those ceramic complexes. They are associated with Puuc Slate Ware basins (4, a–e; 16, d, g; 26, b, 6, 7, 10), jars (5, e, z), and a flaring-side bowl (6, x); with Puuc Unslipped Ware storage jars (2, i–k, m; 26, a, 2–4; 60, c), hourglass censers (3, g), basins (cf. 3, r–t for form), and a deep bowl (3, p); with Cauich Coarse-cream Ware water jars (10, j); with Thin Slate Ware basins (7, v); and with Puuc Red Ware basins (GWB, fig. 52, f, 11). In Sotuta this bolster type forms 23.5 per cent at Chichen Itza and 1.4 per cent at Mayapan of all bolsters encountered in those ceramic complexes. They are linked with Chichen Slate Ware water jars (14, h–j, p), restricted-orifice basins (16, b; 27, h, i), and tripod dishes (19, b, d); with Chichen Unslipped Ware jars (11, d), and with a Chichen Red Ware jar (27, f). In Hocaba at Mayapan these rounded bolsters total 8.1 per cent of all bolsters. They are associated with Mayapan Unslipped Ware cooking jars (cf. 28, a, 9), huge or large size jars (cf. 28, c, 1, 4–6), and a restricted-orifice bowl (no illustration); with Mayapan Red Ware storage jars (cf. 38, a, 14, 15, 18), water jars (38, a, 5, 7; 74, d), and drums (GWB, fig. 25, a, 3); and with Peto Cream Ware water jars (cf. 52, b, d; 75, l). In Hocaba-Tases at Mayapan the rounded bolster forms 19.3 per cent of all bolsters. They are linked with Mayapan Red Ware storage jars (cf. 38, a, 5, 7), basins (46, b, 1), and restricted-orifice bowls (41, a, 1; 74, e); with Mayapan Unslipped Ware huge and large size storage jars (cf. 28, c, 1, 3–7); with San Joaquin Buff Ware storage jars (cf. 53, a, 1, 6); and with Peto Cream Ware water jars (52, b, d; 75, l) and a restricted-orifice bowl (no illustration). In Tases at Mayapan the rounded bolster totals 44 per cent of all bolsters. This form is connected with Mayapan Red Ware restricted-orifice bowls (41, a, 5), basins (46, b, 4), storage jars (38, a, 14, 15, 18, b, 8), water jars (no illustration), and a tripod dish (no illustration); with Mayapan Unslipped Ware huge or large size storage jars (28, c, 1, 4–6), effigy censers (no illustration), cooking jars (28, a, 9), tripod dishes (29, t), and restricted-orifice bowls (no illustration); with San Joaquin Buff Ware storage jars (53, a, 1, 6) and a basin (53, b, 4); and with Peto Cream jars (cf. 52, b, d; 75, l), basins (cf. 51, l), and a restricted-orifice bowl (51, j for vessel form).

Square bolsters are moderately well represented in Hocaba through Tases but appear rarely in Cehpech and are verified by two examples in Sotuta. In Cehpech at Kabah they total 7.8 per cent of all bolsters, 1.2 per cent at Uxmal, and .8 per cent at Mayapan. This bolster form is linked with Puuc Unslipped Ware storage jars (2, n; 26, a, 7) and basinlike censers (3, t), and with Puuc Slate Ware basins (4, i, j). In Sotuta the two examples of the square bolster occur on a Chichen Unslipped Ware storage jar (11, g) and a Chichen Red Ware restricted-orifice bowl (21, a). In Hocaba at Mayapan the square bolster totals 11 per cent of all bolsters. This bolster form is associated with Mayapan Red Ware water jars (23, i; 38, a, 11) and storage jars (cf. 38, b, 5); with Peto Cream Ware water jars (cf. 51, a, h); and with Mayapan Unslipped Ware huge or large storage jars (cf. 28, c, 1, 3–6). In Hocaba-Tases at Mayapan this type of bolster forms 8.5 per cent of all bolsters. This bolster form is used on Mayapan Unslipped Ware huge and large size storage jars (28, c, 2; 60, m), effigy censers (no illustration), tripod jar censers (no illustration), and a deep bowl (no illustration); on Mayapan Red Ware storage jars (38, c, 4), basins (cf. 46, b, 3, 5, 8), and restricted-orifice bowls (no illustration); on Peto Cream Ware water jars (51, a); and on San Joaquin Buff Ware storage jars (cf. 53, a, 4). In Tases at Mayapan the square bolster totals 12.5 per cent of all bolsters. This bolster type is associated with Mayapan Unslipped Ware huge or large size storage jars (28, c, 3, 10), effigy censers (no illustration), restricted-orifice bowls (no illustration), and a tripod dish (29, t); with Mayapan Red Ware storage jars (38, b, 5), basins (no illustration), bowl clusters (37, b, c for vessel form), drums (no illustration), and a restricted-orifice bowl (GWB, fig. 27, j, 7), with San Joaquin Buff Ware storage jars (53, a, 4) and a basin (53, b, 4 for vessel form); and with Peto Cream Ware basins (GWB, fig. 27, j, 26), storage jars (ibid., fig. 24, c, 22), and water jars (51, h; GWB, 19, i, 13).

Triangular bolsters are moderately well represented throughout but show greatest strength in the Cehpech Ceramic Complex at Mayapan and least strength in Sotuta at Chichen Itza. In Cehpech at Mayapan they total 51.2 per cent of all bolsters, 11.2 per cent at Uxmal, and 7.5 per cent at Kabah. This bolster form is linked with Puuc Slate Ware basins (4, f, h, k; 16, c, f), water jars (26, b, 1, 2), and tripod dishes (26, b, 17); with Cauich Coarse-cream Ware basins (GWB, 53, c, 15, 17, 21); with Puuc Unslipped Ware storage jars (2, o; 26, a, 5) and basinlike censers (3, s); and with Puuc Red Ware basins (GWB, 52, e, 4, f, 6, 13, 14). In Sotuta at Mayapan they form 9.6 per cent and at Chichen Itza 3.6 per cent of all bolsters. The triangular bolster is present in association with Chichen Slate Ware basins (15, c) and jars (27, a). In Hocaba at Mayapan triangular bolsters total 17.6 per cent of all bolsters. They are used on Mayapan Red Ware storage jars (cf. 38, b, 2–4, c, 6) and tripod dishes (no illustration); on Mayapan Unslipped Ware cooking jars (GWB, fig. 22, a, 27), and on Peto Cream Ware jars (ibid., figs. 20, b, 5; 24, c, 23) and restricted-orifice bowls (ibid., fig. 20, b, 15, f, 8). In Hocaba-Tases at Mayapan this bolster type forms 7 per cent of all bolsters. It is associated with Mayapan Red Ware storage jars (38, c, 6), basins (46, b, 6, 7), and restricted-orifice bowls (no illustration) and with Mayapan Unslipped Ware huge jars (cf. 28, c, 8). In Tases at Mayapan triangular bolsters total 8.3 per cent of all bolsters. They are used on Mayapan Red Ware storage jars (38, b, 2–4, c, 6), basins (46, b, 6, 7), and restricted-orifice bowls (GWB, figs. 25, p, 2; 27, j, 9); on Mayapan Unslipped Ware cooking jars (ibid., fig. 22, a, 28) and huge or large size storage jars (28, c, 8); and on San Joaquin Buff Ware storage jars (53, a, 5, 7, 8) and a basin (53, b, 4 for vessel form).

Bulging rim. This rim form does not protrude far enough to be considered a bolster; it is more than a thickening and is connected with the vessel lip, i.e., the edge of the rim. It is represented in most ceramic complexes, more abundantly in Hocaba through Tases than in the earlier ceramic complexes. In Cehpech at Uxmal the bulging rim forms .8 per cent of all rim sherds and is associated with Cauich Coarse-cream Ware vertical-neck jars (10, d); at Kabah .2 per cent with the same jar form and ware. In Sotuta no bulging rim forms are noted. In Hocaba this rim form totals 3.6 per cent of all rim sherds and is linked with Mayapan Unslipped Ware cooking jars (GWB, fig. 22, a, 1) and Fine Orange Ware, Matillas Group tripod dishes (cf. 55, a, 4–6, 8). In Hocaba-Tases it forms 2.2 per cent of all rim sherds, deducting those of effigy censers, and is connected with Mayapan Unslipped Ware cooking jars (GWB, fig. 22, a, 1) and a small-mouth, high-neck jar (no illustration) and with Fine Orange Ware, Matillas Group tripod dishes (cf. 55, a, 4–6, 8). In Tases the bulging rim totals 1.7 per cent of all rim sherds, deducting those of effigy censers. It is found on Mayapan Unslipped Ware cooking jars (GWB, fig. 22, a, 1) and on Fine Orange Ware, Matillas Group tripod dishes (55, a, 4–6, 8).

Everted rim. This rim form includes both slightly everted and widely everted rims. The latter are rare and more often associated with the Middle and Late Preclassic periods. The everted rim is well represented throughout, with a high point

in the Sotuta Ceramic Complex. In Cehpech at Uxmal it totals 2.3 per cent of all rim sherds; at Kabah .9 per cent, and at Mayapan 7.4 per cent. It is used on Puuc Slate Ware taper-neck jars (5, u–w), flaring-side tripod dishes (6, u, v; 26, b, 14–16), and high-neck jars (5, dd); on Puuc Unslipped Ware storage jars (2, b, c; 26, a, 8, 10, 11) and hourglass censers (3, b, f, j); and on Fine Orange Ware, Altar Group cylindrical vases (27, l). In Sotuta at Chichen Itza this rim form totals 10.7 per cent of all rim sherds and at Mayapan 7.3 per cent. It is associated with Chichen Unslipped Ware hourglass censers (12, d), storage jars (11, k), and ringstand vases (30, u); with Chichen Slate Ware water jars (14, a–d, f) and tripod dishes (19, a, c, e); with Chichen Red Ware water jars (20, d), tripod dishes (21, cc, ff, gg), and a rounded-side bowl (21, x); and with Fine Orange Ware, Silho Group tripod dishes (22, s–u). In Hocaba at Mayapan the everted rim forms 1.7 per cent of all rim sherds. It is used on Mayapan Red Ware water jars (38, a, 6), tripod dishes (GWB, fig. 94, h, 9), and a storage jar (cf. 38, b, 1), and on Peto Cream Ware jars (cf. 51, b) and tripod dishes (GWB, fig. 24, a, 10). In Hocaba-Tases at Mayapan this rim form totals .4 per cent of all rim sherds, deducting those of effigy censers. It is linked with Mayapan Red Ware storage jars (38, a, 16), tripod dishes (GWB, fig. 94, h, 9), and a water jar (cf. 38, a, 6); with Peto Cream Ware water jars (51, b); with San Joaquin Buff Ware storage jars (no illustration); with Mayapan Unslipped Ware cooking jars (no illustration) and a huge storage jar (no illustration); and with Tulum Red Ware jars (48, c, e). In Tases at Mayapan the everted rim forms .4 per cent of all rim sherds, deducting those of effigy censers. It is used on Mayapan Red Ware storage jars (38, b, 1, 6) and water jars (cf. 38, a, 6); on Mayapan Unslipped Ware tripod dishes (29, u) and a huge jar (no illustration); on San Joaquin Buff Ware storage jars (no illustration); on Peto Cream Ware storage jars (51, f); and on Tulum Red Ware jars (48, a, b).

Incurving rim. This is a rim that turns inward either in a gentle curve or more abruptly. The incurving rim dates back to Preclassic times (RES, fig. 16, e, 4–8), but then seems to disappear until Tepeu 2 times (ibid., fig. 48, b). It is also well represented in Tepeu 3 at Uaxactun (ibid., fig. 48, c; 49, a, 9–12; 50, b, 1–6). In Cehpech at Uxmal the incurving rim totals .3 per cent of all rim sherds and at Kabah 1.1 per cent. It is associated with Puuc Slate Ware jars (5, x) and with Puuc Unslipped Ware flaring-side bowls (3, q) and an hourglass censer (3, k). In Sotuta at Chichen Itza this rim type forms .3 per cent of all rim sherds. It is linked with Chichen Slate Ware grater bowls (no illustration) and with Chichen Unslipped Ware comals (GWB, fig. 97, *k, 9*). *Remarks*: the incurving rim seems to have been discontinued, at least in the Yucatan Peninsula section of the Maya area, after the Sotuta Ceramic Complex.

Inset rim. This type rim is extremely rare. Only two examples have been noted in these collections. Both occur in Tases and one is definitely made for a fitted cover. This is a Mayapan Red Ware effigy double-boiler vessel (45, *a*). The other belongs to a Fine Orange Ware, Matillas Group deep bowl (55, *a, 7*). Another type has an inner ledge on which a cover might rest. This rim form is exemplified in Cehpech on a Puuc Red Ware jar (26, *e, 6*). The same vessel form appears, however, at Labna (GWB, fig. 3, *b*), decorated with Late Classic figure painting and presumably belonging to that era. *Remarks*: it is interesting to note that here we have examples of two different kinds of cover rest; one a slipcover exterior type, the other an interior set-in rest.

Overhanging rim. This rim form may at times be confused with the everted rim, except that basically the overhanging rim droops downward, hanging close to rim wall and the everted rim forms a near right angle with the body. The overhanging rim is fairly well represented in Cehpech but then jumps to Hocaba-Tases and Tases for a modest revival. In Cehpech at Uxmal this rim form totals 1.5 per cent of all rim sherds and at Mayapan 1.1 per cent. It is associated with Puuc Unslipped Ware storage jars (2, *a*) and with Puuc Slate Ware high-neck jars (5, *ee*). In Hocaba-Tases at Mayapan it forms .1 per cent of all rim sherds after deducting the effigy censers. The overhanging rim is used on Mayapan Red Ware restricted-orifice bowls (no illustration), a basin (no illustration), and a storage jar (cf. 38, *b, 7, 9*), and on a Mayapan Unslipped Ware cooking jar (cf. GWB, fig. 14, *e, 9*). In Tases at Mayapan this rim type totals .1 per cent of all rim sherds after deducting the effigy censers. It is associated with Mayapan Red Ware storage jars (38, *b, 7, 9*).

Parenthesis rim. This rim form derives its name from the resemblance it bears to the two upright curves that limit a parenthetical phrase. It also suggests a bicycle tire profile. There is an intimation of this form in Cehpech associated with Puuc Slate Ware taper-neck jars (5, *v, w*) which are everted but have a very slight parenthesis aspect. It first appears at Mayapan in its true form in Hocaba-Tases, where it totals .2 per cent of all rim sherds, deducting those from effigy censers. The

parenthesis rim is studied under jars with this rim form earlier in this chapter. It is associated with San Joaquin Buff Ware water jars (53, *a, 20*); with Tulum Red Ware water jars (cf. 48, *k*); and with Mayapan Red Ware high-neck jars (cf. 38, *d, 1–3*). In Tases at Mayapan it forms .2 per cent of all rim sherds, deducting those from effigy censers. The parenthesis rim is linked with Mayapan Red Ware water jars (38, *d, 1–3*); with San Joaquin Buff Ware water jars (53, *a, 18, 21*); and with Mayapan Unslipped Ware wide-mouth, high-neck jars (31, *g*).

Pinched rim. This category has a tendency to blend into what has been termed a slightly triangular rim bolster. Pinched rims are rare and appear to be confined to the Cehpech Ceramic Complex. At Uxmal they total .9 per cent of all rim sherds; at Mayapan only 1 sherd was found. They are associated with Puuc Unslipped Ware storage jars (2, *h, l*; 26, *a, 6*).

Rim molding. This rim treatment consists of a flat raised band encircling the upper exterior of a vessel. It is used sparingly in Cehpech but increases in popularity in Sotuta through Tases. In Cehpech at Uxmal rim moldings are used on .17 per cent of all rim sherds and at Mayapan on a single sherd. They are linked to Puuc Unslipped Ware storage jars (2, *e*) and to a Thin Slate Ware rounded-side bowl (7, *p*). In Sotuta at Chichen Itza this rim type forms 1.7 per cent of all rim sherds and at Mayapan 3.4 per cent. It is associated with Chichen Slate Ware restricted-orifice basins (16, *a*) and cylindrical tripods (13, *l*); with Plumbate Ware, Tohil Group standard jars (23, *a*) and restricted-orifice bowls (23, *b*); with Fine Orange Ware, Silho Group pyriform vases (22, *g*), a jar (22, *a*), a hemispherical bowl (22, *q*), and a cylindrical vase (27, *j*); and with Chichen Red Ware pyriform vases (20, *r–t*), a flaring-side dish (21, *u*), a cylindrical vase (GWB, fig. 86, *f*), and a restricted-orifice bowl (cf. 21, *a*, for vessel form). In Hocaba at Mayapan the rim molding totals 3.4 per cent of all rim sherds. It is associated with Mayapan Red Ware water jars (cf. 38, *a, 9*) and with Mayapan Unslipped Ware pedestal-base jar censers (no illustration). In Hocaba-Tases at Mayapan this rim form totals 1.5 per cent of all rim sherds, deducting those from effigy censers. It is used on Mayapan Red Ware water jars (GWB, fig. 25, *c, 1–5*) and drums (39, *h*) and on Mayapan Unslipped Ware pedestal-base jar censers (no illustration). In Tases at Mayapan rim moldings total .8 per cent of all rim sherds deducting those from effigy censers. They are associated with Mayapan Red Ware water jars

(GWB, fig. 25, c, 1–5) and with Peto Cream Ware water jars (cf. 52, a).

Scalloped rim. Another term for this is pie-crust lip or rim, made by indenting the lip with the finger or a tool. In the collections used for this report a number of scalloped flanges are recorded, but only one scalloped rim, and that linked with a comal of uncertain chronology (cf. 18, h). Considering its position and association at Chichen Itza, however, it might belong in the Sotuta Ceramic Complex.

T-shape rim. This is a very special rim form principally confined to Yucatan and the Cehpech Ceramic Complex. It was not encountered in any ceramic complexes postdating Cehpech, but its beginning was in the Preclassic Period or Formative Stage (GWB, fig. 5, b, 1). In Cehpech at Uxmal it totals 1.3 per cent of all rim sherds; at Kabah .7 per cent, and at Mayapan 15.9 per cent. The T-shape rim is used on Puuc Slate Ware jars (5, d, j) and basins (GWB, fig. 43, d, 1, 12, 15, 16, 21, 27, 28, 45, 46); on Cauich Coarse-cream Ware basins (10, a) and jars (GWB, fig. 53, a–d); and on Puuc Unslipped Ware storage jars (26, a, 9, 12) and hourglass censers (3, j).

Thickened rim. This rim form consists of a thickening of the upper part of the vessel as it approaches and includes the lip or edge. It is lightly distributed throughout. In Cehpech at Uxmal it totals 3.7 per cent of all rim sherds; at Kabah 2.9 per cent, and at Mayapan 1 sherd. Thickened rims are associated with Puuc Unslipped Ware storage jars (2, p) and hourglass censers (3, a); with Cauich Coarse-cream Ware jars (10, i), and with Puuc Slate Ware water jars (5, f, h, i, y). In Sotuta at Chichen Itza they form .1 per cent of all rim sherds. These few sherds are connected with Chichen Unslipped Ware comals (18, h). In Hocaba at Mayapan this rim form totals .3 per cent of all rim sherds. It is associated with Peto Cream Ware jars (52, c, f) and with Mayapan Red Ware storage jars (38, c, 1, 3). In Hocaba-Tases at Mayapan a single example is present, connected with a Mayapan Red Ware basin (no illustration). In Tases at Mayapan thickened rims total .2 per cent of all rim sherds, deducting those from effigy censers. They are linked with Mayapan Red Ware tripod dishes (GWB, fig. 94, h, 13), drums (39, b, e, g, i, k), and storage jars (38, b, 22) and Peto Cream Ware storage jars (cf. 52, f).

DECORATIVE TECHNIQUE MODES

In Chapter V on methods of decoration and in Tables 25–40 all the techniques involved are listed and described. Surely the generic terms for these techniques, such as carving, incising, and painting, to name a few, are too general to be effective as modes. Therefore if these are separated into their more specific parts, the subdivisions take on a stronger modal significance. For instance, carving subdivides into plano-relief, flat-carving, modeled-carving, and gouged-incising, each of which may be handled as a mode with rewarding results. The same is true of incising, which may be separated into sharp-incising, groove-incising, slant-grooving, light-incising, fine-incising, and scratching. Add to these subdivisions a further separation, based on when the incising was made, the result is a group of specific and useful modes. In the case of painting much the same classificatory process is followed. There are two main divisions: positive and negative painting. In the positive category both prefire and postfire painting are used. Positive prefire painting needs further refinement. This might be

accomplished by using line treatment: fine or thick, light or bold. Positive postfire painting is separated into three categories: 1) design painting on a primary white calcareous coating; 2) the simple addition of blue, green, or red paint; and 3) the application of stucco which is then painted. In the negative category, which may be prefired or refired, there are two principal techniques: resist and reserve space. Sometimes, especially in figure painting, positive and negative painting are combined on the same vessel. This is true of the early resist painting at Teotihuacan, which at times is combined with positive painting. Note, however, that the Late Classic figure painting is coupled with the reserve-space negative technique, whereas the Patlachique or Protoclassic combination is with negative resist. Resist at Teotihuacan, apparently a refired and smoked technique, has a range from Tezoyuca through Tzacualli. In any event it is resist (possibly more than one kind) and reserve space techniques that are successfully used as modes, not those of negative painting or positive painting.

DESIGN MODES

In Chapter VI on types of design, all the designs used on the pottery under consideration are listed, illustrated, and described. If general terms such as circles, scrolls, or terraces, to name but a few, are used, their usefulness as modes is extremely vague; the more specific approach is most likely to bear fruit. For instance, the circle, either simple or concentric, can be used as a filler, as part of a figure such as the eye or ear ornament, as one of several devices in a design, or linked with other circles to form a chain. The scroll has many varieties: angular, hook, "ram horn," simple curvilinear, or spiral. And these are often combined with other devices to make a design such as the step-fret or the scroll meander, to mention only two. The terrace may be plain or solid black, split or combined with some other design element such as a right angle, a scroll, or a U-shape. And these terraces are often used in bands. Thus when reduced to more specific entities, designs become useful modes.

Another approach to handling specific design forms is by arranging them in a special way. Here we refer to symmetry. An interesting example of this is found in the band designs of Fine Orange Ware, Silho Group associated with the pyriform vessel form. In this connection the painted black bands are normally done in translation or serial repetition, whereas those that are gouged-incised are usually developed in slide reflection.

PART THREE

Ceramic Distribution at Mayapan

VIII

Ceramic Association Within the
Wall at Mayapan

The Mayapan ceramic diagnostics are described in Part Four below. The percentage changes by early, middle, and late lots are listed in Table 7. Here, however, we are interested in the pottery associated with different civic or ceremonial groups and the attendant structure types. The fundamental ceramic divisions most adaptable to, and most helpful for, an understanding of the relationship of pottery to these groups and structures are utilitarian as opposed to ceremonial and jars as opposed to bowls. Certain vessels normally serving a utilitarian purpose on occasion may be used ceremonially, and vice versa. Actually the very few that are used for a function other than originally intended would not appreciably alter the percentages set forth in Tables 8–23. Other categories might have been used such as wares: kitchen, fine, ritualistic, special, and trade, with a collection of forms for each. Such a breakdown, however, would only have complicated the problem without clarifying it.

Parts of this chapter are admittedly impressionistic; although I have tried to make all my assumptions and analyses as clear as possible, I may even be liable to the charge of circularity. I hope, however, that the clarity of presentation will underscore those places where circularity may have slipped into the discussion. In spite of these reservations, I feel that some of the results discussed here are of sufficient interest to warrant their inclusion in this report. This feeling is reinforced by the fact that sufficient data on sherd counts, associations, and other information, have been included in various chapters to enable other scholars to rework and amplify my material, if they are so inclined.

UTILITARIAN POTTERY

This class of pottery is found in unslipped wares, red ware, black ware, cream ware, or buff ware and includes certain forms, some of which may be artistic as well as utilitarian and serve a purpose other than ceremonial. These forms, whether purely utilitarian or artistic but serviceable, comprise the following: jars for carrying water, storage, and cooking; basins or large bowls used for storage or cooking; tripod flaring-side or rounded-side bowls, including graters; small bowls; deep bowls; vases; molds; miniature vessels; candle-flame shields; bowl clusters; and stands. The function of these vessels is determined not by the fact that they are found in a kitchen or common dwelling but by the way they are made, by evidence of burning, and by the fact that in many cases the same vessel form is used today in Mesoamerica for one or more specific services.

Jars for carrying water have a narrow mouth and neck which makes for easier pouring and less chance of spilling; they are small enough in size, weight, and capacity for easy carrying, and the opposed handles provide convenient attachments for lifting and carrying; similar vessels are used to carry water in many parts of contemporary Mesoamerica (R. Thompson, 1958, p. 59). Jars for storage have a wide mouth and are usually too large in size, weight, and capacity for easy carrying. Most do not have handles. The large orifices facilitate the removal of contents and they have the appropriate size and capacity for storage purposes. Furthermore, similar vessels serve as storage containers, especially of water, in many parts of contemporary Mesoamerica (ibid., p. 60). Jars for cooking are globular with broad, low bodies, very thin walls, low necks, well-marked shoulders, and probably rounded bodies. Amazingly, no certain bottoms were found, perhaps because they were burned sufficiently for them to crumble into ashes. The few lugs and handles present might be functionally related to suspension, but most are too small to serve this purpose effectively. This form also is similar to the standard cooking pot used over the fire throughout Mesoamerica today (ibid., p. 61).

Large bowls or basins may be used as storage containers or cooking pots. They are large in size and capacity and usually quite heavy, which makes them hard to carry. Very few have fire-blackened bottoms, but similar vessels are used for both storage and cooking throughout modern Meso-america (*ibid.*, p. 61).

Tripod flaring-side dishes, found in large quantity and in many sizes at Mayapan, are quite shallow and flat-bottomed, which makes them good for serving food. The great quantity and serviceability of these vessels, considering the dearth of small serving dishes at Mayapan, is a good negative reason for assigning at least a fair share of them to that function. It is, of course, a fact that this service could be equally well used ceremonially. At Mayapan a very small number of these dishes were found in graves or caches, while a large number were dredged up from the Sacred Cenote at Chichen Itza. For this reason my placement of this form entirely in the utilitarian category may have been inaccurate.

Tripod rounded-side bowls or dishes are used for both serving and grating. The serving function is closely allied to that of the flaring-side dishes which are at times hard to differentiate in form. The grating function is assumed when the bowl floor shows scoring. If these so-called graters served some other purpose, possibly ceremonial, I am not aware of it. That this form has been known to be employed for grating chillies is well known and quite feasible.

Small flat-base bowls, some of which have a restricted orifice while others are hemispherical, are also considered to be utilitarian. Because of their size they have a small capacity, which suggests a food dish rather than a storage vessel. The form follows that of the gourd, which is extensively used for eating and drinking throughout tropical America. The restricted-orifice form has often been referred to as a seed bowl in the literature. Deep bowls may have a pedestal base, a ringstand base, or three feet. In this report the plain bowls, without spikes, buttons, and decorated fillets, are considered as serving some utilitarian function, possibly eating and drinking.

Vases, usually with a pedestal base but sometimes having three feet, are of small size and capacity and considered to have been used as household containers for food or drink. Similar vessels are used for these purposes throughout contemporary Latin America (*ibid.*, p. 62). Molds most assuredly serve to reproduce certain forms in quantity. Miniature vessels function as paint-pots, since red and blue paint has been noted

in some examples, as perfume flasks, a suggestion not necessarily proved, and presumably as toys. A small collection of forms has been included under utilitarian because the only function logically attributable to them falls in that category. These are candle-flame shields, bowl clusters, and stands. Candle-flame shields are discussed as to their function in Chapter XVI under Telchaquillo Brick Ware. Bowl clusters and stands are examined as modes in Chapter VII, and their possible usefulness is reviewed.

The large quantity of these forms found in certain groups of buildings would indicate that these groups had a domestic rather than ceremonial function. Types of domestic structure would be those which A. L. Smith (1962) has called kitchens, ordinary dwellings, elaborate dwellings, etc., on a strictly nonceramic (i.e., architectural) basis.

CEREMONIAL POTTERY

This includes special forms associated with many of the same wares as utilitarian pottery such as unslipped, red, black, cream, and buff. I also include fine orange and plumbate, which may have had little ritualistic significance but as luxury trade ware items most certainly formed part of vessels used on very special occasions and in that sense were ceremonial. These special forms comprise the following: censers including effigy, ladle, tripod jars, and pedestal-base jars; cups which may be tripod, pedestal-base, and rarely flat-base; effigy vessels; figurines; pedestal-base vases; drums and masks.

The effigy censer has vents in floor or side wall and nearly always shows floor-burning and sometimes adhering copal. The ladle censer handle usually opens into a bowl, making it possible to blow on the embers. The tripod jar censer shows fire-burning on floor which has many perforations, while the pedestal-base censer jars lack the floor vents and few identifiable base sherds show floor-burning. Both the tripod jar censer and the pedestal-base jar censer were decorated with painting, appliqué buttons, and impressed fillets, although the latter had less painting and had spikes added.

Quite small cups are found in both burials and caches and may occasionally have served a utilitarian purpose, although none suggests itself. Many have modeled heads on one side, often representing the god Chac. Effigy vessels are many and varied, but nearly all suggest worship of some god. These effigy vessels are associated with caches, rarely with burials. Figurines, often included in burials, rarely in caches, in some instances were toys and whistles, and perhaps more often were small personal idols. Pedestal-base vases when decorated with paint and appliqué spikes, buttons, and impressed fillets are considered as ceremonial pottery, although they do not appear to have been used as censers. Masks are quite clearly ceremonial, as are drums. At Mayapan the greater part of ceremonial pottery is associated with Mayapan Unslipped Ware; even in this ware it does not become dominant until the Tases Phase (Table 10).

The widespread existence of these forms of the wares noted above in certain groups of structures would indicate that these structures had a ceremonial rather than a domestic function. Included under the term ceremony would be those structure types which T. Proskouriakoff (1962a) has called shrines, colonnades, temples, etc., on a strictly nonceramic (i.e., architectural) basis. Some assemblages of structures, like quadrangles, may have served more than one purpose, while structures such as oratories may have at times taken on more importance and thus changed from

nonceremonial or semiceremonial into fully ritualistic. Therefore it is often the character of these associated ceramics that reveals as clearly as do the architectural features the uses of structure at any given time.

JARS AND BOWLS
(Table 23)

In like manner jars and bowls may indicate a more specific function for a utilitarian or domestic architectural location. A high percentage of water jars would lead one to suspect a cenote as the source of the material, whereas an abundance of cooking and storage vessels including bowls, basins, and wide-mouthed jars would suggest a kitchen or midden. A preponderance of bowls of various forms combined with many shapes and types both utilitarian and to a much lesser degree ceremonial, would infer a dwelling, whereas the same combination with a preponderance of censers, effigy vessels, and other special forms and types would suggest a ceremonial structure.

POTTERY ASSOCIATED WITH
THE BASIC CIVIC DIVISIONS AT MAYAPAN

For easier handling of the material excavated at Mayapan, four divisions were made and described in the introduction to this report. Three were most important and separated the site into the following lots or units: A, the dwelling places; C, the ceremonial structures, and D, the cenotes. The fourth category, B, concerned the great wall encircling the city, and was omitted from the present study because of the extremely small amount of sherd material involved (782 sherds from 5 cuts).

DWELLING LOTS (A)

The ceramic-dwelling association is listed in Table 8; the total sherd count in this group is 149,-052 or 37.4 per cent of the total number of sherds found within the confines of the wall of Mayapan. In the same table the utilitarian sherds encountered in dwellings form 73.1 per cent, as compared to 44.3 per cent for ceremonial structures. Table 2 lists the findings from a stratigraphic pit in a typical dwelling (J–49b). Here the utilitarian pot-

tery formed 92.1 per cent and jars 72.6 per cent. In this table the Hocaba Ceramic Complex is predominant (92.3%), Mayapan Red Ware strongly represented (63.5%), and Mayapan unslipped ware poorly (29.9%). At this point someone may well ask why the Table 8 finding of 73.1 per cent utilitarian pottery differs so markedly from the 92.1 per cent finding in J–49b pit or the 78.7 per cent combined results of Tables 12 and 13 dealing with ordinary and elaborate dwellings. The answer is simply that Table 8 includes all buildings, even shrines and oratories, associated with dwellings and dwelling groups.

CEREMONIAL LOTS (C)

The ceramic-ceremonial type structure association is also listed in Table 8, and in this context the sherd count totals 194,654 or 48.8 per cent. In the same table the utilitarian sherds found in ceremonial structures comprise 44.3 per cent, the ceremonial 55.7 per cent. This is a complete reversal of the dwelling lot results. In Table 3 are listed the detailed findings of a stratigraphic trench cut through the accumulated refuse deposited between two ceremonial structures, Q–77 and Q–162. Once again the preponderance (70.8%) of the Hocaba Ceramic Complex is apparent. In this trench collection, utilitarian pottery formed 81.1 per cent and jar forms totaled 65.7 per cent. This is comparable to what we find in the combination elaborate dwelling ceremonial type midden (Table 22, Q–127, 127a). A true ceremonial image is represented in Str. Q–151, a colonnade. The results listed in Table 18 show that the ceremonial pottery totals 85.1 per cent and jars form only 9.7 per cent out of a total of 44.373 sherds.

CENOTE LOTS (D)
(Table 9)

The ceramic-cenote association in Table 8 shows a total sherd count of 55,255 or 13.8 per cent. In this same table the cenotes show a utilitarian content of 86.7 per cent, as compared to a ceremonial sherd participation of 13.3 per cent. This high percentage of utilitarian pottery was to be expected in cenotes primarily used as a source of water. Here is proof that most cenotes played a small part in the ceremonial activities of the city life, even though the only cenotes excavated within the great wall of Mayapan were located in ceremonial centers. In Table 4, comprising a detailed examination of an isolated stratified column in Cenote Chen Mul, once again the Hocaba Ceramic Complex proved to be dominant, 51.4 per cent, but the Tases Ceramic Complex was beginning to show some strength, 23.8 per cent. Weathering played a strong part, resulting in a high percentage (22.7) of unidentifiable sherds. In this column utilitarian pottery comprised 76.9 per cent, ceremonial pottery 23.1 per cent, and jars 45.3 per cent. Undoubtedly the large proportion of weathered material cut down both the utilitarian and jar percentages. Ordinarily jars were far more numerous in cenote context than the above percentage indicated. Percentage of jars associated with cenotes was 63.4. This disparity may be due to the fact that the stratigraphic column was situated directly below the mouth of the cenote, which was surrounded by ceremonial structures and quite far removed from any of several water holes within Cenote Chen Mul. Jars were found in greater numbers near the main water holes (Table 21), while censers were far more abundant near the mouth of this cenote. The location of the column under the mouth also explains the considerable quantity of weathered and unidentifiable sherds which were found there.

POTTERY ASSOCIATED WITH RESIDENTIAL, CIVIC, AND RELIGIOUS STRUCTURES

In examining the relationship between pottery and the associated structures, the utmost care was taken to avoid mixed or contaminated sherd lots. Only surface collections immediately involved with a certain building or special room were used. It would have been interesting to distinguish the fall from the material resting on the floor of a room or platform at the time of collapse, but this separation was rarely made. Indeed it is extremely difficult to make, especially if the fall is light. Burial, burial vault, ossuary, and cache materials were used because they were associated with the function of the structure, while fill deposits were omitted because they had nothing to do with use of the building. In spite of a number of problems, we feel that a fairly accurate ceramic-architectural picture has been obtained.

The various types of structure at Mayapan have been well studied and presented in the Carnegie Institution publication *Mayapan, Yucatan, Mexico* (Pollock et al. 1962). In that publication T. Proskouriakoff handled the "Civic and Religious Structures of Mayapan" as they occur in ceremonial groups: their composition, building construction, architectural ornament, and associated sculpture, whereas A. L. Smith in the same publication described the "Residential and Associated Structures" emphasizing dwellings, their supplementary buildings including kitchens, platforms, shrines, and oratories. Together these buildings formed dwelling groups. The platform with its variety of function has been omitted for lack of excavation. Residential structures, except for a few in the Main Group, are mostly to be found in other than the three principal ceremonial groups located within the walled city of Mayapan. When present, they tend to be more elaborate than the ordinary dwelling. Kitchens, oratories, and shrines may be associated with either dwelling or ceremonial groups.

KITCHENS
(Table 11)

A. L. Smith (1962, p. 220) tells us "There can be little doubt that all groups must have had at least one kitchen." There were several possible kitchen types: the corner room, Str. R–86a; exterior platforms or benches at the end of houses, Strs. K–67c and P–23c; small separate platforms, Str. Q–208a; and certain indefinite constructions behind colonnades, Strs. Q–86, Q–145a, Q–212a. Table 11 lists eight kitchens with associated surface pottery totaling 94.4 per cent utilitarian, nearly 80 per cent in the jar category. Of this selection, Str. R–86a is without question a kitchen (*ibid.*, p. 219); its pottery is 98.9 per cent utilitarian pottery and 93.2 per cent jar forms of which 70 per cent were for cooking or storage and only 30 per cent for water. These results are what one would expect. Other unexcavated but possible kitchens include structures A–3f, C–15c, E–26, H–27a, H–30, J–86a, K–79c, L–114a, P–28b, P–143, R–142c, S–53a, S–96, T–53a, U–2b, X–43, Y–1b, Y–8b, Y–111c, all of the exterior platform or bench type; A–3b, S–26c, both separate platforms with two walls.

DWELLINGS

In a broad sense dwellings may be separated into ordinary and elaborate, the former used by the poor or unimportant, the latter by the rich or important.

Ordinary dwellings (Table 12). These houses were of the simplest type, rarely consisting of more than two rooms, one in front, one in back, supported by a low platform and covered by a thatch roof. According to Smith (*ibid.*, p. 217) "Occasionally these two-room houses have a small altar placed against the back wall of the rear room in line with the doorway (fig. 5, c, Str. S–30c)." Burials were found in these houses, but rarely caches. The percentage of utilitarian pottery is high, averaging 88.8; and jars of all kinds total 66.4.

Elaborate dwellings (Table 13). These more imposing dwellings are nearly always found in a group, and most of the pretentious groups are in the vicinity of the Main Group. Besides being generally bigger and more elaborate than the ordinary dwellings, these houses usually have beam-and-mortar roofs (as witness 14 out of the 20 listed in Table 13), masonry walls, stone columns, and often more than two rooms. Some had a shrine room centered in the rear room area or projected from the center of the house rear. The ceramic findings would differ in no way from those of ordinary dwellings, were it not for three structures R–86, R–88, and Y–2d. These three had a total sherd count of 4,141 with 62.9 per cent ceremonial, 37.1 per cent utilitarian; jars totaled 23.6 per cent. This result is very similar to that of temples; in other words, these particular elaborate dwellings appear to have a strong ceremonial flavor. Just why these few, architecturally much like the rest of this group, should have more ceremonially oriented pottery, and therefore presumably served a different purpose, is not at all clear.

ORATORIES
(Table 14)

Throughout Mayapan many groups had what may be called a family oratory. This was usually a single-room structure, although four out of approximately 50 had an adjoining room. Of the 14 listed in Table 14, 9 had beam-and-mortar roofs and 5 had thatch roofs. All had altars placed against the center of the back wall. Usually oratories had benches extending around three sides of the room, but sometimes they were lodged only against the length of the back wall and one end wall. Caches and burials were found in most excavated oratories.

No single feature mentioned above identifies a building as an oratory, but a combination of several does, yet the ceramic association tends to separate them. Three, including Q–82, Q–153, and R–91, have a much stronger ceremonial pottery character than the rest. The pottery of these three, Type B in Table 14, is 65.3 per cent ceremonial as compared to 23 per cent for the others, Type A. Thus our initial separation is based on ceremonial ceramic content. Closely allied to this quantitative factor, however, is the basic function of the oratory, worship involving prayer and offerings.

In the case of the Type A Oratory usually an ordinary single family is implied, with the oratory serving for the conducting of special services. The abundance and quality of the ceremonial material may be directly related to the importance of the family. Thus three of the oratories, Q–37a, Q–172, and Y–8b, classified as Type A, have a larger ceremonial pottery content than is normal for this type. All form part of family groups, but each has a different plan and setting. Q–37a, a single building, is one of a group of two constructions. Q–172, a two-room building, forms part of a group dominated by Q–169, an elaborate dwelling, and includes Q–171, another dwelling; Q–170 is a shrine; Q–173a is a warehouse; and Q–173 is possibly the house of the Caluac (Thompson and Thompson, 1955, pp. 242–243). Y–8b, a room with attached kitchen, is the central building of a group of three. There are other single-room oratories and others with attached kitchens, but why are these listed above more heavily stocked with ceremonial pottery? One suggestion is that oratories Q–37a and Y–8b served a number of neighboring families too small to have their own. On the other hand Q–172, a two-room type oratory and service room combination, was associated with a fairly large, important family group, possibly presided over by a member of the priesthood or the nobility. Most likely an oratory in such a setting would be well stocked for the practice of an ancestral cult. Structure Q–172 with its combination service room and oratory is somewhat similar to Structure R–88, where the north room could be for service and the south room the oratory. This oratory, also, had a very high ceremonial pottery content (69.9 per cent). Perhaps Structure R–88 served the same purpose for its associated quadrangle as Structure Q–172 did for its smaller group of buildings.

The Type B oratories separate into those including Strs. Q–82 and Q–153, linked with a ceremonial group and in this case the Main Group (Square Q) or those with a single oratory, Str. R–91, associated with a quadrangle, known as a residential group which comprises Strs. R–85 to R–90. In either case these ritualistic or distinguished surroundings would tend to increase the normal ceremonial accumulation. And since two of these three Type B oratories, Q–82 and Q–153, have no dwellings within their groups, it is likely that they served not a particular family, but rather a particular cult. Perhaps the men were housed in the group colonnaded hall to assure their freedom from contamination during certain periods; at this time they may have used the group oratory for prayer and offerings. The oratory, Structure R–91, on the other hand, was used for much the same purpose but by men from the quadrangle, which is composed of three elaborate dwellings, a spacious kitchen, three shrines, and a possible oratory (Str. R–88). It is assumed because of the con-

siderable amount of ceremonial type pottery recovered from this quadrangle, the size and quality of the residences, the separate shrines, and even a possible oratory within its walls that it housed people of importance. The oratory set apart, Str. R–91, may have been used like those in the ceremonial group to give greater isolation to the men participating.

There are a number of oratories not excavated and therefore not listed in Table 14. These are as follows: Type A, located in dwelling groups, K–79b, L–140c, Z–22c; Type B, located in ceremonial groups, H–14, J–109, Q–55, Q–88, Q–142a (?), Q–158, Q–202, and Q–217.

SHRINES

As defined by Proskouriakoff (1962a, p. 90):

The word "shrine" is applied to small cell-like enclosures usually containing an altar or a statue. At Mayapan we distinguish three major kinds: *interior shrines*, such as enclose the altars of colonnaded halls; *statue shrines*, which are usually just large enough to house a stucco figure and which often occur on stairways or on low platforms in front of temples; and *raised shrines*, which stand on independent substructures, some being quite elaborate and resembling small temples.

The first two are closely linked to either colonnaded halls or temples; the third is a freestanding, usually single-room structure set on a platform or high substructure with one or more stairways. Both group and ceremonial shrines belong to this third category, while the first two are purely ceremonial.

Group shrines (Table 15). These shrines according to A. L. Smith (1962, p. 222) are "small individual structures on a platform . . . usually placed in the center of the [domestic group] court. . . ." Three examples are listed in the table of which one has two rooms and one a beam-and-mortar roof, both most unusual adjuncts for group shrines. None has a stairway but an altar bench is usually present. Caches rather than burials are associated with these shrines. In fact, except for ossuary shafts, burials are lacking in all shrines. The group shrine ceramic picture consists of a high utilitarian percentage (84.1) and a fairly strong jar showing (56.7).

Ceremonial shrines (Table 16). These single-room shrines are placed on a fairly high substructure requiring at least one stairway. They may have beam-and-mortar or thatch roofs. All but one of those listed in Table 16 appear to have had an associated statue and four out of seven had ossuary shafts; the others had caches. All those located in the Main Group have a strong ceremonial pottery percentage, but Strs. H–18 and T–70 situated in smaller ritualistic groups are linked with more utilitarian pottery. Possibly H–18 served both as shrine and temple, but in any case it is a strikingly ritualistic type structure and there is no satisfactory explanation for the preponderance of utilitarian material. In the case of T–70, if the large number of unidentified sherds is eliminated, the result is reversed, giving the edge to the ceremonial pottery (54.4 per cent).

Quadrangle shrines (Table 17). These three shrines, R–85a, R–89, and R–90, all located in the quadrangle consisting of structures R–85 through R–90, have some group shrine traits and some ceremonial shrine traits, but they are in most respects more closely related to the former. This is essentially true of the pottery, but with a somewhat stronger ceremonial aspect. The pottery of R–89 is more utilitarian, that of R–90 is strongly utilitarian, and the material in R–85a is more ceremonial although fairly evenly divided between the two types.

Although, as mentioned earlier, kitchens, oratories, and shrines occur in both dwelling groups and ceremonial centers, colonnades and temples belong strictly to the latter.

COLONNADED HALLS
(Table 18)

Proskouriakoff refers (1962a, p. 89) to "two assemblage types, which appear to be standard." She goes on to say: "These will be referred to as the 'basic ceremonial group' and the 'temple assemblage.'

In both, an important, if not the principal, unit is a colonnaded hall, which we think probably served as living quarters for unmarried boys being trained in the arts of war and ritual." The colonnaded halls of Mayapan are buildings complete in themselves. None was vaulted, but some

had beam-and-mortar, others thatch-roof construction. Some possessed one or two end rooms; one, Str. Q–81, had no end room. The pottery clearly demonstrates the ritualistic character of the colonnades with an 84.2 per cent ceremonial content and only 10.2 per cent jars. All three independent colonnaded halls listed in Table 18 were associated with caches rather than burials.

Not counting the three listed in Table 18, there are 22 colonnades located in the Main Group and 4 in other groups. These unexcavated colonnades include: H–12, H–15, H–16, J–111, Q–54, Q–64, Q–70, Q–72, Q–87, Q–87a, Q–88a, Q–99, Q–129, Q–142, Q–144, Q–145, Q–156, Q–161, Q–163, Q–164, Q–212, Q–213, Q–220 (?).

TEMPLES
(Table 19)

Most temples have three doorways and a centrally located interior altar. Only the round temples, Q–126 and Q–214, and Platform Temple, Q–80, differ. The round temples have a single doorway and no interior altar but rather a stairway shrine; the platform temple has 7 rooms, 10 doorways, and 13 niches but no altar. In addition all three of these unusual temples have vaulted instead of beam-and-mortar roofs. All the temples listed in Table 19 have one stairway except Str. Q–162, which has four. Mayapan temples fall into four principal types: serpent column (Q–143, Q–159, Q–162, Q–218); round (Q–126, Q–152, Q–214); pyramid (Q–58, Q–141); and platform (Q–80, Q–95). The ceramic association shown in Table 19 favors the ceremonial kind of pottery, with 61.7 per cent in that category and only 22.4 per cent jar content. Considered by types (Table 20), the serpent column temples have the largest ceremonial pottery accumulation (77.8 per cent), the platform temples the next largest (69.8 per cent), followed by pyramid temples with 65.3 per cent; round temples have the least, only 48.5 per cent. Actually only one of the round temples, Str. Q–126, has less ceremonial than utilitarian pottery, and this structure is in the thinned out, eastern fringe of the Main Group.

POTTERY ASSOCIATED WITH SPECIAL DEPOSITS

In addition to the pottery that was linked with the different basic civic divisions and that which was connected with residential, civic, and religious

structures, there is also the pottery associated with the cenote, midden, and stratigraphic cuts. These we choose to refer to as special deposits.

CENOTES
(Table 21)

Although cenotes have been discussed briefly in the Carnegie Institution's *Current Reports* (Smith, 1953, pp. 67–81; 1954a, pp. 222–223) and the *Final Report* (*Mayapan, Yucatan, Mexico*, 1962, Pollock, p. 2 and A. L. Smith, pp. 210–211), a brief review at this time seems in order. These deep wells or sinkholes, called cenotes from the Maya word *dzonot*, have been studied by various people and institutions, notably H. C. Mercer (1896), L. J. Cole (1910), Carnegie Institution of Washington (see A. S. Pearse and others, 1936), G. W. Brainerd (1940–42), S. K. Lothrop (1952), R. T. Hatt and others (1953), and A. M. Tozzer (1957). These studies have been primarily geological, hydrographic, and zoological, the archaeological aspect being treated only by Mercer, Brainerd, Lothrop, Tozzer, and A. L. Smith. In this present study the ceramic association has been emphasized. At this time, however, let us examine the number and kinds of cenotes located within the wall at Mayapan. In all, this wall enclosed 22 named cenotes, 17 of which gave access to water, although in most instances a very small amount subject to seasonal variation. These cenotes included at least three of the four types normally found in Yucatan: A, the jug-shaped cenote; B, the vertical-walled cenote; C, the aguada-like cenote; and D, the cavelike cenote (Hall, 1936, fig. 1, pp. 5–7). Within the wall of Mayapan examples of Types A, B, and D are respectively X-Coton Cenote (Smith, 1953, pp. 67–75; figs. 1, 3, 4), Itzmal Chen Cenote (no illustration but definitely Type B), and Chen Mul Cenote (Smith, 1954a, pp. 222–225; figs. 2 and 5, a; GWB, p. 348, Map 11). Type C, the aguada-like cenote, is rare at Mayapan if present at all. There are several possible examples of this type at Chichen Itza, especially the great aguada or depression (Ruppert, 1952, Map 6B) in which an ancient well is located.

Within the Great Wall at Mayapan the vast majority of cenotes were situated in the southwestern corner of the city, which may be divided into the northwestern section, squares A–D, K–N, with no cenotes; the northeastern section, squares E–J, with 4 cenotes; the southeastern section, squares S–U, W, X, with 2 cenotes; and the southwestern section, squares O–R, Y–FF, with 16 cenotes. This last section, as might be expected, contained the greatest concentration of dwellings, ceremonial structures, and miscellaneous buildings. Cenotes served the community not only as the source of water but also as a place of worship of the Chacs, the gods of rain and agriculture. Only a few of the Mayapan cenotes were directly associated with a ceremonial group and undoubtedly were used in the ritual concerning the intercession for rain and the forecasting of future crops. Only three groups could be called ceremonial, the large Main Group, and two small groups, one in Square H, the other in Square T. The Main Group in Square Q had two cenotes, Chen Mul and Chen Chooch, the latter really a sascabera. Square H had a small ceremonial group closely linked to Cenote Itzmal Chen, and Square T also contained a few ceremonial structures associated with Major Gate T and Cenote X-Coton. The only cenotes where pottery was found were X-Coton and Chen Mul within the walled city and Telchaquillo and Santa Cruz outside but nearby.

A ceramic review of these cenotes (Tables 9 and 21), excluding Cenote Santa Cruz which was very lightly sampled, presents a picture different from that offered by both the dwelling and ceremonial lots (Table 8). In Table 8 under D, sascaberas are included, which, being primarily refuse deposits, tend to cloud the picture. Nevertheless the D Lots resemble more closely the A or dwelling lots than the C or ceremonial lots. In fact, the D Lots register considerably more utilitarian pottery, and therefore less ceremonial, than do the dwelling lots. The principal difference, however, is the greatly increased percentage of water jars over cooking and storage jars in the cenotes. Omitting the sascabera sherds from the D Lots, we find that water jars form 48.8 per cent of the total sherds, whereas in the A Lots they comprise only 16.1 per cent. The only cenote that appears to have been used primarily as a source for water is Cenote Telchaquillo, with 91 per cent water jars. Nearest to this is a water hole within Cenote Chen Mul (Table 21), where water jars formed 86.9 per cent of the total.

In Cenote Chen Mul, besides the pottery from the water hole is that from the surface soil mostly directly beneath the opening. Here is a larger percentage (33.4) of ceremonial material than in any other cenote ceramic lot, clearly resulting from the washing in of debris from the surrounding ceremonial buildings, Group Q–151 (Proskouriakoff, 1962a, p. 113), presumably after the abandonment. Other special lots (Table 21) noted in Cenote Chen Mul include the soil differentiations, namely, red, brown, and black. The red soil or *kancab*, earliest accumulation within the cenote, appears to have been removed in sections (Smith, 1954a, fig. 3) and used as coloring matter for pottery and for dwelling walls (Hatt *et al.*, 1953,

p. 23). This kancab may originally have been void of pottery but over the years has taken on small amounts via root channels or other openings made by animals. The large amount listed in Table 21 may result from mixing with the adjacent brown soil while digging. The only red section (Smith 1954a, fig. 3) not mixed with the brown or black soils was Section b–b¹, lots D–65–68, which contained a total of 171 relatively small sherds. This large section is about one-sixth of the total red soil area examined, but the total number of red soil sherds came to 4,518, much more than should be expected. However, this small lot has much the same percentage classification as shown in the larger in Table 21, namely, utilitarian 87.7, ceremonial 12.3, and water jars 40.9. In turn the brown soil located in the cutout red sections had to be later than the red soil, but there is little difference in the ceramic content (probably due to mixing) except for a lessening in the number of water jars. Black soil pottery, on the other hand, is far more utilitarian and has a greater percentage (56.8 compared to 38.4 and 29.6 for red and brown soils, respectively) of water jars. The black soil is found at the bottom and on occasion underlying the red soil.

In Cenote X-Coton the few sherds found associated with the water hole were principally utilitarian, but the water jars formed only 40 per cent, which is below the general average of 50.5 per cent for cenotes. This is undoubtedly due to the fact that many non-water jar sherds were washed down the stairway into the water hole area. The general surface sherds had a higher water jar content, while the fill used to level off a large ceremonial area had the largest, and the platform associated sherds the next to largest. The reason why these last two sherd groups, mostly fill, had such a comparatively high percentage (69.4 and 59.5) of water jars may be that the material for these constructions was gathered from the neighborhood of the water hole. The two principal caves found within Cenote X-Coton had the lowest percentage (38.9) of water jars, even though the larger cave at one time probably was a source of water later blocked up (Smith, 1953, pp. 71–72; figs. 1 and 2).

There is no need to include Cenote Telchaquillo in Table 21, since it was used primarily as a source for water including drinking, cooking, washing, and bathing. In Table 9 this is very apparent; water jars formed 91 per cent of the total sherds recovered. On the other hand, it is clear that both Chen Mul and X-Coton served at least two functions. They were a source of water, but they also were used ceremonially, even though the total

amount of ceremonial pottery is quite small in each case. Chen Mul had more ceremonial pottery than X-Coton and fewer water jars.

MIDDENS
(Table 22)

These are defined variously as dunghills, accumulations of refuse about a dwelling place, or as a heap of refuse. The last definition is more what we have in mind. In our usage, however, refuse signifies more than general debris. It consists of discarded food leavings in the form of animal, bird, and fish bones, artifacts of all kinds, and pottery. The difference between a midden and a collection of general debris is the high percentage of food leavings and useful artifacts in the former. The pottery is generally high in utilitarian vessels. When the midden is supplied from a ceremonial structure or structures the pottery contains a larger proportion of ritualistic vessels, the bones average high in human variety, and artifacts include adornments.

There may be deposits difficult to identify as middens, but those listed in Table 22 are considered to fit the requirements fairly easily. In our opinion three main types of midden were encountered at Mayapan: the house type with refuse from a house or houses; the service type with refuse from kitchens or other service areas often associated with the space in back of colonnades; and the ceremonial type with refuse from ritualistic structures.

It is of interest to note that in proportion to the number of associated sherds the following percentages were found: house type 3.9 bones, 4.5 artifacts, 31.1 cooking-storage jars; service type 3.5 bones, 1.3 artifacts, 43.6 cooking-storage jars; ceremonial type .8 bones, .3 artifacts, 8.9 cooking-storage jars; ceremonial and service combination 5.5 bones, 1.5 artifacts, 23.7 cooking-storage jars; house and ceremonial combination 4.5 bones, .2 artifacts, 40.9 cooking-storage jars. Some of the bone and artifact percentages which may appear very low are only relative, because in most non-midden debris they would be either far less numerous or absent. It is of prime interest that cooking-storage jars, like bones and artifacts, have a low percentage in the ceremonial type refuse. Jar totals follow much the same pattern as those of cooking-storage jars, only at higher percentages.

These findings suggest that house and service middens, alone or combined with ceremonial middens, are in fact kitchen middens. All have a preponderance of utilitarian pottery with quite high percentages of jars, considerable quantities of animal, bird, and fish bones but no human bones except a very few actual burials, and many artifacts, mostly useful rather than ornamental. Ceremonial middens, on the other hand, present a quite different picture. The pottery is more ceremonial than utilitarian including many censers, the bone material is more of the human than animal variety, and the artifacts include more of the adornment type than in the other middens. In other words, in the ceremonial type midden we find more ritualistic than utilitarian leavings.

STRATIGRAPHIC CUTS
(Table 24)

The archaeologist working at the site is greatly dependent on stratified ceramic cuts for his study of pottery development. Stratigraphy may be vertical or horizontal; it may have to do with accumulated refuse deposits, or with the gradual expansion of a building each addition to which represents a possible later manifestation of pottery fill. Stratigraphy can be artificial or natural. Artificial stratigraphy is used in cutting a trench into a refuse deposit or digging a test pit by arbitrarily selecting 20 cm. or 30 cm. levels as a means of determining pottery change. This is not necessary once a profile of the trench or pit has been obtained showing natural divisions which can be followed. In addition a series of floors laid one above the other with intervals of fill between, or one structure added to another either vertically or horizontally, offer natural stratigraphic possibilities. Many of these stratigraphic arrangements were present at Mayapan, and most have been put to profitable use. Deep middens of long tenure were scarce.

There are four principal ceramic time markers within the early (Hocaba) and late (Tases) Postclassic periods at Mayapan. Two of these involve distinctive wares, Peto Cream and San Joaquin Buff, the former belonging strictly to the Hocaba, the latter to the Tases, Ceramic Complex. Another Tases marker is the unslipped-exterior variety of the Mama Red Type; and most abundant and most characteristic of the Tases Ceramic Complex is the Chen Mul Modeled Type.

In Table 24, which includes eight stratigraphic cuts, several facts emerge. In the early lots Tases Ceramic Complex types are absent, Hocaba types are predominant except in the Cenote X-Coton cut (D 80–82, 86–88), and the unidentifiable sherds total 15.6 per cent. Actually the early lot pattern is quite clear, whether we make use of the eight selected stratigraphic cuts or the total early lot findings listed at the end of Table 24. In either case Hocaba types predominate, forming 72 per cent, with the addition of pre-Hocaba at 12 and 15 per cent and unidentifiable sherds at 16 and 13 per cent for stratigraphic cuts or total early lots, respectively. The early lots truly represent the Hocaba Ceramic Complex. Two important facts stand out in the early lot delineation: the large amount of weathered unidentifiable sherds and the relatively small number of Sotuta Ceramic Complex specimens. The high percentage of unidentifiable sherds suggests that these sherds were exposed to weathering for a long time. We suspect a considerable interval of abandonment towards the end of the Sotuta Phase and before occupancy by Middle Postclassic people about the middle of the Hocaba Phase. To a certain extent this would account for the small amount of recognizable Sotuta Phase pottery, a mere .4 per cent of the total as compared to 1.6 per cent for the preceding Cehpech Phase. A third factor important to the Hocaba Ceramic Complex is the relatively small part played by Peto Cream Ware. This ware which was found in large quantities at Chichen Itza and Dzibilchaltun in a phase immediately following the Sotuta, forms only 1.4 per cent of all sherds found at Mayapan and 8.5 per cent of the total early lot sherds. This in turn suggests that early Hocaba is largely lacking at Mayapan and that the Hocaba people settled there closer to middle Hocaba when Peto Cream Ware was on the wane.

The middle lots as portrayed in the stratified cuts vary somewhat from the picture presented in the total middle lot accounting. The Hocaba sherd percentage remains relatively constant at 74.8 and 71.2 for the stratified and total middle lots, respectively. The same is true for unidentifiable sherd percentages, 11.3 and 9.1, respectively. However, the pre-Hocaba content is 7 per cent for the stratified lots as compared to only 1.9 per cent for the total middle lots. On the other hand, the Tases sherds at 6.9 per cent for the stratified lots are less by far than the 17.8 per cent shown for the total middle lots. In any event the middle lots demonstrate a clear picture of the fading out of pre-Hocaba pottery, the continued supremacy of Hocaba types, the beginnings of the Tases Ceramic Complex, and an approximate 10 per cent admixture of unidentifiable sherds. The Peto Cream Ware percentage diminishes considerably in both stratified and total middle lots, while the Chen Mul Modeled Type has a modest beginning of 5.7 and 13.8 per cent in stratified and total middle lots, respectively.

Finally, the late lots like the early lots have a well marked pattern. The Hocaba Ceramic Complex types continue with comparative vigor at 39 per cent, Tases Types advance to 50 per cent, and unidentifiable sherds comprise approximately 10 per cent. Peto Cream Ware drops to below 1 per cent, while Joaquin Buff Ware remains at about 1 per cent and Mama Red Type, unslipped-exterior variety at 2 per cent of the total late lot sherds. The most important single type associated with the late lots either stratified or in total sherd count is Chen Mul Modeled which forms approximately 46 per cent in both cases.

In summary, Hocaba Ceramic Complex types, although off to a rather late beginning at Mayapan, dominate the early and middle lots and show strength in the late lots. The pre-Hocaba sherds, never very plentiful, decline progressively in the middle and late lots, while Tases Ceramic Complex sherds, lacking in the early lots, have a modest beginning in the middle lots and reach their peak in the late lots. The unidentifiable sherds from both stratified cuts and total counts diminish progressively from early through late lots. This is likewise true of Peto Cream Ware. While San Joaquin Buff Ware and the Mama Red Type, unslipped-exterior variety, although diagnostic of the Tases Ceramic Complex, are found in about the same percentage in both the middle and late lots. The Chen Mul Modeled Type, another Tases diagnostic, is markedly more abundant in the late than in middle lots.

Although the middle lots do not suggest a special Ceramic Complex, they are of importance as the high point for the Hocaba Ceramic Complex, the birthplace of the Tases Ceramic Complex, and the fading out point of the pre-Hocaba pottery and Peto Cream Ware sherds.

Finally, let us remember that the Tases Ceramic Complex types may never have reached their peak at Mayapan, since the city was sacked and occupation cut off before this complex had run its full course.

IX

Burials, Burial Vaults, and Ossuaries

This chapter continues the discussion on burials and burial vaults initiated by A. L. Smith (1962, Chapter IV, pp. 232–255). Smith gave numbers 1–40 to the burials and 1–18 to the burial vaults found in residential buildings and other structures associated with them. Here we add 13 burials, bringing the total to 53, no new burial vaults, and 8 ossuaries. These additional burials were found for the most part in ceremonial centers, less frequently in cenotes.

Repeating A. L. Smith's definitions with additions, we find that the term *burial* includes everything connected with an interment: grave, skeletal material, and associated objects. The term *grave* is used as a general heading for various types of resting places for the dead: simple, cist, and crypt.

Simple. A grave without any definite outline, with one or more bodies, in the fill of a building or under the floor of a court or plaza.

Cist. A grave with definite outlines that may be the sides of an excavation into structural fill, masonry walls, bedrock, or a combination of any of the three. The floor of the cist can be of plaster, leveled fill, or bedrock. Cists have no capstones and are filled with earth.

Crypt. Usually a more carefully walled grave, more elaborate, and always roofed with either capstones, a corbeled vault, or wooden beams supporting the masonry above. Crypts were not filled with earth. Earth has occasionally been found in crypts that had been opened or where roofs were partly or completely collapsed, but it never went as high as the roof.

Total burials have been given numbers 1 to 53.

The term *burial vault* is employed for a place apparently prepared for interment of the dead but never so used. The two types of burial vaults are cist and crypt. The definitions of these two terms given above for graves apply to burial vaults. Burial vaults are numbered 1 to 18.

The term *ossuary* is assigned to those graves used as mass depositories. The two types of ossuary are *cist* and *shaft*. The definition of cist has

been given above. Shaft is a deep, well-like pit, sometimes bottle-shaped, erected much like a smoke stack or well casement and centrally placed in the pyramid or shrine. While ossuary shafts are usually associated with pyramid-temple construction, ossuary cists are found in shrines. Ossuaries are numbered 1 to 8. In the descriptions below, CR stands for Current Reports of the Carnegie Institution.

BURIALS

Burial 41 (CR 14, p. 258 figs. 1 2).

Location: cut through latest plaza floor abutting against the North stairwall of Str. Q–58, a serpent-column temple (Proskouriakoff, 1962a, p. 100).

Grave: shallow cist.

Skeletal material: one male adult skeleton with articulated body minus the head.

Furniture: none.

Burial 42 (33, 40; CR 14, pp. 259–260, figs. 1, 2, 9, 10).

Location: below plaza floors, deep in circular cist forming part of square platform Q–59a, the first addition east of Str. Q–58 (CR 14, figs. 1 and 2, a, 8).

Grave: circular cist, a shaft but used for formal burials rather than for mass sacrificial depositories as were the ossuary cists. It consisted of a circular shaft of roughly trimmed stones.

Skeletal material: three adult skeletons placed one above the other, articulated with legs flexed at knees, making possible the extended east-west position of the torsos in the confined space. The condition of the central skeleton suggests that the body had been placed on a pyre and partially cremated.

Furniture: two Mayapan red basal-break tripods (40, a, 2; CR 14, fig. 10, u), 8 ladle censers (33, a, e; CR 14, fig. 10, t); burned copal; charcoal; six fragments of stucco, one obsidian flake-blade; one jade bead (CR 14, fig. 9, i); two limestone manos; sherds from middle lot C–15.

Burial 43 (CR 14, p. 260, figs. 1; 2, a).

Location: on plaza floor within a ring of stone masonry approximately 75 cm. high, with an interior diameter of 80 cm., set inside a small round platform, Q–59b. This platform is built on the plaza floor between Strs. Q–58 and 59a.

Grave: circular cist, a shaft but used for a formal burial rather than a mass sacrificial depository as were the ossuary cists. Once ceremony was over, the grave was filled with stones tightly packed in lime and earth.

Skeletal material: one adolescent skeleton was placed in a tightly flexed position.

Furniture: no formal mortuary furniture, but charcoal, one obsidian flake-blade, one stone basin, three fragments of painted stucco, and middle lot sherds, C–19, were found.

Burial 44 (CR, 14, p. 262, figs. 1; 2, a).

Location: on plaza floor within a small rectangular shaft associated with platform Q–60. This platform was built on the plaza floor due east of Str. Q–59.

Grave: rectangular cist, long axis east-west, constructed of roughly cut stones laid horizontally in mud mortar.

Skeletal material: one adult male, tightly flexed due to the limited space, was placed on floor in an east-west position (?); then the shaft was filled with loose rock without mortar.

Furniture: none.

Burial 45 (CR 9, p. 157, fig. 4, a, c).

Location: under earliest floor in a small niche in the bedrock near north stairway of Str. Q–77, a probable dance platform.

Grave: simple type.

Skeletal material: two partially disarticulated skeletons of nine- or ten-year-old children.

Furniture: no furniture but small collection of early lot sherds, C–43.

Burial 46 (CR 20, p. 91, fig. 2, a, 2).

Location: in brown earth below Str. Q–77.

Grave: shallow simple, cut into brown earth prior to construction of platform Str. G–77.

Skeletal material: one child (4–6 years old) skeleton placed in a flexed position with head to the north.

Furniture: none.

Burial 47 (CR 9, p. 145, figs. 1, 11).

Location: in fill beneath uppermost floor north of the unidentified Str. Q–79 (CR 9, fig. 1, a).

Grave: simple type, resting on large, flat stone.

Skeletal material: child skeleton tightly flexed.

Furniture: one perforated shell pendant (CR 9, fig. 11, a) and some middle lot sherds, C–9.

Burial 48 (CR 9, p. 160, fig. 5).

Location: about 10 cm. below the surface in the fill of the southeast extension of Str. Q–84, a circular platform.

Grave: simple type.

Skeletal material: one adult; fragmentary remains.

Furniture: none. The associated pottery, C–44, including one restorable tripod jar (31, aa; 62, f), is of late lot.

Burial 49 (CR 9, p. 160, fig. 5).

Location: in sandy fill of a thick-walled cist south of west stairway of monument platform, Str. Q–84.

Grave: circular cist sunk to bedrock. Plastered on interior.

Skeletal material: burned and unburned fragments of at least two human skeletons.

Furniture: none. May have been subjected to later looting (?). Presence of much charcoal and many large sherds (not fitting to form restorable pots) is inconclusive evidence of its having been a true burial rather than a repository for rubbish. The sherds, C–49, are of the middle lots.

Burial 50 (CR 14, p. 269, figs. 4, 9, 10).

Location: centrally located beneath Str. Q–95, temple with a burial shaft (CR 14, fig. 4, b).

Grave: oval crypt, an enlarged cavity or subterranean chamber in porous limestone, sealed with a capstone.

Skeletal material: two adult skeletons, male and female, lay on the floor. The female skull was greatly deformed. Heaped over them was midden rubbish containing the disarticulated skeletons of two young children, both with artificially deformed skulls.

Furniture: other midden material included ashes and charcoal intermingled with an extraordinary number of animal and bird bones; jade bead (CR 14, fig. 9, h); 12 obsidian flake-blades; 3 limestone manos (CR 14, fig. 10, a, b); hammerstone (CR 14, fig. 10, c); 2 shell ornaments (CR 14, fig. 10, j); 5 unworked shells; perforated animal tooth (CR 14, fig. 10, o); 2 Mayapan Red grater bowls (46, a, 1, 2; CR 14, fig. 10, v), and a number of middle lot sherds, C–30.

Burial 51 (CR 16, p. 19, fig. 1, b).

Location: in postconstruction midden on west

side of round temple Q-214.

Grave: simple type.

Skeletal material: two adult flexed skeletons.

Furniture: none. The upper midden, however, contained animal and bird bones; red-painted plaster; three stalactites from modeled stucco figures; 2 obsidian flake-blades; flint chip; unworked univalve shell, and many late lot sherds, C-74.

Burial 52 (CR 5, pp. 71–72, figs. 1, 2, 6).

Location: Cave 1 in Cenote X-Coton at a depth of 1 m. (CR 5, fig. 1).

Grave: simple type.

Skeletal material: remains of at least twelve skeletons (CR 5, fig. 2, c) including an infant, a child of six or seven years, and adults. The bones, scattered promiscuously and mixed with sherds, dirt, and rocks, appeared to have been secondarily buried save for one seemingly articulated arm found near the surface.

Furniture: one Puuc Slate bowl (26, *b*, 23; 60, *d*; CR 5, fig. 6, *f*). Many sherds were found associated with the bones. These belong to early lot D-7.

Burial 53 (CR 5, p. 72, fig. 1, *g*).

Location: at western end of Cave 2 in Cenote X-Coton.

Grave: simple type.

Skeletal material: one adult skeleton found in a limestone pocket covered with rocks.

Furniture: none. Late lot sherds, D-14, were associated with the burial.

OSSUARIES

Ossuary 1 (Year Book 54, p. 283; Proskouriakoff, 1962a, fig. 1).

Location: off center in subsidiary shrine H-13.

Grave: ossuary cist, whose narrow rectangular shaft reaches down 2 m.

Skeletal material: badly scattered and decayed bones of at least three adults and one child.

Furniture: none; but middle lot sherds, C-133, were present.

Ossuary 2 (CR 34, pp. 446–447, fig. 1).

Location: north side of the substructure of Str. H-18.

Grave: ossuary cist without protecting capstone. This cist was built by using a balustrade and wall of the earlier substructure, the wall of the later substructure, and a specially built end wall for its four sides. This last wall was constructed of stones laid in mortar. The dimensions were roughly 1 m.

long, 50 cm. wide, and 1 m. deep.

Skeletal material: remains of fourteen well-articulated adult skeletons and one adolescent boy. The skulls of most had occipital flattening, and two were missing.

Furniture: none. The ossuary cist, however, was filled with debris including animal, bird, and fish bones; large conch shell; obsidian flake-blade; broken stone carving; 5 fragments of modeled and painted stucco; painted stalactite, and middle lot sherds, C-126.

Ossuary 3 (CR 9, p. 151, fig. 2, a).

Location: in Shrine Q-69.

Grave: ossuary cist, 90 × 60 × 120 cm. deep, capped by east jamb stone.

Skeletal material: seven articulated skeletons, six of them adult. Presumably each body was not introduced from above until its predecessors had decomposed and settled.

Furniture: none; but middle lot sherds C-28 were present.

Ossuary 4 (31, 63; CR 9, p. 153, figs. 3, 7, 9, 11).

Location: in Shrine Q-71.

Grave: ossuary cist, 50 × 80 × 125 cm. deep, capped by a large rectangular stone.

Skeletal material: one adolescent and six adult skeletons squeezed into an inadequate space, suggesting a period of decomposition between burials. One filed tooth was recovered (Fry, 1956, p. 552; fig. 2, c, left).

Furniture: one Navula Unslipped Type tripod censer jar (31, *q*); one Hunacti Appliqué Type tripod censer jar (CR 9, fig. 7, *f*); one Hunacti Appliqué Type tripod censer bowl (CR 9, fig. 7, *e*); one Chen Mul Modeled Type effigy cup (63, *j*; CR 9, fig. 9, c right); greenstone celt fragment, 3 broken chipped flint points, broken chipped chert implement, rubbing stone, perforated bone needle, 3 circular shell beads, 2 tubular jade beads, 2 rectangular white shell beads, and 3 broken bone needles (CR 9, fig. 11, *b*); 3 unretouched obsidian blade fragments; painted stucco fragments; 8 fragments unworked univalve shell; fragment unworked bivalve shell, and numerous middle lot sherds, C-22.

Ossuary 5 (CR 9, p. 155, fig. 2, *b*).

Location: centrally placed in shrine, Str. Q-90.

Grave: ossuary cist, 45 by 45 cm. with an estimated depth of 185 cm.

Skeletal material: three adult and two adolescent skeletons.

Furniture: chipped flint point; unretouched obsidian blade; fragments of painted and modeled stucco; charcoal; and a few middle lot sherds, C–37.

Ossuary 6 (CR 14, pp. 254–256, figs. 2, 9).

Location: centrally placed within the core of the pyramid of Str. Q–58, reaching from below temple floor to bedrock (CR 14, fig. 2, a).

Grave: ossuary shaft, a slender bottle-shaped repository roughly 7.3 m. deep. The shaft was constructed at the same time as the primary structure and its masonry casement consisted of roughly trimmed blocks and slabs set in lime mortar (CR 14, fig. 2, a, 4). The shaft had been disturbed in modern times.

Skeletal material: presumably dropped into shaft from the temple floor. Recovered were bones and teeth of more than four children and adults, some showing evidence of burning.

Furniture: mixed with these bones were animal and bird bones; charcoal and ashes; celt-shaped jade bead (CR 14, fig. 9, l); 12 obsidian-flake blades; 2 fragments of unworked shell; and numerous middle lot sherds, C–20.

Ossuary 7 (CR 14, pp. 269, 271, figs. 4, 9, 10).

Location: placed well forward in the core of the temple platform, Str. Q–95 (CR 14, fig. 4, a, b).

Grave: ossuary shaft, founded on bedrock, was constructed in the form of a tall-necked bottle, with the narrow upper part square in plan (CR 14, fig. 9, f). The opening at terrace level presumably had been covered with a capstone, removable when necessary.

Skeletal material: shaft filled with over forty skeletons of children, adolescents, and adults of both sexes.

Furniture: mixed with these skeletons were bones of animals and birds; charcoal and ashes; 2 jade beads (CR 14, fig. 9, k); 44 obsidian flake-blades; obsidian "thumbnail" scraper; 2 flint points (CR 14, fig. 9, p, r); 8 flint chips; 3 fragments of unworked shell; 3 perforated (CR 14, fig. 10, i, l) and small tinkler (CR 14, fig. 10, k) shell; 2 shell pendants (CR 14, fig. 10, f); 14 small shell beads; 5 tubular bone beads; fragment of gold (CR 14, fig. 10, q); copper disk (CR 14, fig. 10, p) and numerous middle lot sherds, C–29.

Ossuary 8 (CR 11, pp. 207–209, fig. 2, a).

Location: in the center of the temple chamber of Str. T–72.

Grave: ossuary shaft, circular and about 1 m. deep, constructed of uncut limestone rocks laid without mortar. May have had a removable stone cover.

Skeletal material: charred bones of cremated adults and children.

Furniture: mixed with these bones were animal bones; obsidian flake-blade; obsidian chip; 17 flint chips, and numerous late lot sherds, C–2.

DISCUSSION

All of the thirteen burials described above were associated with ceremonial structures or cenotes. Seven, however, were simple burials connected with miscellaneous types of construction or natural entities, including 2 dance platforms, 1 monument platform, 1 round temple, 1 unidentified building, and 2 caves situated inside a cenote; 5 were cist burials, of which 4 were associated with platforms and 1 with a temple substructure; and 1 was a crypt burial located in the limestone below a temple. Although more simple burials than cists or crypts were found associated with ceremonial structures, the cist type burial predominated over the simple and crypt types in association with dwellings. In the overall picture combining dwelling and ceremonial structure burials, the order was as follows: 24 cist, 20 simple, and 9 crypt. For burial orientation see A. L. Smith, 1962, p. 251.

A few burials are found outside ceremonial structures but associated with them, under plaza floor (Burials 41, 45, and 47), under structures laid down prior to construction (Burials 46 and 50), and in postconstruction midden on west side of Q–214 (Burial 51).

The burials located within ceremonial structures are found inside platforms either in cists (Burials 42–44 and 49) or in the fill (Burial 48).

Two burials were discovered in Cenote X-Coton inside caves; both are the simple type (Burials 52 and 53).

Of 11 burials located in, or directly associated with, ceremonial structures, 7 had only one skeleton and 4 had two or more. The largest number of individuals found in a single grave was 3. In many instances sex information was not included. An adult male and female, possibly man and wife, were found in one grave (Burial 50). Of 19 skeletons involved, 13 were adult and 6 children.

There were at least 13 skeletons associated with cenote burials. Of these, eleven represent adults, one a child, and one an infant. Sex was not reported.

In many burials the skeletal remains had been disturbed or were in such poor condition that it was impossible to determine their original positions. Information as to the exact position of the bodies in the graves is sparse. Of the 32 (19 associated with ceremonial structures and 13 with cenotes) skeletons involved, 9 were reported flexed, usually to fit in the grave (Burials 42–44, 46, 47, 51), 14 disarticulated or partially disarticulated (Burials 45 and 52), 8 without mention of position (Burials 41, 48–50), and 1 was removed by laborers before position had been recorded (Burial 53). The better than 12 disarticulated skeletons found in Cave 1 of Cenote X-Coton most likely represent secondary burials. According to A. L. Smith (1962, p. 252) "there does not seem to have been any fixed rule as to which way the bodies headed or faced, although more headed east than any other direction." Three adult skeletons flexed at knees headed east (Burial 42), and a child also flexed headed north (Burial 46). There was no evidence of total cremation but in one instance (Burial 49) some bones were burned and some unburned, and in another instance (Burial 42) the position of the central skeleton suggests that the body had been placed on a pyre and partially cremated.

Cranial deformation was noted in three skeletons, all from Burial 50. The skull of an adult female showed strong nuchal crest; anteroposterior and superior deformation, and very large Inca bone (Fry, 1956, p. 558). The skulls of two young children exhibited some lambdoid flattening (ibid.).

No filed or inlaid teeth were recovered from any of these burials and only three instances of tooth filing were reported: one from Burial 4 associated with dwellings (ibid., pp. 552–553), one from a midden connected with Str. J–50a, and one from Ossuary 4.

According to A. L. Smith (1962, p. 253), there is no definite evidence that sacrificial victims were buried in dwellings. This is true of ceremonial structures as well, with the exception of ossuaries, either cist or shaft types. Burial 52 might well be considered a natural ossuary since the limestone formed a sort of deep cone-shaped shaft (R. E. Smith, 1953, fig. 2, c). But were these sacrificial victims or were they displaced from their original burials and piled into this natural repository?

There is one possible example of husband and wife sharing the same grave (Burial 50), but Dr. Fry (1956, p. 558) questions whether the skeleton presumed to be female actually was. Family burials certainly did occur in dwellings but probably not customarily in ceremonial structures.

As mentioned by A. L. Smith (1962, p. 253), the furniture found in graves of dwellings, group oratories, and religious structures in ceremonial groups was sparse and of little value. This is no doubt largely due to the graves having been opened and robbed, either in pre- or post-Conquest times. For each burial, the objects found in graves are listed under "Furniture." However, only one of the graves (Burial 49) found associated with ceremonial structures might have been robbed and this is unlikely, considering the absence of any surface disturbance (R. M. Adams, 1953, p. 160).

Based on pottery association, 2 burials belonged to the early, 5 to the middle, 3 to the late lot period, and 3 lacked pottery.

There are 8 ossuaries: 5 cist and 3 shaft burials. Invariably the cist type is associated with shrines and the shaft type with pyramid temples. Practically, this is due to the fact that a higher structure is required to enclose a deeper shaft than is needed for the enshrining of a relatively small cist.

The question arises as to the purpose of these ossuaries. Certainly one possibility is that they served as sacrificial repositories. There may even be a correlation between the particular cist or temple and the god to whom the victims were being sacrificed. Obviously we lack sufficient evidence to establish definitely that these were sacrificial repositories, but a few clues tend to support this theory: one shaft (Ossuary 6) was the repository for cremated human and animal bones; in nearly all of the ossuaries the individuals of all ages and both sexes were inserted at intervals, giving the preceding bodies time to decompose between burials, thus making possible the closely packed, often crushed result; rare use of true grave furniture (found only in Ossuary 4); the inclusion of swept-in debris; the importance of the location is at variance with uncouth manner of burial. It would seem quite in order to sacrifice to certain gods various individuals and place them in shrines or temples dedicated to these gods; thus as sacrificial offerings quantity could be more important than manner of burial. Whereas in the case of high ranking individuals, instead of sacrificial victims, the prominence of the burial place was excellent but not the manner in which they were put to rest.

Capstones can be connected definitely only with Ossuaries 3 and 4 but others, including Ossuaries 6 and 8, probably had removable stone covers thrown out when graves were disturbed.

Ossuary 6 was a repository for the cremated bones of humans and animals. Three ossuary shafts (Ossuaries 6–8) and one ossuary cist (Ossuary 2) were well supplied with animal and bird bones. All the ossuaries contained a fairly good collection of sherds and usually a few other objects. Other items found in the ossuaries have been listed under "Furniture."

The total number of individuals identified in ossuaries was 82: 64 adult and 18 children. In all graves the skeletons were flexed with the exception of Ossuary 1, in which the bones were scattered and decayed, and Ossuary 6, where the bones had been cremated. Skull deformation was noted only in Ossuary 2, wherein most of the skulls showed occipital flattening.

Based on pottery association, 7 ossuaries belonged to the middle, and 1 to the late period. However, Shook (CR 14, p. 271) suggests that the pottery from the lower part of the shaft of Ossuary 8 belonged to the early period and the pottery from the upper part to the middle or late period. The ceramic evidence, although not conclusive, indicates that all material in the shaft belongs to the middle period. Naturally the lowest items were thrown in first, but apparently not during the earlier period, because in the sealed grave (Burial 50) directly beneath Ossuary 8 shaft, middle lot sherds (C–30) were found, including effigy censer fragments.

In a few instances human skeletons were disposed of in such a way as to exclude the concept of their having been buried formally or even informally. These instances include three different dispositions: 1) recovered from just below ground surface north of Str. Q–79; 2) thrown on a refuse dump in a narrow passage between Strs. Q–151 and 152; and 3) found in building fall (?) above bench at northwest side of Str. Q–151.

In the first instance, according to R. M. Adams (CR 9, pp. 145–146; fig. 1, b),

. . . five adult skeletons were exposed in the debris above the uppermost floor at a depth of less than 30 cm. below the surface, and scattered fragments of two additional individuals occurred at the same level elsewhere in the trench . . . three large, crudely chipped flint knives which were found within the ribcages of two of the individuals and against the pelvis of a third

must represent the weapons with which they were killed. The lack of consistent pattern in the disposition of the limbs strongly suggests that they were flung down or left without ceremony rather than formally arranged for burial.

Just how the preservation of these articulated skeletons resting at this shallow depth can be accounted for is a mystery. Certain happenings, however, are clear. The death of these individuals must have occurred near the end of the occupation of Mayapan; some form of covering must have existed; the lack of furniture and the lack of arrangements strongly oppose the idea of a formal burial; proximity to an apparent northern entrance to the court of the Castillo and failure to extract three still-usable blades suggest a fight to protect this gateway.

The second instance, according to Shook and Irving (CR 22, pp. 145–146; figs. 2, c, e; 7, c–f), involves the intermittent filling of the narrow passage between Strs. Q–151 and 152 with refuse and sascab. This filling process continued from the early to the late period of the occupation of Mayapan. In excavating this area by means of a 6-m.-long trench, six arbitrary stratigraphic levels of 50 cm. thickness were uncovered. These show a complete ceramic sequence (CR 22, fig. 2, e) where Level 5 to bedrock includes early lots C–86 and C–87; Levels 3–5, middle lots C–88, C–89, and C–90; Levels 1–2, late lots C–91 and C–92. Besides the very large (23,615 sherds) pottery collection, many other artifacts common to refuse deposits were encountered. Furthermore, there were disarticulated human bones of at least five adult individuals. Heads appear to have been severed and these skulls and long bones were scattered throughout Levels 2 and 3. Shook and Irving state, "The implication is that the bodies were beheaded, the jaws removed, and perhaps were further dismembered before they were thrown into the passage. No evidence of burial rites was seen. It seems likely that the passage was filled with rubble and mortar in order to cover the putrifying corpses or bones."

The third instance as described by Shook and Irving (CR 22, pp. 146–148, 154; figs. 2, d; 5, j, k) concerns the finding of a child's skull in the surface debris (fall?) above bench at the northwest side of Str. Q–151. Shook (p. 154) calls it "burial of a child's skull." If the surface accumulation is fall, then the skull could hardly have been buried in it. If not fall, what is it?

X

Caches

This chapter deals with 24 caches found in ceremonial structures, continuing A. L. Smith's (1962, pp. 256–263) study of caches which reviewed 27 caches in dwellings and the structures associated with them.

The term *cache* [p. 256] is applied to one or more objects that appear to have been buried as a votive or dedicatory offering and not to have been associated with a burial. The two types of repositories for caches are simple and cist.

Simple: Cache, without definite outline, in the fill of a building or of an altar in a building, or under the floor of a terrace or court.

Cist: Repository with definite outlines that may be the sides of an excavation into structural fill or bedrock.

There is also a different kind of cache repository or container, namely, a pottery vessel which has been used to hold one or more objects Several examples have been found. Sometimes the vessel contained nothing. In this report the pottery vessel has been considered one of the objects of the cache and not merely a storage place for a cache, the reason being that the vessel often contains only one or two beads and is itself the most important object.

Some repositories were found with nothing in them. They have been considered caches, and included, as there is little doubt that they once contained objects that have been removed.

The total of all caches has been given numbers 1 to 51.

CACHES (28–51)

Cache 28 (64, *i*; CR 2, p. 11; figs. 1, 18).

Location: in a shallow hole in the bedrock just north of and outside the portal of Gate D (CR 2, fig. 1, *d*).

Objects: turtle effigy vessel filled with ashes and covered with a small flat lid (64, *i*; CR 2, fig. 18, *c*). Late lot B–1.

Repository: simple.

Cache 29 (61, *a*, 1; *d*, 1; CR 14, pp. 261–262; figs. 1, 2, 10).

Location: in shallow hole cut through the uppermost plaza floor (CR 14, figs. 1; 2, *a*) along the west side of platform, Str. Q–59.

Objects: two unslipped vessels, a Yacman Striated Type jar (61, *a*, 1; CR 14, fig. 10, *r*, left), and a Navula Unslipped Type miniature bowl with restricted orifice (61, *d*, 1; CR 14, fig. 10, *r*, right). The smaller vessel was found inside the larger and they form part of late lot C–17.

Repository: simple.

Cache 30 (30, *d*; CR 20, p. 91; fig. 2, *a*, 3).

Location: in the upper portion of the dry rock fill of the west side of the dance platform, Str. Q–77 (CR 20).

Objects: one noneffigy censer, a Hunacti Appliqué Type vase with pedestal base (30, *d*) containing ashes and burned copal incense. It belongs with late lot C–39a.

Repository: simple.

Cache 31 (46, *a*, 3; 51, *o*; 75, *k*; CR 20, p. 92; figs. 2, 5).

Location: placed on bedrock at the foot of the dance platform, Str. Q–77 (CR 20, fig. 2, *a*, 7), just prior to the laying of Floor 3.

Objects: an upright bowl containing ashes covered by an inverted bowl. The lower vessel was a Kukula Cream Type hemispherical bowl (51, *o*; 75, *k*; CR 20, fig. 5, *k*), the covering vessel a Mama Red Type grater bowl (46, *a*, 3; CR 20, fig. 5, *l*), both belonging to early lot C–64.

Repository: simple.

Cache 32 (49, *g*; 64, *d*; CR 31, pp. 383–384; figs. 1, 2, 3).

Location: in a pocket formed by the removal of a stone from the wall under the altar in shrine of Str. Q–81, a colonnaded hall and the excavation of a shallow depression in Floor 2 (CR 31, figs. 1, 8; 2, *d*, *e*). Also in the fill behind an additional wall built across the pocket (CR 31, fig. 1, 9).

Objects: two vessels consisting of a Chen Mul Modeled Type turtle effigy vessel (64, *d*; CR 31, fig. 3, *q*, *r*), and a Mama Red Type miniature jar with neck and handles removed and covered by a reused Mama Red Type jar fragment cut to form a circular disk (49, *g*; CR 31, fig. 2, *i*). Beneath the turtle effigy vessel was a subspherical bluish stone bead (CR 31, fig. 2, *h*, 2) and inside it was a small piece of white shell. These all belong to middle lot, C–71a.

Repository: simple.

Cache 33 (31, *ee*; CR 31, p. 384; figs. 1; 2, *d, e*).

Location: under altar in shrine of the colonnaded hall, Str. Q–81, was an empty cist. If looting took place, it occurred before the collapse of the roof, since roof debris lay undisturbed on top of the altar. Perhaps two small greenish-blue tripod cups found on the west bench originally came from the cist and formed part of an altar cache.

Objects: two Cehac Painted Type tripod cups (31, *ee*) belonging to late lot C–72.

Repository: cist.

Cache 34 (CR 14, pp. 266, 268; figs. 3, 9, 10).

Location: in masonry altar placed in center of rear chamber of the oratory, Str. Q–82 (CR 14, fig. 3, *c* and *e*, 6), against the back wall.

Objects: cache was probably looted (CR 14, p. 268), but two items found just outside the cist possibly were dropped there by the looters. These were a large jade bead (CR 14, fig. 9, *g*), and a small but complete tripod cup (CR 14, fig. 10, *s*), Navula Unslipped Type. Both objects belong to late lot C–32.

Repository: small square cist.

Cache 35 (40, *b*, 9; CR 9, p. 161; figs. 5, 9, 11).

Location: in the fill about 30 cm. below the surface of the monument platform, Str. Q–84 (CR 9, fig. 5).

Objects: two basal-break tripod dishes, Mama Red Type, Mama Variety (40, *b*, 9; CR 9, fig. 9, *a, b*), and three very large flint and obsidian chipped blades (CR 9, fig. 11, *d*), all from middle lot C–49.

Repository: simple.

Cache 36 (61, a, 3; CR 22, p. 130; figs. 1, 7).

Location: on bedrock below primary court floor and a shrine room of the colonnaded hall, Str. Q–97 (CR 22, fig. 1, *c, i*).

Objects: charcoal and burnt animal bones deposited in large jar covered by a smaller jar (61, a, 3; CR 22, fig. 7, *h*). Both jars are unslipped, Yacman Striated Type, early lot C–35c.

Repository: simple.

Cache 37 (CR 22, pp. 130–131; figs. 1, 7).

Location: below dais in shrine of colonnaded hall, Str. Q–97 (CR 22, fig. 1, *d*), in a shallow, ragged hole.

Objects: cache was probably looted before the collapse of the shrine roof and more than likely at the time of the destruction and abandonment of Mayapan. A small unbroken tripod cup (CR 22, fig. 7, *j*) found on the shrine floor next to the dais may have formed part of the cache and been discarded. It is a Navula Unslipped Type vessel belonging to late lot C–35.

Repository: Cist.

Cache 38 (31, *hh*; 63, *i*; CR 21, pp. 119–120; figs. 1, 3).

Location: in altar of shrine, Str. Q–148 (CR 21, fig. 1, *e, f*), which doubtless had been looted before destruction and abandonment of Mayapan.

Objects: overlooked by the looters was an effigy (Chac, the long-nosed god), flat-bottom cup, Chen Mul Modeled Type (31, *hh*; 63, *i*; CR 21, fig. 3, *h*), which contained two jade and three shell beads (CR 21, fig. 3, *e*, 9), a tiny fleck of copper, and a jadelike flake possibly from a mosaic, all from late lot C–81.

Repository: simple.

Cache 39 (CR 22, p. 144; figs. 2, 6).

Location: in carved stone, turtle (CR 22, fig. 6, *a, b*) covering hole dug through the floor into the bench of shrine in colonnaded hall, Str. Q–151, presumably in search of a cache (CR 22, fig. 2, *c,B*).

Objects: the turtle had a cavity on one side containing fragments of sting-ray spines and two obsidian flake-blades. This cavity was covered by a stone disk and sealed by mortar. These objects belong to late lot C–93a.

Repository: simple.

Cache 40 (43, *j*; 44, *g*; 74, *y*; CR 22, p. 144; figs. 2, 7).

Location: inside altar block of shrine in colonnaded hall, Str. Q–151, apparently placed there after Altar Stage 3 (CR 22, fig. 2, *c*, A).

Objects: two pottery vessels, one a Papacal Incised Type tripod deep bowl (43, *i*; CR 22, fig. 7, *a*), the other a Mama Red Type restricted orifice bowl (44, *g*; 74, *y*; CR 22, fig. 7, *b*). These vessels (middle lot C–85b), nested one inside the other, contained two obsidian flake-blades, a sting-ray spine, a flake of clear obsidian or rock crystal, and a small rectangular piece of jadelike green stone with slightly convex sides. A small shell tinkler, a convex obsidian end scraper, and several obsidian flake-blades were in the fill around the cache.

Repository: simple.

Cache 41 (CR 21, p. 112; figs. 1, a, b; 2, f).

Location: in the center of an altar built on a bench of the oratory, Str. Q–153.

Objects: a ball of copal between two small tripod basal-break dishes, Mama Red Type (late lot C–79c), placed lip to lip.
Repository: simple.

Cache 42 (38, *b*, 20; 74, *h*; CR 20, p. 98; figs. 2, 3, 5).
Location: in a cist under a round masonry altar centrally placed in front (north) of the Castillo, Str. Q–162. The cache rested between Plaza Floors 8 and 4 (CR 20, figs. 2, *a*, *q*; 3, *j*, *k*).
Objects: a high-necked jar, Mama Red Type (38, *b*, 20; 74, *h*; CR 20, fig. 5, *n*), containing animal tooth, burned shells, coral, and other marine objects, belonging to middle lot C–63.
Repository: cist.

Cache 43 (63, *a*; CR 22, fig. 7, *m*; Proskouriakoff, 1962a, p. 119).
Location: from cache in central altar of the colonnaded hall, Str. Q–164 (Proskouriakoff, 1962a, Plan of the Main Group at Mayapan).
Objects: effigy (Chac, the long-nosed god) cup, Chen Mul Modeled Type, with two covers, consisting of an inner circular disk made from an unslipped jar sherd and a Mama Red Type disk-shaped lid originally made for another vessel (63, *a*). The late lot is C–1.
Repository: simple.

Cache 44 (CR 16, p. 17; figs. 1, 2).
Location: below raised level in stairway shrine upon which rests a feminine idol, a dedicatory cache was placed (CR 16, fig. 1, *d*). This is associated with round temple, Str. Q–214, east stairway.
Objects: a small tripod effigy (Chac, the long-nosed god) cup, (CR 16, fig. 2, *j*) Chen Mul Modeled Type, containing 1 jade fragment, 3 jade and 2 shell beads (late lot C–76).
Repository: simple.

Cache 45 (64, *b*; CR 16, p. 17, figs. 1, 2).
Location: placed in a small hole cut through the final plaza floor in the corner formed by the platform and the south stairwall (CR 16, fig. 1, c) of round temple, Str. Q–214.
Objects: a small effigy vessel, Chen Mul Modeled Type (64, *b*; CR 16, fig. 2, *i*), representing a warrior crouching on one knee bearing a shield in the left hand and a poised spear in the right. This specimen belongs to late lot C–76.
Repository: simple.

Cache 46 (63, *e*; CR 32, p. 406; figs. 2, 4, 5).
Location: in center of rectangular altar (CR 32,

figs. 2, *a*; 5, *j*) behind the columns in serpent-column temple, Str. Q–218.
Objects: an effigy tripod cup, Chen Mul Modeled Type (63, *e*; CR 32, fig. 4, *o*), representing the head of Chac, the long-nosed god. The vessel contained 3 small shell beads, two of them disk-shaped, one rectangular. All objects belong to late lot C–96b.
Repository: simple.

Cache 47 (CR 32, p. 408; figs. 2, 4).
Location: at the base of and between two sculptured stones (CR 32, fig. 4, *n*) located 30 cm. from the west side of the statue platform, Q–218b (CR 32, fig. 2, *a*).
Objects: two small frog effigy jars, Chen Mul Modeled Type (cf. 64, *l*; CR 32, fig. 2, *b*). These vessels belong to late lot C–98b.
Repository: simple.

Cache 48 (CR 34, p. 452; figs. 1, 3).
Location: under sculptured stone slab associated with shrine, H–18a (CR 34, fig. 1, c–c'), located 1 m. southwest of Str. H–18.
Objects: two jade beads and a tiny piece of copper (CR 34, fig. 3, *g*), all belonging to middle lot C–137.
Repository: simple.

Cache 49 (CR 11, pp. 211; fig. 2, *c*, 4).
Location: unassociated with the stela and perhaps the altars placed below the primary plaza floor between the circular and middle altar west of Str. T–70.
Objects: an unslipped jar, Yacman Striated Type (cf. 28, *a*, 12), possibly belongs to a middle lot.
Repository: simple.

Cache 50 (43, *q*; 74, *z*; CR 11, pp. 211–212; figs. 1, *c*; 2, *c*, 5; 3, *a–e*, *k–m*, *r*).
Location: placed where altar of older single shrine had been when fourth major renovation of Str. T–70, took place (CR 11, figs. 1, *c*; 2, *c*, 5; 3, *a–e*).
Objects: two pottery vessels and 5 jade beads (CR 11, fig. 3, *k–m*). One vessel was a deep bowl, Mama Red Type (43, *p*; 74, *z*; CR 11, fig. 3, *r*), the other a fragmentary tripod dish, Matillas Orange Type (cf. 55, *a*, 5). All these objects belong to early lot C–4.
Repository: simple.

Cache 51 (44, *h*; CR 11, pp. 212–213; figs. 1, *d*; 2, *c*, 6; 3, *s*).
Location: under altar supporting a seated human idol modeled in stucco (CR 11, fig. 1, *d*) in shrine

of Str. T–70 (CR 11, fig. 2, c, 6).

Objects: one pottery vessel, Mama Red Type restricted-orifice bowl (44, *h*; CR 11, fig. 3, *s*) with

jade and shell beads. All objects belong to early lot C 4.

Repository: simple.

DISCUSSION

Dedicatory or foundation offerings in ceremonial structures as well as in buildings and under stelae were common practice among the Maya (A. L. Smith, 1962, p. 261). At Mayapan 24 caches were found in connection with ceremonial structures.

Of the 24 repositories found, 20 were of the simple type and 4 were cists. Eleven of the simple repositories belong to the late lot; five to the middle lot, and four to the early lot category.

Caches were found in altars associated with colonnaded shrines (Caches 32, 33, 39, 40, 43), shrines (Caches 38, 50, 51), oratories (Caches 34, 41), stairway shrines (Caches 37, 44), a temple (Cache 46), the Castillo (Cache 42), and under primary floor between two altars (Cache 49), or encountered in or near platforms including platform fill (Caches 30, 35), below plaza floor fronting platforms (Caches 29, 31), below plaza floor in corner formed by stairwall and temple platform (Cache 45), and below plaza floor on west side of platform (Cache 47), or in a variety of places, such as outside Gate D (Cache 28), below plaza floor fronting colonnaded hall (Cache 36), and under stone slab of shrine (Cache 48).

If there is any specific location for caches associated with ceremonial structures and, for that matter, with buildings, it is along the central axis. This is no doubt true, but it is also true that most of the investigation occurred along the central axis. Of the 24 caches connected with ceremonial structures, 21 were located along the central axis (Caches 29–44, 46, 47, 49–51).

A variety of objects were cached. On occasion they were simply placed in the fill, but frequently they were put in a pottery vessel. There were 22 caches which contained one or two pottery vessels that may have held cache objects. Of these, 9 actually contained objects, 2 had copal, 2 were filled with ashes, and 2 others had probably contained objects found nearby that may have spilled out. The other 7 may have had their contents removed or have contained something that had disintegrated or disappeared, such as food or a liquid. The cache vessels were of various forms including 9 effigy vessels, 5 jars, 4 tripod cups, 4 tripod dishes, 3 restricted bowls, 2 deep bowls, and a hemispherical bowl, a grater bowl, a noneffigy

censer, and a miniature jar. The effigy vessels depicted gods (Chac), turtles, frogs, and a warrior. Other objects found were: a stone turtle; jade beads, flakes, and ornaments; shell beads, a fragment, and burned shells; obsidian chipped blades, flake blades, and fragments; flint chipped blades; a spherical bluish stone bead; coral and other marine objects; sting-ray spines; tiny pieces of copper; charcoal; burnt animal bones; and an animal tooth. Objects most frequently found in caches comprise 13 jade beads in five repositories, 8 shell beads in three, and 5 obsidian chipped blades in three.

In all, 5 of 24 caches associated with ceremonial structures appear to have been looted. This is not as large a percentage of looting or removal as occurred in caches connected with buildings, which total 8 of 27 caches. There is little doubt that most of these, if not all, were robbed or removed by the ancient Maya themselves (see Proskouriakoff and Temple, CR 29, p. 300; A. L. Smith, 1962, p. 262).

As Smith states (1962, p. 262) "most of the caches were probably placed as dedications to the buildings with which they were associated, but it is likely that some, such as those found in altars in buildings, may have been votive offerings rather than having been dedicatory." This may also be said of the caches connected with ceremonial structures.

Possible cache locations or objects were noted in seven instances, four having to do with ceremonial structures and three with buildings. The four instances associated with ceremonial structures all refer to disturbed altars, whereas the three cases involving dwellings refer to pottery vessels found under floors in a possible midden area, or placed there as a late offering, above fall of a structure. These last may or may not represent caches but are mentioned here simply as a record. There follows a list of the seven possible caches which have been left unnumbered.

POSSIBLE CEREMONIAL CACHES

Q–143 (CR 32, p. 399; figs. 1, *a*; 3, *g*).

Location: in disturbed rectangular altar centrally placed against the rear wall of the shrine room of Str. Q–143.

Objects: none.
Repository: simple.

Q–149 (CR 21, p. 116; figs. 1, *c*, *d*; 2, *g*).

Location: in ripped out altar which was centered on the back wall of shrine in Str. Q–149. Evidently the shrine had been looted, for a hole had been dug below the base of the altar, perhaps in the search for a cache.

Objects: none.
Repository: simple.

Q–162 (CR 20, p. 96; figs. 1; 2, *a*, *c*).

Location: in rectangular altar located against the rear wall and centered opposite the entrance, later covered by a somewhat larger renovation. Both altars had been destroyed by a pit dug through them to a depth of 50 cm. below floor level.

Objects: none forming with certainty part of a cache.

Repository: simple.

Q–162 (CR 20, p. 98; figs. 2, *a*, 10; 3, *i*).

Location: in square altar built on the eleventh floor north of the Castillo, Str. Q–162. This altar continued in use during the final stages and was badly damaged either by the elements or by pillaging at the time Mayapan was abandoned.

Objects: none.
Repository: simple.

POSSIBLE BUILDING CACHES

Q–166–167a (CR 33, p. 432; fig. 1, A–A[1]; Proskouriakoff, 1962a, Plan of the Main Group of Ruins).

Location: below the floor level in the area north of Str. Q–167 and east of Str. Q–167a. This may be a kitchen midden and therefore possibly not a cache.

Objects: two large jars, Yacman Striated Type, broken in place, resting in a deposit of ash (late lot A–251).

Repository: simple.

Q–167–168 (CR 33, p. 432; fig. 1, A–A[1]).

Location: below plastered floor between Strs. Q–167 and Q–168.

Object: one large jar, Yacman Striated Type, broken in place (late lot A–253).

Repository: simple.

Q–172 (CR 25, p. 233; figs. 1, *a*, *d*; 2, *h*; 3, *h*, *i*).

Location: in mixed earth and mortar above the mass of roof-fall in Room A of Str. Q–172 (CR 25, figs. 1, *a*, *d*; 2, *h*).

Objects: a ritualistic vessel in the form of a pottery turtle with human head in mouth (CR 25, fig. 3, *h*, *i*), Chen Mul Modeled Type. Marked as belonging to late lot A–406 but actually placed on top of that lot.

Repository: simple, an offering made after the collapse of the roof and presumably after the fall of Mayapan.

XI

A Summary of Intrasite Distribution and Association

Part III has been concerned with Ceramic Distribution in Mayapan. In this chapter, ceramic repositories, ceramic association with buildings, ceramic findings in cenotes, and stratigraphy as an important factor in any ceramic classification will be reviewed. Repositories are many and varied, embracing middens, burials, and caches. The buildings are numerous and of many types serving a number of functions, such as kitchens, living quarters, places of worship, and halls for training. Cenotes are also found in some quantity within the walls at Mayapan and they served more than one purpose. Finally, in reviewing the results of the stratigraphic cuts, a short chronological summary is attempted. In addition, typological and modal distributions are discussed.

CERAMIC REPOSITORIES

Middens or refuse repositories include all classes of refuse such as pottery and other artifacts, plus food leavings in the form of animal, bird, and fish bones, and some human bones. Three principal types of midden are reported from Mayapan: the house type with refuse from a house or houses; the service type with refuse from kitchens or other service areas often associated with the space in back of colonnades, and the ceremonial type with refuse from ritualistic structures. Checking quantities of bone, artifact, and ceramic types found in the different middens, the results show that kitchen middens (house types, service types, and combinations of these with ceremonial types) have a preponderance of utilitarian pottery with relatively high percentages of jars, sizable amounts of animal, bird, and fish bones, and many artifacts nearly all useful rather than ornamental. In contrast, the purely ceremonial middens contain more ceremonial than utilitarian pottery including many censer fragments along with human bones and artifacts of the adornment category.

Graves as a ceramic repository are considered

under burials, of which 53 were found. These have association with both residential and ceremonial (civic or religious) structures and rarely with cenotes. Of the 40 residential burials, 23 are linked with dwellings, 12 with oratories, 2 with platforms, and one each with a shrine, a court floor, and the outside of a large dwelling group. As to kind of burial, 19 are cist, 13 simple, and 8 crypt. The ceramic complex association places 30 with middle lots, 5 with late lots, and 5 without pottery. In all, 6 may have been either robbed or had furniture removed, 2 may have been family graves, and 1 is a cremation. The ceramic furniture totals 83 objects not counting a couple of thousand effigy censer fragments which may or may not have truly formed part of the grave. These objects include 30 figurines (20 human, 10 animal), 25 flaring-side tripod dishes, 8 cups (5 regular and 3 effigy), 3 ladle censers, 3 storage jars, 3 small effigy censers, 2 restricted-orifice ringstand bowls, 1 effigy vessel, and 8 miscellaneous vessel forms. The ceremonial structure burials total 11, involving 7 platforms, 3 temples, and 1 unidentified building. Of these 5 are simple, 5 are cist, and 1 is a crypt and 5 are associated with middle lots, 2 with late lots, and 1 with early lots. The remaining 3 lacked pottery. In all, 1 may have been robbed and 1 is partially cremated. The ceramic furniture totals 11 objects comprising 8 ladle censers, 2 flaring-side tripod dishes, and 1 tripod deep bowl. A distinctive ceremonial burial is that in an ossuary. There are 8 of these, 5 called cists and 3 shafts. All are associated with middle lot pottery. Only one ossuary, however, a cist, contained any complete vessels. This is Ossuary 4, which had 2 tripod jar censers, 1 tripod bowl censer, and 1 effigy cup. Cenotes are associated with but 2 burials, and these are located in Cenote X-Coton. The only other excavated cenote within the Mayapan wall is Cenote Chen Mul where no certain burials were uncovered. Both Cenote X-Coton burials came from caves. One may have contained more than one burial including one of the Hocaba Ceramic Complex and another of the Cehpech, which had the only complete vessel recovered, a Puuc Slate Ware beveled-rim ringstand bowl. The second cave burial belongs to the Tases Ceramic Complex. These findings establish that burials are more prevalent in residential than in ceremonial structures, although possibly less excavation was undertaken in the latter. An item of interest concerning ceramic furniture is that figurines lead the list for residential structures and ladle censers for ceremonial. The insufficient data from ceremonial burials however precludes any meaningful comparisons. Ossuaries occur only in the ritualistic centers and contain very little ceramic furniture.

Cache repositories are also found in both residential buildings and ceremonial structures. In all, 51 caches were found: 27 from residential and 24 from ceremonial structures. Of the 27 residential caches, 14 are associated with dwellings, 6 with shrines, 4 with oratories, and 1 each with a group altar, a platform, and a storage room. Two kinds of cache are involved; the simple represented by 20 and the cist by 7. Most of these caches, a total of 18, belong to the middle lots, and only 4 to the late lots, leaving 5 without pottery. It would appear that more caches than burials were looted; probably 8 residential. The ceramic furniture totals 27 objects: 8 effigy vessels including 5 turtles; 4 cups; 4 covers; 2 jars; 2 restricted-orifice bowls; 2 animal figurines, and 5 miscellaneous vessel forms. Eight of the 24 ceremonial structure caches are linked with platforms, 7 with colonnaded halls, 4 with temples, 2 with shrines, 2 with oratories, and 1 with a gate. The simple cache type is represented by 20, and the cist type by 4. Considering chronological position, 14 belonged to late lots, 6 to middle lots, and 4 to early lots. In all probability 5 caches were robbed. The furniture totals 35 objects: 8 cups; 6 effigy vessels including 2 turtles; 5 jars; 4 flaring-side tripod dishes; 3 restricted-orifice bowls; 2 covers, and 7 miscellaneous forms but no figurines.

Caches appear to be more evenly distributed than are burials with respect to residential and ceremonial structures. The burial-structure-association, however, is not very different from the cache-structure-association. Burials occur in 23 dwellings, 12 oratories, 9 platforms, 3 temples, and 6 miscellaneous structures, while caches are found in 14 dwellings, 9 platforms, 8 shrines, 7 colonnaded halls, 6 oratories, 4 temples, and 3 miscellaneous structures. Only caches were encountered in shrines or colonnaded halls. Burials are more abundant in the middle lots, caches in the late lots. Of a possible total of 20 robbed offerings, 13 are from caches. Finally, graves contained more ceramic objects than caches: 83 objects from 53 graves, 35 from 51 caches. The two outstanding grave items are 30 figurines and 25 flaring-side tripod dishes; caches had no figurines and only 4 flaring-side tripod dishes. Otherwise many items are common to both.

ARCHITECTURAL CERAMIC ASSOCIATIONS

The salient facts that emerge from an architectural-ceramic-association study are the following. The principal structures used in this study are kitchens, dwellings both ordinary and elaborate; oratories, shrines including group, ceremonial, and quadrangle types, colonnaded halls, and temples. At the two extremes are kitchens with 94 per cent utilitarian pottery and colonnaded halls with 84 per cent ceremonial pottery. In the kitchen collections jars total 80 per cent compared to 10 per cent in those of the colonnaded halls. The utilitarian pottery percentage in ordinary dwellings, 89 per cent, and in elaborate dwellings, 76 per cent, is much what one would expect. Oratories, on the other hand, present a curious problem. Architecturally, although by no means exactly alike, they are hard to separate, but ceramically three out of fourteen labeled Oratory B stand apart. All others are Oratory A. The A category has a utilitarian sherd content of 77 per cent as compared to 35 per cent for the B category. The best available explanation, not completely satisfactory, is that those oratories with more ceremonial pottery, even in the A category, serve a larger group of people in a ritualistic capacity. This is especially true of B category, where two are in the main ceremonial group which have a greater ritualistic accumulation. The third Oratory B example is associated with a quadrangle but set apart, possibly for special services and offerings. Shrines also show a considerable variance in class of pottery according to the three shrine types: group, ceremonial, and quadrangle. The group shrines have 84 per cent, the ceremonial 32 per cent, and the quadrangle 59 per cent utilitarian pottery. Naturally the ceremonial shrines, located in ceremonial groups, enjoy a high ritualistic ceramic content contrasted with the group shrines serving small domestic dwelling groups where utilitarian pottery, for whatever purpose it was used, far surpasses the ceremonial. The quadrangle shrines, on the other hand, although essentially within a residential setting, are linked to a high ranking, more elaborate clientele and therefore show a more modified (60–40% utilitarian-ceremonial pottery) content. Finally, the temples, which one might presume to be highly ritualistic in function, surprisingly are associated with only 62 per cent ceremonial pottery. Considered by temple types, the serpent-column temples have the largest ceremonial pottery accumulation at 78 per cent, the platform temples follow with 70 per cent, the pyramid temples with 65 per cent, and the round temples with the least at 49 per cent. Actually only one of the round temples has less ceremonial than utilitarian pottery; it is located in the thinned out eastern fringe of the Main Group.

CENOTE CERAMIC ASSOCIATION

A special place for pottery accretion is the cenote, the Maya water source in Yucatan. The findings in the two most thoroughly investigated cenotes, Chen Mul and X-Coton, are that utilitarian pottery formed 87 per cent and jars 51 per cent of some 38,100 sherds involved. The jar total would be considerably greater, as witness 87 per cent at the Cenote Chen Mul water hole, if cenotes had been considered solely as a source for water. Other uses are as a source for Kancab used in building or slipping for pottery, and as a place for worshiping the rain god, Chac, including sacrificing to the same rain god. At Mayapan the cenotes seem to have served more extensively practical than ritualistic uses.

STRATIGRAPHY

Stratigraphic cuts, especially long-term deep ones, are the life blood of ceramic analysis. But whether vertical cuts or horizontal additions to a building, whether arbitrary or natural divisions are used, the important thing is stratigraphy. At Mayapan many types of stratigraphy were present and used, but deep middens of long tenure were scarce.

The results of these cuts show that Hocaba Ceramic Complex types, although late in coming to Mayapan, dominate the early and middle lots, and retain some strength in the late lots. The pre-Hocaba sherds form a meager percentage in the early lots, declining progressively in the middle and late lots. Although Tases Ceramic Complex sherds, not present in the early lots, enjoy a modest beginning in the middle lots, they attain their peak in the late lots. Peto Cream Ware diminishes progressively from early through late lots; whereas San Joaquin Buff Ware and Mama Red Type, unslipped-exterior variety, although diagnostic of

the Tases Ceramic Complex, have about the same percentage in both middle and late lots. On the other hand, the Chen Mul Modeled Type, another Tases diagnostic, gains momentum in the late over the middle lots. Even though the middle lots (Hocaba-Tases) are not considered to be a ceramic complex, they serve as an intermediate level where the Hocaba Ceramic Complex attains its full strength, where the Tases Ceramic Complex starts, and where both pre-Hocaba pottery and Peto Cream Ware begin to fade out of the picture. Let us also remember that the sacking and abandonment of Mayapan cut short the development and perhaps final chapter of the Tases Ceramic Complex at that site.

TYPOLOGICAL AND MODAL DISTRIBUTION

Types and modes are both derived from attributes. A type as used in the type-variety system, particularly in this report, is based on the attributes of decorative technique and form. From types and the varieties which distinguish them, groups evolve. A group is a collection of closely related types that demonstrate a consistency in range of variation of form and color. Along with the group the ware develops as the exponent of the technological aspect. Each ware has a number of types and varieties, but while a ware may range over any number of cultural phases, a type is usually linked with only one, as is a group. Based on types and their stratigraphic position a ceramic sequence is established, which is the development aspect. This permits the forming of a ceramic complex — the assemblage of all the varieties, types, groups, and wares that conform stratigraphically to one cultural phase and, therefore, to one period in time. This is the temporal aspect. When assigning types, the whole vessel is taken into consideration, even though only sherds are used. Types make possible a taxonomic organization of the pottery so as to attain more easily the goals of determining cultural development and function. A mode is a selected attribute or cluster of attributes that displays significance in its own right. Thus a mode may be a special foot form, a rim type, an entire vessel, temper, a surface texturing process, a decorative technique, a design device, or even an entire motif. From mode analysis as opposed to type-variety analysis it is possible to determine mode tradition, to make temporal unit studies resulting in a mode complex, and to develop horizon styles by means of cultural trait distribution through space.

Therefore, by using the type-variety method of

analysis in this ceramic study, it has been possible to establish six ceramic complexes: the Cehpech, the latest Puuc area complex; the Sotuta, the latest surely recognized complex at Chichen Itza and associated with the Toltec regime; the Hocaba, the earliest complex connected with the walled city of Mayapan and belonging to Brainerd's Middle Mexican substage; the Tases, the latest complex at Mayapan, but not in Yucatan; and two complexes of periods established after the fall of Mayapan. These are Chikinchel of Protohistoric times, of which at Mayapan only the fine-orange Cunduacan Group is represented, and Chauaca of the Colonial Period with a small collection of surface sherds. In addition, there is the transitional ceramic complex between Sotuta and Hocaba noted at Dzibilchaltun and vaguely indicated at Chichen Itza; this is a Peto Cream Ware complex. At Mayapan between the Hocaba and Tases complexes a middle level collection of sherds is sometimes referred to as Hocaba-Tases but is not considered a ceramic complex. The sequence formed by these ceramic complexes has been achieved through stratigraphy. Through trade certain types are distributed over a very wide area, thus establishing intersite relationship and, therefore, contemporaneity. Furthermore, in intrasite development ceramic types serve to identify the character of an architectural assemblage or group as well as the actual function of its different structures.

By using mode classification, on the other hand, a number of important findings emerge. These include ceramic trends such as the increasing use of ritualistic pottery which reaches its peak in the Tases Ceramic Complex. An important adjunct to this ritualistic assemblage is the effigy censer which develops gradually, possibly from Cehpech times as suggested by the findings of slateware examples at Xcaret in Quintana Roo to the Chikinchel Ceramic Complex with fine-orange Cunduacan specimens from Tamulte, Tabasco. The early use of the black tricklelike painted decoration which attained great popularity in both Cehpech and Sotuta, finally fading out in the Hocaba Ceramic Complex, is another Yucatan area mode. The utilization of a waxy finish found on Mamom and especially Chicanel slipped wares of the Peten has a strong revival during the Cehpech and Sotuta ceramic complexes. These two complexes are also marked by the abundant use of volcanic ash temper in a nonvolcanic region. The ash may have been wind blown and located in pockets but more likely brought in through trade from vol-

canic areas. The grater bowl, adopted in Yucatan in Sotuta times, continues through the Tases Ceramic Complex. Drums are present in Cehpech and persist through Tases. Certain vessel parts are strongly Yucatecan and, although they may occur sporadically elsewhere, do immediately suggest the Yucatan Peninsula. These are strap handles, bolster rims, and rim moldings, which are well represented in all complexes from Cehpech through Tases. In some instances these attributes carry on into modern pottery making.

Other modes identify a certain period of time. These may be called single complex modes. To name only a few in each complex beginning with Cehpech, there are beveled-rim ringstand bowls, flaring-side basal-Z-angle tripod dishes, flutes, stamped cylindrical feet, bead rims, T-shape rims, modeled-carving, deep coarse striations, and vertical crazing. In Sotuta are found ladle-handle tripod censer jars, rounded-side flat-base dishes, lamp-chimney pedestal-base vases, pyriform vases, bell-shape feet, bulbous feet, gadrooning, light-fine striation, and designs including the crosshatch, figure-eight arrangement, scroll meander, spatter, and black-painted birds. There is no mode solely identified with Hocaba except the Xcanchakan Black-on-cream Type. Other modes linked with Hocaba are also equally well represented in Tases: huge storage jars, low-neck wide-mouth cooking jars, light-coarse striation, and roughening of the surface, all associated with utilitarian pottery. Moldmade effigy feet have a beginning in Hocaba and attain greater popularity in Tases. Tases has its own quite distinctive modes. These are bowl clusters, candle-flame shields, deep bowls either ringstand or tripod, Mayapan Red Ware flaring-side tripod dishes or bowls with unslipped exterior, high-neck tripod jars, masks, parenthesis-rim jars, and designs including the circle chain, fish, and eye associated devices.

Thus, through mode analysis, certain traditions involving each complex and associated cultural phase are established, as well as certain trends spanning long time periods. When more is known, it will be possible not only to establish mode complexes but to evolve horizon styles.

Finally, whether one deals with types or modes, the degeneration of Maya pottery following the Sotuta Ceramic Complex is very clear. The paste is generally coarser, which is partially due to the lack of ash temper. The finish is inferior because of careless smoothing and poor firing. Often a fairly pleasing result was attained by high polishing. The decoration is simple and not very exciting. One of the few Tases contributions that stand out is the modeled and painted work of the effigy censers and effigy vessels. These are colorful and arresting even though the artistic quality leaves much to be desired.

PART FOUR

Analysis by Ceramic Complex

INTRODUCTION

A description of all wares together with their associated groups, types, and varieties is given in Chapter IV where for easy reference the wares are presented alphabetically. In Chapters XII through XVII these wares, types, and varieties are analyzed minutely and critically as they appear in the different ceramic complexes. Below (pp. 133–135) for purposes of clarity and quick reference are listed the ware, the ceramic group, and the type-variety content of the Yucatan ceramic complexes which are observed and studied in this report.

THE FULL COMPLEMENT OF WARES, CERAMIC GROUPS, TYPES, AND VARIETIES LISTED CHRONOLOGICALLY BY CERAMIC COMPLEX

ECAB CERAMIC COMPLEX
(?? B.C.–?? B.C.)

Homun Unslipped Ware
  Unslipped Yotolin Group
    Yotolin Pattern-burnished Type: Yotolin Variety

TIHOSUCO CERAMIC COMPLEX
(800 B.C.–A.D. 100)

Xcanatun Unslipped Ware
  Unslipped Saban Group
    Saban Unslipped Type: Saban Variety
    Chancenote Striated Type: Chancenote Variety
Yucatan Opaque Ware
  Red Nolo Group
    Nolo Red Type: Nolo Variety
    Kiba Incised Type: Kiba Variety (sharp-incised)
    Kiba Incised Type: groove-incised variety
    Kini Composite Type: Kini Variety
  Black Ucu Group
    Ucu Black Type: Ucu Variety
    Yaxkukul Composite Type: Yaxkukul Variety
Tutul Xiu Red Ware
  Red Tipikal Group
    Tipikal Red-on-striated Type: Tipikal Variety

COCHUAH CERAMIC COMPLEX
(A.D. 300–600)

Ware (?)
  Cetelac Fibre-temper Type: Cetelac Variety
Usil Red Ware
  Red Xanaba Group
    Xanaba Red Type: Xanaba Variety
    Caucel Black-on-red Type: Caucel Variety
Yucatan Chalky Ware
  Brown Chuburna Group
    Chuburna Brown Type: Chuburna Variety
Yucatan Gloss Ware
  Red Batres Group
    Batres Red Type: Batres Variety
  Buff Maxcanu Group
    Maxcanu Buff Type: Maxcanu Variety
  Orange Timucuy Group
    Timucuy Orange-polychrome Type: Timucuy Variety
    Valladolid Incised-dichrome Type: Valladolid Variety
    Tituc Orange-polychrome Type: Tituc Variety
    Popola Gadrooned Type: Popola Variety

MOTUL CERAMIC COMPLEX
(A.D. 600–800)

Dzibilchaltun Ware
  Red Conkal Group
    Conkal Red Type: Conkal Variety
Yucatan Gloss Ware
  Teya Black-on-orange Type: Teya Variety
Fine Black Ware
  Black Yalcox Group
    Yalcox Black Type: Yalcox Variety
    Tekanto Incised Type: Tekanto Variety
    Tekanto Incised Type: red-decorated variety
    Xnoria Fluted Type: Xnoria Variety
    Xtab Composite Type: Xtab Variety
Fine Gray Ware
  Gray Chablekal Group
    Chablekal Gray Type: Chablekal Variety
    Chicxulub Incised Type: Chicxulub Variety
    Cholul Fluted Type: Cholul Variety
    Telchac Composite Type: Telchac Variety
Fine Orange Ware
  Fine-orange Dzibilchaltun Group
    Dzibilchaltun Orange Type: Dzibilchaltun
      Variety
    Xlacah Incised Type: Xlacah Variety
    Xlacah Incised Type: red-slip variety
    Xlacah Incised Type: black-slip variety
Thin Black Ware
  Black Uman Group
    Uman Black Type: Uman Variety
    Bokaba Incised Type: Bokaba Variety

CEHPECH CERAMIC COMPLEX
(A.D. 800–1000)

Puuc Unslipped Ware
  Unslipped Chum Group
    Chum Unslipped Type: Chum Variety
    Yokat Striated Type: Yokat Variety
    Yokat Striated Type: neck-interior variety
    Oxkutzcab Appliqué Type: Oxkutzcab Variety
    Halacho Impressed Type: Halacho Variety
    Yiba Modeled Type: Yiba Variety
    Tepakan Composite Type: Tepakan Variety
Puuc Slate Ware
  Slate Muna Group
    Muna Slate Type: Muna Variety
    Muna Slate Type: notched variety
    Sacalum Black-on-slate Type: Sacalum Variety
    Tekit Incised Type: Tekit Variety
    Akil Impressed Type: Akil Variety
    Chumayel Red-on-slate Type: Chumayel Variety
    Chumayel Red-on-slate Type: modeled variety
    Chumayel Red-on-slate Type: incised variety
    Yaxnic Modeled Type: Yaxnic Variety
    Nohcacab Composite Type: Nohcacab Variety
    Xaya Gouged-incised Type: Xaya Variety

Thin Slate Ware
  Thin-slate Ticul Group
    Ticul Thin-slate Type: Ticul Variety
    Xul Incised Type: Xul Variety
    Tabi Gouged-incised Type: Tabi Variety
    Tikihal Circle-shading Type: Tikihal Variety
Puuc Red Ware
  Red Teabo Group
    Teabo Red Type: Teabo Variety
    Becal Incised Type: Becal Variety
    Becal Incised Type: groove-incised variety
    Opichen Gouged-incised Type: Opichen Variety
    Tekax Black-on-red Type: Tekax Variety
    Tekax Black-on-red Type: orange variety
    Sahcaba Modeled-carved Type: Sahcaba Variety
    Yaxumha Composite Type: Yaxumha Variety
    Sitpach Modeled Type: Sitpach Variety
Fine Orange Ware
  Fine-orange Altar Group
    Altar Orange Type: Altar Variety
    Pabellon Modeled-carved Type: Pabellon Variety
    Trapiche Groove-incised Type: Trapiche Variety
    Cedro Gadrooned Type: Cedro Variety
    Tumba Black-on-orange Type: Tumba Variety
  Fine-orange Balancan Group
    Balancan Orange Type: Balancan Variety
    Caribe Incised Type: Caribe Variety
    Caribe Incised Type: red-paint variety
    Caribe Incised Type: groove-incised variety
    Canizan Gadrooned Type: Canizan Variety
    Palizada Black-on-orange Type: Palizada Variety
    Provincia Plano-relief Type: Provincia Variety
    Tenosique Red-on-orange Type: Tenosique Variety
Cauich Coarse-cream Ware
  Cream Holactun Group
    Holactun Black-on-cream Type: Holactun Variety
    Holactun Black-on-cream Type: cinnamon-slip variety

SOTUTA CERAMIC COMPLEX
(A.D. 1000–1200)

Chichen Unslipped Ware
  Unslipped Sisal Group
    Sisal Unslipped Type: Sisal Variety
    Piste Striated Type: Piste Variety
    Espita Appliqué Type: Espita Variety
    Tibolon Blue-on-red Type: Tibolon Variety
    Cumtun Composite Type: Cumtun Variety

Chichen Slate Ware
  Slate Dzitas Group
    Dzitas Slate Type: Dzitas Variety
    Balantun Black-on-slate Type: Balantun Variety
    Balam Canche Red-on-slate Type: Balam Canche Variety
    Chacmay Incised Type: Chacmay Variety
    Chacmay Incised Type: groove-incised variety
    Tekom Gouged-incised Type: Tekom Variety
    Mopila Gadrooned Type: Mopila Variety
    Nenela Modeled Type: Nenela Variety
    Timak Composite Type: Timak Variety
    Timak Composite Type: sharp-incised variety
Chichen Red Ware
  Red Dzibiac Group
    Dzibiac Red Type: Dzibiac Variety
    Chan Kom Black-on-red Type: Chan Kom Variety
    Chan Kom Black-on-red Type: sharp-incised variety
    Chan Kom Black-on-red Type: cream-slip variety
    Xuku Incised Type: Xuku Variety
    Xuku Incised Type: groove-incised variety
    Xuku Incised Type: cream-slip variety
    Xuku Incised Type: black-slip variety
    Holtun Gouged-incised Type: Holtun Variety
    Holtun Gouged-incised Type: cream-slip variety
    Holtun Gouged-incised Type: black-slip variety
    Tiholop Gadrooned Type: Tiholop Variety
Fine Orange Ware
  Fine-orange Silho Group
    Silho Orange Type: Silho Variety
    Calkini Gadrooned Type: Calkini Variety
    Champan Red-on-orange Type: Champan Variety
    Cumpich Incised Type: Cumpich Variety
    Cumpich Incised Type: black-paint variety
    Kilikan Composite Type: Kilikan Variety
    Kilikan Composite Type: black-slip variety
    Kilikan Composite Type: cream-slip variety
    Kilikan Composite Type: polychrome variety
    Nunkini Modeled Type: Nunkini Variety
    Nunkini Modeled Type: black-paint variety
    Nunkini Modeled Type: polychrome variety
    Pocboc Gouged-incised Type: Pocboc Variety
    Pocboc Gouged-incised Type: black-slip variety
    Pocboc Gouged-incised Type: cream-slip variety
    Pomuch Polychrome Type: Pomuch Variety
    Yalton Black-on-orange Type: Yalton Variety

Fine Buff Ware
  Fine-buff (?) Group
    Cerro Montoso Polychrome Type: Cerro Montoso Variety
Plumbate Ware
  Plumbate Tohil Group
    Tohil Plumbate Type: Tohil Variety
    Tumbador Incised Type: Tumbador Variety
    Porvenir Gadrooned Type: Porvenir Variety
    Malacatan Modeled Type: Malacatan Variety
Ware (?)
    Tinum Red-on-cinamon Type: Tinum Variety
Ware (?)
    Libre Union Red-on-buff Type: Libre Union Variety
Ware (?)
    Tunkas Red-on-gray Type: Tunkas Variety
Ware (?)
    Cenotillo Gray-polychrome Type: Cenotillo Variety

HOCABA CERAMIC COMPLEX
(A.D. 1200–1300)

Mayapan Unslipped Ware
  Unslipped Navula Group
    Navula Unslipped Type: Navula Variety
    Yacman Striated Type: Yacman Variety
    Hoal Modeled Type: Hoal Variety
    Hunacti Appliqué Type: Hunacti Variety
    Cehac Painted Type: Cehac Variety
    Kanasin Red-on-unslipped Type: Kanasin Variety
    Cehac-Hunacti Composite Type: Cehac-Hunacti Variety
Mayapan Red Ware
  Red Mama Group
    Mama Red Type: Mama Variety
    Chapab Modeled Type: Chapab Variety
    Dzonot Appliqué Type: Dzonot Variety
    Papacal Incised Type: Papacal Variety
Mayapan Black Ware
  Black Sulche Group
    Sulche Black Type: Sulche Variety
    Conil Plano-relief Type: Conil Variety
    Pacha Incised Type: Pacha Variety
    Sacmuyna Modeled Type: Sacmuyna Variety
Peto Cream Ware
  Cream Kukula Group
    Kukula Cream Type: Kukula Variety
    Xcanchakan Black-on-cream Type: Xcanchakan Variety
    Xcanchakan Black-on-cream Type: sharp-incised variety
    Pencuyut Incised Type: Pencuyut Variety
    Cusama Plano-relief Type: Cusama Variety
    Mataya Modeled Type: Mataya Variety

Fine Orange Ware
Fine-orange Matillas Group
    Matillas Orange Type: Matillas Variety
    Chilapa Gouged-incised Type: Chilapa Variety
    Grijalva Incised-polychrome Type: Grijalva Variety
    Nacajuca Black-on-orange Type: Nacajuca Variety
    Salto Composite Type: Salto Variety
    Sayula Polychrome Type: Sayula Variety
    Villahermosa Incised Type: Villahermosa Variety

TASES CERAMIC COMPLEX
(A.D. 1300–1450)

Mayapan Unslipped Ware
Unslipped Panaba Group
    Panaba Unslipped Type: Panaba Variety
    Chen Mul Modeled Type: Chen Mul Variety
    Buleb Striated Type: Buleb Variety
    Huhi Impressed Type: Huhi Variety
    Thul Appliqué Type: Thul Variety
    Acansip Painted Type: Acansip Variety
    Chenkeken Incised Type: Chenkeken Variety
    Acansip-Thul Composite Type: Acansip-Thul Variety
    Chenkeken-Acansip Composite Type: Chenkeken-Acansip Variety
Mayapan Red Ware
Red Panabchen Group
    Panabchen Red Type: Panabchen Variety
    Mama Red Type: unslipped-exterior variety
    Mama Red Type: black-and-red-on-unslipped variety
    Mama Red Type: black-on-unslipped variety
    Mama Red Type: red-on-unslipped variety
    Dzitxil Openwork Type: Dzitxil Variety
    Pustunich Incised Type: Pustunich Variety
    Yobain Plano-relief Type: Yobain Variety
    Tixua Gadrooned Type: Tixua Variety
    Tzitz Red Type: Tzitz Variety
San Joaquin Buff Ware
Buff Polbox Group
    Polbox Buff Type: Polbox Variety
    Kimbila Incised Type: Kimbila Variety
    Tecoh Red-on-buff-Type: Tecoh Variety
    Tecoh Red-on-buff Type: outline-incised variety
    Pele Polychrome Type: Pele Variety

Telchaquillo Brick Ware
Red Moyos Group
    Moyos Red Type: Moyos Variety
    Cozil Incised Type: Cozil Variety
Mayapan Coarse Ware
Unslipped Uayma Group
    Uayma Modeled Type: Uayma Variety
Fine Orange Ware
Fine-orange Matillas Group
    Matillas Orange Type: Matillas Variety
    Chilapa Gouged-incised Type: Chilapa Variety
    Grijalva Incised-polychrome Type: Grijalva Variety
    Nacajuca Black-on-orange Type: Nacajuca Variety
    Salto Composite Type: Salto Variety
    Sayula Polychrome Type: Sayula Variety
    Villahermosa Incised Type: Villahermosa Variety
Tulum Red Ware
Red Payil Group
    Payil Red Type: Payil Variety
    Palmul Incised Type: Palmul Variety
    Kanlum Plano-relief Type: Kanlum Variety

CHIKINCHEL CERAMIC COMPLEX
(A.D. 1450–1550)

Fine Orange Ware
Fine-orange Cunduacan Group
    Cunduacan Orange Type: Cunduacan Variety
    Buey Modeled Type: Buey Variety

CHAUACA CERAMIC COMPLEX
(A.D. 1550–1800?)

Ochil Unslipped Ware
Unslipped Yuncu Group
    Yuncu Unslipped Type: Yuncu Variety
    Tetis Appliqué Type: Tetis Variety
    Kinchil Composite Type: Kinchil Variety
Abala Red Ware
Red Sacpokana Group
    Sacpokana Red Type: Sacpokana Variety
    Choolac White-on-red Type: Choolac Variety
Bolon Brown Ware
Brown Oxcum Group
    Oxcum Brown Type: Oxcum Variety

XII

Pre-Cehpech Ceramic Complexes

In this monograph we are attempting not to delineate or analyze the early sherd occurrences, but merely to list them with as much description as the fragmentary condition of the sherds permits. As mentioned earlier, our purpose is to set down clearly and analytically our findings pertaining to four late ceramic complexes; namely, Cehpech, Sotuta, Hocaba, and Tases, which form a preponderant part of the Mayapan ceramic assemblage. In addition there are two later complexes, Chikinchel and Chauaca, that are poorly represented and not definitely fixed in time. The pre-Cehpech sherds are listed under the ceramic complex (local: Cupul, Tihosuco, Cochuah, and Motul; or trade: Mamom, Chicanel, Tzakol, and Tepeu) to which they belong and the site at which they were found. These sites, Uxmal, Kabah, Chichen Itza, and Mayapan, are described under the ceramic complex which is best represented: Uxmal and Kabah with the Cehpech Ceramic Complex, Chichen Itza with the Sotuta, and Mayapan with the Hocaba, Tases, Chikinchel, and Chauaca complexes.

It is interesting to note that no examples of the Chakan Ceramic Complex, which follows the Tihosuco and immediately precedes the Cochuah, were found. The Chakan Ceramic Complex and the Matzanel Ceramic Complex are presumed to be contemporaneous. It is the contents of the Chakan Ceramic Complex that are in doubt here. Clearly a part of Brainerd's (1958) Formative Monochrome (pp. 48–49) and his Flaky Redware (pp. 49–50) belong in Chakan, and perhaps his Flaky Dichrome (p. 50), but the last I prefer for the Cochuah Ceramic Complex.

Numbers in brackets following geographic areas and ware listings in Chapters XII–XVII refer to quantities of rim sherds. As mentioned before, "figure" or "fig." is not used before numbers referring to illustrations from this study.

MAMOM CERAMIC COMPLEX

MAYAPAN [2]

Oddly enough it is at Mayapan rather than at Uxmal, Kabah, or Chichen Itza that two sherds of the Middle Preclassic, Mamom Ceramic Complex were found in an early lot.

Flores Waxy Ware.
Dish, flaring sides, medium-thick walls, direct rim, flat base. Slipped and polished all over. *Types and decoration. Joventud Red Type:* 2 rim, no body sherds. No illustration, but compare Smith (1955a, fig. 14, a, 3).

TIHOSUCO CERAMIC COMPLEX

UXMAL–KABAH

At Uxmal no Preclassic sherds were uncovered; at Kabah a single body sherd was found.

Yucatan Opaque Ware.
Dish, flaring sides, medium-thick to thick walls, flat base. Slipped black and burnished all over.

Types and decoration. Yaxkukul Composite Type: Uxmal, none; Kabah, no rim, 1 body sherd. Horizontal incised and punctate lines (10, *n*). S temper.

CHICHEN ITZA [1]

All the Preclassic pottery except one rim sherd was found in the lower to middle strata of Cut 1.

The rim sherd came from the lowest level of Cut 16.

Yucatan Opaque Ware.

Dish, wide-everted rim. Flaring medium-thick to thick sides, flat base. Badly weathered but traces of red slip. *Types and decoration. Nolo Red Type:* 1 rim, no body sherds. No illustration but compare Brainerd (1958, figs. 65, c, *12*; 107, a, *5*).

Tutul Xiu Red Ware.

Jars. Globular body. Slipped and burnished red over striations on exterior only. *Types and decoration. Tipikal Red-on-striated Type:* no rim, 4 body sherds. No illustration but compare Brainerd (1958, fig. 31, e, *19, 20, 26, 27*).

MAYAPAN [14]

At Mayapan in the Late Preclassic Period a total of 63 Tihosuco Ceramic Complex sherds were encountered, including 55 from D Lots, 7 from A Lots, and 1 from C Lots.

Xcanatun Unslipped Ware.

Jars. Wide mouth, low to medium-high outcurving neck, globular body, base not encountered, medium-thick to thick walls. Imperfectly smoothed surface. *Types and decoration. Chancenote Striated Type:* 7 rim, 27 body sherds (middle and late A and D Lots). No illustration but see Brainerd (1958, figs. 12, a; 65, a).

Yucatan Opaque Ware.

Jars, continuous curve. Wide mouth, outcurving neck, pear-shape (?) body, base not encountered. Medium-thick walls. Slipped and burnished light brownish red on exterior and neck interior. *Types and decoration. Nolo Red Type:* 1 rim (24, c), no body sherds. *Kiba Incised Type:* no rim, 7 body sherds (early D Lots). No illustration, but see Brainerd (1958, fig. 31, e).

Dishes, basal break. Flaring medium-thick to thick sides, direct rim, flat base (?). Slipped and burnished red to brownish red all over. *Types and decoration. Nolo Red Type:* 3 rim, 7 body sherds (early D Lots). No illustration but form same as 24, g. *Kiba Incised Type, Kiba Variety:* no rim, 4 body sherds (early D Lots). Form is same as above. *Kiba Incised Type,* groove-incised variety: 2 rim (24, j), no body sherds.

Bowl, lateral flange. Small vessel, flaring medium-thick sides, direct rim, flange located just below lip, base presumably flat. Slipped and burnished all over. *Types and decoration. Ucu Black Type:* 1 rim (24, i), no body sherds.

Tutul Xiu Red Ware.

Jars. Wide mouth, low to medium-high outcurving neck, direct rim, globular body with medium-thick to thick walls. Slipped and burnished over a striated surface. Slip is a deep red. *Types and decoration. Tipikal Red-on-striated Type:* no rim, 4 body sherds. No illustration but see Brainerd's Red Slip over Striated Ware (1958, fig. 31, e, *19, 20, 26, 27*).

CHICANEL CERAMIC COMPLEX

MAYAPAN [30]

At Mayapan in the Late Preclassic Period a total of 42 Chicanel Ceramic Complex sherds were found including 39 from D Lots, 2 from C Lots, and 1 from A Lots.

Paso Caballo Waxy Ware.

Jars. Wide mouth, low flaring thick neck, direct or thickened rim, globular body with medium-thick to thick walls. Slipped and polished light brownish red on exterior and neck interior. Surfaces have a waxy feel. *Types and decoration. Sierra Red Type:* 6 rim (24, a, b), 2 body sherds. *Alta Mira Fluted Type:* no rim, 2 body sherds (no illustration). *Lagartos Punctate Type:* 1 rim, 1 body sherd. For illustration see Smith (1955a, fig. 70, a, *15, 16*).

Bowls, basal break. Flaring or outcurving medium-thick to thick sides, direct rim, flat base. Slipped and polished red to brownish red all over. Surfaces have waxy feel. *Types and decoration. Sierra Red Type:* 10 rim, 7 body sherds (24, d, g).

Bowls, recurving side. Direct rim, flat base, medium-thick to thick walls. Slipped and polished red to brownish red all over. Surfaces have waxy feel. *Types and decoration. Sierra Red Type:* 4 rim, no body sherds (24, h).

Bowl, lateral-Z-angle. Direct rim, Z-angle just below lip, flat base, thick walls. Slipped and polished red all over. Surface has waxy feel. *Types* and decoration. *Sierra Red Type*: 1 rim, no body sherds. No illustration but see Smith (1955a, fig. 70, *a*, 43).

Dishes, basal break. Flaring medium-thick to thick sides, wide-everted [5], and everted [3] rims, flat base. Slipped and polished red to brownish red all over. Surfaces have waxy feel. *Types and decoration. Sierra Red Type*: 7 rim, no body sherds. No illustration but see Smith (1955a, fig. 16, *c*, 2, 3). *Laguna Verde Incised Type*: 1 rim, no body sherds. No illustration but see Smith (1955a, fig. 16, *c*, 6).

COCHUAH CERAMIC COMPLEX

UXMAL [0]–KABAH [1]

At Uxmal no Cochuah Ceramic Complex sherds were found, whereas Kabah was responsible for 17.

Yucatan Chalky Ware.
Jars. Wide mouth, flaring medium-high neck, direct rim, globular body with thin to medium-thick walls. Slipped and polished a reddish brown, somewhat streaky, and applied to body exterior only. *Types and decoration. Chuburna Brown Type*: Uxmal, none; Kabah, no rim, 10 body sherds. For description and illustration see Smith (1955b, p. 255, Lustrous Streaky Brown, fig. 3, *qq*).

Yucatan Gloss Ware.
Jars. Wide mouth, flaring medium-high neck, direct rim, globular body with thin to medium-thick walls. Glossy slip on exterior and neck interior (when present). *Types and decoration. Timucuy Orange-polychrome Type*: Uxmal, none; Kabah, no rim, 1 body sherd. Too fragmentary to be certain of exact shape or design (10, *m*) but it is clearly Regional Polychrome (three-color polychrome) as described and illustrated by Brainerd (1958, p. 50; fig. 63, *b–d*) and as Tzakol 1 red-and-black-on-orange polychrome by Smith (1955a, p. 128, fig. 24, *a*, 1–4; see also T. and M. Gann, 1939, pl. 2, fig. 2). *Valladolid Incised-dichrome Type*: Uxmal, none; Kabah, 1 rim, 5 body sherds. For description and illustration see Brainerd (1958, p. 50; figs. 1, *g, i*; 6; 17, *g, 1–9*; 64; 66, *a*; 107, *b, 1, 3, 5, 8, 9*).

CHICHEN ITZA

The pottery of the Maya Classic Period prior to the Cehpech Ceramic Complex was very scarce at Chichen Itza in the five cuts used in this study. Only 12 Cochuah Ceramic Complex body sherds were found.

Yucatan Chalky Ware.
Jars, low neck. Wide mouth, low flaring neck, direct rim, globular body with medium-thick walls, concave base. Slipped and polished on exterior and neck interior. *Types and decoration. Chuburna Brown Type*: no rim, 5 body sherds. No illustration but this form is described by Smith (1955b, p. 254, fig. 3, *qq*) under the name Lustrous Streaky Brown Ware.

Bowl, hemispherical. Rounded, medium-thick sides, direct rim, flat base. Slipped and polished reddish brown on interior and exterior, base uncertain. *Types and decoration. Chuburna Brown Type*: no rim, 1 body sherd. No illustration and no precedent for this form.

Yucatan Gloss Ware.
Jars, high neck. Wide mouth, high outcurving necks, bolster rim, globular body, medium-thick walls, deeply striated on interior. Glossy orange slip on exterior and partway down neck interior. *Types and decoration. Valladolid Incised-dichrome Type*: no rim, 1 body sherd. No illustration but this type is described and illustrated by Brainerd (1958, p. 50; figs. 1, *g*; 6, *a*; 64; 66, *a*). *Popola Gadrooned Type*: no rim, 2 body sherds. No illustration. Gadrooning done from exterior.

Usil Red Ware
Jars. Medium-wide to wide mouth, usually high outcurving neck, direct, thickened or bolster rim, globular medium-thick walls, concave base. Slipped and polished on exterior and on neck interior when present. *Types and decoration. Xanaba Red Type*: no rim, 3 body sherds. This forms part of Flaky Redware (GWB, pp. 49–50; figs. 4; 6, *a, 8–15, 22–29*; *b*; *c*; 17, *f*). *Remarks*: Usil Red Ware refers to those reds which are uniform in attributes such as coarse textured paste, lustrous relatively thick slip, and a strong red (2.5 YR 5/6 and 10 R 5/6) color. This ware is primarily associated with the Cochuah Phase. Further data may

extend its range to the Motul Phase, in which event specimens may be distinguished as to their horizon by their shapes.

MAYAPAN [163]

At Mayapan in the Early Classic Period a total of 466 Cochuah Ceramic Complex sherds was found, including 436 from D Lots, 21 from C Lots, and 9 from A Lots.

Usil Red Ware.

Jars. Wide mouth, low medium-high to high flaring or outcurving neck, direct or thickened rim, globular body, usually concave base. Walls are medium-thick to thick. Slipped and polished on exterior and generally on neck interior, at least the upper part. The slip has a tendency to flake or spall in areas from a smooth, fine, powdery, cream-colored undersurface. *Types and decoration.* Xanaba Red Type: 5 rim, 19 body sherds (25, *a;* early C and D Lots, middle C Lot, and late D Lot). *Caucel Black-on-red Type:* 1 rim, 2 body sherds (no illustration).

Yucatan Gloss Ware.

Jars. Wide mouth, tapering neck, everted rim, flaring lower sides incurving at body-neck junction. Glossy buff slip on exterior and on everted-rim interior. Surface lumpy with imperfectly smoothed temper particles. *Types and decoration.* Maxcanu Buff Type: 13 rim, 88 body sherds (GWB, fig. 11, *a*).

Jars. Medium-wide to wide mouth, medium-high to high outcurving neck, direct or bolster rim, globular to pear-shape body, concave base. Glossy orange slip on exterior and neck interior. Usually the interior body is deeply striated (*ibid.,* fig.

64, *b*). *Types and decoration.* Valladolid Incised-dichrome Type: 15 rim, 56 body sherds (25, *c, d*). *Timucuy Orange-polychrome Type:* 37 rim, 106 body sherds (25, *e–o*). *Tituc Orange-polychrome Type:* 13 rim, 33 body sherds (no illustration).

Bowls, basal-Z-angle. Flaring or outcurving medium-thick sides, direct rim, basal-Z-angle, and probably a ring base since ring bases were found but no mammiform feet. They had an allover orange gloss slip which was decorated with red and black designs, mostly horizontal lines and bands. *Types and decoration.* Timucuy Orange-polychrome Type: 8 rim, 15 body sherds (25, *v*).

Bowls, basal flange. Flaring or outcurving medium-thick sides, direct rim, ring base. At juncture of base and side a flange pointing diagonally downward. Glossy slip on interior and exterior down to and including flange. The orange slip is decorated with red and black geometric design. *Types and decoration.* Tituc Orange-polychrome Type: 12 rim, 20 body sherds (GWB, figs. 9, *a, f;* 19, *g, 3;* 30, *a;* 60, *b;* 63, *a, 12*).

Bowls, lateral flange. These bowls are large and may be considered basins. Flaring medium-thick sides, thickened rim, lateral flange high on vessel side, probably ring base (*ibid.,* fig. 8, *e*). Glossy red slip on interior and exterior down to and including flange below which the walls are striated. *Types and decoration.* Batres Red Type: 3 rim, 1 body sherd (25, *b*).

Yucatan Chalky Ware.

Jars. Wide mouth, low flaring medium-thick neck, direct rim, globular body with medium-thick walls, concave base. Slipped reddish brown and polished on exterior to within a few centimeters of base and on neck interior. *Types and decoration.* Chuburna Brown Type: 10 rim, 9 body sherds (25, *bb;* 60, *a*).

TZAKOL CERAMIC COMPLEX

UXMAL–KABAH

At Uxmal, 3 Tzakol Ceramic Complex body sherds were encountered, at Kabah, 6. No rim sherds were found.

Peten Gloss Ware.

Jar. No rim, globular body, medium-thick walls. Glossy slip on exterior only. *Types and decoration.* Aguila Orange Type: Uxmal, no rim, 1 body sherd; Kabah, none. Similar to orange gloss jars

illustrated by Smith (1955a, fig. 17, *c*, 7–10).

Bowls, hemispherical. Rounded medium-thick sides, direct rim, flat base. Glossy slip on interior and exterior, sometimes on base. *Types and decoration.* Balanza Black Type: Uxmal, no rim, 2 body sherds; Kabah, no rim, 2 body sherds. For description and illustration compare with Tzakol Gloss Ware, plain black (RES, pp. 80 and 136, fig. 10, *k, m*).

Bowls, basal flange. Flaring medium-thick sides, direct rim, probably ring base. Glossy slip on interior and exterior above flange. *Types and decoration.* *Aguila Orange Type:* Uxmal, none; Kabah, no rim, 3 body sherds. For description and illustration see Smith (1955a, p. 135, fig. 18, c).

Bowl, basal break. Flaring medium-thick sides, direct rim, flat base. Glossy slip on interior and exterior but not on base. *Types and decoration.* *Aguila Orange Type:* Uxmal, none; Kabah, no rim, 1 body sherd. Similar to cache bowls of Tzakol Phase (RES, p. 96, fig. 19, b).

CHICHEN ITZA [2]

The Tzakol Ceramic Complex sherds encountered at Chichen Itza totaled 3.

Peten Gloss Ware.

Bowls, hemispherical. Rounded, medium-thick sides, direct rim, flat base. Glossy orange slip on interior and exterior, base uncertain. *Types and decoration.* *Aguila Orange Type:* 1 rim, 1 body sherd. Like orange examples illustrated by Smith (1955a, fig. 23, a, 4–7) but without decoration.

Bowl, flaring side. Medium-thick walls, direct rim, rest of form not known. It could be a Tzakol basal-break cache-type vessel or a basal-flange or basal-Z-angle bowl with ring base. *Types and decoration.* *Aguila Orange Type:* 1 rim, no body sherds (not illustrated).

MAYAPAN [46]

At Mayapan in the Early Classic Period a total of 244 Tzakol Ceramic Complex sherds were found, including 219 from D Lots, 19 from C Lots, and 6 from A Lots.

Thin Black Ware.

Bowl, cylinder tripod. Slightly outcurving thin sides, direct rim, presumably flattish base, and three feet. Glossy slip all over. Black on exterior, orange on interior. *Types and decoration.* *Catzim Incised Type:* 1 rim, no body sherds. Abstract design, no illustration.

Peten Gloss Ware.

Jars. Small mouth, high vertical neck, direct rim, globular body, flat base. Glossy slip on exterior and neck interior. *Types and decoration. Boleto Black-on-orange Type:* no rim, 2 body sherds.

Jars. Small mouth, medium-high flaring or outcurving neck, direct rim, globular body, bases uncertain. Glossy slip on exterior and neck interior. *Types and decoration. Aguila Orange Type:* 9 rim, 131 body sherds (no illustration). *Boleto Black-on-orange Type:* no rim, 2 body sherds.

Bowls, hemispherical. Rounded medium-thick sides, direct rim, flat base. Glossy slip on interior and exterior. *Types and decoration. Aguila Orange Type:* 2 rim, no body sherds (no illustration). *Pita Incised Type:* 6 rim, 8 body sherds. Designs are geometric (25, q–s; 60, f). *Boleto Black-on-orange Type:* 1 rim, 5 body sherds (no illustration).

Bowls, basal-Z-angle. Flaring or outcurving medium-thick sides, direct rim, basal-Z-angle, ring base. All over glossy orange slip. *Types and decoration. Aguila Orange Type:* 9 rim, 23 body sherds (25, w). *Pita Incised Type:* 3 rim, 1 body sherd. These have horizontal incised lines on exterior (no illustration).

Bowls, basal flange. Flaring or outcurving medium-thick sides, direct rim, ring base or tripod. At juncture of base and side a flange pointing diagonally downward. Glossy slip on interior and exterior but seldom below flange. *Types and decoration. Aguila Orange Type:* 9 rim, 15 body sherds. Undecorated and no illustration but see Smith (1955a, fig. 18, c). *Pita Incised Type:* 1 rim, no body sherds. Horizontal groove on exterior (25, t). *Delirio Plano-relief Type:* 1 rim, 1 body sherd with plano-relief abstract design (25, p). *Dos Arroyos Orange-polychrome Type:* 3 rim, 9 body sherds with geometric designs (cf. RES, figs. 25, b; 26).

Bowls, cylinder tripod. Vertical or slightly outcurving, medium-thick sides, direct rim, somewhat convex base, and three feet. Glossy slip on interior and exterior except base. *Types and decoration. Aguila Orange Type:* no rim, 1 body sherd (undecorated and no illustration). *Pucte Brown Type:* 1 rim, no body sherds (undecorated and no illustration).

MOTUL CERAMIC COMPLEX

MAYAPAN [79]

At Mayapan a total of 357 Motul Ceramic Complex sherds was found. This includes 304 sherds from cenotes (D Lots), 23 from residential and associated structures (A Lots), and 30 from ceremonial structures (C Lots).

Thin Black Ware.

Jars. Wide mouth, low to medium-high flaring neck, direct rim, globular body with thin walls, base not known. Glossy slip on exterior and neck interior. *Types and decoration. Uman Black Type:* 2 rim, 1 body sherd. No illustration but for ware and form see Brainerd (1958, fig. 53, *g*).

Bowls, side angle. Outcurving thin sides angling to a flat base, direct rim. Slipped and glossy all over. Occasional reddish areas and some crazing. *Types and decoration. Bokoba Incised Type:* 6 rim, 7 body sherds which are preslip incised (25, *y–aa*).

Dzibilchaltun Ware.

Jars. Wide mouth, low flaring neck, direct rim, globular or barrel-shape body, concave base. Slipped and burnished on exterior to, and often overlapping, groove below which it is lightly striated, and on neck interior. Slip color ranges from red to brown or orange and even gray. *Types and decoration. Conkal Red Type:* 68 rim, 258 body sherds (25, cc–ee; 60, *b*).

Fine Black Ware.

Jars. No lip or neck sherds; globular body, concave base. Matte to slight luster; slipped jet black on body exterior. *Types and decoration. Yalcox Black Type:* no rim, 4 body sherds (no illustration).

Bowls, side angle. Inward sloping thin sides angling to flat base, direct rim. Slipped and burnished jet black all over after careful smoothing. *Types and decoration. Tekanto Incised Type, red-decorated variety:* 3 rim, 4 body sherds (25, *x*). Postslip, prepolish incised abstract design plus a horizontal red line defining lower limit or incised band. The incisions may have been red-filled.

Fine Gray Ware.

Bowls, basal flange. Flaring or outcurving medium-thick sides, often everted rim, tripod (?). At juncture of base and side a flange pointing diagonally downward. Seemingly unslipped, but well smoothed; usually a matte finish. Color throughout is a deep gray. *Types and decoration. Chablekal Gray Type:* no rim, 4 body sherds (no illustration but for form compare Berlin, 1956, fig. 5, *gg*).

TEPEU 1 CERAMIC COMPLEX

UXMAL [1]–KABAH [1]

Late Classic Period pottery is extremely rare at both Uxmal and Kabah. Actually only one rim sherd was found at Uxmal and one at Kabah, and no body sherds at either site. Nor were any certainly identifiable Motul Ceramic Complex sherds.

Peten Gloss Ware.

Bowls, rounded side. Medium-thick sides, direct rim, pointed lip, probably flat base. Glossy slip on interior and exterior. *Types and decoration. Bejucal Brown-on-buff Type:* Uxmal, 1 rim, no body sherds; Kabah, none. Brown rim stripe on interior; brown semidisk rim band on exterior (10, *p*). The brown used on a Uaxactun cylindrical vase (RES, fig. 72, *a*) is applied very thinly and streaked with black, as is the case with this specimen. *Saxche Orange-polychrome Type:* Uxmal, none; Kabah, 1 rim, no body sherds. Interior and exterior have red rim stripe; exterior broad horizontal black stripe (10, *l*).

MAYAPAN [4]

At Mayapan a total of 35 Tepeu sherds were encountered: 7 Tepeu 1 and 28 Tepeu 2. This includes 30 sherds from A Lots and 5 from D Lots.

Peten Gloss Ware.

Bowls, hemispherical. Rounded medium-thick sides, direct rim, flat base. Glossy orange slip all over. *Types and decoration. Saxche Orange-poly-chrome Type*: 2 rim, no body sherds (no illustration, design not clear). *Uacho Black-on-orange Type*: 1 rim, no body sherds (no illustration).

Plates, tripod, basal ridge. Flaring medium-thick sides, direct rim, basal ridge, three feet. Glossy orange slip on interior; exterior generally unslipped but smoothed. *Types and decoration. Saxche Orange-polychrome Type*: 1 rim, 3 body sherds (no illustration).

TEPEU 2 CERAMIC COMPLEX

MAYAPAN [7]

Peten Gloss Ware.

Jars, medium-wide mouth. Flaring, medium-high neck, direct rim, globular body with medium-thick walls; base not known. Glossy slip on exterior and neck interior. Crazing sometimes present. *Types and decoration. Yuhactal Black-on-red Type*: 1 rim, 15 body sherds. Slip color is dark red and decoration black (no illustration). *Chantuori Black-on-orange Type*: no rim, 2 body sherds. Slip color is orange, decoration black (no illustration).

Bowls, side angle. Outcurving thin to medium-thick sides angling to a flat base, direct rim. Slipped and glossy all over. *Types and decoration. Infierno Black Type*: 4 rim, 4 body sherds (no illustration). *Geronimo Incised Type*: 1 rim, no body sherds (25, *u*; 60, *e*).

Vase, cylindrical. Slightly outcurving medium-thick sides, direct rim, probably flat base. Glossy black slip on interior and exterior. Red medium-coarse textured paste. *Types and decoration. Carmelita Incised Type*: 1 rim, no body sherds. Preslip horizontal and vertical grooving on exterior. No illustration but compare Berlin (1956, fig. 4, *ll*) for color, form, and decoration.

XIII

Cehpech Ceramic Complex

UXMAL AND KABAH [6,242]

These two sites are located in the Puuc, a hilly region in western Yucatan extending in a generally northwest and southeast direction. Many other important sites, including Sayil and Labna, to name only two of the more important, are to be found in this once extensively populated area. Uxmal and Kabah were selected for this study not only because they were the most accessible, but because previous ceramic testing led us to believe that best results for our purposes could be achieved there.

Uxmal appeared to be the site likely to give us the most complete picture of the Cehpech Ceramic Complex, as well as some knowledge of the Chakan, Cochuah, and Motul Ceramic complexes. We were successful in getting an excellent sample of Cehpech Phase pottery from the seven cuts (1–6, 8) used in this study. We did not encounter more than three examples of the Tzakol Ceramic Complex and one of the Tepeu Ceramic Complex (10, p), although many sherds of these complexes and earlier had been found under the great platform supporting the Palace of the Governor. The Sotuta Ceramic Complex, which we thought might be moderately represented, accounted for only one sherd out of a total of 33,467 collected; three others were marked as possibly of the Tases Ceramic Complex. Also included in the Cehpech total are 1,342 unidentifiable sherds. Thus Uxmal could supply us with a substantial sample of Cehpech Phase pottery only. It would not be logical to assume from our findings that the Toltec people ever occupied Uxmal. The meager late ceramic sample noted, as well as the few late decorated elements such as the feathered serpent motif, are insufficient to warrant the idea of an occupation by Toltec peoples but do suggest some contact and influence.

Kabah, according to the ceramic findings of H. B. Roberts (1935, p. 127), has produced in the lowest strata of two trenches polychrome sherds of the same general type as those from Holmul V and

Tepeu at Uaxactun. Roberts says that "the polychrome wares were found in direct association with the earliest of the Puuc wares and rim forms."

The pottery collection resulting from the five cuts (1–5) made for this report contained a total of 13,337 sherds including 1 Tihosuco Ceramic Complex specimen (10, n), 17 Cochuah, and 6 Tzakol (10, l, m, p), 1 Motul example, and 1 Sotuta, a Tohil Plumbate specimen. The rest, including 482 unidentifiable sherds, belong to the Cehpech Ceramic Complex. Again we find a ceramic situation very similar to that encountered at Uxmal. Clearly the Cehpech Ceramic Complex is well represented at Kabah and Uxmal; the main differences appear to be areal rather than temporal.

As indicated above, we were greatly surprised to find only 28 sherds of Chakan-Cochuah-Motul pottery and scanty numbers of Tihosuco, Sotuta, and Hocaba-Tases Ceramic Complex sherds from the combined Uxmal-Kabah pottery collections. It was, however, most gratifying to learn that our material represented an almost unmixed collection of Cehpech Phase ceramics. The Cehpech pottery may be separated into five wares (the Brainerd equivalents in parentheses), Puuc (Florescent) Unslipped, Puuc (Florescent Medium) Slate, Thin Slate, Puuc Red (Florescent Medium and Thin Red), and Cauich Coarse-cream (Holactun Slateware); each of these wares is represented by a number of types. Puuc Unslipped Ware includes the following types: Chum Unslipped, Yokat Striated, Halacho Impressed, Oxkutzcab Appliqué, Tepakan Composite, Yiba Modeled. Puuc Slate Ware has seven types: Muna Slate, Sacalum Black-on-slate, Chumayel Orange-on-slate, Tekit Incised, Xaya Gouged-incised, Akil Impressed, Yaxnic Modeled. Thin Slate Ware embraces four types: Ticul Thin-slate, Xul Incised, Tabi Gouged-incised, Tikihal Circle-shading. Puuc Red Ware includes six types: Teabo Red, Tekax Black-on-red, Becal Incised, Opichen Gouged-incised, Yaxumha Modeled, Sahcaba Modeled-carved. Cauich Coarse-cream Ware has one type: Holactun Black-on-cream.

Closely associated with this ceramic complex is Fine Orange Ware of which two groups are present, fine-orange Balancan (Puuc Fine Orangeware: Z-type, GWB, p. 54) and fine-orange Altar (Y Fine Orange, Smith, 1958b), both trade wares. Each group is composed of one or more types. The fine-orange Balancan Group includes five types: Balancan Orange, Caribe Incised, Provincia Plano-relief, Palizada Black-on-orange, Tenosique Red-on-orange. The fine-orange Altar Group at present can claim but one type from the Yucatan collections, Pabellon Modeled-carved.

Besides types there are varieties. In this report the variety is for the most part the established variety and bears the same name as the type. In

a few instances, however, other varieties have been recorded. This is true for the Yokat Striated Type which has the established Yokat Variety including jars striated on exterior, but when jars carry striations on the neck interior as well, they are listed under neck-interior variety. The Muna Slate Type has two varieties including Muna, the established variety, and the basal-notched variety. The Chumayel Red-on-slate Type has two varieties besides the Chumayel established variety: the incised variety and the modeled variety. The Tekax Black-on-red Type includes the Tekax or established variety and the orange-slip variety. The Holactun Black-on-cream Type, in addition to the Holactun established variety, has the orange-slip variety, which occurs rarely. The fine-orange Balancan Group includes a Caribe Incised Type which besides the Caribe established variety has the red-band variety.

PUUC UNSLIPPED WARE [771]

Forms, Types and Varieties	Uxmal Rim	%	Kabah Rim	%	Total Rim & body
Jars: Yokat Striated Type, neck-interior variety	304	49.4	10	6.4	600
Yokat Striated Type, Yokat Variety	150	24.4	133	85.3	14,505
Chum Unslipped Type, Chum Variety	0		0		1,052
Halacho Impressed Type, Halacho Variety	0		0		2
Censers, hourglass: Oxkutzcab Appliqué Type	85	15.6	5	3.8	207
Tepakan Composite Type	6		1		15
Halacho Impressed Type	4		0		35
Censers, basin: Halacho Impressed Type	27	4.5	2		46
Chum Unslipped Type	1		0		1
Censers, ladle: Chum Unslipped Type	17	2.8	0		50
Bowls, flaring side: Chum Unslipped Type	9	1.5	2		19
Oxkutzcab Appliqué Type	1		0		3
Bowls, rounded side: Chum Unslipped Type	7	1.1	3		17
Bowls, restricted orifice: Chum Unslipped Type	3		0		8
Flageolets: Yiba Modeled Type	1		0		12
Figurines: Yiba Modeled Type	0		0		21
Total	615		156		16,593

Jars, interior neck striated (2, a–g, s, u). Medium-wide to wide mouth, high outcurving or flaring medium-thick to thick neck, thin to medium-thick body, overhanging (a), everted (b, c), or direct (d, f), rim, some with rim flange (g) or rim molding (e), pointed, rounded, beveled, or flat lip, globular body. *Size:* lip diam. 18–50 cm., av. 29.8 cm., most common of 51 measured are 32 cm. [19], 26 cm. [10], and 36 cm. [6]; neck ht. 4.5–12.8 cm., av. 7.6 cm., most common of 5 measured is 7.2 cm. [2]. *Surface:* smoothed on exterior and neck interior; light-coarse horizontal striations on neck interior and light-coarse or medium-coarse stria-

tions on body exterior. A few (c) have vertical light-coarse striations on neck exterior. In some cases the edge of a shell was used. There are three main varieties of Cehpech coarse striation: s, u, light; t, v, medium; w–aa, deep. A small percentage of the Uxmal jars had a white calcareous coat. Color commonly light, of which beige (10 YR 7/3, 7/4) is predominant; others are gray (10 YR 6/2), cream (10 YR 8/3), and fawn (5 YR 6/4). *Paste:* coarse texture. Color much the same as surface but sometimes pink (5 YR 7/6) or rarely light reddish brown (5 YR 5/4). *Types and decoration:* Perhaps it is an exaggeration to think of striation as a decoration. However, it does alter the surface and therefore we shall consider it here. *Yokat Striated Type, neck-interior variety*: Uxmal, 304 rim, 286 body sherds surely associated with this variety; Kabah, 10 rim, no body sherds. Many other striated body sherds belong with this variety, but there is no way of separating them from those belonging with the Yokat Variety, so they will all be listed under Yokat. *Remarks*: these jar shapes with light surface color and distinctive raking (striation) methods form a definite Uxmal Variety rarely found at Kabah. Occasionally the normal Uxmal shape will not have interior neck striations and somewhat more frequently Kabah jar shapes will have interior neck striations.

Jars, interior neck not striated (fig. 2, h–p, t, v, w–aa). Small to medium-wide mouth, low to medium-high outcurving or flaring medium-thick to thick neck, medium-thick to thick body, rounded rim bolster (*i, k, m*), pinched rim (*h, l*), triangular rim bolster (*o*), thickened rim (*p*) or square rim bolster (*n*), rounded, beveled, or pointed lip, globular body. *Size*: lip diam. 16–33 cm., av. 23.3 cm., most common of 61 measured are between 20 and 26 cm. [52]; neck ht. 3.5–6.5 cm., av. 5.1 cm., most common of 24 measured is 6 cm. [10]. *Surface*: smoothed on exterior and neck interior; coarsely striated body exterior; usually the deep (w–aa) striation but occasionally the medium or spaced (*t, v*) is used. Color cinnamon (7.5 YR 7/4), beige (10 YR 7/3), or fawn (5 YR 6/4. *Paste*: coarse texture. Color commonly brown (5 YR 4/6, 7.5 YR 5/4) or buff (10 YR 6/4). *Types and decoration*. *Yokat Striated Type*: Uxmal, 150 rim, 7,341 body sherds; Kabah, 133 rim, 6,881 body sherds. *Chum Unslipped Type*: Uxmal, no rims surely identified with unslipped jar bodies, 1,052 body sherds; Kabah, none. *Halacho Impressed Type*: Uxmal, 2 body sherds; Kabah, none. Rarely thumb-impressed fillet (*q, z*) encircling neck-shoulder junction. *Remarks*: this group of jars is found at both Uxmal and Kabah but in different proportions: *h* and *l* are predominantly from Uxmal, whereas *i–k, m–o* are quantitively far more important at Kabah, and *g, p* are almost entirely from Kabah. In general the Uxmal specimens run lighter in color than those from Kabah. A small disk cover made from a reused sherd from Uxmal is included with the jars (2, r).

Censers, hourglass (3, a–k). Medium-thick to thick sides, thickened (*a, b*), T-shape (*j, k*), everted (*f, i*), bolster (*c, g*), or direct (*e*) rim, pointed, rounded, flat, or beveled lip; some have a flange or flanges (*d–f, i*) and one has a circular hole in wall (*k*, possible censer cover), flat to convex bases,

and all have pedestal supports. *Size*: lip diam. 9–48 cm., av. 28.7 cm., most common of 26 measured are 22 cm. [7], 24 cm. [6], and 48 cm. [5]. For other measurements see illustrations. *Surface*: all interiors carefully smoothed and exteriors imperfectly smoothed. Many have white calcareous coat on exterior; otherwise the surface is brown (2.5 YR 5/4, 5 YR 5/4, 7.5 YR 6/4, 10 YR 5/3) or beige (10 YR 7/4). *Paste*: coarse texture. Color brown (2.5 YR 5/6), pink (5 YR 7/6), or fawn (5 YR 6/4). *Types and decoration*. *Oxkutzcab Appliqué Type*: Uxmal, 85 rim, 114 body sherds; Kabah, 5 rim, 3 body sherds. Nearly all are embellished with spikes (*a, f, i–k*). *Tepakan Composite Type*: Uxmal, 6 rim, 8 body sherds; Kabah, 1 rim, no body sherds. These examples have both appliqué spikes and thumb-impressed fillet (*b, c, g*). *Halacho Impressed Type*: Uxmal, 4 rim, 29 body sherds; Kabah, no rim, 2 body sherds. Reed-impressed flanges (*e*), a nail-impressed band (*d*), and a raised band resembling overlapping tiles (*h*). *Remarks*: censers of any type are rare in the Kabah collection. Brainerd (1958, fig. 39) illustrates most of the above Cehpech "hourglass" censer forms and in some instances more completely. He says, "Our earliest recognized incensarios are of the 'hourglass' form typical of this collection and come from the Regional-Florescent deposits (fig. 19, a–c). This general form lasted through the Florescent and part of the Mexican stage; see figs. 22, 23 for latest examples." An example occurs in the Rio Frio Cave group in British Honduras (Mason, 1928, fig. 30).

Censers, basin (3, r–t). Medium-thick to thick walls, ovoid, rounded, triangular, or square bolster rim, basinlike body, flat or possibly pedestal base. *Size*: lip diam. 38–48 cm., av. 40.8 cm., most common of 6 measured is 38 cm. [4]. *Surface*: exterior obliquely striated (*r, s*), or smoothed and coated white; interior well smoothed and usually fire-blackened. Color commonly beige (10 YR 7/4, 7/3). *Paste*: coarse texture. Color cinnamon (7.5 YR 7/4) and pinkish cinnamon (2.5 YR 6/6 to 5 YR 7/6). *Types and decoration*. *Halacho Impressed Type*: Uxmal, 27 rim, 16 body sherds; Kabah, 2 rim, 1 body sherd. Thumb-impressed (*r, t*) or reed-impressed (*s*) bolster. *Chum Unslipped Type*: Uxmal, 1 rim, no body sherds; Kabah, none. Undecorated bolster, no illustration. *Remarks*: this form occurred rarely at Kabah. Brainerd (1958, fig. 39, f, 10) shows an example from Sayil with reed-impressed bolster. This might be a basin and not a pedestal-base censer.

Censers, ladle (3, n, o). Thin to medium-thick rounded (*o*) or possibly flaring sides, direct rim, beveled lip, and tubular handle opening into bowl. *Size*: lip diam. 19 cm. (one specimen). *Surface*: smoothed, especially interior which is fire-blackened. Some have calcareous white coat all over (*n*). Color obscured by white coat or fire-blackening. *Paste*: coarse texture. Color of one pinkish buff (2.5 YR 7/4). *Types and decoration. Chum Unslipped Type*: Uxmal, 17 rim, 33 body sherds; Kabah, none. Some may have spikes on body or handle, *n* has button on handle, a number have blue rim band (*o*). *Remarks*: Brainerd (1958, fig. 39, *d, 1, 2; f, 1; g; h, 7*) illustrates this form.

Bowls, flaring side (fig. 3, *l, q*). Medium-thick flaring sides, direct (*l*) or sharply incurved (*q*) rim, rounded or beveled lip, concave or flat base. *Size*: lip diam. 14–16 cm. (only two measured); ht. 4.5 cm. *Surface*: exterior imperfectly smoothed, interior usually well smoothed. Some have white calcareous coat. One blackened all over (*q*). Color of *l*, cream (10 YR 8/4). *Paste*: coarse texture. *Types and decoration. Chum Unslipped Type*: Uxmal, 9 rim, 8 body sherds; Kabah, 2 rim, no body sherds. Undecorated (*q*) except for some with evidence of blue paint. *Oxkutzcab Appliqué Type*: Uxmal, 1 rim, 2 body sherds; Kabah, none. A few (*l*) have spikes on exterior, others have evidence of blue paint. *Remarks*: some of these may belong to the hourglass-type censer.

Bowls, rounded side (3, *p, u, v*). Medium-thick walls, direct (*u, v*) or bolster (*p*) rim, beveled or flat lip, presumably flat base. *Size*: lip diam. 15 cm. for two examples. *Surface*: exterior usually striated, interior well smoothed. Some have both interior and exterior calcareous white coat (*u*). Color beige (10 YR 7/3, 7/4). *Paste*: course texture. *Types and decoration. Yokat Striated Type*: Uxmal, 6 rim, 6 body sherds; Kabah, 3 rim, 1 body sherd. *u, v*, no other decoration. *Chum Unslipped Type*: Uxmal, 1 rim, no body sherds; Kabah, none. *p* is the only example with blue paint on exterior. *Remarks*: some of these may well have been ladle-type censers.

Bowls, restricted orifice (3, *w*). Thin walls, direct rim, beveled lip, globular body. *Size*: lip diam. 12 cm. *Surface*: well smoothed all over. Color light brown (2.5 YR 6/4). *Paste*: coarse texture. Color same as surface. *Types and decoration. Chum Unslipped Type*: Uxmal, 3 rim, 5 body sherds; Kabah, none. Exterior painted blue. *Remarks*: Brainerd (1958, fig. 39, *d, 3; h, 6*) illustrates two restricted bowls.

Flageolets (3, *x, y, bb*), musical instruments resembling flutes, but blown from the end instead of from the side. Here we have a multiple-mouthed type with three mouth holes besides a number of stops along the tube. *Surface*: well smoothed. Color light brown or gray. *Paste*: medium-fine texture. Color light brown or beige. *Types and decoration. Yiba Modeled Type*: Uxmal, 1 rim, 9 body sherds; Kabah, no rim, 2 body sherds. Blue used on adornos which include buttons and effigy heads possibly moldmade (*bb*). Red paint also used (*y*). *Remarks*: the total number of flageolet fragments is 12. Brainerd (1958, figs. 54, *a, ff*; 56) illustrates several flageolets. His figures 54, *ff* and 56, *u* are especially suggestive of our *x, y*. On the other hand Smith (1936, fig. XVI, 18) shows an example reminiscent of *bb*.

Figurine fragments (3, *z, aa*). Mostly jointed limbs and other modeled figurine fragments such as bodies, whistle mouthpieces, and a moldmade head which may belong to a flageolet. *Types and decoration. Yiba Modeled Type*: Uxmal, no heads, 18 body sherds; Kabah, no heads, 3 body sherds. The total number of jointed limbs (*z, aa*) is nine (8 Uxmal, 1 Kabah), and other figurine fragments are twelve including 9 body pieces, 2 whistle mouthpieces, and 1 head, all from Uxmal save for 2 body pieces found at Kabah. These figurine fragments sometimes show both modeling and appliqué, but since the appliqué is secondary rather than an equal part of the manufacturing technique we have placed them under the Yiba Modeled Type rather than the Tepakan Composite Type. *Remarks*: it is possible that *z* and *aa* are not jointed limbs. *z* may represent a bar pendant and *aa* some kind of perforated charm end similar to that illustrated by Brainerd (1958, fig. 56, *a*).

Summary. We find a notable difference between the Uxmal and Kabah unslipped jars. This is seen in the use of horizontal striation on the interior neck of most of the Uxmal jars which have a wide mouth and high neck. Only a few of this type were found at Kabah. The Kabah small-mouth, medium-high neck unslipped jar is also found in fair quantity at Uxmal. In both cases the jar bodies are coarsely striated, less coarsely in the case of those with interior neck striation, but in either case more coarsely than on the Chichen Unslipped Ware jars. The latter also have a different rim treatment which calls for an ovoid or flat bolster rim as compared to the Uxmal-Kabah rounded bolster, overhanging or everted rim. A most interesting bit of data is the disproportionate number of unslipped jars found at Kabah, 52.7 per cent of all sherds, compared to 27.3 per cent and 21.3 per cent at Uxmal and Chichen Itza, respectively. The only reasonable explanation that suggests itself is that at Kabah we unwittingly dug into a ceremonial kitchen midden rather than the usual general refuse deposits of ceremonial centers as at Uxmal and Chichen Itza. This suggestion is based on the lack of censers, figurines, or flageolets at Kabah (.2 per cent) as compared to a small percentage (1.2) at Uxmal and a larger percentage (14.1) of just censers at Chichen Itza. Of course the Chichen Itza material, having to do with a different cultural phase, may and probably does indicate that in Yucatan censers were in greater demand during Sotuta than in Cehpech times.

This brings us to the chief censer diagnostics noted at the three sites in their respective ceramic complexes. In effect we can omit the material from Kabah save to say that the few sherds found coincided in every way with the forms encountered at Uxmal. The hourglass and ladle censers of the Sotuta Ceramic Complex from Chichen Itza and of the Cehpech Ceramic Complex from Uxmal differ as to form in only minor details, but in all other respects they are usually quite dissimilar. The temper (Tables 41–43) is completely different. The surface finish is much the same in both instances, but the color of the Uxmal-Kabah specimens runs more to beige, light brown, and cinnamon rather than to gray and buff, which seem to predominate in the Chichen Itza examples. The decorative techniques, especially on the hourglass censers, are much the same at Chichen Itza and Uxmal, but the method of using these techniques and the design styles achieved are very different. Chichen Itza has a tripod censer not found in the Uxmal-Kabah collections.

A matter of great interest is the paste-temper and surface-color relationship of Puuc Unslipped Ware jars and censers. Jars have a preponderance of clear calcite with some gray limestone temper and a beige, cream, or gray surface color, while censers are dominated by potsherd temper and a light brown or cinnamon surface color.

Flageolets and whistles are not present in the Sotuta Ceramic Complex material from Chichen Itza but do occur sparsely in the Cehpech collections from Uxmal and Kabah. Flageolets and whistles seem to be a part of the Classic and especially the Late Classic tradition as noted in the Peten and other lowland Maya regions. The flageolet may belong more in Tepeu 3 than in 2.

PUUC SLATE WARE

For descriptive listing, see page 149.

Dishes, tripod (6, a–x, z–ee, gg, hh, kk) which by form may be separated into three main categories: 1) basal break (a–k, m, n, x, z–ee), 2) basal-Z-angle (o–q, gg, hh, kk), and 3) basal flange (l, r–w). x seems to be a special form but presumably is a tripod.

1) Basal break [1,465], a shape described by Brainerd (1958, p. 47), is here descriptive of a tripod dish with medium-thick to thick, flaring or outcurving sides, direct rarely everted rim, rounded, beveled or pointed lip, rarely strap handles (x), slightly convex to flat base, three solid conical (a–d) or hollow oven-shape (f, dd), rarely solid slab (bb, cc; GWB, fig. 58, b), or hollow cylindrical (ee, kk) feet. *Size:* lip diam. 22–32 cm., av. 24.4 cm., most common of 80 measured is 24 cm. [43]; base diam. 15–24 cm., av. 17 cm., most common of 80 measured 17 cm. [34], 16 cm. [22], and 18 cm. [12]; vessel ht. 4.5–8.5 cm., av. 5.5 cm., most common of 52 measured 6 cm. [21], 5 cm. [14], and 5.5 cm. [9]. *Surface:* slipped and polished all over (f, j, k), on interior and exterior and partially over base and feet (a, c), or on interior and exterior but not on base or feet (b, d, e, g–i, m, n, z–ee). Well smoothed and with waxy feel. A few have striated base. Often rootlet-marked, occasionally crazed, some with purple veins, but rarely fire-clouded. Color is commonly gray (10 YR 7/2, 5 YR 7/2), beige (10 YR 7/3, 7/4), or brown (5 YR 4/6, 3/4; 7.5 YR 5/4), and less frequently drab (10 YR 6/3). *Paste:* medium texture. Color usually reddish, but a fair number are buff to light brown. *Types and decoration. Muna Slate Type, Muna Variety:* Uxmal, 1,241 rim, 2,805 body sherds; Kabah, 170 rim, 559 body sherds. a–d, f, g, undecorated examples. *Muna Slate Type, notched variety:* Uxmal, 1 rim, 2 body sherds; Kabah, none. Notched wall-base angle (m). *Tekit Incised Type:* Uxmal, 12 rim, 26 body sherds; Kabah, 17 rim, 29 body sherds. Preslip sharp-incising includes band of vertical lines (j) or geometric band (k) on exterior wall; postslip sharp-incising (e) appears once on interior wall as cross-hatched band. *Akil Impressed Type:* Uxmal, 7 rim, 34 body sherds; Kabah, 1 rim, 8 body sherds. This type involves the impressing of basal fillets (h; 58, b). *Xaya Gouged-incised Type,* represented by a single rim sherd example (x) from Uxmal, differs in form primarily because of a vertical strap handle and rim bolster. Presumably it was a tripod. The stepfret exterior band was gouged-incised. Brainerd (1958, fig. 45, g, 14) illustrates a similar form from Uxmal. A body sherd also from Uxmal had a gouged-incised basal guilloche band. *Sacalum Black-on-slate Type,* familiar elsewhere, is extremely rare in this form at Kabah where 4 body sherds were found and is absent from our collections at Uxmal. Brainerd (1958, fig. 47, a–i),

PUUC SLATE WARE [3,465]

Forms, Types, and Varieties	Uxmal Rim	%	Kabah Rim	%	Total Rim & body
Dishes, tripod:		46		33.4	
Muna Slate Type, Muna Variety	1,271		173		4,902
Muna Slate Type, notched variety	6		0		11
Tekit Incised Type	27		17		149
Akil Impressed Type	9		2		67
Xaya Gouged-incised Type	1		0		1
Sacalum Black-on-slate Type	0		0		4
Chumayel Red-on-slate Type	2		3		7
Nohcacab Composite Type	1		5		8
Basins:		41.2		41.9	
Muna Slate Type	1,021		232		9,372
Tekit Incised Type	6		0		8
Sacalum Black-on-slate Type	144		19		765
Chumayel Red-on-slate Type, Chumayel Variety	4		0		20
Chumayel Red-on-slate Type, incised variety	6		0		6
Chumayel Red-on-slate Type, modeled variety	1		0		1
Jars:		10.8		11.7	
Muna Slate Type	264		67		4,333
Tekit Incised Type	31		3		84
Akil Impressed Type	6		0		59
Sacalum Black-on-slate Type	7		0		255
Chumayel Red-on-slate Type	1		1		93
Bowls, beveled rim, ringstand:		1.3		10.5	
Muna Slate Type	37		62		274
Sacalum Black-on-slate Type	0		1		1
Bowls, rounded side:		.6		2.3	
Muna Slate Type	16		14		154
Tekit Incised Type	2		0		2
Sacalum Black-on-slate Type	1		0		1
Miscellaneous forms:					
Vase, cylindrical (?); Xaya Gouged-incised Type	1		0		1
Dish, flat base; Chumayel Red-on-slate Type	0		1		1
Censers, effigy (?); Yaxnic Modeled Type	0		0		6
Flute (?); Yaxnic Modeled Type	0		0		1
Total	2,865		600		20,586

however, encountered examples at Uxmal as well as elsewhere. Black designs are found on the vessel floor (z), where a possible scroll and dab design is used, and simpler designs on inner wall and rim. *Chumayel Red-on-slate Type*: Uxmal, 1 rim, 1 body sherd; Kabah, 3 rim, 1 body sherd. The designs (aa) are much the same as those of Sacalum Black-on-slate. *Nohcacab Composite Type*: Uxmal, 1 rim, no body sherds; Kabah, 4 rim, no body sherds. This type embraces two techniques of decoration: incising and impressing. The incising is usually preslip and the motif an exterior wall band of vertical lines; the impressing may be by thumb or finger of basal fillet (i) or by reed of basal molding (n, u). Both n and u have red-painted basal moldings. Another, not illustrated, has red lip band and incising on exterior wall. *Remarks*: the Kabah basal-break tripod dishes are

nearly identical to those from Uxmal with the exception of those with notched wall-base angles which were not encountered at Kabah. The solid slab foot is rare at both sites but more prevalent at Kabah than Uxmal; actually most common at Yaxuna (GWB, fig. 10 d, f, g). Brainerd gives us a very complete picture of this form as found in the Puuc area (*ibid.*, figs. 45 and 46). He also illustrates a few with black-painted decoration (*ibid.*, figs. 47 a–i) showing rim dabs and floor designs including both the scroll and dab (b, i) and the Tlaloc-like head (c).

The form x, fully described in the legend, is unique in the Cehpech Ceramic Complex material for having a gouged-and-incised design. Brainerd illustrates a similar form from Uxmal (*ibid.*, fig. 45, g, 14).

2) Basal-Z-angle [36] is much the same as the

basal break save for angle and feet. It has medium-thick to thick flaring or outcurving sides, direct rim, rounded, beveled, or pointed lip, sharp Z-angle at juncture of base and side, convex base, and hollow ovoid, cylindrical (o), or anthropomorphic (p) feet. *Size*: lip diam. 26–40 cm., av. 32 cm., most common of 18 measured is 34 cm. [8]; base diam. 17–27 cm., av. 23 cm., most common of 18 measured 23–25 cm [10]; wall ht. 4.4–8.8 cm., av. 5.5 cm., most common of 18 measured is 5.8 cm. [7]. *Surface*: much the same as basal break. Color beige (10 YR 7/4), gray (5 YR 7/2), or brown (5 YR 4/6). *Paste*: medium texture. Color mostly reddish. *Types and decoration. Muna Slate Type, Muna Variety*: Uxmal, 15 rim, 52 body sherds; Kabah, 3 rim, 13 body sherds. p, undecorated example. *Muna Slate Type, notched variety*: Uxmal, 5 rim, 2 body sherds; Kabah, no rim, 1 body sherd. Notched Z-angle, no illustration. *Tekit Incised Type*: Uxmal, 12 rim, 43 body sherds; Kabah, no rim, 4 body sherds. Preslip incised basal bands (o, q). *Akil Impressed Type*: Uxmal, no rim, 1 body sherd; Kabah, none. Reed-impressed Z-angle, no illustration. *Chumayel Red-on-slate Type*: Uxmal, 1 rim, no body sherds; Kabah, none. Red basal band covering lower part of exterior wall and Z-angle, no illustration. *Remarks*: rarely found at Kabah. Brainerd illustrates and discusses this form right along with the basal-break dishes (1958, figs. 18, *k, 11*; 45, e, *29–30*; h, *5*; 46, c, *26, 29–32*; d, *8, 12–15*; e, *1, 2, 10, 11*; f, *22*; 58, c; 62, n). He also illustrates two principal types of hollow cylindrical stamped feet: those with flat bottom and full-length human figure with a distinctive hairdo and others having rounded bottoms, decorated with fat-cheeked head or obese full-length figure. This latter is a representation of the "fat god."

3) Basal flange [22], medium-thick to thick flaring or outcurving sides, direct or everted (often grooved) rim, rounded, beveled, or pointed lip, at juncture of base and side a flange (usually terraced) pointing diagonally downward, often a ridge above flange, convex base, and three presumably hollow feet (no complete examples). *Size*: lip diam. 30–34 cm., av. 31.7 cm.; mostly small fragments. *Surface*: usually slipped and burnished all over save on base. Sometimes rootlet-marked. Color gray (10 YR 7/1, 7/2, 5 YR 7/2) or beige (10 YR 7/3). *Paste*: medium texture. Color commonly reddish. *Types and decoration. Muna Slate Type*: Uxmal, 15 rim, 20 body sherds; Kabah, no rim, 9 body sherds. Undecorated examples in one instance (*l*) had a stepped flange. *Tekit Incised Type*: Uxmal, 3 rim, 3 body sherds;

Kabah, none. Preslip incised ladder triangle (r) band on exterior wall. *Akil Impressed Type*: Uxmal, 2 rim, 11 body sherds; Kabah, 1 rim, 2 body sherds. Reed-impressed (t) or stamped (w) basal molding. *Nohcacab Composite Type*: Uxmal, no rim, 1 body sherd; Kabah, 1 rim, 1 body sherd. This type embraces three techniques of decoration: painting, incising, and impressing. The basal moldings are painted red and reed-impressed, and the lower exterior wall has a preslip incised band of vertical lines (s, v). Flanges may be notched or terraced. *Remarks*: this form is more abundant at Uxmal [20] than at Kabah [2] and the body sherds total 35 and 9, respectively. Brainerd illustrates what he calls basal-break bowls with a basal ridge and skirt (1958, figs. 45, e, *19*; 46, f, *23, 24*; 58, a, b, d, i, *4*, j; 67, g, *2, 6, 8, 9*) showing a considerable variety of decoration as well as some variation in form.

Basins (4, a–k) may be divided into three shape categories: 1) rounded rim bolster, a few (g) of these may be ovoid; 2) triangular rim bolster (f, h, k); and 3) square rim bolster (i, j).

1) Rounded rim bolster [1,301] and 2) triangular rim bolster [115] basins may be reviewed together, since the only marked difference is in the rim treatment. Medium-thick to thick rounded sides, rounded (occasionally ovoid) or triangular rim bolster, pointed or rounded lip, vertical strap handles, slightly concave base. *Size*: lip diam. 26–64 cm., av. 38.3., most common of 124 measured 33–42 cm. [73]; bolster thickness 1.8–3.8 cm., av. 2.6 cm., most common of 124 measured 2.2–2.7 cm. [77]. *Surface*: slipped and polished all over save under strap handles. Rootlet-marking usually purple; fire-clouding and rarely crazing have been noted. a has the extra smooth finish and C–1 temper suggestive of Thin Slate, but the paste seems a little less fine than usual for Thin Slate and the color too brown. Color commonly gray (10 YR 6/2), brown (7.5 YR 6/4, 5 YR 5/6), and buff (7.5 YR 7/2, 6/2); less frequently cream (10 YR 8/3) and drab (10 YR 6/3). *Paste*: medium texture. Color usually reddish. *Types and decorating. Muna Slate Type*: Uxmal, 1,015 rim, 5,897 body sherds; Kabah, 232 rim, 2,222 body sherds. a, b, h, k, undecorated examples. *Tekit Incised Type*: Uxmal, 2 rim, no body sherds; Kabah, none. Preslip incised geometric rim band (c). *Sacalum Black-on-slate Type*: Uxmal, 144 rim, 476 body sherds; Kabah, 19 rim, 126 body sherds. Black, actually gray, trickle on exterior from rim to base (g). *Chumayel Red-on-slate Type, Chumayel Variety*: Uxmal, 4 rim, 11 body sherds; Kabah, no rim, 5 body sherds. Orange and cinnamon-col-

ored trickle from rim to base (e, f). *Chumayel Red-on-slate Type, modeled variety*: Uxmal alone had a rim sherd (d) of this variety with red bolster and modeled raised areas. *Remarks*: Brainerd (1958, figs. 43, a–c; 44, b, c) illustrates a good range of this shape.

3) Square rim bolster [16] basins, found only at Uxmal, have medium-thick rounded sides, pointed or flat lip, vertical strap handles, slightly concave base. *Size*: lip diam. 26–34 cm., av. 30.3 cm., most common of 15 measured 34 cm. [4], 29 cm. [3], 28 cm. [3]; bolster thickness 1.5–2.8 cm., av. 1.9 cm., most common of 15 measured is 1.8 cm [9]. *Surface*: slipped and burnished on interior and exterior. May be crazed, rootlet-marked, and sometimes fire-clouded. Color sometimes dark brown on interior, but exteriors usually gray (10 YR 6/2). *Paste*: medium texture. Color commonly reddish. *Types and decoration. Muna Slate Type*: Uxmal, 6 rim, no body sherds that can be separated from those listed under basins with rounded and triangular bolsters; Kabah, none. j, undecorated example. *Tekit Incised Type*: Uxmal, 4 rim, 2 body

sherds; Kabah, none. Preslip incised rim and rim band, no illustration. *Chumayel Red-on-slate Type, incised variety*: Uxmal, 6 rim, no body sherds; Kabah, none. Preslip incised red rim and an incised red band just below bolster (i). *Remarks*: Brainerd (1958, fig. 44, a) shows us a few of this form with a variety of decoration including incised, one plano-relief carved, and one with hollow reed impressions. The latter is from Kabah and is reminiscent of the unslipped basinlike censers (3, r–t).

Jars (5, a–hh) may be separated into six form categories for purposes of study; namely, 1) the small-mouth, relatively low-neck jars with vertical strap handles (except for z which has lug handles) closely associated with the neck (a–j, q, y–bb), 2) the wide-mouth, high-neck jars or drums (k–n, r–t), 3) the taper-neck, everted rim jars (u–w), 4) the wide-mouth, medium-high-neck jars with rounded body (p), 5) the small-mouth, vertical neck, incurved rim jars (x), 6) a miscellaneous group (cc–hh).

PUUC SLATE WARE JAR VARIATIONS

	Uxmal		Kabah		
Jar Forms	Rim	%	Rim	%	Total Rims
1) a–j, q, y–bb	158	50.8	39	54.3	197
2) k–n, r–t	72	23.3	17	24.3	89
3) u–w	41	13.3	3	4.3	44
4) p	15	4.9	0		15
5) x	5	1.6	10	14.3	15
6) cc–hh	18	6.1	2	2.8	20
Total	309		71		380

1) Small-mouth jar [197] with relatively low to medium-high thick neck, direct (a, b, g, q, bb), inner bulge (c, aa), exterior bolster (e, z), T-shape (d, j), or thickened (f, h, i, y) rim, rounded, flat, beveled, or pointed lip, barrel-shape body with medium-thick to thick walls, and a slightly concave base. Although the mouth measurement averages small, it is rather large in relation to the narrow barrel-shape body. *Size*: lip diam. 9–22 cm., av. 13.8 cm., greatest concentration of 56 measured is 11–14 cm. [43]; neck ht. 2.5–7 cm., av. 5 cm., most common of 39 measured 3 cm. [8], 6 cm. [8], 5 cm.[5], 5.5 [5]. *Surface*: slipped and polished on exterior and neck interior (a, c, e, i, j, q, aa, bb), just over lip on neck interior (b, d, h), or not at all on neck interior (f, g, y, z). All slipped surfaces have waxy feel. Some necks (f, h) are rootlet-marked, some (b, q) fire-clouded, both true of many body sherds. Color commonly

buff (7.5 YR 6/2, 7/2), beige (10 YR 7/4), or gray (10 YR 6/2, 7/2), sometimes brown (7.5 YR 5/6). *Paste*: medium texture. Color commonly reddish but may be buff or drab or have dark core and reddish edges. *Types and decoration. Muna Slate Type*: Uxmal, 158 rim, 2,575 body sherds; Kabah, 38 rim, 1,378 body sherds. a–j, q, y–aa, undecorated examples among which some of the rims may have belonged with trickle-decorated bodies because normally these rims are not decorated. *Sacalum Black-on-slate Type*: Uxmal, no rim, 179 body sherds; Kabah, no rim, 68 body sherds. Black trickle on exterior body only, no illustration. *Chumayel Red-on-slate Type*: Uxmal, no rim, 83 body sherds; Kabah, 1 rim, 8 body sherds. Like Sacalum Black-on-slate, the Chumayel Red-on-slate jars usually show trickle on body only but one rim sherd (bb) has red trickle from lip on down the exterior. *Remarks*: this jar form is fairly well represented in all its rim varieties at both sites. At Uxmal this class of jar forms 50.8 per cent and at Kabah 54.3 per cent of all Puuc Slate jars collected. Brainerd (1958, figs. 40; 41, a, b; 42, c–f, g, 9–11; 105, g) illustrates a considerable number from both Uxmal and Kabah as well as other Puuc sites. This jar form includes the "chultun jar."

2) Wide-mouth jar [89], high thick flaring or outcurving neck, direct rim, rounded, beveled, or flat lip, no handles noted, globular (?) or barrel-shape (?), medium-thick to thick body, slightly concave base. Size: lip diam. 28–46 cm., av. 36.3 cm., most common of 27 measured 32 cm. [5], 36 cm. [5], and 38 cm. [4]; neck ht. (all broken) greater than 10 cm. Surface: slipped and polished on exterior and partway down neck interior (k, m), all over neck interior (l, n), and not at all on neck (r, s, t). May be rootlet-marked, crazed, or fire-blackened. Color has wide range including beige (10 YR 7/3, 7/4), gray (10 YR 7/1), buff (7.5 YR 7/2), drab (2.5 YR 7/2), fawn (5 YR 6/4), or light brown (7.5 YR 6/4). Paste: medium texture. Colors closely follow slip save that some have reddish paste. Types and decoration: Muna Slate Type: Uxmal, 35 rim, 21 body sherds; Kabah, 14 rim, no body sherds surely associated. l–n, undecorated examples. Tekit Incised Type: Uxmal, 31 rim, 43 body sherds; Kabah, 3 rim, 7 body sherds. Incised exterior neck, diagonally (s) or horizontally and diagonally (r), but rarely body (gg) incising. Akil Impressed Type: Uxmal, 6 rim, 53 body sherds; Kabah, none. Nail-impressed (k, r) and thumb-impressed fillets (o, t) on shoulder. Remarks: at Kabah k–n is more abundantly represented than r–t, whereas at Uxmal both forms are equally important. Brainerd (1958, fig. 37, c) illustrates what he calls drums from Uxmal. He also shows some Florescent Medium Slateware (Puuc Slate) jars with nail-impressed bands and thumb-impressed fillets (ibid., figs. 41, b, 54; 42, f, 2, 3). Most of category 2 may be drums.

3) The taper-neck jar [44] with medium-thick to thick neck, everted, often slight parenthesis rim, rounded or flat lip, and body similar to that of the Oxkintok Coarse Monochrome jar (ibid., fig. 11, a). Size: lip diam. 11–17 cm., av. 13.2 cm., most common of 34 measured is 13 cm. [24]; neck ht. 4.5–9 cm., av. 6.9 cm., most common of 17 measured 5.5 cm. [6] and 9 cm. [5]. Surface: slipped and polished on exterior and just below rim on neck interior. Some fire-clouding. Color buff (7.5 YR 6/2) or brown (7.5 YR 5/4). Paste: medium texture. Color is about the same as slip. Types and decoration. Muna Slate Type: Uxmal, 40 rim

sherds; Kabah, 3 rim sherds. No body sherds surely associated with this form. v, w, undecorated examples. Sacalum Black-on-slate Type: Uxmal, 1 rim, 1 body sherd; Kabah, none. A single example (u) of black trickle occurred on this form. Remarks: this form is rare at Kabah. Actually these may represent an attempt to copy the Oxkintok jar form which presumably belongs to an earlier ceramic phase. Brainerd (1958, figs. 40, c 4; 41, a, 35, 40, 47, b, 3, 33, 49; 42, e, 8, 9) illustrates a number of these jar forms from Sabacche, Uxmal, Sayil.

4) The wide-mouth, low to medium-high-neck jar [15], thick flaring neck, direct rim, beveled lip, rounded medium-thick sides. Size: lip diam. 36.0 cm., neck ht. 5–7 cm., only two measured. Surface: slipped and polished all over. Fire-clouding present. Color of one specimen is fawn (5 YR 6/4). Paste: medium texture. Color about same as slip. Types and decoration. Muna Slate Type: Uxmal, 15 rim, 19 body sherds; Kabah, none. p, undecorated example. Possibly some of the body examples with trickle belong to this form but none could be surely associated. Remarks: none present in the Kabah collection. Brainerd (1958, fig. 44, b, 41, 43), possibly correctly, has placed this form with basins. It is true that they are slipped on interior as well as exterior but they also have a neck.

5) The small-mouth, vertical neck, incurved rim jar [15], medium-high thick neck, rounded lip, medium-thick barrel-shape body, slightly concave base. Size: mostly fragmentary. Surface: slipped and polished on exterior only. Color range much the same as no. 1 category. Paste: medium texture. Types and decoration. Muna Slate Type: Uxmal, 5 rim, 9 body sherds; Kabah, 10 rim, no body sherds. x, undecorated example. Sacalum Black-on-slate Type: Uxmal and Kabah, none surely identifiable but some very probably had trickle. Remarks: more abundant at Kabah than Uxmal. Brainerd (1958, figs. 40, c, 16, d, 7, 16, 29, 32, 44, e, 17, 18; 41, b, 22, 24, 26, 64; 42, e, 20, 24) illustrates a number of this jar form from Sabacche, Kabah, Labna, Uxmal, and Sayil.

6) Miscellaneous collection of Puuc Slate jars and jar covers [20]. Examples of these jars are described in the legends for cc–hh. Two other jar forms, presumed to be of this ceramic complex and located in Merida Museum, are illustrated (58, g, h). The disk (hh) and flanged covers are illustrated by Brainerd (1958, figs. 40, c, 10, 11, d, 64; 41, b, 19, c; 42, g, 1–6) from Kabah, Uxmal, and Sayil. Types and decoration. Muna Slate Type: Uxmal, 11 rim, no body sherds; Kabah, 2 rim, no

body sherds. cc–ee, *hh*, undecorated examples. *Sacalum Black-on-slate Type*: Uxmal, 6 rim, no body sherds; Kabah, none. Black trickle on exterior of neck and body, no illustrations. *Chumayel Red-on-slate Type*: Uxmal, 1 rim, no body sherds; Kabah, none. Exterior has orange trickle from lip down (*ff*). *Tekit Incised Type*: Uxmal, none; Kabah, 1 body sherd. Preslip incised geometric design on body exterior (*gg*).

Bowls, beveled rim, ringstand (4, *l, m*). Thin to medium-thick rounded sides, usually exteriorly beveled and slightly incurved rim, pointed lip, ringstand base either plain or stepped. *Size*: lip diam. 17–21 cm., av. 20.1 cm., most common of 20 measured 20–21 cm. [17]; base diam. 9–11 cm., av. 9.7 cm., most common of 16 measured 10–10.7 cm. [13]; ht. of one 8.2 cm. *Surface*: slipped and polished all over save ringstand which may be slipped on exterior. Some are rootlet-marked, some fire-clouded. Color gray (10 YR 7/1) or brown (7.5 YR 6/4). *Paste*: medium texture. Color range about same as other Puuc Slate vessels. *Types and decoration. Muna Slate Type*: Uxmal, 37 rim, 135 body sherds; Kabah, 62 rim, 40 body sherds. Undecorated except for seven which have stepped ringstands. *Sacalum Black-on-slate Type*: Uxmal, none; Kabah, 1 rim, no body sherds. Black dabs on rim. *Remarks*: this form is more abundant as to rims at Kabah than Uxmal. Brainerd (1958, fig. 49, *a–i*) uses nearly a full page to depict the variations of this form.

Bowls, rounded side (6, *ff, ii, jj*). Thin to medium-thick walls, direct rim, pointed or flat lip, probably flat base. *Size*: lip. diam. 5–19 cm., av. 15.8 cm., most common of 6 measured is 18 cm. [3]. *Surface*: slipped and polished all over. May be crazed. Colors noted are gray (10 YR 7/1) and dark brown. *Paste*: medium texture. Colors follow closely those of slip. *Types and decoration. Muna Slate Type*: Uxmal, 16 rim, 100 body sherds; Kabah, 14 rim, 24 body sherds. *ii, jj*, undecorated examples. *Tekit Incised Type*: Uxmal, 2 rim, no body sherds; Kabah, none. One example (*ff*) has prepolish incised and punctate rim band. *Sacalum Black-on-slate Type*: Uxmal, 1 rim, no body sherds; Kabah, none. Black dabs at rim, no illustration. *Remarks*: this is a form rarely associated with Puuc Slate. Probably these few examples are copies of the Thin Slate hemispherical bowl. Brainerd (1958, fig. 49, *d, 9–15, e, 1–3*) illustrates a few from Sayil and Uxmal together with the beveled-rim, ringstand bowl.

Miscellaneous forms, including a Xaya Gouged-incised Type cylindrical vase (6, *nn*) from Uxmal, a Chumayel Red-on-slate Type bowl with flaring sides and flat base (6, *y*) from Kabah, and Yaxnic Modeled Type possible effigy censer fragment (6, *mm*), a possible flute fragment (6, *ll*), and five mold-pressed foot fragments (6, *gg, hh, kk*), from Uxmal. Examples of these unusual Puuc Slate Ware forms are described in the legends. *Remarks*: y is clearly a Puuc Slate Ware vessel with the typical paint finger dabs on rim, in this case reddish. Perhaps other examples will turn up at sites so far not excavated. The vase is most likely a copy of a Thin Slate Ware cylindrical vase for which it has all the qualifications except that the paste is coarser and a reddish color. Brainerd (1958, figs. 50, *i, 2*; 61, *e*) depicts several Thin Slate vessels with a similar twist rim band, possibly deep bowls or even a cylindrical vase.

Summary. Puuc Slate Ware as found at Uxmal and Kabah seems to be representative of the Puuc as a whole. It is synonymous with Brainerd's (*ibid.*, pp. 52, 53) Florescent Medium Slateware which he describes at some length. The Uxmal-Kabah differences are for the most part minor, usually associated with the rims of jars and basins or the base-body angle of tripod dishes. The most distinguishing diagnostic of Puuc and Chichen Slates is form. There are virtually no exactly matching forms in the slate wares of these two ceramic complexes. Otherwise the differences are less pronounced. In both cases the finish is smooth and waxy, perhaps less waxy for the Chichen examples. The slip is probably equally translucent, but Chichen Slate Ware is more apt to reflect the uniformly contrasting red paste, giving the gray to beige slip a slightly pinkish hue. Furthermore, Puuc Slate Ware slip runs to brown as well as beige and gray, and the paste is not uniformly red but more inclined to follow the slip color, thus reducing the contrast and producing an effect of less translucence. Brainerd feels that Puuc Slate is more translucent than Chichen Slate, but I do not agree. In both wares the use of trickle paint seems identical save for the added U and S bands on Chichen Slate vessels. Other forms of decoration, such as incising and impressing, are Cehpech rather than Sotuta traits. The solid conical foot appears to be distinctive of the Cehpech Ceramic Complex.

An offshoot of Puuc Slate Ware is Thin Slate Ware, which is a very distinct entity in itself. This entity is in no way represented in, or associated with, Chichen Slate Ware.

THIN SLATE WARE [934]

Forms and Types	Uxmal Rim	%	Kabah Rim	%	Total Rim & Body
Bowls, hemispherical: Ticul Thin-slate Type	530	64.5	78	83.9	2,189
Xul Incised Type	1		0		1
Tabi Gouged-incised Type	7		0		7
Tikihal Circle-shading Type	3		0		3
Dishes, tripod: Ticul Thin-slate Type	104	12.5	13	15.1	326
Xul Incised Type	1		1		10
Vases, cylindrical: Ticul Thin-slate Type	88	10.8	1		446
Tabi Gouged-incised Type	3		0		42
Basins: Ticul Thin-slate Type	83	10.0	0		256
Tabi Gouged-incised Type	1		0		1
Bowls, deep: Xul Incised Type	19	2.1	0		52
Cover, disk: Ticul Thin-slate Type	1		0		2
Jars (?): Ticul Thin-slate Type	0		0		12
Total	841		93		3,347

Bowls, hemispherical (7, *a–h, k, p*) may be separated into four categories; namely, 1) direct rim, flat base (*a–c, p*); 2) bead rim, tripod (*h*) or flat base (*f–g, k*); 3) direct rim, restricted orifice (*d*); 4) direct rim, ringstand base (*e*). *Surface:* there is a definite uniformity of surface treatment which includes careful smoothing, allover slipping and polishing, and a waxy feel less pronounced than in Puuc Slate Ware. Most pieces have vertical crazing, some are rootlet-marked, often purplish, a few have fire-clouding. Slip color commonly a light gray (10 YR 7/1, 8/2, 6/2; 2.5 Y 7/2) or beige (10 YR 7/3), less frequently cream (2.5 Y 8/2) or light brown (10 YR 6/3). This last color is more common for the light brown kind of Thin Slate as found at Chichen Itza but does occur at Uxmal. *Paste:* fine texture but has temper usually saccharoidal calcite (Tables 41 and 42). Color approximately same as slip.

1) Direct rim [387], rounded thin sides, pointed lip, flat base. *Size:* lip diam. 14–20 cm., av. 17.2 cm., most common of 43 measured concentrated between 16–18 cm. [34]; ht. ca. 7–8 cm. *Types and decoration. Ticul Thin-slate Type:* Uxmal, 318 rim, 705 body sherds; Kabah, 61 rim, 243 body sherds. *a*, undecorated example, is most common. Two examples some time after firing were decorated with painted stucco. *Tabi Gouged-incised Type:* Uxmal, 7 rim, no body sherds; Kabah, none. These gouged-incised specimens have either a step-fret (*b, c*; 58, *e*) or braid (*p*) band; occasionally the excised areas are red-filled (*c*; 58, *e*). *b* also has broad shallow vertical grooves. *Remarks:* this form is almost as well represented at Kabah as at Uxmal. It is the predominant Thin Slate form

at both sites. Brainerd (1958, figs. 50, *a, 1–4, 19–26, b, 9–14, k, 2–30;* 51, *b, 18–21, c, 3, 4*) illustrates a number of this form from Kabah, Labna, Uxmal, and Sayil. A possible example from Tancah (10, *k*) has gouged-incised braid bands.

2) Bead rim, flat base or tripod [195], rounded thin sides, rounded lip, flat base (*f*) or three nubbin feet (*h*). *Size:* lip diam. 12–23 cm., av. 17.4 cm., most common of 43 measured concentrated between 16–19 cm. [35]; ht. 6.3–8.2 cm., av. 7.8 cm., most common of 9 measured is 8.2 [7]. *Types and decoration. Ticul Thin-slate Type:* Uxmal, 179 rim, 552 body sherds; Kabah, 12 rim, 20 body sherds. *h*, undecorated example, is most common. *Xul Incised Type:* Uxmal, 1 rim, no body sherds; Kabah, none. *k*, the only example, has preslip sharp-incised oblique geometric band on exterior. *Tikihal Circle-shading Type:* Uxmal, 3 rim, no body sherds; Kabah, none. *f, g* have two darkened circular areas penetrating clear through wall, which because of spacing, size, and position suggest that they are not accidental. *Remarks:* this form is well represented at both sites but more abundantly at Uxmal. Brainerd (1958, figs. 50, *a, 5–15, b, 5–8, k, 32, 33, 35–49;* 51, *b, 5–8*) illustrates it from Kabah, Labna, Uxmal, and Sayil.

3) Direct rim, restricted orifice [31], rounded thin sides, pointed lip, probably flat base. *Size:* lip diam. 13–23 cm., av. 16 cm., most common of 7 measured 13–15 cm. [5]. *Types and decoration. Ticul Thin-slate Type:* Uxmal, 26 rim, 17 body sherds; Kabah, 5 rim, 2 body sherds. *d*, undecorated example, may be more abundant than recorded because in very small sherds the restriction is hard to identify. One example is stuc-

coed-and-painted. *Remarks*: Brainerd (1958, figs. 50, *a*, *18*, *o*, *8–10*; 51, *b*, *1*, *4*) shows a few of this form from Kabah, Uxmal, and Sayil.

4) Direct rim, ringstand [7] bowls, rounded thin sides, direct rim, pointed lip, terraced ringstand. *Size*: lip diam. 18–20 cm., av. 18.2 cm., most common of 10 measured is 18 cm. [9]; ht. 7 cm. *Types and decoration. Ticul Thin-slate Type*: Uxmal, 7 rim, 42 body sherds; Kabah, none. No decoration observed save for terracing of ringstand (*e*). *Remarks*: actually there are probably many more of this shape than recorded because without the base the rim sherds are indistinguishable from the flat-base hemispherical bowl. Brainerd (1958, figs. 50, *h*; *j*; *k*, *1*; *m*, *1*, *2*) illustrates a few examples from Uxmal.

Dishes, tripod (7, *o*, *r*, *s*, *u*, *w–aa*). Thin to medium-thick flaring or outcurving sides, direct or everted rim, rounded, beveled, or flat lip, flat or slightly convex base, and three solid conical (*r*), hollow moldmade (*o*, *aa*), or hollow flat-bottom cylindrical (*z*) feet. *Size*: lip diam. 17–39 cm., av. 27.3 cm., most common of 43 measured concentrated between 22–28 cm. [28]; base diam. 13–23 cm., av. 18.5 cm., most common of 26 measured concentrated between 18–21 cm. [15]; overall ht. one example (*r*) 6.2 cm., wall ht. 3.8–6.8 cm., av. 5.2 cm., most common of 28 measured concentrated between 4.5–5.5 cm. [21]. *Surface* and *paste* the same as described for hemispherical bowls. *Types and decoration. Ticul Thin-slate Type*: Uxmal, 104 rim, 193 body sherds; Kabah, 13 rim, 16 body sherds. *o*, *r*, *s*, *u*, undecorated examples, are predominant. *o* has moldpressed feet and another example is stuccoed-and-painted. *Xul Incised Type*: Uxmal, 1 rim, 4 body sherds; Kabah, 1 rim, 4 body sherds. Only one incised flaring-sided tripod dish example (*y*), which has postslip sharp-incised crosshatched band. The others are either basal-Z-angle tripod dishes with preslip sharp-incised basal band of horizontally hatched triangles (*w*) or basal-flange tripod dishes with postslip sharp-incised basal band of obliquely hatched triangles (*x*). *Remarks*: included in the above group of essentially basal-break tripods are a few basal-Z-angle (*w*) and basal-flange (*x*) tripods. Brainerd does not include the basal-break, basal-Z-angle, or basal-flange tripods in his Thin Slate shape assortment. Perhaps they are not normal, but they have all the qualifications save that they are averagely medium-thick. They are very well smoothed, somewhat waxy, polished, many have vertical crazing, and nearly all examined had saccharoidal calcite temper (see Tables 41 and 42) except at Kabah where other tempers are present.

In the cases where tempers other than saccharoidal calcite are present, we may have an instance of poor judgment in sorting. In certain borderline cases I may have thrown into the Thin Slate pile an example which more properly belonged in the Puuc lot. In any event, it would seem that this is a case where the Thin Slate potter was copying Puuc Slate forms rather than the Puuc Slate potter borrowing Thin Slate temper, although neither possibility can definitely be eliminated.

Vases, cylindrical (7, *i*, *j*, *m*, *n*). Thin walls, direct, bead or everted rim, pointed or flat lip, pedestal or flat base. *Size*: lip diam. 11–20 cm., av. 14.7 cm., most common of 42 measured is 14 cm. [22]; base diam. 11–14 cm., av. 12.3 cm., most common of 13 measured is 12 cm. [8]; ht. 15–15.5 cm., most common of 13 measured is 15 cm. [8]. *Surface* and *paste* the same as described for hemispherical bowls. *Types and decoration. Ticul Thin-slate Type*: Uxmal, 88 rim, 349 body sherds; Kabah, 1 rim, 8 body sherds. *i*, *j*, *n*, undecorated examples, are most common. *Tabi Gouged-incised Type*: Uxmal, 3 rim, 39 body sherds; Kabah, none. A few examples have a postpolish gouged-incised braid rim band (*m*). A few body sherds have vertical grooving (GWB, fig. 50, *f*, from Kabah). *Remarks*: 93 per cent of this shape have vertical crazing. Only one rim sherd was found at Kabah. Brainerd (1958, figs. 50, *c–g*; 51, *b*, *9*, *10*, *13*, *15*, *c*, *14–16*) illustrates a number of this form from Kabah, Labna, Uxmal, Sayil, and Oxkintok. One of Brainerd's examples from Uxmal has a perforated rattle base (*ibid.*, fig. 50, *c*). A fine example (58, *f*) is recorded from a private collection in Merida.

Basins, bolster rim (7, *t*, *v*; 58, *c*). Rounded thin to medium-thick sides, usually ovoid bolster rim, vertical strap handles, flat or slightly concave base. *Size*: lip diam. 23–40 cm., av. 32.8 cm., most common of 40 measured concentrated between 30–35 cm. [33]; base diam. 14 cm.; ht. one specimen 20 cm. *Surface* and *paste* the same as described for hemispherical bowls. *Types and decoration. Ticul Thin-slate Type*: Uxmal, 83 rim, 173 body sherds; Kabah, none. *v* (58, *c*) undecorated example. *Tabi Gouged-incised Type*: Uxmal, 1 rim, no body sherds; Kabah, none. *t*, the only embellished example, has postslip gouged-incised braid band. *Remarks*: this shape in Thin Slate seems to be absent at Kabah. Brainerd does not include the basin in his Thin Slate shape assortment. The same remarks could be made here as were made under tripod dishes. In other words, I believe that the Ticul Thin Slate potters may on occasion have copied this Muna Slate form.

Bowls, deep (7, l, q). Thin recurving or nearly vertical sides, direct rim, flat lip, and presumably flat base. *Size*: lip diam. 18–21 cm., av. 19.8 cm., most common of 9 measured concentrated between the small range offered. *Surface* and *paste* the same as described for hemispherical bowls. *Types and decoration. Xul Incised Type*: Uxmal, 19 rim, 32 body sherds; Kabah, no rim, 1 body sherd. Postpolish single horizontal sharp-incised line about 3.5 cm. below lip on exterior. One has groove-incised horizontal line. This same sherd (q; 58, d) at some time after firing was decorated with painted stucco. *Remarks*: found mostly at Uxmal. Brainerd (1958, fig. 50, e, 1–4, 10–12) shows a few of this form from Uxmal.

Disk, cover (7, bb). Medium-thick, grooved edge, flat. *Size*: diam. 8 cm. *Surface* and *paste* the same as described for hemispherical bowls. *Types and decoration. Ticul Thin-slate Type*: Uxmal, 1 rim; Kabah, none. No decoration. *Remarks*: has one suspension hole showing, which may mean that the disk was used as an ornament. Only this one example noted in either our collections or Brainerd's.

Jars (cf. GWB, fig. 50, n, 1–8). Very rare. Only body sherds found. *Types and decoration. Ticul Thin-slate Type*: no rim, 12 body sherds all from Uxmal. No illustration but see Brainerd.

Summary. Thin Slate is a very distinctive ware, as a rule easily differentiated from Puuc Slate. The principal diagnostics are thinness of wall, smooth surface, vertical crazing, close similarity of slip and paste color, uniformity of temper, saccharoidal calcite, relative scarcity in other types of the Cehpech Ceramic Complex, and, last but by no means least, a different assortment of shapes including hemispherical bowls, cylindrical vases, sometimes cups, and deep bowls. Other forms, such as tripod dishes and bolster-rim basins, may have been copied. Certain forms, such as the cylindrical vase or cup, may be derived from fine gray and fine or thin black wares. The hemispherical bowl, the most abundant Thin Slate form, is also common in the contemporaneous Puuc Red Ware and fine-orange Balancan Group. This form occurs rarely in Puuc Slate and was probably copied.

PUUC RED WARE [582]

Forms, Types, and Varieties	Uxmal Rim	%	Kabah Rim	%	Total Rim & Body
Bowls, hemispherical: Teabo Red Type	288	61.9	25	63.5	985
Becal Incised Type, groove-incised variety	1		0		7
Opichen Gouged-incised Type	22		2		59
Sahcaba Modeled-carved Type	7		0		12
Tekax Black-on-red Type, Tekax Variety	7		6		43
Tekax Black-on-red Type, orange variety	3		0		4
Dishes, tripod: Teabo Red Type	152	30.8	9	30.8	485
Becal Incised Type, Becal Variety	7		3		79
Opichen Gouged-incised Type	2		0		9
Yaxumha Composite Type	2		4		10
Vases, cylindrical: Teabo Red Type	18	3.8	2	3.8	35
Becal Incised Type, Becal Variety	2		0		11
Bowls, beveled rim, ringstand: Teabo Red Type	11	2.0	0		14
Basins: Teabo Red Type	7	1.3	0		15
Jars: Teabo Red Type	1		1		22
Total	530		52		1,790

Bowls, hemispherical (8, a–f, h, i, m, o) may be separated into three categories: 1) direct rim, flat base (a, b, f, h, i, m); 2) bead rim, tripod (c–e); 3) direct rim, ringstand base (o). *Surface*: there is a uniformity of surface treatment which includes careful smoothing, allover slipping and polishing except bases of tripod dishes and ringstand bowls. All have a waxy feel. Blemishes are rare but do include occasional fine pitting, black spots, or

crazing. Slip color red (2.5 YR 4/8, 4/6; 10 R 4/4, 4/8), reddish orange (2.5 YR 5/8, 10 R 5/8), and reddish brown (2.5 YR 5/6). *Paste*: medium to fine texture, but always has temper. Unlike Thin Slate, Puuc Red demonstrates the use of a number of different tempers (Tables 41 and 42). Color closely approximates that of slip.

1) Direct rim, flat base [234], thin to medium-thick rounded sides, pointed or rounded lip. *Size*:

lip diam. 15–21 cm., av. 18.3 cm., most of 65 measured concentrated between 17–20 cm.; ht. 6.5–9 cm., av. 7.3 cm., most common of 14 measured 7 cm. [9]. *Types and decoration. Teabo Red Type*: Uxmal, 195 rim, 461 body sherds; Kabah, 16 rim, 101 body sherds. *a*, undecorated examples. *Sahcaba Modeled-carved Type*: Uxmal, 7 rim, 5 body sherds; Kabah, none. Uncommon but typical of Uaxactun Carved Ferruginous (RES, fig. 86, *i*) is *m*, embellished on exterior with a mold-made frieze of seated figures. *Tekax Black-on-red Type, Tekax Variety*: Uxmal, 7 rim, 9 body sherds; Kabah, 6 rim, 21 body sherds. Well represented is black painting, including exterior rim band of half disks (*f*), interior and exterior rim stripe (10, *o*), interior dot and bar design, exterior large scroll (*h*), and exterior reserve-space decoration (*i*). *Tekax Black-on-red Type, orange variety*: Uxmal, 3 rim, 1 body sherd; Kabah, none. The only decoration consists of vertical parallel lines (*b*). *Remarks*: Brainerd (1958, figs. 51, *d*; *e*, *1–7, 9*; *h*, *2*; *k*, *6–8*; *l*, *21 25, 47–52*; 60, *d*, *4*) illustrates a considerable collection of this form from Sabacche, Sayil, and Uxmal. His possibly Pabellon Modeled-carved Type or Carved Ferruginous sherd (*ibid.*, fig. 60, *d*, *4*) is much like *m* and the fine-orange Altar Group bowls depicted by Smith (1955a, fig. 86, *d–h*). Actually, both the Pabellon Modeled-carved Type and Carved Ferruginous (Sahcaba Modeled-carved Type) were found at Uxmal.

2) Bead rim, tripod [103], thin to medium-thick rounded sides, flat base, and three solid nubbin feet. *Size*: lip diam. 14–20 cm., av. 18.2 cm., most common of 41 measured concentrated between 17–20 cm. [35]; ht. 7.6 cm. [12]. *Types and decoration. Teabo Red Type*: Uxmal, 93 rim, 99 body sherds; Kabah, 9 rim, 11 body sherds. *d*, undecorated example. *Becal Incised Type, groove-incised variety*: Uxmal, 1 rim, 6 body sherds. *c*, preslip grooved concentric diamond band (cf. Brainerd, 1958, 51, *g*, from Labna). *Remarks*: a duplicate of this form is found in Ticul Thin Slate (7, *h*). Brainerd (*ibid.*, fig. 51, *e*, *9–15*; *g*; *h*, *1*; *k*, *4*, *5*; *l*, *1–20*) depicts examples of this form from Kabah, Labna, Sayil, and Uxmal.

3) Direct rim, ringstand base [24], thin to medium-thick rounded sides, pointed lip, sometimes terraced ringstand. *Size*: lip diam. 20–22 cm., av. 20.1 cm. most common of 12 measured is 20 cm. [11]. Approximate ht. 7.4 [11]. *Types and decoration. Opichen Gouged-incised Type*: Uxmal, 22 rim, 34 body sherds; Kabah, 2 rim, 1 body sherd. *o*, preslip gouged-incised under white-slipped exterior band below a horizontal black stripe. *Remarks*: Brainerd (*ibid.*, figs. 52, *d*, *1–3*;

60, *k*, *1–4*) shows a number of examples suggestive of this form and decorative style from Uxmal, or provenience is not specified.

Dishes, tripod (8, *j–l, n, p–t*) may be separated into three categories; namely, 1) basal break, flat base (*j–l, n, s, t*); 2) basal flange, convex base (*p–r*); and 3) basal-Z-angle (cf. GWB, fig. 52, *i, k*). *Surface* and *paste* same as described for bowls with rounded sides.

1) Basal break, flat base [168], medium-thick to thick flaring or outcurving sides, direct rim, rounded, beveled, sometimes grooved (*l*), or pointed lip, rarely notched medial flange (*n*), flat or slightly convex base, three hollow oven-shape or cylindrical with rounded-bottom feet. *Size*: lip diam. 24–48 cm., av. 29.2 cm., most common of 35 measured concentrated between 24–30 cm. [27], base diam. 16–38 cm., av. 21.5 cm., most common of 24 measured concentrated between 16–18 cm. [11] and 23–24 cm. [8]; wall ht. 4.8–7.2 cm., av. 5.8 cm., most common of 26 measured concentrated between 4.8–5.2 cm. [14] and 6.8 and 7.2 cm. [7]. *Types and decoration. Teabo Red Type*: Uxmal, 150 rim, 298 body sherds; Kabah, 6 rim, 7 body sherds. *j–l*, undecorated examples, most common. *Becal Incised Type*: Uxmal, 3 rim, 5 body sherds; Kabah, 2 rim, no body sherds. A few are preslip incised on exterior (no illustration), and one (*n*) besides incising has a black rim stripe on interior. *Opichen Gouged-incised Type*: Uxmal, 2 rim, 7 body sherds; Kabah, none. *t*, gouged-incised step-fret basal band on exterior and black rim band of semicircles on interior. *Yaxumha Composite Type*: Uxmal, 2 rim, 4 body sherds; Kabah, 3 rim, no body sherds. *s*, preslip gouged-incised white medial braid band plus red-coated and impressed basal molding. *Remarks*: this form is twice as abundant in Puuc Red Ware as in Thin Slate Ware. Brainerd (1958, fig. 52, *j*, *5*; *m*, *2–8, 11, 12, 15–17, 19–21*) illustrates a considerable number of this form from Kabah and Uxmal, but none shows decoration. *n* and *t* both have black decoration on interior as well as the main decorative techniques used on exterior. At some time in the future, when more examples have been found, it may be advantageous to have a black-painted variety in both cases.

2) Basal flanged [8], medium to thick outcurving sides, direct rim, beveled and grooved lip, a flange (*p, r*) or apron (*q*), convex to flat base, and three hollow feet (none more than indicated but identifiable by means of welding marks). *Size*: lip diam. 30–31 cm., only two measured. *Types and decoration. Teabo Red Type*: Uxmal, 1 rim, 2 body sherds; Kabah, 2 rim, 4 body sherds. No il-

lustration for undecorated sherds. *Becal Incised Type*: Uxmal, 3 rim, 11 body sherds; Kabah, 1 rim, 15 body sherds. Preslip incised basal bands including crosshatched (*p*) and vertical lines (*q*). *Yaxumha Composite Type*: Uxmal, none; Kabah, 1 rim, no body sherds. *r*, preslip incised basal band of vertical lines and stamped basal molding. *Remarks*: Brainerd (1958, fig. 52, *m*, 14) shows only one example of this form.

3) Basal-Z-angle [3], medium to thick flaring to outcurving sides, direct or everted and grooved rim, rounded lip, flat base. *Size*: approximately same as basal-flange form. *Types and decoration*. *Teabo Red Type*: Uxmal, 1 rim, 9 body sherds; Kabah, 1 rim, 4 body sherds. No illustration but similar in shape to Muna Slate Type (6, *p*). *Becal Incised Type*: Uxmal, 1 rim, 31 body sherds; Kabah, no rim, 7 body sherds. No illustration but a number have preslip incised basal band of horizontally hatched triangles. *Remarks*: Brainerd (1958, fig. 52, *i*; *j*, 3; *k*; *l*; *m*, 1, 9, 10, 13, 14, 18) shows a number of this form of which *k*, 16 has black floor decoration.

Vases, cylindrical or barrel-shape (8, *u*, *v*). Thin walls, direct or bead rim, flat, pointed, or rounded lip, flat base, rarely three solid nubbin feet (*v*). *Size*: lip diam. 11–19 cm., av. 15.7 cm., most common of 7 measured 19 cm. [3], 12 cm. [2]. *Surface* and *paste* the same as described for bowls with rounded sides. *Types and decoration*. *Teabo Red Type*: Uxmal, 18 rim, 15 body sherds; Kabah, 2 rim, no body sherds. No illustration but shapes are same as found in Ticul Thin-slate Type (7, *i*, *j*, *n*). *Becal Incised Type*: Uxmal, 2 rim, 9 body sherds; Kabah, none. *u* has preslip horizontal grooving and *v* has an undecorated white basal band above which is a preslip incised black band with presumably human figure motif. *Remarks*: Brainerd (1958, fig. 51) illustrates the barrel-shape, direct (*l*, 35–37) or bead (*l*, 26–34) rim, and cylindrical vase with bead rim (*l*, 41–46). He also shows a tripod vase with hollow oven-shape feet (*f*) from Kabah, although we found no Puuc Red vases of this form at that site.

Bowls, beveled rim, ringstand (cf. 4, *l*, *m*, for shape). Rounded medium-thick sides, beveled-out rim, pointed lip, plain or terraced ringstand base. *Size*: lip diam. 18–24 cm., av. 20.7 cm., most common of 7 measured is 20 cm. [3]. *Surface* and *paste* the same as described for bowls with rounded sides. *Types and decoration*. *Teabo Red Type*: Uxmal, 11 rim, 3 body sherds; Kabah, none. No decoration observed save terracing of ringstand. *Remarks*: this shape seems to be lacking in Puuc Red Ware at Kabah, although it is more abundant

in Puuc Slate Ware at that site than at Uxmal. Brainerd (1958, fig. 51, *h*, 3; *i*; *n*, 1–7) illustrates examples of this ware and form from Labna, Oxkintok, and Uxmal.

Basins, bolster rim (cf. 4, *a–k* for shape). Medium-thick to thick rounded sides, rounded or triangular bolster rim, rounded or pointed lip, vertical strap handles, slightly concave base. *Size*: lip diam. 31–36 cm., av. 32.3 cm., most common of 6 measured is 31 cm. [4]; bolster thickness 1–2.1 cm., av. 1.3 cm., most common of 6 measured is 1 cm. [4]. *Surface* and *paste* the same as described for bowls with rounded sides. *Types and decoration*. *Teabo Red Type*: Uxmal, 7 rim, 8 body sherds; Kabah, none. No decoration observed save for one with grooved rim bolster. *Remarks*: this form extremely rare in Puuc Red at Uxmal and not encountered in our collections from Kabah. Brainerd (1958, fig. 52, *c*, 1, 3, 4; *e*, 1–4; *f*, 2, 4–18), however, did find a few examples from Kabah as well as Uxmal.

Jars (8, *g*) include only two possible rim sherds and a few [20] body sherds and therefore provide little data, save that the *surface* and *paste* are the same described for bowls with rounded sides, although they are slipped and polished on exterior only. *Types and decoration*. *Teabo Red Type*: Uxmal, 1 rim, 14 body sherds; Kabah, 1 rim, 6 body sherds. *g*, undecorated example. *Remarks*: Brainerd (1958, fig. 52, *a*, *b*) illustrates a few jars from Sabacche and Uxmal.

Summary. In form Puuc Red Ware is very similar to Thin Slate Ware, but the surface treatment is much the same as that of Chichen Red Ware. The identical shapes found in Puuc Red and Thin Slate are hemispherical bowls with direct or bead rim and flat base or three solid nubbin feet, and direct with ringstand base; tripod dishes with hollow oven-shape or cylindrical round-bottom feet; cylindrical vases with direct or bead rim and flat base; basins with rounded bolster rim. Shapes not found in the Thin Slate group are the beveled rim, ringstand bowl, barrel-shape vase, and jar. The chief difference in surface treatment between Puuc Red and Chichen Red is that the former has fewer blemishes and a somewhat more waxy feel. As for decoration, Puuc Red follows both Thin Slate and Puuc Slate but also has its own, such as black reserve space and moldmade modeled carving, the latter being a copy of the same technique and design used in the fine-orange Altar Group, and probably the same type as Carved Ferruginous (RES, p. 34); namely, the Sahcaba Modeled-carved.

CAUICH COARSE-CREAM WARE [373]

Forms and Types	Uxmal Rim	Kabah Rim	Total Rim & body
Jars: Holactun Black-on-cream Type	199	3	1,338
Basins: Holactun Black-on-cream Type	170	1	929
Total	369	4	2,267

Jars (10, *d, f–j*) are of two principal neck forms: 1) vertical (*d, h, j*); 2) outcurving (*f, g, i*); otherwise they differ very little. *Surface:* imperfectly smoothed; slipped and lightly burnished, leaving a matte finish on exterior, base, and just below lip on neck interior. The cream (5 YR 8/2) or grayish (5 YR 8/1) and even the rarer cinnamon (5 YR 7/6, 7.5 YR 7/4) slips are opaque and tend to peel off. *Paste:* coarse texture. Predominantly sherd tempered. Color may be buff, drab, cinnamon, or pinkish. *Types and decoration. Holactun Black-on-cream Type:* Uxmal, 199 rim, 1,131 body sherds; Kabah, 3 rim, 5 body sherds. Strong black vertical stripes (trickle) on body exterior and usually black dabs on rim including lip (*d, f–h*). Many bases evince black decoration (*g*).

1) Vertical [121] neck with bulging rim (*d*), rounded rim bolster (*j*) or thickened rim (*h*), rounded or flat lip, pear-shape body, two vertical strap handles (*h*), and flat base. *Size:* lip diam. 8–13 cm., av. 11.6 cm., most comon of 27 measured is 12 cm. [20]; neck ht. 3–8 cm., av. 7.3 cm., most common of 16 measured 8 cm. [8] and 7.5 cm. [5]; necks are medium-thick to thick and bodies medium-thick. *Remarks:* Brainerd (1958, fig. 53, *a, 12–14, 17–20; b, 1, 3–5*) shows a number of this form.

2) Outcurving [81] neck with direct (*f*) or everted and thickened (*g, i*) rim, beveled lip rarely with groove (*g*), pear-shape body, and flat base. *Size:* lip diam. 16–20 cm., av. 16.8 cm., most common of 25 measured 16 cm. [10] and 17 cm. [8]; neck ht. 5–7.2 cm., av. 6.2 cm., most common of 18 measured 6–6.6 cm. [14]; neck and body thickness is medium-thick to thick. *Remarks:* Brainerd (1958, fig. 53, *a, 7–10, 15; b, 2, 6–16*) illustrates quite a few of this form.

Basins (10, *a–c, e*) may be separated into three main categories: 1) large ovoid rim bolster, globular body (*c*); 2) medium size ovoid to triangular rim bolster, egg-shaped body (*b*); 3) T-shape rim, flaring sides (*a*). *Surface* and *paste* same as jars; interiors unslipped and coarse texture paste; *a* is a rare cinnamon-slip color variety and *e* is an unusual basin form with rim flange and rounded lip.

1) Large ovoid rim bolster, globular body [69], medium-thick to thick walls, restricted orifice, rounded lip, horizontal strap handles, flat or slightly concave base. *Size:* lip diam. 28–46 cm., av. 37.5 cm., most common of 20 measured concentrated between 32–36 cm. [9] and 40–42 cm. [7]; bolster thickness 3–4.4 cm., av. 3.6 cm. *Types and decoration. Holactun Black-on-cream Type:* Uxmal, 69 rim, 304 body sherds; Kabah, none. Strong black dabs on bolster rim and black horizontal and vertical stripes below bolster covering two-thirds of exterior wall, lower third remaining unslipped but striated. *Remarks:* restricted orifice, large bolster, strap handles, and nontrickle decoration set these large basins apart from the other two Holactun Black-on-cream basin categories. Brainerd (1958, fig. 53, *c, 2, 4, 10, 12–17, 19, 21*) gives us quite a few rim varieties of this form.

2) Medium-size ovoid to triangular rim bolster, egg-shaped body [57], thin to thick walls, incurved rim, rounded or pointed lip, flat or slightly concave base. *Size:* lip diam. 15–38 cm., av. 24.7 cm., most common of 30 measured concentrated between 22–25 cm. [15] and 30–32 cm. [6]; ht. (*b*) 20.5 cm.; bolster thickness 1.4–3.1 cm., av. 2.2 cm. *Types and decoration. Holactun Black-on-cream Type:* Uxmal, 57 rim, 250 body sherds; Kabah, none. Black vertical lines thickened at bolster and coming to an abrupt end midway down vessel exterior wall where slip also ends. *Remarks:* this form is actually intermediary between categories 1 and 3 but closest to 3 in all respects save shape of bolster. However, when the T-bolster becomes less of a T and the ovoid bends a bit towards the horizontal, they become difficult to differentiate. Brainerd (1958, fig. 53, *c, 1, 18; d, 1–4, 8, 11, 12, 23–25*) illustrates this form.

3) T-shape rim, flaring sides [45], thin to medium-thick walls, rounded or pointed lip, flat or slightly concave base. *Size:* lip diam. 23–28 cm., av. 26.2 cm., most common of 18 measured is 26 [14]; ht. (*a*) 14 cm.; bolster breadth 2–2.9 cm., av. 2.7 cm. *Types and decoration. Holactun Black-on-cream Type:* Uxmal, 44 rim, 194 body sherds; Kabah, 1 rim, 10 body sherds. Much the same as

category 2 but the vertical stripes may be joined to form a solid band at bolster. The vertical stripes end abruptly about midway down exterior body where slip also terminates. Sometimes this lower unslipped area carries a horizontal striated band. *Remarks*: this is perhaps the form that first comes to mind at the mention of Holactun Black-on-cream (Brainerd's Holactun Slateware, 1958, p. 54), even though it is the least abundant of the three basin categories. The T-shape bolster is so distinctive that it overshadows all else. Brainerd (1958, fig. 53, *c, 3, 5, 7; d, 5–7, 13, 26*) shows a number of this form. *e* is a unique form of which there is just one example. It may be that instead of a rim flange it has a deeply grooved rim bolster.

Summary. Holactun Black-on-cream Type is very scarce at Kabah but reasonably abundant at Uxmal. The most distinctive trait, other than the T-rim bolster for the basin, is the fact that basins are unslipped on interior, thus making it difficult to distinguish basin from jar body sherds unless the fact that the black trickle on jars, extending to base, in contrast to the black trickle or decoration on basins, terminating well above base, is considered. Another unusual trait of the Holactun Black-on-cream basin is the restricted orifice or incurved rim, which is a factor usually associated with the Chichen Slate Ware basin. This basin form may be a precursor of the Chichen Slate form. In addition the Holactun Black-on-cream Type strikes me as a likely precursor of the Xcanchacan Black-on-cream Type. Jars on the other hand are closely associated in form with Puuc Slate Ware jars and have little if any similarity to Chichen Slate Ware jars. Some vessels have a cinnamon to orange slip. This is the cinnamon-slip variety, not emphasized because of its rarity and often just off cream coloring.

FINE ORANGE WARE [117]

Forms, Types, and Varieties	Uxmal Rim	%	Kabah Rim	%	Total Rim & body
Fine-orange Balancan Group		88.6		91.7	
Bowls, rounded sides:					
Balancan Orange Type	17		2		96
Caribe Incised Type, Caribe Variety	3		0		5
Caribe Incised Type, red-paint variety	3		0		4
Provincia Plano-relief Type	28		7		78
Canizan Gadrooned Type	0		2		2
Tenosique Red-on-orange Type	38		0		122
Vases, cylindrical: Caribe Incised Type, groove-incised variety; Table 30	3		0		6
Dish, tripod:					
Provincia Plano-relief Type	1		0		1
Fine-orange Altar Group		11.4		8.3	
Bowls, rounded sides:					
Tumba Black-on-orange Type	7		1		38
Pabellon Modeled-carved Type	3		0		6
Bowl, pear-shape:					
Tumba Black-on-orange Type	1		0		1
Vase, barrel-shape:					
Pabellon Modeled-carved Type	1		0		2
Total	105		12		361

In the above inventory two fine orange groups are listed, Balancan and Altar, because presumably they are contemporaneous and represent trade specimens at Uxmal and Kabah. For a more detailed understanding of these fine orange groups, consult a report by Smith (1958b, pp. 151–160).

Fine-orange Balancan Group.

Bowls, rounded side (9, *a, c–e, g*; 58, *i–k*). Thin walls usually basal break (*a, c*), some rounded to a flat base (*e, g*), direct rim, pointed or flat lip, flat base. Usually these bowls have slightly rounded sides but some are more rounded and almost attain the hemispherical; others are more flaring, rounding to a flat base. *Size*: lip diam. 14–24 cm., av. 22.6 cm., most common of 42 measured concentrated between 18–22 cm. [39]; ht. 6–7.5 cm., av. 6.7 cm., most common of 12 measured 6 cm.

[6] and 7.5 cm. [5]. *Surface*: smooth but not lustrous. Some examples (*d, e, g*) are partially coated with a clear, opaque white slip thinly applied and bearing a high gloss. Slip or surface color orange (5 YR 6/6, 6/8, 10 R 5/8) or brown (5 YR 4/4, 2.5 YR 5/6, 7.5 YR 5/6). *Paste*: fine texture. All those examined proved to be untempered. Color nearly matches surface. *Types and decoration. Balancan Orange Type*: Uxmal, 17 rim, 62 body sherds; Kabah, 2 rim, 15 body sherds. Undecorated, no illustration. *Caribe Incised Type, Caribe Variety*: Uxmal, 3 rim, 2 body sherds; Kabah, none. No illustration but simple horizontal and vertical lines. *Caribe Incised Type, red-paint variety*: Uxmal, 3 rim, 1 body sherd; Kabah, none. *a*, interior broad red rim stripe; exterior horizontal and vertical grooving with three-pointed implement. *Provincia Plano-relief Type*: Uxmal, 28 rim, 38 body sherds; Kabah, 7 rim, 5 body sherds. 9, *e, g* and 58, *j, i* have plano-relief exterior designs, often with human figure motif. *d* (58, *k*) has geometric motif enhanced by the cursive M. *Canizan Gadrooned Type*: Uxmal, none; Kabah, 2 rim, no body sherds. Gadrooning is rare and horizontal, but not illustrated because too fragmentary. *Tenosique Red-on-orange Type*: Uxmal, 38 rim, 84 body sherds; Kabah, none. *c*, interior red scalloped border, exterior may have fire-clouding. *Remarks*: the Cehpech fine-orange Balancan Group and Altar Group are easily distinguished from each other and from the Sotuta fine-orange Silho Group by shape, save for the rounded-side bowl. Although this form varies little in the three fine-orange groups, the decoration does vary both in techniques and designs. The painting technique has its place in both the Balancan and Altar groups: the former with red exterior and red or black interior scalloped borders wherein a strong black is used; the latter with a black scalloped exterior border decoration, but the black is so lightly applied that the orange slip shows through. In the case of the Silho rounded-side bowls, an irregular orange or reddish border is achieved by fire-clouding to gray or brown the entire vessel, interior and exterior, below this rim border. The Provincia Plano-relief Type ringstand bowl shown in 58, *a*, found at Moxviquil, Chiapas, is an excellent example of another variation of this round-sided bowl form which, although not certainly identified in our Uxmal and Kabah collections, may well have been present. At least the plano-relief technique of decoration and the cursive M style of design is ample assurance that this specimen belongs to the Provincia Plano-relief Type, notwithstanding that vessels of this same shape (Brainerd, 1941, p. 166,

fig. 1, *b*) are recognized as forming part of the fine-orange Silho Group shape assemblage. It is also true that this form is present in the Cehpech Ceramic Complex shape assemblage in Thin Slate and Puuc Red wares.

Vases, cylindrical (9, *m*). Thin to medium-thick slightly outcurving sides, direct rim, beveled lip, probably flat base. *Size*: lip diam. 10 cm. *Surface*: smooth, but not lustrous. Slipped and burnished. Color reddish orange. *Paste*: fine texture. Apparently untempered. Color orange. *Types and decoration. Caribe Incised Type, groove-incised variety*: Uxmal, 3 rim, 3 body sherds; Kabah, none. Preslip grooved design suggestive of feathers. *Remarks*: this is an unusual form for the fine-orange Balancan Group. Brainerd does not illustrate any examples of this form unless it belongs to the cup shape which he depicts from Dzibilchaltun (1958, fig. 59, *g*) and in that case the grooved type of decoration is not in keeping.

Dish, tripod (?) (9, *k*). Outcurving thin to medium-thick sides, direct rim, flat lip. *Size*: lip diam. 20 cm., wall ht. 3 cm. *Surface*: slipped and burnished on interior and exterior. Color reddish brown on interior, white on exterior. *Paste*: fine texture. Apparently untempered. Color orange. *Type and decoration. Provincia Plano-relief Type*: Uxmal, 1 rim, no body sherds; Kabah, none. Plano-relief and preslip incising; actually the excised areas were covered by white slip. *Remarks*: this is a most unusual form for the fine-orange Balancan Group, but the plano-relief decoration with white slip is in keeping.

Fine-orange Altar Group.

Bowls, rounded side (9, *b, h–i*). Thin to medium-thick walls, direct rim, rounded or flat lip, flat base. *Size*: very fragmentary. *Surface*: slipped and burnished all over. Color brown (5 YR 5/6, 2.5 YR 5/6) and orange (2.5 YR 5/8). *Paste*: fine texture. Apparently untempered. Color nearly matches that of slip. *Type and decoration. Pabellon Modeled-carved Type*: Uxmal, 3 rim, 3 body sherds; Kabah, none. Moldmade including glyphlike rim bands and human figure motif below. *Remarks*: these are typical of the Uaxactum examples illustrated by Smith (1955a, fig. 86, *b–h*). *Tumba Black-on-orange Type*: Uxmal, 7 rim, 27 body sherds; Kabah, 1 rim, 3 body sherds. *b*, black scalloped exterior border.

Bowl, pear-shape (9, *f*). Thin walls, restricted orifice, direct rim, pointed lip. *Size*: lip diam. 4 cm. *Surface*: slipped and burnished on exterior only. Possible black smudging on exterior. Color orange. *Paste*: fine texture. Apparently untempered. Color orange. *Types and decoration.* *Tumba Black-on-orange Type:* Uxmal, 1 rim, no body sherds; Kabah, none. No decoration unless black smudging is residue of vertical black striping. *Remarks:* this form has not been noted in any of the fine orange types save in the Marquez Collection of fine-orange Silho Group vessels described by Smith (1957b, fig. 5, *a, b*). Possibly this is a fine-orange Silho Group piece.

Vase, barrel-shape (9, *l*). Thin to medium-thick sides, direct rim, pointed lip. *Size:* lip diam. approximately 8 cm. *Surface:* slipped and burnished on exterior and just below lip on interior. Color brown (7.5 YR 5/6). *Paste:* fine texture. Apparently untempered. Color same as slip. *Types and decoration. Pabellon Modeled-carved Type:* Uxmal, 1 rim, 1 body sherd; Kabah, none. Horizontal grooving on exterior and probably modeled-carved panels on body. *Remarks:* this may be the same shape as those from Uaxactun illustrated by Smith (1955a, fig. 86, *i–p*), some of which are of the fine-orange Altar Group.

Summary. The fine-orange Balancan Group is moderately represented at Uxmal (.9 per cent of all sherds) and less so (.3 per cent) at Kabah. This fine-orange group is definitely contemporaneous with the Cehpech Phase but did not originate in Yucatan; more likely it originated in southwestern Campeche or eastern Tabasco. The most important form is the flaring-side bowl often rounding to a flat base or having a ringstand base. Sometimes this bowl form is nearly hemispherical and is difficult to differentiate from the Silho hemispherical bowl save for the difference in surface treatment. The decorative techniques used on the fine-orange Balancan Group vessels are red or black painting, incising, gadrooning, and plano-relief, as compared to black painting, grooving, modeling, and gouging-and-incising on the Silho Group specimens. The styles of design are also quite different in the two groups. In the fine-orange Balancan Group we find scrolls, circles and dots, cursive M-like device, and human figure motif, whereas in the Silho Group we encounter braids, step-frets, terrace and other elements, scroll meanders, black birds, and floral designs.

The fine-orange Altar Group is found in very small quantity at Uxmal and not at all at Kabah. This is presumably a Peten type of fine orange found sparsely at Uaxactun and more abundantly at Altar de Sacrificios and Seibal. The two principal forms are the rounded-side bowls and the barrel-shaped vases, the latter differing from the rare occurrence of this form in the fine-orange Balancan Group usually by having a pedestal base. The rounded-side bowl is the same in form but has a different decorative treatment. This is basically black painting of borders, often scalloped, where the black is so lightly applied that the orange slip shows through. This same kind of black application is used on the barrel-shape and pear-shape vessels with gadroonlike broad vertical striping. The decorative techniques noted in the fine-orange Altar Group are grooving, black painting, and carving, actually reproduced on the vessel by impressing in a mold. The design motifs associated with carving consist mostly of human figures and hieroglyphs.

CHICHEN ITZA [75]

At Chichen Itza a relatively small percentage (2.1) of Cehpech Ceramic Complex sherds was found in the five cuts used for determining the component parts of the Sotuta Ceramic Complex.

PUUC UNSLIPPED WARE

Jars (cf. 2, *a–g*). Yokat Striated Type, neck-interior variety: 1 rim, 2 body sherds.

PUUC SLATE WARE

Basins (16, *c–g*). Rounded sides, triangular (*c, f*), rounded (*d, g*), or ovoid (*e*) rim bolster, rounded, pointed, or beveled lip, vertical strap handles, medium-thick walls, globular body, flat or concave base. *Size:* lip diam. 22–42 cm., av. 33 cm., most common of 24 measured 35 cm. [7], 29 cm. [6], and 32 cm. [4]. *Surface:* slipped and polished all over save under strap handles. Waxy feel. Color commonly gray (10 YR 6/1, 8/2) or buff (10 YR 7/3, 7.5 YR 7/2), less frequently light brown (7.5 YR 6/4) and pinkish yellow (10 YR 8/6). *Paste:* medium texture. Color commonly brown (2.5 YR 5/6, 10 YR 4/4, 5 YR 6/4 to 4/6) less frequently pinkish cinnamon (2.5 YR 6/8) or combinations such as edges red (2.5 YR 4/6) and core drab (10 YR 6/3), edges drab (10 YR 6/3) and core red (2.5 YR 4/6), and edges red (2.5 YR 4/8) and core pinkish cinnamon (5 YR 6/6). *Types and decoration. Muna Slate Type:* 4 rim, 70 body sherds. (For illustration cf. 4, *a, b*). *Sacalum Black-on-slate Type:* 40 rim, 203 body sherds. Some of these specimens are illustrated (16, *c–g*). *c, f, g* have brown, orange, and black vertical stripes, respectively, on interior and exterior; *d, e* have beige vertical stripes on exterior only. Probably all trickle (vertical stripes) was intended to be black.

Dishes, tripod, basal break (19, *g–m*). Outcurving or flaring medium-thick sides forming an angle with a flat or slightly convex base, everted (*g, i, k*), direct (*h*), or thickened (*j*) rim, rounded or beveled lip, and three feet of various forms including hollow oven, solid slab (*l*), and solid terraced slab (*m*). *Size:* lip diam. 18–30 cm., av. 24.3 cm., most common of 16 measured 26 cm. [5], 18 cm. [4], and 30 cm. [3]; ht. without feet 5.1–7 cm., av. 6.4 cm. *Surface:* slipped and polished all over except on flat bases; the convex bases have slip as do hollow oven-shape feet, but slab feet are unslipped. Waxy feel. One specimen has purple veins (*k*). Color commonly gray (10 YR 7/1, 7/2, 6/2), less frequently drab (10 YR 6/3) and brown (7.5 YR 6/4). *Paste:* medium texture. Color commonly reddish brown (2.5 YR 5/6, 5 YR 5/6), red (2.5 YR 4/6), orange (5 YR 6/8), and gray (10 YR 5/1), less frequently drab (10 YR 6/3) or combinations such as edges brown (10 YR 4/4, 5/4) and core reddish brown (5 YR 4/4). *Types and decoration. Muna Slate Type, Muna Variety:* 14 rim, 25 body sherds. Undecorated examples (*i–k*). *Muna Slate Type, basal-notched variety:* no rim, 2 body sherds. Usually slab feet (*l*). *Sacalum Black-on-slate Type:* 2 rim, 6 body sherds. None illustrated but compare Brainerd (1958, fig. 47, *a–i*). *Tekit Incised Type:* 2 rim, no body sherds. One example (*g*) illustrates a rare case of both interior and exterior incising. *Akil Impressed Type:* 1 rim, 2 body sherds. Nail-impressed (double row) basal band (*h*). *Remarks:* these specimens from Chichen Itza are very like those from Uxmal and Kabah (6).

Bowls, beveled rim, ringstand (cf. 4, *l, m*). Medium-thick rounded sides, beveled and slightly incurved rim, ringstand base. *Surface:* slipped and polished all over except ringstand. Waxy feel. Color gray. *Paste:* medium texture, grayish color. *Types and decoration. Muna Slate Type:* 3 rim, no body sherds.

Drums (?) or jars (14, *o, p*). Wide (*o*) or medium-wide (*p*) mouth, high outcurving neck, direct (*o*) or slightly bolster (*p*) rim, rounded and grooved (*o*) or pointed (*p*) lip. *Size:* lip diam. 25 and 16.5 cm., respectively. Thick (*o*) and medium-thick (*p*) walls. *Surface:* slipped and polished on neck below incising. Slip color for *p* is cream (10 YR 8/4). *Paste:* medium texture. Color, *p* orange (2.5 YR 6/8), *o* cinnamon (7.5 YR 7/4). *Types and decoration. Tekit Incised Type:* 2 rim, 1 body sherd. *o* deeply incised vertically and diagonally forming a chevron pattern, *p* incised vertically. *Remarks:* these differ slightly from the Cehpech examples (5, *r, s*), but I now believe that *o* probably belongs with that ceramic complex rather than with the Sotuta. Brainerd (1958, fig. 37, *c, 3, 6*) illustrates two which he calls unslipped; actually most of the neck is unslipped but slip begins on neck just below the incised zone. He (*ibid.*, fig. 40, *e, 2, 20*) illustrates two more under Florescent Medium Slateware (Puuc Slate Ware) which he calls drums. They may be drums because complete drums to which *p* might well belong have been noted in the Marquez Collection in Merida. The wide-mouth, thick-neck type I believe can belong not to the drum category but more likely to a storage jar form.

PUUC RED WARE

Bowls, beveled rim, ringstand (cf. 4, *l, m*). These bowls conform in shape to the examples given in the above-mentioned figure and are described earlier in this chapter. *Types and decoration. Teabo Red Type:* 2 rim, 5 body sherds. No illustration.

THIN SLATE WARE

Bowsl, hemispherical (cf. 7, *a, h*). These bowls conform in all respects to the examples given in the above-mentioned figure and are described earlier in this chapter. *Types and decoration. Ticul Thin-slate Type:* 3 rim, 11 body sherds. *Remarks:* no certain bead lip sherds noted.

Dishes, tripod (cf. 7, *o, r*). These dishes are described earlier in this chapter. *Types and decoration. Ticul Thin-slate Type:* 1 rim, 2 body sherds.

Jars (no illustration). These rare jar forms are mentioned earlier in this chapter and illustrated by Brainerd (1958, fig. 50, *n*). *Type and decoration. Ticul Thin-slate Type:* no rim, 3 body sherds.

MAYAPAN [1,047]

At Mayapan a smaller percentage (1.6) of Cehpech Ceramic Complex sherds was found than at Chichen Itza. The Sotuta Ceramic Complex findings at Mayapan, however, represented an even smaller percentage (.3).

PUUC UNSLIPPED WARE

Jars (26, a). Wide mouth, low to medium-high flaring or outcurving neck with bolster [139 including 80 rounded, 47 triangular, 9 flat, 3 square], T-shape [78], direct [40], everted [16], overhanging [11], or pinched [1] rim, globular body with medium-thick walls and probably flat base. *Surface:* well smoothed and striated on body exterior, rarely on neck. Color brownish red, cinnamon, buff, and gray. *Paste:* coarse texture. Color normally follows that of surface. *Types and decoration. Yokat Striated Type:* 284 rim, 2,259 body sherds. Excellent whole specimens are illustrated by Brainerd (1958, figs. 38, a; 65, d; 68, a, e, d).

Jar. Wide mouth, medium-high outcurving neck, overhanging rim, globular body with medium-thick walls, and probably flat base. *Surface:* well smoothed and striated on body exterior and neck interior. Color cinnamon. *Paste:* coarse texture, cinnamon color. *Types and decoration. Yokat Striated Type, neck-interior variety:* 1 rim, no body sherds (cf. 2, a).

Jar. Wide mouth, medium-high outcurving neck, direct rim, globular body, base not present. *Surface:* well smoothed all over exterior and neck interior, gray color. *Paste:* coarse texture, gray color. *Types and decoration. Chum Unslipped Type:* 1 rim, 1 body sherd (no illustration).

Bowls, basal break. Flaring medium-thick sides, direct rim, flat lip, flat base. *Surface:* well smoothed on interior and exterior, color cinnamon. *Paste:* coarse texture, cinnamon color. *Types and decoration. Chum Unslipped Type:* 2 rim, no body sherds (cf. 3, q). *Yokat Striated Type:* 2 rim, no body sherds. These have oblique exterior striations (cf. 3, v).

Bowls, hemispherical. Rounded medium-thick sides, direct rim, flat base. *Surface:* smoothed all over, color brown. *Paste:* coarse texture, brown color. *Types and decoration. Chum Unslipped Type:* 2 rim, no body sherds (cf. 3, u for shape).

Censers, hourglass form. Flaring medium-thick to thick sides, thickened or everted rim, pedestal base. *Surface:* well smoothed on interior, imperfectly on exterior, color cinnamon. *Paste:* coarse texture, cinnamon color. *Types and decoration. Chum Unslipped Type:* 1 rim, no body sherds. Undecorated, no illustration. *Yokat Striated Type:* 1 rim, 1 body sherd. This has a notched flange (cf. 3, i). *Halacho Impressed Type:* no rim, 1 body sherd. Has impressed fillet (cf. 3, c, g).

Flute, head adorno. Fragment of flute consisting of a modeled human head applied to the flute tube. *Surface:* unslipped, weathered but evidence of green-blue and red paint. *Paste:* coarse texture, reddish brown color. *Types and decoration. Yiba Modeled Type:* no rim, 1 body sherd (26, c, 1).

PUUC SLATE WARE

Jars (26, b, 1–5). Small (1–3) or wide (4–5) mouth, medium-high to high, vertical, tapered, flaring or outcurving neck, direct or bolster rim, rounded, pointed, flat or beveled lip, globular or pear-shape body with medium-thick walls, flat to slightly concave base. *Surface:* slipped and polished on exterior and neck interior (except in rare cases, 26, b, 3). Occasional crazing. Waxy feel. Color follows normal Puuc Slate Ware color range (Chapter IV). *Paste:* medium texture including variety of tempers (calcite, ash, clay lump, and sherd), gray through buff and even red color. *Types and decoration. Muna Slate Type:* 201 rim, 1,765 body sherds. Excellent whole vessels are illustrated by Brainerd (1958, figs. 10, a; 40, a, b; 42, d). *Sacalum Black-on-slate Type:* 3 rim, 240 body sherds. For complete specimens see Brainerd (1958, figs. 32, a; 36, a, c; 42, c). *Tekit Incised Type:* 11 rim, 16 body sherds. These sherds have deep vertical or oblique incisions on neck exterior which often is unslipped, whereas rest of exterior is slipped (see 5, r, s). *Akil Impressed Type:* no rim, 1 body sherd. This sherd has two parallel horizontal bands, one nail-impressed, the other reed-impressed. *Remarks:* the Tekit Incised Type and Akil Impressed Type sherds may belong to drums.

Basins (26, b, 6–10). Rounded sides, rounded, ovoid and triangular bolster, or thickened rim, vertical strap handles, medium-thick walls, globular body, flat or slightly concave base. *Surface:* slipped and polished all over save under strap handles. Waxy feel. Color gray or buff, less frequently light brown. *Paste:* medium texture, brown or pinkish cinnamon color. *Types and decoration. Muna Slate Type:* 176 rim, 132 body sherds. A whole vessel is illustrated by Brainerd (1958, fig. 43, b). *Sacalum Black-on-slate Type:* 5 rim, 18 body sherds. For complete specimens see Brainerd (1958, figs. 41, f; 43, a).

Dishes, tripod, basal break (26, b, 11–22). Flaring or outcurving medium-thick sides, direct, everted or slight bolster rim, flat or slightly convex base, and three feet of various forms including solid conical, solid slab, and solid terraced slab; a few have notched (26, b, 21) or terraced (26, b, 22) flanges. *Surface:* slipped and polished all over except on flat bases. Waxy feel. Color commonly gray, less frequently brown. *Paste:* medium texture, reddish brown, red, orange, and gray color. *Types and decoration. Muna Slate Type:* 139 rim, 350 body sherds. Various complete vessels are illustrated by Brainerd (1958, figs. 10, g, 1, 6, 14; 45, b–d; 46, a, b; 48, a, 42). *Sacalum Black-on-slate Type:* 1 rim, 5 body sherds. Several complete specimens are illustrated by Brainerd (1958, fig. 35, i–m; 47, a–i). *Tekit Incised Type:* 1 rim, 7 body sherds (cf. 6, j, k, o). *Akil Impressed Type:* 3 rim, 4 body sherds (26, b, 16, 21, 22). *Nohcacab Composite Type:* 1 rim, no body sherds (26, b, 20).

Bowls, beveled rim, ringstand (26, b, 23). Rounded medium-thick sides, usually beveled and slightly incurved rim, ringstand base. *Surface:* slipped and polished all over save ringstand. Color gray or brownish. Waxy feel. *Paste:* medium texture, gray and brown color. *Types and decoration. Muna Slate Type:* 90 rim, 107 body sherds. *Sacalum Black-on-slate Type:* 1 rim, no body sherds (60, d).

Flutes (26, c, 2, 4). Long tube with three or more stops and mouthpiece at end. Near mouth end a modeled figure is applied. *Surface:* slipped and polished over most of surface. Waxy feel. Color originally gray now fire-blackened. *Paste:* medium texture, gray color. *Types and decoration. Yaxnic Modeled Type:* 1 rim, no body sherds.

THIN SLATE WARE

Bowls, hemispherical (26, d). These may have direct rim or bead lip, flat or tripod (nubbin feet) base. The sides are rounded and thin to medium-thick. *Surface:* carefully smoothed before slipping

and polishing all over. Slight waxy feel. Most sherds have vertical crazing, some are rootlet-marked, often purplish color, usually a light gray, sometimes cream or light brown. *Paste:* fine texture with saccharoidal calcite temper (temper of these specimens not checked but saccharoidal calcite is very uniform for all thin slate specimens examined — see Tables 41 and 42). Color approximately same as slip. *Types and decoration. Ticul Thin-slate Type:* 47 rim, 80 body sherds (see also 7, a, h). *Xul Incised Type:* no rim, 1 body sherd (cf. 7, k). *Tabi Gouged-incised Type:* no rim, 1 body sherd (cf. 7, b, c).

Bowls, deep (cf. 7, l for shape). Recurving thin sides, direct rim or rim with molding, flat lip, and presumably flat base. *Surface and paste* the same as described for hemispherical bowls. *Types and decoration. Ticul Thin-slate Type:* 2 rim, no body sherds.

Bowls, ringstand (cf. 7, e). Rounded thin sides, direct rim, ringstand base which may be terraced. *Surface and paste* the same as described for hemispherical bowls. *Types and decoration. Ticul Thin-slate Type:* no rim, 1 body sherd (nonterraced type).

Vases, cylindrical (cf. 7, i, j, m, n). Nearly vertical sides, direct rim, flat or pedestal base. *Surface and paste* the same as described for hemispherical bowls. *Types and decoration. Ticul Thin-slate Type:* 2 rim, 5 body sherds. *Xul Incised Type:* 1 rim, no body sherds.

Dishes, tripod (cf. 7, o, r). Flaring or outcurving thin to medium-thick sides, direct rim, flat or slightly convex base, and three feet. *Surface and paste* the same as described for hemispherical bowls. *Types and decoration. Ticul Thin-slate Type:* 4 rim, 3 body sherds.

Jars (cf. GWB, fig. 50, n, 1–8). Very rare and in this case fragmentary. *Types and decoration. Ticul Thin-slate Type:* no rim, 1 body sherd.

PUUC RED WARE

Bowls, hemispherical (cf. 8, a–i). Rounded thin to medium-thick sides, direct or bead rim, flat base or tripod (nubbin or hollow oven feet). *Surface:* carefully smoothed before all over slipping and polishing. Blemishes are rare but include occasional fine pitting, black spots, or crazing. Color red or reddish orange. *Paste:* medium to fine texture, but always with temper. Color closely approximates that of slip. *Types and decoration. Teabo Red Type:* 14 rim, 50 body sherds. (cf. 8, a, d). *Tekax Black-on-red Type, orange variety:* 1 rim, 1 body sherd (cf. 8, b).

Bowls, beveled rim, ringstand (cf. GWB, fig. 51, *m, n*). Rounded medium-thick sides, beveled-out rim, ringstand base. *Surface* and *paste* the same as described for hemispherical bowls. *Types and decoration. Teabo Red Type:* 3 rim, 5 body sherds.

Dishes, tripod (26, e, 1, 2, 4, and 1 is more bowl than dish). Flaring or outcurving medium-thick sides, direct rim; some have basal-Z-angle; most have convex base with three feet usually hollow oven or cylindrical. *Surface* and *paste* the same as described for hemispherical bowls. *Types and decoration. Teabo Red Type:* 13 rim, 33 body sherds (cf. 8, *j–l*). *Becal Incised Type:* 4 rim, 7 body sherds (26, e, 2, 4).

Vases, cylindrical (26, a, 3, 5). Slightly flaring thin to medium-thick sides, direct rim, flat base. *Surface* and *paste* the same as described for hemispherical bowls. *Types and decoration. Teabo Red Type:* 1 rim, 1 body sherd. *Becal Incised Type:* 1 rim, no body sherds.

Basins (cf. GWB, fig. 52, e, 3). Rounded medium-thick to thick sides, rounded bolster rim, probably two vertical strap handles, slightly concave base. *Surface* and *paste* the same as described for hemispherical bowls. *Types and decoration. Teabo Red Type:* 1 rim, 1 body sherd.

Jars (26, e, 6; for shape cf. GWB, fig. 3, b, 2). Wide mouth, high, vertical thick neck, everted rim with inner cover rest, globular body, no base sherds present. *Surface* and *paste* the same as described for hemispherical bowls. *Types and decoration. Teabo Red Type:* 2 rim, 10 body sherds (see also GWB, fig. 52, b).

Figurine, whistle (26, c, 3). Monkey figure, modeled with mouthpiece at tail. *Surface:* slipped and polished over most of surface. Waxy feel. Color is a deep red. *Paste:* medium texture, red color.

Types and decoration. Sitpach Modeled Type: no head, 1 body fragment.

FINE ORANGE WARE

Fine-orange Balancan Group.

Bowls, hemispherical (cf. 9, a–e, g–j). Rounded thin sides, direct rim, flat base. *Surface:* smooth but not lustrous. Slip or surface color orange or brown. *Paste:* fine texture, and appears to be untempered. Color nearly matches surface. *Types and decoration. Balancan Orange Type:* 13 rim, 55 body sherds. *Caribe Incised Type:* 5 rim, 11 body sherds. *Provincia Plano-relief Type:* no rim, 1 body sherd.

Fine-orange Altar Group.

Vases, cylindrical (27, l; see also Smith, 1958b, fig. 4, f and Woodbury and Trik, 1953, fig. 82). Nearly vertical thin to medium-thick sides, slightly everted and grooved rim, rattle bottom which presumably contained pellets. *Surface:* slipped and burnished on exterior only. Red-orange color. *Paste:* fine textured, appearing untempered. See legend for figure 27 for further data. *Types and decoration. Pabellon Modeled-carved Type:* 5 rim, 34 body sherds.

Bowls, hemispherical (cf. RES, figs. 64, b, 5; 86, b–h). Rounded thin to medium-thick sides, flat base. *Surface:* well smoothed and burnished, lacking the high luster associated with Peten Gloss Ware. May be lightly slipped. *Paste:* fine texture, appears untempered. Color orange, like surface. *Types and decoration. Pabellon Modeled-carved Type:* no rim, 2 body sherds. *Tumba Black-on-orange Type:* 1 rim, no body sherds.

CEHPECH CERAMIC COMPLEX SUMMARY

In the Cehpech Ceramic Complex Uxmal and Kabah have two principal wares, Puuc Unslipped and Puuc Slate, and three, Thin Slate, Puuc Red, and Cauich Coarse-cream, less important numerically but obviously much used and well thought of in the Puuc area. These are the wares that belong in the Puuc region and, although not all manufactured in the same center, were used to some degree at all sites.

The pottery of this complex might possibly be broken down into subcomplexes, but not on the basis of the stratigraphic trench findings at Uxmal and Kabah, where no important changes were noted from top to bottom. There are, however, a number of very important differences, which are almost always quantitative, between the two sites. The culinary vessels are far more abundant at Kabah, as explained in an earlier section of this report, possibly due to our having dug in kitchen rather than in ceremonial middens at that site. If this is the case, it would account for the greater quantity of Thin Slate Ware, Puuc Red

Ware and fine-orange Balancan Group at Uxmal as opposed to the predominance of Puuc Un-slipped and Puuc Slate wares at Kabah. Cauich Coarse-cream, reasonably abundant at Uxmal, is quite scarce at Kabah; although it can hardly be considered a fine ware, it might have had a cere-monial significance.

There is also the question of areal distribution, the movement of pottery from different centers of manufacture within the Puuc. Obviously some sites, through proximity or selection, favored the wares of certain centers of manufacture over those of other centers. It is my opinion that each of the three less important above-mentioned wares was manufactured at a different center. In some cases, notably Thin Slate and Cauich Coarse-cream, this opinion is borne out by the technological findings (Tables 41 and 42). It is based on a number of visible factors.

First, Thin Slate is quite distinct from Puuc Slate. In fact the only real similarity is in the waxy finish, but the Thin Slate vessels are more perfectly smoothed, have a lighter slip color, and a more finely textured paste than the Puuc Slate. Further-more, the principal Thin Slate forms, hemispherical bowl and cylindrical vase, are virtually unknown in Puuc Slate Ware. It is true that two other forms, the tripod dish and basin, which are predominant in Puuc Slate, do occur in the Thin Slate form as-semblage, but in a secondary capacity. This ap-pears to me to be a case of the Thin Slate potters copying a Puuc Slate form, rather than the Puuc Slate potters importing the very distinctive tem-pering ingredients to improve the paste of ves-sels they were also turning out by the thousands. It must also be remembered that they would have to impart a smoother finish, use a generally thin-ner wall, in fact turn out a finer product, where-as all the Thin Slate potter would have to copy would be the form. Another point in favor of Thin Slate manufacture of basins is the fact that trickle decoration was not used.

Puuc Red has a mixture of Puuc Slate Ware, Thin Slate Ware, and fine-orange Balancan and Altar Group traits. The Puuc Slate traits are mainly of form: tripod dishes, beveled rim ringstand bowls, and a few basins with rounded or triangular bol-ster. The paste texture may be medium but often gravitates toward the fine, bringing it close to Thin Slate in texture. Other Thin Slate traits are extreme smoothness, lack of blemishes, thinness of wall, and a few important shapes like the hemi-spherical bowl including direct rim with flat or ringstand base, and bead rim tripod, and the cylindrical vase. The traits held in common with

the fine-orange Balancan and Altar groups have nothing to do with paste composition or surface finish but considerable to do with form as wit-ness the Puuc Red hemispherical bowl which closely approximates the Balancan and Altar bowl with rounded sides. In fact a certain num-ber are identical. Another form, the barrel-shape vase was found in both groups. The decorative techniques associated with these fine-orange groups, however, were rarely found on Puuc Red Ware. The exceptions are the moldmade repro-ductions of carved human figures and a single ex-ample of plano-relief.

As for the Cauich Coarse-cream Ware, except for the use of black trickle decoration and pot-sherd temper there is little similarity between it and Puuc Slate Ware. Cauich Coarse-cream has a coarse textured paste, roughish finish, and a good polish as compared to the medium textured paste, smooth finish, and waxy feel of Puuc Slate Ware. Furthermore, the two shapes noted in Cauich Coarse-cream — jars and basins — differ radical-ly from those of Puuc Slate. The jars have high necks, either vertical or outcurving; the basins have large ovoid, medium ovoid, or T-shape rim bol-sters. The temper used in Cauich Coarse-cream is nearly uniformly potsherd, while less than one-third of the Puuc Slate jars and basins have pot-sherd temper. The main differences, therefore, are paste texture, surface finish, and form.

The two principal Cehpech Ceramic Complex wares, Puuc Unslipped and Puuc Slate, appear to have had various centers of manufacture. This is suggested by the variety of shapes and minor variations within shapes, sometimes accompanied by a distinctive temper. This is true of the Puuc Unslipped ladle censer and for a large percentage of the "hourglass" censer with potsherd temper. However, in the Puuc Slate Ware aggregate as found at Uxmal and Kabah (Tables 41 and 42), certain shapes accompanied by certain tempers may dominate but, in view of the small quantities involved, not enough warrant more than a casual investigation until more material is available. Ex-amples of shape-temper predominance are found in the following associations: ringstand bowls with exterior rim bevel and ash temper; tripod flaring-sided dishes and cryptocrystalline calcite temper; basins with rounded rim bolster and ash temper; and basins with triangular rim bolster and pot-sherd temper. Thus our present position concern-ing Puuc Unslipped jars and all Puuc Slate vessels is that they may have been, and probably were, manufactured at a number of different centers upon which the different Puuc sites drew, but with varying degrees of emphasis.

It is interesting to note that each of the five wares included in the Cehpech Ceramic Complex has a different set of decorative techniques and sometimes different styles of design. In this report decorative techniques are the main factor used in establishing types. The decorative techniques associated with Puuc Unslipped Ware are striation, impressing of fillets, flanges, or rim bolsters with thumb or reed, notching of flanges, application of spikes, effigy heads, buttons and overlapping tiles, modeling, and painting with blue and red colors. These techniques are represented in order by the following types: Yokat Striated, Halacho Impressed, Oxkutzcab Appliqué, Yiba Modeled, and Tepakan Composite (equal use of appliqué and impressing). The addition of paint on these vessels has not been considered adequate as a type distinction principally because it is so easily dissipated. As for Puuc Slate Ware, the various associated techniques are painting, usually black including trickle, dabs and scrolls, impressing of flanges, basal moldings and fillets with thumb, reed, or stamp, notching of wall-base angle, gouged-incised, preslip and less frequently postslip incising usually geometric, and modeling. These techniques are represented, respectively, by eight types: Sacalum Black-on-slate and Chumayel Red-on-slate; Akil Impressed; Muna Slate, notched variety; Xaya Gouged-incised; Tekit Incised; Yaxnic Modeled; and Nohcacab Composite (equal use of incising and impressing). Thin Slate includes preslip and postslip incising, vertical grooving, gouging-incising including step-fret and braid bands and darkening of areas. These techniques are represented in order by three types: Xul Incised, Tabi Gouged-incised, and Tikihal Circleshading. Stucco-painting and terracing of ringstands have been included under Ticul Thin-slate Type, normally undecorated. Puuc Red Ware potters decorated their vessels with preslip incising, but besides geometric designs they used the human figure motif, usually incised through a black band and grooving of diamond bands as well as horizontal line grooving. Other Puuc Red techniques are gouging-incising of geometric designs through a white secondary slip, moldmade modeled carving involving human figures, and black painting of geometric designs in both positive and reserve space techniques. These techniques are represented in order by the following types: Becal Incised; Opichen Gouged-incised; Sahcaba Modeled-carved, and Tekax Black-on-red, Tekax Variety and orange variety. A further type is Yaxumha Composite, a combination of incising, impressing, and rarely gouging-incising. Positive black painting is the only technique used on Cauich Coarse-cream Ware and the usual decorations are a broad trickle, rim dabs, or horizontal and vertical striping forming a sort of fencelike motif. This is the Holactun Black-on-cream Type. A rare variety is that with an orange slip.

Next let us consider the influence on the four Cehpech Ceramic Complex slipped wares, described above, by the decorative techniques associated with a fine orange trade ware of the Balancan and Altar groups. Plano-relief, a trait closely associated with the Balancan Group and deriving from Early Classic tradition, is used once on a Puuc Red Ware tripod dish in a stepfret band, and more often on Thin Slate hemispherical bowls. This clearly appears to be a borrowing of ideas rather than a general practice. Another technique used on Balancan vessels and generally not elsewhere is incising which frequently depicts the cursive M, a motif so far not encountered on any other ware with the possible exception of one Puuc region specimen (58, h) of uncertain ware and red-painted interior scalloped rim bands. Altar Group traits are variously distributed: modeled-carving reproduced by a mold, here found on Puuc Red vessels; horizontal and vertical grooving; and a weak, gossamery black paint used to form scalloped bands and horizontal and vertical black striping. A stronger black version of this is found on Puuc Red bowls.

Thus we find that each of the five Cehpech Ceramic Complex wares has its own set of decorative techniques with little borrowing one from the other. We note that the fine-orange Balancan and Altar groups have contributed new ideas in decorative techniques and some vessel forms, such as the rather shallow bowl with rounded sides. But curiously enough these new and distinctive traits seem to have been borrowed exclusively by the Puuc Red and Thin Slate potters, thus establishing an even closer relationship between these two wares than is indicated by similarity of paste texture, surface finish, and form. It is nevertheless presumed, because of the radically different tempering materials used in these two wares, that they were manufactured in separate sites.

Cehpech pottery is abundant at all Puuc sites of which Uxmal and Kabah are representative. It is quite well established at Chichen Itza in levels underlying the Sotuta Ceramic Complex horizon and in small percentages within that ceramic complex. At Mayapan it is present but forms only 1.6

per cent of the total sherds collected. The evidence from many other sites suggests that the Cehpech Ceramic Complex was the most widespread and proliferous of any within the confines of the northern half of the Yucatan Peninsula.

XIV

Sotuta Ceramic Complex

UXMAL [2] — KABAH

At Uxmal and Kabah a very few Sotuta Ceramic Complex sherds were found.

CHICHEN RED WARE

Dishes, rounded sides. Medium-thick walls, direct rim, rounded lip, flat base. Slipped and polished all over. *Types and decoration. Dzibiac Red*

Type: Uxmal, 2 rim, 2 body sherds; Kabah, none.

PLUMBATE WARE

Jar (?). Body fragment. Presumed to belong to the plumbate Tohil Group, but too fragmentary and plain for certain identification. *Tohil Plumbate Type:* Uxmal, none; Kabah, 1 body sherd.

CHICHEN ITZA [2,968]

Chichen Itza, located in north central Yucatan, is one of the most important sites in the peninsula and the only site where any sizable collection of Sotuta Ceramic Complex pottery has been unearthed. Since it also had an extremely long occupancy, we hoped to find there a prolonged stratigraphic sequence. We did not find the sequence, but we did find ceramic types from the Tihosuco through the Tases ceramic complexes. Perhaps the most rewarding discovery was that of five Sotuta deep refuse deposits with 19,217 sherds including 962 unidentifiable fragments and with a small percentage (.02) of earlier and an even smaller percentage (.01) of later material. These earlier and later finds are recorded in Chapter XII, Chapter XV, and Chapter XVI, and in Table 1, *b*. Indeed, out of a total of 25,716 sherds collected from all the nineteen cuts excavated in 1954, only 80 Hocaba and Tases sherds or .003 per cent were found. These late sherds all came from within or close to the surface levels.

The evidence presented by the few late sherds can hardly be construed to suggest an occupation of people taking over from the Sotuta Phase people or Toltecs. Even when we examine the material taken from nine house-type constructions (Ruppert, Shook, Smith, and Smith, 1954, p. 286) and find truly Late Mexican types, and an increase

in the percentage (.177) of all late pottery recovered from above floors, the facts suggest that people were reusing the houses in late times. These people may have been pilgrims who occupied the better-preserved houses during their visits, leaving behind some broken utilitarian pottery as well as censers. That people returned to an abandoned and ruined Chichen Itza to worship is made clear by Morris *et al.* (1931, pp. 179–180) in describing the pottery, mostly of the large effigy-censer variety but including some red ware tripod plates, found "in the vegetable mold just beneath the surface, most plentiful in front of the doorways and strewn down the stairs."

As mentioned above, Chichen Itza contained pottery illustrative of all the Yucatan ceramic complexes from the Ecab through the Tases and it seems likely that, with careful trenching through great plaza platforms and into building construction (which we were not able to do in this brief survey), a worthwhile ceramic sequence could be found. But it was not strictly necessary to find such a sequence in order to solve our immediate and most pressing problem, a better understanding of the pottery pertaining to the Sotuta Ceramic Complex. Brainerd (1958, fig. 71, legend) states, "The sorting of the Medium Slateware at Chichen Itza suffers as does all sorting there, from lack of pure deposits of Florescent date. The Puuc collections were substituted for such a standard in the sorting and non-Puuc-like Medium Slateware assumed to be Early Mexican." We have approached the problem somewhat differently. Instead of worrying about not finding pure deposits of Chichen Itza Cehpech pottery, we felt that at a site where the principal part of the visible architecture was Sotuta Phase, there must exist refuse dumps containing pottery representative of this cultural phase, unencumbered by earlier or later sherds in any quantity.

Nineteen cuts (see Appendix A) or trenches were dug in preparation for this study, but only five are used in this report. Thanks to these five cuts (1, 10, 14, 16, 17) into sizable refuse dumps located in different parts of the site, we were able to amass a large collection of 19,217 sherds descriptive of the ceramic complex of the Sotuta Cultural Phase. These five cuts produced as nearly pure deposits of pottery of that phase as could be sought. The pottery may be separated into three wares: Chichen Unslipped, Chichen Slate, and Chichen Red. Closely associated with this ceramic complex are two important trade groups: namely, fine-orange Silho and plumbate Tohil. Less important, and probably trade wares are six types — at least I shall call them types for the present: Tinum Red-on-cinnamon; Libre Union Red-on-buff which may be a Tinum Red-on-cinnamon variety; Uayma Brown, a heterogeneous lot held together by color and thinness of slip; Cerro Montoso Polychrome; Tunkas Red-on-gray; and Cenotillo Gray-polychrome.

CHICHEN UNSLIPPED WARE [1,217]

Forms, Types, and Varieties	Rim	%	Total Rim & Body
Jars:		25.5	
Piste Striated Type	310		3,699
Sisal Unslipped Type	0		391
Censers, hourglass:		46.5	
Sisal Unslipped Type	361		1,737
Cumtun Composite Type	203		244
Espita Appliqué Type, striated variety	2		7
Censers, tripod:		17.8	
Sisal Unslipped Type	181		324
Espita Appliqué Type	31		101
Cumtun Composite Type	4		27
Censers, ladle:		8.1	
Sisal Unslipped Type	57		104
Tibolon Blue-on-red Type	42		68
Espita Appliqué Type	0		1
Bowls, flaring sides: Sisal Unslipped Type	12	1.0	16
Comals: Sisal Unslipped Type	6		6
Bowls, rounded sides: Sisal Unslipped Type	5		5
Bowls, restricted orifice: Sisal Unslipped Type	3		3
Total	1,217		6,733

Jars (11, a–g, i–m). Usually have medium-wide mouth, low to medium-high outcurving or nearly vertical neck, various rim forms including 155 rim moldings or ovoid rim bolsters (a–c, l), 78 rounded rim bolsters (d), 35 direct rims (f, i, m), 28 medial rim bolsters (e) which constitute a distinct brand, 9 everted rims (k), 4 inner rim grooved (j), 1 square rim bolster (g), rounded pointed, flat or beveled lip, mostly globular body with medium-thick sides, and probably flat base. Size: a–d, f, g, i–m, lip diam. 9–27 cm., av. 19 cm., most common of 48 measured 18 cm. [14] and 20 cm. [11]; neck ht. 2–6.5 cm., av. 4.6 cm., most common of 42 measured 4 cm. [11] and 5 cm. [11]; e, lip diam. 26–28 cm., av. 27.3 cm., only 3 measured; neck ht. 3–4 cm., av. 3.33 cm., only 2 measured. Surface: smoothed but not polished. Very occasionally had white calcareous coat. Color commonly gray (10 YR 7/2, 6/2, 6/1), beige (10 YR 7/4), or cream (10 YR 8/4), and less frequently drab (10 YR 6/3), brown (7.5 YR 5/4), fawn (5 YR 6/4), and buff (7.5 YR 6/2). Paste: coarse texture and usually clear calcite or gray limestone for temper. Color commonly gray (2.5 YR 7/2, 10 YR 4/1, 5/1, 6/1, 7/1, 6/2, 7/2) and less frequently brown (5 YR 4/4, 10 YR 5/4), fawn (5 YR 6/4), cinnamon (7.5 YR 7/4, 2.5 YR 6/8), drab (10 YR 6/3), buff (10 YR 6/4), orange (5 YR 6/6), and red (5 YR 5/6).

Types and decoration. No decoration other than medium-coarse body striations, which may be quite light (*n–p*), medium-deep (*q, s, u*), sometimes spaced (*r, t, v*). *Piste Striated Type:* 310 rim, 3,389 body sherds (933 medium-deep striation; 2,436 quite light striation; 20 spaced striation). *Sisal Unslipped Type:* no certain rim, 391 body sherds. *Remarks:* e is unusual in having a very distinctive rim form, in its distinctive paste composition including a white carbonate temper enjoying a fine lamellar structure, and in its occurrence in middle to upper levels of cuts located only in the southwestern part of the site. Twenty-eight rim sherds of this form were found.

Censers, hourglass (12, *a–e*). Have flaring, medium to thick sides, direct or everted rim, beveled lip, pedestal base, and sometimes flanges (*b, d, e*). *Size:* lip diam. 32–50 cm., av. 41.4 cm., most common of 29 measured 42 cm. [8] and 36 cm. [6]; overall ht. of one specimen was 24.8 cm. with diameter of 46.4 cm. *Surface:* smoothed all over. Some show fire-blackening on interior. Color commonly beige (10 YR 7/4) and cream (7.5 YR 8/4, 10 YR 8/3), less frequently gray, drab, and cinnamon. *Paste:* coarse texture and usually gray limestone temper. Color commonly gray (5 YR 8/1, 7.5 YR 6/0, 10 YR 7/2), less frequently cinnamon (7.5 YR 7/4) and brown (2.5 YR 6/4). *Types and decoration. Sisal Unslipped Type:* 361 rim, 1,376 body sherds. a undecorated example. *Cumtun Composite Type:* 203 rim, 41 body sherds. b, e decorated with scalloped horizontal rim flanges, thumb-impressed fillets, ropelike fillets, and staggered buttons, and c embellished with appliqué figures. These Cumtun examples usually are painted in red, blue, and yellow or any combination of these colors. *Espita Appliqué Type, striated variety:* 2 rim, 5 body sherds (*d*). *Remarks:* some (*d, e*) of the decorated censers have vertical side flanges. d has very light vertical striations on exterior.

Censers, tripod (12, *f, g*) have flaring medium-thick to thick sides rounding (*f*) or sharply angled (*g*) to flat base, bolster or direct rim, beveled lip, vertical strap handles, and three large hollow bulbous feet with circular front vent. *Size:* lip diam. 36–48 cm., av. 45.2 cm., most common of 12 measured 48 cm. [9], ht. of one specimen approximately 25 cm. *Surface:* smoothed all over. Some have calcareous white coat. Many show interior fire-blackening. Color commonly cinnamon (7.5 YR 7/6), less frequently gray, drab, or red. *Paste:* coarse texture and usually gray limestone temper. Color commonly cinnamon (2.5 YR 6/8), less frequently brown (2.5 YR 5/6), gray, or drab. *Types and decoration. Sisal Unslipped Type:* 181 rim, 143 body sherds. g undecorated example. *Espita Appliqué Type:* 31 rim, 70 body sherds. No illustration. Generally exterior adorned with clusters of 9 appliqué buttons in three parallel rows. *Cumtun Composite Type:* 4 rim, 23 body sherds. f shows the entire cluster area painted blue. *Remarks:* some had pedestal base, but none assembled in this collection (GWB, figs. 69, c; 70, a).

Censers, ladle (12, *h, j, k*). Flaring medium-thick sides, direct rim, rounded, pointed, or beveled lip, hollow tubular handle opening into bowl (one example did not and one had appliqué bird), flat base. *Size:* lip diam. 16–21 cm., av. 19 cm., most common of 25 measured 18 cm. [14] and 21 cm. [9]; ht. 5–5.5 cm., av. 5.2 cm., most common of 6 measured 5 cm [4]. *Surface:* smoothed more perfectly on interior than exterior. A few show fire-blackening on interior. Some have white calcareous coat. Most [57] are buff or drab, but a lot [42] are painted red (10 R 4/4) all over. *Paste:* coarse texture and usually gray limestone temper. Color commonly gray (10 YR 7/1, 7/2; 2.5 Y 7/2). *Types and decoration. Sisal Unslipped Type:* 57 rim, 47 body sherds. j undecorated example. *Tibolon Blue-on-red Type:* 42 rim, 26 body sherds. Those painted red all over usually have a blue rim stripe (*k*). *Espita Appliqué Type:* no rims, 1 body sherd. h, a handle with bird (?) adorno. *Remarks:* some of these either plain or painted red may have been simple bowls. A few red vessels had circular vents in the base and these may have served as censer covers (*k*). Brainerd (1958, fig. 70, *f*) shows one with handle.

Bowls, flaring sides (12, *i*). Medium-thick walls, direct rim, rounded lip, flat base. *Size:* approximately the same as ladle censers. *Surface:* well smoothed on interior and exterior. Like ladle censers some have white calcareous coat. The one nearly complete specimen (*i*) was fire-blackened on exterior. *Paste:* coarse texture and usually gray limestone temper. Color cream (10 YR 8/4) or gray (2.5 Y 7/2). *Types and decoration. Sisal Unslipped Type:* 12 rim, 4 body sherds. No decoration observed.

Comals (18, *h*), or griddles. Flaring, thick sides rounding to flat base, thickened, incurved, or scalloped rim, flat or beveled lip. *Size:* one specimen, lip diam. 50 cm., ht. 3 cm. *Surface:* more carefully smoothed on interior than exterior. *Paste:* coarse texture. *Types and decoration. Sisal Unslipped Type:* 6 rim, no body sherds. No decoration observed. *Remarks:* these comals were found in the surface level and might therefore belong to the Tases Ceramic Complex or even later. Their thickness and size (great diameter and low height) excludes them from the ladle censer category. Brainerd (1958, figs. 66, *g*; 97, *k*, *1*, *2*, *5–9*) illustrates several comals from Chichen Itza. I believe they are either of the Tases Phase, perhaps even of more recent manufacture, or were made in Sotuta Phase times and are precursors of the more recent griddle (R. H. Thompson, 1958, p. 109). Actually comals did not come into extensive use in Yucatan until after the conquest.

Bowls, rounded sides (12, *l*). Medium-thick walls, direct rim, rounded lip, flat base. *Size:* lip diam. 9 cm., ht. 2.9 cm. *Surface:* smoothed all over. Some have fire-clouding on exterior. One specimen (*l*) shows deposit of purple paint on floor, probably used as paint pot. Color dark drab. *Paste:* medium-fine texture. Color dark drab. *Types and decoration. Sisal Unslipped Type:* 5 rim, no body sherds. No decoration observed.

Bowls, restricted orifice (12, *m*). Fairly thick walls, direct rim, rounded or pointed lip, base not observed. *Size:* lip diam. 15 cm. and 32 cm. Only two measured. *Surface:* smoothed, sometimes imperfectly. One may have had a white calcareous coat. Color light brown (2.5 YR 6/4). *Paste:* medium-coarse texture. Color red (10 R 5/4). *Types and decoration. Sisal Unslipped Type:* 3 rim, no body sherds. No decoration observed.

Summary. The form is the most important stylistic diagnostic of Chichen Unslipped Ware: jars with medium-high outcurving to vertical neck with generally ovoid to flat rim bolsters; hourglass censers differing in minor details of form and body thickness from those of the Cehpech Ceramic Complex found at Uxmal; ladle censers not easily distinguished from the Chum Unslipped Type save by temper (gray limestone for former and potsherd for latter); tripod censers apparently peculiar to the Sotuta Ceramic Complex. Surface finish plays a definite but less striking part. Gray is the most common surface color for jars and hourglass censers, but the tripod censers are usually cinnamon and ladle censers buff or drab. Paste composition, including the tempering material used (Table 43), is sometimes a most informative factor; although both calcite and limestone prevail, there is a special white carbonate temper with a fine lamellar structure which is associated exclusively with jars with medial bolster, a very special form. Color of paste is commonly gray for jars and ladle censers, but cinnamon prevails for the tripod censers. The methods of decorating the unslipped vessels are three: raking (striating), appliqué (flanges, adornos, fillets, modeled figures), and positive postfire painting (RES, pp. 41, 48–51, 53, 54, respectively). All these methods are used on the Uxmal Cehpech vessels, but differently. The raking is generally lighter, finer, and differently spaced from that used in the Cehpech Ceramic Complex, but generally not as fine as that used later. The Sotuta Ceramic Complex type of spikes, buttons, fillets, and flanges and the manner of their application as found at Chichen Itza differ considerably from either the Puuc-Cehpech or Mayapan-Tases types. In the Sotuta Ceramic Complex, spikes are commonly clustered and painted blue; buttons, lacking in Cehpech, are frequently used in Sotuta and later; Sotuta fillets are often ropelike, and Sotuta flanges may be horizontal and scalloped or vertical and painted. In addition the Sotuta style of effigy censer, a form not used in Cehpech, is not unlike the Tases effigy censer in general vessel form but has thinner walls and a lower pedestal. However, the figures, or more exactly the features, usually of the head, are applied in low relief and painted in blue, red, and yellow. The yellow is a rather startling innovation.

CHICHEN SLATE WARE [1135]

Forms, Types, and Varieties	Rim	%	Total Rim & Body
Dishes, rounded sides:		35.3	
Dzitas Slate Type	320		972
Balantun Black-on-slate Type	81		228
Bowls or basins, restricted, bolster rim:		27.1	
Dzitas Slate Type	101		852
Balantun Black-on-slate Type	155		1,143
Chacmay Incised Type	13		38
Timak Composite Type	1		1
Bowls, restricted, direct rim: Dzitas Slate Type	20		45
Balantun Black-on-slate Type	14		73
Balam Canche Red-on-slate Type	3		3
Chacmay Incised Type	1		1
Bowls, grater:		15.6	
Chacmay Incised Type	156		347
Timak Composite Type, sharp-incised variety	21		37
Jars, small mouth:		16.3	
Dzitas Slate Type	139		2,397
Balantun Black-on-slate Type	6		1,615
Balam Canche Red-on-slate Type	18		107
Jars, wide mouth, tripod: Dzitas Slate Type	11		26
Tekom Gouged-incised Type	2		10
Nenela Modeled Type	0		4
Chacmay Incised Type	0		3
Jars, wide mouth, tripod: Mopila Gadrooned Type	0		2
Jars, wide mouth: Balantun Black-on-slate Type	6		6
Chacmay Incised Type	2		2
Timak Composite Type	1		1
Dishes, tripod, convex base:		4.8	
Dzitas Slate Type	44		148
Balantun Black-on-slate Type	10		36
Censers, ladle: Balam Canche Red-on-slate Type	5	0.4	11
Bowls, cylinder tripod (?): Dzitas Slate Type	3	0.3	7
Covers, disk: Dzitas Slate Type	2	0.2	2
Total	1,135		8,117

Dishes, rounded sides (13, a–g). Medium-thick walls, direct rim, beveled, rounded, or pointed lip, flat or slightly concave base. *Size:* lip diam. 23–32, cm., av. 27.7 cm., most common of 45 measured concentrated from 27–30 cm. [29]; ht. 5–6–5 cm., av. 6.3 cm., most common of 7 measured 6.5 cm. [6]. *Surface:* slipped and polished all over including base. Waxy feel; a few show peeling of slip. Color commonly gray (10 YR 7/1, 7/2), less frequently brown (2.5 YR 4/3), drab (10 YR 6/3), and yellowish cream (10 YR 8/6). *Paste:* medium-fine texture. Color commonly orange (2.5 YR 5/8), red (2.5 YR 4/6), brown (2.5 YR 5/6, 5 YR 5/8), less frequently cinnamon (2.5 YR 6/8), cream (10 YR 8/4), and buff (10 YR 6/4). *Types and decoration. Dzitas Slate Type:* 320 rim, 652 body sherds. *a, b,* undecorated examples. *Balantun Black-on-slate Type:* 81 rim, 147 body

sherds. Mostly black design on interior consisting of wall trickle (d), rim dabs (e, f), and floor spatter (c, d). This spatter may be the result of running together of trickle plus some actual scattering of paint drops over floor surface. Some (b) have lip groove not considered as decoration, more likely functional. *Remarks:* a few (g) have flaring sides rounding to flat base. Brainerd (1958, fig. 74, a, c, d) illustrates a considerable range of form and decoration in this category.

Bowls or basins, restricted (13, h–k; 15, a–j; 16, a, b). A form which for clarity may be divided into 1) those with bolster [270] and 2) those with direct [38] rim.

1) The bolster type (15, a–j; 16, a, b), medium-thick to thick walls, globular body, ovoid (15, a–j), rounded (16, b) rim bolster, or rim molding (16, a), rounded or pointed lip, two strap handles,

and a slightly concave base. *Size*: lip diam. 25–54 cm., av. 34.7 cm., most common of 46 measured 25 cm. [10], 32 cm. [10], 30 cm. [6], 40 cm. [5] and 34 cm. [4]; ht. 26–38 cm., only 2 measured. *Surface*: slipped and polished on interior, exterior, and generally on base, but not under handles. A few like those in figure 15, *h* and most with grooved bolster (15, *i*, *j*) are slipped and polished on exterior and just over lip on interior. Many of bolster rim type have purple veins. Slip color commonly gray (10 YR 8/1, 7/2; 2.5 Y 7/2, 8/0, 8/2) and buff (7.5 YR 6/2; 10 YR 7/3), and less frequently orange (5 YR 6/6), drab (2.5 Y 6/2), and pinkish yellow (10 YR 8/6). *Paste*: medium-fine texture. Color commonly orange (2.5 YR 5/8), brown (2.5 YR 5/6, 5 YR 4/6), pinkish cinnamon (2.5 YR 6/8, 7/6), and less frequently red (2.5 YR 4/8, 4/6), buff (10 YR 6/4), and beige (10 YR 7/4); in some cases the core is black between reddish brown (2.5 YR 5/6); brown (10 YR 5/3) between red (2.5 YR 4/6); and buff (10 YR 6/4) between reddish brown (5 YR 5/6). *Types and decoration. Dzitas Slate Type*: 101 rim, 751 body sherds. No illustration for undecorated. *Balantun Black-on-slate Type*: 155 rim, 988 body sherds. Black vertical stripes (trickle) beginning at or near exterior base running up to and over lip where it broadens out (15, *j*) and then down onto vessel floor. Often these black stripes are accompanied by a black spatter which becomes more pronounced near floor and in general on interior rather than exterior (15, *a–c*). *Chacmay Incised Type*: 13 rim, 25 body sherds. Rim bolsters (15, *i*, *j*) were grooved horizontally; usually two or three grooves per bolster (GWB, fig. 73, *d*, 13–26). *Timak Composite Type*: 1 rim, no body sherds. Rim bolsters were grooved and both interior and exterior had black tricklelike decoration (15, *f*).

2) The direct rim type (13, *h–k*), thin to medium-thick walls, globular or barrel-shape body, direct rim save for one with inset rim (*i*), beveled, rounded, or pointed lip, flat to concave base. *Size*: lip diam. 8–19 cm., av. 17.7 cm., most common of 15 measured is 19 cm. [13]; ht. 14 cm. (8 rim and 54 body sherds of one vessel). *Surface*: slipped and polished all over including base, except *j* which usually has exterior slip only. Slip color gray (5 YR 7/2). *Paste*: medium-fine texture. Color commonly brown (5 YR 4/4, 4/6; 2.5 YR 5/6) or less frequently orange (2.5 YR 5/8). *Types and decoration. Dzitas Slate Type*: 20 rim, 25 body sherds. *j*, *k* undecorated examples. *Balantun Black-on-slate Type*: 14 rim, 59 body sherds. Many (13, *h*, *i*) have black trickle on both interior

and exterior. *Balam Canche Red-on-slate Type*: 3 rim, no body sherds. Streaky red exterior designs including pendent triangle or zig-zag rim band (17, *d*), floral (17, *e*), and disks (17, *f*). *Chacmay Incised Type*: 1 rim, no body sherds. No illustration of horizontal incised line on exterior. *Remarks*: this form with trickle or undecorated was not encountered in the Cehpech Phase collections at either Uxmal or Kabah but did occur in some quantity in the Sotuta Phase deposits at Chichen Itza. Therefore I believe that Brainerd (1958, fig. 73, *a*, 7–14; *c*, 25–33) may be wrong in placing this form in the Cehpech Ceramic Complex. The Balam Canche Red-on-slate Type examples of this form with various designs are illustrated by Brainerd (1958, fig. 75, *k*).

Bowls, grater (13, *m*, *n*). Tripod, medium-thick rounded sides, direct rarely incurved rim, rounded, pointed or beveled lip, slightly convex or flat base, and three hollow oven-shape feet with slit, circular, or rarely no vent. *Size*: lip diam. 18–24 cm., av. 20.1 cm., most common of 28 measured concentrated between 18–22 cm. [27]; ht. 7–7.5 cm., av. 7.1 cm., most common of 5 measured is 7 cm. [4]. *Surface*: slipped and polished all over including feet. Waxy feel. Slip color commonly gray (2.5 Y 7/2, 8/2; 10 YR 8/1), cream (5 YR 9/2), and beige (10 YR 7/4). *Paste*: medium to rather fine texture. Color orange (5 YR 4/8), dark brown (5 YR 4/6), and reddish brown (5 YR 5/8). *Types and decoration. Chacmay Incised Type*: 156 rim, 191 body sherds. No illustration for unpainted. *Timak Composite Type, sharp-incised variety*: 21 rim, 16 body sherds. Black step-fret (*m*) and curvilinear (*n*) design on interior. The floor grids may be crosshatched or quartered and hatched. *Remarks*: it is not certain that all the grids were originally slipped, but some definitely were. Brainerd (1958, fig. 74, *h*, *i*) has illustrated his Early Mexican Medium Slateware (Chichen Slate Ware) grater bowls and shown the different grid types (*ibid.*, fig. 74, *j*, 1–3). Also note Brainerd's discussion of graters in time and space (*ibid.*, fig. 74, legend).

Jars (14, *a–n*, *q*; 17, *a–c*) may be divided into three principal form categories: 1) small mouth, medium-high to high neck, flat base (14, *a–j*; 17, *a–c*), 2) wide mouth, tripod (14, *q*), 3) wide mouth, low thick neck with trickle or grooving (14, *k–n*).

1) Small mouth [163]. Medium-high to high vertical or outcurving neck, medium-thick walls, globular and pear-shape body, direct, slightly everted, or bolster rim which may have triangular, beveled, pointed, or rounded lip, two horizontal strap handles, slightly concave or flat base. *Size*:

lip diam. 9–18 cm., av. 14.4 cm., most common of 53 measured 16 cm. [11], 14 cm. [10], and 12 cm. [7]; neck ht. 3.7–12.5 cm., av. 7.5 cm., most common 7 cm. [13], 10–12 cm., [13], and 4 cm. [10]. *Surface*: slipped and polished on exterior and just over lip on neck interior (14, a–j; 17, a–c) or all over neck interior (17, b). Waxy feel. Slip color commonly gray (5 YR 7/2, 7/1; 5 Y 7/2, 8/1; 2.5 YR 8/0; 10 YR 7/2, 6/1, 6/2, 8/1), less frequently cinnamon (5 YR 7/4, 7.5 YR 7/6), buff (10 YR 7/3), beige (10 YR 7/4), and drab (10 YR 6/3). *Paste*: medium-coarse texture. Color commonly orange (2.5 YR 5/8, 10 R 5/8) and red (2.5 YR 6/8), less frequently brown (2.5 YR 5/6), gray (2.5 YR 8/0), or beige (2.5 Y 7/4) with reddish brown (5 YR 5/8) core. *Types and decoration*. *Dzitas Slate Type*: 139 rim, 2,258 body sherds. Undecorated examples (14, e, g). *Balantun Black-on-slate Type*: 6 rim, 1,609 body sherds. Body embellished with black (sometimes orange, red, or brown) vertical stripes called trickle (14, c, d, i, j) and may have horizontal band of black S's (14, a, h) or dots (14, f) just below neck; neck may have black decoration (14, b). *Balam Canche Red-on-slate Type*: 18 rim, 89 body sherds. Red spiral scroll and disk (17, a). Interior red rim stripe and exterior broad red stripe at body-neck juncture with vertical red body stripes (17, b) or horizontal, red angular scroll band (17, c). The red (2.5 YR 4/6, 10 R 5/6) is quite streaky as if from brush strokes. *Remarks*: 14, a and 59, a represent the same vessel. Brainerd (1958, fig. 71, a, c, 1–5, 19–26) illustrates the high-neck examples of the Dzitas Slate and Balantun Black-on-slate types which he feels confident belong in the Early Mexican Substage, but about others with medium-high neck (*ibid*., fig. 71, b, 11–16, 23–30) he is doubtful. Actually, although the high-neck shape is predominant, the medium-high neck (14, e; 17, a–c) does form part of the Sotuta Ceramic Complex jar tradition. This shape has close relationship in neck and rim to a similar form in the fine-orange Silho Group, formerly X Fine Orange type (Smith, 1957b, fig. 4, b; GWB, fig. 76, a). In form the Balam Canche Red-on-slate Type jars are more like the Dzibiac Red Type than the Dzitas Slate Type.

2) Wide mouth, tripod [13]. Gently outcurving, continuous curve, low to medium-high neck, direct or slightly everted rim, rounded or pointed lip, globular body, thin to medium-thick walls, three hollow bulbous feet. *Size*: lip diam. 9–10 cm., av. 9.4 cm., most common of 7 measured is 9 cm. [4]; overall ht. 15.5 cm. [3]. *Surface*: slipped and polished on exterior including base

and feet and on neck interior. Slip color commonly gray (10 YR 7/2); one with metallic appearance (not plumbate) is brown (7.5 YR 5/4). *Paste*: medium-fine texture. Color commonly orange (2.5 YR 5/8), but may be drab (10 YR 6/3, metallic specimen) or pinkish cinnamon (2.5 YR 6/6). *Types and decoration*. *Dzitas Slate Type*: 11 rim, 15 body sherds. No undecorated examples illustrated and possibly all of this form had decoration of some kind on a small part of body. *Tekom Gouged-incised Type*: 2 rim, 8 body sherds. Five of the bodies have a metallic appearance. Usually gouged-incised, horizontal shoulder band (14, q), in this case a braid. *Nenela Modeled Type*: no rim, 4 body sherds. No illustration. *Chacmay Incised Type*: no rim, 3 body sherds. These have incised concentric triangle shoulder band. *Mopila Gadrooned Type*: no rim, 2 body sherds. Two jar body sherds possibly of this form are gadrooned, apparently done from exterior. *Appendages*: one foot decorated with Greek cross deeply incised on exterior. One body fragment shows evidence of possible tubular spout. *Remarks*: this is a shape commonly associated with the fine-orange Silho Group, formerly X Fine Orange (Smith, 1957b, fig. 1, b, 2; GWB, fig. 77, jj) but in this case more closely with Chichen Red Ware (*ibid*., fig. 85, b, 8, 9, and probably others).

3) Wide mouth, low thick neck with trickle or grooves [9]. Medium-thick to thick walls, globular to pear-shape body, direct rim, flat, rounded or pointed lip, flat or concave base. *Size*: lip diam. 16–27 cm., av. 22.8 cm., most common of 4 measured is 27 cm. [2]; neck ht. 5 cm. *Surface*: slipped and polished on exterior and just over lip on neck interior. Waxy feel. Color commonly gray (2.5 Y 7/2, 10 YR 7/2). *Paste*: medium-coarse texture. Color either orange (2.5 YR 5/8) or pinkish cinnamon (2.5 YR 6/8) with gray (2.5 Y 8/0) core. *Types and decoration*. *Balantun Black-on-slate Type*: 6 rim, no body sherds. Vertical black trickle beginning at lip (14, m) and presumably extending down body. *Chacmay Incised Type, groove-incised variety*: 2 rim, no body sherds. Horizontal grooves (14, k, n) on neck exterior. *Timak Composite Type*: 1 rim, no body sherds. Black trickle on body as well as horizontal neck grooves (14, l). *Remarks*: compare same vessel form shown by Brainerd (1958, fig. 71, d) and see use of black S band (59, i).

Dishes, tripod, convex base (19, a–f). Recurving or outcurving medium-thick sides rounding to base, slightly everted (a, c, e), slight bolster (b, d) or direct (f) rim, flat (a, c), pointed (b, d), or beveled (f) and grooved (e) lip, three hollow bulbous feet with single circular vent. *Size*: lip diam. 22–31 cm., av. 25.4 cm., most common of 24 measured 22–26 cm. [17]; ht. without feet 4.5–6.5 cm., av. 5.8 cm., most common of 9 measured 6.2 cm. and 6.5 cm. [6]; overall ht. 7 and 9.5 cm. for only examples present. *Surface*: slipped and polished all over including base and feet. Waxy feel. Color commonly gray (10 YR 7/1, 7/2, 8/1, 8/2; 7.5 YR 8/0; 5 Y 8/1), less frequently cream (10 YR 8/3). *Paste*: medium texture. Color commonly reddish brown (2.5 YR 5/6; 5 YR 4/6), red (2.5 YR 4/6), and orange (5 YR 6/6; 2.5 YR 5/8), less frequently combinations such as edges drab (2.5 Y 6/2) and core red (2.5 YR 4/6). *Types and decoration*. Dzitas Slate Type: 44 rim, 104 body sherds. *a* is undecorated example. *Balantun Black-on-slate Type*: 10 rim, 26 body sherds. Decoration mostly on interior; usually black trickle lines thick near rim and thinning out as they approach floor (*b–d*); some have trickle plus floor design (*e, f*). *Appendages*: commonly hollow bulbous feet [85], but some of these are close to oven-shape. *Remarks*: Brainerd (1958, fig. 74, *a, b*) illustrates quite a few of this shape.

Censers, ladle, or possibly dishes (17, *g, h*). Outcurving or flaring medium-thick sides rounding to flat base. *g* may be a ladle censer (cf. GWB, fig. 75, *e*). *Size*: lip diam. 24–30 cm., av. 27.3 cm.; approximate ht. 6 cm. *Surface*: slipped and polished all over. Waxy feel. Color cinnamon (7.5 YR 7/4) or beige (10 YR 7/4). *Paste*: medium texture. Color reddish brown (2.5 YR 5/6) or pinkish cinnamon (2.5 YR 6/8). *Types and decoration*. *Balam Canche Red-on-slate Type*: 5 rim, 6 body sherds. Red finger dabs (*g*) or part disks (*h*) as interior rim bands. *g* has red disk on exterior and *h* has red ovoid on interior wall. *Remarks*: Brainerd (1958, fig. 75, *i, 1–4; j, 1, 2*) shows several sections that might be of this shape besides the ladle mentioned (*ibid.*, fig. 75, *e*).

Bowls, cylinder tripod (?) (13, *l*). Nearly vertical medium sides, rim molding, flat lip, convex base with indication of feet. *Size*: lip diam. 13 cm.; ht. without feet 23 cm. *Surface*: slipped and polished on exterior and just over lip on interior. Waxy feel. Slip, upper part buff (7.5 YR 6/2); lower part dark buff (2.5 Y 5/2). *Paste*: medium texture. Color, upper part reddish brown (5 YR 5/6); lower part reddish brown (2.5 YR 5/6). *Types and decoration*. Dzitas Slate Type: 3 rim, 4 body sherds. *l* is only undecorated example. *Remarks*: this is a very doubtful category but the reconstruction as illustrated is plausible. The upper part could and may have belonged to a high-neck jar since it appears to be slipped on exterior and just

over lip on interior. As sometimes occurs with cylindrical bowls, however, a substance might have been deposited in the vessel which removed the slip from all but the interior rim area. The two fragments (base and upper section) seem to belong to the same or a like vessel, having the same slip and paste color and same temper, which is volcanic ash.

Covers, disk (13, *o*), beveled edge. *Size*: lip diam. 12 cm.; thickness .7–1 cm. *Surface*: slipped and polished all over. Waxy feel. The beveled edge may not be slipped, in which case this may be a reused sherd from flat-based dish. Fire-clouded. *Paste*: medium texture. Color reddish brown (5 YR 5/8). *Types and decoration*. Dzitas Slate Type: 2 rim, no body sherds.

Summary. Shape, as in Chichen Unslipped Ware, is the outstanding slate ware diagnostic for this complex. Some dishes with rounded sides are wide and shallow without supports, others are more flaring and round to a slightly convex base supported by hollow bulbous feet. This type foot is typical of the Sotuta Ceramic Complex and is particularly linked with fine-orange Silho Group pyriform vessels. Restricted bowls are distinctive to this complex, especially those with grooved bolsters. In the Yucatan Peninsula the grater bowl appears for the first time in the Sotuta Phase unless certain specimens mentioned by Brainerd (1958, fig. 80, legend) from Xpuhil, Campeche are found to belong to the Cehpech Phase. Jars differ from earlier jar forms in their high, slightly outcurving neck and somewhat everted rim; a few have distinctive, low grooved or corrugated necks, and a small percentage are tripods closely resembling a shape found in the fine-orange Silho Group. Shape-wise most of these jars may be found in the Hocaba Ceramic Complex but with a radical change in ware. The surface finish of Chichen Slate Ware is not easily differentiated from Puuc Slate. Brainerd does differentiate, calling the Chichen Slate opaque and not soapy and the Puuc Slate translucent and soapy. To me they both have a soapy feel, the Chichen Slate perhaps less so, and both appear to be translucent. The difference in translucency depends on paste-slip contrast: Chichen Slate having a nearly uniform reddish paste and Puuc Slate having more variety of paste color with grays and buffs predominating over red and orange. Thus, when paste and slip are nearly alike translucence is less apparent, but when paste and slip show a sharp contrast, as in the Chichen Slate with reddish paste and grayish cream to gray slips, the result is a slightly pinkish tinged slip, a rare occurrence in Puuc Slate. Chichen Slate like Puuc Slate paste is of medium texture but differs in color as mentioned above and even more in temper; the former sherds have a nearly uniform volcanic ash temper and the latter a wide variety of calcites and volcanic ash. The ceramic complex of a slate sherd having red paste, volcanic ash temper, and no distinguishing decorative features can only be recognized by its shape. This brings us to the methods of decoration and styles of design used on Chichen Slate Ware.

Painting is the most common and is usually in the form of black (rarely orange, red, or brown) trickle. Other designs in black include semidisks, a series of hooks, step-frets, U's, S's, and floor scrolls. Restricted bowls besides having trickle sometimes are black spattered. Red painting, not trickle, is moderately used. This is the Balam Canche Red-on-slate Type characterized by streaky brush (?) strokes. Incising is rarely used, but rim grooving is employed for both jars and restricted bowls.

CHICHEN RED WARE [553]

Forms, Types, and Varieties	Rim	%	Total Rim & Body
Dishes, rounded sides:		72.2	
Dzibiac Red Type	381		1,133
Chan Kom Black-on-red Type	14		32
Xuku Incised Type, Xuku Variety	1		2
Xuku Incised Type, cream-slip variety	2		5
Holtun Gouged-incised Type	1		1
Jars, small mouth, high neck:		11.0	
Dzibiac Red Type	54		876
Chan Kom Black-on-red Type, Chan Kom Variety	0		27
Chan Kom Black-on-red Type, cream-slip variety	0		1
Xuku Incised Type, Xuku Variety	0		6
Xuku Incised Type, groove-incised variety	1		5
Xuku Incised Type, cream-slip variety	0		14
Holtun Gouged-incised Type, Holtun Variety	0		13
Holtun Gouged-incised Type, cream-slip variety	0		1
Tiholop Gadrooned Type	0		3
Jars, wide mouth, low neck: Dzibiac Red Type	6		231
Bowls, restricted, direct rim:		5.8	
Dzibiac Red Type	31		87
Xuku Incised Type, Xuku Variety	1		1
Xuku Incised Type, cream-slip variety	0		1
Bowls, grater:		3.4	
Xuku Incised Type	13		21
Xuku Incised Type, black-paint variety	6		10
Dishes, tripod:		3.4	
Dzibiac Red Type	8		67
Chan Kom Black-on-red Type	4		4
Xuku Incised Type, cream-slip variety	3		5
Holtun Gouged-incised Type, Holtun Variety	1		1
Holtun Gouged-incised Type, cream-slip variety	3		9
Vases, cylindrical:		1.6	
Dzibiac Red Type	8		18
Xuku Incised Type, groove-incised variety	1		2
Dishes, flaring sides:		1.4	
Dzibiac Red Type	5		8
Xuku Incised Type	2		2
Holtun Gouged-incised Type, cream-slip variety	1		1
Vases, pyriform:		1.1	
Dzibiac Red Type	6		12
Holtun Gouged-incised Type, cream-slip variety	0		1
Holtun Gouged-incised Type, Holtun Variety	0		1
Total	553	99.9	2,601

Dishes, rounded sides (21, *g, h, n–r, w, x, hh, ii, kk*). Medium-thick walls, direct or everted (*x*) rim, rounded, pointed, or beveled lip, flat or concave base. Vessels may have walls of even thickness, taper from thickish at base to thin at lip, or be thickish at lip and taper to thin base. *Size*: lip diam. 16–38 cm., av. 27.8 cm., most common of 70 measured 27 cm. [27], 32 cm. [13], 28 cm. [12]; ht. 5–9 cm., av. 6.2 cm., most common of 37 measured 5–7 cm. [34]. *Surface*: well smoothed before slipping and polishing all over. Slight waxy feel. Some fire-clouding on both interior and exterior of many sherds. Some have gray bases and floors as the result of firing in a reducing atmosphere. Color red (10 R 4/6, 4/8, 5/6). *Paste*: medium texture. Color commonly orange (2.5 YR 5/8), less frequently red (2.5 YR 4/8). *Types and decoration. Dzibiac Red Type*: 381 rim, 752 body sherds. Usually undecorated (*h, n–p*; 59, *k*). *Chan Kom Black-on-red Type*: 14 rim, 18 body sherds. A few have black painted vertical lines (trickle) on the interior (*q, r*). *Xuku Incised Type, Xuku Variety*: 1 rim, 1 body sherd. Preslip incised angular scroll on exterior (*x*). *Xuku Incised Type, cream-slip variety*: 2 rim, 3 body sherds. Postslip incised design through cream (*w*; cf. fig. 59, *p*). *Holtun Gouged-incised Type*: 1 rim, no body sherds (no illustration). *Remarks*: scratching or doodling is present on the exterior wall in the form of a kan cross (*p*) or on floor of bases in various designs (*hh, ii, kk*). Brainerd (1958, pp. 55–56) discusses this ware and illustrates a few examples of this form (*ibid.*, fig. 88, *a, 10–13*). See our photographs of an undecorated (59, *k*) and a decorated example (59, *p*).

Jars (20, *a–e, g–q*) may be separated into two categories: 1) small mouth (*a–d, g–o, q*), 2) wide mouth (*e, p*).

1) Small mouth, medium-high vertical, outcurving or flaring neck, direct or slightly everted rim, rounded, flat or beveled lip, pear-shape or globular body, concave or flat base. *Size*: lip diam. 8–12 cm., av. 9.7 cm., most common of 21 measured 9 cm. [9], 10 cm. [7]; neck ht. 3.5–5.5 cm., av. 4.6 cm., most common 4.5 cm. *Surface*: well smoothed. Slipped and polished on exterior and neck interior save for some with slip only part way down the neck interior. Slight waxy feel. Color commonly red (10 R 4/6, 4/8; 2.5 YR 4/6), less frequently reddish brown (2.5 YR 5/6). *Paste*: medium texture. Color commonly orange (2.5 YR 5/8), less frequently brown (2.5 YR 5/6, 5 YR 4/4). *Types and decoration. Dzibiac Red Type*: 54 rim, 822 body sherds. Usually undecorated. (*a–d, j, p*). *Chan Kom Black-on-red Type, Chan*

Kom Variety: no rim, 27 body sherds. Some (*h*) have black-painted dots, circles, and crescents. *Chan Kom Black-on-red Type, cream-slip variety*: no rim, 1 body sherd. Black-on-cream band over red slip with geometric design (*i*). *Xuku Incised Type, groove-incised variety*: 1 rim, 4 body sherds. Horizontally grooved neck (*g*). *Xuku Incised Type, Xuku Variety*; no rim, 6 body sherds. Postslip, prepolish design (*n*); preslip deeply incised horizontal and vertical lines (*o*). *Xuku Incised Type, cream-slip variety*: no rim, 14 body sherds. Incised through cream band (*m, q*). *Holtun Gouged-incised Type, Holtun Variety*: no rim, 13 body sherds. Preslip gouged-incised floral (?) design (*l*). *Holtun Gouged-incised Type, cream-slip variety*: no rim, 1 body sherd. Preslip gouged-incised through cream band (*k*). *Tiholop Gadrooned Type*: no rim, 3 body sherds. No illustration. *Remarks*: one (*j*) otherwise undecorated has scratching or doodling on shoulder. Brainerd (1958, fig. 85) illustrates a number of jar forms and a greater variety and more complete designs which include many typical of the fine-orange Silho Group style. He also shows a gadrooned specimen (*ibid.*, fig. 85, *b, 6*), whose melon shape was attained by pushing out the wall.

2) Wide mouth, low flaring neck, direct rim, rounded lip, globular body, medium-thick walls, horizontal strap handles, probably flat base, but one (*p*) has three hollow bulbous feet. The tripod is reminiscent of a Chichen Slate specimen (14, *q*). *Size*: lip diam. 26 cm.; neck ht. 1.2 cm. *Surface*: slipped and polished all over. Color red (2.5 YR 4/6). *Paste*: medium texture. Color orange (2.5 YR 5/8) edges, dark gray core. *Types and decoration. Dzibiac Red Type*: 6 rim, 225 body sherds. Undecorated example (*e*).

Bowls, restricted (21, *a–f*). Square rim bolster (*a*) or direct (*c–f*) rim, beveled (*a*), pointed (*c–e*), or rounded (*f*) lip, pear-shape (*a, b*) or globular (*c–f*) body, medium-thick walls, vertical strap handles (*f*), flat (*d*) or slightly concave (*e, f*) base. *Size*: *a–e*, lip diam. 5–10 cm., av. 7 cm., *f*, lip diam. 18 cm., base diam. 7 cm., max. diam. 21 cm., ht. 13.5 cm. *Surface*: slipped and polished on exterior and just over lip (*a*), all over (*b, f*), exterior only (*c–e*); *f*, fire-clouded quite evenly around exterior rim and down deep on interior but not on base or floor. Waxy feel present but not as pronounced as usual, nor is surface as well smoothed. Color red (*a, b*, 2.5 YR 4/6; *c*, 2.5 YR 4/8; *d*, 10 R 4/6; *e*, weathered) and reddish brown (*f*, 2.5 YR 5/6). *Paste*: medium texture. Color reddish brown (*a*), orange (*c*, 2.5 YR 5/8), and pinkish cinnamon (*f*, 2.5 YR 6/8). *Types and decoration. Dzibiac Red*

Type: 31 rim, 56 body sherds. Several undecorated examples (*c–f*). *Xuku Incised Type, groove-incised variety*: 1 rim, no body sherds. *a* has horizontal grooving. *Xuku Incised Type, cream-slip variety*: no rim, 1 body sherd. The single example illustrated (*b*) has an incised through cream geometric band on upper body. *Remarks*: Brainerd, (1958, fig. 86) virtually our only source of comparison for these types, illustrates a form apparently not present in our sample, although *b* may be a possible exception. This form he calls a churn shape (*ibid.*, fig. 86, *a–c*) with stepped basal flange or skirt, most reminiscent of a shape found at Mayapan (43, *i*; Shook and Irving, 1955, fig. 7, *a*) belonging to the Tases Ceramic Complex and with different foot form and style of design. Brainerd's examples have hollow bulbous feet and a design style typical of fine-orange Silho, a group whose traits so often seem to have been copied by the Sotuta Phase potters. Brainerd (1958, fig. 86, *h*, 2–5, 8–10) does, however, depict some of the forms shown here (*c–e*). This leaves *a* and *f* without representation in Brainerd's collection.

Bowls, grater (21, *j–m*). Tripod, medium-thick rounded sides, slightly restricted orifice, direct rim, rounded lip, convex base, three hollow bulbous (*j*) or Turkish slipper (*m*) feet usually with a slit vent. *Size*: lip diam. 16–22 cm., av. 19.4 cm., most common of 10 measured 20 cm. [7]; ht. without feet 3.5–6.5 cm., av. 5.4 cm., most common of 5 measured 5 cm. [2]; ht. with feet 8–8.5 cm., av. 8.3 cm. *Surface*: slipped and polished all over. In some cases slip seems to have worn off over the grid area. Waxy feel. Color red (2.5 YR 4/8, 10 R 5/6). *Paste*: medium to fine texture. Color orange (2.5 YR 5/8), reddish brown (2.5 YR 5/6), or reddish brown (2.5 YR 5/6) edges with gray (10 YR 6/2) core. *Types and decoration. Xuku Incised Type*: 13 rim, 8 body sherds. Undecorated examples (*j*, *m*). *Xuku Incised Type, black-paint variety*: 6 rim, 4 body sherds. A few have black trickle on interior (*k*, *l*). The grid patterns are the same as those found on Dzitas Slate graters. *Remarks*: Brainerd does not record this form in Early Mexican Redware (Chichen Red Ware).

Dishes, tripod (21, *y–gg*). Flaring or outcurving medium-thick sides, direct (*y–bb*) and everted (*cc–gg*) rim, rounded, pointed, or beveled lip, flat or rarely convex base, and three hollow bulbous feet with diagonal slit vent, or questionably hollow cylindrical feet with flat (*ee*) or rounded (*dd*) bottom (may belong with Cehpech material), and very rarely hollow bell-shaped feet. The bulbous and bell-shaped feet are not illustrated because

the sherds were very fragmentary and only suggested these shapes. *Size*: lip diam. 21–26 cm., av. 22.7 cm., most common of 4 measured 21 cm. [2]; ht. without feet 4.5–5 cm., av. 4.6 cm. *Surface*: slipped and polished all over, save for some (*y–bb*) not slipped on base. Waxy feel. Color red (10 R 4/8, 5/6; 2.5 YR 4/6, 4/8), reddish brown (2.5 YR 5/6, 6/6; 5 YR 5/6), and orange (2.5 YR 5/8). *Paste*: medium to fine texture. Color red (2.5 YR 4/6), orange (2.5 YR 5/8), and pinkish cinnamon (2.5 YR 6/8). *Types and decoration. Dzibiac Red Type*: 8 rim, 59 body sherds. Undecorated example (*y*). *Chan Kom Black-on-Red Type*: 4 rim, no body sherds. Black interior trickle (*z*). *Xuku Incised Type, cream-slip variety*: 3 rim, 2 body sherds. Cream-slipped exteriors may have post-slip step-fret band (*cc*; cf. 59, *o*) or preslip incised curvilinear band (*gg*). *Holtun Gouged-incised Type, Holtun Variety*: 1 rim, no body sherds. No illustration. *Holtun Gouged-incised Type, cream-slip variety*: 3 rim, 6 body sherds. A number (*aa*, *bb*, *ff*, *gg*) have cream (10 YR 7/4, 8/2, 8/4, 8/6; 2.5 Y 9/4) on exterior wall. These usually have a preslip gouged-incised braid band (*aa*) or other gouged-incised designs (*bb*, *ff*; 59, *l–n*). *Remarks*: Brainerd (1958, figs. 86, *j*; 87, *a–s*) illustrates a greater number of these tripods showing a greater variety of design, including many typical of the fine-orange Silho style. He also points out the rare use of black paint on Red Dzibiac Group vessels (*ibid.*, fig. 87, legend).

Vases, cylindrical (21, *i*). Medium-thick sides, direct rim or rim molding, flat, rounded, or pointed lip, flat or pedestal (?) base. *Size*: lip diam. 8–10 cm., av. 8.7 cm. *Surface*: slipped and polished on exterior and just over lip on interior. Color red (2.5 YR 4/8, 10 R 4/6). *Paste*: medium to fine texture. Color red (2.5 YR 4/8), pinkish cinnamon (2.5 YR 6/8). *Types and decoration. Dzibiac Red Type*: 8 rim, 10 body sherds. *Xuku Incised Type, groove-incised variety*: 1 rim, 1 body sherd (21, *i*). *Remarks*: Brainerd (1958, p. 258, fig. 86) says "*f–h* demonstrate the range through bulbous to cylindric vessels which characterizes these forms." An example taken from Brainerd (fig. 86, *g*, 8) is a Holtun Gouged-incised Type vase or deep bowl (59, *q*).

Dishes, flaring sides (21, *s–v*). Flaring medium-thick sides rounding to flat or concave base, direct rim (*s*, *t*, *v*) or rim molding (*u*), rounded or pointed lip. *Size*: lip diam. 16–34 cm., av. 23.3 cm., only 3 measured, mostly fragmentary, ht. of 1 specimen, 7 cm. (lip diam. 34 cm.). *Surface*: slipped and polished on interior and exterior, often with added cream band on exterior. Red waxy but cream not. Color commonly red (10 R 4/6, 4/8, 5/6; 2.5 YR 4/8), less frequently orange (2.5 YR 5/8) and reddish brown (2.5 YR 5/6). *Paste:* medium to fine texture. Color pinkish cinnamon (2.5 YR 6/8), brown (2.5 YR 5/6, 5 YR 4/6), orange (2.5 YR 5/8), and edges orange (2.5 YR 5/8) with drab (10 YR 6/3) core. *Types and decoration. Dzibiac Red Type:* 5 rim, 3 body sherds. Undecorated examples (*t, u*). *Xuku Incised Type:* 2 rim, no body sherds. Preslip incised design on exterior (*v*). *Holtun Gouged-incised Type, cream-slip variety:* 1 rim, no body sherds. Gouged-incised scroll and related elements (*s*) through cream band. *Remarks:* this form is hard to differentiate from rounded-side dishes or tripod dishes when the sherds are very fragmentary. It does not have a basal break and the sides are flaring rather than rounded. Possibly this form should have been included with dishes with rounded sides. A possible censer handle (18, *e*), similar to Balam Canche Red-on-slate censer (GWB., fig. 75 *e*), may belong with this general form group. *Xuku Incised Type, cream-slip variety* is present at Chichen Itza (59, *o, p*; GWB., figs. 86, *j, 5; 87, aa*).

Pyriform vases (20, *f, r–u*). Tapering neck, rim molding, flat lip, pear-shape body, medium-thick walls, probably three hollow bulbous feet. *Size:* lip diam. 9–10 cm., av. 9.2 cm., ht. without feet ca. 16 cm. for 1 specimen. *Surface:* slipped and polished on exterior including base and feet and partway down neck interior. Color red (10 R 4/8, 2.5 YR 4/6) or reddish brown (2.5 YR 5/6). *Paste:* medium to fine texture. Color orange (2.5 YR 5/8) or brown (10 YR 5/3). *Types and decoration. Dzibiac Red Type:* 6 rim, 6 body sherds. Undecorated examples (*r–t*). *Holtun Gouged-incised Type.* cream-slip variety: no rim, 1 body sherd. *f* is the one decorated specimen that surely belongs to this form. This has a gray-slipped sunken circular band with gouged-incised design made up of simple and "ram horn" scrolls and other elements. *Holtun Gouged-incised Type, Holtun Variety:* no rim, 1 body sherd. *u* probably belongs to pyri-

form vase and has gouged-incised braid band. *Remarks:* Brainerd (1958, figs. 85, *b, 9; 86, d, e*) illustrates some excellent examples of the tripod pyriform, especially in his figure 86, *d* and *e*.

Summary. Shape, as in the Chichen Unslipped and Chichen Slate wares, is the outstanding diagnostic in Chichen Red ware for this complex. Similar to Chichen Slate, Chichen Red Ware has medium-high to high-neck jars, dishes with rounded sides, restricted-orifice bowls, graters, tripod dishes and, in addition, dishes with flaring sides, and pyriform vessels. Chichen Red like Chichen Slate has a waxy feel and is well smoothed. The decoration closely resembles that of Chichen Slate save that black trickle is rarely used and only on bowls or dishes rather than jars, basins, and restricted bowls as in Chichen Slate. Gouging-incising as well as preslip and postslip incising are used, and many of the designs are typical of those associated with the fine-orange Silho Group. Brainerd (1958, p. 56) says,

This ware is certainly grounded in Florescent tradition, the Thin Redware of the Puuc sites. Slip and paste of the two wares show marked similarity. However, the style of shape and decoration of Mexican Medium Redware shows more influence from X Fine Orange ware than does the style of Mexican Medium Slate (see figs. 85–88 and captions). Forms seem to be X Fine Orange copies, save perhaps for fig. 86, *a–c*, as does the decoration, save perhaps for fig. 85, *a*, although there are various suggestions throughout of influence of the local tradition in shape and design. This strong influence of the Mexican mainland imported fine wares is not surprising; this ware, like its Florescent predecessor, was fabricated into medium-sized and small vessels, many of which are decorated and which must have had a restricted "upper class" use. The "upper class" people of this period were culturally oriented toward the Mexican mainland.

This statement agrees with my observation except for the reference to the mainland, because I believe northwestern Campeche to be the center from which the fine-orange Silho Group originates.

FINE ORANGE WARE [37]

Forms, Types, and Varieties	Rim	%	Rim & Body
Fine-orange Silho Group		58.7	
Jars, standard form, flat base: Silho Orange Type	3		50
Yalton Black-on-orange Type	2		23
Cumpich Incised Type	4		21
Calkini Gadrooned Type	0		4
continuous curve, tripod: Kilikan Composite Type	3		40
Bowls, hemispherical: Silho Orange Type	10		13
Yalton Black-on-orange Type	1		1
Dishes, tripod: Yalton Black-on-orange Type, Yalton Variety	2		5
Yalton Black-on-orange Type, cream-slip variety	1		1
Cumpich Incised Type, black-paint variety	1		1
Pocboc Gouged-incised Type	1		1
Kilikan Composite Type, cream-slip variety	2		8
Vases, pyriform: Silho Orange Type	0		9
Yalton Black-on-orange Type	4		50
Pocboc Gouged-incised Type	0		6
Kilikan Composite Type	0		2
Bowls, restricted: Silho Orange Type	1		1
Yalton Black-on-orange Type	2		2
Total	37		238

Fine-orange Silho Group (22 and 59, b–h). Includes jars, hemispherical bowls, tripod dishes, pyriform vessels, restricted bowls, and some miscellaneous sherds.

Jars (22, a–f) are of two principal forms: 1) a–d, f, the standard and most common form which has a sharp neck-shoulder junction and concave base (see also 59, b, c), and 2) e, the continuous-curve jar with relatively low neck and probably three hollow bulbous feet. Naturally the body sherds of these two globular forms as well as the body sherds of the more globular pyriform vessels and restricted bowls are hard to differentiate. The estimated total jar body count is 126.

1) a–d, f [9], small (a–d) or relatively wide (f) mouth, low vertical (a), medium-high outcurving (c) or vertical (d, f) neck, direct rim, flat (a, f) or rounded (c, d) lip, globular body, medium-thick sides thickening at base-side junction, concave base. *Size:* lip diam. 10–12 cm., av. 11 cm., most common of 4 measured 11 [2]; neck ht. 2.5–4 cm., av. 3.5 cm., most common of 4 measured 3.7 cm. [2]. *Surface:* slipped and lightly burnished on exterior including base and feet and on neck interior. One specimen (a) has an iridescent or metallic appearance. Color orange (2.5 YR 5/8), reddish brown (2.5 YR 5/6, 5 YR 4/3), red (2.5 YR 4/6), and brown (2.5 YR 5/4). *Paste:* fine texture. All examined were untempered. Color orange (5 YR 6/6, 6/8), pinkish cinnamon (2.5 YR 6/8), and cinnamon (7.5 YR 7/4). *Types and decoration. Silho Orange*

Type: 3 rim, 47 body sherds. Undecorated examples illustrated (c, d). *Yalton Black-on-orange Type:* 2 rim, 21 body sherds. These have black curvilinear (b; 59, c) designs often representing the serpent or black geometric patterns (f; 59, b). *Cumpich Incised Type:* 4 rim, 17 body sherds. Horizontal grooving of body (a). *Calkini Gadrooned Type:* no rim, 4 body sherds. The gadrooning is worked from exterior and is vertically placed on body (no illustration but compare Smith, 1957b, fig. 13, b). *Remarks:* this form is well illustrated by Brainerd (1958, fig. 76, a–e) who says, "decoration in black painted designs alone." Smith (1957b, fig. 4, a–d) shows four jar forms presumably belonging to the fine-orange Silho Group. Two (a, d) are grooved horizontally and two (b, c) have black-painted design.

2) e [3], low vertical neck forming continuous curve with body, direct rim, flat lip, globular body, medium-thick walls, three hollow bulbous feet. *Size:* lip diam. 7.4 cm.; neck ht. 3 cm.; max. diam. 22.5 cm., overall ht. 22 cm. *Surface:* slipped and burnished on exterior and just over lip on neck interior. Color orange (2.5 YR 5/8). *Paste:* fine texture. Untempered. Color pinkish cinnamon (2.5 YR 6/8). *Types and decoration. Kilikan Composite Type:* 3 rim, 37 body sherds. Black-painted horizontal stripes and snout design and a gouged-incised scroll meander band. *Remarks:* Brainerd (1958, fig. 76, f–t) portrays a number of vessels of this shape but does not suggest that generally

they are tripods. Smith (1957b, fig. 5, *d*) illustrates one of this form with horizontal and vertical grooving; some of the more globular pyriforms (*ibid.*, fig. 6) might also be considered as belonging to this form group.

Bowls, hemispherical (22, *o–q*; 59, *d, e*) rounded thin to medium-thick sides, direct rim (*q* has molding), pointed, rounded, or flat lip, flat base. *Size*: lip diam. 13–20 cm., av. 17.2 cm., most common of 10 measured 17 cm. [7]; ht. 6.7 cm. (1 example). *Surface*: slipped and burnished all over. Most are all over gray (5 YR 7/1, 2.5 Y 8/0) save rim area on interior and exterior which remains orange. Color orange (2.5 YR 5/8), pinkish cinnamon (2.5 YR 6/8), red (2.5 YR 4/8), or brown (7.5 YR 5/4, 5/6, 5/8). *Paste*: fine texture. Those tested were untempered. Color orange (5 YR 6/6), cinnamon (7.5 YR 7/6), pinkish cinnamon (2.5 YR 6/6), and buff (10 YR 6/4). *Types and decoration. Silho Orange Type*: 10 rim, 3 body sherds. Usually have gray fire-clouded bodies (*o*; 59, *d*) leaving an orange rim band. A few (*p, q*; 59, *e*) are without fire-clouding. *Yalton Black-on-orange Type*: 1 rim, no body sherds. Extremely rare (no illustration). *Remarks*: Brainerd (1958, fig. 79, legend) says "a; b; c: Belong to a sharply marked type which never shows painted or incised decoration. Shape and color variation on surface (orange rim and smudged gray body) are distinctive. . . ." This variation in color seems to me to indicate a fully oxidized orange rim and an unoxidized gray lower section. In both areas the same color is found clear through the vessel wall. In other words, the gray is not just a surface phenomenon.

Dishes, tripod (22, *r–v*), outcurving medium-thick sides, direct (*r, s, v*) or everted (*t, u*) rim, flat lip, convex base, three hollow bell-shaped feet with single rectangular side vent or hollow bulbous feet (*v*). *Surface*: slipped and lightly burnished all over including base and feet. The cream slip when present is well polished and on exterior. Color orange (2.5 YR 5/8), pinkish cinnamon (2.5 YR 6/8), reddish brown (2.5 YR 5/6). *Paste*: fine texture. Those tested were untempered. Color orange (5 YR 6/6), pinkish cinnamon (2.5 YR 6/8). *Types and decoration. Yalton Black-on-orange Type, Yalton Variety*: 2 rim, 3 body sherds. These include black-painted designs on orange slip, such as terrace (?) and U (*t*), "handbells," dots and hook (*u*), and a band of steps, hooks, and associated elements (59, *f*). *Yalton Black-on-orange Type, cream-slip variety*: 1 rim, no body sherds. Scroll and related elements on cream slip (*s*). *Cumpich Incised Type, black-paint variety*: 1

rim, no body sherds. Exterior decorated with a band of black birds (*v*), interior floor probably crosshatched for grating. *Pocboc Gouged Incised Type*: 1 rim, no body sherds (cf. 59, *q*). *Kilikan Composite Type, cream-slip variety*: 2 rim, 6 body sherds. Exterior has gouged-incised scroll meander band through cream, and interior has black-painted decoration (cf. 59, *h*, and GWB, fig. 81, *i*). *Remarks*: actually *v* may be a grater bowl. Brainerd (1958, fig. 80, *l–p*) illustrates a near duplicate (*l*) which is a grater bowl and says "The grater bowl bottoms shown here, *l*; *n*; *o*; *p*, originally suggested that this feature had been introduced with X Fine Orangeware, presumably from the Vera Cruz littoral. The likelihood that the grater bowl existed earlier in this area has been mentioned elsewhere (fig. 74, caption)." It must be noted, however, that the shape of this grater bowl differs radically from the normal Sotuta Ceramic Complex form (13, *m, n*) which usually has a slightly incurved rim. The more common tripod dish or plate (*r–u*) with outcurving sides, flat or slightly convex base, and bell-shaped feet is amply illustrated by Brainerd (1958, fig. 81, *a–x*) as to form, decorative techniques, and design motifs (see also 59, *f–h*).

Pyriform vases (22, *g–k*), tripod, usually rim molding (*g*) or rim grooves, flat or pointed lip, pear-shape body, flat or convex base with hollow bulbous feet. *Size*: lip diam. 4.8–11 cm., av. 8.6 cm., most common of 4 measured 11 cm. [2]; ht. without feet of *g*, a small specimen, 10.8 cm. *Surface*: slipped and lightly burnished on exterior only, including base and feet. Color commonly reddish brown (2.5 YR 5/6) and orange (2.5 YR 5/8), less frequently red (2.5 YR 4/8) and pinkish cinnamon (2.5 YR 6/8). *Paste*: fine texture. Presumably untempered. Color commonly pinkish cinnamon (2.5 YR 6/8), less frequently brown (5 YR 4/4) and orange (5 YR 6/6). *Types and decoration. Silho Orange Type*: no rim, 9 body sherds. No illustration but compare examples illustrated by Smith (1957b, figs. 6, *n*; 13, *c*; 15, *a*). *Yalton Black-on-orange Type*: 4 rim, 46 body sherds. Black-painted terrace and U central band framed by horizontal black lines and lowermost band of black U's (*g*) or black banding including U's (*h*). *Pocboc Gouged-incised Type*: no rim, 6 body sherds. Gouged-incised banding including ovoid and circles (*i*). *Kilikan Composite Type*: no rim, 2 body sherds. Both body sherds (*j, k*) are illustrated, showing the combination of black design banding and gouged-incised banding on the same vessel. A common practice is combining the black bird band and the gouged-incised scroll meander band (*k*; Smith, 1957b, figs. 10, *m*; 11, *a*, *c–j*; GWB, fig. 77, *x*, *z*). The floral motif (*j*), usually gouged-incised, is also commonly used in bands on this form (Smith, 1957b, figs. 9, *m*; 10, *a*, *b*, *d*, *l*; 11, *q–s*; GWB, fig. 77, *f*, *i*, *m*). *Remarks:* the black is normally a strong black. The pyriform with its seven-shape variations (Smith, 1957b, pp. 136, 137) is certainly one of the most characteristic fine-orange Silho Group forms, but is not well represented in this collection. *e*, placed here with the jars, is my number 2 form in the list of seven variations.

Bowls, restricted (22, *l–n*) orifice, globular or pear-shaped body, thin to medium-thick walls, direct (*l*), flat bolster (*m*), or bead (*n*) rim, rounded, flat, or pointed lip; bases may be flat, convex, and may have pedestal or three hollow bulbous feet. *Size:* lip diam. 11–13 cm., av. 11.7 cm. *Surface:* slipped and lightly burnished on exterior only. Color reddish brown (2.5 YR 5/6, 5 YR 5/6). *Paste:* fine texture. Those examined were untempered. Color orange (5 YR 6/8) or cinnamon (7.5 YR 7/4). *Types and decoration. Silho Orange Type:* 1 rim, no body sherds. Illustrated example (*m*). *Yalton Black-on-orange Type:* 2 rim, no body sherds. One example (*l*) has black circle and dot design. *n*, a specimen from Tecolpan, Chiapas, was found by Heinrich Berlin. This might be a fine-orange Balancan Group specimen because of the figure-painted motif, but the shape is more like the fine-orange Silho Group form here shown. *Remarks:* this form is not too common but Smith (1957b, fig. 5, *a–c*) shows a few with a variety of decoration and form, and Brainerd (1958, fig. 80, *z–gg*) also illustrates a direct rim, globular type with a considerable range of design.

Summary. The fine-orange Silho Group is associated with the Sotuta Ceramic Complex but is definitely an import insofar as Yucatan is concerned. Smith (1958b, p. 154) suggests "On the basis of frequency of occurrence it would appear that X Fine Orange was probably made some-

where along the coast of Campeche." Brainerd (1958, p. 57) says,

The Chichen Itza collection of this ware is the largest in existence (1,053 sherds and 11 whole vessels), unless the scattered collections from Isla de Sacrificios, Veracruz, be considered as one. The predominant types from Isla de Sacrificios are not found at Chichen Itza, and the types of the Chichen Itza collections are not found predominant among the decorated wares of any other site. On the other hand, there is no doubt that the Fine Orangeware of the Early Mexican subphase at Chichen Itza was not made in Yucatan, and little doubt that it was made somewhere in coastal Veracruz or in Tabasco.

The subject under discussion here, however, is Silho as a fine-orange group and not fine orange as a ware. Isla de Sacrificios, it is true, was the repository for very large collections of fine orange but actually harbored a relatively small quantity of the fine-orange Silho Group as it is recognized today, whereas the fine-orange collections found at Chichen Itza contained virtually nothing but fine-orange Silho Group sherds.

The Chichen Itza fine-orange Silho Group collection discussed in this report totaled 238 sherds or 1.2 per cent of a selected collection of presumed Sotuta Ceramic Complex deposits. Brainerd did not have the wherewithal to make such a selection. He could only use the rough total [200,000] of all sherds collected up to 1940 at Chichen Itza and the total [1,064] of the fine-orange Silho Group sherds and whole vessels to determine the percentage (.5) of the fine-orange Silho Group. The small percentage in either case would not bar this as a local fine ware group, but the unusual paste and very different form and design styles strongly suggest it to be a trade group. Whether Brainerd is correct in assuming coastal Veracruz or Tabasco, or Smith in selecting coastal Campeche as the region of origin, cannot be decided without further investigation; the excavations resulting in Berlin's 1956 publication, however, tend to eliminate Tabasco as a possible source because of its very rare occurrence there.

FINE BUFF WARE [1]

Form and Type	Rim	%	Rim & Body
Fine-buff (?) Group		1.6	
Vases, pedestal base: Cerro Montoso Polychrome Type	1		7

Fine-buff Group (23, *e*). Lamp-chimney vase with pedestal base, thin walls, direct rim, flat lip. *Size:* lip diam. 6 cm. *Surface:* slipped and polished on exterior only. Color brown (10 YR 5/3). *Paste:*

fine texture. Untempered. Color cinnamon (7.5 YR 7/4) edges and gray (5 Y 7/2) core. *Types and decoration. Cerro Montoso Polychrome Type:* 1 rim, 6 body sherds. Four color polychrome, red, black, and white on brown to buff slip. Geometric rim and basal bands; scroll meander (?) and terrace and hook, respectively. Central motif not clear but an ahau is present. *Remarks*: compare this example with similar vase illustrated by Brainerd (1958, fig. 89, a). I believe some of these fragments are pieces of the same vase. All come from the same location at Chichen Itza, my trench paralleling that of Henry Roberts (1931–1935). A similar vase is illustrated by Du Solier (1943, p. 78, *n, o*). Both Brainerd's and Du Solier's examples are figure painted.

Summary. Clearly this is a trade ware.

PLUMBATE WARE [11]

Forms and Types	Rim	%	Rim & Body
Plumbate Tohil Group		17.5	
Jars, standard form: Tohil Plumbate Type	8		18
Tumbador Incised Type	1		4
Porvenir Gadrooned Type	0		3
Bowls, restricted: Tumbador Incised Type	2		2
Total	11		27

Plumbate Tohil Group (23, *a–d*). As found in this collection, it may be separated into two forms: jars and bowls.

Jars (*a, c, d*) are representative of Shepard's (1948) standard jar form with high, nearly cylindrical neck, globular body, thin to medium-thick walls (thickest at base and neck), rim molding (*a, d*), direct rim (*c*), rounded or pointed lip, and usually flat base. *Size*: lip diam. 7–11 cm., av. 9.8 cm., most common of 6 measured 11 cm. [3]; neck ht. 5–8 cm., av. 6.8 cm. (only 3 measured). *Surface*: imperfectly smoothed, slipped all over, probably dipped, glazed, and usually shows crazing. Color commonly gray (5 Y 5/1, 6/1; 10 YR 5/2), less frequently reddish brown (2.5 YR 5/6, 5 YR 5/6), brown (7.5 YR 5/4, 5/6), olive (2.5 Y 4/2), orange (2.5 YR 4/8), mottled red (10 R 5/6), and black. *Paste*: fine texture. Usually has microscopic inclusions. Color dark gray (2.5 YR 4/0), black, light gray (2.5 YR 6/0), pinkish cinnamon (2.5 YR 6/8), pinkish cinnamon (2.5 YR 6/6) edges with gray core, and light brown (7.5 YR 6/6). *Types and decoration. Tohil Plumbate Type*: 8 rim, 10 body sherds. Several illustrated undecorated specimens (23, *a, d*). *Tumbador Incised Type*: 1 rim, 3 body sherds. Grooved neck (*c*), and of the three grooved body examples one has additional punctation. *Porvenir Gadrooned Type*: no rim, 3 body sherds. Gadrooning on body worked from exterior in two cases, the other from interior. *Remarks*: these standard jars (*a, d*) are like Shepard's (1948) figure 8, *a*; and *c* is similar to her figure 10, *c*.

Bowl (23, *b*), restricted orifice, rim molding, rounded lip, thin walls. *Size*: lip diam. 8.5 cm. *Surface*: imperfectly smoothed, slipped all over, probably dipped, glazed, and shows crazing. Color beige with gray areas producing a mottled effect. *Paste*: fine texture, but has fine temper particles. Color gray. *Types and decoration. Tumbador Incised Type*: 2 rim, no body sherds. Vertical grooving on exterior. *Remarks*: this shape was not noted in Shepard's (1948) plumbate study.

Summary. Plumbate is another certain trade ware.

TYPES OF UNIDENTIFIED WARES [14] *

* These include four named and two unnamed brown types listed below, all presumably belonging to the Sotuta Ceramic Complex.

Forms and Types	Rim	%	Rim & Body
		22.2	
Ladle-handle jar censers: Tinum Red-on-cinnamon Type	8		53
Tripod jars: Libre Union Red-on-buff Type	4		12
Cylindrical vases: Cenotillo Gray-polychrome Type	0		4
Pedestal-base jars: Tunkas Red-on-gray Type	0		8
Low-neck, wide-mouth jars: Unnamed Brown Type	1		5
Rounded-side bowls: Unnamed Brown Type	1		1
Total	14		83

Tinum Red-on-cinnamon Type (11, *h, w, y*) probably ladle-handle jar censers with wide mouth, low outcurving (*w*) or flaring (*h, y*) neck, direct rim, rounded or pointed lip, thin to medium-thick walls, two hollow cylindrical (*y*) feet, and probably a third foot, shaped as a hollow tubular handle. *Size:* lip diam. 8–13 cm., av. 10.2 cm., most common of 6 measured 10 cm. [4]; neck ht. 1.2–3.8 cm., av. 2.3 cm., most common of 5 measured 2.3 cm. [3]. *Surface:* slipped and polished, save for perforated areas, on exterior and neck interior. Color cinnamon (7.5 YR 7/4). *Paste:* medium texture. Color pinkish cinnamon (2.5 YR 6/6, 6/8). *Quantity and decoration:* 8 rim, 45 body sherds. Broad red (10 R 4/4) rim stripe on exterior (*h*) or interior (*w, y*). All have perforated decoration on body, some on neck and body, and all have red stripe on neck interior. *w* has red vertical stripes joined in arc at top on body exterior. In addition some (*w*) have incised design. Blue paint sometimes covers the unslipped neck (*y*). In some instances the red used is specular hematite red. *Remarks:* Brainerd (1958, fig. 97, *h–j*) illustrates several of this form. Wauchope (1948, pp. 148–150) calls this form "Mixtec type."

Libre Union Red-on-buff Type (11, *x*) jars or possibly ladle-handled censers with wide mouth, low flaring neck, medium-thick walls, direct rim, rounded lip, basal molding, three hollow, somewhat elongated bulbous feet, and no evidence of a ladle handle. *Size:* lip diam. 14 cm.; neck ht. 3 cm:; reconstructed overall ht. 19 cm. *Surface:* slipped and burnished on the exterior down to

and including the basal ridge, lower part and feet unslipped; neck interior slipped and burnished. Color buff (10 YR 6/4). *Paste:* coarse texture. Color gray (10 YR 8/1), buff (10 YR 7/3), or beige (10 YR 7/4). *Quantity and decoration:* 4 rim, 8 body sherds. Generally have horizontal red (10 R 3/6) stripe medially placed on neck exterior. *Remarks:* these examples have a surface finish, lustrous but lumpy, similar to that of Oxkintok Coarse Monochrome as described by Brainerd (1958, p. 50, fig. 11, *b, 7*), and even the neck form corresponds. Neither the basal molding nor the hollow elongated bulbous feet, however, have any equivalent in the Oxkintok collection as presented by Brainerd. I believe it possible that these are fragments of the ladle-handled censer, presumably of the Sotuta Ceramic Complex.

Cenotillo Gray-polychrome Type (23, *f*) thinwalled cylindrical vase. *Surface:* slipped and polished all over. Smooth finish. Color gray (10 YR 8/1). *Paste:* medium texture. Quartz temper. Color pinkish cinnamon (2.5 YR 6/6). *Quantity and decoration:* no rim, 4 body sherds. Painted red, orange, and black on gray slip. Design consists of vertical and horizontal lines and stripes plus some sort of panel enclosed motif. *Remarks:* no precedent for this type.

Tunkas Red-on-gray Type (23, *g*) thin-walled pedestal-base restricted bowl or jar. *Size:* base diam. 17 cm. *Surface:* slipped and polished all over including underside of pedestal. Color primary slip gray (10 YR 8/1), secondary slip red (10 R 4/8). *Paste:* medium texture. Quartz temper. Color pinkish cinnamon (2.5 YR 6/6) edges and brown (7.5 YR 5/4) core. *Quantity and decoration*: no rim, 8 body sherds. Reserve space (negative painting), horizontal thin gray line on exterior. *Remarks*: no precedent for this type.

Unnamed Brown Types (18, *a, b*). The two forms, jar (*a*) and bowl (*b*), included in this category are not necessarily of the same ware, but they all have a thin brown slip.

Jar, low flaring neck, direct rim, rounded lip. *Size*: lip diam. 9.4 cm. *Surface*: thinly slipped and burnished on exterior only. Body exteriors have traces of adhering blue or red paint, and the interiors have a thick accumulation of blue or red paint, suggesting that this type was used as a paintpot. Slip color light brown to cinnamon (10 YR 7/6, 7.5 YR 7/4). *Paste*: medium-coarse texture with C-2 temper. Color drab (10 YR 6/3) or gray (10 YR 7/1). *Quantity and decoration*: 1 rim, 4 body sherds. No decoration observed.

Bowl, rounded medium-thick to thick sides, direct rim, pointed lip. *Size*: lip diam. 19 cm. *Surface*: slipped (?) and burnished on interior and exterior. Color brown (7.5 YR 5/4). *Paste*: medium-coarse texture with Q-1 temper. Color brown (7.5 YR 4/2). *Quantity and decoration*: 1 rim, no body sherds. No decoration observed.

Summary. It is more than likely that the Tinum Red-on-cinnamon and Libre Union Red-on-buff ladle-handle censers are also trade pieces because this censer form is typical of late horizons in Oaxaca (Wauchope, 1948, pp. 148–150), but there is always the possibility that they are local copies. Brainerd (1958, fig. 97, legend) suggests that some are of local manufacture and others imported. The thinly slipped unnamed brown jar, is probably local since it is not a fine ware; it may even belong to some ceramic complex other than the Sotuta. Unfortunately there is not enough material to judge. The thinly slipped unnamed brown bowl is probably a trade piece because of its quartz sand temper (18, *b*).

Finally, Tunkas Red-on-gray and Cenotillo Gray-polychrome are probably both imported types, but I know of no comparable types at present. Although each is the only example found, these two specimens in my opinion have a sufficient number of distinctive attributes to be given type names. They not only have quartz sand temper which immediately marks them as imports but they have diagnostic surface finishes, styles of decoration, and vessel forms. I believe that when encountered elsewhere these types will be readily recognizable and therefore may be given type names, whereas in the case of the brown specimens neither surface finish or color nor vessel form are distinctive enough to separate them from other brown jars or bowls with thin slip. The quartz sand temper of the brown bowl sets it apart as an import but as the only diagnostic attribute is not sufficient basis for giving this bowl a type name.

MAYAPAN [261]

CHICHEN UNSLIPPED WARE

Jars (cf. 11, *a, b, d, e, j–m*), medium-wide mouth, medium-high outcurving neck, bolster or direct rim, continuous-curve neck-body junction, globular body with thin to medium-thick sides, flat or concave base. *Surface*: smoothed, a few with white calcareous coat. Color commonly gray, beige, or cream. *Paste*: coarse texture. Color range much the same as surface. *Types and decoration. Piste Striated Type*: 10 rim, 148 body sherds. Striation covers exterior body only.

Censer, hourglass (cf. 12, *a*), flaring medium-thick sides, direct rim, beveled lip, pedestal base. *Surface*: smoothed all over. Color commonly beige. *Paste*: coarse texture, beige color. *Types and decoration. Sisal Unslipped Type*: 1 rim, no body sherds.

Censer, tripod (cf. 12, *f*), flaring medium-thick to thick sides rounding to flat base, bolster rim, vertical strap handle, and three hollow bulbous feet (in this case not present). *Surface*: smoothed all over. Color is cinnamon. *Paste*: coarse texture, cinnamon color. *Types and decoration. Espita Appliqué Type*: 1 rim, no body sherds. Buttons applied probably in clusters.

Censers, ringstand-base vase (cf. 30, *u*), flaring medium-thick to thick sides, everted rim, flat lip, flat base, and possibly a terraced ringstand (cf. GWB, fig. 104, *c, 1* and Acosta, 1945, fig. 20, *N*). *Surface*: well smoothed with exterior calcareous coat. *Paste*: coarse texture, unidentified temper, gray color. *Types and decoration. Cumtun Composite Type*: 4 rim, 13 body sherds. These have upper and lower thumb-impressed fillets framing rows of appliqué spikes.

CHICHEN SLATE WARE

Jars (27, *a, b*), small or medium mouth, medium-high to high outcurving neck, direct, everted, or slightly triangular bolster rim, globular or pear-shape body, concave base. *Surface:* slipped and polished on exterior and just over lip or all over neck interior. Waxy feel. Slip color commonly gray. *Paste:* medium-coarse texture and orange, red, or brown color. *Types and decoration. Dzitas Slate Type:* 42 rim, 341 body sherds. *Balantun Black-on-slate Type:* 1 rim, 22 body sherds.

Basins (27, *h, i*), rounded, medium-thick to thick walls, bolster rim, restricted orifice, globular body, two vertical strap handles, slightly concave base *Surface:* slipped and polished on interior, exterior, and generally on base. Slip color gray or buff. Waxy feel. *Paste:* medium texture, orange, brown, or red color. *Types and decoration. Dzitas Slate Type:* 119 rim, 91 body sherds. *Balantun Black-on-slate Type:* 3 rim, 1 body sherd (cf. 15).

Bowls, restricted (cf. 13, *j, k*), rounded thin to medium-thick sides, restricted orifice, direct rim, globular body, slightly concave base. *Surface:* slipped and polished all over including base. Color gray. Waxy feel. *Paste:* medium texture, orange and brown color. *Types and decoration. Dzitas Slate Type:* 3 rim, 3 body sherds.

Dishes, rounded sides (cf. 13, *a, b*), medium-thick walls, direct rim, flat or slightly concave base. *Surface:* slipped and polished all over including base. Waxy feel. Color gray or brown. *Paste:* medium texture, orange, red, or brown color. *Types and decoration. Dzitas Slate Type:* 2 rim, 1 body sherd.

Dishes, tripod (cf. 19, *a*), outcurving medium-thick sides rounding to a convex base, direct, slightly everted, or slight bolster rim; feet are hollow bulbous. *Surface:* slipped and polished all over including base and feet. Waxy feel. Color gray or cream. *Paste:* medium texture, reddish brown, red, and orange color. *Types and decoration. Dzitas Slate Type;* no rim, 8 body sherds.

CHICHEN RED WARE

Dishes, rounded sides (cf. 21, *n–r*), medium-thick walls, direct rim, flat or concave base. *Surface:* well smoothed before slipping and polishing all over. Slight waxy feel. *Paste:* medium texture, red and reddish orange color. *Types and decoration. Dzibiac Red Type:* 15 rim, 45 body sherds. *Chan Kom Black-on-red Type:* 1 rim, no body sherds (cf. 21, *q, r*).

Dishes, tripod (cf. 21, *cc, gg*), outcurving or flaring medium-thick sides, direct or everted rim, flat or convex base, and three hollow bulbous or cylindrical feet. *Surface:* slipped and polished all over, rarely base left unslipped. Waxy feel. Color is red, reddish brown, or orange. *Paste:* medium texture, red and orange color. *Types and decoration. Xuku Incised Type:* 1 rim, 1 body sherd.

Bowls, restricted (cf. 21, *a, c–e*), rounded medium-thick sides, direct or slight bolster rim, globular or pear-shape body, bases not present. *Surface:* slipped and polished on exterior and just over lip on interior, exterior only, or all over. Slight waxy feel. Color red or reddish brown. *Paste:* medium texture, reddish brown and orange color. *Types and decoration. Dzibiac Red Type:* 4 rim, no body sherds. *Xuku Incised Type:* 1 rim, no body sherds (cf. 21, *b*).

Jars (27, *f;* cf. 20, *a–d*), small mouth, outcurving medium-high to high neck, direct or slight bolster rim, globular or pear-shape body, no bases present. *Surface:* slipped and polished on exterior and neck interior (one has blue paint on interior and exterior). Color is red or reddish brown. Waxy feel. *Paste:* medium texture, reddish brown color. *Types and decoration. Dzibiac Red Type:* 6 rim, 71 body sherds. *Xuku Incised Type:* no rim, 2 body sherds (cf. 20, *g, n, o*).

FINE ORANGE WARE

Fine-orange Silho Group.

Jars (cf. 22, *a–d, f*). Small mouth, low or medium-high outcurving or vertical neck, direct rim, globular body with medium-thick walls, flat base. *Surface:* slipped and lightly burnished on exterior and neck interior. Color orange, reddish brown, and red. *Paste:* fine texture, apparently untempered, orange color. *Types and decoration: Silho Orange Type:* no rim, 2 body sherds. *Yalton Black-on-orange Type:* 1 rim, no body sherds. *Pocboc Gouged-incised Type:* no rim, 5 body sherds. *Nunkini Modeled Type:* 2 rim, 5 body sherds (27, *k*).

Vases, pyriform (cf. 22, *g;* see GWB, fig. 77, *m, p, gg, jj*). These are mostly of the tripod, not pedestal base, variety. Neck tapers up in a continuous curve from a pear-shape or globular body, thin walls, rim often with molding, convex base and hollow bulbous feet. *Surface:* slipped and lightly burnished all over exterior. Color is orange or reddish brown. *Paste:* fine texture, apparently untempered, orange color. *Types and decoration. Silho Orange Type:* 9 rim, 78 body sherds. One body sherd has painted stucco coating — too fragmentary to judge design. *Yalton Black-on-orange Type*: 3 rim, 38 body sherds. *Cumpich Incised Type*: 1 rim, 10 body sherds. *Pocboc Gouged-incised Type*: 3 rim, 9 body sherds. *Pomuch Polychrome Type*: no rim, 1 body sherd. *Kilikan Composite Type*: no rim, 1 body sherd.

Plates, tripod (cf. 22, *r–u*). Outcurving medium-thick sides, direct or everted rim, convex base, three hollow bell-shape feet. *Surface:* slipped and lightly burnished all over. Color is orange or reddish brown. *Paste:* fine texture, apparently untempered, orange color. *Types and decoration. Silho Orange Type*: 2 rim, 2 body sherds. *Yalton Black-on-orange Type*: no rim, 3 body sherds.

Vases, cylindrical (27, *j*). Somewhat barrel-shape, thin to medium-thick sides, grooved rim molding, base not present. *Surface:* slipped and burnished on exterior only. Color reddish brown. *Paste:* fine texture, apparently untempered, pinkish cinnamon color. *Types and decoration. Yalton Black-on-orange Type*, grooved variety: 1 rim, 3 body sherds. *Pomuch Polychrome Type*: no rim, 1 body sherd. *Kilikan Composite Type*: 1 rim, 3 body sherds. These sherds have both black-painted and gouged-incised decoration (no illustration).

Bowl, subhemispherical (cf. Smith, 1957b, fig. 4, *k*, for shape only). Rounded thin sides, direct rim, flat base, three hollow conical feet. *Surface:* slipped and burnished all over. Color orange. *Paste:* fine texture, apparently untempered, orange color. *Types and decoration. Silho Orange Type*: no rim, 1 body sherd.

Mold, figurine. Very fragmentary. No apparent slip and appears untempered. Pale orange color. *Types and decoration. Nunkini Modeled Type*: 1 rim, no body sherds.

FINE BUFF WARE

Jar or vase (60, *g*). Thin sides, possibly jar or pyriform vase, direct rim, possibly high pedestal base. *Surface:* slipped and polished on exterior only. Not certainly polychrome; may be dichrome; only brown design on dirty cream slip is visible. *Paste:* fine texture, apparently untempered, buff color. *Types and decoration.* Unnamed type: 10 rim, 7 body sherds.

PLUMBATE WARE

Plumbate Tohil Group.

Jars (60, *h–k*), probably all standard jar forms, but only body sherds present. These have thin to medium-thick walls. *Surface:* imperfectly smoothed, slipped all over, glazed, most show crazing. Color gray, gray with orange edging, or orange. *Paste:* fine texture but has microscopic inclusions, dark gray or black color. *Types and decoration. Tohil Plumbate Type*: no rim, 4 body sherds. *Tumbador Incised Type*: no rim, 2 body sherds. *Porvenir Gadrooned Type*: no rim, 3 body sherds.

UNIDENTIFIED WARE

Jars, censer (27, *d, e*; cf. GWB, fig. 97, *h*), wide mouth, low flaring neck, direct rim, globular body with thin to medium-thick sides, 2 hollow bulbous feet, and a third hollow elongated foot to be used as a handle. *Surface:* slipped and polished on exterior and neck interior (*d*) or on exterior only except neck (*f*). Slip color red, unslipped areas cinnamon. *Paste:* medium texture, pinkish cinnamon color. *Types and decoration. Tinum Red-on-cinnamon Type*: 10 rim, 5 body sherds. Bodies have geometric openwork design.

Jars, tripod (cf. 11, *x*), this form is not certain and might even be a jar censer form with third foot-handle. It has wide mouth, low flaring neck, direct rim, globular body with medium-thick walls, base missing. *Surface:* slipped and polished on exterior and neck interior. Color is buff. *Paste:* course texture, gray to beige color. *Types and decoration. Libre Union Red-on-buff Type*: 3 rim, no body sherds.

SOTUTA CERAMIC COMPLEX SUMMARY

The Sotuta Phase-associated pottery found at Chichen Itza has proved reasonably adequate for our present aims: to establish a clear understanding of the pottery to be included in the Sotuta Ceramic Complex and to determine the origins of the characteristic traits of this pottery.

The first aim has been presented in detail and discussed at some length in the preceding pages but here I propose to review briefly this material, which appears to belong to a single cultural phase. At least our stratigraphic trenching failed to indicate any significant ceramic changes from bottom to top except in Cut 1 where about 30 per cent of the sherds in the lowest levels belonged to the Cehpech Ceramic Complex. Perhaps future digging will bring to light certain early to late modifications within the Sotuta Ceramic Complex, but I feel they are bound to be minor. As collected, the pottery of the Sotuta Ceramic Complex embodies three presumably indigenous wares: Chichen Unslipped, Chichen Slate, and Chichen Red. The types associated with these wares, usually established because of a distinctive decorative technique or the lack of same, are as follows: Chichen Unslipped Ware includes Sisal Unslipped, Piste Striated, Espita Appliqué, Tibolon Blue-on-red, and Cumtun Composite; Chichen Slate Ware has Dzitas Slate, Balantun Black-on-slate, Balam Canche Red-on-slate, Chacmay Incised, Tekom Gouged-incised, Mopila Gadrooned, Nenela Modeled, and Timak Composite; Chichen Red Ware embraces Dzibiac Red, Chan Kom Black-on-red, Xuku Incised, Holtun Gouged-incised, and Tiholop Gadrooned. Furthermore, a number of trade wares are associated with this ceramic complex, of which the best known are Fine Orange, Tohil Plumbate, and Fine Buff. These wares in turn are represented by a number of types: namely, Fine Orange Ware by Silho Orange, Yalton Black-on-orange, Pomuch Polychrome, Pocboc Gouged-incised, Nunkini modeled, Cumpich Incised, Calkini Gadrooned, and Kilikan Composite, all of which types form the fine-orange Silho Group; Plumbate Ware by Tohil Plumbate, Tumbador Incised, and Porvenir Gadrooned which together comprise the plumbate Tohil Group; Fine Buff Ware by Cerro Montoso Polychrome. Other types without ware designation, some trade pieces and some unusual or special local products, have been recognized for the first time in this report. These types include Tinum Red-on-cinnamon, Libre Union Red-on-buff, Tunkas Red-on-gray, and Cenotillo Gray-polychrome.

Each of the local Sotuta Ceramic Complex wares has its own range of paste composition, type of surface finish, set of forms, group of decorative techniques, and styles of design. This does not mean that certain attributes are not common to two or more wares, or that different types do not share similar characteristics. Some have many traits in common. Chichen Unslipped Ware has coarse paste, various types of calcite temper, imperfectly smoothed surface, and its own set of forms, decorative techniques, and styles of design quite different from any of those used in the slipped wares, Chichen Slate Ware and Chichen Red Ware. Both of these wares, on the other hand, have medium-coarse paste, usually volcanic ash temper, and well-smoothed surface with a waxy feel.

Concerning form, there are some interesting differences and similarities found in association with the various Sotuta Ceramic Complex wares. Chichen Unslipped Ware jars, censers, bowls, and comals have no counterpart in any of the slipped wares. On the other hand similar slipped forms are often reproduced in both Chichen Slate and Chichen Red wares: dishes with rounded sides and an average height-diameter index of 22.6, restricted bowls, jars with small mouth and medium-high or high, vertical outcurving neck, grater bowls, and tripod dishes. Certain slipped forms, however, occur in only one local ware: Chichen Red pyriform vessels, cylindrical bowls, and ringstand bowls; Chichen Slate disk covers and jars and possible ladle censers, both the latter belonging to the Balam Canche Red-on-slate Type. It is noteworthy that the first five slipped forms listed, the predominant forms, are all well represented in both Chichen Slate and Chichen Red, whereas most of the others are usually found in a single ware. These latter in some instances (Chichen Red pyriform vessels and ringstand bowls, and Chichen Slate, the Balam Canche Red-on-slate Type jars) are copies of fine-orange Silho Group forms. The trade or unusual type forms will be discussed later.

With reference to techniques of decoration, the Sotuta Ceramic Complex has a considerable variety and, as in the case of form, the techniques (striation, impressing, appliqué, and postfire painting) of Chichen Unslipped are lacking in the slipped wares. In the latter certain techniques such as black painting, especially trickle, gouging-incising, incising, gadrooning, postslip incising or doodling, and horizontal grooving are found in both Chichen Slate and Chichen Red wares. Other techniques like incising and gouging-incising through a secondary cream slip or band, painting dark red on lighter red, and the use of specular hematite red occur only on Chichen Red. Red-painted decoration is the only technique found in these cuts associated with the Balam Canche Red-on-slate Type of Chichen Slate Ware.

In connection with design, the Sotuta Ceramic Complex has mostly abstract motifs, some of which are common to both slipped wares; others pertain to only one. Braid design, usually gouged-incised, is found on both Chichen Slate and Chichen Red vessels, as are the step-fret motif, painted black on Chichen Slate and incised on

Chichen Red vessels, and the Greek or kan cross postslip incised on both wares. Finger dabs, dots or disks, in black or red are used on Chichen Slate, including Balam Canche Red-on-slate Type dishes. The angular scroll, incised or painted red, occurs on Chichen Red and Chichen Slate, including Balam Canche Red-on-slate Type bowls and jars. The designs associated with only one of the local Sotuta Phase wares are quite numerous. Chichen Unslipped Ware has postfire area painting, the contrasting of colors for decoration rather than any specific design, and the use of appliqué to create different motifs such as the rope or grotesque figures, and geometric bands. Chichen Slate potters utilized two decorative devices not observed in the other Sotuta Phase wares: the black-paint spatter on restricted bowls and the black S band on jars. Chichen Red potters, often copying fine-orange Silho Group motifs, decorated their vessels with a variety of bands including gouged-incised simple curvilinear scroll, usually in a scroll meander, "ram horn" scroll, floral, circle and rectangle, black circle, black dot, incised terrace and rectangle, and incised concentric circle, hook and cross. The makers of Balam Canche Red-on-slate Type vessels decorated jars with red spiral scrolls, red striping, or red zigzag.

The second aim, to determine the origin of the characteristic traits, is more perplexing. As a matter of fact, the principal wares, unslipped, slate and red, changed but little from the Cehpech Phase, and we therefore may assume that the potters continued to be Maya rather than Toltec. The shapes, however, do change, although in some cases only in minor details, such as slight alterations of jar necks and rims. This may be due to natural progress. On the other hand, new forms appear, including shallow, flat-based dishes with rounded sides, tripod dishes with hollow bulbous feet, grater bowls, and pyriform vessels. Techniques rarely used in the Cehpech Ceramic Complex become important in the Sotuta Ceramic Complex, and design styles are usually different. Some of these new forms, techniques, and designs are more than likely derived from the fine-orange Silho Group. Others cannot certainly be placed as to origin.

Of the forms which have no counterpart in the Cehpech Ceramic Complex three may have been borrowed from the fine-orange Silho Group: grater bowls and tripod dishes with hollow bulbous feet associated with both Chichen Slate and Chichen Red wares, and Chichen Red pyriform vessels. This leaves only the shallow flat-based dish with rounded sides, the form with most recorded rim sherds, that does not seem to derive from any form in particular, except a much used form from Tula found in different wares.

Nearly all the techniques used in the Sotuta Ceramic Complex were used in the Cehpech; the only exceptions noted were gadrooning and the use of specular hematite red. In like manner many of the designs utilized by the Sotuta potters had been used earlier, but a number appear to have been borrowed from the fine-orange Silho Group. These are the S motif, the scroll meander band, and the floral motif. It is likely that the only truly Silho motif is the scroll meander because both the S device and the floral representation go back at least to the Early Classic Period.

Some of the trade types and forms other than Silho Orange, Tohil Plumbate, and Cerro Montoso Polychrome have unusual ceramic traits to offer. Tinum Red-on-cinnamon Type is represented by a single form, the bulbous foot tripod jar-shape censer, and has areas decorated with incising, openwork, and red slip or blue paint. This censer is usually known as the Mixtec-type censer and belongs in the time span represented by such cultural phases as Zacualpa–Tohil, Chixoy Drainage–Chipal 2, Zaculeu–Qankyake, and Chichen Itza–Sotuta. Tunkas Red-on-gray, since the form is in doubt, has simply two distinctive traits to offer: the use of quartz temper and the technique of negative (reserve-space) painting. Cenotillo Gray polychrome gives the impression, at first glance, of being decorated with figure-painted panels and of belonging to the Late Classic Period, which may well be the case. There is just a chance, however, that it may be included in the Early Postclassic Period, although the quartz temper suggests that it was manufactured outside the normal centers supplying Chichen Itza during the Sotuta Phase.

Analyzing each ware as to its place in the complex, we find that most were manufactured either at Chichen Itza or at a place nearby, and there was influence both from earlier pottery and from contemporary trade wares.

Chichen Unslipped Ware seems, because of a difference in temper, to have at least two sources, the jars coming from one, the censers from another. If, however, this temper difference relates to the special use of the vessels, the jars for storage, the censers for burning incense, both forms could have been made by the same potters using different tempers.

Chichen Slate Ware is much like Puuc Slate Ware save in form, decorative techniques, and style of design. In other words, the paste composition in some instances is much the same, the surface finish in both cases is smooth, polished, and has a waxy feel, and many of the jars and basins in both types are decorated with a trickle-like application of black, rarely orange, red, or brownish vertical stripes. Here we have a type that seems to have evolved out of an earlier type with the natural changes expected for a new era. Most likely it was manufactured at Chichen Itza.

In part this is true of Chichen Red which has much the same paste composition, many of the same forms, decorative techniques, and styles of design as Chichen Slate. As for form, a few vessel shapes are reproduced in both Chichen Slate and Chichen Red. Only jars have different characteristics in the two wares. In Chichen Slate the jar with high outcurving neck and slightly everted rim predominates; in Chichen Red the medium-high-neck variety prevails. In traits other than form, however, the makers of Chichen Red leaned more heavily on the fine-orange Silho Group for their inspiration than did the Chichen Slate potters.

Of three wares of the Sotuta Ceramic Complex, Chichen Slate is the only one that has a type, Balam Canche Red-on-slate Type, without counterpart in the Cehpech Ceramic Complex. Its forms also are not only quite distinct from anything noted in the Puuc but even different from forms found in the other Sotuta types. The red-painted (Balam Canche Red-on-slate Type) decoration embraces different designs including spiral scrolls and disks. These differences suggest an independent manufacturing center.

The fine-orange Silho Group undoubtedly influenced the Sotuta Phase potter. In form we find the pyriform, a typical Silho shape, used in Chichen Red, the tripod jar used in Chichen Slate, and the grater used in both. The hollow bulbous foot, much used by the Silho potters, occurs in both Chichen Slate and Chichen Red. In decorative techniques we encounter gouging-incising and gadrooning, strong Silho traits, applied to both Chichen Slate and Chichen Red vessels. In design also we find the step-fret with angular scroll used in all three wares, although it cannot be said that this device is typical of the fine-orange Silho Group.

Where many of the new traits found in the Sotuta Ceramic Complex came from, other than those possibly derived from the fine-orange Silho Group, acquired in trade, is hard to say. It is quite possible that they are normal, natural changes uninfluenced by the Toltec people. At least I cannot trace any definite connections with Tula ceramics, except for shallow flat-based dishes with rounded sides. Nor have I been able to suggest any centers of manufacture other than Chichen Itza for any of the three wares, although different centers seem likely for some of the Chichen Unslipped forms and the Balam Canche Red-on-slate Type; but Chichen Slate and Chichen Red may well have been made at the same center, presumably Chichen Itza.

XV

Hocaba Ceramic Complex

UXMAL [1]—KABAH

At Uxmal, three, and at Kabah two sherds of this complex turned up on or near the surface.

MAYAPAN UNSLIPPED WARE

Jar, low neck, wide mouth. Medium-thick to thin walls. *Types and decoration. Yacman Striated Type:* Uxmal, 1 rim, no body sherds; Kabah, none.

MAYAPAN RED WARE

Jars. Exact jar form not determinable but one typical Hocaba Ceramic Complex strap handle is included. *Types and decoration. Mama Red Type:* Uxmal, no rim, 2 body sherds; Kabah, no rim, 2 body sherds.

CHICHEN ITZA [4]

At Chichen Itza many sherds of the Hocaba Ceramic Complex were encountered on or near the surface together with the later Tases Ceramic Complex pottery. Only 21 sherds of the Hocaba Ceramic Complex, however, were found in the five trenches used to establish the Sotuta Ceramic Complex. These occurred on or near the surface.

MAYAPAN RED WARE

Bowls. Rounded, medium-thick sides, direct rim, possibly tripod base (cf. 41, *b*, 1). *Surface:* slipped and burnished all over. Color red. *Paste:* coarse texture, pinkish color. *Types and decoration. Mama Red Type:* 2 rim, no body sherds.

Jars. Quite fragmentary material recognizable because of surface finish and paste texture. *Types*

and decoration. Mama Red Type: 1 rim, 8 body sherds.

Bowls, flaring-side, tripod (cf. 40, *b*). Flaring, medium-thick sides, direct rim, slightly convex base, three solid conical feet. *Surface:* slipped and burnished all over except on base and feet. *Color* red. *Paste:* coarse texture, pinkish color. *Types and decoration. Mama Red Type:* 1 rim, 7 body sherds.

PETO CREAM WARE

Jars (cf. 52, *f*). Very fragmentary material recognizable because of surface treatment and paste texture. *Types and decoration. Xcanchakan Black-on-cream Type:* no rim, 2 body sherds. Evidence of black tricklelike decoration is typical.

MAYAPAN [2,131]

At Mayapan a very sizable collection of Hocaba Phase pottery types was found mostly in the lower levels. These Hocaba Ceramic Complex types continue in the middle levels and peter out in the upper levels or late assemblage which comprises the Tases Ceramic Complex.

The Maya people responsible for the Hocaba Phase pottery probably came to Mayapan some time — perhaps fifty to sixty years — after the inception of this pottery style. One reason for entertaining this theory is the presence at Mayapan of Peto Cream Ware and the Xcanchakan Black-on-cream Type always associated with Mayapan Red Ware, while at Dzibilchaltun, according to Andrews (1960, p. 256) "we find ceramics in this 'black-on-cream' tradition first in pure samples, later mixed with, and finally giving way to, the redwares of the Decadent Period. We have, without question, a clear period of transition, marked by the rise and fall of a distinctive pottery tradition, which again must be spliced into currently accepted chronological frameworks."

Andrews and I differ on the interpretation of his findings. He believes that for a period of time what he calls the "black-on-cream" tradition was the sole ceramic ware used at certain sites, particularly at Dzibilchaltun. My contention is that there are not enough shapes in the "black-on-cream" collection and no unslipped utilitarian types present to warrant the hypothesis of a ceramic complex. Rather, I believe that the "black-on-cream" is a type pertaining to a cream ware which like Thin Slate Ware was made at a single (?) manufacturing center and distributed over a large region where it was used in conjunction with other wares. Actually this appears to be the normal procedure in the Maya area at all times. Even the widely spread and abundant Mayapan Red Ware is never, to my knowledge, found alone. It is always accompanied by Mayapan Unslipped Ware and some examples of other local wares such as Peto Cream and San Joaquin Buff, plus a variety of trade wares. In earlier periods even a ware as important as slate is not found entirely by itself in normal stratified levels but is associated with other wares and types.

Perhaps this is a good place to redefine a ceramic complex. A ceramic complex is the total ceramic manifestation present in a single cultural phase. Usually it is made up of utilitarian and fine wares, both locally made and trade. Under certain conditions, as in a kitchen midden, one would not be surprised at the lack of trade wares or even locally made fine wares. But one would expect to find both unslipped and slipped utilitarian wares with most types represented, not just one type (black-on-cream) of a single ware (cream).

In considering the Hocaba and Tases ceramic complexes at Mayapan we have to deal with three stratigraphic divisions consisting of the lower, middle, and higher levels. In the text these levels are usually referred to as early, middle, and late lots. The early material is clear-cut and embodies the Hocaba Ceramic Complex, nothing later. The late material is also uncomplicated; it amply characterizes the Tases Ceramic Complex. These two ceramic complexes are analyzed and presented in the same manner as the previous complexes (Cehpech and Sotuta) with one variation. This change involves the omission of measurements and ware summaries in connection with the early or Hocaba Ceramic Complex material, since such matters can jointly be handled far better under the late or Tases Ceramic Complex exposition. The material of the middle levels, however, usually called Hocaba-Tases, from which no definite ceramic complex has been evolved, does not lend itself to the usual procedure. We are circumventing this problem by simply showing a list (Appendix C), as in the other cases, tabulating the complete sherd occurrence by wares, forms, and types. These wares, forms, and types are all described in the early and late lot analyses.

MAYAPAN UNSLIPPED WARE [715]

Forms and Types	A Rim	C Rim	D Rim	%	Total Rim & body
Jars, wide mouth, low neck:				62.9	
Yacman Striated Type	183	132	71		3,348
medium-high neck: Yacman Striated Type	2	16	4		265
huge size, high neck: Navula Unslipped Type	1	12	6		96
Kanasin Red/unslipped Type	1	0	0		2
large size, high neck: Navula Unslipped Type	0	9	13		122
Censers, effigy:				21.5	
Hoal Modeled Type	4	37	0		562
tripod jar: Cehac-Hunacti Composite Type	2	24	2		138
pedestal vase or jar: Cehac-Hunacti Composite Type	0	12	5		109
ladle: Navula Unslipped Type	50	14	4		110
Dishes, flat base, bolster rim:				7.7	
Navula Unslipped Type	8	36	7		55
flat base, lug handles: Navula Unslipped Type	2	2	0		4
Basins, bolster rim: Yacman Striated Type	0	44	0	6.2	51
Bowls, restricted: Navula Unslipped Type	3	3	2	1.4	8
deep: Yacman Striated Type	1	0	0		1
small, paintpot: Navula Unslipped Type	1	0	0		1
grater: Chenkeken Incised Type	0	0	0		2
Cups, tripod: Cehac Painted Type	1	0	0		1
Figurines: Hoal Modeled Type	1	0	0		3
Pestle (?): Hoal Modeled Type	0	0	0		1
Total	260	341	114		4,879

Jars, wide mouth, low neck (28, a, 14; 61, a, 3; cf. 28, a, 1–13, 15–25; 61, a, 1, 2, 4). These may be flaring or vertical and have direct or bolster rim, rounded, beveled, pointed, or flat lip, globular body with thin to medium-thick walls, flat or convex base. *Size:* included in Tases measurements. *Surface:* well-smoothed neck interior and exterior below which body is lightly striated. About 40 per cent have a thin calcareous coat. Relatively few have exterior fire-blackening. *Paste:* coarse texture, generally calcite temper. The color is much the same as on surface where cinnamon predominates over gray. *Types and decoration:* here we are considering striation as a form of decoration as well as functionally utilitarian. Yacman Striated Type: 386 rim, 2,962 body sherds. *Remarks:* normally these early cooking jars lack a shoulder angle below which the striation begins. Adornos are not present and cinnamon color is predominant. One example has crack-lace mending hole. Brainerd (1958, fig. 93, a, b) illustrates two complete specimens.

Jars, wide mouth, medium-high neck (cf. 28, b, 1, 3). These may be flaring or vertical and have direct rim, rounded or beveled lip, pear-shape or globular body with medium-thick walls, two horizontal strap handles, flat or slightly concave base. *Surface:* well smoothed with body striation begin-

ning from 1 to 2.5 cms. below neck. Usually has calcareous coating. *Paste:* coarse texture, calcite temper, and generally gray color. *Types and decoration.* Yacman Striated Type: 22 rim, 243 body sherds. *Remarks:* probably these are storage jars.

Jars, huge size, wide mouth, high neck (cf. 28, c, 1; 60, l). Flaring or outcurving neck, bolster or direct rim, rounded or flat lip, two vertical strap handles set on opposite sides of shoulder, pear-shape body with medium-thick to thick walls, convex base. *Surface:* exterior well smoothed and usually completely covered with a thick coat of plaster hiding handles and bolster. Some have as many as three coats of plaster. *Paste:* coarse texture, calcite temper, and gray color. *Types and decoration:* usually undecorated. *Navula Unslipped Type:* 19 rim, 77 body sherds. *Kanasin Red-on-unslipped Type:* 1 rim, 1 body sherd. In the late lots, these huge storage jars often have red interior necks and bolsters, but here only two were found.

Jars, large size, wide mouth, high neck (cf. 28, c, 2–11). Flaring or outcurving necks, bolster or direct rim, rounded or flat lip, two opposite vertical strap handles set on shoulder, pear-shape or globular body, convex (?) base. These vessels are smaller but otherwise much the same as the huge jars in surface finish and paste. They also are coated with plaster in most instances. *Types and decoration*: no decoration noted on these specimens. *Navula Unslipped Type*: 22 rim, 100 body sherds. *Remarks*: probably these are storage jars.

Censers, effigy (cf. 32, b–d; 68, a). Cylindrical vessel with pedestal base, medium-thick to thick sides, direct rim, rounded lip. *Surface*: well smoothed and covered with a white coat usually used as a background for painted decoration. *Paste*: coarse texture, calcite temper, gray or cinnamon color. *Types and decoration*: these early effigy censers have low-relief modeling on the cylinder wall embellished with some appliqué ornaments (only 9 found) and a variety of color. Even a "diving god" effigy is represented. *Hoal Modeled Type*: 41 rim, 521 body sherds.

Censers, tripod jar (cf. 31, e, h, i; 62, e). High flaring, outcurving or nearly vertical neck, direct or bolster rim, pointed, beveled, or rounded lip, globular body with medium-thick sides, convex base sometimes perforated with five vent holes, and three feet, which may be hollow or solid oven-shape, or hollow cylindrical with rounded bottom. *Surface*: well smoothed, and exterior usually covered with a white calcareous coat. *Paste*: coarse texture, calcite temper, gray or cinnamon color. *Types and decoration*: nearly all are painted and carry appliqué finger-impressed fillets and buttons; sometimes nail-impressed bands take the place of fillets. *Cehac-Hunacti Composite Type*: 28 rim, 110 body sherds.

Censers, pedestal vases or jars (30, k, n–q; cf. 31, a–c). High flaring or outcurving neck, direct or bolster rim, pointed, beveled, or rounded lip, globular body with medium-thick sides, pedestal base, and a few (30, n–q) have horizontal lateral flanges. *Surface*: smoothed, and exterior usually covered with a white calcareous coat. *Paste*: coarse texture, calcite temper, gray or cinnamon color. *Types and decoration*: most are painted as well as embellished with appliqué ornaments consisting of spikes, buttons, and impressed fillets. *Cehac-Hunacti Composite Type*: 17 rim, 92 body sherds.

Censers, ladle (33, f; also cf. 33, a–e). Flaring medium-thick sides rounding to a flattish base, direct rim, rounded, beveled, or pointed lip, and a tubular handle opening into or closed off from bowl interior. *Surface*: better smoothed on interior than exterior. Two examples have rim groove. A few have fire-blackened interiors. Some have rasp-like finish on exterior. *Paste*: coarse texture, calcite temper, gray or cinnamon color. *Types and decoration*: none is embellished except a few which have a white calcareous coat. *Navu-*

la *Unslipped Type*: 68 rim, 42 body sherds. *Remarks*: it is most likely that some of these were basal-break dishes and not censers.

Dishes, flat base, bolster rim (cf. 29, dd; 61, c, 2). Flaring medium-thick sides, flat bolster rim, rounded, pointed, or beveled lip, flat, concave, or impressed-circle base. *Surface*: better smoothed on interior than exterior which may have a rasp-like finish. *Paste*: coarse texture, calcite temper, gray or cinnamon color. *Types and decoration*. *Navula Unslipped Type*: 51 rim, 4 body sherds.

Dishes, flat base, lug handles. Flaring medium-thick sides, direct rim, rounded, beveled, and pointed lip, lugs attached to either side, flat base. *Surface*: better smoothed on interior than exterior. *Paste*: coarse textured, calcite temper, gray or cinnamon color. *Types and decoration*. *Navula Unslipped Type*: 4 rim, no body sherds.

Basins, bolster rim (29, f). Flaring medium-thick sides, flat bolster rim, beveled lip, two vertical strap handles, flat base. *Surface*: well-smoothed interior, lightly striated exterior. Many have white calcareous coat on exterior. *Paste*: coarse texture, calcite temper, gray and cinnamon color. *Types and decoration*. *Yacman Striated Type*: 44 rim, 7 body sherds.

Bowls, restricted (cf. 29, k, l, n, o, q; 61, c, 1). Rounded medium-thick sides, direct [5] or bolster [3] rim, globular body, slightly concave or flat base. *Surface*: generally interiors better smoothed than exteriors. *Paste*: coarse texture, calcite temper, cinnamon or gray color. *Types and decoration*. *Navula Unslipped Type*: 8 rim, no body sherds.

Bowls, deep (cf. 31, v). Nearly vertical medium-thick sides rounding to a presumably flat base which may or may not have feet, direct rim, flat lip. *Surface*: better smoothed on interior than exterior which is lightly and vertically striated. *Paste*: coarse texture, gray color. *Types and decoration*. *Yacman Striated Type*: 1 rim, no body sherds.

Bowl, small paintpot (no illustration). Rounded thick sides, direct rim, grooved flat lip, flat base. *Surface*: better smoothed on interior than exterior. Traces of blue paint adhering to both interior and exterior. *Paste*: coarse texture, gray color. *Type and decoration*. *Navula Unslipped Type*: 1 rim, no body sherds.

Bowls, grater (cf. 33, j). Medium-thick to thick rounded sides, direct rim, probably rounded lip, three solid oven-shape feet. *Surface*: interior better smoothed above scoring than exterior. This scored area not delimited by an encircling groove. *Paste*: coarse texture, no temper readings, gray color. *Types and decoration*: very fragmentary. *Chenkeken Incised Type*: no rim, 2 body sherds. *Remarks*: Chenkeken Incised is considered to be a Tases type and therefore may be intrusive in this instance.

Cup, tripod (61, e, 3). Slightly flaring thin to medium-thick sides, direct rim, flat lip, flat base, three solid conical feet. *Surface*: smoothed all over exterior and covered with a white calcareous coat. *Paste*: coarse texture, gray color. *Types and decoration*: traces of painted turquoise design. *Cehac Painted Type*: 1 rim, no body sherds.

Figurines (no illustration). All human, one modeled and quite crudely made. Others moldmade including a turban headdress. *Surface*: probably painted but badly weathered. *Paste*: coarse texture, gray and cinnamon color. *Types and decoration*. *Hoal Modeled Type*: 1 head, 2 body sherds.

Pestle (?) fragment or possibly adorno. The knoblike end is covered with punctation. It is modeled. *Paste*: coarse texture, cinnamon color. *Types and decoration*. *Hoal Modeled Type*: no finished end, 1 body sherd.

MAYAPAN RED WARE [1,186]

Forms and Types	A Rim	C Rim	D Rim	%	Total Rim & body
Jars, water, high neck:				26.3	
Mama Red Type	26	72	167		7,493
Papacal Incised Type	10	12	25		510
Chapab Modeled Type	0	0	0		3
storage, low neck:				13.1	
Mama Red Type	50	69	7		2,836
Dzonot Appliqué Type	0	1	0		1
storage, high neck: Mama Red Type	4	13	11		737
Dishes, tripod, flaring side:				44.4	
Mama Red Type	51	160	47		825
Papacal Incised Type	22	27	22		179
tripod, rounded side: Mama Red Type	58	114	26		431
Bowls, restricted orifice:				14.8	
Mama Red Type	29	63	30		137
tripod grater: Papacal Incised Type	11	36	2		161
deep, tripod: Mama Red Type	3	1	0		17
Papacal Incised Type	0	0	0		4
deep, cuspidor shape: Mama Red Type	0	1	0		1
Basins, bolster rim: Mama Red Type	0	1	4	0.4	5
Cups: Mama Red Type	0	4	0	0.3	5
Miniature jar: Mama Red Type	0	0	0		1
Vases, cylindrical: Mama Red Type	0	2	0	0.2	20
Drums: Papacal Incised Type	0	3	2	0.4	7
Vessels, effigy: Chapab Modeled Type	0	0	0		1
Total	264	579	343		13,374

Jars, water, high neck (38, a, 1, 4–9, 11, 22, 23) nearly vertical, flaring or outcurving with direct or everted rim, rounded, flat, or square bolster, rounded, pointed, or flat lip, two horizontal strap handles, 9 examples of tubular spouts (38, a, 23), pear-shape body, medium-thick walls, slightly concave base. *Surface*: slipped and burnished on exterior and partway down neck interior. Many of bases show evidence of slip. The color is usually predominantly red but on any given vessel the red blends into orange, reddish brown, and brown, and in many cases there are gray fire-clouded areas. *Paste*: coarse texture, generally calcite tem-

per (see Mayapan Red Ware, Chapter IV), and pink to pale red color. *Types and decoration*: for the most part these jars remain undecorated. *Mama Red Type*: 265 rim, 7,228 body sherds. *Papacal Incised Type*: 47 rim, 463 body sherds. Mostly this form of decoration is associated with the inner rim and consists of one, two, or three (cf. 38, a, 2, 10; 74, a, b) horizontal groove-incised lines. *Chapab Modeled Type*: no rim, 3 body sherds. These examples consist of a modeled animal head forming part of jar shoulder (38, a, 22).

Jars, storage, low neck (38, b, 12, 13; c, 1–3). Sometimes medium-high outcurving neck, flaring, or vertical with wide mouth, direct or thickened rim, slight triangular or square bolster, flat, pointed, or rounded lip, globular or squat body which may have two horizontal strap handles, usually flat to concave base. A few have sharp-angle shoulders. *Surface:* slipped and burnished on exterior and neck interior. A few are crazed. Color is more uniformly red than those encountered in water jar category. *Paste:* coarse texture, generally calcite temper, and pink color. *Types and decoration:* usually undecorated. *Mama Red Type:* 126 rim, 2,710 body sherds. *Dzonot Appliqué Type:* 1 rim, no body sherds.

Jars, storage, high neck (38, *a*, 17; cf. 38, *a* and *b*). Also medium-high neck, outcurving or flaring with wide mouth, ovoid, rounded or flat bolster rim, rounded, beveled, flat, or pointed lip, two horizontal strap handles, pear-shape or globular body, slightly concave base. *Surface:* slipped and burnished on exterior and neck interior, or on exterior and partway down neck interior. The color is predominantly red, but on most vessels the red blends into orange, reddish brown, and brown. Usually there are gray fire-clouded areas. *Paste:* coarse texture, calcite temper, beige and gray color. *Types and decoration:* no decoration noted. *Mama Red Type:* 28 rim, 709 body sherds.

Dishes, tripod, flaring sides (cf. 40, *b*, *c*). Also outcurving and medium-thick sides, direct rim, rounded, pointed, or beveled lip, convex base. Some [5] have basal flange which may be terraced or notched, and all have three feet which may be hollow oven [93], hollow bulbous [17], solid conical [14], hollow effigy [2], or hollow cylindrical [1]. *Surface:* slipped and burnished on interior and exterior. Color is quite uniformly red with some fire-clouding. Rootlet-marking is common and crack-lace mending holes occur. A few are postfire coated with blue paint on exterior as well as interior, suggesting that some may have been used as paint pots. *Paste:* coarse texture, generally calcite temper, and pink, beige, or cream color. *Types and decoration:* rarely is this vessel shape decorated, then mostly on the interior rim in the form of horizontal grooving or on the flange when present. *Mama Red Type:* 258 rim, 567 body sherds. *Papacal Incised Type:* 71 rim, 108 body sherds. The horizontal interior rim grooves may consist of one, two, or three parallel lines. A number of decorated flanges of which *c*, 3, 5 are early examples.

Dishes, tripod, rounded sides (41, *b*, 7; cf. 41, *b*, 5, 6, 8, 9, 11), which are medium thick, direct rim, rounded, beveled, or pointed lip, convex base, and three feet usually hollow oven, sometimes

solid, either conical or oven shape. *Surface:* slipped and burnished all over. Color is somewhat more uniform with respect to each vessel than is the case with jars. Red and reddish brown are the prevailing colors. One body sherd had blue paint adhering to the interior; another showed crack-lace mending holes. *Paste:* coarse texture, generally calcite temper, and pink or gray color. *Types and decoration:* no decoration observed. *Mama Red Type:* 198 rim, 233 body sherds.

Bowls or basins, restricted orifice (41, *a*, 7, 8; 44, *h*; cf. 41, *a*, 1–6, 9; 44, *f*, *g*, *i–m*). Direct [40] or flat bolster [82] rim, rounded, beveled (sometimes flat), or pointed lip, medium-thick globular body, some with lugs, others with two horizontal strap handles, flat or slightly concave base, rarely convex base with pedestal (cf. 44, *l*, *m*). *Surface:* slipped and burnished on exterior only, on interior and exterior, or on interior only and bolster when present. Color is red, reddish brown, or orange. *Paste:* coarse texture, generally calcite temper, and cream, gray, beige, and pinkish cinnamon color. *Types and decoration:* no decoration observed. *Mama Red Type:* 122 rim, 15 body sherds.

Bowls, tripod, grater (46, *a*, 3; cf. 46, *a*, 1, 2, 4). Medium-thick rounded sides, direct rim, rounded, beveled, or pointed lip, convex base, and three oven-shape feet. *Surface:* slipped and burnished all over but frequently slip has worn off grid. Some fire-clouding is present. Scoring on floor is alternately vertical and horizontal by arc. The scored area may be limited by a single encircling groove, left open or closed by two parallel encircling grooves. Slip color may be red, orange, or reddish brown. *Paste:* coarse texture, generally calcite temper, and cream, gray, or pinkish color. *Types and decoration:* no decoration other than floor scoring observed. *Papacal Incised Type:* 49 rim, 112 body sherds.

Bowls, tripod, deep (43, *h*; cf. 43, *a–g*, *i–o*, *r–t*). Medium-thick recurving or nearly vertical sides, direct rim, rounded or beveled lip, occasionally a basal apron flange either terraced or notched, convex base, and three hollow oven to cylindrical with rounded-bottom or solid conical feet. *Surface:* slipped and burnished on interior and exterior or on exterior and just over lip on interior. Mostly the slip is a good uniform red with few blemishes. *Paste:* coarse texture, generally calcite temper, and cinnamon or pinkish cinnamon color. *Types and decoration:* rarely decorated. *Mama Red Type:* 4 rim, 13 body sherds. *Papacal Incised Type:* no rim, 4 body sherds. The incised decoration may be on flange (cf. 43, *n*, *o*) or on both flange and body (cf. 43, *i*).

Bowls, deep, cuspidor shape (43, *p*; 74, *z*; cf. 43, *c*, *q*). Medium-thick recurving sides, direct rim, rounded lip, flat base. *Size:* lip diam. 13 cm., max. diam. 14.7 cm., base diam. 5 cm., height 8.4 cm. *Surface:* slipped and burnished all over including base. Color is variegated including red, reddish orange, light brown, dark reddish brown, with considerable fire-clouding on both interior and exterior. This specimen, illustrated in figure 43, *q*, must have contained something besides three jade beads to account for the slip on the vessel floor being eaten away. *Paste:* coarse texture, probably calcite temper, pinkish cinnamon color. *Types and decoration:* no decoration observed. *Mama Red Type:* 1 rim, no body sherds.

Basins, bolster rim (cf. 46, *b*, 1–10). Medium-thick to thick rounded or flaring sides, flat or ovoid bolster, flat lip, may have two solid slab lug or two vertical strap handles, usually flat or concave base. *Surface:* slipped and burnished on interior and partway down exterior, or on interior and bolster. Unslipped exteriors may be striated, but mostly just smoothed. Slip color is red, orange, or reddish brown. One specimen has coat of blue paint on interior. *Paste:* coarse texture, probably calcite temper, and gray or cream paste color. *Types and decoration:* no decoration observed. *Mama Red Type:* 5 rim, no body sherds.

Cups (cf. 45, *d*; 75, *g*). Barrel-shape with pedestal base (?), medium-thick sides, direct rim, rounded lip. *Surface:* slipped and burnished on exterior only. Slip color is red. *Paste:* coarse texture, probably calcite temper, color not identified. *Types and decoration:* most of these particular sherds not decorated. *Mama Red Type:* 4 rim, 1 body sherd.

Miniature jar (49, *h*). Globular body, medium-thick sides, probably two lug handles, thick flat base 3.5 cm. in diameter. *Surface:* slipped and burnished on exterior only. Color is variegated including red, orange, and light brown. *Paste:* coarse texture, probably calcite temper, and color not identified. *Types and decoration. Mama Red Type:* no rim, 1 body sherd.

Vases, cylindrical (cf. 44, *a–d*). Medium-thick cylindrical or outcurving sides, direct rim, rounded lip, flat base [16] or convex base with pedestal [2]. *Surface:* well smoothed, slipped and burnished on exterior only. Slip color is predominantly red but may be mixed with reddish brown and gray fire-clouded areas. *Paste:* coarse texture, probably calcite temper, and pinkish or buff color. *Types and decoration:* no evidence of decoration. *Mama Red Type:* 2 rim, 18 body sherds.

Drums (cf. 39, *a–o*) or jars. Medium-thick to thick walls. Smaller opening at one end than at the other. High vertical or outcurving neck, direct rim, flat or rounded bolster rim, flat, rounded, or pointed lip. Bodies may be like the reconstruction (39, *a*) or like a high-neck jar form. *Surface:* slipped and burnished all over exterior, except where worn off, or only below grooving. Slip color is red; some are variegated. *Paste:* coarse texture, probably calcite temper, and cream or pinkish color. *Types and decoration:* all have vertical or diagonal rim groovings, possibly to give a rough holding surface for tying on skin. The grooving may also be a form of decoration. *Papacal Incised Type:* 5 rim, 2 body sherds..

Vessel, effigy (45, *g*), animal head which may belong on the shoulder of a jar or other type vessel such as that in 45, *b*. *Surface:* slipped and burnished. Color is red. *Paste:* coarse texture, probably calcite temper, color not observed. *Types and decoration. Chapab Modeled Type:* no rim, 1 body sherd.

MAYAPAN BLACK WARE [0]

Forms and Types	A Rim	C Rim	D Rim	Total Rim & body
Jars, water (?): Sulche Black Type	0	0	0	36
Bowls, hemispherical: Sulche Black Type	0	0	0	5
Total	0	0	0	41

Jars, water (no illustration), medium-thick to thick sides, pear-shape or globular body, concave base. *Surface:* slipped and burnished on exterior only. Same as Mayapan Red Ware except for color which varies from a strong black to a brownish black, or may have dark red areas. *Paste:* coarse texture, usually calcite temper similar to Mayapan Red Ware, and gray or pink color. *Types and decoration:* no evidence of decoration. *Sulche Black Type:* no rim, 36 body sherds. *Remarks:* all from D Lots.

Bowls, hemispherical (?). Medium-thick rounded sides and flat base. *Surface:* slipped and burnished all over. Color is a strong black. *Paste:*

coarse texture, probably calcite temper, and gray or pink color. *Types and decoration*: no evidence of decoration. *Sulche Black Type*: no rim, 5 body sherds. *Remarks*: all from D Lots.

PETO CREAM WARE [213]

Forms, Types, and Varieties	A Rim	C Rim	D Rim	%	Total Rim & body
Jars, water:				46.9	
Xcanchakan Black/cream Type	7	50	34		2,069
Kukula Cream Type	5	4	0		87
Mataya Modeled Type	0	0	0		1
Storage:				2.3	
Kukula Cream Type	0	2	1		59
Xcanchakan Black/cream Type	0	1	1		2
Dishes, tripod, flaring side:				40.4	
Xcanchakan Black/cream Type	2	24	4		66
Kukula Cream Type	0	2	6		13
tripod, rounded side: Xcanchakan Black/cream Type	2	24	6		55
Kukula Cream Type	0	15	1		30
Bowls or basins, restricted orifice:				9.9	
Xcanchakan Black/cream Type	0	11	9		66
tripod, grater: Xcanchakan Black/cream Type,					
sharp-incised variety	0	0	1		1
Vase, cylindrical: Kukula Cream Type	1	0	0	0.5	1
Total	17	133	63		2,450

Jars, water (52, c, g, i, y; cf. 51, a, b, d–h; 52, a, b, d, h, j, k; 75, l, m). Small to medium-wide mouth high (51, g, h; 52, a–c; 75, l, m), medium-high (51, a, b, d–f; 52, k), or low (52, d) neck which may be outcurving (51, a, d, h; 52, a–d; 75, l, m), vertical (51, b, f; 52, k), flaring (51, g), or bulging (51, e), flat bolster (51, g; 52, a; 75, m), rounded bolster (52, b, d; 75, l), square bolster (51, a, h), thickened (52, c), everted (51, b, e, f), and direct (51, d; 52, k) rim, flat, pointed, rounded, or beveled lip, medium-thick walls, pear-shape body, usually two horizontal strap handles placed on opposite sides of body at point of greatest diameter, slightly concave base. *Surface*: slipped and burnished on exterior and neck interior (51, a, b; 52, c, j), on exterior and partway down neck interior (51, e; 52, a, b; 75, l, m), on exterior only (52, k), or all over (cf. 52, e). Slip color is cream, beige, gray, or cinnamon. *Paste*: coarse texture, usually calcite temper, and beige, gray, pink, drab, cinnamon, or reddish brown color. *Types and decoration*: only about 5 per cent of this form is undecorated. *Kukula Cream Type*: 9 rim, 78 body sherds. *Xcanchakan Black-on-cream Type*: 91 rim, 1,978 body sherds. The decoration consists of black painted designs on both neck and body. The necks carry finger dabs on interior rim (52, a–d) and triangles (52, a; 75, m), parallel vertical tricklelike stripes (52, c), finger rim dabs (52, d), or parallel vertical rectangles (52, k) on exterior.

The shoulder is embellished with encircling bands including S's and dots (52, a, b; 75, l, m), S's and scrolls (52, g, j), sloppy taus and scrolls (52, h), and S's and a U chain (52, i). The bodies are usually decorated with broad vertical stripes, called trickles, thicker at upper end. *Mataya Modeled Type*: no rim, 1 body sherd (52, y).

Jars, storage (51, c; 52, e, f). Wide mouth, low or medium-high outcurving neck, triangular or flat bolster, and direct or thickened rim, pointed, flat, or rounded lip, medium-thick to thick globular body, probably concave base. *Surface*: slipped and burnished on exterior and neck interior. Rarely slipped all over (52, e). Slip color cream or beige. *Paste*: coarse texture, probably calcite temper, and beige color. *Types and decoration*: usually without decoration. *Kukula Cream Type*: 3 rim, 56 body sherds. *Xcanchakan Black-on-cream Type*: 2 rim, no body sherds. Necks may have finger dabs on rim interior (52, f). Shoulders are embellished with encircling bands including "sausages" (52, e) and crescents (52, f). *Remarks*: Brainerd (1958, figs. 20, a, 2, 3, 6; 92, f, 11–13) illustrates low-neck jars with horizontal neck grooving similar to that found in the Sotuta Ceramic Complex, Chacmay Incised Type, groove-incised variety.

Dishes, tripod, flaring-sides (52, w, x; cf. 51, s–u; 52, t–v). Sometimes outcurving or recurving sides, direct rim, beveled, rounded, pointed, and flat lip, convex base, three hollow oven-shape or cylindrical feet. *Surface*: slipped and burnished all over, but sometimes not on base; rarely crazed. Slip color may be cream, beige, or light brown. *Paste*: coarse texture, probably calcite temper, and cinnamon or beige color. *Types and decoration*: only about 18 per cent are without decoration. *Kukula Cream Type*: 8 rim, 5 body sherds. *Xcanchakan Black-on-cream Type*: 30 rim, 36 body sherds. Black-painted decoration on interior includes parallel vertical stripes (cf. 52, *v*), trace of a hook on floor (52, *w*), and a kin-like sign as part of wall band (52, *x*).

Dishes, tripod, rounded side (52, *p, q*; cf. 51, *q*; 52, *o, r*). Medium-thick walls, direct or flat bolster rim, beveled, flat, rounded, or pointed lip, convex base, and three hollow oven-shape feet. *Surface*: slipped and burnished all over. Rarely these have an interior rim groove. Slip color may be cream or beige. *Paste*: coarse texture, probably calcite temper, and gray color. *Types and decoration*: approximately 35 per cent are undecorated. *Kukula Cream Type*: 16 rim, 14 body sherds. *Xcanchakan Black-on-cream Type*: 32 rim, 23 body sherds. *Remarks*: 52, *p, r* may be hemispherical bowls.

Bowls or basins, restricted orifice (cf. 52, *l–n*). Medium-thick globular body, direct [1] rim, flat or triangular bolsters [19], beveled lip, probably slightly concave base. *Surface*: slipped and burnished all over. Slip color is cream or beige. *Paste*: coarse texture, probably calcite temper, and beige or cream color. *Types and decoration*: apparently all specimens of this shape are decorated. *Xcanchakan Black-on-cream Type*: 20 rim, 46 body sherds. *Remarks*: Brainerd (1958, fig. 19, *i, 7, 8*) illustrates two examples of exterior rim grooving similar to that found in the Sotuta Ceramic Complex, slate Dzitas Group.

Bowl, tripod, grater (52, *s*; cf. 51, *r*). Medium-thick rounded sides, direct rim, beveled lip, convex base, probably three hollow oven-shape feet. *Surface*: slipped and burnished all over. Evidence of scoring on floor. Slip color is cream. *Paste*: coarse texture, probably calcite temper, paste color not recorded. *Types and decoration*: altogether a rare form in this ware. *Xcanchakan Black-on-cream Type, sharp-incised variety*: 1 rim, no body sherds. Black-painted decoration on interior includes vertical stripes and dot chain beginning on lip, also rim dabs. Scoring on floor badly worn.

Vase, cylindrical (51, *v*). Medium-thick walls, direct rim, rounded lip, probably slightly convex base with pedestal support. *Size*: lip diam. 11 cm., overall ht. ca. 22 cm., thickness .6–.9 cm. *Surface*: slipped and burnished on exterior only, color apparently cream but badly weathered. The pedestal has traces of red (?) and is actually counted with red ware although used in this reconstruction. *Paste*: coarse texture, no other data recorded. *Types and decoration*: no decoration. *Kukula Cream Type*: 1 rim, no body sherds.

FINE-ORANGE MATILLAS GROUP [17]

Forms and Types	A Rim	C Rim	D Rim	%	Total Rim & body
Dishes, tripod:				88.2	
Matillas Orange Type	0	0	0		1
Nacajuca Black/orange Type	0	2	0		7
Villahermosa Incised Type	0	0	0		1
Salto Composite Type	0	1	0		1
tripod, basal flange: Matillas Orange Type	1	0	0		2
tripod, with or without flange:					
Matillas Orange Type	3	0	0		44
Villahermosa-incised Type	0	3	1		4
Chilapa Gouged-incised Type	1	2	0		3
Nacajuca Black/orange Type	0	1	0		2
Jars, high neck: Matillas Orange Type	0	0	0		12
Villahermosa Incised Type	0	0	0		2
Bowls, restricted, direct rim:				11.8	
Matillas Orange Type	1	0	0		1
Nacajuca Black/orange Type	1	0	0		1
Total	7	9	1		81

Dishes, tripod (cf. 55, *a*, 6, 8; *b*, 3; *c*, 2; 75, *o*). Medium-thick to thick flaring sides, interior and exterior rim bulge or slight exterior rim bulge, rounded or flat rim, no flange, convex base, and three hollow feet. *Surface*: slipped and burnished all over. Slip color usually darker than paste and includes orange, red, reddish brown, light brown, and cinnamon. *Paste*: fine texture, no temper, and color usually orange but may include cinnamon, pinkish cinnamon, and light brown. *Types and decoration*: in this shape category, the undecorated sherds form only a small percentage: *Matillas Orange Type*: no rim, 1 body sherd. *Nacajuca Black-on-orange Type*: 2 rim, 5 body sherds. Horizontal striping on interior and exterior (cf. 55, *d*, 2) is most common. *Villahermosa Incised Type*: no rim, 1 body sherd. *Salto Composite Type*: 1 rim, no body sherds. This specimen had black on interior and gouged-incised decoration on exterior.

Dishes, tripod, basal flange (cf. 55, *a*, 4, 5; *b*, 1, 2, 4; *c*, 1; *d*, 5; 75, *p*). Medium-thick flaring sides, interior and exterior slight rim bolster, rounded lip, notched flange, convex to flat base, and three hollow feet. *Surface*: slipped and burnished on interior and not below flange on exterior. Color is orange. *Paste*: fine texture, no temper, color orange slightly lighter than the slip. *Types and decoration*: no decoration observed. *Matillas Orange Type*: 1 rim, 1 body sherd.

Dishes, tripod, with or without flange (cf. 55, *c*, 3, 4; *d*, 2, 3; 75, *q*), medium-thick flaring sides, interior, exterior, or interior and exterior rim bulge, rounded, beveled, or flat rim, convex or more rarely flat base, and three hollow feet, sometimes oven-shape, but usually moldmade effigy, either zoomorphic (cf. 56, *a*) or anthropomorphic (cf. 56, *c*). Flanges if present could be plain, notched, or terraced. *Surface*: slipped and burnished on interior and exterior. Color is usually darker than that of paste and includes orange, red, reddish brown, light brown, and cinnamon. *Paste*: fine texture, no temper, and color, usually orange, may include cinnamon, pinkish cinnamon, and light brown. *Types and decoration*: the undecorated sherds of this shape category comprise 64 per cent of the total. *Matillas Orange Type*: 3 rim, 41 body sherds. *Villahermosa Incised Type*: 4 rim, no body sherds. Most of these are incised on exterior, some preslip incised on interior. The most common interior design is the chevron (cf. 55, *b*, 1, 3, 4). *Chilapa Gouged-incised Type*: 3 rim, no body sherds. These include exterior decoration for the most part but they are hard to identify because of the fragmentary condition of the material. *Nacajuca Black-on-orange Type*: 1 rim, 1 body sherd.

Jars, high neck (cf. 55, *a*, 1), medium-wide mouth, direct rim, rounded lip, medium-thick globular body, flat base. *Surface*: slipped and burnished on exterior and neck interior. Slip color orange or red. *Paste*: fine texture, no temper, and orange or cinnamon color. *Types and decoration*: most of these are undecorated. *Matillas Orange Type*: no rim, 12 body sherds. *Villahermosa Incised Type*: no rim, 2 body sherds. It is the body rather than the neck which is decorated.

Bowls, restricted, direct rim (55, *d*, 1), thin to medium-thick rounded sides, pointed lip, probably flat base. *Surface*: slipped and burnished on exterior only. Color is orange. *Paste*: fine texture, no temper, and pink or cinnamon buff color. *Types and decoration*: this shape is usually decorated. *Matillas Orange Type*: 1 rim, no body sherds. *Nacajuca Black-on-orange Type*: 1 rim, no body sherds. The design is made up of black parallel horizontal and oblique lines (55, *d*, 1).

HOCABA CERAMIC COMPLEX SUMMARY

In the Hocaba Ceramic Complex (A.D. 1200–1300 but at Mayapan possibly only 1250–1300) as established at Mayapan, three principal local wares were identified: Mayapan Red (54.3%), Mayapan Unslipped (19.8%), and Peto Cream (10%), in order of quantitative precedence. Another local ware of minor importance is Mayapan Black (.2%). The only trade ware significantly associated with this ceramic complex is Fine Orange of the Matillas Group (.3%). Oddly enough, the early lots, the source of the Hocaba Ceramic Complex, had the largest number of unidentifiable sherds (15.4%) of the various ceramic complexes under consideration. One would normally expect the surface lots, the repository for most of the Tases Ceramic Complex, to excel in this capacity.

Not all the Hocaba local wares may have been manufactured in the same center, any more than modern Yucatan pottery which as R. H. Thompson (1958) has demonstrated is made in such places as Izamal, Mama, Maxcanu, Merida, Ticul, Uayma, and Valladolid. Although no systematic study of the paste composition of Mayapan pottery was made; as was done for the Kabah, Uxmal, and Chichen Itza collections, the small sample examined and referred to by Brainerd (1958, pp. 54, 57) suggests a uniformity greater even than that found at Chichen Itza for the Sotuta Ceramic Complex.

Mayapan Red Ware does not develop naturally from Chichen Red Ware. Actually they have nothing in common except that they are both red, and even the red color is different. Chichen Red has a uniformity of color vessel by vessel, whereas Mayapan Red vessels are more often variegated in color. For a description of Mayapan Red Ware see Chapter IV. The red-slipped pottery that is Mayapan Red Ware, when associated with the Hocaba Ceramic Complex becomes the red Mama Group which includes the following forms: jars, both water and storage; dishes, tripod with either flaring or rounded sides; bowls, some having restricted orifice, others tripod grater, or deep; basins with bolster rim; cups; miniature vessels; vases; drums; and an effigy vessel. In addition it has certain types and varieties: Mama Red Type, Mama Variety; Papacal Incised Type, Papacal Variety or groove-incised variety; Dzonot Appliqué Type, Dzonot Variety; and Chapab Modeled Type, Chapab Variety. The vast majority of the sherds involved are undecorated. Most of the incised examples, forming only 4 per cent of all red Mama Group sherds associated with the Hocaba Ceramic Complex, are groove incised. These have horizontal parallel grooves just below lip. A mere handful are sharply incised, and a few of these may be classified as postfire doodling. The Dzonot Appliqué Type is extremely rare, one rim sherd with some sort of attachment being the only example. Chapab Modeled has four specimens including a modeled bird or animal head placed on jar shoulder.

The next most important ware is Mayapan Unslipped. This differs in many respects from both Puuc Unslipped Ware and Chichen Unslipped Ware (Table 25). The principal ware attributes that differ are temper, smoothness, and kind of striation. Mayapan Unslipped Ware sherds examined have cryptocrystalline calcite temper (Chapter IV), as compared to the usual clear calcite for Puuc Unslipped Ware jars and potsherd temper for the censers, whereas the majority of Chichen Unslipped Ware jars are tempered with clear calcite

some have a white carbonate temper with a fine lamellar structure, and most of the censers have a gray limestone temper. Considering smoothness, we find that Mayapan Unslipped Ware like the two earlier wares is generally medium well smoothed, but unlike the others quite a few basins and bowls have an exterior roughness often called a sandpaper finish or, if more coarsely done, a wood rasp finish. Finally we come to the matter of striation which, as used on wide-mouth, low-neck storage or cooking jars and rarely on other vessels of Mayapan Unslipped Ware, is light and rather fine. On Chichen Unslipped jars the striations are usually medium, rarely fine, and on Puuc Unslipped jars the striations are coarse and deeper than on either of the others.

The unslipped group associated with Mayapan Unslipped Ware in the Hocaba Ceramic Complex is the unslipped Navula Group. The forms associated with this group are: jars, cooking or storage; censers including the effigy, tripod, or pedestal jar and ladle types; dishes having flat base and bolster rim and a few with lugs; bowls, most with a restricted orifice, others deep, grater, or even with a small paintpot; cups; figurines; and a possible pestle. The types and varieties linked to this group include: Yacman Striated Type, Yacman Variety; Hoal Modeled Type, Hoal Variety; Navula Unslipped Type, Navula Variety; Cehac-Hunacti Composite Type, Cehac-Hunacti Variety; Kanasin Red-on-unslipped Type, Kanasin Variety; Chenkeken Incised Type, Chenkeken Variety; and Cehac Painted Type, Cehac Variety. Only 16.7 per cent of the unslipped Navula Group is decorated, and the majority of these are modeled, the Hoal Modeled Type, which in general involves the decoration of early style effigy censers, rarely figurines. The Cehac-Hunacti Composite Type embraces both painting and appliqué and is found on censers, both tripod and pedestal jar forms. The painting consists of red or blue designs, and the appliqué involves fillets, spikes, and buttons. Kanasin Red-on-unslipped Type is rare in this complex. It is associated with huge jars, and usually the bolster and neck interior are painted red. Incising is uncommon and of the sharp variety associated with grater bowls. Painting, Cehac Painted Type, by itself rare in this ceramic complex, is found once on a tripod cup.

A ware that is distinctive and that belongs in the Hocaba Ceramic Complex is Peto Cream Ware. The paste composition consists of coarse texture, usually calcite temper, and most commonly beige and gray color. The surface finish was attained by means of smoothing, but due to the coarseness of the paste a lumpy effect persisted. This is true in spite of the addition of a fine-textured slip which was lightly burnished. This slip is opaque and usually cream in color, except for a few having a dull orange tint. The only group associated with this ware is the Kukula Cream Group. The forms used are: jars, both water and storage; dishes tripod with either flaring or rounded sides; bowls with restricted orifice; tripod grater; and a cylindrical vase. The types and varieties connected with this group include: Xcanchakan Black-on-cream Type, Xcanchakan Variety and incised variety; Kukula Cream Type, Kukula Variety; Mataya Modeled Type, Mataya Variety; and Cusama Plano-relief Type, Cusama Variety. The vast majority of sherds belong with the Xcanchakan Black-on-cream Type. Much of the black decoration consists of a quasi trickle. Other designs found are dots, hooks, scrolls, S's, U's, "sausages," loops, finger dabs, concentric circles, triangles, and even a human head. The Mataya Modeled Type has a single example — an applied human head. Another sole example, made up of one rim and two body sherds, belongs to the Cusama Plano-relief Type. This specimen (51, *n*), a deep bowl, was found with the middle lots. The design represents a probable quatrefoil. A number of quite thin sherds (51, *d, e, i, m, n, q*) included with Peto Cream Ware may, when a large collection is available and more is known about them, be classified under a different ware name, such as Thin Cream Ware. Besides thinness, some of these sherds differ in form and in having a somewhat higher polish.

Mayapan Black Ware in the Hocaba Ceramic Complex is identical to Mayapan Red Ware except for slip color and the fact that only two forms have been noted, jars and hemispherical bowls. Only one group, the black Sulche Group, and one type, the Sulche Black Type, is represented in the early lots. The other types wil be discussed with the Tases Ceramic Complex.

Fine Orange Ware is intermingled with the Hocaba Ceramic Complex by means of the fine-orange Matillas Group, formerly called V Fine Orange. This is a pottery acquired through trade from Tabasco (Berlin, 1956, and R. E. Smith, 1958b). The paste has a very fine texture, is untempered, and is orange to cinnamon in color. The surface is well smoothed, thinly slipped and burnished, rarely attaining a high sheen and sometimes almost matte. Besides the orange or reddish slip, usually a shade darker than the paste, some sherds have a black or white slip. These slips rarely cover the entire vessel but are used

in bands or on sections of the pot. Fine Orange Ware has a number of forms, some quite distinctive. These include tripod dishes with or without basal flange, jars with high necks, and restricted-orifice bowls. The types here represented are: Matillas Orange Type, Matillas Variety; Nacajuca Black-on orange Type, Nacajuca Variety; Villahermosa Incised Type, Villahermosa Variety; Chilapa Gouged-incised Type, Chilapa Variety; and Salto Composite Type, Salto Variety. The Matillas Orange Type forms 74.1 per cent of the fine-orange Matillas Group sherds in the Hocaba Ceramic Complex. The other types follow in the order listed, with 12.3, 8.7, 3.7, and 1.2 per cent, respectively. The Nacajuca Black-on-orange Type is usually decorated with horizontal and oblique parallel lines. The Villahermosa Incised Type has postslip incising as a rule, but in some instances where the slip is much the same as the paste the incising may be preslip. The designs include chevron bands with centrally placed circles and others, but the sherds are too small for certain identification. The Chilapa Gouged-incised Type, involving only three sherds all very fragmentary and therefore doubtful as to design, has examples of both preslip and postslip gouging and incising. The Salto Composite Type embraces both the gouged-incised and painted techniques. The single example present had a black band on interior and gouged-incised decoration on exterior.

An interesting observation concerning the fine-orange Matillas Group is that it seems to have had little if any influence on the other Hocaba Ceramic Complex wares or groups. The use of effigy feet is the only common component.

Is the Hocaba Ceramic Complex Influenced in any way by the preceding Sotuta Ceramic Complex?

The answer to this question is yes, but largely through the cream Kukula Group of Peto Cream Ware. Only occasionally is the red Mama Group affected. Certain traits are carried over into the Hocaba Ceramic Complex by means of the slate Dzitas Group usually to the cream Kukula Group. This is true of certain forms: jars with wide mouth and low grooved neck, jars with narrow mouth, high outcurving neck, two horizontal strap handles, and a pear-shape body; bowls with restricted orifice and direct horizontally grooved rim, bowls with restricted orifice and flat bolster rim (also the red Mama Group) which may have horizontal grooving, tripod grater bowls with oven feet (also the red Mama Group); tripod dishes with flaring sides and hollow bulbous feet (also the red Mama Group), tripod dishes with recurving sides and hollow oven-shape feet; and pot-stands with flat top and pedestal base, found only in Brainerd's 1958 publication. This is likewise true of certain decorative techniques associated with the slate Dzitas Group and also found in the cream Kukula Group. These are the use of black paint and of modeling. Incising occurs in both complexes, especially in connection with the red Dzibiac Group and the red Mama Group. The designs common to both the slate Dzitas and the cream Kukula groups include the "sausage," spiral scroll, and tricklelike device. Others that form part of both the fine-orange Silho and cream Kukula groups comprise plain rectangles, hooks, "ram horn" scrolls, the U-shape device, naturalistic human figures, flower-like quatrefoils, and possible kin signs. Plain rectangles, "ram horn" scrolls, and flowerlike quatrefoils are also found in the red Dzibiac as well as the cream Kukula Group.

Thus it is clear that without the cream Kukula Group very little of the makeup of the Sotuta Ceramic Complex would be found in the Hocaba Ceramic Complex.

Some traits found in the Hocaba and Tases complexes, however, have their beginnings in the Cehpech Ceramic Complex and even earlier. Forms include hemispherical bowls, cylindrical vases, and ladle censers. In addition certain form accessories persist: lateral flanges; hollow cylindrical feet with flat or rounded base; ringstands; and pedestals both bell-shape and cylindrical. These forms are associated with many different wares and groups. This is equally true of certain decorative techniques such as postfire dichrome and polychrome painting, sharp-incising both preslip and postslip, groove-incising, impressing with thumb or finger, carving of the gouged-incised type, and modeled-and-appliqué buttons and heads. The same may also be said of various design devices: chevrons, circles and concentric circles, crescents or semicircles, crosshatching, dots or dotted lines, lines either vertical, horizontal, or diagonal, the guilloche or braid, part or semidisks, S-shapes or reverse curves, scrolls either simple or angular, step-frets (angular type), taus, triangles, and zigzag lines. Miscellaneous traits,

found at least as early as the Cehpech Phase and through the Tases Phase, include the use of Maya blue and a calcareous white coating usually associated with the unslipped wares; certain rim forms, including everted rims and rounded, triangular, square, and flat bolster rims; and a variety of blemishes such as rootlet-marking, fire-clouding, crazing, and fire-blackening both on interior and exterior of the vessel.

On the other hand, new traits abound in the Hocaba Ceramic Complex that have no apparent connection with the immediately preceding complexes. These consist of jars with tubular spout; huge storage jars with a thick coating of plaster covering the entire vessel; flat-base basins with flat bolster rim and horizontal strap handles or lug handles; restricted-orifice bowls with triangular bolster rim, restricted-orifice bowls with direct rim and ringstand or pedestal base, cuspidor-shape bowls, tripod deep bowls with hollow oven-shape, or solid conical feet, deep bowls with ringstand or pedestal base, some deep bowls either tripod or pedestal-base have a basal-flange; tripod basal-break dishes with flat base and flat bolster rim or lug handles; tripod dishes with rounded sides and solid conical, solid oven, or hollow oven feet; tripod or pedestal-base cups which may be undecorated, painted, or effigy; drums essentially jar-shape; miniature jars with high vertical neck; censers with attached human figure (some evidence of a similar type in Puuc Slate), tripod jar-shape censers, or pedestal-base vase or jar-shape censers; and figurines (rare) including both mold-made and crudely modeled humans. This completes the list of new forms introduced to the Hocaba Ceramic Complex with the exception of moldmade hollow animal feet and lug handles, which apparently appear for the first time in this area. Other firsts are a new finishing technique involving a sandpaper or rasplike appearance, and in design the corkscrew scroll which has been missing since Late Classic times.

Where these new ceramic traits come from is still uncertain. The answer perhaps may be waiting discovery on the east coast of the Yucatan Peninsula or deep in the Peten of Guatemala.

Tases Ceramic Complex

Any attempt to describe the Tases Ceramic Complex without a review of the known sources of this material would be inadequate. According to our present knowledge, the provenience is spread over most of Quintana Roo, Yucatan, and Western Campeche, parts of Tabasco and Chiapas, and rarely the Peten of Guatemala. Future excavation, however, may unearth more Tases-like pottery from the Peten than has already been noted at the ruins of Topoxte, Lake Yaxha, Tikal, and the Town of Flores. Present knowledge suggests that these late ceramic manifestations were the result of copying northern specimens rather than of trade.

Other than Mayapan, the only site from which Tases pottery is described in this report is Chichen Itza, and then only a few surface specimens from otherwise pure Sotuta Phase trenches. In point of fact Chichen Itza harbored a very large collection of Tases Phase pottery, most of which was found not only on the surface but for the most part on top of fallen construction.

CHICHEN ITZA [1]

At Chichen Itza four sherds of the Tases Ceramic Complex were found on or near the surface in the five trenches used to establish the Sotuta Ceramic Complex.

MAYAPAN UNSLIPPED WARE

Censers, effigy or possibly effigy vessels. One a scalloped lip, the other a painted blue jaguar earlike adorno. *Surface:* imperfectly smoothed, color gray with added blue paint. *Paste:* coarse texture, grayish color. *Types and decoration. Chen Mul Modeled Type:* 1 rim, 1 body sherd.

TULUM RED WARE

Jar. Possibly an upper neck fragment. *Surface:* slipped and polished on exterior only. *Paste:* medium textured, buff colored. *Types and decoration. Payil Red Type:* no rims, 1 body sherd. *Bowl* (?). Very fragmentary. Badly weathered. *Types and decoration. Payil Red Type:* no rims, 1 body sherd.

MAYAPAN [29,332]

Here we begin the study of the Tases Ceramic Complex as found at Mayapan. This is a complex marked by the abundance of effigy censers. The censers which belong essentially to the Chen Mul Modeled Type are found in many parts of the ruins, often on the surface and especially in association with colonnades. The number of Chen Mul Modeled Type effigy censers found in the Tases Ceramic Complex totaled 128,118 or 45.9 per cent of all sherds in that complex, while those from middle lots totaled 9,936 or 11.5 per cent of all middle lot sherds.

The other important types representative of the Tases Ceramic Complex include Mama Red Type, unslipped-exterior variety; Pustunich Incised Type, Pustunich Variety; and Chapab Modeled Type. Of these only the Mama Red Type, unslipped-exterior variety forms any measurable percentage of the late lot total and that a mere 1.9 per cent. There are also certain wares that attain their peak in this ceramic complex: San Joaquin Buff, Telchaquillo Brick, and Tulum Red. The fine-orange Matillas Group is represented equally in the middle and late lots at 1 per cent of the slipped wares which is double the percentage it attained in the early lots.

Actually 41.4 per cent of the ceramic material found in the Tases Ceramic Complex is a carry-over from the Hocaba Ceramic Complex. This carry-over includes the following wares and percentages: Mayapan Unslipped Ware, 12.5; Mayapan Red Ware, 27.8; Peto Cream Ware, .5; Mayapan Black Ware, .3; and fine-orange Matillas Group, .3.

In the surface levels mixed with Tases types are found a few (115) sherds belonging to later ceramic complexes. Sixteen of these are of the fine-orange Cunduacan Group, which forms part of the Chikinchel Ceramic Complex and Protohistoric Period. The remainder, 99 sherds, are of the Chauaca Ceramic Complex associated with the Colonial Period. A question immediately arises as to why 16 Chikinchel Fine Orange Ware fragments were found above the floors of an elaborate dwelling, Q-244b. Possibly they were part of a post-abandonment offering destroyed by falling walls. The later Chauaca sherds could have been deposited any time after the evacuation but most probably in early colonial times.

MAYAPAN UNSLIPPED WARE

For descriptive listing, see pages 208–209.

Jars, wide mouth, low neck (28, a, 1–11, 13, 15–18, 20–24). These may have vertical or slightly flaring, direct or bolster rim, rounded, beveled, grooved, flat, or pointed lip, globular body, a few with plain [24] or bird head [10] lug handles (28, a, 16, 18), others with plain [3], or bird head [2] lugs (28, a, 17, 20–23) and a few [8] with a flange, often notched (cf. 28, a, 25), flat or convex base. *Size:* lip diam. 11–36 cm., av. 23.4 cm., most common of 182 measured 22 cm. [40], 25 cm. [32], and 20 cm. [20]; neck ht. 1.5–3.5 cm., av. 2.4 cm., most common of 224 measured 2 cm. [52], 2.3 cm. [50], 2.5 cm. [39], and 2.8 cm. [29]; thickness .3–.5 to .7–1.2 cm., most common .5–.8. *Remarks:* modern vessels similar to these are called *cooking pots* (R. H. Thompson, 1958, pp. 113–117, figs. 34, 35). These jars may have been used for purposes other than cooking be-

cause few show fire-blackening. *Surface:* well smoothed on interior and neck exterior, including a short distance on shoulder just below neck which varies from 1 to 2.5 cm., in many cases just the width required for thumb smoothing. The remainder of vessel exterior is lightly striated, probably raked with dried grass or the like. A few examples, smoothed all over, lack striation. Numerous sherds evidence the use of a white calcareous coating. Color is 63 per cent gray (10 YR 6/1 and 10 YR 5/1) and 37 per cent cinnamon (5 YR 6/6 and 10 YR 7/3). *Paste:* coarse texture, generally calcite temper. The color is much the same as on surface where gray predominates over cinnamon. *Types and decoration:* here we are considering striation as a form of decoration. *Yacman Striated Type:* 3,866 rim, 18,743 body sherds. *Thul Appliqué Type:* 18 rim, 35 body sherds. These have shoulder lugs. *Panaba Unslipped Type:* 4 rim, 28 body sherds. *Acansip Painted Type:* 3 rim, 2 body sherds. This form is rarely painted and even the few (28, a, 13, 15) recorded here may more properly belong with the small deep tripod bowls or jars (31, z, aa). *Chenkeken Incised Type:* no rim, 1 body sherd. This has two wavy, horizontal incised lines.

Jars, wide mouth, medium-high neck (28, b, 2, 3), may have flaring or nearly vertical, direct rim, rounded, beveled, or flat lip, pear-shape body, two opposite horizontal strap handles placed at maximum body diameter, concave base. *Size:* lip diam. 24–31 cm., av. 28.3 cm., most common of 9 measured 26 cm. and 31 cm. [3 each]; neck ht. 4–6.5 cm., av. 5.4 cm., most common of 8 measured 6.5 cm. [3], 4 cm. [2]; thickness .4–.9 to .5–1.1 cm., most common .4–.9 cm. *Surface:* well smoothed all over for about 51 per cent; the rest have body striation similar to that found on the jars with lower necks. Many have a white calcareous coat. *Paste:* coarse texture, probably calcite temper, gray (10 YR 6/1, 10 YR 5/1, 10 YR 8/1) or cinnamon (5 YR 6/6, 10 YR 7/3) color. *Types and decoration:* no decoration encountered other than striation. *Panaba Unslipped Type:* 104 rim, 324 body sherds. *Yacman Striated Type:* 39 rim, 376 body sherds.

Jars, large size, high neck (28, c, 8–11), which may be outcurving or flaring, bolster (rounded, flat, square, or triangular) or direct rim, rounded, beveled, or flat lip, usually carry vertical strap handles set on opposite shoulders, pear-shape or globular body, probably flat or slightly concave base. *Size:* lip diam. 13–36 cm., av. 23.8 cm., most common of 33 measured 20–25 cm. [17]; neck ht. 6.5–9 cm., av. 7.7 cm., most common of 8

MAYAPAN UNSLIPPED WARE

Forms and Types	A Rim	C Rim	D Rim	%	Total Rim & Body	
Jars, wide mouth, low neck:				23.5		
Yacman Striated Type	1,988	1,599	279		3,866	18,743
Thul Appliqué Type	9	9	0		18	35
Panaba Unslipped Type	4	0	0		4	28
Acansip Painted Type	3	0	0		3	2
Chenkeken Incised Type	0	0	0		0	1
Jars, wide mouth, medium-high neck:				0.9		
Panaba Unslipped Type	11	93	0		104	324
Yacman Striated Type	30	0	9		39	376
Jars, huge size, high neck:				2.6		
Navula Unslipped Type	241	122	15		378	4,167
Kanasin Red/unslipped Type	47	1	0		48	251
Jars, large size, high neck:				1.8		
Navula Unslipped Type	129	141	28		298	1,992
parenthesis rim: Panaba Unslipped Type	2	0	0		2	0
Censers, effigy, large and medium size:				50.8		
Chen Mul Modeled Type	1,416	6,705	295		8,416	119,633
Hoal Modeled Type	0	0	0		0	3
Censers, effigy, small size:						
Chen Mul Modeled Type	0	5	0		5	64
Censers, ladle:				9.3		
Navula Unslipped Type	698	743	106		1,547	548
Chenkeken Incised Type	0	1	0		1	0
Censers, jar, tripod:				1.4		
Cehac-Hunacti Composite Type	16	173	44		233	1,212
Huhi Impressed Type	0	0	0		0	27
Acansip Painted Type	1	0	0		1	1
Censers, jar, pedestal base:				1.1		
Cehac-Hunacti Composite Type	14	149	2		165	355
Huhi Impressed Type	1	7	2		10	65
Acansip-Thul Composite Type	0	1	0		1	0
Censers, jar, tripod or pedestal base:				0.1		
Cehac-Hunacti Composite Type	9	10	0		19	389
Bowls, restricted, direct rim:				1.1		
Navula Unslipped Type	100	70	8		178	37
Yacman Striated Type	0	5	0		5	12
Huhi Impressed Type	0	2	0		2	1
Bowls, restricted, bolster rim:				0.3		
Navula Unslipped Type	18	19	5		42	12
Bowls, deep, tripod:				0.8		
Panaba Unslipped Type	46	14	1		61	29
Huhi Impressed Type	4	28	1		33	45
Thul Appliqué Type	10	10	0		20	29
Acansip Painted Type	20	0	0		20	10
Chenkeken Incised Type	1	0	0		1	0
Bowls, grater: Chenkeken Incised Type	3	4	1		8	14
Bowl, thick: Panaba Unslipped Type	1	0	0		1	0
Dishes, flat base, flaring side:				1.0		
Navula Unslipped Type	59	90	21		170	10

MAYAPAN UNSLIPPED WARE (Continued)

Forms and Types	A Rim	C Rim	D Rim	%	Total Rim & Body	
Dishes or bowls, tripod, flaring side:				0.9		
Panaba Unslipped Type	52	53	21		126	46
Chenkeken-Acansip Composite Type	0	18	0		18	7
Chenkeken Incised Type	1	4	0		5	2
Acansip Painted Type	0	0	1		1	0
Dishes or bowls, tripod, rounded side:				0.2		
Panaba Unslipped Type	14	14	0		28	17
Acansip Painted Type	1	0	0		1	0
Cups, tripod:				1.1		
Panaba Unslipped Type	93	41	15		149	164
Cehac Painted Type	4	10	0		14	12
Chen Mul Modeled Type	2	11	0		13	7
Cups, pedestal base:				0.1		
Acansip-Thul Composite Type	9	0	0		9	2
Chen Mul Modeled Type	6	1	0		7	5
Panaba Unslipped Type	1	1	3		5	15
Acansip Painted Type	0	0	1		1	1
Cups, flat base:						
Chen Mul Modeled Type	0	5	0		5	1
Basins, flat base:				0.9		
Navula Unslipped Type	27	34	12		73	32
Yacman Striated Type	27	35	11		73	31
Chenkeken Incised Type	12	0	0		12	3
Vases, pedestal base:				0.9		
Panaba Unslipped Type	1	80	0		81	38
Thul Appliqué Type	0	32	0		32	10
Cehac-Hunacti Composite Type	0	31	0		31	10
Acansip Painted Type	0	8	0		8	4
Figurines: Chen Mul Modeled Type	27	24	10	0.4	61	123
Vessels, effigy:				0.2		
Chen Mul Modeled Type	18	22	0		40	411
Plates, ringstand:				0.2		
Panaba Unslipped Type	14	25	1		40	5
Molds: Chen Mul Modeled Type	12	2	0	0.1	14	0
Miniature, bowls, restricted:						
Panaba Unslipped Type	0	5	0		5	0
Miniature, bowls, hemispherical:						
Panaba Unslipped Type	0	2	0		2	0
Miniature, jars:						
Panaba Unslipped Type	1	3	1		5	1
Covers, disk-shape sherd:						
Buleb Striated Type	4	0	0		4	1
Covers, disk shape:						
Panaba Unslipped Type	1	2	0		3	0
Masks: Chen Mul Modeled Type	4	0	0		4	0
Stands: Panaba Unslipped Type	1	0	0		1	2
Total	5,213	10,464	893		16,570	149,365

measured 7.5–9 cm. [4]; thickness .5–.8 cm. to .9–1.4 cm., av. .7–.95 cm., most common of 22 measured .7–.9 cm. [17]. *Surface:* well smoothed on exterior and neck interior. Many have calcareous white coating and a few have thick plaster covering. Relatively few have exterior fire-blackening. Generally gray in color. *Paste:* coarse texture, probably calcite temper, cinnamon (5 YR 6/6, 10 YR 7/3) or gray (10 YR 6/1, 10 YR 5/1, 10 YR 7/1, 10 YR 8/1) color. *Types and decoration:* no decoration associated with this form other than painted-red neck interior and bolster rim when present. *Navula Unslipped Type:* 298 rim, 1,992 body sherds.

Jars, large size, high neck, parenthesis rim (31, *g*), an unusual jar form, wide mouth, nearly vertical neck, rounded bolster rim, rounded lip. There is a slight groove in bolster. *Size:* lip diam. 34 cm., neck ht. ca. 8 cm., thickness .8–1.1 cm. *Surface:* well smoothed all over, badly weathered — could possibly have been a red-slipped jar but no evidence of slip. *Paste:* coarse texture, probably calcite temper, gray color. *Types and decoration:* no evidence of decoration. *Panaba Unslipped Type:* 2 rim, no body sherds.

Jars, huge size, high neck (28, *c*, 1, 3–7; 60, *l*), wide mouth, flaring or outcurving neck, rounded, oval, or square bolster rim, rounded or flat lip, pear-shape body, usually carry vertical strap handles set on opposite shoulders, convex base. *Size:* lip diam. 19–46 cm., av. 33.9 cm., most common of 103 measured 40–42 cm. [36] and 28–32 cm. [27]; neck ht. 8.5–15 cm., av. 12.8 cm., most common of 19 measured 12.5 cm. [9]; thickness .8–1 to 1.3–1.4 cm., av. .87–1.13 cm., most common of 26 measured .8–1 cm. [8], .9–1.2 cm. [6]. *Surface:* well smoothed on exterior and neck interior. A few have red slip on neck interior and bolster. Most of these vessels show evidence of having been completely and heavily coated with plaster involving one, two, or three layers and so complete that it concealed strap handles and at times even the mouth. A number of specimens show textile imprint on lowest of three layers (Proskouriakoff, 1962, p. 404, "Impressions of Woven Fabrics.") *Paste:* coarse texture, probably calcite temper, gray (10 YR 6/1, 10 YR 5/1) or cinnamon (5 YR 6/6, 10 YR 7/3) color. *Types and decoration:* no decoration other than the red-slipped neck specimens. *Navula Unslipped Type:* 378 rim, 4,167 body sherds. *Kanasin Red/unslipped Type:* 48 rim, 251 body sherds.

Censers, effigy, large and medium size (32, *e–u*, *w*, *x*, *bb–kk*; 67; 68, *b*, 1, 2, 4–6, 8, 9, 11, 12; 69; 70, *a*, 1–3, 5–27, *b*, 1–3, 5–15; 71, *a*, 1, 3–5, 7–11, *b*, 1–3, 5–9, *c*, 1–6, *d*, 1–12; *e*, 1–10; 72, *a–ff*, *hh–pp*; 73, *a*, 1–9, *b*, 1, 3–7, *c*, 1–8, *d*, 1–5, 7, 8; cf. middle lot specimens in figs. 32, *v*, *aa*; 66, *d*, 7; 68, *b*, 3, 7, 10; 70, *a*, 4, *b*, 4, 16, 17; 71, *a*, 2, 6, *b*, 4, *c*, 7; 72, *gg*; 73, *b*, 2, 8, *d*, 6). These censers consist of a pedestal-based cylindrical vase and an effigy figure attached to the front of the vessel, in an upright position. Both the vase and the pedestal have thick vertical, slightly flaring, or outcurving sides, direct or bolster rim, rounded or flat lip; the vase has a concave floor. In many instances it is not possible to distinguish individual pedestal rims from vase rims, although on the average the former may be smaller in diameter. Holes in vase and pedestal sides and vase floors provided draft, presumably for the burning of copal; all the vessel floors as well as many side fragments were fire-blackened. *Size:* lip diam. 11–30 cm., av. 19.3 cm., most common of 242 measured 18–21 cm. [109]; pedestal diam. 10–22 cm., av. 15.4 cm., most common of 131 measured 15–17 cm. [55]; overall ht. of 3 vessels 40.5, 42.6, 43.5 cm.; thickness .5–1.2 cm., most common .8–1.2 cm. *Surface:* well smoothed all over vessel, sometimes a calcareous coat, rarely a white or black design on exterior. Fire-blackening is mostly on interior, especially on the floor where copal remains have occasionally been found. The entire front of the attached effigy was painted in many colors (red, orange, yellow, blue, green, turquoise, white, and black; less commonly gray, purple, and brown; both brown and gray may at times have been accidental). Density of paint produces different color tones. The usual color of the vessel is gray or cinnamon. *Paste:* coarse texture, generally calcite or gray limestone temper. The color is much the same as on surface where gray predominates over cinnamon. *Types and decoration:* since all have an attached effigy, they belong to the Chen Mul Modeled Type: 8,416 rim, 119,633 body sherds, or the Hoal Modeled Type: no rim, 3 body sherds (32, *c*, *d*; 68, *a*). *Remarks:* the Chen Mul Modeled Type effigies are attached to the base of the vase at approximately the buttocks, the hollow torso and head being joined to the vase at the back, the headdress of the effigy commonly rising 10 to 15 cm. above the rim of the vase. The free-standing legs, modeled and hollow, are usually quite straight or slightly flexed and set apart, the feet pointing directly ahead. The arms, also modeled and hollow, usually hang close to the body, elbows forming a right angle, with well-shaped hands terminating in long, tapering fingers, habitually showing fingernails and extended a short distance in front of the body palms upward, ready to offer some object. This position is almost invariable for the right hand, except when it grasps a spear-thrower (70,*a*, 24) or holds a spear (?). Normally the left arm and hand are found in the same offering position as the right, but occasionally the arm although flexed appears to be carrying a shield (67, *e*; 70, *a*, 19) and the hand, palm down, may be holding some object (67, *e*). Both right and left arms and hands show a variety of positions (70, *a*,) the same being true for legs and feet (70, *b*). Usually the hands are made with long tapering fingers, but sometimes they are shown clenched without visible fingers (70, *a*, 15, 16). Feet, likewise, are normally modeled with care, revealing all five toes with well-indicated toenails. A few, however, are less carefully made or are not human: toes suggested by means of incised lines (70, *b*, 5, 9, 12, 15), toenails not shown (70, *b*, 5–7, 9–15, 17), only four toes represented signifying some animal (70, *b*, 11–13, 15), or without toes (70, *b*, 10).

Finally, there is the modeled head with special attention to the moldmade face. The head is adorned with a wide range of headdresses welded to head and covered with appliqué ornaments. It has four principal forms: bonnet from which a funnel-shaped crown arises (32, *g*, *k*; 67, *b*, *c*; 68, *b*, 2, 4, 7, 8, 10, 11; 69, *b*, *h*, *l*, *m*, *q*; 71, *a*, 3); helmet representing unidentified birds (32, *e*, *f*, *m*; 67, *f*; 68, *b*, 6, 9; 69, *a*, *i*), jaguar or puma (67, *a*, *e*; 69, *j*, *k*), serpent (32, *n*; 67, *d*), alligator (32, *l*), and the leaf-nosed bat (69, *c*); skullcap (66, *d*, 7; 68, *b*, 5; 71, *a*, 5); and rectangular box from which a funnel-shaped crown arises (71, *a*, 1, 4; Lothrop, 1924, pl. 9, *g*).

The face, possibly the most important part of these figures, was made in a mold, and the four basic types may be embellished by painting or appliqué to represent different gods. First there is the youthful face [117] with straight nose [75], of which 54 portray the maize god (32, *g*; 67, *b*; Thompson, 1957, pp. 615–616), 4 (2 doubtful as to nose type) whiskered gods (R. M. Adams, 1953, fig. 10, *c*, left and right; Thompson, 1957, p. 611), 3 Quetzalcoatl-Kukulca (67, *a*; 69, *k*; Thompson, 1957, p. 617), 3 Mexican goddess Tlazolteotl (69, *b*; D. E. Thompson, 1955, fig. 2, *p*; Thompson, 1957, pp. 613–615), and 11 unidentified youthful gods (68, *b*, 12; 69, *l*; Thompson, 1957, fig. 2, *g*, p. 619); youthful face with Roman nose [26] including 8 whiskered gods (32, *e*; 68, *b*, 6; Thompson, 1957, fig. 1, *i*, *j*, pp. 610–611), 2 gods of merchants or god M (32, *j*, *m*; 67, *f*; Thompson, 1957, fig. 1, *f*, *h*, pp. 608–610), 1 possible Venus god (69, *h*; Thompson, 1957, fig. 2, *e*, pp. 616–617),

and 15 *unidentified* youthful gods (32, *l*; 68, *b*, 11; 69, *a*, *c*, *f*, *g*, *m*, *n*, *t*; Thompson, 1957, figs. 2, *f–i*; 4, *k*; p. 619); and youthful face with upturned nose [16] all representing the god of merchants or god M (32, *h*; 68, *b*, 9; Thompson, 1957, figs. 1, *e*; 4, *h*, *i*; pp. 608–610). Second, there is the old face [51] with markedly Hebraic nose [30], represented by 21 old gods such as god D, Itzamna (32, *k*; 67, *c*, *e*; 68, *b*, 2, 4, 5, 8; 69, *j*; Thompson, 1957, fig. 4, *e*, *f*; pp. 618–619), 6 old gods with cleft chin (69, *d*, *e*; Thompson, 1957, fig. 4, *e*, *f*), and 3 miscellaneous old gods not included with Itzamna (32, *f*; 69, *i*, *p*; Thompson, 1957, p. 622). Third comes the representation of the death face [9] including 7 full face skulls (69, *r*, *s*; Thompson, 1957, fig. 4, *d*; p. 618), and 2 heads showing one side treated naturalistically and the other half displaying the features of a skull (69, *u*; Thompson, 1957, p. 618). Fourth, there is the face covered by a yellow mask of human skin [3] which characterizes Xipe Totec, a Mexican god of vegetation (32, *i*; 68, *b*, 3; Thompson, 1957, figs. 2, *a*, *b*; 4, *g*, all Thompson's examples from middle lots). In addition to the four basic face types listed above there are a few that do not conform; one has an unusually prominent nose and bulging eyes (69, *o*). It is not intended to suggest that each of the basic face types came from the same mold or even that each of their varieties was so reproduced. It is clear, however, that many of these varieties were repeated from the same mold. For instance, using two examples of the straight-nosed youthful-faced type made in the same mold, one may be embellished to represent god E, the maize deity (32, *g*; 67, *b*), the other Quetzalcoatl (67, *a*); or employing two specimens of the Roman-nosed youthful-faced deity resulting from a common mold; one may be made to represent the whiskered god (32, *e*), the other the merchant god (32, *m*) by merely changing the painting of the face and adding more whiskers.

In the study made of the face, the nose has figured prominently but eyes, mouth, and chin are also very important. The noses totaling 179 have been listed: 75 straight (32, *g*; 67, *a*, *b*, *f*; 68, *b*, 10, 12; 69, *b*, *c*, *l*, *n*, *t*), 30 Hebraic (32, *k*; 67, *c*; 68, *b*, 2, 4, 5, 8; 69, *d*, *e*, *i*, *j*, *p*), 26 Roman (32, *e*, *f*, *j*, *l*, *m*; 66, *d*, 7; 68, *b*, 6, 11; 69, *f–h*, *m*), 21 long (32, *n*; 67, *d*; 69, *q*), 16 turned up or Pinocchio (32, *h*; 68, *b*, 9), 9 skeletal or death's head (68, *b*, 7; 69, *r*, *s*), 1 flat, a Xipe Totec specimen (68, *b*, 3), and 1 prominent example (69, *o*). Eyes, totaling 136, fall into various types including: 84 natural (32, *e–g*; 67, *a*, *b*; 68, *b*, 6, 10, 11; 69, *a–c*, *f–i*, *k–n*, *t*), 21 perforated (14 the entire eye, 32, *h*, *j*, *m*; 67, *f*; 68, *b*, 7, 9, 12; 69, *s*; 7 just the pupil,

69, *h*), 14 old man with heavy lid (32, *k*, *n*; 67, *c*, *d*; 68, *b*, 2, 5; 69, *d*, *e*, *p*), 6 Tlaloc (Thompson, 1957, fig. 1, *a*), 4 central punch for pupil (69, *o*), 4 bulging which are appliqué (69, *j*, *o*), and 3 closed usually Xipe Totec (32, *i*; 68, *b*, 3). Most of the natural type eyes as well as the heavy-lidded old man type have black painted pupils. These represent the predominant Mayapan eye type. Checking effigy censer eyes from elsewhere, it would appear that the east coast of Yucatan favors the perforated eye pupil (Gann, 1918, fig. 67, and pl. 20; Gann, 1926, frontispiece; WTS, 1960, figs. 16, *k*, *l*; 17, *b*, *e*). This is also true of British Honduras as found at Santa Rita (Gann, 1900, pl. XXXII) and Benque Viejo (Gann, 1925, p. 92) and other sites, specimens from which were examined in the Peabody Museum of Harvard University. However, a small group of effigy censer figures obtained from Topoxte, Peten, Guatemala by W. R. Bullard, Jr., and now on exhibit in the Peabody Museum of Harvard University favor the eye with punched pupil. The punching was done so vigorously that when the punch accidentally went clear through the vessel wall the hole was blocked by an added piece of clay. The mouth is usually partially open, and this is true of all facial types. One type, however, that of the upturned nose, seems always to have a protruding lower lip. The chin may be normal, strong, or cleft. The normal or medium strong chins are found associated with the youthful face; the strong or outjutting chin is characteristic of the old face, as is the cleft chin.

The wearing apparel, jewelry, and adornments pertaining to the figures are described in Chapter V; processes involving additions to the surface, appliqué (Table 37).

Censers, effigy, small size (66, *d*, 4–6, 8, 9, 11–13; cf. middle lot specimens in 64, *a*; 66, *d*, 1–3, 10). These small censers do not have the uniformity associated with the medium and large size. This is true for both the vessel and attached godlike figure. The vessel may be a cylindrical vase with pedestal base (66, *d*, 1, 2) much like the larger specimens or may have a quite different form such as that of a barrel-shape vase with ringstand base (64, *a*). The godlike figures are less elaborate than their larger counterparts and fewer in number. *Size*: based on middle lot findings. Pedestal-base vase, lip diam. 6.8–7 cm., most common of three measured is 7 cm. [2]; vase ht. 9.5–12.5 cm, most common 12–12.5 cm. [2]; overall ht. 12.9–18.5 cm., only two complete vessels; thickness .5–.6 cm. for two of complete specimens. Restricted vase with ringstand base,

lip diam. 5.5 cm., vase ht. 9.8 cm., overall ht. 14.2 cm., only one complete vessel. *Surface*: well smoothed all over vessel, may have a calcareous coat. The entire front of the attached effigy was painted white, and on this primary coat many colors were used including red, blue, yellow, orange, green, and black. The usual color of the vessel is gray or cinnamon. *Paste*: coarse texture, temper not tested. The color is much the same as on surface. *Types and decoration*: since all have or had an attached effigy they belong to the *Chen Mul Modeled Type*: 5 rim, 64 body sherds. The effigies are more closely attached to the front of the vase than they are on the larger effigy censers. The position of the legs, arms, feet, and hands varies in each example, thus lacking the greater uniformity of the bigger censers. The gods represented include three complete specimens belonging to the middle lots, the old god, Izamna (66, *d*, 2), and two examples of the god of merchants (64, *a*; 66, *d*, 1), also two possible maize-god likenesses (66, *d*, 10, 11), other youthful gods (66, *d*, 4, 8, 9), and two reproductions of the old god (66, *d*, 5, 6), all of which are portrayed by means of disconnected heads.

Censers, ladle (33, *b*, *c*; also cf. middle lot forms in figures 33, *a*, *d*, *e*; 62, *g–i*). Medium-thick to thick rounded or flaring sides, direct rim, beveled, rounded, or pointed lip, flat to slightly convex base, and hollow tubular handle opening into bowl, rarely closed off from bowl (33, *e*). *Size*: lip diam. 10–34 cm., av. 22.4 cm., most common of 133 measured 21–27 cm. [74], 16–18 cm. [31]; ht. 3–8 cm., av. 6.3 cm., most common of 34 measured 5.5–6.5 cm. [26]; overall length 13–31.5 cm., av. 16 cm., most common of 9 measured 13 cm. [5]; thickness .5–1 cm., av. .64–.96 cm., most common of 38 measured .7–1 cm. [16], .6–1 cm. [15]. *Surface*: better smoothed on interior than on exterior, which may be partially striated or have a rasplike finish. Fire-blackening on some interiors and calcareous white coating on some exteriors. *Paste*: coarse texture, probably calcite temper, gray and cinnamon color. *Types and decoration*: most appear to be undecorated. *Navula Unslipped Type*: 1,547 rim, 548 body sherds. *Chenkeken Incised Type*: 1 rim, no body sherds. This type has a lip groove.

Censers, jar, tripod (31, *e*, *f*, *h*, *i*, *k*; 62, *e*) which have high flaring, outcurving, or nearly vertical neck, direct rim, rounded, flat, or beveled lip, globular body, three hollow oven-shaped feet without vent or rattle. Many base fragments as well as a few whole vessels have from 5 (the most common number) to 11 holes perforated through floor. A few (cf. 31, *j*) have lateral moldings and may belong to this form rather than that of the jar with pedestal base. *Size*: lip diam. 15–22 cm., av. 20.6 cm., most common of 45 measured 21–22 cm.; neck ht. 4–7.5 cm., av. 6.8 cm., most common of 42 measured 6.5 cm. [17], 7.5 cm. [9]; overall ht. 25–28 cm., av. 26.8 cm., most common of those measured 28 cm. [9]; thickness .7–1 cm. to .8–1.4 cm., av. .7–1.2 cm., most common of 45 measured .7–1.1 cm., .7–1.3 cm., and .7–1.4 cm. (each 9 times). *Surface*: smoothed on interior and exterior. The latter has a primary white calcareous coating extending to base of neck on interior. The interiors were usually heavily stained from copal burning. *Paste*: coarse texture, probably calcite temper, gray, rarely cinnamon color. *Types and decoration*: no plain vessels were noted. *Cehac-Hunacti Composite Type*: 233 rim, 1,212 body sherds. These were usually embellished with appliqué thumb nail, or reed-impressed fillets and buttons or disks which might be reed-impressed. *Huhi Impressed Type*: no rim, 27 body sherds. Rarely were nail or thumb-impressed horizontal bands rather than fillets used. *Acansip Painted Type*: 1 rim, 1 body sherd. These have painted designs superimposed on the primary calcareous white coat in a variety of colors, but different shades of blue and green were most commonly employed.

Censers, jar, pedestal base (31, *d*, ringstand base; for others with pedestal base cf. 31, *a–c*; 62, *a–c* all belonging to middle lots). These have high flaring, outcurving, or nearly vertical neck, direct rim, rounded, flat, or beveled lip, globular or barrel–shaped body, and flaring or outcurving-sided pedestal base, rarely ringstand base. *Size*: lip diam. 12–21 cm., av. 15.9 cm., most common of 58 measured 18 cm. [19] and 13.5 cm. [14]; overall ht. 15–31 cm., av. 19.6 cm., most common of 39 measured 15–15.5 cm. [20]; neck ht. 3–8.5 cm., av. 5.6 cm., most common of 20 measured 5–5.5 cm. [13]; pedestal ht. much the same as neck ht. except for ringstands which range 1.5–2.2 cm.; thickness .4–1 cm., av. .56–.86 cm., most common of 32 measured .6–.9 cm. [19]. *Surface*: almost identical to that of tripod jar censers except that this form had less painted decoration and more appliqué spike adornment. *Paste*: coarse texture, probably calcite temper, more gray than buff or cinnamon color. *Types and decoration*: no plain vessels were noted. *Cehac-Hunacti Composite Type*: 165 rim, 355 body sherds. These were usually adorned with appliqué thumb, nail, or reed-impressed fillets, buttons or disks which might be reed-impressed, and spikes arranged in various

systems. *Huhi Impressed Type*: 10 rim, 65 body sherds. The use of thumb or nail impressions in horizontal bands directly applied to vessel wall rather than on fillets was comparatively rare. *Acansip-Thul Composite Type*: 1 rim, no body sherds (31, *d*).

Censers, jar, tripod or pedestal base (31, *l–p*). These conform in every way to the two preceding form categories except for the lack of bases for exact identification. *Types and decoration*: only those with appliqué embellishment were noted. *Cehac-Hunacti Composite Type*: 19 rim, 389 body sherds. Most of these had appliqué thumb, nail, or reed-impressed fillets, buttons, or disks sometimes reed-impressed, and spikes. *Chenkeken-Acansip Composite Type*: no rim, no body sherds (found in middle lots, 32, *a*).

Bowls, restricted, direct rim (29, *l–p*; also cf. middle lot forms in 29, *k, q*; 61, *c*, 1), restricted orifice, medium-thick globular body, rounded, beveled, and rarely flat lip, flat or concave base, some have slab or bird lugs, others, strap handles. *Size*: 12–36 cm., av. 22.2 cm., most common of 46 measured concentrated between 17 cm. and 22 cm. [30]; ht. 11.5–14.8 cm., av. 12.2 cm., only 5 measured; thickness .5–1.2 cm., av. .7–.9 cm., mostly medium thick. *Surface*: smoothed on interior and partway down exterior. The lower section of the exterior may be lightly striated or roughly rasped, leaving a coarse sandpaper appearance. A few have white calcareous coating on exterior. *Paste*: coarse texture, probably calcite temper, cinnamon or gray color. *Types and decoration*: possibly a larger number than recorded of the near base sherds were lightly striated. *Navula Unslipped Type*: 178 rim, 37 body sherds (29, *k, l, n, o, q*; 61, *c*, 1). *Yacman Striated Type*: 5 rim, 12 body sherds (29, *m, p*). *Huhi Impressed Type*: 2 rim, 1 body sherd. A few have a horizontal thumb or nail-impressed band a short distance below lip on exterior (no illustration).

Bowls, restricted, bolster rim (no illustration, but see GWB, fig. 22, *c*, 9 for an excellent example). Restricted orifice, medium-thick globular body, rounded or beveled lip, flat or concave base. *Size*: similar to those with direct rim. *Surface*: smoothed on interior and partway down exterior. Lower section of some exteriors may be either lightly striated or rasped, leaving a coarse sandpaper appearance. *Paste*: coarse texture, probably calcite temper, cinnamon or gray color. *Types and decoration*: no striated sherds certainly identified with bolster rims. *Navula Unslipped Type*: 42 rim, 12 body sherds.

Bowls, deep, tripod (31, *r–x, z–bb*; 61, *c*, 5; 62,

f; also cf. middle lot forms in 31, *q, y* and 61, *c,* 4), which in certain instances (31, *q–u, z, aa*; 62, *f*) are clearly jars and in others (31, *v, w, bb*; 61, *c,* 4, 5) are clearly deep bowls, while a few remain doubtful (31, *x, y*). Therefore all have been handled under one heading as deep bowls which change gradually into jars, first with gently out-curving necks growing into sharply angled necks. Medium-thick sides, wide mouth, direct rim, rounded, beveled, pointed, or flat lip, globular body for jars, vertical or recurving sides for bowls, convex base, and three solid conical feet, except for one (31, *r*) with three solid cylindrical feet. Some have lug handles (fig. 31, *r, t, u, aa*). *Size:* lip diam. 7–20 cm., av. 11.1 cm., most common of 60 measured 10–13 cm. [44]; overall ht. 8–18 cm., av. 11.6 cm., most common of 9 measured 10–11 cm. [4]; thickness .4–1.1 cm., av. .55–.86 cm., most common of 30 measured .5–.7 cm. [9], .5–.8 cm. [6], and .5–1 cm. [3]. A few of the jars have neck hts. 1.2–4 cm., av. 2.7 cm., most common of 16 measured 3 cm. [9]. *Surface:* smoothed all over and usually fire-blackened on interior. Some less perfectly smoothed have white calcareous coating on exterior, which in some instances was decorated in a variety of colors including blue, green, red, yellow, and black. The designs are not very clear. One middle lot example (31, *q*) has a lightly striated body. In general, interiors were more carefully smoothed than exteriors. *Paste:* coarse texture, probably calcite temper, gray, cinnamon, dark brown, and beige color. *Types and decoration:* some are undecorated (31, *q, v, w, y*; 61, *c,* 4, 5). *Panaba Unslipped Type:* 61 rim, 29 body sherds. *Huhi Impressed Type:* 33 rim, 45 body sherds. These have horizontal thumb- or nail-impressed band on the exterior body or neck (31, *s*). *Acansip Painted Type:* 20 rim, 10 body sherds. These few have a painted decoration (31, *x,* blue, yellow, and black) without other embellishments. *Thul Appliqué Type:* 20 rim, 29 body sherds. This lot may have painted decoration as well as appliqué, thumb-impressed fillets sometimes with buttons often reed-impressed, or other adornments (31, *r, t, u, z–bb*; 62, *f*). *Chenkeken Incised Type:* 1 rim, no body sherds. No illustration but decoration consists of a horizontal band of vertical incisions.

Bowls, grater (cf. 33, *j*; 61, *c,* 3, middle lot), tripod, medium-thick to thick rounded sides, direct rim, pointed or rounded lip, three solid oven-shape feet. *Size:* only one measured, lip. diam. 18 cm., overall ht. 8.8 cm.; thickness .5–1 cm. *Surface:* smoothed on exterior and interior above scoring. Exterior occasionally rasped, leaving a

coarse sandpaper appearance. A few had white calcareous coating on exterior and down to scored area on interior. In most cases this scored area was not delimited by an encircling groove. *Paste:* coarse texture, probably calcite temper, usually gray color. *Types and decoration:* no decoration other than scoring which is functional. *Chenkeken Incised Type:* 8 rim, 14 body sherds.

Bowl, thick (no illustration). Shape uncertain, but has direct rim, rounded lip. *Size:* fragmentary. *Surface:* smooth all over this small piece. *Paste:* coarse texture, probably calcite temper, gray color. *Types and decoration:* no embellishments. *Panaba Unslipped Type:* 1 rim, no body sherds.

Dishes, flat base, flaring side (29, *dd–ff*). Medium-thick to thick walls, flat bolster [123] or direct [47] rim, beveled, pointed, or rounded lip, flat or slightly concave base. *Size:* lip diam. 17–34 cm., av. 22.9 cm., most common of 24 measured 21 cm. [10]; ht. 3–4.4 cm., av. 4 cm., most common of 5 measured 4.4 cm. [2]. *Surface:* smoothed on interior and exterior. A few are smoothed partway down exterior, the lower part having a rasped or coarse sandpaper finish. Many have a white calcareous coat on exterior. *Paste:* coarse texture, probably calcite temper, cinnamon or gray color. *Types and decoration:* mostly undecorated. *Navula Unslipped Type:* 170 rim, 10 body sherds (29, *dd–ff*).

Dishes or bowls, tripod, flaring side (29, *r–w, y–cc*), medium-thick to thick walls, direct [108], bolster [27], or everted [15] rim, rounded, flat, beveled, or pointed lip, flat to convex base, and three conical feet, rarely solid slab (29, *z*) or hollow (29, *y*). One specimen (29, *cc*) found at Chichen Itza was a square tetrapod with solid tau-shaped slab feet. *Size:* lip diam. 9–34 cm., av. 18.9 cm., greatest concentration of 43 measured 15–23 cm. [25]; ht. without feet 3–6 cm., av. 5.3 cm., most common of 16 measured 6 cm. [11]; thickness .4–1.2 cm., av. .6–.9 cm., most common of 23 measured .7–.8 cm. [6]. *Surface:* smoothed on interior and exterior; occasionally exterior has a rasped appearance beginning about 3 cm. below lip. A few specimens show interior burning. *Paste:* coarse texture, probably calcite temper, cinnamon or gray color. *Types and decoration:* mostly undecorated but both painting and incising do occur. *Panaba Unslipped Type:* 126 rim, 46 body sherds. A few may be very lightly striated low down on exterior, which more generally is plain or rasped (29, *r–u, w*). *Chenkeken-Acansip Composite Type:* 18 rim, 7 body sherds. No illustration but decoration consists of interior horizontal grooving and postfire painting on both interior and exterior. *Chenkeken Incised Type*: 5 rim, 2 body sherds. These have interior horizontal grooving. No illustration. *Acansip Painted Type*: 1 rim, no body sherds. Usually these were painted blue all over (29, *y–bb*) in solid color except *y*, which had vertical blue stripes on exterior.

Dishes or bowls, tripod, rounded side (29, *x*; 33, *i*). Medium-thick to thick walls, direct rim, rounded lip, convex base, and three solid or hollow conical feet. *Size*: lip diam. 9–15 cm., av. 10.7 cm., most common of 7 measured 9 cm. [5]; ht. without feet 3–4.5 cm., av. 3.7 cm., most common of 4 measured 3.6 cm. [2]; thickness .5–.8 cm., av. .58–.76 cm., most common of 5 measured .5–.7 cm. [2] and .7–.8 cm. [2]. *Surface*: smoothed on interior and partway down exterior; lower exterior often has rasped finish. *Paste*: coarse texture, probably calcite temper, gray or cinnamon color. *Types and decoration*: generally undecorated. *Panaba Unslipped Type*: 28 rim, 17 body sherds (no illustration). *Acansip Painted Type*: 1 rim, no body sherds. This specimen has painted vertical red stripes on interior, applied after firing (29, *x*).

Cups, tripod (31, *cc, ee, ff*; 61, *e*, 2; 63, *e, g, h*; cf. early lot, 61, *e*, 3 and middle lots, 31, *dd*; 61, *e*, 1; 63, *f*). Medium-thick to thick walls, cylindrical or pear-shaped body, direct rim, flat, rounded, beveled, or pointed lip, convex base, and three solid conical feet. *Size*: lip diam. 2.2–6 cm., av. 4.5 cm., most common of 51 measured 4–5 cm. [41]; overall ht. 6–11.5 cm., av. 7.9 cm., most common of 32 measured 7–8.5 cm. [23]; thickness .4–.6 cm. to .7–.8 cm., av. .5–.7 cm., most common of 28 measured .5–.7 cm. [17]. *Surface*: smoothed on exterior only. Many have a white calcareous coating. *Paste*: coarse texture, probably calcite temper, cinnamon or gray color. *Types and decoration*: probably many of these had a painted embellishment which weathered off. *Panaba Unslipped Type*: 149 rim, 164 body sherds (no illustration, but same form as painted). *Cehac Painted Type*: 14 rim, 12 body sherds (31, *cc–ee*; 61, *e*, 1–3). *Chen Mul Modeled Type*: 13 rim, 7 body sherds. These include representations of Chac, the long-nosed god (31, *ff*; 63, *e, f, h*), and a face covererd by a vertical braid nose and most of the eyes (63, *g*).

Cups, pedestal base (30, *b, y*; 63, *a, c, d*; cf. middle lots, 30, *v, w*; 61, *e*, 4, 5; 63, *b*), medium-thick to thick walls, cylindrical, pear-shaped, barrel-shaped, or jar-shaped vessel, direct rim, flat, rounded, or beveled lip, flaring to nearly vertical pedestal base. *Size*: 5–8.7 cm., av. 6.1 cm., most

common of 12 measured 5 cm. [5]; overall ht. 7.6–20.5 cm., av. 10.3 cm., most common of 13 measured 8–11 cm. [10]; thickness .5–.8 cm. to .7–.9 cm., av. .59–.84 cm., most common of 10 measured .5–.8 cm. to .6–.8 cm. [6]. *Surface*: smoothed on exterior only. Many have a white calcareous coating. *Paste*: coarse texture, probably calcite temper, gray or cinnamon color. *Types and decoration*: doubtless many unslipped had some form of painted decoration. *Acansip-Thul Composite Type*: 9 rim, 2 body sherds (30, *v, y*). *Chen Mul Modeled Type*: 7 rim, 5 body sherds. These include representations of Chac, the long-nosed god (30, *y*; 63, *a, b*), a possible Ehecatl (63, *c*), and a death's head (63, *d*). *Panaba Unslipped Type*: 5 rim, 15 body sherds (no illustration). *Acansip Painted Type*: 1 rim, 1 body sherd (30, *w*; 61, *e*, 4, same vessel).

Cups, flat base (31, *hh*; 63, *i*; cf. middle lots, figs. 31, *gg*; 63, *j*). Medium-thick to thick walls, cylindrical body, direct rim, flat or rounded lip, flat base. *Size*: lip diam. 3.2–5.1 cm., av. 4.4 cm., only 3 measured, the third is 4.8 cm.; ht. 3.2–8 cm., av. 6.2 cm., only 3 measured, the third is 7.3 cm.; thickness .5–1.4 cm., av. .57–1.1 cm., most common of 3 measured .6–1.4 cm. [2]. *Surface*: smoothed on exterior only which usually has a white calcareous coating. *Paste*: coarse texture, probably calcite temper, gray color. *Types and decoration*: only undecorated specimen illustrated is one from middle lots (Panaba Unslipped Type, 31, *gg*). *Chen Mul Modeled Type*: 5 rim, 1 body sherd. One represents Chac, the long-nosed god (31, *hh*; 63, *i*); another resembles the god of merchants (middle lot, 63, *j*).

Basins, flat base (29, *a, d–g, i–j*; cf. middle lots, 29, *b, c, h*). Medium-thick to thick flaring sides, direct [129] or flat bolster [29] rim, beveled, rounded, or pointed lip, lugs [45:27 slab, 8 hook, 6 spike, 4 twist], flat or slightly concave base, a few with two vertical strap handles placed high on opposite sides of exterior wall. *Size*: lip diam. 20–44 cm., av. 30 cm., most common of 36 measured 28 cm. [7], 30 cm. [6], and 35 cm. [5]; ht. 8–17.3 cm., av. 13.3 cm., most common of 8 measured 16.8 cm. and 12 cm. [3 each]; thickness .7–.9 cm. to 1.2–1.4 cm., av. 83–1.08 cm., most common of 15 measured .8–1 cm. [8]. *Surface*: well smoothed on interior and partway down exterior. The lower exterior area may be rasped [81] or striated [77]. *Paste*: coarse texture, probably calcite temper, cinnamon or gray color. *Types and decoration*: the majority of plain unslipped vessels were undoubtedly rasped on lower exterior. *Navula Unslipped Type*: 73 rim,

32 body sherds (29, a–e, g–i). Yacman Striated Type: 73 rim, 31 body sherds (29, f, j). Chenkeken Incised Type: 12 rim, 3 body sherds. No illustration but these may have one [4] or two horizontal interior rim grooves [8].

Vases, pedestal base (30, a, c–j, l, r–t; 62, d; cf. middle lot, m). Medium-thick to thick vertical or recurving sides, direct or bolster rim, flat or rounded lip, flaring or vertical pedestal base. A small group (30, l–t) have a lateral flange; one (l) has in addition a broad hollow molding between flat lip and flange. *Size:* lip diam. 11–16 cm., av. 14.5 cm., most common of 37 measured 16 cm. [15] and 14 cm. [12]; ht. 18.5–26 cm., av. 21.6 cm., most common of 9 measured 18.5 cm. [4]; thickness .4–.6 to .7–.9 cm., av. .6–.8 cm., most common of 23 measured .7–.9 cm. [7]. *Surface:* imperfectly smoothed interior, often coarse sandpaper texture on exterior; rarely fire-blackened on interior; most have white calcareous coating on exterior. *Paste:* coarse texture, probably calcite temper, cinnamon or gray color. *Types and decoration:* many fragments are undecorated, but probably most whole vessels had some form of decoration. *Panaba Unslipped Type:* 81 rim, 38 body sherds (30, a, n, p, q, s). *Thul Appliqué Type:* 32 rim, 10 body sherds (30, c, g–j, o, r, t). *Cehac-Hunacti Composite Type:* 31 rim, 10 body sherds (30, d, e, k, l; 62, d). *Acansip Painted Type:* 8 rim, 4 body sherds (30, f).

Figurines (35, a, 1–3, 7, 12, 15; b, 3; c, 3; 65, e, j–m, o; cf. middle lots, 35, a, 4–6, 8–11, 13, 14, 16, 17; b, 1, 2, 4–9; c, 1, 2; 65, a–d, f–i, n, p). These total 184, including 171 hollow and 13 solid, or 152 human and 32 animal. The hollow figurines may be open at base to top of head with moldmade front and undecorated flat back welded on (35, a, 1–3, 15; 65, e; cf. 35, a, 4; 65, g), often supplied with suspension holes drilled in back of shoulders; in some cases the base may be closed and a vent placed in back (cf. 65, h); in others there may be two or more hollow compartments (cf. 35, a, 10, 16). One hollow specimen (cf. 65, f) is seated. The solid figurines are of two main classes: those [6] with stationary limbs (35, b, 3; cf. 35, b, 1, 2, 4, 6–9; 65, a–d) and those [7] with articulated limbs (cf. 35, b, 5; 65, p). The humans, hollow or solid, may represent females [12] or males [6] with a variety of headdress or hairdo including crown (35, a, 1–3; cf. 35, a, 4–6; b, 5; 65, a, b, h) or turban (35, a, 7, 12; b, 3; cf. 35, a, 8–11; b, 1, 2, 4; 65, c, d, f g) headdress and parted-in-middle hairdo (35, a, 15; 65, e), or bald (cf. 35, b, 6, 7); also animals: jaguars (65, j, m; cf. 35, a, 9; b, 8; 65, g), pisotes (35, c, 3; cf. 35, c, 1), deer

(65, l), bat (71, c, 6), possible dog (65, k), and iguana (cf. 65, g), also birds (cf. 35, c, 2; 65, g, a dove and an owl, and a fish (65, o). *Size:* ht. of humans 6–30.5 cm., av. 11.3 cm., most common of 20 measured 8.5–9 cm. [8], 10–12.5 cm. [7]; ht. of animals 3–16.5 cm., av. 8.8 cm., most common of 8 measured 3–3.5 cm. [3], 8.5–9 cm. [2], and 13.2 cm. [2]. *Surface:* all probably had painted decoration on a calcareous white background. *Paste:* coarse texture, not tested for temper, gray or cinnamon color. *Types and decoration:* the painting added to these moldmade figurines embodied face, body, and clothing embellishment. The colors used included for humans blue, green, black, red, yellow, orange, and white; for animals red, blue, black, and yellow. Many of the examples, however, were too badly weathered for color to be noted. The modeling is generally mediocre. *Chen Mul Modeled Type:* 61 head, 123 body fragments.

Vessels, effigy (32, ll; 64, b, e–i, l, m, p; cf. middle lots, 32, mm–pp; 64, a, c, d, j, k n, o), include bowls: shallow with turtle-shape (cf. 64, d, j, k, n, o); deep, portraying merchant god resting on one knee (cf. 64, a); deep, representing diving god with animal-shaped pedestal base (64, e, f, h); deep, representing warrior (64, b) or old god, Itzamna (cf. 64, c); and restricted formed like turtle (64, i), and jars shaped like a frog, a rabbit, and a turtle (64, l, m, p, respectively). *Size:* bowls, turtle-shaped [9], lip diam. 4.4–8.3 cm.; av. 6 cm. (only 4 measured); vessel ht. 8.3–10 cm., av. 8.9 cm. (only 3 measured); max. length 15–23.4 cm., av. 18.4 cm.; most common of 7 measured 17–20 cm. [4]. Bowls with pedestal base [8], lip diam. 14–14.5 cm.; overall ht. 22.5 cm. Miscellaneous jars [9], lip diam. 3.5 cm. for one example; ht. 11–13.5 cm. for two specimens. *Surface:* smoothed on exterior and covered after firing with a primary white calcareous coat which is often followed by a secondary coat of blue or green paint upon which details of face or design are depicted in blue, green, red, orange, yellow, and black. Further, many parts were modeled and applied, and some figures were moldmade. *Paste:* coarse texture, temper readings not taken, gray, or cinnamon color. *Types and decoration:* since all are modeled at least in part, as was the case with the effigy censers, this is the term given to the type. *Chen Mul Modeled Type:* 40 rim, 411 body sherds. Subjects represented are as follows: turtles, often with human head in mouth, 12 rim, 74 body sherds; toads, 8 rim, 133 body sherds; diving god, 8 rim, 15 body sherds; birds, 3 rim, 53 body sherds; jaguars, 3 rim, 50 body sherds; warriors, 1 rim, 16 body sherds; rabbit, 1 rim, 1 body sherd; miscellany including miniature altar, 4 rim, 69 body sherds. *Remarks*: many of these effigies served as cache vessels (64, *b–d, i–k, m–o*).

Plates, ringstand (29, *gg*), medium-thick to thick flaring sides rounding to a ringstand base, direct rim, beveled, pointed, or rounded lip. *Size*: lip diam. 15–29 cm., av. 20.3 cm., most common of 17 measured 18–20 cm. [9]; base diam. 8–11 cm., av. 8.8 cm., most common of 4 measured 8 cm. [3]; ht. 3.5–5 cm., av. 4 cm. (3 measured); thickness .6–.7 cm. to .8–1.4 cm., av. .7–1.1 cm. *Surface*: smoothed all over save ringstand. Several covered with white calcareous coat. *Paste*: coarse texture, probably calcite temper, gray or cinnamon color. *Types and decoration*: all appear to be undecorated. *Panaba Unslipped Type*: 40 rim, 5 body sherds.

Molds (66, *a*, 1, 2; cf. middle lots, 66, *a*, 3, 4, and 5 from Cenote TA). Since large, medium, and small size censer heads, both bodies and heads of figurines, effigy vessel heads, and adorno heads found on large and medium size effigy censer arms or headdresses are made in molds, the various representations and sizes are numerous. Considering the number of moldmade objects involved, however, not too many molds were found. *Size*: head ht. 4.8–10 cm., av. 6.7 cm., most common of 5 measured 4.8–7 cm. [4]. *Surface*: smoothed and several had white calcareous coat on exterior. *Paste*: coarse texture, no tempers tested, paste gray or dirty cream color. *Types and decoration*: since these molds were made from an originally modeled figure, they have been grouped under modeled types. *Chen Mul Modeled Type*: 14 heads, no body fragments.

Miniature bowls, restricted (33, *h*; 61, *d*, 1, 2). Thin to medium-thick sides, restricted orifice, direct rim, pointed or rounded lip, globular or barrel-shaped body, flat or ringstand base. *Size*: lip diam. 2.4 cm. (33, *h*); ht. 3.5–5.5 cm., av. 4.3 cm. (3 measured). *Surface*: smoothed on exterior. One (33, *h*) was fire-blackened on exterior. *Paste*: coarse texture, no temper test made, gray or beige color. *Types and decoration*: all lacked embellishment. *Panaba Unslipped Type*: 5 rim, no body sherds.

Miniature bowls, hemispherical (no illustration). Medium-thick rounded sides, direct rim, flat base. *Size*: fragmentary. *Surface*: better smoothed on interior than exterior. *Paste*: coarse texture, probably calcite temper, gray color. *Types and decoration*: lacked any embellishment. *Panaba Unslipped Type*: 2 rim, no body sherds.

Miniature jars (33, *g*; cf. middle lot, 28, *a*, 12).

Thin to medium-thick globular sides, wide mouth, direct rim, rounded or pointed lip, flat or pedestal base. *Size*: lip diam. 3.5–3.9 cm., av. 3.7 cm.; ht. 4–4.4 cm., av. 4.2 cm. (only 2 measured). *Surface*: smoothed on exterior, and those with pedestal base [3] all over. Some have a thin white calcareous coat. *Paste*: coarse texture, probably calcite temper, gray color. *Types and decoration*: no embellishment noted for these specimens, although a middle lot example (28, *a*, 12) is lightly striated on exterior. *Panaba Unslipped Type*: 5 rim, 1 body sherd.

Covers, disk-shape sherd (29, *jj*). Thin to medium-thick slightly concave walls, direct rim, jagged lip, roughly circular form. Made from unslipped jar body sherd. *Size*: lip diam. 4–6.5 cm., av. 5.7 cm., most common of 4 measured 4 cm. [2]. Thickness .4–.5 to .5–.7 cm., av. .45–.6 cm., most common of 4 measured .4–.5 cm. [2]. *Surface*: smoothed and striated on exterior. *Paste*: coarse texture, probably calcite temper, gray color. *Types and decoration*: all are striated. *Buleb Striated Type*: 4 rim, 1 body sherd.

Covers, disk shape (29, *ii*). Medium-thick to thick slightly concave walls, direct rim, beveled lip, circular form. *Size*: only 3 specimens, lip diam. 8.2 cm., 10 cm., and 11 cm., thickness .5–.8 cm., .6–.7 cm., and 1.2–1.5 cm. *Surface*: smoothed on exterior, sometimes on interior. One has thick plaster coat. *Paste*: coarse texture, probably calcite temper, two gray and one cinnamon color. *Types and decoration*: other than plaster no ornamentation was noted. *Panaba Unslipped Type*: 3 rim, no body sherds.

Masks (34, *d, e*; cf. middle lots, 34, *a–c, f*). Medium-thick to thick walls, often heart-shaped head, representing death, humans, animals, or grotesques. *Size*: 6–16.8 cm., av. 8.7 cm., most common of 6 (including several from middle lots) measured 6–8 cm. [5]. *Surface*: well smoothed and usually covered with a white calcareous coat added after firing. This primary coating in turn was frequently embellished with paint in various colors including red, blue, green, yellow, and black. *Paste*: coarse texture, not tested for temper, gray or cinnamon color. *Types and decoration*: all these moldmade specimens are included under a modeled type because the original had to be modeled and a mold made from it. *Chen Mul Modeled Type*: 4 head fragments.

Stands (no illustration). Medium-thick walls, flat platelike slab resting on a thick flaring pedestal. These may have some connection with "pedestals" from Chichen Itza illustrated by Brainerd (1958, fig. 71, *e–i*), which he was unable to place accurately in time. The Brainerd specimens are of Slate Ware, whereas these are unslipped. *Size*: fragmentary, no measurements taken. *Surface*: smoothed on the top side. *Paste*: coarse texture, not tested for temper, gray color. *Types and decoration*: no evidence of any embellishment. *Panaba Unslipped Type*: 1 rim, 2 body sherds.

SUMMARY

The diagnostic attributes which identify Mayapan Unslipped Ware are paste composition, form, techniques and style of decoration, and to a lesser degree surface finish. Temper was not thoroughly examined, but the relatively small number of sherds checked appeared to be unusually homogeneous and uniform in paste composition, The unslipped examples as well as the slipped being tempered with a form of calcite.

It may be said that Mayapan Unslipped Ware had a uniform paste composition consisting of coarse texture, usually calcite temper, and gray to cinnamon color. The chief diagnostic difference in paste between Mayapan Unslipped Ware, Chichen Unslipped Ware, and Puuc Unslipped Ware is temper: Chichen, mostly clear calcite and gray limestone, and Puuc, clear limestone and potsherd, neither having the same kind of calcite temper used for Mayapan Unslipped Ware.

Form, however, is a most important mark of identification. Although jars and censers are strongly represented in the Cehpech, Sotuta, Hocaba, and Tases phases, it is often possible to distinguish by form alone to which phase a jar or censer specimen belongs. Another interesting aspect of form is the shift in predominance from one phase to another.

In comparing the quantitative occurrence of one form to another, a study of the rim sherds is apt to be more revealing and therefore more rewarding than a study of the total sherds involved. There are several reasons for this: *a*, rims offer more certainty as to exact form; *b*, rims break up into a reasonably predictable sherd quantity range according to vessel form, size, and ware; and *c*, rim sherds give a somewhat more accurate picture of the number of different vessels found. The most exact method for reaching total vessel count, however, is by weight — that is, by weighing whole vessel examples in the different wares, forms, and sizes and then weighing the total sherds corresponding to these wares, forms, and sizes and dividing by the weight of the key example.

Therefore, in Table 23 we find that according to rim sherd count Sotuta Phase, Chichen Unslipped

Ware jars are less abundant than censers, but more so when the total sherd count is used. Since the ware is the same in both instances, and since different sizes are present in both jars and censers, the real difference focuses on the forms. Jars had medium-wide mouth, rather high neck, and a large globular body with medium-thick sides, resulting in a rim-body ratio of 1:12.2. Censers, which vary in form including hourglass (1:2.5), tripod bowl (1:1.1), and ladle (1:3.1), as a unit have a rim-body ratio of 1:2. The Early Mayapan Hocaba Phase Mayapan Unslipped Ware jars have a rim-body ratio of 1:7.8 and the censers (all forms) a rim-body ratio of 1:5.9, which are closer than was the case with similar material from the Sotuta Phase. Nevertheless, there were nearly three times the number of jar rims as compared to censer rims, a reversal of the Sotuta Phase findings and four times the number of jar total sherds to censer total sherds as compared to less than two to one in the Sotuta Phase. Rims show that unslipped censers were used more than unslipped jars in the Sotuta Phase and that unslipped jars were more used than censers in the Hocaba Phase. Total sherds, however, indicate that jars were most abundant in both phases to a greater or lesser degree. The rim story is the closest to being correct. It is interesting to note that in the Tases Phase the findings closely follow those of the Sotuta rim count. In other words, the censer form is predominant. It is also interesting to note the complete movement (Table 23) of jar and censer rims throughout the Middle and Late Postclassic Period at Mayapan: jar rims gradually lessen, whereas censer rims increase in importance. Other forms that are diagnostic of the Hocaba Phase unslipped ware are dishes with bolster rim, restricted bowls, deep bowls, cups, and figurines. These forms continue to be used in the Tases Phase some, like the dishes with bolster rim and basins, decreasing considerably in popularity, others becoming more popular. But even more important as Tases Ceramic Complex markers are the new forms: jars with high neck and parenthesis rim, tripod deep bowls, thick bowls, cups with pedestal or flat base, disk-shape covers, tripod dishes with flaring or rounded sides, basins without bolster rim, vases with pedestal base, effigy vessels, ringstand plates, miniature vessels, potstands, molds, and masks.

The style of decoration associated with Mayapan Unslipped Ware does indeed set it apart in many instances, although the decorative techniques employed were much the same as those used in previous phases. These techniques included striating, painting, modeling, appliqué, incising, and impressing.

The kind of striation, especially on jars, was lighter and usually finer than that found on Cehpech or Sotuta unslipped vessels. This same kind of striation had its beginning in the Hocaba Phase (Yacman Striated Type) and continued without change throughout the Tases Phase (Buleb Striated Type). It was mainly associated with jars but was used on other vessels such as basins and bowls, deep or restricted.

The painting of Mayapan Unslipped Ware, done after firing on a white calcareous coating, as encountered in both the Hocaba and Tases ceramic complexes, was more a matter of contrasting colors than it was the manipulation of design, except in the simplest geometric form. For instance, the figures attached to the normally undecorated effigy censer vessel were vividly painted in red, blue, green, orange, yellow, brown, black, and white. The only designs noted occurred on the faces, headbands, shields, fans, aprons, or capes, in other words as details of facial characterization, dress, armament, or other equipment. In the Hocaba Phase, besides Hoal Modeled Type effigy censers, the jar-form censers although mostly weathered may have been painted, and a single example of a tripod cup had traces of blue design, Cehac Painted Type. Painting, Acansip Painted Type, was less rare in the Tases Phase, where in addition to the prolific effigy censer count, censer jars were often painted either with a single color or two-tone vertical striping; deep bowls, flat-based dishes, and vases usually enjoyed a single color; cups, although normally painted blue, were occasionally decorated with polychrome geometric designs, and jars, usually undecorated except for striation, in rare instances were embellished with polychrome designs.

Modeling, meaning shape, embraced the reproduction of human bodies, animals, birds, shells, and other objects. The heads, usually moldmade, belonged to effigy censer figures, effigy vessel figures, and figurines, or were used as adornos on larger figures. The vessel forms coupled with modeling, Hoal Modeled Type in the Hocaba Phase, were effigy censers and figurines. These same forms with slight modifications continued on in the Tases Phase as the Chen Mul Model Type and new forms were added, including cups, effigy vessels, molds, and masks. In general the quality of workmanship linked with both the Hoal Modeled Type and the Chen Mul Modeled Type was tolerable. It was only with the rare Uayma Modeled Type, Tases Phase examples, that crude craftsmanship was evidenced.

Appliqué, a much used technique especially in the Tases Phase, is the embellishment of a vessel or figure by the application of pieces of clay, fashioned by hand or moldmade, often representing facial features or parts of the body, either human or animal, but in some instances as simple adornos. In rare cases, especially in association with the Hoal Modeled Type effigy censer, much of the modeling was done directly on the figure and little appliqué ornamentation was used. By contrast, appliqué adornment formed a major part of the Chen Mul Modeled Type effigy censer. Appliqué decoration was not only used with modeling but was frequently coupled with painting in the Tases Phase, as witness the Acansip-Thul Composite Type. The forms associated with this technique, Hunacti Appliqué Type (Hocaba Phase) and Thul Appliqué Type (Tases Phase), are censer jars for the former and censer jars, deep bowls, cups, vases, and jars for the latter.

Incising, a little-used technique not noted in connection with the Hocaba Phase unslipped vessels, is the reproduction of lines by means of a pointed implement. The Tases Chenkeken Incised Type associated with ladle censers, tripod dishes, and basins occasionally has one or two horizontal incised lines just below rim on interior; a jar body exterior has two wavy horizontal incised lines, a deep bowl has a slit band or band of deeply incised short vertical lines just below lip on exterior, and a vase or censer has an incised S band between the lateral molding and the flange.

Impressing, associated more with the Tases than the Hocaba Ceramic Complex, was accomplished by pressure of various sorts upon the wet clay. This technique was used to create bands by thumb or nail impressions either directly on the vessel wall or on an appliqué fillet. Another way of impressing was by reed in the center of buttons.

The surface finish of Mayapan Unslipped Ware was much the same throughout the Hocaba and Tases phases. This includes a moderately careful smoothing, the frequent use of a white calcareous coating, and the rare use of one, two, or three plaster coats. Mayapan Unslipped Ware surface finish is less well smoothed than Chichen Unslipped Ware, and about the same as Puuc Unslipped Ware. All three unslipped wares were at times covered with a white calcareous coat, but only Mayapan Unslipped Ware was occasionally thickly coated with plaster.

MAYAPAN RED WARE

Forms, Types, and Varieties	A Rim	C Rim	D Rim	%	Total Rim & body	
Jars, water, high neck:				12.1		
Mama Red Type	474	506	218		1,198	24,851
Papacal Incised Type	123	46	22		191	3,737
Chapab Modeled Type	8	0	0		8	43
Jars, storage, low neck:				2.3		
Mama Red Type	83	107	68		258	5,633
Papacal Incised Type	5	3	0		8	141
Dzonot Appliqué Type	1	0	0		1	0
Jars, storage, high neck:				7.0		
Mama Red Type	463	263	67		793	15,530
Papacal Incised Type	1	10	0		11	216
Jars, parenthesis rim:				0.3		
Panabchen Red Type	24	2	6		32	685
Pustunich Incised Type	3	0	0		3	0
Jars, tripod, high neck:				0.7		
Tzitz Red Type	55	1	4		60	481
with central bulge: Tzitz Red Type	9	2	0		11	53
with three necks: Tzitz Red Type	4	0	0		4	20
Dishes, tripod, flaring side:				56.0		
Mama Red Type	2,447	1,798	338		4,583	7,652
Papacal Incised Type	283	112	34		429	692
Mama Red Type, unslipped-exterior variety	457	842	120		1,419	3,498
Mama Red Type, black-and-red-on-unslipped variety	1	0	1		2	0
with flange: Mama Red Type	0	7	0		7	16
Papacal Incised Type	0	0	0		0	1
Dishes, tripod, rounded side:				6.5		
Mama Red Type	159	277	81		517	478
Papacal Incised Type	1	0	0		1	1
Mama Red Type, unslipped-exterior variety	60	131	35		226	214
Bowls or basins, restricted orifice:				6.8		
Mama Red Type	323	394	53		770	432
Pustunich Incised Type	1	0	0		1	1
Yobain Plano-relief Type	1	0	0		1	0

Jars, water, high neck (38, a, 3, 19–21; cf. early lot specimens in 38, a, 1, 4–9, 11, 22, 23 and middle lot specimens in 38, a, 2, 10, 12; 74, a–d). Some have medium-high nearly vertical, flaring or outcurving neck with direct or everted rim, rounded, flat, or square bolster, rounded, pointed, or flat lip, two horizontal strap handles, a single possible example of a tubular spout (cf. 38, a, 23) connected to neck, pear-shape body, medium-thick walls, slightly concave base. *Size:* lip diam. 5–28 cm., av. 13.9 cm., most common of 137 measured fall within the 11–17 cm. range; neck ht. 3.2–9 cm., av. 7.3 cm., most common of 79 measured fall within the 6.5–8 cm. range; thickness .5–.9 to .7–1.7 cm., av. .66–1.08 cm., most common of 43 measured .7–1.2 cm., [8], .6–1 cm. [7], .7–1.1 cm. [7], and .7–.9 cm. [6]. *Surface:* slipped and burnished on exterior and partway down neck interior. Bases often show slip. The slip color is usually predominantly red (10 R 4/8, 2.5 YR 4/8), but on any given vessel the red blends into orange (2.5 YR 5/8, 5 YR 6/8), reddish brown (5 YR 5/6, 5/8), and brown (2.5 YR 5/6, 7.5 YR 5/6, 5/8). Fire-clouding and rootlet-marking are common but crazing is rare. *Paste:* coarse texture, generally calcite temper (see Mayapan Red Ware, Chapter IV), and pink to pale red color. *Types and decoration:* a large proportion of these jars remains undecorated. *Mama Red Type:* 1,198 rim, 24,851 body sherds. *Papacal Incised Type:* 191 rim, 3,737 body sherds. Mostly associated with the inner rim, this form of decoration consists of one, two, or three (cf. 38, a, 2, 10; 74, a, b) horizontal groove-incised (preslip) lines. *Chapab Modeled Type:* 8 rim, 43 body sherds. These are really effigy jars with a bird, rarely animal head

MAYAPAN RED WARE (Continued)

Forms, Types, and Varieties	A Rim	C Rim	D Rim	%	Total Rim & Body	
Bowls, tripod, grater:				1.6		
Papacal Incised Type	66	102	13		181	389
Papacal Incised Type, scratched variety	0	0	0		0	2
Bowls, deep, tripod:				0.7		
Mama Red Type	49	17	9		75	18
with basal flange: Panabchen Red Type	3	0	0		3	9
Bowls, cluster, pedestal:				0.3		
Panabchen Red Type	26	0	0		26	41
Dzitxil Openwork Type	8	0	0		8	12
Bowls, hemispherical: Panabchen Red Type	16	9	0	0.2	25	7
Basins: Mama Red Type	144	277	18	3.8	439	410
Vases, cylindrical:				0.7		
Mama Red Type	5	76	2		83	199
Pustunich Incised Type	0	0	1		1	1
Drums: Papacal Incised Type	18	34	6	0.5	58	64
Vessels, effigy: Chapab Modeled Type	0	21	0	0.2	21	39
Miniature vessels, jars:				0.2		
Mama Red Type	15	4	2		21	6
Pustunich Incised Type	2	0	0		2	0
Dzonot Appliqué Type	1	0	0		1	0
bowls, tripod: Mama Red Type, unslipped-exterior	1	0	0		1	3
Covers, disk:				0.1		
Panabchen Red Type	5	9	0		14	1
scutate: Panabchen Red Type	0	0	1		1	0
Cups, tripod: Mama Red Type	0	4	0		4	10
pedestal: Chapab Modeled Type	2	0	0		2	6
Plate, pedestal: Panabchen Red Type	6	0	0		6	6
Figurines: Chapab Modeled Type	1	0	0		1	3
Total	5,354	5,054	1,099		11,507	65,601

on the shoulder (38, a, 19–20; 42, a). One specimen had some sort of modeling on vessel neck.

Jars, storage, low neck (38, b, 7, 9, 21, c, 7; cf. 38, b, 11–13; c, 1–6) flaring or outcurving with wide mouth, direct or thickened rim, slight triangular or square bolster, flat, pointed, or rounded lip, globular or squat body which may have two horizontal strap handles, usually flat to concave base. A few have a sharp-angle shoulder (cf. 38, b, 11, 12). One appears to have had a spout and another may have had three hollow feet. *Size:* lip diam. 8–32 cm., av. 20.3 cm., most common of 35 measured are 24 cm. [8], 23 cm. [4], 27 cm. [4], 21 cm. [3], 11 cm. [3], and 12 cm. [3]; neck ht. 1.1–5 cm., av. 3.5 cm., most common of 46 measured are 3 cm. [13], 5 cm. [11], 3.5 cm. [7], and 2.5 cm. [7]; thickness .4–.6 cm. to .8–1.1 cm., av. .64–.89 cm., most common of

39 measured are .6–.9 cm. [8], .7–1.1 cm. [8], .7–1 cm. [5], .6–.7 cm. [4], and .6–.8 cm. [4]. *Surface:* slipped and burnished on exterior and neck interior, sometimes on exterior and just over lip on neck interior, and rarely on neck interior only. A few are crazed and a few are rootlet-marked. The color is more uniformly red than those of the water jar category. The most used reds are 10 R 4/6, 4/8 and reddish brown 2.5 YR 3/6; less common are red 2.5 YR 4/8 and reddish brown 5 YR 5/6. *Paste:* coarse texture, generally calcite temper (see Mayapan Red Ware, Chapter IV), and pink color. *Types and decoration:* mostly undecorated. *Mama Red Type:* 258 rim, 5,633 body sherds. *Papacal Incised Type:* 8 rim, 141 body sherds. These comprise preslip sharp-incised exterior decoration (47, c, h, i, k, l) including scrolls, a diamond band, hooks, vertical and hori-

zontal lines, and interlocking lines. Others are postslip sharp incised (47, *b, e*) with vertical lines and S's, and a few (47, *p, s, t*) have postfire doodling. *Dzonot Appliqué Type*: 1 rim, no body sherds. This specimen has an impressed and appliqué fillet (38, *b*, 9).

Jars, storage, high neck (38, *a*, 13–15, 18; *b*, 1–6, 8, 10, 16–19, 22; 74, *l*; cf. 38, *a*, 16, 17; *b*, 20; 74, *j, k*). Some have outcurving or flaring neck with wide mouth, rounded, flat, triangular or square bolster rim and some everted and overhanging rim, rounded, pointed, beveled, or flat lip, two horizontal strap handles, pear-shape or globular body, slightly concave base. *Size*: lip diam. 14–43 cm., av. 28.5 cm., most common of 197 measured range from 20 cm. to 37 cm. [184]; neck ht. 3.7–12.5 cm., av. 6.9 cm., most common of 143 measured range 5–9 cm. [123]; thickness .4–.5 cm. to 1.1–2 cm., av. .7–1.02 cm., most common of 110 measured are .6–.8 cm. [20], .7–1 cm. [13], .6–.9 cm. [9], .8–1.1 cm. [7], .8–1 cm. [6], .7–1.2 cm. [6], and .8–1.6 cm. [6]. *Surface*: slipped and burnished on exterior and neck interior, rarely all over interior. Both rootlet-marking and crazing occur. The color is predominantly red (10 R 3/6, 2.5 YR 4/8, 10 R 4/6, 4/8, 2.5 YR 4/6), but on most vessels the red blends into orange (10 R 5/8, 2.5 YR 5/8), reddish brown (5 YR 5/6), and brown (2.5 YR 5/4, 5 YR 4/4). Usually gray fire-clouded areas not present. *Paste*: coarse texture, calcite temper (see Mayapan Red Ware, Chapter IV), and generally pink to pale red, rarely beige or gray color. *Types and decoration*: rarely decorated. *Mama Red Type*: 793 rim, 15,530 body sherds. *Papacal Incised Type*: 11 rim, 216 body sherds. These include interior horizontal rim grooving with one, two, or three parallel lines and exterior preslip sharp-incised decoration (38, *b*, 8).

Jars, parenthesis rim (38, *d*, 1–3), high vertical, bulbous or angular neck, rounded, rarely beveled lip, globular body, no bases associated but probably slightly concave. *Size*: lip diam. 16–19 cm., av. 18.1 cm., most common of 11 measured are 18 cm. [5] and 19 cm. [4]; neck ht. 7.5–9 cm., av. 8.5 cm., most common of 6 measured are 9 cm. [4] and 7.5 cm. [2]; thickness .7–1 cm. to .7–1.3 cm., av. .75–1.15 cm., most common of 6 measured are .8–1.2 cm. [3] and .7–1 cm. [2]. *Surface*: slipped and burnished on exterior and on rim, leaving interior neck usually unslipped. Some are crazed and some rootlet-marked, but most are weathered. Slip color is commonly red (10 R 4/8, 3/6), rarely reddish brown (2.5 YR 3/6). *Paste*: coarse texture, calcite temper (see Maya-

pan Red Ware, Chapter IV), and generally pink to pale red color. *Types and decoration*: usually undecorated. *Panabchen Red Type*: 32 rim, 685 body sherds. *Pustunich Incised Type*: 3 rim, no body sherds.

Jars, tripod, high neck (38, *d*, 4–7; 42, *b–d*), which may be outcurving, have central bulge, or involve three nearly vertical necks. The latter may have been some sort of triple-mouthed drum. All had direct rim, rounded or pointed lip, and, except for the three-necked specimen (42, *d*) which lacked base, globular bodies with three hollow oven-shape feet. *Size*: all except drum: lip diam. 20–24.7 cm., av. 22.3 cm., most common of 39 measured are 20.3 cm. [18] and 24.7 cm. [13]; neck ht. 13–17 cm., av. 15.1, most common of 38 measured are 17 cm. [13], 14 cm. [9], and 13 cm. [9]; thickness .5–1 cm., of which necks run .6–1 cm., bodies .5–.8 cm. Drums (?): lip diam. 13.6 cm., neck ht. 14.8 cm., thickness .4–.7 cm. *Surface*: slipped and burnished on exterior and neck interior, except for drumlike specimens which are unslipped on neck interior. Most are crazed and some rootlet-marked. Slip color is darker red (10 R 3/6) than is normally associated with Mayapan Red Ware. *Paste*: coarse texture, calcite temper (see Mayapan Red Ware, Chapter IV), and generally pink to pale red color. *Types and decoration*: usually undecorated. *Tzitz Red Type*: jars, 71 rim, 534 body sherds, and possible three-necked jars or drums, 4 rim, 20 body sherds.

Dishes, tripod, flaring side (40, *a*, 1, 3, 4, 6; *b*, 1–8, 10–12, 14, 16, 17; *c*, 1, 2, 6, 8, 10–15, 17–20; 74, *p–t*; cf. 40, *a*, 2, 5; *b*, 9, 13, 15; *c*, 3–5, 7, 9, 16; 74, *m–o, v*) also outcurving sides and medium-thick walls, direct rim, rounded, pointed, beveled, or flat lip, slightly convex base, and three feet. These last may be solid conical [1210] hollow oven [531], hollow effigy [193], hollow miscellaneous [166], hollow cylindrical [147], solid oven [58], hollow bulbous [37], solid cylindrical [10], hollow conical [8], and nubbin [1]. Associated with hollow feet are 21 pellets. A few (7 rim, 17 body sherds) of these tripods have a basal flange which may be terraced (40, *c*, 1–3, 6–8), plain (40, *c*, 4), or notched (40, *c*, 5, 9, 10), and some are also incised (40, *c*, 3, 5, 8, 10). *Size*: lip diam. 8–37 cm., av. 21.9 cm., most common of 292 measured fall within the 20–26 cm. range and these total 239 sherds; overall ht. 3–12 cm., av. 7.3 cm., most common of 104 measured fall within the 5.5–9 range totaling 80 sherds; thickness .4–.9 cm. to .6–1.6 cm., av. .64–.91 cm., most common of 145 measured fall largely within two thickness groups .6–.8 cm. to .6–.9 cm. [66] and .7–.8 to

.8–1.2 cm. [59]. *Surface*: slipped and burnished on interior and exterior, sometimes on base or just over edge of base. More often the base is scored and not slipped, but even then the feet in general are partially slipped and only lightly polished. This is the Mama Variety. The unslipped-exterior variety is slipped and polished on interior only. Color is usually uniformly red (10 R 4/8, 3/6, 4/6; 2.5 YR 4/8, 4/6), orange (5 YR 4/8, 10 R 5/8, 2.5 YR 5/8), reddish brown (2.5 YR 5/6, 5 YR 5/6), or brown (10 YR 7/6). Occasionally there is blending of these colors, and frequently fire-clouding is present. Rootlet-marking is common and crack-lace mending holes occur. Crazing is rare. A few sherds, some of which may belong to paint pots, are coated with blue [24] or green [6] paint, usually on the interior. *Paste*: coarse texture, generally calcite temper (see Mayapan Red Ware, Chapter IV), pink to pale red (5 YR 7/6, 8/2, 8/3 to 10 YR 6/1), cream (10 YR 8/3, 8/4), or gray (2.5 Y 8/2) color. *Types and decoration*: rarely is this vessel shape decorated. *Mama Red Type, Mama Variety*: 4,590 rim, 7,668 body sherds. *Papacal Incised Type*: 429 rim, 693 body sherds. Most of the incising consists of preslip horizontal interior rim grooves involving one, two, or three parallel lines (40, *b*, 11, 14). In addition, one has exterior preslip groove-incised complicated curvilinear design (cf. 47, *r*). Another, a basal-flange dish, has preslip incising on exterior wall (no illustration). *Mama Red Type, unslipped-exterior variety*: 1,419 rim, 3,498 body sherds. These are slipped and polished on the interior only (40, *a*, 1–5). *Mama Red Type, black-and-red-on-unslipped variety*: 2 rim, no body sherds.

Dishes, tripod, rounded side (41, *b*, 1, 6, 8–11; cf. 2–5, 7), medium-thick, direct rim, rounded, pointed, beveled, or flat lip, convex base, and three feet, either solid conical, hollow oven, or solid cylindrical. *Size*: lip diam. 8–34 cm., av. 17.4 cm., most common of 120 measured are 20 cm. [26], 14 cm. [22], 10 cm. [12], 12 cm. [10], 18 cm. [10], 23 cm. [9] and 24 cm. [9]; overall ht. 3.2–8.9 cm., most common of 31 measured are 6 cm. [10], and 5.5 cm. [7]; thickness .3–.5 to .8–1.2 cm., av. .59–.79 cm., most common of 116 measured are .7–.8 cm. [18], .6–.8 cm. [17], .5–.7 cm. [15], .5–.6 cm. [12], .6–.7 cm. [9], .5–.8 cm. [8], .6–1 cm. [8], and .6–.9 cm. [6]. *Surface*: Mama Variety sherds are slipped and burnished all over, whereas the unslipped-exterior variety specimens are slipped and burnished on the interior; the unslipped exterior often has a sand-paper finish but may be vertically, diagonally, or horizontally striated. Color is usually red (2.5 YR

4/8, 10 R 4/6, 4/8, 3/6), rarely orange (2.5 YR 5/8), and is more uniform with respect to each vessel than is the case with jars or even the tripod dishes with flaring sides. A number of sherds have interior fire-blackening and others show floor areas that are eaten away, possibly by food. Fire-clouding is present and rootlet-marking common. A few [13] sherds of the unslipped-exterior variety are coated with blue paint on the unslipped exterior. *Paste*: coarse texture, generally calcite temper (see Mayapan Red Ware, Chapter IV), pink to pale red (5 YR 7/6, 8/2, 8/3 to 10 YR 6/1), cream (7.5 YR 8/4), or gray (10 YR 8/1, 8/2) color. *Types and decoration*: usually undecorated. *Mama Red Type, Mama Variety*: 517 rim, 478 body sherds. *Papacal Incised Type*: 1 rim, 1 body sherd (no illustration). *Mama Red Type, unslipped-exterior variety*: 226 rim, 214 body sherds. These are unslipped on exterior.

Bowls or basins, restricted orifice (41, *a*, 2–5, 9; 44, *f, j, o, r, u, v*; cf. 41, *a*, 1, 6–8; 44, *g–i, k–n, q*; 47, *n*; 74, *e, u, w–y, aa, bb*), direct [360] rim and rounded, flat, or triangular bolster [412], rounded, pointed, beveled, or flat lip, medium-thick sides, some with lugs, others with two horizontal strap handles, flat or concave base, rarely convex base with pedestal (cf. 44, *l, m*; 74, *aa, bb*). *Size*: lip diam. 6–40 cm., av. 22.2 cm., most common of 155 measured fall within the 19–22 cm. [62], 25–29 cm. [39], and 10 cm. [10] range; overall ht. with flat base 5.6–10.8 cm. av. 10.3 cm., most common of 11 measured is 10.8 cm. [9], with pedestal base 9.8–13.8 cm., av. 10.8 cm., most common of 6 measured is 10.2 cm. [3]; thickness .4–.7 to .9–1.1 cm., av. .69–.8 cm., most common of 110 measured are .6–.7 cm. [35], .7–.8 cm. [30], and .8–1 cm. [10]. *Surface*: slipped and burnished on exterior only, on interior and exterior, or on interior only and bolster when present. Color is red (10 R 4/6, 4/8, 2.5 YR 4/8) or orange (2.5 YR 5/8, 10 R 5/8). *Paste*: coarse texture, generally calcite temper (see Mayapan Red Ware, Chapter IV), and cream (10 YR 8/3, 8/4), gray (10 YR 8/2), beige (10 YR 7/4), or pinkish cinnamon (2.5 YR 6/8) color. *Types and decoration*: rarely decorated. *Mama Red Type*: 770 rim, 432 body sherds. *Pustunich Incised Type*: 1 rim, 1 body sherd. No illustration but compare 47, *n*. *Yobain Plano-relief Type*: 1 rim, no body sherds. No illustration.

Bowls, tripod, grater (cf. 46, *a*). Medium-thick rounded sides, direct rim, rounded, pointed, beveled, or flat lip, convex base, and three feet (21 hollow oven, 21 solid conical, 10 solid oven). *Size*: lip diam. 18–23 cm., av. 20.6 cm., most common of 32 measured is 22 cm. [12]; over-all ht. 8.2–10.5 cm., av. 9.4 cm., only 3 measured and third is 9.4 cm.; thickness .4–.7 cm. to .7–1.4 cm., av. .63–.83 cm., most common of 32 measured are .6–.8 cm. [12] and .6–.7 cm. [6]. *Surface*: slipped and burnished all over including base and feet, but often slip has worn off scored floor area. The scoring was done before slipping and may be deep or shallow, close together or fairly wide apart. It usually forms a grid, that is, a quartered circle, each quarter containing parallel grooves at right angles to those in the adjoining quarter. The circle may be bounded by a single groove, left free, or encircled by a pair of grooves. Some fire-clouding is present. Slip color is red (10 R 5/6, 2.5 YR 4/8), reddish brown (2.5 YR 3/6, 5/6; 5 YR 5/6), or orange (2.5 YR 5/8, 10 R 5/8). *Paste*: coarse texture, generally calcite temper (see Mayapan Red Ware, Chapter IV), and cream or gray color. *Types and decoration*: rarely decorated other than by scoring. *Papacal Incised Type*: 181 rim, 389 body sherds. *Papacal Incised Type, scratched variety*: no rim, 2 body sherds. Both specimens are bases with crude postfire incised designs on under side, one in the form of crosshatching. No illustration.

Bowls, deep, tripod (43, *a, b, e, g, k, r, s*; cf. *d, f, j, l*). Medium-thick recurving or nearly vertical sides, direct rim except for one T-shape (*s*), rounded, beveled, or pointed lip, globular body, convex (*e, g*) or flat (*d, f, j*) base, and three feet which may be solid conical, hollow oven, or solid oven. A few pedestals occur (43, *a, l*). *Size*: lip diam. 8–20 cm., av. 12.8 cm., most common of 17 measured are 12 cm. [6], 13 cm. [3], and 14 cm. [3]; overall ht. 10.5–12.4 cm., av. 11.9 cm., most common of 8 measured is 12.4 cm. [6]; thickness .5–.6 cm. to .8–1 cm., av. .58–.73 cm., most common of 4 measured is .5–.6 cm. [2]. *Surface*: slipped and burnished all over, on exterior and just over lip on interior, or partway down exterior and interior. The slip is almost always a good uniform red with few blemishes. Color is red (10 R 4/8, 4/6) or orange (10 R 5/8). Many sherds are weathered. *Paste*: coarse texture, generally calcite temper (see Mayapan Red Ware, Chapter IV), and cream, gray, or cinnamon (7.5 YR 7/6) color. *Types and decoration*: no decoration noted. *Mama Red Type*: 75 rim, 18 body sherds.

Bowls, deep, with basal flange (cf. 43, *h, i, m–o*). Medium-thick recurving sides, direct rim, rounded lip, slightly globular lower body, flange either notched or terraced, and convex base with three feet or pedestal. Feet are usually hollow cylin-drical with rounded bottoms. One form herein included is more jarlike, having a low neck (43, *m*), but otherwise conforms. *Size*: lip diam. 10.3–20 cm., av. 13.8 cm., only 3 measured and third is 11.2 cm.; overall ht. 11.9–16 cm., av. 13.8 cm., third of 3 measured is 13.5 cm.; thickness .4–.8 cm. to .7–1 cm., av. .5–.87 cm., most common of 3 measured is .4–.8 cm. [2]. *Surface*: slipped and burnished on interior and exterior except base below flange. The jarlike form is slipped and polished on exterior and neck interior. It has considerable crazing. Many sherds are badly weathered. Besides notching, some flanges have postslip, prepolish incising. Slip color is red (10 R 4/8). *Paste*: coarse texture, generally calcite temper (see Mayapan Red Ware, Chapter IV), and gray or cream to pink color. *Types and decoration*: usually undecorated except for flange. *Panabchen Red Type*: 3 rim, 9 body sherds.

Bowl cluster, pedestal (37, *b, c*; 75, *c*; cf. 37, *a*). This is a cluster of four rounded-side deep bowls surrounding and attached to a similar centrally placed bowl, all of which are supported by a single large pedestal. This latter may be flaring or nearly vertical and usually has a bolster rim at base. The flaring pedestal has a rounded bolster, the vertical a square bolster. *Size*: one reconstructed example, overall top diam. 19.5 cm.; base diam. 16 cm.; overall ht. 13.5 cm. Sherds, lip diam. 6–10 cm., av. 7.7 cm., most common of 16 measured 6.5 cm. [5] and 9 cm. [4]; bowl ht. 4.8–6.5 cm., av. 6 cm., most common of 10 measured is 6.5 cm. [5]; thickness .3–.7 cm. to .5–.9 cm., av. .48–.76 cm., most common of 15 measured are .5–.7 cm. [8] and .5–.9 cm. [4]; flaring pedestals, base diam. 16 cm. [18]; ht. 6.8 cm.; thickness .6–.8 cm. [18]; vertical pedestals, base diam. 13–16 cm., av. 13.6 cm., most common of 4 measured is 13 cm. [3]; ht. 8.6 cm.; thickness .5–.6 cm. to .7–.8 cm., av. .54–.64 cm., most common of 5 measured is .5–.6 cm. [4]. *Surface*: slipped and burnished on exterior of bowls and pedestal and just over lip of bowl interior, but not on pedestal interior. In 75, *c*, central bowl of cluster has green paint on rim, on interior, and over sides on exterior. None of the additional four bowls in this cluster shows evidence of green or any other color paint. Nearly all these bowl fragments, except the central bowl of the cluster, are burnt on interior and partway down on exterior. Slip color is red (2.5 YR 4/8, 10 R 3/6), reddish brown (5 YR 5/6, 2.5 YR 3/6), and brown (5 YR 5/4). *Paste*: coarse texture, generally calcite temper (see Mayapan Red Ware, Chapter IV), and cinnamon color. *Types and decoration*: most of fragments evidence no decoration. *Panabchen Red Type*: 26 rim, 41 body sherds. *Dzitxil Openwork Type*: 8 rim, 12 body sherds. The openwork design involves circles and U's. In one instance incising accompanies openwork.

Bowls, hemispherical (41, *c*, 1, 2; cf. 3, 4) with medium-thick rounded sides, direct rim, pointed or rounded lip, slightly concave base. *Size*: lip diam. 12–21.3 cm., av. 18 cm., most common of 18 measured are 21.3 cm. [9] and 14 cm. [4]; ht. 4.2–8 cm., av. 7.5 cm., most common of 11 measured is 8 cm. [9]; thickness .3–.6 cm. to .5–1 cm., av. .48–.8 cm., most common of 11 measured is .5–.8 cm. [9]. *Surface*: slipped and burnished all over including base. Usually crazed and fire-clouded. Slip color is red (2.5 YR 4/8) or orange (2.5 YR 5/8), which may be found on the same vessel. *Paste*: coarse texture, generally calcite temper (see Mayapan Red Ware, Chapter IV), and gray (10 YR 8/1, 8/2) color. *Types and decoration*: no decoration noted. *Panabchen Red Type*: 25 rim, 7 body sherds.

Basins (46, *b*, 2–10; cf. *b*, 1). Medium-thick to thick flaring to rounded sides, rounded, flat, triangular, or square bolster rim, and one example of a direct rim, rounded, beveled, or flat lip, two solid slab lugs or two vertically placed strap handles, usually flat or slightly concave base. *Size*: lip diam. 25–48 cm., av. 38.8 cm., most common of 75 measured are 29–36 cm. [30], 40–43 cm. [20], and 48 cm. [11]; ht. 15 cm. (for 9 fragments); thickness .6–.7 cm. to .8–1.6 cm., av. .79–1.54 cm., most common of 31 measured are .8–1.6 cm. [9] and .7–.8 cm. [9]. *Surface*: slipped and burnished on interior and partway down exterior, on interior and bolster, or in some instances all over. Unslipped exteriors may be striated or, more often, just smoothed. Slip color is red (10 R 4/8), orange (2.5 YR 5/8, 5 YR 4/8), or reddish brown (2.5 YR 3/6, 5 YR 4/8). A couple of sherds have crosshatched scratching or doodling. *Paste*: coarse texture, generally calcite temper (see Mayapan Red Ware, Chapter IV), and gray (10 YR 8/1, 8/2) or cream (10 YR 8/3) color. *Types and decoration*: no formal decoration. *Mama Red Type*: 439 rim, 410 body sherds.

Vases, cylindrical (44, *a*, *b*, *e*; cf. *c*, *d*). Medium-thick cylindrical or outcurving sides, direct rim, flat, beveled, or rounded lip, convex base with pedestal or three solid conical feet, and flat base (rare). Actually 31 pedestals and 7 solid conical feet were found associated with this form, that is, attached to cylindrical vases. *Size*: lip diam. 7–13 cm., av. 10.5 cm., most common of 10 measured is 10 cm .[6]; ht. overall of one tripod specimen

24.3 cm.; ht. without pedestal of three examples 23 cm., 29.2 cm., and 31.2 cm.; thickness .6–.7 cm. to .9–1.1 cm., av. .68–.9 cm., most common of 8 measured .6–.9 cm. [4]. *Surface*: well smoothed, slipped, and burnished on exterior and often just over lip on interior. Blemishes include rootlet-marks, some flaking, and rarely crazing. Slip color rarely a uniform red, but more like jars where each vessel has a blending of red, orange, and brown. Variations are red (10 R 4/6, 4/8 and 2.5 YR 4/8), orange (2.5 YR 5/8; 5 YR 6/6), and brown (7.5 YR 5/6). *Paste*: coarse texture, generally calcite temper (see Mayapan Red Ware, Chapter IV), and light buff, cream, or gray color. *Types and decoration*: usually undecorated. *Mama Red Type*: 83 rim, 199 body sherds. *Pustunich Incised Type*: 1 rim, 1 body sherd. Fragmentary, no illustration.

Drums (39, *d–g*, *i–o*; cf *a–c*, *h*). or possibly jars. Medium-thick to thick walls. Smaller opening at one end than the other. High vertical or outcurving neck, direct rim, and flat or square bolster rim, flat, beveled, rarely rounded or pointed lip. Form may be like reconstruction (39, *a*) or like a high-neck jar with pear-shape body. *Size*: lip diam. 9–24 cm., av. 18.4 cm., most common of 16 measured ranges from 16–24 cm. [14]; thickness .6–.8 cm. to 1–1.8 cm., av. .8–1.2 cm., most common of 16 measured .9–1.2 cm [5] and .7–.8 cm. [4]. *Surface*: slipped and burnished all over exterior except where worn off near rim, very rarely on neck interior. An apparently unslipped or worn exterior rim strip may be where the stretched skin was fastened to the playing end of the drum. The vertical, diagonal, or crosshatched grooving or sharp-incising associated with this same upper area may have been a roughening process to facilitate the fastening of the skin. The slip color usually red (2.5 YR 4/8, 10 R 3/6) or orange (2.5 YR 5/8), occasionally variegated. *Paste*: coarse texture, generally calcite temper (see Mayapan Red Ware, Chapter IV), and cream or gray color. *Types and decoration*: all appear to have grooving or sharp-incising near drum-playing end. This grooving or incising is generally postslip, prepolish, rarely preslip or postslip, postfire. *Papacal Incised Type*: 58 rim, 64 body sherds. The decoration — and sometimes the incisions do represent a design — may be vertical (39, *e–g*, *i*, *k*, *l*, *o*), diagonal (39, *d*, *j*), or crosshatched (39, *e*, *n*) lines some of which may have been purely functional. *m*, in 39, appears surely to be decorative.

Vessels, effigy (45, *a*, *f*; 75, *e*; cf. 45, *b–e*, *g*; 75, *f*) are of several forms, including a handleless double-boiler type (45, *a*; 75, *e*), jars (45, *b*, *c*, *e*, g; 75, f), possibly small effigy censers (45, f, h), and cups (45, d). The last, however, are discussed under cups. Form descriptions are given in figure legends. *Size*: the double boiler, overall ht. 24.5 cm.; thickness .4–1 cm.; upper part, lip diam. 15 cm.; ht. 10 cm.; lower part, lip diam. 12 cm.; ht. 16 cm.; jars, using the humpback effigy as an example, lip diam. 9.8 cm., ht. 14.2 cm.; effigy censer very fragmentary. *Surface*: double boiler, slipped and burnished all over except in areas of of modeling and appliqué; slip color is red to buff; the after-firing paint colors used on "diving god" are yellow, orange, blue, green, and red, with black details; the jar and censer forms are slipped and burnished on exterior only; the color is red (2.5 YR 4/8). The effigy jar representing a humpback (45, b) is slipped and burnished on exterior and neck interior, the color is red but mostly fire-blackened, and the ornaments, eyes, and mouth were painted (colors badly weathered) after firing. *Paste*: coarse texture, generally calcite temper (see Mayapan Red Ware, Chapter IV), cream or gray color. *Types and decoration*. *Chapab Modeled Type*: 21 rim, 39 body sherds.

Miniature vessels, jars (49, a, c, e, f, i, j, l; cf. b, d, g, h, k). Globular body, medium-thick sides, flaring, vertical, or outcurving medium-high neck, direct rim, rounded, beveled, flat, or pointed lip, often two lug handles, rather thick flat base. Two specimens (49, a, i) have suspension holes in neck. Another jar probably had a spout (49, l). *Size*: lip diam. 3.5–10 cm., av. 5.8 cm., most common of 15 measured are 4.5 cm. [5] and 8 cm. [3]; ht. 1.2–3 cm., av. 2.6 cm., most common of 12 measured is 3 cm. [6]; thickness .4–.5 cm. to .7–.9 cm., av. .52–.58 cm., most common of 13 measured are .5–.5 cm. [6] and .5–.6 cm. [3]. *Surface*: slipped and burnished all over, on exterior and just over lip on interior, and on exterior only. Slip color is red (10 R 4/8 and 2.5 YR 4/8). Some are badly weathered. *Paste*: coarse texture, generally calcite temper (see Mayapan Red Ware, Chapter IV), cream or gray color. *Types and decoration*: usually undecorated. *Mama Red Type*: 21 rim, 6 body sherds. *Pustunich Incised Type*: 2 rim, no body sherds. Preslip incised decoration on body (49, a). *Dzonot Appliqué Type*: 1 rim, no body sherds. Appliqué thumb-impressed fillet (49, c).

Miniature vessels, bowls, tripod (41, b, 10). Medium-thick rounded sides, direct rim, rounded lip, convex base, and three feet (usually missing). *Size*: too fragmentary for measurement. *Surface*: slipped and burnished on interior only. Color is red but weathered. *Paste*: not recorded. *Types*

and decoration. *Mama Red Type, unslipped-exterior variety*: 1 rim, 3 body sherds.

Covers, disk [14] or scutate [1] (37, g; cf. f). The disk cover is of two types, either flat, well made, rarely having a handle [10] or slightly convex and made from a used jar body sherd [4]. The scutate cover is similar to the one illustrated (37, f). *Size*: well-made disk measured, lip diam. 7.5–10.5 cm., av. 9 cm., two reused sherd disks measured are 8 and 10 cm.; thickness .6–.6 cm. to .9–1.2 cm., av. .7–.9 cm., two reused measured are .7–.7 and .6–1.1 cm. *Surface*: slipped and burnished on exterior only, some fire-clouding. Color red, many weathered. *Paste*: not recorded. *Types and decoration*: no decoration noted. *Panabchen Red Type*: 15 rim, 1 body sherd.

Cups (30, x, z–bb; cf. 45, d). These may have tripod [4] or pedestal [2] supports. Barrel-shape, medium-thick sides, direct rim, rounded lip, convex base supported by solid conical feet or flaring pedestal. *Size*: similar to unslipped types. *Surface*: slipped and burnished on exterior only except in modeled and appliqué areas, and the figures portrayed are usually painted after firing. Those specimens are too weathered to identify colors used. Slip color is red. *Paste*: not recorded. *Types and decoration*: tripods are undecorated. *Mama Red Type*: 4 rim, 10 body sherds. *Chapab Modeled Type*: 2 rim, 6 body sherds. These are pedestal cups (30, x, z–bb; cf. 45, d) with godlike effigy faces modeled on one side.

Plate, pedestal (41, d), thick flaring sides, direct rim, rounded lip, slightly convex base, vertical pedestal support. *Size*: lip diam. 21 cm., base diam. 9 cm., overall ht. 7.2 cm., pedestal ht. 4.5 cm., thickness .7–1.3 cm. *Surface*: slipped and burnished all over including pedestal exterior. Considerable fire-clouding, especially on interior. Rootlet-marks but no crazing noted. Slip color is red (10 R 4/8). *Paste*: not recorded. *Types and decoration*: no decoration noted. *Panabchen Red Type*: 6 rim, 6 body sherds.

Figurines (37, d; 45, i). Only three fragments and one complete figurine found: one piece forms part of a female body (45, i), another is a whistle mouthpiece probably placed at tail, and the third is a disk adorno or possibly a shield (cf. 64, b). The complete specimen represents a male god, possibly Xipe Totec. It is hollow and moldmade with open base. *Size*: ht. 14.7 cm. *Surface*: slipped red and burnished all over exterior. *Paste*: not recorded. *Types and decoration*: all are modeled and some may have been painted. *Chapab Modeled Type*: 1 complete, 3 body fragments.

SUMMARY

Mayapan Red Ware is thoroughly identified and described in Chapter IV. Here let us consider the salient characteristics that differentiate it from other red wares using the attributes associated with paste composition and surface finish.

Under paste composition we find that Mayapan Red Ware has a uniformly coarse texture, an apparently fairly stable type of calcite temper, and a color range including pinks and pale reds, creams, and grays. Compared with Puuc Slate Ware, for instance, it shows marked standardization of paste.

Considering surface finish, Mayapan Red Ware is actually inferior to many of the preceding slipped wares: Puuc Slate, Chichen Slate, Puuc Red, and Chichen Red. The inferiority is not based on the same imperfection in each instance, however. In general, Mayapan Red Ware is poorly smoothed and in this respect markedly different from both Puuc Red and Chichen Red wares but not greatly subordinate to either Puuc Slate or Chichen Slate wares. The luster is produced by burnishing, which is also true of the Slate wares, but the Puuc and Chichen Red wares are lightly polished, giving them a somewhat higher luster. All of the above named wares have a relatively thin slip but feel different to the touch. The slates have a distinctly waxy feel, the Puuc and Chichen reds a slightly waxy feel, while Mayapan Red Ware is sleek and slippery. Blemishes are associated with Mayapan Red Ware and the Slate wares. The former has fire-clouding, popping or spalling, and rootlet-markings; Puuc Slate Ware includes fire-clouding, occasional crazing, and rootlet-markings; and Chichen Slate Ware has fire-clouding, rootlet-markings, and peeling of slip in a few cases. The Puuc and Chichen reds, on the other hand, are relatively free from blemishes except for some fire-clouding and occasional rootlet-markings.

An outstanding difference is in the contrast of slip and paste color ever present in Mayapan Red Ware and usually in Chichen Slate Ware, lacking in Puuc Red Ware and Thin Slate Ware, and rarely present in Puuc Slate Ware. Actually the surface or slip color involves much the same red range in all three red wares (Mayapan, Puuc, and Chichen). The difference, however, lies in the fact that the Mayapan Red Ware slip is usually a blending of reds, oranges, and browns on a single vessel, while Puuc Red Ware has an outstandingly uniform red slip, as does Chichen Red Ware except for fire-clouding.

Form, of course, is a major means of identification. It is true that jars, both water and storage, bowls, dishes, and plates with flaring, outcurving, or rounded sides are found associated with most wares. It is the often slight change given to the rim, neck, base, or supports of a vessel, however, that help to place it as to ware or even type. But rarely will form alone make possible an exact identification. For such a purpose all available attributes must be examined and brought to bear upon the problem.

Jars, both storage and water, form 70 per cent of all the Mayapan Red Ware sherds found in late lots as compared to 86.6 per cent in early lots. Actually the late forms differ little from those found in early lots. There are a few new types including jars with parenthesis rim, tripod jars with high outcurving neck or neck with central bulge, and jars or drums with three necks. There is little similarity in form between Mayapan Red Ware jars and those of either Puuc Red Ware or Chichen Red Ware. As a matter of fact, those of the former are extremely rare, and jars of the latter, although forming 45.3 per cent of all Chichen Red Ware sherds found in the five cuts made at Chichen Itza and used in this report, are quite unrelated except for the basic jar form.

Tripod dishes, usually with solid conical feet, make up 17.9 per cent of all Mayapan Red Ware sherds found in late lots as compared to 10.7 per cent in early lots. In the Tases Ceramic Complex foot types including solid oven, solid cylindrical, and hollow conical are added, but the greatest innovation is in the types most used. In the Hocaba Ceramic Complex foot type, percentages are as follows: hollow oven 73.2, hollow bulbous 13.4, solid conical 11, and hollow effigy 1.6. These may be compared to those in the Tases Ceramic Complex comprising solid conical 51.3, hollow oven 22.5, hollow effigy 8.2, hollow cylindrical 6.2, and hollow bulbous 1.6. Here the greatest shift of emphasis is from hollow oven to solid conical feet with a considerable increase in the use of hollow effigy feet. This vessel form, called basal break by Brainerd, differs in Puuc Red Ware primarily because it tends to have outcurving sides and hollow oven or hollow cylindrical feet, whereas in Chichen Red Ware it is relatively rare, often has everted rim, and always hollow bulbous feet. In size range and mode it differs comparatively little, although far more small sized tripod dishes are associated with the Tases Ceramic Complex.

The other vessels which constitute the full complement of Mayapan Red Ware as found in the

Tases Ceramic Complex are restricted, tripod grater, or deep bowls, basins, cylindrical vases, drums, effigy vessels, miniature vessels, covers, cups, and pedestal-base plates. The only Tases forms not found in the Hocaba Phase are covers, pedestal-base plates, and figurines. In the Tases Ceramic Complex these other vessels total 4.4 per cent of all Mayapan Red Ware as compared to 2.7 per cent in the Hocaba Ceramic Complex. Basins, cylindrical vases, drums, effigy and miniature vessels increase in importance in later times, while bowls remain about the same.

Finally let us examine the matter of decoration, including both techniques and design styles. Little decoration is used on Mayapan Red Ware in either the Hocaba (5.3 per cent) or Tases (7.4 per cent) phases, and most of this is embraced by the Papacal Incised Type in the form of horizontal grooving on rim interiors. The sparse incising on exterior of vessels from middle and late lots is illustrated in figure 47. This form of decoration is even rarer in the early lots. It comprises preslip incised scrolls, a diamond band, hooks, S's, stepfrets, vertical and horizontal lines, and interlocking lines suggesting a meander. Postfire doodling is shown in the same figure (p, q, s, t). In addition

two rather complicated designs are portrayed: o, done in plano-relief (Yobain Plano-relief Type) and r, groove-incised. Another technique of decoration is modeling (Chapab Modeled Type), which is even less used than incising but does include vessels representing a "diving god" and a humpback, or having a bird, animal, or godlike head attached to the side or shoulder. The Dzitxil Openwork type of decoration is used exclusively on cluster bowl pedestals. Only one example of an appliqué (Dzonot Appliqué Type) fillet is recorded. Painting is extremely rare, occurring on the unslipped exterior of two Mama Red Type black-on-red unslipped variety and black-on-unslipped variety tripod dishes. The motif of one consists of a black glyph, red border, and oblique red lines; the other has vertical black lines.

Whether or not the Mama Red Type, unslipped-exterior variety can be considered in any sense a decorative device when the vessel interior is slipped red and the exterior is left in the unslipped paste beige, buff, or cinnamon color, is questionable. But that this treatment was used in the Tases Phase as contrasted with allover slip in the Hocaba Phase is well founded.

SAN JOAQUIN BUFF WARE

Forms, Types, and Varieties	A Rim	C Rim	D Rim	%	Total Rim & body	
Jars, storage:				34.2		
Tecoh Red-on-buff Type	155	58	9		222	918
Pele Polychrome Type	14	0	0		14	86
bulging neck: Tecoh Red-on-buff Type	7	5	0		12	30
Jars, water:				13.7		
Polbox Buff Type	74	2	1		77	248
Tecoh Red-on-buff Type	6	3	4		13	38
Kimbila Incised Type	0	0	0		0	8
parenthesis rim: Tecoh Red-on-buff Type	6	1	2		9	22
Dishes, tripod, flaring side:				49.0		
Tecoh Red-on-buff Type	190	77	15		282	325
Pele Polychrome Type	70	0	0		70	49
Polbox Buff Type	3	0	0		3	3
Bowls, hemispherical: Tecoh Red-on-buff Type	6	1	2	1.2	9	9
Bowls, restricted orifice:				0.6		
Tecoh Red-on-buff Type	2	1	0		3	2
Kimbila Incised Type	1	0	0		1	0
Bowls, deep: Tecoh Red-on-buff Type	0	1	0	0.1	1	2
Potstands: Tecoh Red-on-buff Type	4	0	0	0.6	4	2
Basins: Tecoh Red-on-buff Type	2	1	0	0.4	3	0
Vases, cylindrical:				0.1		
Tecoh Red-on-buff Type	1	0	0		1	1
tripod: Tecoh Red-on-buff Type, outline-incised variety	0	0	0		0	1
Covers: Tecoh Red-on-buff Type	1	0	0	0.1	1	0
Total	542	150	33		725	1,744

Jars, storage (53, a, 1–14, 17). Wide mouth, medium to high outcurving or flaring neck, flat [114], triangular [29], rounded [24], and square [20] bolster, direct [28] or everted [7] rim, rounded, flat, beveled, or pointed lip, medium-thick, pear-shape or globular body, two horizontal strap handles attached at point of maximum diameter, flat or slightly concave base, and a few have globular body and three hollow feet (53, a, 17). *Size:* lip diam. 25–42 cm., av. 33 cm., most common of 47 measured are 32 cm. [9], 36 cm. [9], 37 cm. [6], 30 cm. [5], and 25 cm. [5]; overall ht. one specimen 42 cm.; neck ht. 6.5–11 cm., av. 9.3 cm., most common of 40 measured are 10 cm. [17], 8.5 cm. [8], and 11 cm. [6]; thickness .5–1 cm. to .7–1.3 cm., av. .64–1.1 cm., most common of 5 measured .7–1 cm. [2]. *Surface:* lightly slipped and burnished on exterior and slipped and burnished on neck interior and bolster; occasionally exterior slip extends only partway down body, or piece is slipped and burnished on exterior and neck interior. Usually the exterior body has a buff (7.5 YR 7/4, 5 YR 6/6) through beige (2.5 YR 8/4, 10 YR 7/4, 7/3) to cream (7.5 YR 8/6, 8/2, 10 YR 8/4, 2.5 Y 9/4) slip, whereas the neck interior and bolster rim have a red (10 R 3/6, 4/6, 4/8, 4/4, 3/4; 2.5 YR 4/6), reddish brown (5 YR 5/6; 2.5 YR 5/6), or brown (7.5 YR 5/4) slip and the same reds are used in the decoration. *Remarks:* buff has been selected as the most constant slip color, but the range includes gray, cream, beige, buff, pinkish cinnamon, cinnamon, and very light brown. It may emerge that those with gray slip belong to a different ware. The gray-slipped specimens have been retained in Tecoh Red-on-buff because there is a gradual progression from gray through buff, beige, and dirty cream to cream; the grays are rare. *Paste:* coarse texture, generally calcite temper (see Mayapan Red Ware, Chapter IV), and a color which closely follows the buff slip color. In some instances the buff areas may be smoothed and burnished, but not slipped. *Types and decoration:* most lack decoration other than the red neck interior and bolster rim. *Tecoh Red-on-buff Type:* 222 rim, 918 body sherds. A few have exterior decoration (53, a, 10–14, 17) including both curvilinear and rectilinear design. *Pele Polychrome Type:* 14 rim, 86 body sherds. Designs in red and black are placed either on exterior neck or shoulder. Neck motifs, although not too distinct due to weathering and fragmentary condition of sherds, appear to be geometric. One shoulder decoration may represent the body of an animal, possibly a jaguar. No illustration.

Jars, storage, bulging neck (53, a, 19, 22). Wide mouth, high outcurving and bulging neck, direct rim, rounded lip, medium-thick globular body, flat base, and three hollow rounded-bottom cylindrical feet with single circular front vent. *Size:* lip diam. 25 cm., neck ht. ca. 13 cm., vessel ht. ca. 34 cm. Thickness .6–1.1 cm. *Surface:* slipped and burnished on exterior, including base and feet, and neck interior. Slip color is cream (10 YR 8/4) and decoration reddish brown (5 YR 4/8). *Paste:* coarse texture, temper much the same as Mayapan Red Ware, cream color. *Types and decoration:* all have exterior decoration on both neck and body. *Tecoh Red-on-buff Type:* 12 rim, 30 body sherds. The design on neck is geometric and rectilinear and on body more curvilinear.

Jars, water (50; 53, a, 15, 16; 75, i, j). Medium-wide mouth, high nearly vertical or slightly outcurving neck, direct (50, a, b) or flat bolster (50, c) rim, rounded or beveled lip, medium-thick to thick globular body, two horizontal strap handles attached to body at maximum diameter, and flat base. *Size:* lip diam. 11–14 cm., av. 12.1 cm., most common of 36 measured are 11 cm. [14] and 12 cm. [14]; max. diam. 15.2–20.3 cm., av. 18.8 cm., most common of 14 measured are 20 cm. [5] and 19 cm. [5]; base diam. 5.5–8 cm., av. 6.5 cm., most common of 21 measured are 6.5 cm. [9] and 6 cm. [6]; neck ht. 5.5–8.5 cm., av. 7.2 cm., most common of 30 measured are 7.5 cm. [8], 7 cm. [6], 6.5 cm. [6]; overall ht. 21.5–24.8 cm., av. 22.5 cm., most common of 11 measured is 21.5 cm. [5]; thickness, neck .6–.8 cm., body .7–1.4 cm. (the base being thickest). *Surface:* lightly slipped and burnished on exterior including base in some instances. Neck interior may be slipped, partially slipped, or unslipped. Many are too weathered to be certain. Color may be buff (10 YR 7/6, 7/4), cinnamon (7.5 YR 7/6), or brown (7.5 YR 5/6). *Paste:* coarse texture, temper much the same as Mayapan Red Ware, color cream, beige, or gray. *Types and decoration:* most are without embellishment. *Polbox Buff Type:* 77 rim, 248 body sherds. *Tecoh Red-on-buff Type:* 13 rim, 38 body sherds. Simple horizontal red stripes on neck exterior (53, a, 15, 16). *Kimbila Incised Type:* no rim, 8 body sherds. This incising (50, d) is postslip and probably postfire and may be doodling.

Jars, water, parenthesis rim (53, a, 18; cf. 20, 21). Medium-wide mouth, high vertical or possibly bulging (53, a, 19) neck, rounded, flat, or pointed lip, medium-thick to thick walls, possibly globular body, and flat or slightly concave base (no complete vessels or bases definitely associated). *Size:*

230

lip diam. 13–18 cm., av. 15 cm., most common of 5 measured are 13 cm. [3] and 18 cm. [2]; neck ht. 7–8.5 cm., av. 7.8 cm., only two examples measured; thickness .6–1.3 cm., only few measured and this seems to be the range. The thickest point is the juncture of neck and body and the thinnest close to lip. Necks were probably made separately and welded to body, since most of fractures occur at this point. *Surface:* slipped and burnished on exterior only [6], sometimes on neck interior [3]. Exterior slip color is buff ranging from cream (10 YR 8/4) to cinnamon (7.5 YR 7/6); interior slip on neck is red (10 R 4/8). *Paste:* coarse texture, temper much the same as Mayapan Red Ware, color cream or pinkish cinnamon. *Types and decoration:* all have exterior designs in red (10 R 4/8) on both rim and neck. *Tecoh Red-on-buff Type:* 9 rim, 22 body sherds. Frequently the design consists of parallel horizontal and vertical red lines (53, a, 20, 21); these lines may be combined with rectangles, terraces, quatrefoils, and steps (53, a, 18, 19).

Dishes, tripod, flaring side (53, b, 1, 3, 5, 6; 54, a, c, d; 75, n; cf. 53, b, 2; 54, b) thin to thick walls, direct rim, rounded, pointed, beveled, or flat lip, slightly convex base, and three feet usually hollow animal effigy but occasionally hollow cylindrical, solid conical, or hollow conical. One has notched flange, another basal ridge. *Size:* lip diam. 15–31 cm., av. 25.9 cm., most common of 62 measured are 26 cm. [20], 28 cm. [15], 24 cm. [8], and 23 cm. [7]; thickness .4–.8 cm. to .8–1.1 cm., av. .69–1.07 cm., most common of 30 measured are .7–1 cm. [9] and .7–1.1 cm. [9]. One complete specimen measured: lip diam. 28 cm., base diam. 19 cm., bowl ht. 6.3 cm., overall ht. 11.7 cm.; thickness .7–1 cm. *Surface:* slipped and burnished red on exterior and buff on interior, or less frequently buff on exterior and red on interior. Slip usually overlaps base and covers front of feet. It may be buff (7.5 YR 7/2, 2.5 YR 7/4) which includes cream (10 YR 8/4), beige (10 YR 7/4), and cinnamon (7.5 YR 7/6), or red (10 R 4/8, 7.5 R 3/6, 2.5 YR 4/8, 4/6) which embraces reddish brown (5 YR 5/8) and orange (2.5 YR 5/8). *Paste:* coarse texture, temper much the same as Mayapan Red Ware, color similar to that of buff slip. *Types and decoration:* this form in San Joaquin Buff Ware is usually decorated. *Tecoh Red-on-buff Type:* 282 rim, 325 body sherds. The designs include concentric circles, dots, feathers, quatrefoils, "ram horn" scrolls, V's, and horizontal and vertical lines. *Pele Polychrome Type:* 70 rim, 49 body sherds. Designs include painted-black fish motif, triangles, chevrons, and a pos-

sible bat head (54, a–d). *Polbox Buff Type:* 3 rim, 3 body sherds. These have no decoration and are not illustrated but have the same form as the Tecoh Red-on-buff Type.

Bowls, hemispherical (53, b, 7, 8). Medium-thick rounded sides, direct rim, rounded or pointed lip, probably flat base. *Size:* too fragmentary for accurate measurement. *Surface:* slipped red on interior, buff on exterior and burnished. Slip color is red (2.5 YR 4/8) and beige (10 YR 7/4) included in buff range. *Paste:* coarse texture, temper much the same as Mayapan Red Ware, and color cream or beige. *Types and decoration:* all appear to have red design on exterior. *Tecoh Red-on-buff Type:* 9 rim, 9 body sherds. Exterior decorative motifs include horizontal stripes, parallel vertical stripes, and a horizontal triangular band (53, b, 8).

Bowls, restricted orifice (53, b, 9, 12, 15; cf. 53, b, 10). Medium-thick rounded sides, direct or triangular bolster rim, rounded or pointed lip, flat to slightly convex base, may have ringstand or pedestal base. *Size:* mostly too fragmentary for accurate measurement. *Surface:* slipped and burnished buff on exterior, red on interior. Buff slip may be a light brown (7.5 YR 6/6) and red is a reddish orange (10 R 5/8), but more commonly a dark red (10 R 3/6). *Paste:* coarse texture, temper much the same as Mayapan Red Ware, and color cream or beige. *Types and decoration:* usually has red design on exterior. *Tecoh Red-on-buff Type:* 3 rim, 2 body sherds. Decoration may be rectilinear or curvilinear including triangles and scrolls (cf. 53, b, 10). *Kimbila Incised Type:* 1 rim, no body sherds. No illustration, very fragmentary.

Bowls, deep (cf. 43 for form). Medium-thick recurving sides, direct rim, rounded lip, globular body, presumably convex base, and either three feet or a pedestal support. *Size:* too fragmentary for accurate measurement. *Surface:* slipped and burnished all over; red on interior, buff on exterior. No color readings. *Paste:* coarse texture, temper much the same as Mayapan Red Ware, no color readings taken. *Types and decoration:* weathered. *Tecoh Red-on-buff Type:* 1 rim, 2 body sherds.

Potstands (53, b, 14). Medium-thick bulbous body, flaring rims both top and bottom, open at both ends. Three sets of two circular holes, probably for suspension. *Size:* lip diam. both top and bottom 8.2 cm.; overall ht. 6.2 cm.; thickness .5–.7 cm. *Surface:* slipped and burnished all over except on interior of bulge. Slip color is cream (10 YR 8/4), decoration is red (10 R 4/6). *Paste:* coarse texture, temper and color not recorded.

Types and decoration: all have red decoration. *Tecoh Red-on-buff Type*: 4 rim, 2 body sherds. Design consists of horizontal and vertical stripes which frame a vertical twist band, done in reserve-space negative painting.

Basins (53, *b*, 4). Medium-thick rounded sides, rounded bolster rim, rounded, probably flat or slightly concave base. *Size*: too fragmentary for accurate measurement. *Surface*: slipped and burnished buff on exterior and red on interior. Too weathered for color readings. *Paste*: coarse texture, temper and color not recorded. *Types and decoration*: a few examples have red exterior design. *Tecoh Red-on-buff Type*: 3 rim, no body sherds. Motif of decoration consists of horizontal stripes together with an unidentifiable curvilinear design.

Vases, cylindrical, pedestal, or tripod (53, *b*, 12, 13, 15, 16). The only rim sherd is thin-walled, has direct rim, rounded lip, and probably a convex base with a pedestal support; the only tripod example (53, *b*, 16) is also thin-walled, but has flat base. *Size*: too fragmentary for accurate measurement. *Surface*: slipped and burnished on exterior only with buff slip and red decoration. *Paste*: coarse texture, temper and color not recorded. *Types and decoration*: those with pedestal supports have exterior red decoration. *Tecoh Red-on-buff Type, Tecoh Variety*: 1 rim, 1 body sherd. The design on pedestal (53, *b*, 15) is vertical and horizontal red stripes. *Tecoh Red-on-buff Type, outline-incised variety*: no rim, 1 body sherd. This base sherd has painted red decoration leaving rectangular panels in buff background outlined with incising (53, *b*, 16).

Covers (no illustration). Medium-thick rounded sides, direct rim, rounded lip, no handle noted. *Size*: too fragmentary for accurate measurement. *Surface*: slipped and burnished on exterior only, which is the principal reason for considering it a cover. Slip color buff. *Paste*: coarse texture, temper and color not recorded. *Types and decoration*: too fragmentary to identify red design. *Tecoh Red-on-buff Type*: 1 rim, no body sherds.

SUMMARY

San Joaquin Buff Ware is fully described in the chapter on wares. It is a one-phase ware derived from various wares and types. It has much the same surface finish and paste composition as Mayapan Red Ware. In certain instances, however, there is some doubt as to whether the vessel or an area of the vessel was slipped or merely well smoothed and burnished. The paste has

the same coarse texture, apparently the same kind of calcite temper, and a lighter more generally buff to cream, rarely cinnamon color.

Forms follow those of Mayapan Red Ware rather closely, especially the jars, many of which have bolster rims and horizontal strap handles; others have parenthesis rim, and a few have three feet. Other forms that resemble the Mayapan Red Ware aggregate are tripod flaring-side dishes, hemispherical and restricted-orifice bowls, basins, and covers. The only form not found in Mayapan Red Ware is the potstand. The difference insofar as jars are concerned rests primarily on the quantitative shift of emphasis. There are higher percentages of San Joaquin Buff Ware storage jars, tripod jars with central neck bulge, and jars with parenthesis rim than Mayapan Red Ware specimens, whereas the reverse is true of water jars. Flaring tripod dishes differ mostly as to foot types. The San Joaquin Buff Ware foot types are hollow animal effigy (56.5%), hollow cylindrical (21.7%), solid conical (10.9%), and hollow conical (6.5%), as compared to Mayapan Red Ware which has the following foot type percentages: solid conical 51.2, hollow oven 22.5, hollow effigy mostly human 8.2, hollow cylindrical 6.2, and hollow conical .3. Here the greatest shift of emphasis is from red ware solid conical to buff ware hollow effigy. And the effigy changes are from human in the red to animal in the buff. The fine-orange Matillas Group has tripod dishes and plates that bear hollow effigy feet almost exclusively. These may be either human or animal.

The techniques of decoration and design styles differ greatly from others in the Hocaba or Tases Ceramic complexes. The only technique involved is painting. This is separated into two types: Tecoh Red-on-buff and Pele Polychrome. The single instance of incising being added to the Tecoh Red-on-buff Type, thus producing the Tecoh outline-incised variety, is hardly worth mentioning.

The design style has no immediate Yucatan predecessor. It does not occur with contemporary material at Tulum or in any of the other sites in Quintana Roo discussed and illustrated by Sanders (1960). On the other hand, there is a presumably contemporaneous Topoxte Cream Polychrome Type found at Topoxte by W. R. Bullard, Jr. (1960, pp. 370–371, and 1970, pp. 286–292) which has certain design similarities. These are based on the use of a similar color scheme and include such design elements as the "comb" affix, concentric crescents, dots, dot encircled devices, and parallel lines. The closest resemblances, however, appear to be with Maya Peten Classic design. The association is with the Zacatel Cream-polychrome Type and the Narantal Red-on-cream Type, both forming part of Peten Gloss Ware of the Tepeu 2 Ceramic Complex at Uaxactun. The devices common to these types and the Tecoh Red-on-buff Type and the Pele Polychrome Type of San Joaquin Buff Ware are the ahau sign, chevrons, circles and concentric circles, crosses or quatrefoils, crosshatching, dots, fish, the glyph, the guilloche or braid, "ram horn" scrolls, reverse curves or opposed reverse curves, the S-shape, scrolls, squiggles, step-frets or step-and-scrolls, the tau or terrace, triangle bands, and the U-shape. Although these devices or elements are commonly used in both the Tepeu 2 and Tases ceramic complexes, the resulting compositions are sometimes quite different. Nevertheless, the total evidence of color combinations, similarity of design elements, and certain forms suggests a connection, however distant.

PETO CREAM WARE

Forms, Types, and Varieties	A Rim	C Rim	D Rim	%	Total Rim	Total & body
Jars, water:				41.9		
Kukula Cream Type	4	3	0		7	25
Xcanchakan Black-on-cream Type	3	50	2		55	736
Jars, storage:				12.8		
Kukula Cream Type	2	4	1		7	32
Xcanchakan Black-on-cream Type	2	8	2		12	215
Bowls, restricted orifice:				12.8		
Kukula Cream Type	7	0	0		7	3
Xcanchakan Black-on-cream Type	2	8	2		12	18
Bowls, hemispherical:				11.5		
Kukula Cream Type	0	3	0		3	0
Xcanchakan Black-on-cream Type	2	10	2		14	23
Bowls, tripod, recurving side:				0.7		
Xcanchakan Black-on-cream Type	0	0	1			0
tripod, grater: Xcanchakan Black-on-cream Type, incised variety	0	0	0		0	1
Dishes, tripod:				13.5		
Kukula Cream Type	7	2	1		10	0
Xcanchakan Black-on-cream Type	4	5	1		10	14
Basins:				6.8		
Kukula Cream Type	0	0	1		1	0
Xcanchakan Black-on-cream Type	4	3	2		9	6
Total	37	96	15		148	1,073

Jars, water (51, *d–h*; cf. 51, *a, b*; 52, *a–d, g–k*; 75, *l, m*). Small to medium-wide mouth, high, medium-high, or rarely low neck which may be outcurving, vertical, flaring, or bulging, flat, rounded, or square bolster, thickened, everted, and direct rim, flat, pointed, rounded, or beveled lip, medium-thick to thick walls except for 51, *d* and *e* which have thin walls, pear-shape body, usually two horizontal strap handles placed on opposite sides of body at point of greatest diameter, slightly concave base. *Size*: lip diam. 5–18 cm., av. 13.8 cm., most common of 16 measured are 12 cm. [4], and 16 cm. [4]; neck ht. 2.6–8 cm., av. 5.6 cm., most common of 11 measured are 5 cm. [3], 7 cm. [2], and 8 cm. [2], total ht. of two 39 cm. *Surface*: slipped and burnished (51, *d, e*, polished) on exterior and neck interior (51, *a, b, d, f–*

h; 52, *d*) on exterior and partway down neck interior (51, *e*; 52, *a, b*; 75, *l, m*), or on exterior only (52, *k*). Slip color is cream (10 YR 8/4, 8/3; 7.5 YR 8/4), beige (10 YR 7/4), or light gray (10 YR 8/2; 2.5 YR 8/0). *Paste*: coarse texture, temper usually calcite, less frequently gray limestone, and commonly light brown color (7.5 YR 7/4). *Types and decoration*: only a small percentage is undecorated. *Kukula Cream Type*: 7 rim, 25 body sherds. *Xcanchakan Black-on-cream Type*: 55 rim, 736 body sherds. Decoration consists of black-painted designs on both neck and body. The necks carry finger dabs on interior rim (52, *a–d*) and triangles (52, *a*; 75, *m*) or parallel vertical rectangles (52, *k*) on exterior. The shoulder is embellished with encircling bands including S's and dots (52, *a, b*; 75, *l, m*), sloppy tau's, scrolls and dots (52, *h*), and reverse angles and U's (52, *i*). All these bodies have parallel vertical tricklelike stripes.

Jars, storage (cf. 51, *c*; 52, *e, f*). Wide mouth, low or medium-high outcurving neck, triangular and flat bolster or direct rim, pointed, flat, or rounded lip, medium-thick to thick globular body, probably concave base. *Size:* lip diam. 21–35 cm., av. 27.5 cm., most common of 9 measured fall between 21 cm. and 25 cm. [5]. Neck ht. 3.5 cm. (only one specimen). Other measurements not taken due to fragmentary condition of sherds. *Surface:* slipped and burnished on exterior and partway down neck interior or all over. *Paste:* coarse texture, temper same as water jars, color light brown (7.5 YR 7/4). *Types and decoration:* some are undecorated. *Kukula Cream Type:* 7 rim, 32 body sherds. *Xcanchakan Black-on-cream Type:* 12 rim, 215 body sherds. Material very fragmentary. Designs probably much the same as those associated with the Hocaba Ceramic Complex storage jars.

Bowls or basins, restricted orifice (51, *j, p*; cf. 51, *i, k*; 52, *l–n*). Thin to medium-thick globular body, direct [11] or flat and triangular bolster [8] rim, rounded or beveled lip, probably slightly concave base. *Size:* direct rim, lip diam. 10–16 cm., av. 14 cm., most common of 6 measured is 16 cm. [4]; ht. one specimen 8.8 cm.; bolster rim, lip diam. 16–32 cm., av. 24 cm.; only 3 measured and the third is 24 cm.; besides being larger, those with bolster rim are thicker. *Surface:* slipped and burnished all over. Color may be cream (10 YR 8/3), pinkish cream (5 YR 9/2, 10 YR 9/2, 7.5 YR 8/2), beige (2.5 Y 8/4), or light gray (10 YR 8/2, 2.5 Y 8/0). *Paste:* coarse texture, temper probably same as water jars, color beige, cream, or light brown (7.5 YR 7/6, 6/6). *Types and decoration:* some are undecorated. *Kukula Cream Type:* 7 rim, 3 body sherds. *Xcanchakan Black-on-cream Type:* 12 rim, 18 body sherds. The most common design is parallel vertical black stripes (trickle) on both interior and exterior, rarely on exterior only. One example has a tau rim band on the interior and a band of concentric circles on exterior (52, *l*).

Hemispherical bowls (51, *q*; cf. 51, *o*; 52, *p, r*). Thin (51, *q*) to medium-thick rounded sides, direct rim, pointed, flat, rounded, or beveled lip, flat or slightly concave base. *Size:* lip diam. 14–20 cm., av. 17.5 cm., most common of 4 measured is 18 cm. [2]; ht. 8.5 cm. (one with 20 cm. diameter); thickness .3–.4 cm. to .6–.8 cm., av. .47–.65 cm., most common of 4 measured is .5–.7 cm. [2]. *Surface:* slipped and burnished all over, except

for one specimen (51, *q*) which is slipped and polished all over. Color may be cream (10 YR 8/3) or beige (10 YR 7/3). *Paste:* coarse texture except for above thin specimen which has medium texture, temper probably same as water jars, pinkish cream (7.5 YR 8/2) color. *Types and decoration:* a few are undecorated. *Kukula Cream Type:* 3 rim, no body sherds. *Xcanchakan Black-on-cream Type:* 14 rim, 23 body sherds. This includes both interior and exterior painted-black decoration: rims have dabs, squares, or rectangles; interiors have tricklelike stripes or "ram horn" scrolls.

Bowls, tripod, recurving side (cf. 52, *v*). Medium-thick to thick walls, flat bolster rim, flat lip, nearly flat base, probably three hollow ovenshape feet. *Size:* one similar example, lip diam. 19 cm., overall ht. 8 cm., thickness .7–1.1 cm. *Surface:* slipped and burnished all over except for bottoms of feet. Color is cream (10 YR 8/3). *Paste:* coarse texture, temper probably same as water jars, light brown (7.5 YR 6/6) color. *Types and decoration:* only example present is decorated on interior with black paint involving black rim dabs. The illustrated specimen has solid black floor and six sets of three vertical black stripes from rim to floor on interior and slopped over exterior accidently. *Xcanchakan Black-on-cream Type:* 1 rim, no body sherds.

Bowls, tripod, grater (cf. 52, *s*). Medium-thick rounded sides, direct rim, beveled lip, convex base, probably three hollow oven-shape feet. *Size:* too fragmentary for accurate measurement, but using the early example referred to in the illustration, lip diam. 22 cm., overall ht. ca. 8.2 cm., thickness .6–.8 cm. *Surface:* slipped and burnished all over, although usually worn off the scored area of floor. Color is cream (10 YR 8/3). *Paste:* coarse texture, temper probably same as water jars, color not recorded. *Types and decoration:* only 3 Peto Cream Ware fragments noted from Mayapan: one from early lots (52, *s*), another from the middle lots (51, *r*) which is undecorated, and the third from the late lots which is very fragmentary and not illustrated but had indications of black decoration. *Xcanchakan Black-on-cream Type, incised variety:* no rim, 1 body sherd.

Note: two deep bowls found in the middle lots are illustrated (51, *m, n*) and described in the caption.

Dishes, tripod (51, *s, u*; cf. 51, *t*; 52, *o, q, t, u, w, x*) which may be flaring [15], outcurving [4], or slightly rounded [1]. Medium-thick walls, direct rim, rounded, pointed, or beveled lip, convex base and three hollow oven-shape or cylindrical feet. *Size*: lip diam. 20–28 cm., av. 24.4 cm., most common of 11 measured are 26 cm. [4] and 24 cm. [3]; body ht. ca. 5–7.2 cm., av. 6.1 cm., most common of 8 measured are 6.5 cm. [4] and 5 cm. [2]; overall ht. 9.8 cm. (one specimen with hollow cylindrical feet); thickness .5–.6 cm. to .7–.9 cm., av. 56–.78 cm., most common of 12 measured are .5–.7 cm. [4] and .6–.8 cm. [3]. *Surface*: slipped and burnished all over, and a few slipped and burnished on interior and exterior but not on base. Color may be beige (10 YR 7/4, 5 YR 7/4), cream (10 YR 8/4, 8/3; 5 Y 9/2), or gray (2.5 YR 8/0). *Paste*: coarse texture, temper probably same as water jars, color cinnamon (7.5 YR 7/4) or gray (10 YR 8/2). *Types and decoration*: some have no embellishment. *Kukula Cream Type*: 10 rim, no body sherds. *Xcanchakan Black-on-cream Type*: 10 rim, 14 body sherds. The decoration is usually on interior only, consisting of black rim dabs and black tricklelike decoration (cf. 52, *q, t, u*).

Basins (cf. 51, *l*). Rounded medium-thick sides, rounded, square, or flat bolster rim, rounded or flat lip, probably flat to slightly concave base. *Size*: very fragmentary. One example measured. Lip diam. 34.5 cm.; max. diam. 35 cm.; body thickness .8 cm., bolster 1.6 cm. *Surface*: slipped and burnished all over. No color readings taken. *Paste*: coarse texture, temper probably same as for water jars, no color readings taken. *Types and decoration*: rarely undecorated. *Kukula Cream Type*: 1 rim, no body sherds. *Xcanchakan Black-on-cream Type*: 9 rim, 6 body sherds. Black rim dabs noted.

SUMMARY

Peto Cream Ware differs from Mayapan Red Ware principally in color and decorative treatment. Most of the forms are common to both wares and may derive their origin from Chichen Slate ware, particularly the water jars, restricted-orifice bowls, tripod grater bowls, basins, and tripod dishes with flaring or outcurving sides. The surface finish and paste composition appear to be the same as in Mayapan Red Ware. The color of Peto Cream Ware slip, however, may be either cream or beige, and the paste color may be the same plus light brown or cinnamon. Mayapan Red Ware features such decorative techniques as incising, modeling, and appliqué, whereas Peto Cream Ware has only a painted black-on-cream type and a rare incised variety only associated with grater bowls. The design found most often in the Xcanchakan Black-on-cream Type is the trickle, actually painted parallel vertical lines. These lines may be accompanied by rim dabs,

scrolls, U's, and rarely S's. This technique and this design style closely resemble those of the Chichen Slate Ware, Balantun Black-on-slate Type, although the designs associated with the latter run more to S's and dots as accompaniment for the trickle decoration than to the scrolls and dabs found in the Balantun Black-on-cream Type.

Peto Cream Ware is found abundantly at both Chichen Itza and Dzibilchaltun. At the latter site it appears to have a somewhat earlier beginning than it does at Mayapan, and according to Andrews it is found "first in pure samples, later mixed with, and finally giving way to the redwares of the Decadent Period." Be that as it may, at Mayapan it is found always mixed with Mayapan Red Ware, but decreasing in quantity from the Hocaba to the Tases phase. Some forms such as jars maintain their same percentage, ca. 90 per cent, within the ware. Some others, including tripod dishes with both flaring and rounded sides, vases, and deep bowls, decrease, while a few like restricted bowls, tripod grater bowls, and basins increase slightly. Actually Peto Cream as a whole dwindles from 9.9 per cent in the early lots (Hocaba Phase) through 2.1 per cent in the middle lots to .5 per cent in the late lots (Tases Phase).

FINE-ORANGE MATILLAS GROUP

For descriptive listing, see page 235.

Dishes, tripod with flange (55, *a*, 4, 5; *b*, 1, 2, 4; *c*, 1; *d*, 5; cf. 75, *p*). Medium-thick to thick flaring sides, interior, exterior and interior, or exterior rim bulge or direct rim, rounded, beveled, or flat lip, plain, notched, or terraced basal flange, convex or more rarely flat base, and three hollow feet, sometimes oven-shape, but usually mold-made effigy, either anthropomorphic (56, *c*) or zoomorphic (56, *a*). *Size*: lip diam. 20–42 cm., av. 36.3 cm., most common of 24 measured is 42 cm. [15]; body ht. 5.8–8.3 cm., av. 7.8 cm., most common of 21 measured is 8.3 cm. [15]; overall ht. 13 cm. for one specimen with 15 rim fragments; thickness .4–.7 to .6–.9 cm., av. .58–.82 cm., most common of 23 measured is .6–.85 cm. [15]. *Surface*: slipped and burnished on interior only, except for those decorated on exterior which are slipped and burnished all over. The result is usually a matte finish. The unslipped areas are usually well smoothed and lightly burnished. Color may be orange (5 YR 6/8), red (10 R 4/6), or reddish brown (5 YR 5/6). *Paste*: very fine texture, no temper, and pinkish cinnamon (2.5 YR 6/6, 6/8), cinnamon (7.5 YR 7/6), or cinnamon to buff (7.5 YR 7/4) color. *Types and decoration*: most commonly undecorated. *Matillas Orange Type*:

FINE-ORANGE MATILLAS GROUP

Forms and Types	A Rim	C Rim	D Rim	%	Total	Rim & body
Dishes, tripod with flange:				74.4		
Matillas Orange Type	23	43	6		72	136
Villahermosa Incised Type	4	14	0		18	35
Grijalva Incised-polychrome Type	15	0	0		15	16
Chilapa Gouged-incised Type	0	1	0		1	1
Salto Composite Type	1	0	1		2	0
tripod without flange: Matillas Orange Type	36	11	2		49	133
Villahermosa Incised Type	15	3	0		18	12
Chilapa Gouged-incised Type	2	2	0		4	5
Salto Composite Type	0	1	0		1	2
Jars, high neck: Matillas Orange Type	15	4	0	7.9	19	137
Jars, low neck:				1.2		
Matillas Orange Type	0	0	2		2	32
Chilapa Gouged-incised Type	1	0	0		1	0
Bowls, restricted orifice:				6.2		
Matillas Orange Type	1	1	0		2	10
Salto Composite Type	3	2	0		5	19
Chilapa Gouged-incised Type	3	1	0		4	12
Villahermosa Incised Type	2	1	0		3	12
Nacajuca Black-on-orange Type	1	0	0		1	0
Bowls, deep, ringstand base:				6.2		
Matillas Orange Type	2	3	0		5	5
Villahermosa Incised Type	1	3	1		5	14
Chilapa Gouged-incised Type	2	1	0		3	13
Salto Composite Type	1	1	0		2	9
Bowls, hemispherical:				4.1		
Matillas Orange Type	0	3	0		3	7
Chilapa Gouged-incised Type	2	4	0		6	3
Salto Composite Type	1	0	0		1	0
Total	131	99	12		242	613

72 rim, 136 body sherds. *Villahermosa Incised Type*: 18 rim, 35 body sherds. These include preslip incised bands of chevrons and impressed circles (55, *b*, 4) and preslip incised bands of hooks and vertical lines (55, *b*, 2) framed by horizontal lines. *Grijalva Incised-polychrome Type*: 15 rim, 16 body sherds. They comprise the fragments of one vessel (55, *b*, 1) which has an interior decoration consisting of a band of red, black, and white rectangles framed by red upper and black and white lower horizontal stripes. The band of painted rectangles is superimposed upon a preslip incised chevron and impressed circle band. *Chilapa Gouged-incised Type*: 1 rim, 1 body sherd. No illustration, sherds fragmentary. *Salto Composite Type*: 2 rim, no body sherds. In one instance interior has painted black horizontal stripes framing a black geometric band; exterior has a band of gouged-incised scrolls joined by arcs cut through a thin white calcareous coat (55, *c*, 1).

Dishes, tripod without flange (55, *a*, 6, 8; *b*, 3; *c*, 2–4; *d*, 2, 3; 75, *o*, *q*). Medium-thick to thick flaring sides, interior or exterior and interior and

exterior rim bulge or direct rim, rounded, beveled, or flat lip, convex base, and three hollow feet much the same as those found in the preceding flanged dishes. *Size*: lip diam. 17–31 cm., av. 25 cm., most common of 8 measured range between 25 cm. and 28 cm. [5]; body ht. 6.5–8.5 cm., av. 7.5 cm., most common of 5 measured are 6.5 cm. [2] and 8 cm. [2]; thickness .4–.7 cm. to .7–1.1 cm., av. .55–.88 cm.; within the range of 8 measured there is an equal distribution. *Surface*: slipped and lightly burnished all over leaving a matte finish. Slip color may be light brown (7.5 YR 6/6), red (10 R 4/6, 5/6), or reddish brown (2.5 YR 5/6). *Paste*: very fine texture, no temper, and cinnamon (7.5 YR 7/6) color; many are weathered and one has gray (5 YR 6/1) paste. *Types and decoration*: most are undecorated. *Matillas Orange Type*: 49 rim, 133 body sherds (55, *a*, 6, 8). *Villahermosa Incised Type*: 18 rim, 12 body sherds. The most common design used for incising is the chevron band usually accompanied by circles (cf. 55, *b*, 3). The incising is usually done before slipping. *Chilapa Gouged-incised Type*: 4 rim, 5 body sherds. These include vertical and horizontal lines, braid, tau and circle motif plus right angles, and quite complicated designs (55, *c*, 2–4). *Salto Composite Type*: 1 rim, 2 body sherds. Preslip incised chevron bands plus reed-impressed circles separated by horizontal red stripes on interior (55, *b*, 3). *Note*: another type not found with this material but present in early lots (Hocaba Ceramic Complex) and found by Brainerd (1958, fig. 28, *c*, 9, 10) at Mayapan is Nacajuca Black-on-orange. Three of Brainerd's specimens are herein illustrated (55, *d*, 2, 3, 5), the last of which has a flange.

Jars with either high (55, *a*, 1), low (55, *a*, 2; *c*, 8), or bulbous (cf. 55, *a*, 3) neck usually flaring. They have direct or bead rims, rounded or rarely pointed lip, thin to medium-thick globular body, and flat to slightly concave base. *Size*: one high-neck example (55, *a*, 1) is complete; lip diam. 16 cm., max. diam. 21.2 cm., neck ht. 11 cm., overall ht. 27 cm.; thickness .6–.9 cm. The rest are very fragmentary. Low-neck variety, lip diam. 11–15 cm., av. 13.7 cm., only 3 present and 2 measure 15 cm.; max. diam. 12.6–17.1 cm., av. 15.6 cm.; neck ht. 1.9 cm.; thickness .4–.6 to .4–.7 cm., av. .4–.67. Bulbous neck variety found only in middle lots; one specimen measures, lip diam. 11 cm.; max. diam. 13.7 cm.; neck ht. 5.5 cm.; thickness .3–.4 cm. *Surface*: usually slipped and lightly burnished all over, giving a matte finish. A few (55, *a*, 2) are not slipped on interior; others (55, *a*, 1) are slipped on interior and exterior to a point just below the maximum diameter, below which they are smoothed but unslipped. Color may be red (10 R 5/6, 4/6; 2.5 YR 4/6), reddish brown (2.5 YR 5/6, 3/6), or orange (2.5 YR 5/8). *Paste*: very fine texture, no temper, and orange (5 YR 6/6, 6/8), cinnamon (7.5 YR 7/4, 7/6), or light brown (7.5 YR 6/4) color. *Types and decoration*: most are undecorated. *Matillas Orange Type*: high neck, 19 rim, 137 body sherds; low neck, 2 rim, 32 body sherds. *Chilapa Gouged-incised Type*: low neck, 1 rim, no body sherds. This example (55, *c*, 8) has an S-shape neck band and a more complicated body design separated from neck by a molding.

Bowls, restricted orifice (55, *c*, 9, 10, 12, 13, 16, 19; *d*, 6; cf. 55, *b*, 6; *c*, 11, 15; *d*, 1, 4). Thin to medium-thick rounded sides, direct rim, pointed or rounded lip, convex base, probably ringstand support. *Size*: lip diam. 10–15 cm., av. 13.1 cm., most common of 12 measured is 14 cm. [6]; max. diam. 13.5–18 cm., av. 16 cm., most common of 10 measured is 17 cm. [4]; thickness .3–.4 cm. to .4–.7 cm., av. .32–.51 cm., most common of 11 measured are .3–.4 cm. [4] and .3–.6 cm. [3]. *Sur-

face*: slipped and lightly burnished, leaving matte finish, on interior and exterior or on exterior and partway down interior. Color may be red (10 R 5/4, 7.5 R 3/6), cinnamon (7.5 YR 7/6), reddish brown (2.5 YR 5/6, 10 R 4/3), brown (10 YR 5/3, 4/3), or fawn (5 YR 6/4). Other colors used in decoration or background are black, dark brown, and white. *Paste*: very fine texture, no temper, light orange (5 YR 7/8), cinnamon (7.5 YR 7/4, and pink (5 YR 7/6) color; a number have a gray or black core. *Types and decoration*: some are undecorated. *Matillas Orange Type*: 2 rim, 10 body sherds (no illustration). *Salto Composite Type*: 5 rim, 19 body sherds. These combine either preslip gouging-incising or preslip incising with black or white background. The designs include bands of step-frets (cf. 55, *b*, 6), S's and crosshatching (55, *c*, 10), concentric circles and bars (55, *c*, 9), triangles (55, *c*, 13), bars, concentric circles (55, *c*, 16), and more complicated devices (55, *c*, 10, 13; cf. 55, *c*, 15). *Chilapa Gouged-incised Type*: 4 rim, 12 body sherds. The designs used in this type are made up of bands of triangles and circles, concentric circles and crosshatching (cf. 55, *c*, 11), S-shape forming a chain, concentric circles and bars (55, *c*, 12), and more complicated combinations (55, *c*, 19). *Villahermosa Incised Type*: 3 rim, 12 body sherds. No illustration because of fragmentary material. *Nacajuca Black-on-orange Type*: 1 rim, no body sherds. Designs consist mostly of black horizontal and vertical lines and stripes (55, *d*, 6 and cf. 55, *d*, 1, 4).

Bowls, deep, ringstand base (55, *a*, 7; *b*, 8–11; *c*, 5–7, 18; cf. 55, *b*, 5, 7). Tapering or recurving thin to medium-thick sides, direct rim, one inset rim (55, *a*, 7), rounded or pointed lip, convex base, usually a ringstand support, rarely a pedestal. *Size*: lip diam. 10–16.5 cm., av. 13 cm., most common of 11 measured are 11 cm. [4], 16.5 cm. [3], and 15 cm. [2]; overall ht. ca. 6.2–11.5 cm., av. 8.8 cm., most common of 5 measured are 7.5 cm. [2] and 11.5 cm. [2]; overall ht. ca. 7–16.3 cm., av. 11.2 cm., most common of 5 measured are 8.2 cm. [2] and 16.3 cm. [2]; thickness .2–.3 cm. to .4–.7 cm., av. .33–.52 cm., most common of 11 measured is .3–.5 cm. [5]. *Surface*: slipped and lightly burnished all over, on exterior and just over lip on interior, or on exterior only. Color may be red (10 R 5/6, 4/4; 2.5 YR 4/8), cinnamon (5 YR 6/6; 7.5 YR 7/6), reddish brown (2.5 YR 3/6, 5/6), or brown (2.5 YR 5/4). *Paste*: very fine texture, no temper, and orange (10 R 6/6), buff (10 R 6/3), pinkish cinnamon (2.5 YR 6/8), or beige (10 YR 7/3) color. *Types and decoration*: some are undecorated. *Matillas Orange Type*: 5

rim, 5 body sherds (55, a, 7). *Villahermosa Incised Type*: 5 rim, 14 body sherds. Usually postslip, prepolish incising, a few exceptions have preslip incising. Designs include crosshatching, circles, scrolls, loops, horizontal and vertical lines, and some rather complex designs (55, b, 7–10). *Chilapa Gouged-incised Type*: 3 rim, 13 body sherds. Preslip gouging-incising throughout including such designs as the guilloche band (55, c, 7) and a complex design with a variety of elements (55, c, 18). *Salto Composite Type*: 2 rim, 9 body sherds. The principal technique employed here is postslip gouging-incising, through black (55, c, 5) or white (55, c, 6) background. The designs include various bands such as arc and dot, and triangle. There are also complicated motifs (55, c, 5).

Bowls, hemispherical (55, c, 17; cf. 55, c, 14). Thin rounded sides, direct rim, usually pointed lip, flat or slightly concave base. *Size*: lip diam. 14–18 cm., av. 16 cm., only two measured; thickness .3–.4 cm. to .4–.5 cm., most common of 8 measured .3–.4 cm. [4]. *Surface*: slipped and lightly burnished on interior and exterior leaving a matte finish. Color may be orange or reddish brown, mostly badly weathered. One specimen from middle lots has specular hematite red slip. This gouged-incised sherd may belong in the fine-orange Silho Group (55, c, 14). *Paste*: very fine texture, no temper, color readings not taken. *Types and decoration*: some are undecorated. *Matillas Orange Type*: 3 rim, 7 body sherds. No illustration. *Chilapa Gouged-incised Type*: 6 rim, 3 body sherds. Designs may include scroll and block and bars and circle bands (cf. 55, c, 14). *Salto Composite Type*: 1 rim, no body sherds. This example has red rim band and a gouged-incised band of squares with a central device hard to decipher (55, c, 17).

SUMMARY

The fine-orange Matillas Group has little in common with the other fine-orange groups except the basic ware attributes of surface finish and paste composition. The difference is linked with form, techniques of decoration, and design. Form differs quite radically in the various fine-orange groups with the exception of hemispherical bowls and near barrel-shape vessels with possible ring-stand base. The former are associated with the Balancan, Altar, Silho, and Matillas groups, the latter with the Balancan, Altar, and Matillas groups. Certain techniques of decoration are distinctive to individual groups: plano-relief (Provincia) to the Balancan, modeled-carved (Pabellon) to the

Altar, polychrome (Pomuch) and modeled (Nunkini) to the Silho, and incised-polychrome (Grijalva) to the Matillas. Although distinctive, these techniques do not represent that most commonly used, which would be the Tenosique Red-on-orange Type for the fine-orange Balancan Group, the Yalton Black-on-orange Type for the fine-orange Silho Group, and the Matillas Orange Type (undecorated) for the fine-orange Matillas Group. This last formed 71.6 per cent of the fine-orange Matillas Group type. Other types held the following percentages: Villahermosa Incised 13.7, Chilapa Gouged-incised 6.2, Salto Composite 4.8, Grijalva Incised-polychrome 3.6, Nacajuca Black-on-orange .1, and Sayula Polychrome not present in the late lots and forming only .9 per cent of the middle lots. Even more distinctive to each group, however, is the style of design (Smith, 1958b, pp. 151–160). In the fine-orange Balancan Group the design follows the Maya Classic tradition. The human figure is depicted by means of plano-relief and bands of scrolls together with a cursive M-like device are a frequent incised motif. In the fine-orange Silho Group a combination of Maya Classic and Toltec tradition is present. The Classic tradition is usually found in the black banding which includes step-frets with related elements, birds, floral, serpent, and grotesque motifs, while the Toltec usage encompasses gouged-incised scroll meander and floral bands, also modeled effigy vessels representing both animals and humans. In contrast, in the fine-orange Matillas Group abstract patterns are most used including bands of chevrons, triangles, and S's, plus more complicated designs often separated by crosshatched panels.

The fine-orange Matillas Group represents but .3 per cent of the Hocaba and Tases ceramic complexes. It does not appear to have had the strong effect on the other Hocaba or Tases wares, types, and varieties that either the Balancan or Silho groups had on the ceramics of their times.

Actually both these latter groups were an inspiration to the local potters, and copying of forms and designs in the trade ware techniques was quite common. This to a somewhat lesser degree is true of the fine-orange Matillas Group especially with reference to San Joaquin Buff Ware but also to Mayapan Red Ware. A few fine-orange Matillas Group rather special forms appear to have prompted imitation by both the San Joaquin Buff Ware and Mayapan Red Ware local potters. These are jars with bulging necks (42, c; 53, a, 19, 22; 55, a, 3), tripod dishes with flaring sides and usually hollow effigy feet (40, b, 15, 16; 54, a, c, d;

55, *b*, 1), bowls with restricted orifice and ring-stand support (44, *l*, *m*; 53, *b*, 10; 55, *c*, 15), and deep bowls with tapering rim and ringstand support (43, *l*; 55, *c*, 5). Since these forms are for the most part quantitatively negligible in both the local ware aggregates and do represent a substantial percentage of the fine-orange Matillas Group assemblage, it is probable that the copying was done by local potters.

Techniques of decoration associated with the fine-orange Matillas Group are not normally connected with either San Joaquin Buff Ware or Mayapan Red Ware. The latter is rarely decorated except for horizontal rim grooving and occasional incising (47) on jar bodies and bowl exteriors which bear little resemblance to the Villahermosa Incised Type. The San Joaquin Buff Ware decoration, on the other hand, runs almost entirely to red or red and black painting, a technique sparsely used in the fine-orange Matillas Group. Local designs, either incised or painted, have little in common with those associated with the fine-orange Matillas Group barring a few devices, including the guilloche band and scrolls used with a variety of other elements.

MAYAPAN BLACK WARE

Forms and Types	A Rim	C Rim	D Rim	%	Total Rim & body	
Jars, water, medium-high, to high neck:				37.2		
Sulche Black Type	12	0	3		15	722
Pacha Incised Type	1	0	0		1	0
Sacmuyna Modeled Type	0	0	0		0	4
Dishes, tripod, flaring side:				44.2		
Sulche Black Type	1	2	16		19	23
Tripod, rounded side:				11.6		
Sulche Black Type	0	0	4		4	1
Pacha Incised Type	0	0	1		1	0
Bowls, restricted orifice:				4.7		
Sulche Black Type	2	0	0		2	3
Vases, cylindrical:						
Sulche Black Type	0	0	0		0	1
Figurines:				2.3		
Sacmuyna Modeled	1	0	0		1	0
Total	17	2	24		43	754

Jars, water, medium-high to high neck (no illustration, cf. 38, *a*, 1–12) nearly vertical, flaring, or outcurving with direct rim, rounded, pointed, or flat lip, two horizontal strap handles or effigy lug handles, pear-shape body, medium-thick walls, slightly concave base. For size, surface, and paste see Mama Red Type water jars. *Types and decoration*: mostly undecorated. *Sulche Black Type*: 15 rim, 722 body sherds. *Pacha Incised Type*: 1 rim, no body sherd. Horizontal incised lines on neck exterior. *Sacmuyna Modeled Type*: no rim, 4 body sherds. These body sherds consist of 4 effigy lug handles.

Dishes, tripod, flaring side (no illustration, cf. 40, *b*, 1, 2, 4). Medium-thick to thick walls, direct rim, rounded or pointed lip, slightly convex base, and three solid conical feet. For size, surface, and paste see Mama Red Type tripod dishes with flaring sides. *Types and decoration*: no form of embellishment encountered. *Sulche Black Type*: 19 rim, 23 body sherds.

Dishes, tripod, rounded side (no illustration, cf. 41, *b*, 6, 8, 9), which have medium-thick walls, direct rim, rounded, beveled, or pointed lip, convex base, and three feet usually solid conical. For size, surface, and paste see Mama Red Type tripod dishes with rounded sides. *Types and decoration*: rarely embellished. *Sulche Black Type*: 4 rim, 1 body sherd. *Pacha Incised Type*: 1 rim, no body sherds. This specimen has vertical incised lines on exterior.

Bowls, restricted orifice (no illustration, cf. 44, *f*, *j*). Medium-thick globular sides, direct rim, rounded or pointed lip, flat or slightly concave base. For size, surface, and paste see Mama Red Type bowls with restricted orifice. *Types and decoration*: no form of embellishment encountered. *Sulche Black Type*: 2 rim, 3 body sherds.

Vase, cylindrical (no illustration). It has medium-thick sides, a basal molding, and flat base. Possibly not a vase but appears to be because of height-diameter ratio. Only other basal molding in the Tases collection is found in 54, e, a Pele Polychrome Type. *Types and decoration*: no embellishment other than the basal molding. *Sulche Black Type*: no rim, 1 body sherd.

Figurine (no illustration). A black bird whistle with mouthpiece at tail. *Size*: no measurement taken. *Surface*: slipped black and burnished all over exterior. *Paste*: not recorded. *Types and decoration*. *Sacumuyna Modeled Type*: 1 head, no body sherds.

SUMMARY

Mayapan Black Ware is relatively rare, and although some of the fragments are pure black others show reddish areas. This ware follows Mayapan Red Ware very closely; in fact color appears to be the only difference. No complete vessels were found. At times the question arose as to whether a black ware was really intended. Perhaps the black sherds should be considered as a group under a more general ware category such as Yucatan Burnished Ware. Brainerd (1958) does not mention a black ware in his late Mexican substage, only Coarse Red ware which is the equivalent of Mayapan Red Ware.

TELCHAQUILLO BRICK WARE

Forms and Types	A Rim	C Rim	D Rim	Total Rim & body	
Candle-flame shields:					
Moyos Red Type	68	2	0	70	193
Cozil Incised Type	1	0	0	1	32
Total	69	2	0	71	225

Candle-flame shields (36, a–c). These tilelike objects are approximately a half cylinder measuring about 34 cm. in length, 17 cm. in diameter at midsection, thickness 1.9 cm. at base and .7 at top. All edges are flat. A few (36, b) have offset ends at base. The fact that they are wider and thicker at base than at top permitted them to stand firmly. The interior is severely scorched and fire-blackened over all the central part, leaving unburnt about 3.5 cm. at top and 5 cm. at bottom. At first the form and central burning seemed to suggest its use as a conduit section whose overlapping areas were protected. If it served as a conduit, why any burning? A suggestion was made that these objects may have been used as light reflectors, placed behind a candle to focus light on some definite area. Another possibility is that they served as candle-flame shields or deflectors. This latter appears to be the most likely answer. *Size*: lower (thick) lip diam. 14–19 cm., av. 17 cm., most common of 21 measured is 18 cm. [10]; upper (thin) lip diam. 11–15 cm., av. 13 cm., most common of 13 measured are 11 cm. [4] and 15 cm. [4]; ht. of one specimen 34.5 cm.; thickness .7–2 cm., av. .7–1.96 cm., most common of 10 measured are .7–2 cm. [6] and .7–1.9 cm. [4].

Surface: lightly slipped and imperfectly burnished all over. Preslip smoothing shows light vertical striations. The interior or concave surface is often crazed and as mentioned above is centrally fire-blackened. The color is red (10 R 4/4). *Paste*: very coarse texture, no temper readings made, red (2.5 YR 4/6) or orange (2.5 YR 5/8) color. *Types and decoration*: a large proportion of these candle-flame shields remain undecorated. *Moyos Red Type*: 70 rim, 193 body sherds. *Cozil Incised Type*: 1 rim, 32 body sherds. Preslip, groove-incised geometric design covers a large part of exterior, another count against its being used as a conduit, since the design would be concealed.

SUMMARY

Telchaquillo Brick Ware has only one form which served a very special function, possibly as a shield. Since the great majority of these objects were found on the surface, they may belong to a post-Tases Ceramic Complex. If so, they represent 72.2 per cent of such a collection, which seems highly unlikely for so special a product.

TULUM RED WARE

Forms and Types	A Rim	C Rim	D Rim	%	Total Rim & body	
Jars, wide mouth, high neck:				29.4		
Payil Red Type	3	0	0		3	5
Palmul Incised Type	0	2	0		2	4
Jars, wide mouth, low neck:				23.5		
Palmul Incised Type	2	0	0		2	0
Kanlum Plano-relief Type	0	0	2		2	0
Dishes, tripod, flaring:				23.5		
Payil Red Type	0	3	0		3	0
Palmul Incised Type	0	1	0		1	0
Bowls, hemispherical:				11.8		
Palmul Incised Type	2	0	0		2	0
Restricted orifice:				5.9		
Palmul Incised Type	1	0	0		1	0
Basin:				5.9		
Payil Red Type	0	1	0		1	0
Total	8	7	2		17	9

Jars, wide mouth, high neck (48, *b, d, j, k*) or medium-high neck (48, *a, e*) which have direct (*d*), everted (*a, b, e*), and parenthesis (*k*) rim, or rim molding (*j*), rounded, but rarely beveled (*b*) or pointed (*d*) lip, thin to thick walls for both neck and globular body, bases not present. *Size:* lip diam. 18.5–22 cm., av. 20.1 cm., most common of 5 measured is 20 cm. [3]; neck ht. 3.5–9.5 cm., av. 6.4 cm., the medium-high necks range ca. 4 cm., the high necks ca. 9 cm.; thickness .4–.5 cm. to .7–.9 cm., av. .46–.68 cm., most common of 8 measured are .4–.5 cm. [2] and .4–.6 cm. [2]. *Surface:* well smoothed, slipped and burnished on exterior, giving a medium to light luster. Interiors may be slipped and burnished all over (*a, b, e*), just over lip (*d*), or on upper part of neck (*j, k*). Slip color is a uniform red (10 R 4/6, 4/8; 2.5 YR 4/8), varying little on a single vessel or from vessel to vessel. *Paste:* fine texture, probably calcite temper with stray fine grains or quartz, and pale orange color. *Types and decoration:* some are undecorated. *Payil Red Type:* 3 rim, 5 body sherds. *Palmul Incised Type:* 2 rim, 4 body sherds. Usually postfire incised, although one (*a*) may be preslip incised. A distinctive characteristic is that most of the lines are double. The designs include scrolls, circles, and dots. The motifs are not easily classified.

Jars, wide mouth, low neck (48, *i*; cf. 48, *c, f*) which may have flaring (*c, f*) or outcurving (*i*) neck, direct (*f, i*) or everted (*c*) rim, thin to thick walls, globular body. *Size:* lip diam. 24.5–27.5 cm., av. 26 cm., only 2 measured; neck ht. 1.8–2.8 cm., av. 2.3 cm., only 3 measured; thickness .4–.9 cm., av.

.53–.83 cm., most common of 3 measured is .6–.8 cm. [2]. *Surface:* well smoothed, slipped and burnished all over. Slip color is a uniform red (10 R 4/6, 4/8). *Paste:* fine texture, probably calcite temper with stray fine grains of quartz, and pale orange color. *Types and decoration:* no plain unadorned examples. *Palmul Incised Type:* 2 rim, no body sherds. One (*c*) is postfire incised, the other (*f*) is postslip, prepolish incised. The former has an Ilhuitl-like sign motif, the latter a chevron meander band. *Kanlum Plano-relief Type:* 2 rim, no body sherds. The design is a band of blocks separated by vertical bars (48, *i*).

Dishes, tripod, flaring (48, *m–o*; cf. *l*) thin to medium-thick outcurving (*l, m, o*) or flaring (*n*) sides, direct rim which may be slightly thickened (*n*), rounded (*l–n*) or flat (*o*) lip, convex base, and three hollow cylindrical feet (cf. *l*). *Size:* lip diam. 20–27.5 cm., av. 23.9 cm., most common of 4 measured is 24 cm. [2]; overall ht. 8.8 cm. (1 specimen); thickness .4–.6 cm. to .5–.7 cm., av. .45–.65 cm., most common are .4–.6 cm. [2] and .5–.7 cm. [2]. *Surface:* well smoothed, slipped and burnished all over. Slip color is a uniform red (10 R 4/6; 2.5 YR 4/8). *Paste:* fine texture, probably calcite temper with stray fine grains of quartz, and pale orange color. *Types and decoration:* many are unadorned. *Payil Red Type:* 3 rim, no body sherds. *Palmul Incised Type:* 1 rim, no body sherds. Postfire incised geometric and horizontal line banding (48, *o*). Sometimes these vessels have terraced basal flanges (48, *q*). In this case the flange is postfire incised and includes a scroll.

Bowls, hemispherical (cf. WTS, fig. 4, *d*, 9, 12)

with thin to medium-thick sides, direct rim, rounded lip, probably flat base. *Size*: fragmentary. *Surface*: well smoothed, slipped and burnished all over. Slip color is a uniform red (10 R 4/6, 4/8). *Paste*: fine texture, probably calcite temper with stray fine grains of quartz, and pale orange color. *Types and decoration*: only decorated found. *Palmul Incised Type*: 2 rim, no body sherds. Postfire incised geometric bands.

Bowl, restricted orifice (cf. *ibid.*, fig. 4, *d*, 4 for shape), direct rim, rounded lip, rounded thin to medium-thick body. *Size*: fragmentary. *Surface*: well smoothed, slipped and burnished all over. Slip color is a uniform red (10 R 4/6, 4/8). *Paste*: fine texture, probably calcite temper with stray fine grains of quartz, and pale orange color. *Types and decoration*: incised after firing but too fragmentary to determine design motif. *Palmul Incised Type*: 1 rim, no body sherds.

Basin (48, *p*) with bolster rim, rounded lip, and medium-thick rounded body, probably flat base. *Size*: lip diam. 29 cm., thickness .6–.7 cm. *Surface*: well smoothed, slipped and burnished all over. Fire-clouding on interior. Slip color is red but no reading taken. *Paste*: fine texture, probably calcite temper with stray fine grains of quartz, and pale orange color. *Types and decoration*. *Payil Red Type*: 1 rim, no body sherds.

SUMMARY

Tulum Red Ware is not a local pottery but a product of the east coast of the Yucatan Peninsula. As its name suggests, it probably came from Tulum. It is quite easily distinguished from Mayapan Red Ware for a number of reasons: better surface treatment in smoothing and uniformity of slip color, finer paste texture, addition of fine quartz grains to calcite temper, harder consistency, and generally thinner walls. In addition the two most common forms in both wares are jars and tripod dishes. Tulum Red Ware high-neck jars in many instances have parenthesis or everted rims, neither of which are Mayapan Red Ware traits and when found are most likely copies. The low-

neck wide-mouth jars are more alike, as are some of the high-neck jars with flaring or outcurving neck and bolster rim. Perhaps this latter form which at Tulum has thicker walls and coarser paste (*ibid.*, p. 239) is really Mayapan Red Ware. The principal difference in tripod dishes, besides thickness, has to do with depth and foot form. The Tulum Red Ware tripod dishes have more basal convexity and distinctive, hollow flat-bottom cylindrical feet welded to the convex base. Mayapan Red Ware feet are normally solid conical, although many other forms are represented, but seldom the Tulum type, which when it does occur is undoubtedly a copy. Considering decorative techniques we find that Mayapan Red Ware is rarely decorated except with simple horizontal preslip grooving. Tulum Red Ware, although likewise infrequently decorated (both jars and dishes, *ibid.*, figs. 4 and 5), appears to be adorned more often. The form of decoration is mostly postfire incising or scratching, usually done with double lines. Occasionally vessels have plano-relief designs. The decoration is applied in bands to the exterior of basal-break bowls (deep tripod dishes) and to the necks or upper bodies of direct rim jars, usually the low to medium-high neck variety. The designs are geometric involving straight lines, hooks, scrolls, and rarely triangles and wavy lines. The greater part of the rarely decorated Mayapan Red Ware sherds is illustrated in figure 47. Fifty per cent are preslip incised, 25 per cent are postslip incised, and 20 per cent are postfire incised (really doodling); one sherd has plano-relief decoration. In general the designs found on the Mayapan Red Ware vessels are quite distinct from those on the Tulum Red Ware specimens.

Having examined surface treatment, paste composition, vessel form, decorative techniques, and design styles and having found that these attributes as found in Tulum Red Ware differ greatly from those associated with Mayapan Red Ware, we must conclude that except for a general similarity in color the two wares are readily distinguishable one from the other.

MAYAPAN COARSE WARE

Forms and Types	A Rim	C Rim	D Rim	Total Rim & body	
Censers, effigy: Uayma Modeled Type	3	0	0	3	10
Figurines: Uayma Modeled Type	3	3	0	6	0
Total	6	3	0	9	10

Censers, effigy (no illustration). These are fragmentary but approximate the large to medium size of the Chen Mul Type. They also conform in shape and general treatment, although more crudely done. *Size:* too fragmentary. *Surface:* less carefully smoothed than the Chen Mul Type, probably had a white calcareous coat, but no fire-blackening was noted on the few sherds recovered. Nor did any painting show up. *Paste:* very coarse texture, probably calcite temper (but no examination made by Shepard), and reddish brown color. *Types and decoration:* a few modeled fragments were encountered with the vessel rim and body sherds. *Uayma Modeled Type:* 3 rim, 10 body sherds.

Figurines (65, *o*; 66, *c*, 1–3; cf. 35, *a*, 18; 65, *i*). These may be hollow [4] or solid [2], human [4] or animal [2]. All have detached heads (65, *o*; 66, *c*, 2, 3), and two of middle lots are complete figures (65, *i*). Of the animals, one is a fish (65, *o*), the other a possible monkey (66, *c*, 2). The only late lot human head illustrated (66, *c*, 3), like others crudely made, is solid, bald, and has punched eyes. One complete hollow specimen (cf. 35, *a*, 18) of the middle lots has closed base and a vent in back. *Size:* complete specimens, ht. 13.2 cm.; detached heads, ht. 2.8–3.6 cm., av. 3.2 cm., only 3 measured. *Surface:* very carelessly smoothed and crudely modeled. Two of these examples and the two middle lot jaguars (65, *i*) appear to have been merely sunbaked and not fired. No slip was applied but probably in all cases they were painted with a variety of colors. *Paste:* very coarse texture, heavily tempered with what appears to be calcite (not examined by Shepard), and an orange red to reddish brown color. *Types and decoration:* since these are figurines, they were either modeled or moldmade. *Uayma Modeled Type:* 6 head, no body sherds. These are all modeled and most of paint has disappeared with weathering.

SUMMARY

Little can be said of this as a ware except that it is extremely coarse and the objects are crudely fashioned. There may even be two wares involved: the sunbaked and the fired.

TASES CERAMIC COMPLEX SUMMARY

In the Tases Ceramic Complex (A.D. 1300–1450) as established at Mayapan, three principal local wares were identified. These comprise Mayapan Unslipped Ware (59.4%), Mayapan Red Ware (27.6%), and San Joaquin Buff Ware (.9%). The unidentifiable sherds formed a considerable total (10.9%), whereas the remainder grossed less than 2 per cent. These include minor local wares such as Peto Cream (.4%), Mayapan Black (.3%) Telchaquillo Brick (.1%), and Mayapan Coarse (.01%). Only two trade wares are involved: Fine Orange Ware, the fine-orange Matillas Group (.3%), and Tulum Red Ware (.01%). These percentages only refer to the Tases Ceramic Complex.

Mayapan Unslipped Ware may be separated into two groups: one primarily associated with the Hocaba Ceramic Complex and called the Unslipped Navula Group which has already been discussed; the other affiliated with the Tases Ceramic Complex and named the unslipped Panaba Group. The new forms attached to the unslipped Panaba Group are jars with high neck and parenthesis rim, tripod deep bowls, thick bowls, tripod dishes or bowls with flaring or rounded sides, pedestal or flat-based cups, pedestal-based vases, ring-stand plates, miniature vessels, effigy vessels, disk-shape covers, masks, molds, and stands. The types of this ware involving new decorative techniques not found in the Hocaba Ceramic Complex are Chenkeken Incised Type, Chen Mul Modeled Type, and Huhi Impressed Type. Design is extremely rare in this ware except on effigy censers, effigy vessels, and some figurines; painted design is otherwise largely limited to stripes and zonal decoration. The rare incised decoration depicts S's, the guilloche band, and a few hard to decipher curvilinear designs.

Next in importance is Mayapan Red Ware, which may be separated into three groups: one primarily linked with the Hocaba Ceramic Complex and called the red Mama Group, which has been discussed; two others associated with the Tases Ceramic Complex and named the red Panabchen Group and the red Tzitz Group. The new forms attached to the red Panabchen Group are parenthesis-rim jars, deep tripod bowls with basal flange, hemispherical bowls, cluster of bowls on a pedestal, pedestal-base plates, and disk or scutate covers. The new types and varieties affiliated with this group include: Mama Red Type, a variety without exterior slip, which may be undecorated or have red or black decoration; Panabchen Red Type which is the same as the Mama Red Type but linked to the new forms; Pustunich Incised Type, like Papacal but associated with the new forms; Papacal Incised Type, a variety without exterior slip, Dzitxil Openwork Type, and Yobain Plano-relief Type. The new forms attached to the red Tzitz Group are tripod jars with high flaring necks, tripod jars with high bulging necks, and jars or drums possibly having three necks. The only type at present recognized is the Tzitz Red Type. The red Panabchen Group includes a few painted designs such as red or black stripes and a black glyph band placed on the unslipped exterior of basal-break tripod dishes. More often incising is used to depict scrolls, S's, step-frets, guilloches, diamond patterns, the cursive N, and rarely the human figure. Grooving is principally employed in the making of parallel horizontal lines at or near the rim. Parallel vertical grooves or deep incisions, sometimes crosshatched, are placed around the rims of drums, presumably to hold the skin stretched over and tied to that end. Plano-relief is rare and may involve the human figure as well as feathers and other devices. Openwork is the medium used for portraying a guilloche band or circular holes and rectilinear devices. However, design is rare in the red Panabchen Group.

Next in numerical importance, although of small percentage, is San Joaquin Buff Ware. It is found in middle (.2%) and late (.6%) lots, never in early lots. The only group so far associated with this ware is the buff Polbox Group. The forms attached to this group include: storage jars with wide mouth, high outcurving neck, sometimes a bulging neck; water jars with relatively small mouth, high nearly vertical neck, and sometimes a parenthesis rim; tripod flaring-side dishes; hemispherical or restricted-orifice bowls; rarely deep bowls, basins, vases, potstands, or covers. This is a much decorated ware, usually painted. The types are Tecoh Red-on-buff, rarely outlined with incising, Polbox Buff, Pele Polychrome, and Kimbila Incised. The painted designs include such elements as the chevron, circle, concentric circle, concentric U, crescent, dotted line, semidisk, double yoke, guilloche, loop, angular scroll, "ram horn" scroll, scrolls and related elements, scroll and triangle squiggle, step-fret, tau, terrace, triangle, and zigzag; conventionalized devices like the quatrefoil and a possible bat head; natural-

istic forms such as the fish; glyphic forms including the affix "comb," the ahau, and a possible glyph band; or unusual forms like the circle and dot with squiggle tail, and crosshatching used as a filler. The incised designs other than outline incising are most rare; one example shows a pair of angular scrolls, possible doodling.

The number of small, weathered, and therefore unidentifiable sherds is rather large, totaling 10.9 per cent, but to be expected with mostly surface material. That early lots had 15.2 per cent is surprising, but middle lots having 9.3 per cent is normal.

Peto Cream Ware decreases gradually in numerical importance (9.9% early, 2.1% middle, .4% late lots). There is nothing new in decorative technique or design style in the material found in the late lots associated with the Tases Ceramic Complex. A few bolster-rim basins appear in later lots, however, as well as two other shapes not certainly identified in the early lots. These are the hemispherical bowl and the tripod bowl with recurving sides, both of which may have been present in early lot sherds but too small for absolute identification.

Mayapan Black Ware increases gradually from early through middle to late lots, always forming a very small percentage (.16, .3, and .3) of the total. The early vessel shapes appear to have been confined to jars and hemispherical bowls, whereas later tripod dishes with both flaring and rounded sides, bowls with restricted orifice, a cylindrical vase, and even a figurine were found. Besides the original undecorated black (Sulche Black Type), a few incised (Pacha Incised Type) and modeled (Sacmuyna Modeled Type) sherds were encountered. The incised designs consist for the most part in parallel horizontal or vertical lines. Modeling involved lug handles and a figurine head.

Telchaquillo Brick Ware is a relatively late product, since only 7 out of 303 sherds were found in middle lots and none in early lots. Only one form is known, the shield, and a groove-incised (Cozil Incised Type) decorative technique is responsible for the only designs encountered. These latter are essentially geometric.

Another minor local ware is the Mayapan Coarse. It is confined to a few sherds in both the middle and late lots. The forms involved are effigy censers and figurines and these are entirely or in part modeled (Uayma Modeled Type).

The most important of the trade wares is Fine Orange, the fine-orange Matillas Group. This group increases from early to middle, then drops off in the late lots, always forming a very small percentage (.3, .5, and .3). In the middle lots and continuing into the late lots two shapes not found in the early lots appear. These are the deep bowl with recurving sides and ringstand base and the hemispherical bowl. Forms found in all lots include: tripod dishes, tripod dishes with basal flange, jars, and bowls with restricted orifice. The tripod dishes with or without flange usually have hollow effigy feet and are most diagnostic of this group. An aid to identifying rim sherds of this form is the slight rim bulge on interior, exterior, or both. In all, seven decorative techniques are involved with the fine-orange Matillas Group: undecorated but slipped (Matillas Orange Type); sharply incised (Villahermosa Incised Type); gouged-incised (Chilapa Gouged-incised Type); various combination of incised, gouged-incised, or impressed with one color which could be red, black, or white (Salto Composite Type); incising plus polychrome (Grijalva Incised-polychrome Type); painted black on orange (Nacajuca Black-on-orange Type); and polychrome without other embellishment (Sayula Polychrome Type). Grijalva Incised-polychrome occurs only in the middle and late lots and Sayula Polychrome only in the middle lots. All the other techniques mentioned above are found in early, middle, and late lots, usually increasing in occurrence from early to late. The one exception is the Nacajuca Black-on-orange Type which drops down to one sherd in the late lots from 10 to 11 sherds in the early and middle lots, respectively. The three most important types in the late lots as well as in all lots are the Matillas Orange Type (71.6%), the Villahermosa Incised Type (13.7%), and the Chilapa Gouged-incised Type (6.2%). Considering design, horizontal banding on the interior of shallow dishes or on the exterior of bowls or jars is much used. The most diagnostic band associated with the fine-orange Matillas Group is the chevron and circle. Other bands commonly found are the guilloche, the triangle, and the horizontal stripe. Patterns such as the diamond and dot and the crosshatch are employed. There also is evidence of figure design both human and inanimate, plus a number of devices or elements often found at other times and in other places. These include scrolls, hooks, step-frets, brackets, and circles. Many of the above mentioned designs, which are all found in the Tases Ceramic Complex, are also encountered in the Hocaba Ceramic Complex, but too often the fragmentary condition of the earlier material prevents exact identification.

Finally, there is Tulum Red Ware which is not present in the early lots, is strongest in the middle lots, and begins to fall off in the late lots. This might indicate a stronger contact with the east coast in early Tases times. There is some evidence of Tulum Red Ware copying in Mayapan Red Ware. A detailed comparison of these two red wares has been made in the summary of Tulum Red Ware (Chapter IV). This summary also shows how the red Payil Group forms, decorative techniques, and design styles differ from or are similar to those of the red Panabchen Group.

The Tases Ceramic Complex is certainly an outgrowth of the Hocaba Ceramic Complex. Certain of the wares continue, such as Mayapan Unslipped, Mayapan Red, Peto Cream, Mayapan Black, and Fine Orange. However, new wares, groups, types, and varieties are added. The new wares are San Joaquin Buff, Telchaquillo Brick, Mayapan Coarse, and Tulum Red. The new groups and their associated types and varieties include: the unslipped Panaba Group composed of Panaba Unslipped Type, Buleb Striated Type, Thul Appliqué Type, Acansip Painted Type, Chenkeken Incised Type, Huhi Impressed Type, and Chen Mul Modeled Type; the red Panabchen Group formed of Panabchen Red Type, Mama Red Type with interior slip only, Pustunich Incised Type, Papacal Incised Type with interior slip only, Yobain Plano-relief Type, and Dzitxil Openwork Type; the red Tzitz Group; the orange Matillas Group with new types Sayula Polychrome and Grijalva Incised-polychrome.

These additions involve new vessel shapes, new decorative techniques, and new styles of design already listed under the different ware and group summaries. These are new in the sense that they did not occur in the Hocaba Ceramic Complex.

A fair number of the modes linked to the Tases Ceramic Complex also form part of the Hocaba Ceramic Complex. Perhaps the best time-markers for the later complex are the Panabchen Red Type jar with parenthesis rim, the Panabchen Red Type bowl cluster on a pedestal base, the Panabchen Red Type plate with pedestal base, the Chapab Modeled Type double-boiler effigy vessel, the Telchaquillo Brick Ware light shield, the Chen Mul effigy censer, the Dzitxil Openwork Type of decorative technique, and the buff Polbox Group including forms, the red-on-buff decorative technique, and most especially the design style. This last includes a return to the use of glyphs and glyph bands, a circle and dot with squiggle-tail device, and the painted large size naturalistic fish.

The fine-orange Matillas Group is likewise distinctive especially as to vessel shape and design style. In other words, given a Fine Orange Ware sherd, its proper group could be determined easily from its shape and design style.

XVII

Miscellaneous Post-Tases Ceramic Complexes

CHIKINCHEL CERAMIC COMPLEX

MAYAPAN [3]

At Mayapan the Chikinchel Ceramic Complex (A.D. 1450–1550) is poorly represented. Only one ware, Fine Orange, and one group, the Cunduacan Ceramic Group, have been noted. Furthermore, even the sherds assigned to this group are open to question, primarily because of their fragmentary condition. On the other hand some of the other Post-Tases sherds may have had their beginnings in the Chikinchel Phase, although their period of greatest abundance was later in the Chauaca Phase. It is equally possible that the Cunduacan Ceramic Group had its beginning at the end of the Tases Phase.

FINE-ORANGE CUNDUACAN GROUP

Forms and Types	A Rim	C Rim	D Rim	Total Rim & body	
Vessels with thick walls:					
Cunduacan Orange Type	3	0	0	3	13
Total	3	0	0	3	13

Vessels with thick sides (no illustration). The sherds are too fragmentary to be certain of form. Most belonged to large vessels, possibly jars or basins reminiscent of some late Fine Orange ware specimens found by Ruz (1945a) on the coast of Campeche. Otherwise in surface finish and paste composition they conform to Fine Orange Ware and especially to the Cunduacan Ceramic Group as described by Berlin (1956, pp. 136–138) and named U Fine Orange. *Types and decoration*: all sherds are without embellishment. *Cunduacan Orange Type*: 3 rim, 13 body sherds.

SUMMARY

These sixteen sherds were separated from the Matillas Ceramic Group because their thickness made them incompatible with that style of pottery. They have been placed in the Cunduacan Ceramic Group because that group is later and less well established, notwithstanding the lack of vessels of this thickness in the Berlin collection. It is quite possible that they rightly belong to yet another Fine Orange Ware ceramic group located on the Campeche coast and not as yet named, but contemporary with the Cunduacan Ceramic Complex.

CHAUACA CERAMIC COMPLEX

MAYAPAN [44]

The Chauaca Phase is hard to delimit in time; roughly it has been linked to the Colonial Period, approximately 1550–1800. The Chauaca Ceramic Complex comprises a few wares found on the surface, but the total sherds are so inconsiderable that they can hardly represent an orthodox reoccupation of the site. Some of the specimens closely approximate modern pottery from Ticul or Mama. The majority of the examples, however, cannot be found in R. H. Thompson's (1958) article on modern Yucatecan pottery.

OCHIL UNSLIPPED WARE

Forms and Types	A Rim	C Rim	D Rim	Total Rim & body	
Jars, storage, low neck:					
Yuncu Unslipped Type	8	0	0	8	0
Bowls, restricted orifice:					
Kinchil Composite Type	8	0	0	8	7
Total	16	0	0	16	7

Jars, storage, wide mouth, low neck (R. H. Thompson, 1958, fig. 35, a). This form is similar to the cooking or storage vessels found at Mayapan in both the Hocaba and Tases ceramic complexes and called Yacman Striated Type wide-mouth, low-neck jars (28, a, 1–12). The principal differences are that these have a lower neck, a sharper neck-body angle, and a lack of striation. *Size:* too fragmentary. *Surface:* smoothed but unslipped. *Paste:* coarse texture, probably calcite temper, gray color. *Types and decoration:* no embellishment noted. *Yuncu Unslipped Type:* 8 rim, no body sherds.

Bowls, restricted orifice (57, e). Medium-thick to thick sides (thickest at rim), direct rim, pointed lip, no base fragments found. *Size:* lip diam. 52 cm. for three out of 8 sherds, thickness .6–1 cm. *Surface:* well smoothed, weathered, some may have had slip, horizontally and obliquely raked below fillet. *Paste:* coarse texture, probably calcite temper, fawn (5 YR 6/4) color. *Types and decoration:* all have thumb-impressed fillet encircling the upper part of exterior body. *Kinchil Composite Type:* 8 rim, 7 body sherds. These are similar to a specimen illustrated by R. H. Thompson (1958, figs. 11, f; 34, k).

SUMMARY

Little can be said about Ochil Unslipped Ware because of the scarcity of material. It does resemble modern types illustrated by R. H. Thompson, 1958. These examples are not modern, however, but just when they were made between the Tases Phase and modern times is difficult to estimate.

ABALA RED WARE

Forms and Types	A Rim	C Rim	D Rim	Total Rim & body	
Jars, parenthesis rim: Sacpokana Red Type	6	0	0	6	40
Bowls, hemispherical: Sacpokana Red Type	15	0	0	15	7
deep: Sacpokana Red Type	3	0	0	3	0
Total	24	0	0	24	47

Jars, high neck, parenthesis rim (57, a–c; GWB, figs. 33, a; 106, d), wide mouth, rounded lip, medium-thick walls, pear-shape body, probably flat to slightly concave base, and may have two horizontal strap handles located on opposite sides of body at the point of maximum diameter. These jars served to carry water. *Size:* lip diam. 9–14 cm., av. 11.7 cm., most common of 5 measured is 11 cm. [2]; thickness .4–.8 cm., av. .45–.8 cm., very uniform. *Surface:* smoothed but has grainy finish even though it is slipped and burnished. Slip usually covers exterior; some have slip on neck interior. Color is generally red ranging from 2.5 YR 6/6 to 2.5 YR 3/6 and including 2.5 YR 5/6. *Paste:* coarse texture, calcite (type not recorded) temper, gray to buff color. *Types and decoration:* all those examined were undecorated. *Sacpokana Red Type:* 6 rim, 40 body sherds.

Bowls, hemispherical (cf. GWB, fig. 33, f, 1–8) with thin to medium-thick sides, direct rim, flat lip, probably flat base but no fragments present. *Size:* too fragmentary for measurement. *Surface:* smoothed but grainy. Slipped and burnished on interior and exterior. Color is a dark red (2.5 YR 4/2). *Paste:* coarse texture, calcite (type not recorded) temper, gray to buff color. *Types and decoration:* all undecorated. *Sacpokana Red Type:* 15 rim, 7 body sherds.

Bowls, deep (cf. GWB, fig. 33, f, 20–25) with medium-thick slightly recurved sides, direct rim, flat or rounded lip, no base fragments present. *Size:* too fragmentary for measurement. *Surface:* smoothed but grainy. Thinly slipped and burnished on exterior and at least on upper part of interior which is all that remains. Color is a dark red (2.5 YR 4/2). *Paste:* coarse texture, calcite (type not recorded) temper, gray to buff color. *Types and decoration:* all undecorated. *Sacpokana Red Type:* 3 rim, no body sherds.

SUMMARY

It is believed that Abala Red Ware is a colonial product (R. H. Thompson, 1958, figs. 5, b, c; 40, b, c). In most respects, however, it is the same as the modern red ware from Mama (*ibid.*, p. 39; figs. 5, e; 6, a, b; 12, e). Two form differences between the colonial and modern water jars concern the parenthesis rim and the neck-body angle. The colonial parenthesis has a more gentle curve and the body-neck angle is usually a continuous curve instead of a true angle as found in modern examples.

BOLON BROWN WARE

Forms and Types	A Rim	C Rim	D Rim	Total Rim & body	
Comals: Oxcum Brown Type	3	0	0	3	0
Bowl, restricted orifice: Oxcum Brown Type	1	0	0	1	0
Total	4	0	0	4	0

Comals (57, *f*). Nearly flat plate, medium-thick, direct rim, beveled lip, flat base. *Size*: lip diam. 34 cm.; thickness .5–.6 cm. *Surface*: slipped and burnished on interior and exterior, but interior is more carefully smoothed. Exterior shows considerable pitting. Color is brown (7.5 YR 5/4). *Paste*: coarse texture, probably calcite temper, light brown to buff color. *Types and decoration*: all undecorated. *Oxcum Brown Type*: 3 rim, no body sherds.

Bowls, restricted orifice (57, *d*). Medium-thick rounded sides, direct rim, beveled lip, and probably flat base. *Size*: fragmentary. *Surface*: slipped and lightly burnished on exterior only. Color is a reddish brown (2.5 YR 4/4). *Paste*: coarse texture, probably calcite temper, light brown color. *Types and decoration*: undecorated. *Oxcum Brown Type*: 1 rim, no body sherds.

SUMMARY

Bolon Brown Ware is similar to Abala Red Ware except in surface color and finish. Bolon Brown Ware is more brown and the finish is more apt to be matte. Because of the very small sample involved it may be that we are dealing with a single ware of which these specimens are browner and more matte than the norm. In this case we find that the Bolon Brown Ware examples are quite modern in form (R. H. Thompson, 1958, figs. 15, *b*, *d*; 34, *a*, *c*, comals or griddles, and 11, *c*, *e*; 34, *f*; 36, *e*, restricted-orifice cooking pots) but apparently differ as to ware.

LOSA WARE

A single body sherd comprises the entire findings in Losa Ware. This specimen has blue decoration but the fragment is too small to determine either the design or vessel form. It is probably Majolica Ware. William W. Plowden, Jr. (1958, pp. 212–219) describes Majolica at some length and lists two "Blue Periods": 1550 to 1650 and 1700 to the present. Therefore the sherd in question could belong to the colonial period or to a more recent era.

PART FIVE

Conclusions and Reflections

XVIII

The Ceramics of a Declining Culture

THE INFLUENCE OF EARLIER CERAMIC
COMPLEXES ON THE LATE COMPLEXES OF MAYAPAN

In the recently published work on Mayapan, H. E. D. Pollock (1962) has given us in his introduction as clear an understanding of the events leading up to the establishment of that site as an important center as one could desire. This ceramic study has contributed added knowledge, some of which may effect our interpretation of the historical data to some degree. Our knowledge of the two principal ceramic complexes leading up to the Middle Postclassic Period, the Cehpech and the Sotuta, has assumed greater scope through the handling of large and controlled collections. Both these complexes are found at Mayapan in small percentages: 1.6 Cehpech and .3 Sotuta. Perhaps the fact that over five times as many Cehpech as Sotuta sherds were found is significant, especially when the total Mayapan sherd count is nearly 400,000. These large collections of Cehpech pottery came from Uxmal (33,467 sherds) and Kabah (13,337 sherds), however, and the Sotuta from Chichen Itza (19,217 sherds).

Beginning with the Cehpech Ceramic Complex we find a number of important facts. This complex appears to have lasted the longest of any in the Yucatan Peninsula, having its beginning in the Classic Period and enduring until around A.D. 889–987 when the Puuc area was abandoned. It is more widely spread over the entire peninsula than any other complex, for it is found abundantly over all of Yucatan, almost everywhere in northern Campeche, and is well represented all along the east coast as far south as Calderitas. There is a strong link between the Cehpech as found in the Puuc and Tepeu 3 as reported from Uaxactun, at least sufficient to show contemporaneity. The common attributes are the modeled-carved techniques as exemplified by the Pabellon Modeled-carved Type, the bead lip on red ware deep bowls or barrel-shape vases, the basal-Z-angle associated with various wares, and flageolets or flutes.

Although the Puuc was abandoned, Chichen Itza was not, and in the late twelfth century the Toltecs apparently took over. However, it would seem reasonably certain that Maya potters continued manufacturing pottery because there is little change in the Sotuta material. The Cehpech and Sotuta complexes are closely linked through unslipped ware, slate ware, red ware, and fine orange ware. The pottery changes as to form, design, temper to some extent, and decorative techniques, some of which were discarded and others added. Nevertheless, the wares remain much the same. The Sotuta Ceramic Complex also shares a few vessel forms with the Toltec pottery of Tula, Hidalgo. Only one of these, the rounded-side, flat-base dish or plate, is well represented at both sites although not in the same ware. The other common forms are possibly trade types at both places. These are censers, such as the "Mixtec type," the ladle censer which at Tula has red decoration on light brown slip as compared to the Balam Canche Red-on-slate Type from Chichen Itza, and the ringstand-base cylindrical vase covered with spikes (30, *u*; Acosta, 1945, fig. 20, *n*; GWB, fig. 69, *a*). Besides censers, Tohil Plumbate Type vessels have been encountered at both sites. Another trade ware found in some quantity at Chichen Itza and possibly Tula is Silho Fine Orange.

Thus it may be deduced that the Chichen Itza Sotuta pottery was locally made by Maya potters with relatively little influence from Tula or Mexico, but that several censer types and special wares were widely traded. Silho Fine Orange Ware contributed much to the form and decorative motifs of this complex, and in my opinion this ware was manufactured in nearby northwestern Campeche. Finally around 1185–1204 the occupants of Chichen Itza left, not too long after a new style of pottery appeared at the site.

This new pottery is the much discussed Black-on-Cream called Coarse Slateware by Brainerd, who obtained the name from Vaillant (1927). It is called Peto Cream Ware in this report, with

Xcanchakan Black-on-cream as its most prolific type. According to both Brainerd and Andrews it appears to precede the Middle Mexican substage at Dzibilchaltun. Brainerd (1958, p. 57) states, referring to Dzibilchaltun, "At this site there must therefore have been an occupation during which Coarse Slateware was the only slipped pottery — a 'pure' Middle Mexican substage occupation." Andrews (1965, p. 321) speaking of Dzibilchaltun says, "Sealed stratigraphies at two parts of the site started with pure samples of Modified Florescent Slate wares, continued with admixtures of Black-on-Cream, followed by pure sealed deposits, and then by an admixture of and finally a predominance of the later red wares of the Decadent period." At Chichen Itza in the area of the Mercado and Southeast Colonnade a few sherds were found under a floor. Brainerd (1958, p. 57) also found samples of this pottery and he mentions, "This ware occurs only with heavy mixture of Early Mexican potteries in the Chichen Itza collections, and seems limited to surface deposits, save possibly for the Mercado and Southeast Colonnade where it sometimes occurs in about equal quantity in single collections with Medium Slateware."

That Peto Cream Ware as the only slipped ware formed part of a ceramic complex of a transitional phase between the Early Postclassic and Middle Postclassic periods seems most likely. The reasons for this can be found first in the stratigraphic and ceramic association evidence at Dzibilchaltun and Chichen Itza, and second in the very nature of Peto Cream Ware, which clings to most of the vessel shapes and decorative devices of the Sotuta Ceramic Complex while using a new crude method of manufacture. The common form traits are: water jars with outcurving high neck, narrow mouth, and globular body; basins which have ovoid bolster in Sotuta and flat bolster in Hocaba; dishes with outcurving sides, tripod, and convex base whose feet may be bulbous or oven-shape; grater bowls; and stands or pedestals which according to Brainerd are found in both Chichen Slate Ware and Coarse Slateware. The black-painted designs shared by Peto Cream Ware and Chichen Slate Ware, besides the much used trickle, include S's, reverse curves, dots, and U-shape devices. In other words, the vessel form and decoration closely follow the Sotuta style, while the paste composition and surface finish are of Hocaba execution.

THE LATE COMPLEXES OF MAYAPAN: INTERPRETATIONS AND SUMMARY

What we have covered so far is an historical sketch of the ceramic complexes leading up to the beginning of the Hocaba Ceramic Complex at Mayapan. Peto Cream Ware may be considered the opening wedge of a new and certainly decadent era, that period which saw the establishment of Mayapan as an important center. It is decadent not only in its treatment of ceramic art but in all aspects of its culture including sculpture, architecture, customs, and religious practices. To account for this radical change from the relatively high Toltec culture as seen at Chichen Itza, even considering a nonarchitectural Black-on-Cream transitional phase, the advent of new people must be predicated. Perhaps the Peto Cream Ware potters were forerunners who came into northern Yucatan at the end of the Toltec regime and, liking many of the vessel forms and decorative motifs, adapted them to their way of making pottery. Somewhat later the main body of this new group arrived in the Chichen Itza area and later settled Mayapan. The question arises as to who these

people were and where they came from. It may not be of paramount importance to know if they were called Itza. Whoever they were, these Hocaba pottery makers did settle in Mayapan, presumably about A.D. 1250. Where they came from we do not know. They most likely were not the same Itza who reportedly left Chakanputun, possibly Champoton, near the end of the twelfth century for Lake Peten. Later they ventured up the east coast of the Yucatan Peninsula, found Bacalar near Chetumal Bay, and settled at Chichen Itza, all in the space of forty years. This would place them at Chichen Itza about 1210 to 1220. Some forty years later Mayapan was established.

If these Itza peregrinations are followed with the Hocaba Ceramic Complex in mind, the findings would be as follows: well represented at Champoton but otherwise not present at the sites examined along the west coast; traces found at Lake Peten, and a most interesting and closely related lot collected at Topoxte, Lake Yaxha; many figurines and censers including the effigy type unearthed in northern British Honduras; a complete late east-coast pottery assemblage at Ichpaatun in the Chetumal Bay area; an even more closely related collection but still eastcoast style excavated at Tulum; then at Chichen Itza an excellent collection of truly Hocaba wares and types found on the surface overlying the debris of fallen buildings, and finally at Mayapan the model for the Hocaba Ceramic Complex assemblage with Peto Cream Ware and the Xcanchakan Black-on-cream Type forming an integral part. Actually Peto Cream Ware or Sanders' Mayapan Black-on-Cream is found all along the east coast, increasing in quantity from south to north. Percentages to total sherds are: 1.6 Ichpaatun, 4.6 Tulum, 2.6 San Gervasio, 2.6 Mulchi, 2.6 Monte Bravo, and 8.9 Vista Alegre. The percentage at Mayapan in the Hocaba Ceramic Complex to all sherds is 10 and to slipped sherds is 15.4. At Chichen Itza Brainerd reports the percentage of Coarse Slateware to total slipped sherds in a variety of locations as from 32 to 45. Usually at Chichen Itza and always at Mayapan the Peto Cream Ware is accompanied by Mayapan Red Ware and Mayapan Unslipped Ware.

Knowing that Peto Cream Ware is partially inspired by Sotuta forms and decoration it is rather curious to encounter it in quite reasonable quantities along the east coast, an area where Sotuta pottery is almost unknown.

Now that we have traced the beginning and some of the movements of Peto Cream Ware, what about Mayapan Red Ware and the rest of the Hocaba Ceramic Complex? Mayapan Red Ware has the same paste composition as Peto Cream Ware but a more lustrous finish. Hocaba pottery as found at Mayapan, Chichen Itza, Dzibilchaltun, and Champoton differs basically from that of the east coast, and this difference is greater than that produced by the use of different clays and tempering ingredients. It includes forms, decorative techniques, and designs. The similarities are external and general. Most of the trade exchanges occurred in the Tases Ceramic Complex involving principally Tulum Red Ware found at Mayapan and Mayapan Red Ware at Tulum. Another Hocaba ware, Fine Orange of the Matillas Group, originating in an area encompassed by northeastern Tabasco and southwestern Campeche as demonstrated by its abundance at such sites as Tamulte, Juarez, and Atasta. It is also found in relatively small quantities on the east coast. It exerts little influence on the Hocaba pottery, however, with the possible exception of moldmade effigy feet.

But the question of where Mayapan Red Ware and Mayapan Unslipped Ware developed has not been answered. One might see precursors to the effigy censers in the Oaxaca urns which lasted at least into Toltec times. But there does not seem to be anything near at hand that offers a clue, or is there? How about the Cehpech Ceramic Complex and the Puuc people? Where did they go after the Puuc abandonment and what did they do? This is a mystery, but oddly enough the closest likeness to the much used Mayapan Red Ware tripod dish is the Puuc Slate Ware tripod dish. Both normally have solid conical feet but may have hollow cylindrical feet. Other similarities include bolster-rim basins with vertical strap handles common to Mayapan Red Ware and Puuc Slate Ware, and certain unslipped-ware censer jars or vases with pedestal base. This is suggestive but it does not tell us what happened to the Puuc people even if they are responsible for some of the Hocaba vessel forms.

Now let us consider the Tases Ceramic Complex, which is a direct outgrowth of the Hocaba Ceramic Complex. Most of the principal local Hocaba wares, including Mayapan Unslipped, Mayapan Red, and Mayapan Black, continue on in Tases with new types and varieties distinguished by new forms and certain changes in decoration. Three new local wares are added: San Joaquin Buff, Telchaquillo Brick, and Mayapan Coarse. One trade ware, Fine Orange of the Matillas Group, is common to both Hocaba and Tases; the only other, Tulum Red, is linked exclusively with Tases. The most important new feature in Mayapan Unslipped Ware is the Chen Mul Modeled Type including full-figure effigy censers, effigy vessels, effigy cups, and figurines. The effigy vessel is not new in Tases; variations on this form have an early and more or less continuous history, although none is recorded from Hocaba. However, the Chen Mul Modeled Type style is first found in the Hocaba-Tases levels, and increases in production materially during Tases. This increase in production is even more marked for the Chen Mul Modeled Type full-figure effigy censer which totaled 28.7 per cent of all unslipped sherds in the Hocaba-Tases levels and 77.2 per cent in the Tases Ceramic Complex. These full-figure effigy censers are truly idols. They can be traced back at least to Cehpech times where they occur in Puuc Slate Ware at Xcaret and possibly at Mayapan, but these are rare. They also occur somewhat more abundantly in Hocaba through the Hoal Modeled Type. The tremendous increase in the use of the full-figure effigy censer and the effigy vessel in Tases suggests a freshly oriented ceremonial procedure with idolatry (Bullard, 1970, p. 304) in the ascendancy. The idolatrous practice of worshiping stone- and pottery-made idols may reflect the Cocom taking over at Mayapan after a revolution which resulted in the departure of one faction of the Itza and the ascendancy of another about 1382 (Roys, 1962). During Tases several innovations associated with Mayapan Red Ware transpired. These include the manufacture of effigy vessels, increased use of effigy feet as compared to this usage in Hocaba, the appearance of jars with parenthesis rim perhaps copying this feature found in Tulum Red Ware jars, and introduction of the bowl cluster form whose function is not clear. Mayapan Black Ware offers little that is new except a few Sacmuyna Modeled Type effigy jars. Upon examining San Joaquin Buff Ware we find one new form, the potstand, and forms associated with other Tases wares such as the parenthesis-rim jars and effigy feet. Telchaquillo Brick Ware has a single item, the candle-flame shield, a completely new and unique gadget. Mayapan Coarse Ware offers a few more full-figure effigy censers and figurines. The fine orange trade ware of the Matillas Group has a tripod dish form with or without flange which has no counterpart in Mayapan Red Ware except for the prevailing effigy feet. Berlin (1956, fig. 6, *t, u*) illustrates a full-figure effigy censer belonging to U Fine Orange (fine-orange Cunduacan Group of the Chikinchel Ceramic Complex), showing that this form carried on at least up to the Conquest. The Tulum Red Ware trade sherds, although rare, do indicate a definite contact with the east coast, as do the few Mayapan Red Ware sherds encountered at Tulum.

It is apparent that at Mayapan in Tases times there was a modest contact with the east coast and, judging from the findings at Champoton, a much stronger relationship with the west coast. During this time period, however, the most revealing change indicated by this ceramic study was that from a generalized god and nature worship to idol worship as manifested in the vast accumulation of full-figure effigy censers and effigy vessels. Tozzer (1941, p. 23) refers to this conversion to idolatry in a Seler quotation from an ancient manuscript of Motul which reads, "Originally a god had been worshipped here who was the creator of all things, and who had his dwelling in heaven, but that a great prince named Kukulcan with a multitude of people, had come from a foreign country, that he and his people were idolaters, and from that time the inhabitants of this land also began to practice idolatry, to perform bloody sacrificial rites, to burn copal, and the like."

To better understand the source of the Hocaba and Tases pottery and its influence on Yucatan and the peninsula in general, including much of Peten in Guatemala, further digging should be done, preferably of the intensive kind (one site in depth). We still lack detailed knowledge of the west coast ceramic picture. At least two widely separate sites should be excavated, using Alberto Ruz's (1945a) thesis as a guide. We should also excavate along the east coast, using the findings in William T. Sanders' survey of Quintana Roo (1960) to determine one or two late sites for intensive excavation. Nor should the least known north coast be neglected, where possibly a preliminary survey would be advisable. In addition a site somewhere in the southern Quintana Roo and northern British Honduras area should be examined. Thomas Gann's work in part of that region offers illustrations of full-figure effigy censers, effigy vessels, and figurines that are closely allied to like Mayapan forms but lack stratigraphic data and associated material sufficient to anchor them in recognizable ceramic complexes. With the new information from these intensive excavations we may hopefully be able, in the future, to reconstruct a more complete picture of the Middle and Late Postclassic events in Yucatan and perhaps even begin to understand the significance of and reasons for the decline of Maya culture, the numerous migrations recorded in the ethnohistorical literature, and the important change in religious practice which introduces idolatry during the final period at Mayapan.

Appendices A-E

References

Appendix A

LIST OF CUTS

Cuts, which are the equivalent of trenches, are here listed separately by site: Uxmal 10, Kabah 5, Chichen Itza 19. Lot numbers indicate the location of specimens and are here synonymous with levels, the lowest number in P cuts equaling the highest level and the lowest number in G cuts referring to the lowest levels. The letter P placed before a lot number refers to collections made at Uxmal and Kabah, and the letter G stands for collections made at Chichen Itza.

UXMAL
(fig. 1, *b*)

1. South of Palace of the Governor in corner made with Great Pyramid. P1, originally two 25-cm. levels but turned into single lot since there were a number of sherd fits from top to bottom and no change noted. All Cehpech Ceramic Complex.

2. In east slope of Great Pyramid. P2 and P3, upper and lower, respectively, of two 25-cm. levels. All Cehpech Ceramic Complex.

3. In corner formed by west terrace of the Palace of the Governor and the north side of the Great Pyramid. P4, little depth. All Cehpech Ceramic Complex.

4. In north side of House of Palomas. P5, little depth. All Cehpech Ceramic Complex.

5. In line with terrace south of southeast corner of Great Pyramid. The trench, 8 m. long, was partitioned into three sections: 5, 5A, and 5B. Section 5, the southeastern end of the trench (4 m. long), had three levels, P6–P8, each about 25 cm. deep, with P6 at the top level. Section 5A, the northwestern end of trench (4 m. long) abutting on terrace, had five levels, P13–P17, each 25 cm. deep, with P13 the top level. Section 5B, a southwestern extension paralleling section 5A but only 2 m. long, had three levels, P31–P33, each 25 cm. deep, with P31 the top level. All Cehpech Ceramic Complex except for 5 sherds (4 rim and 1 body): 2 Cochuah (1 at top and 1 in middle), 2 Sotuta (next to bottom level), and 1 Hocaba (top level).

6. About 30 m. west of Trench 5 in corner made by south terrace of Great Pyramid and east terrace of pyramid to the southwest. This trench, 6 m. long, was divided into two sections: 6 and 6A. Section 6, the 3-m. southern half, had three levels, P10–P12, each 25 cm. deep, with P10 at top. Section 6A, the 3-m. northern half abutting terrace, had 6 levels, P18–P23, each 25 cm. deep, with P18 at top. All Cehpech Ceramic Complex except 5 body sherds: 3 Cochuah (top level), 2 Sotuta (middle level).

7. In west side of terrace supporting the Palace of the Governor. Two levels, P24 and P25, each about 25 cm. deep. Few badly weathered sherds, checked and discarded. Not used in analysis.

8. Trench 3 m. long into opening between the northwest corner of the Cemetery and the southwest corner of the structure just north of the Cemetery. Five levels, P26–P30, each 25 cm. deep, with P26 at top. All Cehpech Ceramic Complex.

9. In northwest inset corner of the Nunnery. Shallow and little pottery. Not used in analysis.

10. In northeast inset corner of the Nunnery. Shallow and little pottery. Not used in analysis.

KABAH
(fig. 1, *a*)

1. In southeast corner of palace east of the Codz Pop. P34, one level 35 cm. deep. All Cehpech Ceramic Complex.

2. In angle formed by a house platform and a terrace on east side of East Quadrangle. Three levels to bedrock, P35–P37, each 25 cm. deep, with P35 at top. All Cehpech Ceramic Complex.

3. In farthest northeast inset corner of East Quadrangle. The trench had three levels to bedrock, P38–P40, each 25 cm. deep, with P38 at top. All Cehpech Ceramic Complex except for 4 body sherds: 2 Cochuah (top and middle levels), 2 Sotuta (middle and bottom levels).

4. In northeast section of same terrace as Cut 3 but some 30 m. west. Three levels to bedrock, P41–P43, each about 25 cm. deep with P41 at top. All Cehpech Ceramic Complex except 23 sherds (2 rim and 21 body): 1 Cupul (top level); 22 Cochuah (3 top and 19 middle level).

5. In northeast section of same terrace as Cuts 3 and 4 but farther west at corner of terrace and house mound. Four levels to bedrock, P44–P47, each about 25 cm. deep, with P44 at top. All Cehpech Ceramic Complex except one Tohil Plumbate Group body sherd found in top level.

CHICHEN ITZA
(consult Ruppert, 1952, fig. 151, map)

1. Off west edge of terrace of Structure 7B2. Four 25-cm. levels in the south section of cut, the lowest G46 followed by G47, G49, and G50, and two 25-cm. levels in north section, the lowest G48, comparable to G49 and the surface G51, comparable to G50. Lower levels (G46 through G48) have 32.3 per cent Cehpech Ceramic Complex types. Sotuta Ceramic Complex.

2. South of Structure 7B3. Three levels, G1–G3, and a floor sealing off the two lower levels. These lower levels contained nothing later than Cehpech Phase pottery, while the above-floor level yielded mostly Sotuta Phase and a few Cehpech Phase pottery examples. Not used in analysis.

3. In great depression, possibly old cenote, south of structure 7B2. Four levels, G31–G34, each approximately 25 cm. deep. Sherds so fragmentary and water damaged that recording was not attempted.

4. Off southwest corner of terrace west of Structure 5C6 in Grupa de la Fecha. Three levels, G52–G54, ranging from 0–65 cm. at north end and 0–95 cm. at south end. Essentially Sotuta Phase pottery. Not used in analysis.

5. In east side of Structure 5C11 in Grupa de la Fecha. Four levels, G55–G58, each approximately 25 cm. deep. Fair collection of Cehpech Phase sherds in two lowest levels, rest Sotuta Phase. Not used in analysis.

6. In terrace 20 m. east of Structure 5C11 in Grupa de la Fecha. Two levels, G10–G11, each 20 cm. deep. Small collection, all Sotuta Phase pottery. Not used in analysis.

7. In terrace corner behind Structure 5C4 in Grupa de la Fecha. Three levels, G12–G14, each approximately 25 cm. deep. All sherds belong to Sotuta Phase. Not used in analysis.

8. In southeast corner of terrace of Grupa Principal del Suroeste. Three levels: G17 and G16, two upper, each 30 cm.; G15, lowest, 15 cm. deep. Mostly Sotuta Phase pottery but a few Cehpech Phase sherds throughout. Not used in analysis.

9. Pit in southeast corner of terrace floor of Grupa Principal del Suroeste. Two levels, G18 and G19, 30 cm. and 35 cm., respectively. Mostly Sotuta Phase pottery but both levels contained a few sherds of Cehpech Phase pottery, including two examples from the Fine-orange Balancan Group. Not used in analysis.

10. In terrace corner southeast of Structure 5B17. Six levels, G59–G64, partly east end of trench and partly west end. The west end had four levels, G62 upper and G59 lower, each approximately 30 cm. deep; the east end had two levels, 63 upper and 64 lower. Only one Cehpech Phase sherd and three Hocaba Phase examples, the rest of the Sotuta Ceramic Complex.

11. Pit in terrace corner just west of Chultun 1 of Grupa de la Fecha. One level, G20, 10 cm. deep to bedrock. Small collection of Sotuta Phase sherds. Not used in analysis.

12. In depression northeast of Structure 4D1. Two levels, G65–G66, each about 30 cm. deep. Sotuta Phase collection except for four possible Hocaba Phase sherds. Not used in analysis.

13. Pit in dry rock fill between Structures 3D10 and 3D11. Two levels: G22, upper, down 40 cm. to top of Floor 2; G21, lower, below Floor 1 down 90 cm. to bedrock. Nothing between floors. Upper level contained 35 Xcanchakan Black-on-cream sherds, the lower level only two. The remainder belonged to the Sotuta Phase. This is the only cut which had so large a percentage (35%) of Hocaba Phase sherds even in the surface level. Not used in analysis.

14. In great terrace 100 m. west of junction with Sacbe No. 6. Eight levels, G23–G26 east and G27–G30 west, each about 20 cm. deep. All Sotuta Ceramic Complex.

15. In southeast corner of terrace supporting Structure 3C6. Three levels, G67–G69, each 25 cm. deep. Two lower levels have Tihosuco, Cochuah-Motul, and Cehpech Phase sherds and nothing later. The surface level has mixture of Tihosuco, Cehpech, and Sotuta Phase pottery. Not used in analysis.

16. In corner formed by Sacbe No. 1 and terrace upon which Castillo stands. Four levels: G73, surface, 0–30 cm.; G72, 30–75 cm.; G71, 75–90 cm.; G70, lowest, 90–150 cm. One Tihosuco Phase sherd, no Cehpech, the remainder Sotuta Ceramic Complex.

17. In corner made by junction of terrace and Sacbe No. 6. Six levels: G9, surface, 0–55 cm.; G8, 55–85 cm.; G7, 85–120 cm.; G6, 120–155 cm.; G5, 155–185 cm.; G4, lowest, 185–220 cm. Collection includes two Cochuah Phase sherds, one Cehpech, one Tases, the rest Sotuta Ceramic Complex.

18. Surface debris in front of columns of Structure 2C6. One level, G75. Only thirteen sherds, all Fine-orange Silho Group. Not used in analysis.

19. In terrace corner southeast of Structure 2C4. One level, G74, 30–60 cm. to bedrock. Eleven Tihosuco Phase sherds, one Cochuah, 256 Sotuta Phase. Not used in analysis.

Appendix B

LIST OF MAYAPAN EARLY, MIDDLE, AND LATE LOTS

These lots are listed under A, house mound associated material; B, material from the Great Wall; C, ceremonial group and structure findings; and D, artifacts from cenotes or sascaberas.

LATE LOTS

A, A–3, 5, 6, 9, 10, 14, 16, 17, 20–22, 24, 25, 28, 29, 32, 34, 35, 37, 40, 41, 44, 46–52, 56, 57, 59–61, 64, 66, 70–76, 81, 84, 85, 89–91, 94–98, 100, 101, 104, 105, 111, 112, 114, 115, 117, 119, 121, 122, 124, 126, 128, 130, 131, 133, 134, 137, 139, 146, 149–154, 156–159, 165, 166, 171, 175, 176, 201–203, 205–209, 211, 220–223, 228, 231, 234, 235, 238, 241, 250, 251, 255, 256, 259–262, 264, 266–268, 400–410, 426, 431, 434, 436, 437, 439–442, 446, 449, 500–502, 504, 509, 511–514, 517, 521, 527–529, 536, 541–545, 547, 553–555, 559, 561, 565, 567–571, 574, 575, 579, 582–584, 588, 589, 595, 596.

B–1, 2, 4, 6.

C–1, 2, 3, 5, 6, 8, 11–13, 17, 17a, 23, 25, 31, 32, 35f, 36, 39, 44, 50–52, 54, 55, 58–61, 65–67, 67a, 68, 68a, 69, 69a, 72, 74–76, 79, 79a, 79b, 80–82, 92, 93, 93a, 93b, 94, 96a, 97, 98, 98a, 100–103, 107, 108a, 109, 111, 114–122, 125, 127–129, 135, 138, 142–144.

D–1, 2, 4, 9, 12–14, 20–22, 25, 28–32, 34, 37–41, 45, 61, 67, 69, 77, 78, 83, 89, 92, 96.

MIDDLE LOTS

A–1, 2, 4, 7, 8, 12, 13, 15, 18, 23, 26, 27, 36, 39, 45, 53–55, 58, 62, 63, 65, 67–69, 77–80, 82, 83, 86–88, 92, 93, 99, 102, 103, 107, 108, 110, 113, 116, 118, 120, 123, 125, 127, 129, 132, 135, 136, 138, 140–145, 147, 148, 155, 160, 160a, 161–164, 167–170, 172, 173, 195, 204, 210, 212, 213, 215–218, 218a, 219, 224–227, 227a, 229, 230, 232, 233, 236, 237, 239, 240, 242, 243, 253, 257, 258, 263, 265, 269, 411–420, 422, 424, 425, 427–429, 435, 438, 444, 445, 447, 448, 450, 503, 505–508, 510, 515, 516, 518–520, 522–526, 530–540, 546, 548–552, 556, 558, 560, 563, 564, 566, 572, 573, 576–578, 580, 585–587, 590–594.

B–3, 5.

C–7, 9, 10, 14–16, 19–22, 24, 27–30, 33, 35a, 35b, 37, 38, 40, 41, 45–47, 49, 53, 56, 57, 62, 69b, 71, 71a, 73, 77, 83, 85a–d, 88–90, 95, 99, 105, 106, 110, 112, 113, 123, 124, 126, 130–134, 136, 137, 139–141.

D–3, 5, 15, 18, 19, 23, 24, 27, 33, 36, 42–44, 46, 56, 57, 62, 65, 66, 70, 71, 74, 75, 90, 91, 93–95, 97.

EARLY LOTS

A–11, 19, 30, 31, 33, 38, 42, 43, 106, 109, 174, 194, 214, 214a, 252, 254, 421, 423, 430, 432, 433, 443, 451, 557, 562, 581.

C–4, 18, 26, 35, 35c, 35e, 42, 43, 48, 63, 64, 70, 78, 78a, 84, 84a, 85–87, 104, 108.

D–6–8, 10, 11, 16, 17, 26, 35, 47–55, 58–60, 63, 64, 68, 72, 73, 76, 79–82, 84–88.

Appendix C

MAYAPAN MIDDLE LOTS

HOCABA-TASES MATERIAL

MAYAPAN UNSLIPPED WARE

Forms, Types, and Varieties	A Rim	C Rim	D Rim	Total Rim	Body
Jars, wide mouth, low neck:					
Yacman Striated Type	1,637	626	270	2,533	14,937
Acansip Painted Type	2			2	0
Jars, wide mouth, medium-high neck:					
Yacman Striated Type	8	46		54	265
Panaba Unslipped Type	8		14	22	191
Jars, large size, high neck:					
Navula Unslipped Type	12	4	13	29	248
Chenkeken Incised Type			3	3	0
Acansip Painted Type	1			1	0
Jars, huge size, high neck:					
Navula Unslipped Type	66	26	5	97	679
Kanasin Red/unslipped Type	40		12	52	222
Huhi-Thul Composite Type		3		3	29
Jars, small mouth, high vertical neck:					
Panaba Unslipped Type	1			1	1
Censers, effigy, large size:					
Hoal Modeled Type	4	15		19	98
Censers, effigy, large size:					
Chen Mul Modeled Type	408	250	63	721	9,117
Censers, effigy, small size:					
Chen Mul Modeled Type	4	31		35	63
Censers, jar, pedestal:					
Cehac-Hunacti Composite Type	7	365		372	299
Censers, jar, tripod:					
Cehac-Hunacti Composite Type	32	117	14	163	611
Censers, jar, tripod or pedestal:					
Cehac-Hunacti Composite Type	2	0	0	2	1,541
Chenkeken-Acansip Composite Type	0	0	0	0	1
Censers, ladle:					
Navula Unslipped Type	548	340	117	1,005	395
Dishes, flat base, bolster rim:					
Navula Unslipped Type	43	56	9	108	39
Dishes, tripod, direct rim:					
Panaba Unslipped Type	17	24	3	44	9
Chenkeken Incised Type	5	2		7	0
Bowls, restricted orifice, direct rim:					
Navula Unslipped Type	47	28	6	81	5
Bowls, restricted orifice, bolster rim:					
Navula Unslipped Type	9	9	2	20	0
Bowls, restricted orifice, direct or bolster rim: Navula Unslipped Type	0	0	0	0	21
Bowls, deep, tripod:					
Panaba Unslipped Type	3	4	0	7	0
Acansip Painted Type	9	0	0	9	0
Huhi Impressed Type	2	0	0	2	5
Bowls, grater:					
Chenkeken Incised Type	11	1	0	12	19

Forms, Types, and Varieties	A Rim	C Rim	D Rim	Total Rim	Body
Cups, tripod:					
Panaba Unslipped Type	5	4	0	9	23
Cehac Painted Type	5	0	0	5	14
Chen Mul Modeled Type	1	0	0	1	0
Cups, pedestal:					
Acansip Painted Type	2	0	0	2	0
Chen Mul Modeled Type	1	0	1	2	0
Acansip-Thul Composite Type	1	0	0	1	21
Panaba Unslipped Type	1	0	0	1	5
Cups, flat base:					
Chen Mul Modeled Type	0	1	0	1	0
Panaba Unslipped Type	0	0	1	1	0
Basins, flat base:					
Navula Unslipped Type	10	16	4	30	34
Chenkeken Incised Type	0	2	0	2	0
Vessels, effigy:					
Chen Mul Modeled Type	18	1	0	19	22
Plates, ringstand:					
Panaba Unslipped Type	14	0	0	14	11
Miniature jars:					
Panaba Unslipped Type	2	0	2	4	8
Miniature, bowls, deep, tripod:					
Huhi Impressed Type	2	0	1	3	4
Miniature, miscellaneous:					
Panaba Unslipped Type	4	0	1	5	1
Vases, pedestal:					
Acansip Painted Type	3	0	0	3	10
Covers, disk-shaped:					
Panaba Unslipped Type	2	0	0	2	0
Covers, disk-shaped sherd:					
Buleb Striated Type	2	0	0	2	0
Stand: Panaba Unslipped Type	2	0	0	2	1
Figurines: Chen Mul Modeled Type	55	7	2	64	88
Masks: Chen Mul Modeled Type	1	2	2	5	0
Molds: Chen Mul Modeled Type	2	1	0	3	0
Total	3,059	1,981	545	5,585	29,037

MAYAPAN RED WARE

Forms, Types, and Varieties	Rim A	C Rim	D Rim	Total Rim	Body
Jars, water, high neck:					
Mama Red Type	367	200	197	764	15,275
Papacal Incised Type	69	53	30	152	2,979
Tzitz Red Type	7	1	0	8	17
Chapab Modeled Type	0	0	0	0	2
Tixua Gadrooned Type	0	0	0	0	1
Jars, parenthesis rim:					
Panabchen Red Type	5	2	1	8	153
Jars, storage, low neck:					
Mama Red Type	98	103	26	227	4,270
Papacal Incised Type	1	0	0	1	18
Dzonot Appliqué Type	0	1	0	1	0
Jars, storage, high neck:					
Mama Red Type	106	71	15	192	3,566
Panabchen Red Type	31	17	41	89	1,920
Pustunich Incised Type	2	0	0	2	35
Dishes, tripod, flaring side:					
Mama Red Type, Mama Variety	1,416	527	247	2,190	4,147
Mama Red Type, unslipped-exterior variety	303	134	44	481	992
Papacal Incised Type	179	54	49	282	16
Mama Red Type, black/unslipped variety	3	0	0	3	0
Mama Red Type, red/unslipped variety	1	0	0	1	0

Forms, Types, and Varieties	A Rim	C Rim	D Rim	Total Rim	Body
Dishes, tripod, rounded side:					
Mama Red Type, Mama Variety	171	99	77	347	305
Mama Red Type, unslipped-exterior variety	26	49	23	98	61
Papacal Incised Type	2	0	0	2	0
Dishes, flat base, rounded side:					
Panabchen Red Type	13	0	2	15	2
Papacal Incised Type	1	0	0	1	0
Yobain Plano-relief Type	1	0	0	1	1
Bowls or basins, restricted orifice,					
direct rim: Mama Red Type	120	59	18	197	122
Papacal Incised Type	0	1	0	1	1
Bowls or basins, restricted orifice,					
bolster rim: Mama Red Type	87	53	31	171	40
Papacal Incised Type	0	0	1	1	0
Dzonot Appliqué Type	0	0	0	0	1
Bowls, tripod, grater:					
Papacal Incised Type	51	77	15	143	366
Bowls, deep, tripod: Mama Red Type	4	11	12	27	49
Papacal Incised Type	1	0	0	1	4
Bowls, deep, tripod with flange:					
Mama Red Type	9	0	0	9	4
Papacal Incised Type	0	2	1	3	5
Yobain Plano-relief Type	0	0	0	0	1
Bowls, deep, pedestal:					
Panabchen Red Type	0	0	0	0	2
Bowls, deep, pedestal with flange:					
Panabchen Red Type	1	0	0	1	4
Bowls or censers, ladle:					
Panabchen Red Type	3	0	0	3	25
Bowls, fragmentary: Panabchen Red Type	1	0	0	1	5
Pustunich Incised Type	0	0	0	0	1
Bowls, cluster: Panabchen Red Type	3	0	0	3	1
Dzitxil Openwork Type	1	0	0	1	9
Basins, bolster rim: Mama Red Type	24	5	1	30	14
Mama Red Type, unslipped-exterior variety	58	25	0	83	29
Miniature jars: Mama Red Type	8	2	0	10	24
Miniature bowls, deep: Tzitz Red Type	4	0	0	4	3
Panabchen Red Type	3	0	0	3	2
Miniature bowls, restricted:					
Panabchen Red Type	1	0	0	1	0
Cups, pedestal: Mama Red Type	0	5	0	5	2
Chapab Modeled Type	1	0	0	1	6
Figurines: Chapab Modeled Type	4	0	0	4	4
Vases, cylindrical, pedestal:					
Mama Red Type	4	4	0	8	33
Chapab Modeled Type	3	0	0	3	3
Papacal Incised Type	2	0	0	2	0
Vases, cylindrical, tripod:					
Panabchen Red Type	1	2	0	3	8
Vases, barrel-shape:					
Panabchen Red Type	1	0	0	1	0
Drums: Papacal Incised Type	5	13	0	18	46
Vessels, effigy: Chapab Modeled Type	2	0	0	2	14
Covers, disk: Panabchen Red Type	4	0	0	4	1
Covers, scutate: Panabchen Red Type	11	0	4	15	8
Total	3,219	1,570	835	5,624	34,597

PETO CREAM WARE

Forms, Types, and Varieties	A Rim	C Rim	D Rim	Total Rim	Body
Jars, water, high neck:					
Xcanchakan Black/cream Type	22	42	18	82	1,514
Kukula Cream Type	3	7	0	10	71

Forms, Types, and Varieties	A Rim	C Rim	D Rim	Total Rim	Body
Dishes, tripod, flaring side:					
Xcanchakan Black/cream Type	11	10	2	23	14
Kukula Cream Type	6	2	0	8	7
Dishes, tripod, rounded side:					
Xcanchakan Black/cream Type	5	8	3	16	43
Kukula Cream Type	1	2	0	3	1
Bowls or basins, restricted orifice,					
direct rim: Kukula Cream Type	5	0	0	5	8
Xcanchakan Black/cream Type	1	3	0	4	1
Bowls or basins, restricted orifice,					
bolster rim: Kukula Cream Type	1	2	0	3	6
Xcanchakan Black/cream Type	3	0	2	5	2
Bowls, tripod, grater:					
Pencuyut Incised Type	1	0	0	1	3
Xcanchakan Black/cream Type, sharp-incised variety	0	0	0	0	3
Bowls, deep, direct rim:					
Kukula Cream Type	4	0	0	4	0
Bowls, hemispherical:					
Cusama Plano-relief Type	0	1	0	1	2
Vessels, miscellaneous sherds:					
Kukula Cream Type	0	0	0	0	4
Total	63	77	25	165	1,679

SAN JOAQUIN BUFF WARE

Forms, Types, and Varieties	A Rim	C Rim	D Rim	Total Rim	Body
Jars, water, high vertical neck:					
Polbox Buff Ware	4	16	2	22	84
Kimbila Incised Type	1	0	0	1	0
Jars, high neck, parenthesis rim:					
Tecoh Red/buff Type	10	0	0	10	75
Jars, storage, high neck, bolster rim:					
Tecoh Red/buff Type	13	10	1	24	140
direct rim: Tecoh Red/buff Type	2	2	0	4	19
Jars, storage, low neck, direct rim:					
Tecoh Red/buff Type	23	0	0	23	172
everted rim: Tecoh Red/buff Type	5	0	0	5	37
Jars, tripod, bulging neck:					
Tecoh Red/buff Type	0	0	0	0	1
Dishes, tripod, flaring side:					
Tecoh Red/buff Type	79	4	9	92	96
Pele Polychrome Type	32	2	0	34	21
Polbox Buff Type	2	0	0	2	4
Dishes, tripod, rounded side:					
Polbox Buff Type	0	1	0	1	0
Bowls, hemispherical: Tecoh Red/buff Type	2	0	0	2	9
Pele Polychrome Type	1	0	0	1	19
Bowls, restricted orifice, pedestal base:					
Tecoh Red/buff Type	5	0	0	5	11
flat base: Polbox Buff Type	0	0	0	0	4
Bowls, deep, jarlike: Pele Polychrome Type	1	0	0	1	5
Bowls, flaring side, everted rim,					
flat base: Pele Polychrome Type	0	0	0	0	1
Vase, cylindrical:					
Kimbila Incised Type	0	0	0	0	1
Total	180	35	12	227	699

FINE ORANGE WARE: MATILLAS GROUP

Forms, Types, and Varieties	A Rim	C Rim	D Rim	Total Rim	Body
Dishes, tripod, basal flange:					
Matillas Orange Type	9	21	2	32	59
Villahermosa Incised Type	7	7	3	17	21
Salto Composite Type	0	5	0	5	0
Nacajuca Black/orange Type	2	1	0	3	4
Chilapa Gouged-incised Type	0	1	0	1	0
Grijalva Incised-polychrome Type	0	0	0	0	1
Dishes, tripod:					
Matillas Orange Type	21	5	3	29	88
Villahermosa Incised Type	11	0	0	11	8
Nacajuca Black/orange Type	0	1	0	1	2
Chilapa Gouged-incised Type	0	0	0	0	1
Salto Composite Type	0	0	0	0	1
Bowls, deep, restricted orifice:					
Salto Composite Type	5	0	0	5	12
Matillas Orange Type	0	3	0	3	5
Villahermosa Incised Type	0	1	0	1	20
Sayula Polychrome Type	1	0	0	1	3
Chilapa Gouged-incised Type	1	1	0	2	1
Nacajuca Black/orange Type	0	1	0	1	0
Bowls, deep, outcurving side:					
Chilapa Gouged-incised Type	2	0	0	2	5
Bowls, hemispherical:					
Matillas Orange Type	6	0	0	6	8
Villahermosa Incised Type	6	0	1	7	4
Jars, wide mouth, high neck:					
Matillas Orange Type	4	1	0	5	25
bulging neck: Matillas Orange Type	3	0	0	3	8
medium-high neck:					
Matillas Orange Type	1	0	0	1	3
Villahermosa Incised Type	2	0	0	2	5
Total	81	48	9	138	284

MAYAPAN BLACK WARE

Forms, Types, and Varieties	A Rim	C Rim	D Rim	Total Rim	Body
Jars, water, high neck:					
Sulche Black Type	2	0	4	6	247
Dishes, tripod, flaring side:					
Sulche Black Type	3	0	4	7	12
rounded side: Sulche Black Type	2	0	2	4	12
Bowls, restricted orifice, direct rim:					
Sulche Black Type	2	0	0	2	4
Bowls, deep, pedestal base:					
Conil Plano-relief Type	0	0	1	1	1
Bowls, hemispherical: Sulche Black Type	0	1	0	1	1
Drums: Pacha Incised Type	0	0	0	0	1
Covers, disk: Sulche Black Type	0	0	0	0	1
Total	9	1	11	21	279

TULUM RED WARE

Forms, Types, and Varieties	A Rim	C Rim	D Rim	Total Rim	Body
Jars, water, parenthesis rim:					
Payil Red Type	5	2	0	7	12
Kanlum Plano-relief Type	0	0	0	0	2
Palmul Incised Type	0	0	0	0	1

Forms, Types, and Varieties	A Rim	C Rim	D Rim	Total Rim	Body
Jars, storage, medium to low neck, everted rim: Palmul Incised Type	2	0	0	2	4
Jars, storage, medium to low neck, direct rim: Payil Red Type	2	0	0	2	3
Dishes, tripod, flaring side:					
Payil Red Type	3	0	1	4	1
Palmul Incised Type	1	0	0	1	2
basal flange: Palmul Incised Type	0	0	0	0	2
Total	13	2	1	16	27

MAYAPAN COARSE WARE

Forms, Types, and Varieties	A Rim	C Rim	D Rim	Total Rim	Body
Censers, effigy: Uayma Modeled Type	0	0	5	5	20
Figurines: Uayma Modeled Type	0	0	4	4	0
Total	0	0	9	9	20

TELCHAQUILLO BRICK WARE

Forms, Types, and Varieties	A Rim	C Rim	D Rim	Total Rim	Body
Candlestick shields: Moyos Red Type	3	0	0	3	4
Total	3	0	0	3	4

WARE UNKNOWN

	A Rim	C Rim	D Rim	Total Rim	Body
Unidentified sherds	95	171	41	307	7,699
Total of all Hocaba-Tases wares at Mayapan	6,722	3,885	1,488	12,095	74,325

CHAUACA CERAMIC COMPLEX MATERIAL
ABALA RED WARE

	A Rim	C Rim	D Rim	Total Rim	Body
Jars, parenthesis rim: Sacpokana Red Type	3	0	0	3	0
Total of all Mayapan middle lots	6,725	3,885	1,488	12,098	74,325

Appendix D

PASTE COMPOSITION OF THE UXMAL, KABAH, AND CHICHEN ITZA SAMPLES

A. O. Shepard (1958, p. 452)

"spent twelve weeks in the field seeking correlation between stylistic and technical features. From January 10 to February 7 she worked in Merida on R. E. Smith's collections from test cuts at Uxmal, Kabah, and Chichen Itza. A clearcut distribution pattern and definite relations between paste composition, ware, and vessel shape emerged from this review. Some wares, such as the fine-textured, calcite-tempered Thin Slate and the coarse, sherd-tempered Holactun Black-on-cream [herein called Cauich Coarse-cream Ware], are uniform in composition, whereas the more generalized ware Puuc Slate is heterogeneous, including four paste classes: calcite-, volcanic ash-, and sherd-tempered pastes, and lumpy untempered paste. . . . calcite-tempered or volcanic ash-tempered paste is strongly preponderant in some forms, whereas others include a significant representation of the main paste classes. The degree of paste uniformity also differs by site. The two classic Puuc sites, Uxmal and Kabah, have a heterogeneous paste representation; in contrast, the Chichen Itza sample, classed as Toltec by Smith, is exceptionally uniform, the various slipped types running almost exclusively to volcanic ash temper and the unslipped types to calcite temper, with high correlation between classes of calcite and vessel form. We have, then, some good correlations between paste, ware, and shape, some centers showing well established techniques, others exhibiting technical diversity. These occurrences are most simply explained by the hypothesis that pottery-making communities drew on diverse local resources and that there was a lively trade among them, some communities being much more dependent on exchange than others. That is, standardized wares and types may be considered products of pottery-making communities having well established techniques; classes that are variable in composition suggest that style was more widely established than technique; uniformity within a site may reflect self-sufficiency in pottery production; diversity may indicate a community depending in large measure on trade for its pottery. These explanations are without doubt glaring oversimplifications. There are other factors that must be weighed, especially exchange of raw materials, potters of a community practicing a number of different techniques or passing through a period of experimentation, and different degrees of standardization in different centers. These explanations should all be tested as working hypotheses in future explorations, and this season's results hold promise that definite answers can be obtained."

As originally planned Shepard was to have written two sections of this report, one devoted to the study of the paste composition of the Uxmal and Kabah samples, the other to that of the Chichen Itza sample. At her request these sections have been deleted. Also, at her suggestion (letter dated May 20, 1968), however, I wish to state that I have drawn on her analysis especially with regard to her temper findings and temper definitions. Since she has not checked the identification or definitions, responsibility for them is entirely mine. The temper findings are set forth in Chapter IV and in Tables 41–43, which also incorporate the author's ware and form identifications.

CLASSES OF TEMPER

The Uxmal-Kabah-Chichen Itza pottery sample has four paste classes: calcite-, potsherd-, and volcanic ash-tempered pastes, and lumpy clay untempered paste.

Calcite temper has a number of varieties resulting from a wide range in color, texture, particle shape, and degree of opacity. These varieties are described in the order in which they appear in Tables 41 and 42, with the addition of one associated only with Chichen Itza (Table 43).

Clear, crystalline calcite (C), distinguished by the fact that grains are translucent or transparent, is a broad class, the varieties of which are widely distributed in Yucatan. The temper which present-day Yucatan potters call *hip* belongs to this class. Color and clearness indicate that it is a relatively pure form of crystalline calcite. Textures vary from fine to coarse, while grain shape varies from cleavage fragments with plane faces and sharp edges to rounded grains and particles composed of smaller grains. Microcrystalline calcite or limestone is also included in this class. Although it does not appear translucent and may even be gray in color, its crystalline character is shown by the reflectance of light from innumerable minute crystal faces. A small percentage of the temper included in this class contains some opaque grains, but clear grains always preponderate.

Saccharoidal calcite (C–1, C–1A, C–1B), a textural variety of clear calcite, may upon grinding break down into individual grains. They give the paste an exceedingly fine, uniform texture, though a few lumps indicating the original source will remain (Shepard, 1956, p. 382). The term saccharoidal refers to the sugary appearance of stray particles that are aggregates of very fine crystals. In this context it occurs chiefly in a very fine grade which is uniform and identifies one ware — Thin Slate. The texture is so fine that the paste might almost pass as untempered.

Cryptocrystalline calcite temper (C–2) includes all varieties of light-colored submicroscopically crystalline calcite. It is opaque and white or very light gray. The sascab used by present-day potters belongs to this class of temper (R. H. Thompson, 1958, p. 68). Like clear crystalline calcite, it is a widely distributed commodity.

Gray limestone temper (CGL or C–3) is composed of fragments which differ in color from light gray to almost black; dark gray is most typical. In any given paste, particles may be relatively uniform in color or may include a range. Fragments are usually opaque and cryptocrystalline, although stray microcrystalline particles sometimes are found. Fragments are typically angular in shape and dense or massive in appearance.

A white carbonate temper (C–4) having a fine lamellar structure characterizes Chichen Unslipped Ware jars with medial bolster. This temper was not found in any other vessel shape in the Chichen Itza sample, nor did it occur in any of the Uxmal-Kabah sherds. This is a case where a vessel has two distinctive attributes, rim form and temper.

Potsherd temper (S), according to Shepard (1956, p. 383), "is the least distinctive as a class, yet the analyst has resources for differentiating varieties even here. He can detect differences in color and texture of sherd and, most important, he can identify the temper of the sherd temper." In a more recent article Shepard (1964b, p. 518) states,

"Maya pottery of Yucatan presents an interesting contrast to the Puebloan. . . . The sherd temper is often more difficult to identify than in Southwestern pottery. Conspicuous calcite grains are often associated with it; moreover, particles of some limestones superficially resemble sherd fragments. Aside from slip on rare fragments, the distinguishing features of sherd temper are: (1) a range of colors and textures in the fragments and different inclusions in different fragments, because sherds gathered up for temper were not uniform, and (2) irregular, angular particle outline, because sherd does not soften and round in paste preparation as do lumps of clay."

In this context pot-sherd temper is generally medium textured. Fragments are readily distinguished from clay lumps because they are rough, angular, and tempered. The majority are calcite tempered, and free grains of calcite, which could have been separated from the sherds in the course of grinding, occur in the paste. The sherd particles often include a range of colors — grays, reds, and buffs — which give the paste a heterogeneous appearance.

Volcanic ash temper (A) is a fragmental material, not a ground pumice. Shepard (1964a, p. 251) corroborates this in the following statement, "Some years ago Dr. Pollock found pumice being sold in the Mérida market for scouring. It was obtained from the coast where it was washed in by ocean currents. Volcanic glass of corresponding texture, however, has not been found in any of the ash-tempered pottery of the Yucatán Peninsula examined to date." Shepard (1952, pp. 264–

265) casts further light on the character of volcanic ash temper as found in Yucatan:

"A question of primary interest with regard to the ash temper is whether or not more than one source of supply is indicated. All thin sections of this paste have been reviewed in some detail with this question in mind. The ash in all these sections is comparable in form and in sparseness and fineness of mineral inclusions. The paste is distinguished by the occurrence of particles of tuff or indurated ash. The similarity of these examples suggests derivation of the ash from a single source or from similar formations."

The volcanic ash under consideration is composed of fine, flaky, and irregular fragments or shards of clear glass and lumps which are loose aggregates of the shards. The texture of the flakes in some aggregates falls in the range of volcanic dust. The lumps are sometimes stained with ocher or impregnated with calcite. This class of temper varies with respect to the abundance of aggregates and degree of staining or cementation, but distinct varieties were not recognized, and the form and texture of the ash suggest a single mode of origin. Shepard (1964a, p. 251) points out how this differs from the ash temper associated with Uaxactun pottery: "Petrographic analysis of volcanic ash-tempered pottery from Uaxactún reveals several significant facts. First, many different varieties of ash were used. In this respect there is a great contrast between the volcanic ash temper of Uaxactún and that of Yucatán, which is remarkably uniform in character whether it comes from Puuc sites or Chichén Itzá."

Clay lump (L) or lumpy untempered paste is found principally in Puuc Slate Ware at both Uxmal and Kabah (tables 41 and 42). The clay base is dense, almost waxy looking, and contains medium to fine rounded particles of clay which are generally reddish or brown and darker in color than the clay but equally dense and fine. Rarely whitish (L–1) or pale buff lumps occur. In relative quantity, clay lumps range from sparse to abundant.

Pastes with inclusions of more than one material. A minor proportion of sherds contains more than one kind of tempering material. Some of these admixtures may have been intentional, but for the most part they appear to have been accidental.

Key to other temper designations of rare occurrence:

C–5 refers to very coarse, water clear cleavage fragments of calcite. Some medium-textured granular water clear calcite is included.

D? consists of opaque white temper in which rhombic crystals are prominent. This may be dolomite.

Q stands for quartz sand.

FX refers to a fiber temper, similar to Brainerd's (1958, p. 73) Yaxuna specimens but finer.

X attached to any letter means that the specimen has finer than normal temper for that class.

Appendix E

PETEN GLOSS SUBWARES

BANDERA GLOSS SUBWARE
(Tzakol Ceramic Complex)

This subware is divided into the following groups: Polychrome Actuncan (Tzakol 1), orange Aguila* (Tzakol 1–3), dichrome Batellos (Tzakol 2), black Balanza* (Tzakol 2, 3), polychrome Caldero (Tzakol 2, 3), gray Contaro (Tzakol 3), red Dos Hermanos (Tzakol 1), buff Fama (Tzakol 3), resist Japon (Tzakol 3), brown Pucte* (Tzakol 2, 3), and polychrome Yaloch (Tzakol 2, 3). Only a few of these groups and forms (marked with an asterisk) were encountered in these collections and are recorded below. The others are described under color designations by Smith (1955a) and listed by Smith and Gifford (1966).

Orange Aguila Group. *Types and varieties.* Aguila Orange Type, Aguila Variety*; Boleto Black-on-orange Type, Boleto Variety*; Dos Arroyos Orange-polychrome Type, Dos Arroyos Variety*; Milpa Impressed Type, Milpa Variety; Pita Incised Type, Pita Variety*, mostly sharp-incised; San Blas Red-on-orange Type, San Blas Variety; and San Clemente Gouged-incised Type, San Clemente Variety. *Forms.* Jars*; basal-flange bowls*; basal-Z-angle bowls*; hemispherical bowls*; flaring-side bowls*; and a tripod cylindrical bowl*. Other forms not found in these collections are listed by Smith (1955a, pp. 126–160). *Quantity.* Uxmal-Kabah, no rim, 5 body sherds; Chichen Itza, 2 rim, 1 body sherd; Mayapan, 43 rim, 197 body sherds. *Provenience.* Widely spread over the Maya area with considerable concentration in the Alta Verapaz, Quiche, and Peten of Guatemala, British Honduras, and Campeche and Yucatan in Mexico. Reasonably well supplied individual sites include: Coba and Tancah in Quintana Roo; Palenque and Yoxiha in Chiapas; Tiradero in Tabasco; Copan in Honduras; and Kaminaljuyu and Zaculeu in the highlands of Guatemala. *Ceramic complex.* Tzakol 1–3 (A. D. 300–600).

Black Balanza Group. *Types and varieties.* Balanza Black Type, Balanza Variety* and gray-black variety; Delirio Plano-relief Type, Delirio Variety*; Lucha Incised Type, Lucha Variety; Maroma Impressed Type, Maroma Variety; Paradero Fluted Type, Paradero Variety; Positas Modeled Type, Positas Variety; and Urita Gouged-incised Type, Urita Variety. *Forms.* Hemispherical bowls and basal-flange bowls. For other forms not found in these collections see Smith (1955a, pp. 126–160). *Quantity.* Uxmal-Kabah, no rims, 4 body sherds; Mayapan, 1 rim, 1 body sherd. *Provenience.* Much the same as for the orange Aguila Group. *Ceramic complex.* Tzakol 1–3 (A. D. 300–600).

Brown Pucte Group. *Types and varieties.* Pucte Brown Type, Pucte Variety*. *Forms.* Basal-flange bowls; ring-stand rounded-side bowls; pedestal-base rounded-side bowls; cylinder tripods*; jars; apron covers; pitchers; and a rounded-side bowl. *Quantity.* Mayapan, 1 rim, no body sherds. *Provenience.* Mayapan; for other sites see "brown" in the Tzakol Ceramic Complex at Uaxactun (Smith, 1955a). *Ceramic complex.* Tzakol, 2, 3 (A. D. 360–600).

PETIPET GLOSS SUBWARE
(Tepeu 1 Ceramic Complex)

This subware is divided into the following groups: cream Juleki, black Molino, brown San Tomas, buff Sibal*, red Tasital, and orange Veracal.* The groups not described here may be found in Smith (1955a) and Smith and Gifford (1966).

Orange Veracal Group. *Types and varieties.* Desquite Red-on-orange Type, Desquite Variety; Saptam Impressed Type, Saptam Variety; Saxche Orange-polychrome Type, Saxche Variety*; Uacho Black-on-orange Type, Uacho Variety,* and Veracal Orange Type, Veracal Variety. *Forms.* Deep or barrel-shape bowls; tripod basal-ridge plates*; rounded-side bowls*; bowls with flaring sides rounding to flat base; cylindrical vases; drums; and jars. *Quantity.* Kabah, 1 rim, no body sherds; Mayapan, 4 rim, 3 body sherds. *Provenience.* Like the orange Aguila Group, this group is widely distributed over the Maya area with considerable concentration in the Alta Verapaz, Quiche, Motagua Valley, and Peten of Guatemala, much of British Honduras, and Campeche, Quintana Roo, and Yucatan in Mexico. A few sites outside these regions have a fair supply of this pottery; namely, Copan in Honduras, Trinidad in Chiapas, Mexico, and Zaculeu in Guatemala. *Ceramic complex.* Tepeu 1 (A. D. 600–700).

Buff Sibal Group. *Types and varieties.* Bejucal Brown-on-buff Type, Bejucal Variety* and Sibal Buff-polychrome Type, Sibal Variety. *Forms.* Cylindrical vases; tripod basal-ridge dishes; rounded-side bowl*; bowl with flaring sides rounding to flat base; and a drum. *Quantity.* Uxmal, 1 rim, no body sherds. *Provenience.* Uxmal and Uaxactun. *Ceramic complex.* Tepeu 1 (A. D. 600–700).

MARIHUANA GLOSS SUBWARE
(Tepeu 2 Ceramic Complex)

This subware is divided into the following groups. Orange Botifela,* cream Chinos, black Infierno,* red Nanzal,* buff Paixban, brown Tialipa. The groups not described here may be found in Smith (1955a) and Smith and Gifford (1966).

Orange Botifela Group. *Types and varieties.* Botifela

Orange Type, Botifela Variety; Central Farm Composite Type, Central Farm Variety; Chantuori Black-on-orange Type, Chantuori Variety*; Geronimo Incised Type, Geronimo Variety, sharp-incised*; Palmar Orange-polychrome Type, Palmar Variety; Pasos Impressed Type, Pasos Variety; and Salada Fluted Type, Salada Variety. *Forms.* Tripod flaring or outcurving-side plates or dishes; rounded-side, incurved-rim bowls; flaring or outcurving-side bowls or dishes; jars*; tripod plates with notched or stepped flange; cylindrical vases; flaring-side, incurved-rim bowls; rounded-side bowls; side-angle bowls,* and a cover. *Quantity.* Mayapan, 1 rim, 2 body sherds. *Provenience.* This group is well established in the Alta Verapaz, Quiche, and Peten of Guatemala, much of British Honduras, and Campeche and Yucatan in Mexico. Outside of these regions a few sites have this orange-slipped pottery; namely, Huimango, Tabasco, and Trinidad, Chiapas. *Ceramic complex.* Tepeu 2 (A. D. 700–800).

Black Infierno Group. *Types and varieties.* Bambonal Plano-relief Type, Bambonal Variety; Carmelita Incised Type, Carmelita Variety, groove-incised*; Chilar Fluted Type, Chilar Variety and red-interior variety; Infierno Black Type, Infierno Variety.* *Forms.* Tripod flaring-side dishes or plates; flaring-side bowls or dishes; side-angle bowls,* and cylindrical vases.* *Quantity.* Mayapan, 5 rim, 4 body sherds. *Provenience.* In British Honduras at Benque Viejo, San Jose, and Tzimin Kax; in Guatemala at Aintun, Alta Verapaz, Asuncion Mita, Jutiapa, El Baul, Escuintla, and Xacbal and Zacualpa, Quiche; in Honduras at Copen; in Mexico at Acanceh, Dzibilchaltun and Mayapan, Yucatan, and Huaymil,

Jaina, Xpuhil, and Xtampak, Campeche. *Ceramic complex.* Tepeu 2 (A. D. 700–800).

Red Nanzal Group. *Types and varieties.* Batcab Red-polychrome Type, Batcab Variety; Chinja Impressed Type, Chinja Variety; Corozal Incised Type, Corozal Variety; Nanzal Red Type, Nanzal Variety; Reyes Composite Type, Reyes Variety; Rosa Punctate Type, Rosa Variety; and Yuhactal Black-on-red Type, Yuhactal Variety.* *Forms.* Jars*; flaring or outcurving-side plates or dishes; rounded-side, incurved-rim bowls; cylindrical vases; and flaring or outcurving-side bowls or dishes. *Quantity.* Mayapan, 1 rim, 15 body sherds. *Provenience.* In British Honduras at Baking Pot, Benque Viejo, and San Jose; in Guatemala at Tayasal, Tikal, and Uaxactun of the Peten, Chipal and Zacualpa of the Quiche, and Chicuxab and Chipoc of the Alta Verapaz; in Mexico at Acanceh, Dzibilchaltun, and Mayapan of Yucatan; Calderitas and Tancah of Quintana Roo, and at Edzna, Campeche. *Ceramic complex.* Tepeu 2 (A. D. 700–800).

THE CUCAS GLOSS SUBWARE
(Tepeu 3 Ceramic Complex)

This subware includes the following groups: black Achote, orange Asote, brown Maquina, and red Tinaja plus a number of dichromes and polychromes listed by Smith and Gifford (1966). None of these groups is present in the collections concerned with this study with the possible exception of the red Tinaja Group which is very close to the red Teabo Group of Puuc Red Ware.

References

Acosta, J. R.
1945. La cuarta y quinta temporada de excavaciones en Tula, Hgo., 1943–44. *Revista Mexicana de Estudios Antropológicos*, vol. 7, pp. 23–64. Mexico, D.F.

Adams, R. E. W.
1963. The ceramic sequence at Altar de Sacrificios, Guatemala. Unpublished Ph.D. Dissertation, Department of Anthropology, Harvard University.

Adams, R. M., Jr.
1953. Some small ceremonial structures of Mayapan. *Carnegie Institution of Washington, Current Reports*, no. 9. Washington, D.C.

Andrews, E. W.
1960. Excavations at Dzibilchaltun, northwestern Yucatan, Mexico. *Proceedings of the American Philosophical Society*, vol. 104, no. 3. Philadelphia.
1965. Archaeology and prehistory in the northern Maya lowlands. *In: Handbook of Middle American Indians*, vol. 2, *Archaeology of Southern Mesoamerica*, Part 1, pp. 288–330. Austin, Texas.

Berlin, H.
1956. Late pottery horizons of Tabasco, Mexico. *Carnegie Institution of Washington, Publication* no. 606, *Contributions to American Anthropology and History*, no. 59. Washington, D.C.

Brainerd, G. W.
1940–1942. Yucatan pottery. *Carnegie Institution of Washington, Year Book*, nos. 39–41. Washington, D.C.
1941. Fine orange pottery in Yucatan. *Revista Mexicana de Estudios Antropológicos*, vol. 5, pp. 163–83. Mexico, D.F.
1951. Early ceramic horizons in Yucatan. *In:* "Ancient Civilizations of the Americas," S. Tax, editor. *29th International Congress of Americanists, Selected Papers*, vol. 1, pp. 72–78. Chicago.
1953. On the design of the fine orange pottery found at Chichen Itza, Yucatan. *Revista Mexicana de Estudios Antropológicos*, vol. 13, pp. 463–73. Mexico, D.F.
1958. The archaeological ceramics of Yucatan. *University of California, Anthropological Records*, no. 19. Berkeley and Los Angeles.

Bullard, W. R., Jr.
1960. The Maya settlement pattern in northeastern Peten, Guatemala. *American Antiquity*, vol. 25, no. 3, pp. 355–72. Salt Lake City.
1970. Topoxté, a postclassic Maya site in Peten, Guatemala. *Peabody Museum, Harvard University, Papers*, vol. 61, pp. 247–307. Cambridge.

Butler, Mary
1940. A pottery sequence from the Alta Verapaz, Guatemala. *In:* The Maya and their neighbors, pp. 250–67. New York and London.

Coe, M. D.
1961. La Victoria, an early site on the Pacific Coast of Guatemala. *Peabody Museum, Harvard University, Papers*, vol. 53. Cambridge.

Coe, W. R.
1965. Tikal: ten years of study of a Maya ruin in the lowlands of Guatemala. *Expedition*, vol. 8, no. 1, pp. 5–56. Philadelphia.

Cole, L. J.
1910. The caverns and people of northern Yucatan. *American Geographic Society, Bulletin* 42, pp. 321–36. New York.

Dieseldorff, E. P.
1926. Kunst und Religion der Mayavölker im alten und heutigen Mittelamerika. Berlin.
1933. Kunst und Religion der Mayavölker, III: die Datierung der Tempel. Berlin.

Drucker, Philip
1943. Ceramic stratigraphy at Cerro de las Mesas, Veracruz, Mexico. *Smithsonian Institution, Bureau of American Ethnology, Bulletin* 141. Washington, D.C.

Du Solier, M. W.
1943. A reconnaissance on Isla de Sacrificios, Veracruz, Mexico. *Carnegie Institution of Washington, Notes on Middle American Archaeology and Ethnology*, no. 14. Washington, D.C.

Fry, E. I.
1956. Skeletal remains from Mayapan. *Carnegie Institution of Washington, Current Reports*, no. 38. Washington, D.C.

Galíndo y Villa, Jesús
1905. Algo sobre los zapotecas y los edificios de Mitla. *Anales del Museo Nacional de Mexico*. Epoca II: II, pp. 193–258. Mexico, D.F.

Gann, Thomas
1900. Mounds in northern Honduras. *Smithsonian Institution, Bureau of American Ethnology, 19th Annual Report*, pt. 2, pp. 655–92. Washington, D.C.
1918. The Maya Indians of southern Yucatan and northern British Honduras. *Smithsonian Institution, Bureau of American Ethnology, Bulletin* 64. Washington, D.C.
1925. Mystery cities. Exploration and adventure in Lubaantun. London.
1926. Ancient cities and modern tribes. London.

Gann, Thomas and Mary
1939. Archaeological investigations in the Corozal District of British Honduras. *Smithsonian Institution, Bureau of American Ethnology, Bulletin* 123, pp. 1–66. Washington, D.C.

Hall, F. G.
1936. Physical and chemical survey of cenotes of Yucatan. *Carnegie Institution of Washington, Publication* no. 457, pp. 5–16. Washington, D.C.

Hatt, R. T., Fisher, H. I., Langebartel, D. A., and Brainerd, G. W.

1953. Faunal and archaeological researches in Yucatan caves. *Cranbrook Institute of Science, Bulletin* no. 33. Bloomfield.

Joyce, T. A.
1914. Mexican Archaeology. London.

Kidder, A. V., Jennings, J. D. and Shook, E. M.
1946. Excavations at Kaminaljuyu, Guatemala. *Carnegie Institution of Washington, Publication* no. 561. Washington, D.C.

Longyear, J. M., III
1952. Copan Ceramics: A study of southeastern Maya pottery. *Carnegie Institution of Washington, Publication* no. 597. Washington, D.C.

Lothrop, S. K.
1924. Tulum. *Carnegie Institution of Washington, Publication* no. 335. Washington, D.C.
1952. Metals from the Cenote of Sacrifice, Chichen Itza, Yucatan. *Peabody Museum, Harvard University, Memoirs*, vol. 10, no. 2. Cambridge.

Lowe, G. W.
1962. Mound 5 and minor excavations, Chiapa de Corzo, Chiapas, Mexico. *New World Archaeological Foundation, Publication* no. 8, *Papers* no. 12. Provo, Utah.

Lowe, G. W. and Agrinier, Pierre
1960. Excavations at Chiapa de Corzo, Chiapas, Mexico. *New World Archaeological Foundation, Publication*, no. 7, *Papers* no. 8. Provo, Utah.

Marti, Samuel
1955. Instrumentos musicales precortesianos. *Instituto Nacional de Antropología*. Mexico, D.F.

Mason, Gregory
1928. Pottery and other artifacts from caves in British Honduras and Guatemala. *Indian Notes and Monographs, Museum of the American Indian, Heye Foundation*, no. 47. New York.

Medellin Zenil, Alfonso
1955. Exploraciones en la Isla de Sacrificios. Gobierno del Estado de Veracruz, Dirección General de Educación, Departamento de Antropología. Jalapa.

Mercer, H. C.
1896. The hill-caves of Yucatan. The Corwith Expedition of the Department of Archaeology and Palaeontology of the University of Pennsylvania. Philadelphia.

Merwin, R. E.
(1914). Note books on the Eleventh Central American Expedition of the Peabody Museum of Archaeology and Ethnology, Harvard University. Unpublished. Cambridge.

Merwin, R. E. and Vaillant, G. C.
1932. The ruins of Holmul, Guatemala. *Peabody Museum, Harvard University, Memoirs*, vol. 3, no. 2. Cambridge.

Morley, S. G.
1915. An introduction to the study of Maya hieroglyphs. *Smithsonian Institution, Bureau of American Ethnology, Bulletin* 57. Washington, D.C.

Morris, E. H., Charlot, J., and Morris, A. A.
1931. The Temple of the Warriors at Chichen Itza, Yucatan. *Carnegie Institution of Washington, Publication* no. 406. Washington, D.C.

Munsell, A. H.
1949. Munsell Soil Color Charts. Munsell Color Company, Inc. Baltimore.

Navarrete, Carlos
1960. Archaeological explorations in the region of the Frailesca, Chiapas, Mexico. *New World Archaeological Foundation, Publication* no. 6, *Papers* no. 7. Orinda.

Nuttall, Zelia
1910. The Island of Sacrificios. *American Anthropologist*, n.s., vol. 12, pp. 257–95. Lancaster, Pa.

Pearse, A. S., Creaser, E. P., Hall, F. G., et al.
1936. The cenotes of Yucatan: a zoological and hydrographic survey. *Carnegie Institution of Washington, Publication* no. 457. Washington, D.C.

Peterson, F. A.
1963. Some ceramics from Mirador, Chiapas, Mexico. *New World Archaeological Foundation, Publication* no. 11, *Papers* no. 15. Provo, Utah.

Phillips, Philip
1958. Application of the Wheat-Gifford-Wasley Taxonomy to eastern ceramics. *American Antiquity*, vol. 24, no. 2, pp. 117–25. Salt Lake City.

Plowden, W. W., Jr.
1958. Spanish and Mexican Majolica found in New Mexico. *El Palacio*, vol. 65, no. 6, pp. 212–19. Santa Fe, N.M.

Pollock, H. E. D.
1962. Introduction. See Pollock et al. 1962.

Pollock, H. E. D., Roys, R. L., Proskouriakoff, T., and Smith, A. L.
1962. Mayapan, Yucatan, Mexico. *Carnegie Institution of Washington, Publication* no. 619. Washington, D.C.

Proskouriakoff, Tatiana
1957. Middle America. *American Antiquity*, vol. 22, no. 3, pp. 333–34. Salt Lake City.
1962a. Civic and religious structures of Mayapan. See Pollock et al. 1962a.
1962b. The artifacts of Mayapan. See Pollock et al. 1962.

Proskouriakoff, T. and Temple, C. R.
1955. A residential quadrangle: Structures R-85 to R-90. *Carnegie Institution of Washington, Current Reports*, no. 29. Washington, D.C.

Rands, R. L. and B. C.
1957. The ceramic position of Palenque, Chiapas. *American Antiquity*, vol. 23, no. 2, pp. 140–50. Salt Lake City.

Rickards, C. G.
1910. The ruins of Mexico, vol. 1. London.

Ricketson, O. G., Jr. and Ricketson, E. B. et al.
1937. Uaxactun, Guatemala. Group E–1926–1931. *Carnegie Institution of Washington, Publication* no. 477. Washington, D.C.

Roberts, H. B.
1931–1935. Ceramics. *Carnegie Institution of Washington.* Year Books 30–34. Washington, D.C.

Roys, R. L.
1957. The political geography of the Yucatan Maya. *Carnegie Institution of Washington, Publication* no. 613. Washington, D.C.
1962. Literary sources for the history of Mayapan. See Pollock et al. 1962.

Ruppert, Karl
1935. The Caracol at Chichen Itza, Yucatan, Mexico. *Carnegie Institution of Washington, Publication* no. 454. Washington, D.C.

1952. Chichen Itza: architectural notes and plans. *Carnegie Institution of Washington, Publication no. 595.* Washington, D.C.

Ruppert, K. and Smith, A. L.
1952. Excavations in house mounds at Mayapan. *Carnegie Institution of Washington, Current Reports,* no. 4, pp. 45–66. Washington, D.C.

Ruppert, K., Shook, E. M., Smith, A. L., and Smith, R. E.
1954. Chichen Itza, Dzibiac, and Balam Canche, Yucatan. *Carnegie Institution of Washington, Year Book 53.* Washington, D.C.

Ruz L., A.
1945a. La costa de Campeche en los tiempos prehis-panicos: prospeccion ceramica y bosquejo historico. Tesis, Universidad Nacional Autonoma de Mexico.
1945b. Campeche en la arqueología Maya. *Acta Antropológica,* vol. 1, nos. 2–3. Mexico, D.F.
1958. Exploraciones arqueológicas en Palenque: 1953–1956. *Anales del Instituto Nacional de Antropología e Historia,* vol. X. Mexico.

Sanders, W. T.
1960. Prehistoric ceramics and settlement patterns in Quintana Roo, Mexico. *Carnegie Institution of Washington, Publication no. 606, Contributions to American Anthropology and History,* no. 60. Washington, D.C.

Satterthwaite, L., Jr.
1938. Maya dating by hieroglyph styles. *American Anthropologist,* vol. 40, pp. 416–28. Menasha.

Seler, Caecilie
1900. Auf alten Wegen in Mexiko und Guatemala. Berlin.

Seler, Eduard
1904. Gesammelte Ahandlungen zur Amerikanischen Sprach und Alterthumskunde. Vol. 2. Berlin.

Shepard, A. O.
1948. Plumbate, a mesoamerican trade ware. *Carnegie Institution of Washington, Publication no. 573.* Washington, D.C.
1952. Ceramic technology. *Carnegie Institution of Washington, Year Book, no. 51.* Washington, D.C.
1956. Ceramics for the archaeologist. *Carnegie Institution of Washington, Publication no. 609.* Washington, D.C.
1958. Ceramic technology. *Carnegie Institution of Washington, Year Book, no. 57.* Washington, D.C.
1964a. Ceramic development of the lowland and highland Maya. *35th International Congress of Americanists,* vol. 1, pp. 249–62. Mexico, D.F.
1964b. Temper identification: technological sherd-splitting or an unanswered challenge. *American Antiquity,* vol. 29, no. 4, pp. 518–20. Salt Lake City.

Shook, E. M.
1947. Guatemala highlands. *Carnegie Institution of Washington, Year Book, no. 46.* Washington, D.C.
1951. The present status of research on the pre-classic horizons in Guatemala. *In:* "The civilizations of ancient America," Sol Tax, editor. *29th International Congress of Americanists, Selected Papers,* vol. 1, pp. 93–100. Chicago.

1954a. Three temples and their associated structures at Mayapan. *Carnegie Institution of Washington, Current Reports,* no. 14. Washington, D.C.
1954b. The Temple of Kukulcan at Mayapan. *Carnegie Institution of Washington, Current Reports,* no. 20. Washington, D.C.

Shook, E. M. and Irving, W. N.
1955. Colonnaded buildings at Mayapan. *Carnegie Institution of Washington, Current Reports,* no. 22. Washington, D.C.

Shook, E. M. and Kidder, A., II
1961. The painted tomb at Tikal. *Expedition,* vol. 4, pp. 2–7, Philadelphia.

Smith, A. L.
1962. Residential and associated structures at Mayapan. See Pollock *et al.* 1962.

Smith, A. L. and Kidder, A. V.
1951. Excavations at Nebaj, Guatemala. *Carnegie Institution of Washington, Publication no. 594.* Washington, D.C.

Smith, A. L. and Ruppert, K.
1956. Excavations in house mounds at Mayapan: IV. *Carnegie Institution of Washington, Current Reports,* no. 36. Washington, D.C.

Smith, R. E.
1936. Ceramics of Uaxactun: a preliminary analysis of decorative technics and design. *Carnegie Institution of Washington.* Guatemala City.
1944. Archaeological specimens from Guatemala. *Carnegie Institution of Washington, Notes on Middle American Archaeology and Ethnology,* no. 37. Washington, D.C.
1952. Pottery from Chipoc, Alta Verapaz, Guatemala. *Carnegie Institution of Washington, Publication no. 596, Contributions to American Archaeology,* no. 56. Washington, D.C.
1953. Cenote X-Coton at Mayapan. *Carnegie Institution of Washington, Current Reports,* no. 5. Washington, D.C.
1954a. Cenote exploration at Mayapan and Telchaquillo. *Carnegie Institution of Washington, Current Reports,* no. 12. Washington, D.C.
1954b. Exploration on the outskirts of Mayapan. *Carnegie Institution of Washington, Current Reports,* no. 18. Washington, D.C.
1955a. Ceramic sequence at Uaxactun, Guatemala (2 vols.). *Middle American Research Institute, Tulane University, Publication no. 20.* New Orleans.
1955b. Early ceramic horizons at Mayapan and Santa Cruz. *Carnegie Institution of Washington, Current Reports,* no. 26. Washington, D.C.
1957a. Tohil Plumbate and Classic Maya polychrome vessels in the Marquez Collection. *Carnegie Institution of Washington, Notes on Middle American Archaeology and Ethnology,* no. 129. Washington, D.C.
1957b. The Marquez Collection of X Fine Orange and Fine Orange Polychrome vessels. *Carnegie Institution of Washington, Notes on Middle American Archaeology and Ethnology,* no. 131. Washington, D.C.
1958. The place of fine orange pottery in Mesoamerican archaeology. *American Antiquity,* vol. 24, no. 2, pp. 151–60. Salt Lake City.

Smith, R. E. and Gifford, J. C.
   1965. Pottery of the Maya lowlands. *In*: *Handbook of Middle American Indians*, vol. 2, *Archaeology of Southern Mesoamerica*, Part I, pp. 498–534. Austin, Texas.
   1966. Maya ceramic varieties, types, and wares at Uaxactun: supplement to "Ceramic sequence at Uaxactun, Guatemala." *Middle American Research Institute, Tulane University, Publication* no. 28. New Orleans.

Smith, R. E., Willey, G. R., and Gifford, J. C.
   1960. The Type-Variety Concept as a basis for the analysis of Maya pottery. *American Antiquity*, vol. 25, no. 3, pp. 330–40. Salt Lake City.

Spinden, H. J.
   1913. A study of Maya art. *Peabody Museum, Harvard University, Memoirs*, vol. 6. Cambridge.
   1928. Ancient civilizations of Mexico and Central America. *American Museum of Natural History, Handbook Series*, no. 3. New York.

Thompson, D. E.
   1955. An altar and platform at Mayapan. *Carnegie Institution of Washington, Current Reports*, no. 28. Washington, D.C.

Thompson, D. E. and Thompson, J. E. S.
   1955. A noble's residence and its dependencies at Mayapan. *Carnegie Institution of Washington, Current Reports*, no. 25. Washington, D.C.

Thompson, E. H.
   1897a. Explorations of the Cave of Loltun, Yucatan. *Peabody Museum, Harvard University, Memoirs*, vol. 1, no. 2, Cambridge.
   1897b. The Chultunes of Labna, Yucatan. *Peabody Museum, Harvard University, Memoirs*, vol. 1, no. 3. Cambridge.
   1898. Ruins of Xkimook, Yucatan. *Field Columbian Museum, Publication no. 28, Anthropological Series*, vol. 2, no. 3. Chicago.
   1904. Archaeological researches in Yucatan. *Peabody Museum, Harvard University, Memoirs*, vol. 3, no. 1. Cambridge.

Thompson, J. E. S.
   1931. Archaeological investigations in the southern Cayo district, British Honduras. *Field Museum of Natural History, Publication* no. 301, *Anthropological Series*, vol. 17, no. 3. Chicago.
   1939. Excavations at San Jose, British Honduras. *Carnegie Institution of Washington, Publication* no. 506. Washington, D.C.
   1941. A coordination of the history of Chichen Itza with ceramic sequences in Central America. *Revista Mexicana de Estudios Antropológicos*, vol. 5, nos. 2–3. Mexico, D.F.
   1945. A survey of the northern Maya area. *American Antiquity*, vol. 11, pp. 2–24. Menasha.
   1948. An archaeological reconnaissance in the Cotzumalhuapa region, Escuintla, Guatemala. *Carnegie Institution of Washington, Publication* no. 574, *Contributions to American Archaeology*, no. 44. Washington, D.C.
   1950. Maya hieroglyphic writing. *Carnegie Institution of Washington, Publication* no. 589. Washington, D.C.
   1957. Deities portrayed on censers at Mayapan. *Carnegie Institution of Washington, Current Reports*, no. 40. Washington, D.C.
   1962. A catalog of Maya hieroglyphs. University of Oklahoma Press, Norman.

Thompson, R. H.
   1958. Modern Yucatecan Maya pottery making. *American Antiquity*, vol. 23, no. 4, pt. 2. Salt Lake City.

Tozzer, A. M.
   1913. A preliminary study of the prehistoric ruins of Nakum, Guatemala. *Peabody Museum, Harvard University, Memoirs*, vol. 5, no. 3. Cambridge.
   1941. Landa's Relación de las cosas de Yucatan. A translation edited with notes. *Peabody Museum, Harvard University, Papers*, vol. 18. Cambridge.
   1957. Chichen Itza and its Cenote of Sacrifice. *Peabody Museum, Harvard University, Memoirs*, vols. 11 and 12. Cambridge.

Vaillant, G. C.
   1927. The chronological significance of Maya ceramics. MS., doctoral dissertation, Harvard University.
   1935. Chronology and stratigraphy in the Maya area. *Maya Research*, vol. 2, no. 2, pp. 119–43. New York.

Wauchope, Robert
   1948. Excavations at Zacualpa, Guatemala. *Middle American Research Institute, Tulane University, Publication* 14. New Orleans.

Wheat, J. B., Gifford, J. C., and Wasley, W. W.
   1958. Ceramic variety, type cluster, and ceramic system in southwestern pottery analysis. *American Antiquity*, vol. 24, pp. 34–47. Salt Lake City.

Willey, G. R., Bullard, W. R., Glass, J. B., and Gifford, J. C.
   1965. Prehistoric Maya settlements in the Belize valley. *Peabody Museum, Harvard University, Papers*, vol. 54. Cambridge.

Winters, H. D.
   1955. Excavation of a colonnaded hall at Mayapan. *Carnegie Institution of Washington, Current Reports* no. 31. Washington, D.C.

Woodbury, R. B. and Trik, A. S.
   1953. The ruins of Zaculeu, Guatemala (2 vols.). Richmond, Virginia.